The Law of Commons

AUSTRALIA AND NEW ZEALAND
The Law Book Company Ltd.
Sydney : Melbourne : Perth

CANADA AND U.S.A.
The Carswell Company Ltd.
Agincourt, Ontario

INDIA
N.M. Tripathi Private Ltd.
Bombay
and
Eastern Law House Private Ltd.
Calcutta and Delhi
M.P.P. House
Bangalore

ISRAEL
Steimatzky's Agency Ltd.
Jerusalem : Tel Aviv : Haifa

The Law of Commons

by

G. D. Gadsden, Dip. Agric., LL.B., Ph.D.
Lecturer in Law, University College, Cardiff

LONDON

SWEET & MAXWELL

1988

Published in 1988 by
Sweet & Maxwell Limited
11 New Fetter Lane, London
Computerset by Promenade Graphics Ltd., Cheltenham
Printed in Great Britain by
Adlard & Son Ltd., The Garden City Press, Letchworth, Herts.

British Library Cataloguing in Publication Data
Gadsden, G. D.
    The law of commons
    1. Commons—Law and legislation—
England
    I. Title
    344.203'256   KD952

ISBN 0–421–36560–9

Preface

This book has been researched and written during the run up period to comprehensive legislation intended to update the use and management of the common lands. But the approach to new legislation in this area of law tends to be slow and laborious. It is 10 years since an interdepartmental committee report announced governmental interest in planning for a new Act and next year sees the thirtieth anniversary of the Royal Commission report which laid down the guidelines for it. The *Royal Commission on Common Land 1955–1958 Report* recommended the establishment of statutory registers for all common land including a record of the rights exercisable over it and its ownership. It was also proposed that there should be new statutory schemes of management for, and a universal right of public access to, the land. In the event it was decided to proceed in two stages; first, registration and, secondly, management and access provisions. Registration was set in train with the enactment of the Commons Registration Act 1965 and now, some 20 years later, is approaching completion. Unfortunately, it is now widely recognised that the Act was not entirely adequate to effect its purposes. In the Court of Appeal in 1982, Lord Justice Oliver, on finding that the Act deemed land to be waste land of a manor when it was accepted by all the parties that it had never had that status, remarked that the case revealed "what I cannot but think is yet another most unsatisfactory state of affairs created by this Act which, if I may say so, is crying out for amendment . . ." It is now apparent that the second stage of legislation will also have to be concerned with amending the deficiencies, and resolving the anomalies and injustices which have arisen from registration. Thus, there is an additional dimension of complexity added to a subject which was already quite complicated enough. Existing statute law, directly concerned with commons, spans 600 years—the earliest Act still in force is concerned with inclosure of commons—and the common law, at the outset of its development in the twelfth century, dealt with rights of grazing over the land of a feudal lord as one of its main features. I have attempted to show that the common law, at least, is relatively free from ambiguity and that many of the features, which some have thought to be obscure and irrational, are sensible and logical. This is much as one might expect after some 700 years of development. That is not to say that the subject is not complex. The common lands are not one particular type of land but a series of interrelated classes with discrete rules applicable to each class. I hope that I have distinguished all the main classes of land and rights which exist today and described adequately the rules for each class, while at the same time warning against confusing the different classes and rules. The reader will find that some of the issues, which have become live in recent years, of which the permanent or temporary severance of appurtenant rights from the land to which they are attached are typical examples, are dealt with on the basis of principle rather than authority. This is because many of the new issues have not been litigated directly and reference to principles seems the only realistic approach. Until there is statutory enactment or case authority affecting them these issues need to be treated with some caution.

It would be attractive to report that the statutes in force are models of clarity. Unfortunately this is by no means the case. Quite apart from the problems recently posed by the Registration Act of 1965 the earlier Acts are in many cases inconclusive in definition and purpose. Be that as it may, I have attempted to draw together, in outline at least, all the Acts which bear directly on common lands and describe, as best I can, their effects. I should perhaps enter one caveat: the massive Inclosure Act of 1845 is still in force but had its teeth drawn as an instrument for inclosure over a century ago. It is to all intents and purposes defunct and I, therefore, give it scant attention except where some of the subsidiary provisions are still in active use. Needless to say the Commons Registration Act 1965 is accorded pride of place among the statutes considered and I have recorded the major areas of difficulty in interpretation and practice. I am certain that I have not uncovered all the problems but at least those which are apparent from the decisions of the Commons Commissioners, who have been resolving registration disputes for over 15 years, are included. I have also been able to study somewhere between five and 10 per cent. of all the commons registers and the discrepancies which appear on the face of those records are noted. What cannot be discovered from this type of investigation is the scale of totally incorrect registrations. Only time will tell how many are in this category and, while everybody concerned with common land has his own particular horror story, there is no central record to bring them all together.

One direction which the book has taken might seem a little unusual for a text on the law of commons inasmuch as there is more than passing consideration of the liability for straying animals and the connected, and unusual, duty to fence against a common. However, those concerned in practical matters will know that the propensity for animals to stray from commons is a constant source of worry and, liability frequently depends upon the establishment of fencing obligations. I have thought it appropriate to identify and comment upon as many as possible of the practical legal difficulties in these more general areas of law, as well as a few others.

I have written with the intention of providing asistance to those who have to grapple with the various legal problems which occur on the common lands. Clearly most are legal practitioners but I am conscious that there is a wider audience among those with direct interests over the lands, whether public or private. Not all that wider audience is legally qualified and not all legal practitioners are well acquainted with agricultural practice. I have tried, therefore, to simplify the law for laymen and explain agricultural practice for the lawyer. If in so doing I have oversimplified for some readers I hope they will understand the reason. In particular my apologies go to those lawyers who may feel insulted at my apparent ready assumption that they do not understand Latin, Law French or even some of the simpler legal concepts!

I wish to thank all those persons who have helped me in the preparation of this book. In particular my thanks are due to Jack Ellis, of Swansea, whose extensive knowledge of the law and practice of commons inspired me to start my research, the National Farmers Union, and especially James May for providing all the earlier Commissioners' decisions for copying, the staff at the Welsh Office and the Department of the Environment for assistance with the tables, the Department of Education and Science for a studentship which gave me some two and a half years of full time research, my colleagues at University College, Cardiff for their unstinted encouragement and support and, by no means least, the publishers' staff, who gave me such efficient help in the final stages of preparation and also offered sympathetic understanding during a convalescence from illness. I need hardly say that any mistakes are mine alone.

September 30, 1987
                                                        G. D. Gadsden

Table of Contents

Table of Cases

Table of Statutes

Table of Statutory Instruments

Table of Abbreviations

Books

Anon., *Commons*	Anon., *The Law of Commons and Commoners* (1st ed., 1698), (2nd ed., 1702)
Bird	Bird, J.B., *The Law respecting Commons and Commoners* (1st ed., 1801), (2nd ed., 1806).
Cooke's Inclosures	Cooke, G.W., *The Inclosure of Commons* (4th ed., 1864)
Elton	Elton, C.I., *A Treatise on Commons and Waste Lands* (1868)
Fitzherbert's Surveying	Fitzherbert, J., *The Boke of Surveying and Improvments* (1523), published in facsimile 1974
Gale's Easements	Maurice, S.G., *Gale on Easements* (15 editions, 1839–1986)
Glanville Williams	Williams, G., *Liability for Animals* (1939)
Halsbury's Laws	*Halsbury's Laws of England* (4th ed., 1974)
Harris and Ryan	Harris, B. and Ryan, G., *An Outline of the Law relating to Common Land* (1967)
Hunt	Hunt, J.A., *The Law relating to Boundary Walls and Fences* (2nd ed., 1870)
Joshua Williams	Williams, J. *Rights of Commons and Other Prescriptive Rights* (1880)
Megarry and Wade	Megarry, Rt. Hon. Sir Robert and Wade, H.R.W., *The Law of Real Property* (5th ed., 1984)
Scriven's Copyholds	Scriven, J., *A Treatise of the Law of Copyholds* (7th ed., 1896)
Woolrych	Woolrych, H.W., *A Treatise of the Law of Rights of Common* (1st ed., 1824), (2nd ed., 1850)

Journals

C.S.J.	The Journal of the Commons, Open Spaces and Footpaths Preservation Society
O.S.S.	The Journal of the Open Spaces Society

Reports

Common Land Forum Report	*Common Land: The Report of the Common Land Forum*, Countryside Commission C.C.P. 215 (1986)

Royal Commission Report   *Royal Commission on Common Land Report*, Cmnd. 462, (1955–1958)

Unusual case citations

A.L.T.   Agricultural Land Tribunal

D.C.C.   *Decisions of the Commons Commissioners 1972—date*, (17 volumes) compiled by Gadsden and held in the Arts and Social Sciences Library, University College Cardiff

1. The Common Lands

INTRODUCTION

In general terms common land may be described as land over which rights **1.01**
of common are exercised. A right of common is the legal right of one or
more persons to take some part of, the produce of, or the wild animals on
the land of another person.[1] It will become apparent later that this is not an
adequate explanation of all the classes of land involved either under the
common law or in statutes purporting to deal with common land. For
example, one modern statute includes within the definition of common
land a class of land which is subject to no third party rights and is almost
indistinguishable from other unincumbered freehold land except by reference to its physical characteristics.[2] The present work, therefore, makes a
distinction between the common lands which encompass a number of different classes of land and the singular use of common land which describes
only land subject to rights of common. It nevertheless cannot be denied that
the majority of the area of the common lands is common land subject to
rights of common, that is to say it is land which is used in common by a
number of persons who have no claim to the ownership of the land nor do
they hold their rights under the owner of the soil. This agricultural use of
land in common is probably a unique example, so far as this country is concerned, of a shared use of a natural resource where there is neither a direct
legal linkage between the participators nor any public element in the use.

The common lands are best viewed today, for legal purposes, as originating **1.02**
in the manorial system of land tenure. Historically there is now no doubt
that land used in common for agricultural and domestic purposes was
widespread, if not universal, before the Norman Conquest and that the
invaders did little more than take over the existing institutions. However, it
is the common law with which we are concerned and the development of
that legal system did not commence until after the Conquest. As the common law began its development so did the law relating to the common
lands. The important right to graze one's cattle over land belonging to
another person was one of the first matters to be dealt with as a common
law issue. Among the earliest of the writs returnable to the King's Court

---

[1] *Beckett (Alfred F.) Ltd.* v. *Lyons* [1967] Ch. 449 at 482, *per* Winn L.J.: *profit à prendre.*
[2] C.R.A. 1965, s.22(1): "common land" includes waste land of a manor not subject to rights of common.

may be found one for the novel disseisin of common of pasture.[3] The rules governing common land today represent centuries of gradual absorption of manorial custom into a standardised common law—a process which we shall see later has not been entirely completed after some 800 years.

1.03 Not unsurprisingly, as the common law was absorbing, and in turn imposing, a standardised manorial custom as universal law, a model had to be adopted as an exemplar against which competing strains of custom could be assessed. It was the widespread English lowland manor which was used for this purpose. It has been argued[4] that such a model can have no application to most of Wales, for instance, where the Norman influence was less than complete, and the universal English law was not applied until a comparatively late stage.[5] However, it is now clear that the common law rules applicable to a lowland arable system of farming have equal application in Wales and other parts of the country, however inappropriate or unsatisfactory the result may be. Scotland followed an altogether different course and the law as described in this text has no application in that country.

1.04 Following 800 years of development it might be anticipated that the common law rules would be fully developed and well understood. Two factors have conspired to prevent this result. First, the common law courts have proved consistently sensitive to the desirability of upholding a *lex loci*, or in the current context manorial custom, providing it is reasonable and capable of satisfactory proof. It follows that in matters of the common law relating to the common lands it is always necessary to consider the possibility that there is customary law which may prevail. Secondly, the lands used in common within the manorial system were not, and today are not, all subject to rights of common. There are several distinct classes of land involved, each with its own distinguishable set of rules. The law of the common lands far from being well understood has been described as "a rather obscure branch of the law."[6] The obscurity arises from a failure to recognise and distinguish properly the different classes of land involved, with the result that rules which should be discrete within one class of land have become, or have seemed to become, interchangeable with other classes. The obscurity, as will be seen later, is more apparent than real once the various classes of land are properly distinguished.

The manorial model

1.05 Before considering the classes of land and rights which exist, some reference has to be made to the model of a manor which was adopted by the courts to assist in moulding an infinite variety of manorial custom into something

---

[3] *cf.* Hall (ed.), *The Laws and Customs of the Realm of England Commonly Called Glanvill* (1965), p. 169.

[4] *Att.-Gen.* v. *Reveley* (1870) *Karslake's Special Reports*: see answer to original information at pp. 9 *et seq.*

[5] Laws in Wales Act 1535 (27 Hen. 8, c. 26).

[6] *Estler* v. *Murrells* (1959) 173 E.G. 393, C.A., *per* Willmer L.J.

approaching a consistent common law, capable of enforcement in the King's courts. In the early stages of the development of the common law the ground rules were few and the aim was mainly to prevent the customary law of the manor from being abused. As time went on, and the strength of the common law increased, a consistent policy required an exemplar against which conflicting claims under custom might be measured. By the late sixteenth century the reported cases indicate a tendency of the courts to explain and justify the facts before them on the basis that all manors were similarly constituted and subject to similar rules. It is clear from some of the comments made that the institutions within the manor were not all that well understood,[7] but, nevertheless, the manor described by Elizabethan lawyers was the one which became accepted as the legal truth. Today it can be seen to be, if not wholly fictitious, at least inappropriate in many situations. The model is even today sometimes called in aid to explain a decision.[8]

The chosen model was the manor considered to be typical of the broad agri- **1.06** cultural plain of the midlands of England.[9] The first assumption made was that the manor was held by a lord by grant directly or mediately of the King. On the manor was developed a home farm, usually with a manor house, from which the lord took all the produce with the land in hand known as the demesne land of the manor. Around the demesne lands were two or three fields, cultivated in individual arable strips by the tenants holding their land free or by copy of the court roll. The tenants, as one of the services for their land, were required to provide draft animals for the cultivation of the lord's demesne. After the arable crops were harvested the strips were thrown open for intergrazing by all the tenants on a common basis. One year in two or three, each arable field lay fallow to recuperate through grazing by the tenants' livestock. In addition there was a common meadow, held similarly in strips, and cut for hay by the tenants. After the hay was harvested the field was thrown open for grazing in common by the tenants. This usually occurred on Lammas Day, that is August 1. There might also have been a common pasture where the tenants' animals grazed in a communal herd or flock at certain or all times of the year. A grazing cycle existed which extended over all the lands of the manor. From August 1 to the end of the growing season animals grazed on the common meadows supplemented by grazing on the arable fields from the end of September. From about February 1 to April 1, the common meadows provided some grazing. When an arable field lay fallow it provided grazing for the whole year as also did the common pasture if there was one. During the main growing season from April 1 to August 1, when the arable and hay fields were closed, the

---

[7] *Sir Miles Corbet's Case* (1585) 7 Co.Rep. 5a, note at 5b, 77 E.R. 417 at 418: "at first the Court was altogether ignorant of the nature of this common called shack."

[8] *Corpus Christi College* v. *Gloucester County Council* [1983] 1 Q.B. 360 at 365, *per* Lord Denning M.R.

[9] In fact the description bears a considerable resemblance to the manor described by John Fitzherbert in *The Boke of Surveying and Improvments* (1523). It is not inconceivable that it is this book which provided the model. Published in facsimile from the Bodleian Library copy by Theatrum Orbis Terrarum Ltd. (John Fitzherbert was the brother of Sir Anthony Fitzherbert, author of *La Novelle Natura Brevium*, who was much praised by Sir Edward Coke).

animals were turned out on the land which had not been brought into the cultivation of the manor—the so-called waste land of the manor. Associated with the manor there was sometimes park land used by the lord for sporting purposes. Some of the King's manors in hand might be of the same nature but, in addition, he would have resort to the numerous Royal Forests which were, however, governed by entirely distinct law enforceable in special Forest Courts.[10]

1.07 The supposed orderly construction of each manor was probably the exception rather than the rule. The ground plans of a manor were sometimes extraordinarily complex and intermixed with the land of other manors.[11] Nevertheless some manors surviving into the nineteenth century did have a very similar structure.[12] However, in many parts of the country the manorial model not only did not, but could not, apply. The very thought of an arable based system in the uplands of Wales or Cumbria is absurd. In other parts there is little evidence that there ever was an open arable field system or, if there was, it was eliminated at a very early stage.[13] The model therefore takes no account of alternatives or special and localised systems such as the sheep-corn husbandry of Norfolk with its cullet flocks and foldcourses[14] or the transhumance of the *hafod à hendre* system of Wales[15] both of which are well documented. Also, there were developments at a very early stage where land was taken out of the manorial system and controlled by outsiders. Examples may be seen where land was sold away from the manor and used by the new owners in common but, of course, as owners and not as holders of rights in common.[16] Some would challenge the very concept that the manor was the dominant institution and argue that the vill or town was the real basis of much of the institutionalised control.[17] Although little evidence remains today of what might be called town commons there is no doubt that most towns, through their corporations, did have extensive rights, exercisable by inhabitants, over large areas of the surrounding land[18] and this concept does not fit in comfortably with the lowland arable manor model. The significance of many of these differences has subsided but in considering any particular situation today they need to be borne in mind and a too hasty adoption of the manorial model to provide explanation avoided.

[10] *cf.* Manwood, *Lawes of the Forest* (4th ed., 1717).
[11] *cf.* Baker and Francis, *Surveys of Gower and Kilvey*, (1861–1870), *passim*: the manors of the seignory of Gower.
[12] *cf.* Joshua Williams, p. 67: the well-ordered field plan there printed.
[13] Yelling, *Common Fields and Enclosures in England 1450–1850* (1977), p. 27.
[14] *cf.* Allison, "The Sheep-Corn Husbandry of Norfolk in the Sixteenth and Seventeenth Centuries" (1957) 5 Agric.Hist.Rev. 12.
[15] Fleure and Whitehouse, "Early Distribution and Valley-ward movement of Population in South Britain" *Archaeological Cambrensis* 16 (6th Series, 1916) 136–137; Owen, "Arvona Antiqua-Ancient Remains, Hafottai etc." Arch.Camb. 13 (3rd Series, 1867) 106–107.
[16] *e.g.* the "freeholders" of Langfield Moor, West Yorkshire.
[17] See Joshua Williams, Lecture IV, p. 44; for a reconciliation of legal and historical theory, see Scrutton, "The Origins of Rights of Common" (1887) 3 L.Q.R. 370.
[18] *e.g. Johnson v. Barnes* (1872) L.R. 7 C.P. 592; *R. v. Churchill* (1825) 4 B. & C. 750, 107 E.R. 1240.

Historical development

It is difficult without some appreciation of the historical and social back-   **1.08**
ground to understand the law in a modern context and the significance of
current political developments. For the present purposes it will suffice to
identify only the more recent history of the manorial system and the developing attitudes which have led to some measure of public control over the
use of the common lands. The manor as an institution was in a state of
decay almost from its inception and its early history is concerned with the
adaptation of a non-intensive agriculture to an expanding and increasingly
urbanised population. Over the centuries there was a steady movement
towards the engrossment of scattered strips and conversion into ownership
in severalty. From 1700 onwards this was accomplished largely through private Inclosure Acts culminating with the general Inclosure Act of 1845.[19]
Under the provisions of this Act some 650,000 acres were inclosed of which
approximately half was manorial waste land: see Table 1 on Page 6.[20] This
final drive towards inclosure was not carried through to a conclusion.
Within 20 years public attitudes had changed and Parliamentary action
moved towards preservation of the remaining manorial lands with the
intention of ensuring the maintenance of open spaces for amenity and recreational purposes.[21]

The Metropolitan Commons Act 1866[22] forbade any further inclosure of the   **1.09**
common lands situated in the Metropolitan Police District and they have
remained frozen to the present day. The Commons Act 1876,[23] followed
later by the Commons Act 1899,[24] changed the direction of awards under
the 1845 Act so that "regulation" rather than inclosure became the first
priority. Regulation involves maintenance of the existing use coupled,
usually, with some provision for general public rights over the land. In considering whether an application under the Act is expedient, the Commissioners responsible for recommending a scheme to Parliament are required
to take into account whether the proposals will be for "the benefit of the
neighbourhood"—a test fairly easy to satisfy in applications for regulation
but an almost insurmountable hurdle if inclosure is proposed which, self
evidently, is primarily intended to benefit private interests. By the end of
the nineteenth century further inclosure on any scale was at an end: see
Table 2 on Page 6.

In 1913 a Select Committee of the House of Commons[25] concluded that   **1.10**
"regulation of commons as distinguished from inclosure would be every-

[19] Between 1700 and 1845 there were 4,804 private inclosure Acts: *Royal Commission on Common Land Report*, Cmnd. 462, p. 162.
[20] See also the Select Committee on Commons (Inclosure and Regulation) Report
(H.M.S.O., 1913).
[21] For an account of the developing pressures see Lord Eversley, *Commons, Forests
and Footpaths* (1910), *passim*.
[22] See § 12.34.
[23] See § 12.43.
[24] See § 12.64.
[25] See note 20.

TABLE 1

	INCLOSURES 1847–1904*	
	Total number of Awards	
Years	*confirmed*	*Acreage inclosed*
1847–49	41	20,011
1850–59	445	293,003
1860–69	350	218,857
1870–79	108	62,411
1880–89	20	36,730
1890–1904	9	13,939

*Board of Agriculture and Fisheries figures, Report from the Select Committee on Commons (Inclosure and Regulation), (H.M.S.O. 1913), App. 1.

TABLE 2

	CASES COMPLETED UNDER VARIOUS ACTS*					
	METRO-POLITAN COMMONS ACTS	COMMONS ACT 1876		COMMONS ACT 1899		LAW OF COMMONS AMEND-MENT
Years	1866–1898	Inclosure	Regulation	Inclosure	Regulation	ACT 1893
1869	1	—	—	—	—	—
1870–79	8	9	2	—	—	—
1880–89	9	13	16	—	—	—
1890–99	6	3	8	—	—	5
1900–09	7	2	5	16	77	8
1910–19	—	1	4	12	48	10
1920–29	—	—	—	18	49	11
1930–39	1	—	—	59	43	7
1940–55	1	—	—	44	41	4
TOTALS	33	28	35	149	258	45
Total acreage	N/A	30471	44117	441	16935	57
Acreage per case	N/A	1088	1260	3	66	1.26

*Ministry of Agriculture, Fisheries and Food figures: Royal Commission on Common Land 1955–58, Minutes of Evidence, H.M.S.O., Vol. 1, pp. 36–38.

where beneficial to all the interests concerned"[26] and recommended a new Act "complete in itself containing a procedure for regulation."[27] The recommendation was not acted upon although some 70 years later interest had revived and some tentative progress has now been made towards a similar proposal.[28]

The only measures directly affecting the control of the common lands over **1.11** the next 50 years[29] were contained in the L.P.A. 1925. A right of public access was granted to all the metropolitan commons and those common lands and manorial wastes in "urban" areas.[30] In addition the erection of fencing or any other works which prevented or impeded access to land subject to rights of common on January 1, 1926, was made unlawful without the consent of a Minister.[31] In giving or withholding his consent the Minister is required to take into account the same considerations as apply to an application for inclosure, *i.e.* the benefit of the neighbourhood test is applied.

The Act of 1925 was part of the comprehensive reform of real property legis- **1.12** lation which included the abolition of copyhold tenure.[32] With enfranchise-ment of copyholds the need for the remaining customary courts of the manors disappeared and most ceased to sit. Although their jurisdiction remained until 1977[33] inactivity meant that there was a gradual loss of knowledge about the manorial lands. In time the status of both land and rights became increasingly uncertain. A significant acreage of common land self evidently remained and after the Second World War it began to be seen as an important and under used natural resource which could no longer be ignored. In 1955 a Royal Commission was appointed and charged with mak-ing recommendations as to "what changes, if any, are desirable in the law relating to common land in order to promote the benefit of those holding manorial and common rights, the enjoyment of the public, or where at pres-ent little or no use is made of such land, its use for some other desirable pur-pose."[34] The Commission reported in 1958 and recommended a statutory register of common land, rights over it and ownership, a right of public access to all common lands and provision for statutory schemes for improvement and management.[35] The report was widely welcomed and accepted, albeit with some reservations on the part of those persons legally interested in the land and rights regarding the right of public access.

In the event Government decided to implement the report in two stages: **1.13** statutory registration first with a second stage of legislation to follow pro-viding for public access and management schemes. The C.R.A. 1965 was

[26] Select Committee on Commons (Inclosure and Regulation) Report (H.M.S.O., 1913), p. iv.
[27] *ibid.* p. ix.
[28] *cf.* § 1.14.
[29] Apart from such provisions as compulsory purchase powers and planning legis-lation which are of general application.
[30] L.P.A. 1925, s.193; see further § 11.06.
[31] *ibid.* s.194; see further § 9.34.
[32] L.P.A. 1922, s.128, Sched. 12.
[33] Administration of Justice Act 1977; see further § 12.147.
[34] Royal Commission Report, *The Royal Warrant*, p. iii.
[35] *ibid.* paras. 404 *et seq.*

enacted to carry out the registration proposals allowing for registration of land, rights and ownership up to January 2, 1970.[36] After that date unregistered land and rights were deemed not to be common land and became unexercisable respectively. Periods, ending on July 31, 1972, were allowed for objections to any provisional registrations with disputes to be resolved by specially appointed and legally qualified Commons Commissioners. It seems that the number of disputes was expected to be of manageable proportions. In the event there were some 15,000 objections involving 30,000 individual disputes.[37] The first of the Commissioners commenced hearings in 1972 and between one and four have been sitting on a full-time basis ever since. It is difficult to assess how many disputes remain to be resolved but four counties are in the process of reconstituting their registers following procedural irregularities in the original registration.[38] At the time of writing one county has submitted only one major common dispute to the Commissioners for resolution and the inquiry into it is expected to continue until late in 1987. It seems that the Commissioners still have several years work before them. Apart from the protracted nature of dispute resolution the Act of 1965 has proved to be deficient in several respects, and has attracted adverse judicial comment. In a recent case Oliver L.J. felt constrained to remark that "this case reveals what I cannot but think is yet another most unsatisfactory state of affairs created by this Act which, if I may say so, is crying out for amendment. . . ."[39]

1.14   In spite of the delay in completing dispute resolution and the deficiencies in the Act of 1965 there have been movements towards a second stage of legislation. The Department of the Environment published an inter-departmental report in 1977 putting forward suggestions for consideration by interested parties.[40] In 1983 the Countryside Commission established an ad hoc committee, the Common Land Forum, including representatives of the parties legally interested in common land and those with amenity, recreational and institutional interests. The Forum reported in June 1986.[41] Finally, mention must be made of the Dartmoor Commons Act 1985,[42] which makes provision for the management of a very substantial area of common land in Devon. The effect of this Act is probably to take the land concerned outside any second stage of general commons legislation but it may also provide some insight into the form which further legislation may take.

1.15   In order to bring this comment on recent developments up to date it should perhaps be said that since the Royal Commission reported in 1958 there seems to have been a significant shift in public attitude towards the future use of common land. The report seemed to view improved management of

---

[36] See further § 2.02.
[37] H.C. Deb. 934 at 697 (1976–1977).
[38] Commons Registration (Cardiganshire) Act 1978 (c.cviii); Commons Registration (Glamorgan) Act 1983 (c. ix).
[39] *Corpus Christi College* v. *Gloucester County Council* [1983] 1 Q.B. 360 at 378.
[40] *Common Land, Preparations for Comprehensive Legislation,* Report of an Interdepartmental Working Party, 1975–1977, Department of the Environment (1978).
[41] *Common Land: The Report of the Common Land Forum,* Countryside Commission (1986), ref. CCP215.
[42] See further § 12.84.

common land as a means of ensuring better commercial use of the land, *i.e.* recognition of the value of the land as an agricultural and forestry resource. Today there seems to be more public and institutional support for the emphasis to be directed towards preservation of the land as a resource for amenity, recreational, landscape and habitat conservation purposes.

Physical nature and extent

Whether land is common land or one of the analogous classes of land will **1.16** depend upon its legal characteristics. It follows that the physical nature of the land has no bearing on its status.[43] Physical enclosure does not affect legal status nor does lack of enclosure necessarily imply that the land is common land. Nevertheless, much of the common land is unenclosed and of a wild and unkempt nature frequently providing a stark contrast with the contiguous enclosed land held in severalty.

The use of the land depends very much upon its particular location. In the **1.17** more remote upland areas, particularly in the north and west of England and in Wales, common land may be in continuous tracts running into thousands of acres. Usually in the uplands the traditional uses of common land, especially grazing by sheep and cattle, dominate. In this type of area, the grazing provided by the common lands supplements the limited amount of enclosed land available to the farming community. Without this shared use of open grazings many upland farms would cease to be economically viable and it is perhaps not untrue to say that where an upland system of agriculture is the only widespread indigenous industry the common lands not only assist the farming community but underpin the whole local economy. At the other extreme, in many parts of the country, particularly in the lowlands where the inclosure movement resulted in the total extinguishment of the old manorial system, common land is more typically an occasional piece of open and unused land or a village green. This class of land has its own value as a place for exercise and recreation or even as an interlude amongst bricks and mortar in an otherwise completely urbanised environment. On this type of land the traditional uses have totally ceased and new ones have taken their place. Between the two extremes there is an infinite variety of uses and combination of uses. It is perhaps more usual to find multiple use of land than not. Even the more remote upland commons are valued by many members of the general public as places of resort for peace and tranquility. It should not, however, be thought that there is any general right for the public to use common land or even enter it. All common land has an owner who may use it as he wishes subject only to any rights granted away to others and statutory control measures. A right of public access is available only on a minority of the common lands—estimated at perhaps one fifth of the total acreage.[44]

It is not possible to state with any degree of precision the area of common **1.18** land which exists nationally. Probably the best estimates available are still

---

[43] This is not entirely true in the case of waste land of a manor not subject to rights of common as a category of statutory common land: see § 2.36.

[44] Inter Departmental Working Party Report, para. 1.1.

those on which the Royal Commission based its report in 1958.[45] The Commission asked local authorities to provide an estimate of the common lands in their districts and although it is now clear that the returns were inaccurate in detail there is some empirical evidence that the overall estimate was neither an over- nor an under-estimate. The returns indicated that in 1958 there was a little over one million acres in England and a little under half a million acres in Wales.[46] Recently Aitchison and Hughes have carried out survey work on the land registered under the Act of 1965 in eight pre-1974 counties in Wales.[47] The Commission figures for these counties disclosed an estimated 280,000 acres while Aitchison and Hughes found 229,000 acres finally registered in the same counties with a further 67,000 acres still awaiting dispute resolution.[48] Unless all the disputes result in removal of the land from the registers the final total may well be in the region of the 280,000 acres originally estimated.

1.19 The figures for registered common land may, however, seriously underestimate the amount of land in shared agricultural use. Not all land in shared use was registrable for reasons which will be seen later.[49] In one survey carried out in the uplands the sample areas contained 24,434 acres of registered common land and a further 21,656 acres of shared use rough grazings which were not registered.[50]

1.20 As the use made of common land is diverse so is the geographical distribution. The largest areas, both in terms of size of unit and total for the locality, are found in the upland agricultural areas. The northern group of the pre-1974 counties of Cumberland, Westmorland, Lancashire, Northumberland, Durham and the North and West Ridings account for two thirds of all the common land in England with Cornwall, Devon and Somerset providing a further 13 per cent.[51] Wales, as we have already noticed, provides one third of all the common land in England and Wales. In some parts of Wales the proportion of common land to total land area is extraordinarily high—in the old county of Brecon, for example, 28.9 per cent. of the whole county was reported to be common land.[52]

1.21 Another feature of the common lands of considerable diversity is the size of the individual units. The Royal Commission Report gives figures of 4,515 separate units totalling 1,054,661 acres in England with 631 units involving 450,341 acres in Wales. The average size of unit in Wales is clearly much larger than it is in England.[53] In England the number of small units is very high. No less than 2,442 were reported as less than ten acres in size but

---

[45] Royal Commission Report, note the qualifications made about the figures collected at paras. 49 *et seq.*

[46] *ibid.* Table III, p. 25.

[47] Aitchison and Hughes, *The Common Lands of Wales* (1983).

[48] *ibid.* Tables 2b, 2c.

[49] See § 1.56.

[50] Sinclair, *The Upland Landscapes Study,* Environment Information Services (1983) summarised in *The Changing Uplands,* Countryside Commission (1983), p. 36.

[51] Royal Commission Report, para. 68.

[52] *ibid.* para. 67.

[53] *ibid.* para. 65.

accounted for only 0.7 per cent. of the total land area.[54] At the other end of the scale 855 units had an area of over 100 acres each, totalled over a million acres and accounted for 95 per cent. of the total acreage.[55] Perhaps even more significantly 75 per cent. of the total area was accounted for by 221 commons in units over 1,000 acres in extent,[56] and only 10 of these were in lowland areas. Of these ten only four were over 5,000 acres and these were all forest commons: the New Forest, Epping Forest, Ashdown Forest and the Forest of Dean.[57] The overall picture in England seems to be one of a large number of small commons, mostly of the village green type and size, with the majority of the commons of significant acreage mostly confined to the uplands of the north and west of the country, excepting, of course, the old Royal Forests.

The definition of common land

Until the enactment of the C.R.A. 1965[58] there was no statutory definition **1.22** of the term common land. No doubt in the fullness of time the new definition will become recognised as the main if not the only meaning. It suffers from the inherent disadvantage for the present purposes of including categories of land which the common law does not recognise as common land. Further the categories encompassed are totally different from those with which previous commons legislation was concerned. As the previous statutes have not been repealed, nor the common law rules relating to common land purportedly affected by the Act, it follows that for some time at least one has to live with the various common law and statute discreet terms available. In order to avoid excessive confusion this work will refer to land registrable under the 1965 Act as statutory common land.

In colloquial usage, and in many statutes, common land is often referred to **1.23** as "a common" and both terms are well understood as meaning land subject to rights of common. It is necessary in legal considerations, however, to recognise that the term "a common" has a biunial meaning. To the layman a common is the land, whereas to lawyers a common is the right exercisable over the land. Thus possessing a common would to the layman imply owning the land and to the lawyer owning a right over the land. The use of the word associated with rights is frequent in the older texts and law reports although less in use today. It is particularly important in dealing with older materials therefore to be aware of the distinction. The term "common land" is preferred when it is land subject to rights of common which is under consideration but where the context will allow without ambiguity, and it is self

---

[54] Royal Commission Report, para. 66.

[55] *Ibid.* para. 66.

[56] *ibid.* Table I, p. 20.

[57] *ibid.* para. 72; as to the status of the Forest of Dean, see Report of the Forest of Dean Committee 1958 (Cmnd. 686, 1959), para. 105; no owner or occupier within the Forest is entitled to rights of common; no prescription has been possible since 1634; sheep have been run on the Forest not by legal right but by sufferance of the Crown.

[58] See § 1.42 and Chap. 2.

evident that it is the land which is under consideration, the popular usage of "a common" is adopted.

1.24 The present section attempts to describe in outline the various classes of land which exist today and, as the classes concerned are related to, and sometimes dependent upon, the various types of rights which exist, an initial description of those rights is also included. For fuller explanations see Chapter 3.

1. Common law definitions

1.25 Just as until recently there was no statutory definition of common land there has also been no directly attributable common law meaning. Although the colloquial understanding is that it is land subject to rights of common the term is also used in a wider sense to indicate land which is subject to rights of a different nature but which involve use of the land in common. For present purposes the use of the term common land (or a common) is restricted to that class of land which is subject to true rights of common allocating other terms to land subject to distinguishably different rights.

1.26 The common lands as a whole may be divided conveniently into five broad categories dependent largely upon the type of rights exercisable over the land.

(a) Common land

1.27 Common land in a strict and narrow sense is land subject to rights of common. A right of common is one of the two main forms of right, known as *profits à prendre*, which allow the grantee to take some part of the land, the products of the land or the animals *ferae naturae* upon the land of another person.[59] An essential feature of a right of common is that some part of the benefit in the subject matter must remain vested in the owner of the soil, *i.e.* there is a community of use, or commonality, between owner and rights holders.[60] Where all such rights of common cease, whether by extinguishment, release to the owner of the soil or by unity of possession, the land will cease to be common land. A second feature of common land, required for the status to exist, is that at least one of the rights exercisable must be held for an interest equivalent to a fee simple.[61]

(b) Stinted pastures[62]

1.28 The second class of the common lands of most importance is the stinted pastures, which may be found anywhere in the country but are most widespread in the midlands and north of England. They may be distinguished from common land by the single feature that they are subject not to rights of common as described above but to the second main class of *profit à prendre*,

---

[59] *Beckett (Alfred F.)* v. *Lyons* [1967] Ch. 449 at 482, *per* Winn L.J.
[60] See §§ 3.09 *et seq.*
[61] See § 3.11.
[62] See § 1.59.

the sole or several right.[63] In practice the sole right may appear very similar to a right of common but may be distinguished therefrom by one factor—in the case of a sole right there is no community of use between owner of the soil and rights holder as the owner has granted away the entire benefit in the product leaving himself without any share.

(c) Common fields and intercommonage[64]

The third type of land, and one of much less areal significance than the two **1.29** preceding, is land originating in the common fields of the manorial system. It was, and still is in a few places, the practice in common fields for occupiers to take arable or hay crops from parts of the fields held in severalty with grazing in common in an open season when the land is bare of growing crops. This grazing is not a form of *profit à prendre* but is a matter of convenience between adjoining owners to avoid fencing the severalty strips. Such grazing, exercised by owners of land in common fields, is known in the present work by the term intercommonage. Sometimes the land is subject to rights of common or sole profits exercisable by persons with no land in the field. Thus, land of this class, distinguishable by use in severalty for part of the year, may or may not be common land for part of the year.

(d) Land held in undivided shares

Quite frequently, particularly in the north of England, land is encountered **1.30** with the apparent characteristics of a stinted pasture but which on closer examination is found to be owned by the graziers in undivided shares. The grazing entitlement is directly related to the share in ownership. The land is clearly not common land as any rights to graze are derived from ownership of the land and not from rights exercisable over the land of another person. The term used in the present work to describe this class of land is that it is a regulated pasture.[65]

(e) Land held in divided shares

Of a similar nature, but less frequently encountered in practice, is land held **1.31** in divided shares, *i.e.* each owner knows where his own land lies, but there is grazing in common by the owners over the whole.[66] This land is similar to the land described above as common fields with the distinguishing feature that the land is never used in severalty.

2. Some statutory definitions

As has been mentioned already there was no direct statutory definition of **1.32** common land until one was provided by the C.R.A. 1965. Nevertheless "commons" are defined in previous statutes although usually by reference to lands described for the purposes of inclosure in another Act. Occasionally entirely new and undefined expressions have occurred without explanation.

---

[63] See § 3.09.
[64] See § 1.63.
[65] See § 1.75.
[66] See § 1.74.

In the absence of subsequent judicial interpretation ascertaining the assigned meaning is more of an art than a science. In modern statutes there seems to be a tendency developing of relying on the definition in the C.R.A. 1965 which, as will be seen, has its own obscurities. This section considers in outline first the various definitions which are available. Later the Acts are noted, where there is no definition as such but which throw light on the classes of land concerned either by a physical description or by reference to the rights exercisable over the land.

(a) Land subject to be inclosed

1.33 The description of "land subject to be inclosed" described in section 11 of the Inclosure Act 1845, *i.e.* the land eligible for inclusion in an inclosure award, most nearly approximates to the land described in the present work as the common lands.[67] The categories are:

> "(a) all lands subject to any rights of common whatsoever, and whether such rights may be exercised or enjoyed at all times, or may be exercised or enjoyed only during limited times, season, or periods, or be subject to any suspension or restriction whatsoever in respect of the time of enjoyment thereof; . . .
>
> (b) . . . all gated and stinted pastures in which the property of the soil or some part thereof is in the owners of the cattle gates or other gates or stints, or any of them; . . .
>
> (c) . . . all gated and stinted pastures in which no part of the property of the soil is in the owners of the cattle gates or other gates or stints, or any of them; . . .
>
> (d) . . . all land held, occupied, or used in common, either at all times or during any time or season, or periodically, and either for all purposes or for any limited purpose, and whether the separate parcels of the several owners of the soil shall or shall not be known by metes or bounds or otherwise distinguishable; . . .
>
> (e) . . . all land in which the property or right of or to the vesture or herbage, or any part thereof, during the whole or any part of the year, or the property or right of or to the wood or underwood growing and to grow thereon, is separated from the property of the soil; . . .
>
> (f) . . . all lot meadows and other lands the occupation or enjoyment of the separate lots or parcels of which is subject to interchange among the respective owners in any known course of rotation or otherwise . . . "

As might be expected the categories of land correspond to those described already as existing under the common law. The first relates to common land as generally understood while making it clear that the Act applies to the land whether the rights are exercisable at all times of the year or part of the year only. The second and third categories are those described now as regulated and stinted pastures. The fourth is clearly intended to bring into scope

---

[67] With the exception of waste land of a manor not subject to rights of common which is wholly exceptional being a form of unincumbered freehold land which has been included as a statutory form of common land: see C.R.A. 1965, s.22(1).

all common fields which are held, used or occupied in common for all or part of the year whether the individual ownerships are divided or not. The final category makes certain that lot meadows and any analogous lands are included, although generally this type of land would also fall into category four. The fifth category of land described may also overlap the fourth where the land is used in common but additionally will apply where a sole right of vesture, herbage or underwood is held by one person to the exclusion of the owner of the soil. Vesture[68] is a right to take all the herbage on land including the underwood and, herbage[69] is the right to cut grass as well as graze it. A sole owner of vesture or herbage will be unusual today. A right to wood and underwood is a similar right related only to trees large and small and is thought to be now obsolete.

(b) Definitions of "commons"

In later statutes these tend to be by reference to land subject to be **1.34** inclosed under the Inclosure Acts which seems to indicate that all the categories of land included were seen at that time as at least being part of the common lands. The C.R.A. 1965 is an exception.[70]

(i) Metropolitan Commons Acts 1866–1898 The Metropolitan **1.35** Commons Act 1866, s.3 defined a "common" to mean any land subject to rights of common. This was clearly found to be inadequate and by section 2 of the Metropolitan Commons Amendment Act 1869 the words "and any land subject to be included under the provisions of the Inclosure Act 1845" were added. The word "included" almost certainly must be a mistake in substitution for "inclosed" if for no other reason than that *any* land could be included in an inclosure award whether subject to be inclosed or not.[71]

(ii) Commons Act 1876 This Act provides in section 37 that "a com- **1.36** mon means any land subject to be inclosed under the Inclosure Acts 1845 to 1868." This is a direct reference to section 11 of the 1845 Act for although the Act was amended several times the definition remained unchanged.[72]

(iii) Commons Act 1899 This Act provides in section 15 that "the **1.37** expression 'common' shall include all land subject to be inclosed under the Inclosure Acts 1845 to 1882, and any town or village green." The inclusion of town or village greens is to effect the purposes of the Act which are largely protective of the land for public use. It will be noticed that in this Act the definition is inclusive not exhaustive which opens the door to land which is not subject to be inclosed to be regulated under the Act. The purpose of this is possibly to ensure that land, which would have been generally regarded as a "common" because of its historical background but, which

---

[68] *cf.* § 3.92.
[69] *cf.* § 3.96.
[70] C.R.A. 1965, s.22(1) and see §§ 2.24 and 2.36.
[71] Inclosure Act 1845, s.86; Inclosure Act 1848, s.1.
[72] The Inclosure and Commons Acts of the nineteenth century have to be read together.

has ceased to be technically capable of inclosure due to the cessation of rights of common, may still be brought within the scope of the Act.[73]

1.38 **(iv) Commons Act 1908** The term is undefined in this Act and section 1(9) merely states that "the expression 'common' includes commonable land." This is the first use of the word "commonable" in the Commons Acts and it is suggested is a cautious attempt to prevent the word "common" being given only the narrow meaning of land subject to rights of common. Which land is covered by the Act is dealt with later.[74]

1.39 **(v) Law of Property Act 1925** Sections 193 and 194 of this Act provide for public access to all metropolitan commons and manorial wastes and commons situated in urban areas, and protect land subject to rights of common on January 1, 1926, from development, respectively. Metropolitan commons are well understood as those commons affected by the Metropolitan Commons Acts 1866–1898. Neither commons nor manorial waste are defined and the precise meanings are still matters for conjecture.[75]

(c) Earlier commons legislation still in force

1.40 In the earlier statutes definitions were unknown and the land affected is described by its physical nature or the use to which it is put. In the Commons Act 1285, which is concerned with the lord's right to remove land from common land status by the process known as approvement,[76] reference is made only to wastes, woods and pastures. The Inclosure Act 1773 is concerned with "the better cultivation, improvement and regulation of the Common Arable Fields, Wastes and Commons of Pasture" which sounds fairly extensive but there are no definitions and it is left to the description of rights to qualify the various provisions.

(d) Modern legislation

1.41 The definitions of common lands in modern statutes still tend to rely on the well used "land subject to be inclosed" of section 11 of the Inclosure Act 1845.[77] There are exceptions: in the Animals Act 1971, for example, in dealing with liability for livestock straying on to a highway, reduced responsibility is introduced for straying from common land with common land having the same meaning as in the C.R.A. 1965. This rather casual definition by reference to another Act may produce unexpected results particularly when the land may have lost all the attributes which justify special consideration.[78]

---

[73] Thus, land with amenity qualities which has technically ceased to be land subject to be inclosed may, providing the owner does not exercise his power of veto over the proposal, be brought within the Act.
[74] See § 12.77.
[75] See further §§ 11.10 and 11.11.
[76] For which see § 7.47.
[77] *e.g.* the Acquisition of Land Act 1981, s.19(4).
[78] See Animals Act 1971, s.8(2) and § 10.46; *cf.* also the Countryside Act 1968, s.9.

(e) Commons Registration Act 1965

The Act set out to establish public registers of common land (as defined in **1.42**
the Act), rights over it and its ownership. The land which is required to be
registered is land subject to rights of common and waste land of a manor
which is not subject to rights of common.[79] Further, rights of common were
expressed to include certain sole rights.[80] Thus, the previously understood
boundaries of the term common land were crossed in two respects. However, the wording of the Act does not appear to be sufficient to include all
the categories of land formerly understood as being land subject to be
inclosed.[81] Areas of doubt about the scope of land required to be registered
remain[82] and the Common Land Forum have formed the opinion that the
regulated pastures are not within the definition and, where registered, ought
to be removed.[83] Land registered under the Act is referred to in the present
work as statutory common land so as to distinguish it from the common
law meaning of common land.

CLASSIFICATION AND CHARACTERISTICS

This section considers in more detail a modern classification of the various **1.43**
types of common lands which exist and describes the characteristics of each
class. Within each class there may be sub-classes but each has a broadly
similar nature with its own distinctive legal rules. Identification of land as
being within a particular class should indicate immediately the nature of
the associated attributes and, the rights and obligations of the participators.
The classification suggested seems to be valid as judged by examination of a
significant sample of the registers maintained under the Act of 1965, and
the decisions of the Commons Commissioners but, local development or
corruption of particular practices may well have occurred. It follows that
identification of land as being in a particular class does not necessarily
imply that it will have all the characteristics which this analysis suggests
but, on the other hand, variation will be exceptional.

Preliminary considerations

1. Commonable land and rights

Several texts divide the common lands into common land and commonable **1.44**
lands, ascribing to the latter term the characteristic that it is land over
which rights of common are exercisable for part of the year only. While not
denying that such land is properly described as commonable it is suggested
that to use the term in this limited way as a class or sub-class of land is

---

[79] C.R.A. 1965, s.22(1).
[80] *ibid.*
[81] In particular no attempt was made to make it clear that land subject to the rights of
the owners of the land only were registrable.
[82] See the discussion at §§ 2.25 *et seq.*
[83] Common Land Forum Report, Appendix C., paras. 108 *et seq.*

misleading. It is not the way in which it is used in statutes and it has the awkward consequence that *any* type of land, used in common for part of the year only, may fall into the category irrespective of its other characteristics. Additionally, land will change its class as the holders of the rights over the land change their practices from time to time.

1.45   The use of the word commonable abounds in connection with common land. It seems to be used adjectivally to indicate land which is used in common but not necessarily through the medium of rights of common. For example, we find inclosure proposals described as relating to commonable lands (alternatively as applying to open fields) meaning that the land may be subject to rights of common but may also be subject to the right in common of intercommonage, *i.e.* rights between adjoining landowners.[84] It is used to describe animals which are capable of being grazed on a common.[85] Commonable houses or cottages are those with rights of common attached.[86] One statute refers directly to commonable rights when it is rights of common which are under consideration.[87]

1.46   The first statutory example of commonable land seems to be in the Inclosure Act 1854 which deals with compensation for the extinguishment of rights on common and commonable lands.[88] The Act considers two circumstances: where the extinction of commonable rights has taken place and for "lands being common lands, or in the nature thereof, the rights to the soil of which may have belonged to the commoners."[89] It is evident that common land, in this context, is not being used to describe land over which rights are exercisable for the whole of the year. The land concerned is defined by reference merely to the class of owners. Similarly, the term commonable is used in connection with rights exercisable over land owned by a person other than the commoners. It is difficult to escape the conclusion that, in this Act, commonable is used simply as an adjectival description of land and rights, which are, or may be, used in common. Once commonable is understood to mean pertaining to, or in the nature of, common all the statutory references are easily construed. It is unjustified to limit the use of the word commonable to land which is used in severalty for part of any year and problems are compounded if the word is used as a label to be attached to land which is not grazed for part of a year. In both cases the land will move from one class to another according to the practice in any particular year.

1.47   Similarly, commonable seems to have the same breadth of meaning in connection with rights. Under the provisions of the Land Clauses Consolidation Act 1845, the lord of the manor is entitled to compensation for his right in the soil and also for any other commonable or other rights to which he may be entitled.[90] Clearly in this context commonable is being used to describe rights which are not rights of common for none can exist in the

---

[84] See the annual reports of the Board of Agriculture up to 1920 on inclosures.

[85] *Standred* v. *Shorditch* (1620) Cro.Jac. 580, 79 E.R. 496.

[86] *e.g.* Bourne Inclosure Act 1766 (6 Geo. 3, c. iii): an allotment "equal to two cows for each commonable house and toftstead in the said towns."

[87] Copyhold Act 1894, s.22 and marginal note thereto.

[88] Inclosure Act 1854, s.17.

[89] *ibid.* s.15.

[90] Land Clauses Consolidation Act 1845, s.99.

lord. In this context, commonable means rights similar to rights of common, *i.e.* the quasi-rights associated with demesne or purchased freeholds, which are exercised in common with commoners. The other rights mentioned are those such as mineral or gaming rights.

It has to be concluded that commonable means no more than an association **1.48** with use in common and of a similar nature to common land or rights of common. Apart from considerations of classification the term commonable land is used directly for definition purposes in the Commons Act 1908. It is suggested later that it is unduly restrictive to view the term in that Act as applying only to land used for part of the year.[91]

2. Royal forests

In the past, the Royal Forests formed a distinct and entirely separate class of **1.49** common land with their own rules administered through special courts. Since general disafforestation[92] and local statutes which govern the main forests[93] there seems to be little, if any, difference in the way in which the common law now operates over former Forests. One extraordinary difference, hitherto of considerable importance, concerned the extent of rights beyond the normal manorial boundaries.[94] However, the Act of 1965 conclusively recorded the extent of all rights. Where there were differences of nature between ordinary common land and forest land these have now been resolved, and require no further recourse to common law or forestal rules.

Classification

It is convenient first to consider the common lands as falling into three distinct classes all of which are registrable as statutory common land under the Act of 1965. Afterwards we can examine certain other classes of land which may or may not be properly registrable as statutory land.

1. Statutory common land

Although the land now under consideration is termed statutory common **1.51** land it will be seen that it is not all common land within the strict meaning of being subject to rights of common. It is, however, all land which is used in common and the rights are exercisable by persons other than the owner of the soil. The classification now used is of long standing.[95] It is also in direct conformity with some, but not all, of the categories of land described as subject to be inclosed in the Inclosure Act 1845.[96]

[91] See § 12.77.
[92] Wild Creatures and Forest Laws Act 1971, especially s.1(2),(3),(5).
[93] New Forest Acts 1854, 1949, 1970; Epping Forest Acts 1878, 1880 (see also City of London (Various Powers) Act 1977); Ashdown Forest Act 1974.
[94] See *Commissioners of Sewers* v. *Glasse* (1874) L.R. 19 Eq. 134.
[95] This is recognisably described in Fitzherbert's *Surveying* (1523), ff. iii, iv.
[96] *cf.* at § 1.33.

(a) Wastes

1.52 There is no doubt that something in the order of 80 to 90 per cent. of the common lands[97] still in existence originated in waste land of the manors and, as such, is archetypal common land being subject to rights of common. Typically, the land is owned by the lord of the manor and is subject to the rights of successors in title to the original freeholders and copyholders of the manor. In many cases the land is still owned by the lord; in others it is his successor in title following alienation of the land or the manor. It matters little, except in the case of some statutory provisions,[98] whether the land is still owned by the lord and the rights and obligations of owner and commoner are similar in both circumstances.

1.53 Where the structure of the model arable manor was fully developed the picture of the lord's waste is correct. However, it should not be supposed that all the modern wastes originated in the same way. The rules applicable to the model manor are equally relevant to lands which are derived from, say, the *hafod à hendre* transhumance system of Wales or the sheep-corn husbandry systems of East Anglia.[99] The rules will apply to any land which has escaped inclosure and is subject to rights of common and any other land which has become subject to such rights by express or presumed grant.[1]

1.54 The typical waste will consist of an area of open land with rights of common exercisable by the owners or occupiers of enclosed land which most usually, but not necessarily, adjoins it. The rights of common exercised are almost invariably appurtenant to enclosed land but, may exist as rights in gross. Grazing rights, where appurtenant to land are usually limited by the principle of *levancy* and *couchancy*,[2] *i.e.* the quantity is limited to the needs of the dominant tenement, and are usually exercisable at all times of the year. There is no reason, in principle, why the quantum of rights of grazing may not have been granted for a fixed number of animals but on this class of land it seems almost unknown.[3] Although rights in gross are permissable over a waste they are wholly exceptional. The Commons Commissioners have consistently resisted registration of rights in gross where they have had jurisdiction.[4] On most of the wastes it seems that the cus-

[97] In the Royal Commission report at Table II, p. 22 stinted land is said to comprise 33 per cent. of the total, but it seems likely that included within this figure is a substantial proportion of wastes where the quantity of the rights were known. There seems to be no evidence as to the actual acreage of the stinted pastures—the figures in the text are a partially informed guess.

[98] *cf.* the role of the lord and other owners in management at § 7.73.

[99] *cf.* § 1.07, nn. 14 and 15.

[1] *e.g.* in parts of Dartmoor and Brecon the remains of old walling can be seen on land which has now reverted to waste; abandoned demesne land is part of the waste of the manor of Pennard in West Glamorgan: see manorial records reproduced by Francis and Baker in *A Survey of the Seignory or Lordship of Gower*, supplement to Cambrian Archaeological Association volumes for 1861–1870, p. 69.

[2] For which, see § 3.127.

[3] To establish the true nature of rights a distinction must always be made between rights granted for a fixed number and those which have become, by practice recognised, as for a certain number.

[4] *cf. Re The Black Mountain, Dinefwr, Dyfed* (1985) 272/D/441–777, 16 D.C.C. 219, *per* Cmr. Baden Fuller.

tomary obligation for landowners adjoining the waste to maintain their fences against the common applies.[5] This represents a reversal of the usual common law rule that an owner of animals is required to prevent them from straying. Rights of grazing over a waste may have been acquired by privilege of law,[6] express or presumed grant or, may originate from the customary rights of copyhold tenants. They may be appendant, appurtenant, held in gross or be *pur cause de vicinage*.[7] Rights of pasturage are the most importance in economic terms but other rights of common may exist for any of the products which the courts have found acceptable.[8]

One of the principle features of this class of land is that the owner of the soil **1.55** is entitled to any residue of a product which remains after the rights granted away have been satisfied.[9] Very occasionally this residual right has been removed by court decree as part of a settlement of disputes between owner and commoners.[10] The owner of the soil is also entitled to quasi-rights of common in respect of his demesne land and purchased freeholds. The quasi-rights are exercisable *pari passu* with true rights and are compensable upon inclosure or compulsory purchase of the common or part of it.[11] A peculiar feature of current legislation is that upon sale of land with which quasi-rights are exercised it is not possible to convert them into rights of common for an interest equivalent to a fee simple, although a grant of rights in common for a term of years is permissable. Indeed, one of the effects of the Act of 1965 is that no new grants of rights of common are possible over statutory common land.[12]

It seems that there is a considerable acreage of land which is waste land of a **1.56** manor and subject to rights in common but, which is not common land under statute or common law.[13] Prior to the abolition of copyhold tenure under the 1925 property legislation, it was possible for rights of common to be exercised by a lord's copyhold tenants as a matter of custom. However, similar rights exercised by tenants of the lord, holding under a lease or other tenancy, were not, and are not, recognised as being rights of common and it follows that such land is not common land under the common law in spite of identical physical nature and user characteristics.[14] It is not registrable land under the Act of 1965,[15] and has been held by a Commons Commissioner to be demesne land of the lord.[16]

---

[5] For the customary duty to fence against a common, see § 9.05.
[6] As appendant rights: see § 3.28.
[7] For rights of common classified by legal nature, see § 3.26.
[8] For rights of common classified by subject matter, see § 3.58.
[9] Co.Litt. 122a; *cf.* § 3.09.
[10] *e.g. De la Warr (Earl)* v. *Miles* (1881) L.R. 17 Ch.D. 535.
[11] *Musgrave* v. *Inclosure Commissioners* (1874) L.R. 9 Q.B. 162 especially 174–176, *per* Blackburn J.; *cf.* Inclosure Act 1845, s.76 and Land Clauses Consolidation Act 1845, s.99.
[12] See § 4.41.
[13] *cf.* survey cited in § 1.19, n. 50; see also land acquired by water authorities, *e.g.* Birmingham Corporation Water Act 1892 considered in *The Welsh Water Authority* v. *Clayden* (unreported) January 13, 1984, Ch.D.
[14] For further consideration see §§ 3.11 *et seq.*
[15] C.R.A. 1965, s.22(1): excludes from the definition of rights of common rights held for a term of years or from year to year.
[16] *Re Arden Great Moor, Arden, Yorks (N.R.)* (1977) 268/D/209, 6 D.C.C. 415.

1.57 If all the rights of common exercisable over a waste become vested in the owner of the soil, by abandonment or release, the land will cease to be common land but will not necessarily cease to be statutory common land.[17] Such land may also still be subject to other legislation affecting common land. In particular, sections 193 and 194 of the L.P.A. 1925[18] and the Metropolitan Commons Acts 1866–1878,[19] have continuing application.

1.58 One slightly anachronistic feature of the wastes is that if a holder of appurtenant rights of common purchases part of the waste his right is extinguished over the whole waste,[20] whereas if his right is appendant the right of common is apportioned.[21]

(b) Stinted pastures

1.59 Of respectable antiquity[22] and of analogous characteristics to wastes are the stinted pastures. Their origin lies either in an award effecting a statutory inclosure or in express grant by the owner of the soil for freehold or copyhold tenure. In theory acquisition by prescription is possible but the reported cases do not disclose a clear cut example. Where prescription has been successfully claimed it was more to do with proof of the right than acquisition by long user.[23] In all events, a right in gross may not be claimed under the Prescription Act 1832,[24] and, there are now substantial difficulties in the way of any form of prescription for all *profits à prendre*.[25]

1.60 The acreage concerned nationally is very much subservient to that of the wastes but is important in the midlands and north of England. Typically the stinted pasture is separated from other unenclosed land but is often of such scale that it is open land of itself. The distinctive feature of this class of land is that the rights exercisable are those of sole pasture and not rights of common,[26] that is to say the owner of the soil has no residual interest in the grazing. In legal terms, the land is subject to a sole profit and not a profit in common. The principle is that the whole of the grazing has been granted

---

[17] The land may then fall to registration as waste land of a manor not subject to rights of common: see § 2.71.

[18] *cf.* §§ 9.34 and 11.06.

[19] Metropolitan Commons Act, ss.4, 5 and the L.P.A. 1925, s.193 so far as it applies to metropolitan commons.

[20] See § 3.42.

[21] *ibid.* and see § 3.35.

[22] The earliest example encountered in the law reports is described in *R.* v. *Chamberlains of Alnwick* (1839) 9 Ad. & E. 444, 112 E.R. 1279; grant of grazing over a moor to burgesses and their heirs probably during the reign of Henry II but certainly no later than 1290 as evidenced by a deed.

[23] A prescription "time out of mind" was not so much a claim to acquisition by user as a statement that user was so prolonged that its origin need not be examined. The earlier cases on prescription for sole pastures were not concerned with whether the practice existed but whether such a practice could be justified at law; see for example *Potter* v. *North* (1669) 1 Wms.Saund. 346, 85 E.R. 503; *Hoskins* v. *Robins* (1671) 2 Wms.Saund. 324, 85 E.R. 1123.

[24] *Shuttleworth* v. *Le Fleming* (1865) 19 C.B. (N.S.) 687, 144 E.R. 956.

[25] The provisions of the C.R.A. 1965 effectively bar prescription over any land presently registered as common land: see § 4.57.

[26] *cf.* § 3.09.

away as a separate incorporeal hereditament, to one or more persons, which is divided into equal shares known as stints or some other local term, such as beastgates or cattlegates.[27] It seems that a grant of the whole of the product of land may not be created so as to be appurtenant to other land[28] and it follows that the rights over stinted pastures are, usually, held in gross. An exception may occur where the rights have been allotted under an inclosure award as appurtenant to houses, cottages, or toftsteads.[29]

The nature of the sole right of pasture being a divided and fixed share to part **1.61** of an incorporeal hereditament does not readily lend itself to quantification. It is self evidently variable according to the produce of the land available at any time. Nevertheless, most stints have a recognised value in numbers of livestock. In the simplest form a stint may be equivalent to, say, one head of cattle or it may be expressed in alternative classes of animals.

The presumption that adjoining landowners have a customary duty to fence **1.62** against the common does not apply to stinted pastures and the relevant inclosure award, if there is one, needs to be examined to ascertain where the duty lies.[30]

(c) Common fields

The final category into which statutory common land subject to rights may **1.63** be divided is concerned with land having its origin in the common or open fields of the manor. The archetypal arrangement was that each field was divided into strips of land, often as small as three-quarters of an acre each, with tenants of the manor holding and cropping the strips in severalty. After the crops had been harvested the whole field was thrown open for communal grazing in an "open" season. The system also existed as part of town systems, *i.e.* the rights to graze in the open season were vested in the corporation of a town for the benefit of the inhabitants, the freeholders or the burgesses. Many examples are apparent in the case reports.[31] A few seem to have survived to the present day albeit in a somewhat corrupted form.[32] However, as a class of the common lands, open fields today are more of a historical curiosity than an important part of agricultural practice but, where they exist, they are obviously of importance to the remaining participators.

It is clear from study of the Inclosure Commissioners reports that the sys- **1.64** tem survived in exactly the form described until the latter half of the nine-

---

[27] The terms used are not definitive. It is not unusual, for instance, to find wastes described as stinted commons either because the quantity of rights exercisable has become known or, alternatively, to describe land which is closed for part of the year.

[28] *cf.* § 3.17.

[29] See § 3.18 and notes thereto.

[30] See further § 9.28.

[31] *e.g. R. v. Churchill* (1825) 4 B. & C. 750, 107 E.R. 1240; *Johnson v. Barnes* (1872) L.R. 7 C.P. 592.

[32] *Re Swinemoor, Beverley (No. 4)* (1977) 264/D/3, 6 D.C.C. 287; *Re The Severn Ham, Tewkesbury* (1976) 213/D/29–32, 4 D.C.C. 352; *Re North Meadow Common, Sudbury* (1974) 35/D/14–27, 2 D.C.C. 490; *Corfe Common, Dorset.*

teenth century.[33] It is also evident from the same reports that the rights exercised during the open season might be:

(a) by the users of the severalty strips only;
(b) by persons without land in the fields only in which case the rights exercised are rights of sole pasture; or
(c) by both classes of persons together.

1.65 The mere fact that the land is used communally for part of the year will not necessarily create the conditions necessary for common land to exist. A right to graze in common by the owners of the severalty strips clearly arises as an incident of owning or, occupying, the land in the fields and if related to the acreage of land in severalty creates no additional "profit" to the occupier concerned. This right of grazing between adjoining occupiers is clearly distinguishable from rights of common and is referred to in the present work as intercommonage.[34] Whether, therefore, a common field is common land, in the narrow sense of being subject to rights of common, will depend upon whether persons without land in the fields have a right to graze in the open season.

1.66 Although the majority of the surviving common fields originate in the manorial or vill system, there was provision in the Inclosure Acts which allowed individual allotments to be laid together and distinguished by metes and bounds without the necessity of individual fencing.[35] Thus, a form of statutory common field is possible, with the same characteristic of communal grazing between owners, without any rights of common existing. There is a slight indication that some of this class of land still exists.[36] Where established under the Inclosure Act 1845, the land will usually be subject to a right in the severalty owners to enclose whenever they wish[37] and, pending enclosure the land may fall to be treated as a regulated pasture, *i.e.* certain statutory management provisions will apply.[38]

1.67 The rules controlling the use of common fields are inevitably different from those on wastes. The times when fields are open for grazing are a matter of custom and the case reports[39] and inclosure awards[40] indicate a wide variation of practices. Whatever the custom is, it is clear that the severalty

---

[33] A useful illustration is the provisional inclosure order report for certain parishes in Rutland and the East Riding of Yorkshire published as House of Commons Paper No. 282 (1877).

[34] The right between occupiers in common fields was referred to as a right of intercommonage in the major common field inclosure Act of 1836, s.1 (now repealed).

[35] Inclosure (Consolidation) Act 1801, s.13; Inclosure Act 1836, s.27; Inclosure Act 1845, s.80.

[36] *semble Re Tenants Meadow, Duddon, Cumbria* (1975) 262/D/4–7, 3 D.C.C. 214; *Re East Stainmore Regulated Pasture, North Moor, Stainmore* (1986) 262/U/581, 17 D.C.C. 50.

[37] Inclosure Act 1857, s.1.

[38] *ibid.* s.2: applies Inclosure Act 1845, ss.113–120.

[39] *cf. How* v. *Strode* (1765) 2 Wils.K.B. 269, 95 E.R. 804; *Whiteman* v. *King* (1791) 2 H.Bl. 4, 126 E.R. 397; *Hardy* v. *Hollyday* (1792) cited at 4 T.R. 718, 100 E.R. 1264.

[40] *cf.* inclosure order report cited in n. 33.

occupiers may not depart from it so as to defeat the grazing rights.[41] Unlike the rule over wastes where rights are usually appurtenant to dominant land a right of intercommonage is quantified in relation to the land held in the field.[42] This is much as might be expected as intercommonage is an incident of land ownership and occupation.

The presumption that adjoining landowners have a customary duty to fence **1.68** against a waste will almost certainly not apply to common fields. In fact the duty is likely to be firmly on the users of the field to maintain their boundary fences.[43] In Inclosure Acts it is assumed always to be the duty of common field proprietors to fence against what would at the time have been the adjoining wastes.[44]

At this date there is no compelling reason why rights in common fields **1.69** should take precisely the form described. For example, the strips may have been engrossed and enclosed in which case the system will consist of one person using the land in severalty for part of the year with other persons using the land in common in the open season either as rights of common or rights of sole pasture. Another possibility is that the right to use in severalty has been granted as or, has become, a right (known as vesture or herbage[45]), to take all the produce of the land owned by another person. This might be for the entire year or for part only with rights of common or sole rights exercised by others in the open season. A further possibility, which does exist today, is the lot meadow or shifting fee simple where the severalty owners draw lots each year to discover which strips they are to use in that year.[46] Finally, Coke draws attention to the possibility of land being in different several ownership for different parts of the year.[47] Commons Commissioners have found this situation to exist in some cases.[48]

(i) Shack or half year land A common field used for arable cropping **1.70** for half the year and for grazing in common for the remainder is frequently referred to as shack land or, half year land. The first fully reported case on this class of land was *Sir Miles Corbet's Case* (1585)[49] from which the Norfolk term shack is taken. The question before the court was whether the owners in an arable field were entitled to fence their severalties and so put an end to the "common of shack." It was noticed that this type of common, although "in the beginning was but in the nature of a feeding because of

---

[41] *Bruerton* v. *Right* (1672) 1 Freem. 51, 89 E.R. 40: turnips may not be sown; *Anon.* (1702) 12 Mod. 648, 88 E.R. 1578: to plant peas is a "trick."

[42] *Cheesman* v. *Hardham* (1818) 1 B. & Ald. 706 at 712, 106 E.R. 260 at 262, *per* Bayley J. (correcting *Comyn's Digest*, Common E).

[43] See further § 9.28.

[44] Inclosure (Consolidation) Act 1801, s.27.

[45] See §§ 3.92 and 3.96.

[46] *Re Pixey Mead, Gosford and Water Eaton and Yarnton or West Mead, Yarnton, Oxfordshire* (1972) 29/D/5–13, 1 D.C.C. 91; *cf.* Farrer, "Moveable Fee Simple. Lot Meadows" (1936) 1 Conv. 53; Joshua Williams, pp. 90 *et seq.*

[47] Co.Litt. 4a, 165a.

[48] *Re the "open fields" in Chagford, West Devon D., Devon* (1985) 209/D/343–344, 16 D.C.C. 8; *Re the Holmes, the Pound and Broadheath, Shenstone, Staffs* (1982) 233/D/15–19, 13 D.C.C. 461.

[49] (1585) 7 Co.Rep. 5a, 77 E.R. 417.

vicinage for avoiding a suit"[50] had by custom evolved into a right of common appendant or appurtenant with inhabitants of the town grazing the land when uncropped. It was held that the custom of the place must be observed: if there was a custom to inclose into severalty the shack was abolished on the part of the incloser as well as the other owners in the field; if persons with no land in the field had rights of common of shack then there could be no inclosure so as to effect those rights.

1.71 The principle of the right to inclose seems to apply today. Subsequent cases reaffirmed it[51] and the right is expressly preserved in the Inclosure Acts 1773[52] and 1857.[53] If a person incloses part of his land within the field he forthwith deprives himself of any right to graze over the remainder.[54]

1.72 **(ii) Common meadows** The practice on common meadows is use in severalty during the hay growing and harvesting season with grazing in common either by the severalty owners or, others without land in the field, in an open season. The open season frequently commences on Lammas Day, August 12,[55] with the land known as Lammas land or Lammas meadows. In general terms the same conditions and qualifications apply to common meadows as apply to shack land. In practice common meadows are more frequently encountered than land in arable and there are several examples apparent following registration.[56] In addition the lot meadow, or shifting fee simple, still exists.[57]

1.73 *Fitzherbert's Surveying* describes another form of common field where "catell gothe daylye before the herdeman"[58] which seems to be a recognition of a form of common pasture. The practice no longer exists and any land of this class will long have been subsumed into the category of wastes or stinted pastures.

2. Analogous lands

1.74 **(i) Common fields** It has been demonstrated that common fields of arable land and meadow may be subject only to the rights of intercommonage exercisable between owners of contiguous unfenced lands. The rights so exercisable are incidents of the ownership of the land and are in the nature of an agreement between the participants not to sue in trespass. There is no substantive right to take part of the produce of another person's land and a

---

[50] (1585) 7 Co.Rep. 5a, 77 E.R. 418.

[51] *Sir William Hickman* v. *Thorne* (1676) 2 Mod. 104, 86 E.R. 967; *Barker* v. *Dixon* (1743) 1 Wils.K.B. 44, 95 E.R. 483; *Cheesman* v. *Hardham* (1818) 1 B. & Ald. 706 at 710, 106 E.R. 260 at 261, *per* Bayley J.

[52] See s.27.

[53] See s.1, proviso.

[54] *How* v. *Strode* (1765) 2 Wils.K.B. 269 at 274, 95 E.R. 804 at 807 *per curiam.*

[55] August 12 is the "natural day" for Lammas Day instead of August 1 following the change of calendar: Calendar (New Style) Act 1750 (24 Geo. 2, c. 23), s.5.

[56] *e.g. Re Wick Moor, Stogursey, Somerset* (1976) 232/D/19–48, 5 D.C.C. 280; *Re North Ham, etc., Somerset (No. 1)* (1983) 232/D/294, 14 D.C.C. 265.

[57] See § 1.69, n. 46.

[58] *Fitzherbert's Surveying* at f.iii.

right of intercommonage is clearly distinguishable from a right of common. Land of this class may, therefore, be treated as part of the common lands, because of user in common, but is not, in strict terms, common land.

(ii) Regulated pastures Of a similar nature to the stinted pastures **1.75**
described above[59] are the regulated pastures. The land is used in common by a number of persons each with a fixed right to graze a certain number of animals. The distinguishing feature of this class of land is that the graziers own the land, over which the grazing takes place, in undivided shares. The grazing is directly related to the share which each person has in the land ownership. The origin of a regulated pasture may lie in a grant of the land to a number of persons.[60] More frequently it is the product of an inclosure award. It was recognised in statutory inclosure that allotments to some persons were so small as to make it far too expensive to enclose each plot. Under these circumstances provision was made for the small allotments to be thrown together without internal fencing and for the land to be grazed in common.[61] In some of the earlier awards it was unclear whether the allottees held their rights under the lord, *i.e.* the award was for a sole pasture, or, alternatively, they had been allotted the land in fee simple.[62] Whether title to the land was granted with the right to graze under an award can only be established by examination of the award.

Similarly, powers of managing the allotted pastures vary according to the **1.76**
particular award.[63] In an award since the enactment of the Inclosure Act 1845, a regulated pasture will be subject to standard management provisions.[64] Additionally, as we have seen,[65] certain common fields may be treated as though they are pastures regulated under the Act of 1845 pending inclosure into severalty. Where land is a regulated pasture under the Act of 1845 and is subject to the standard management provisions, it is distinguished in the present work from those in earlier awards by referring to it as a statutory regulated pasture.

Since 1925 it has not been possible to hold the legal estate to land in undi- **1.77**
vided shares[66] and in all cases of regulated pastures the legal estate must now be held by trustees or, more usually, the Public Trustee.[67]

A substantial number of regulated pastures exist and a high proportion of **1.78**
them have been registered as statutory common land. As the land is clearly

---

[59] See § 1.59.

[60] *e.g.* Langfield Moor, West Yorkshire.

[61] *cf.* § 1.66, n. 35.

[62] For instance, ever since an award affecting the Great Forest of Brecknock, under provisions contained in the Brecknock Forest Acts 1815 and 1818, there has been dispute as to the ownership of allotments. It cannot be said, even today, that the successors in title to the original allottees are entirely satisfied.

[63] *cf. Paine & Co.* v. *St. Neots Gas and Coke Co.* [1938] 4 All E.R. 592; [1939] 3 All E.R. 812 at 821: powers of allottees to sell sand and gravel (the rights granted by the award are described as "154 common rights or shares of common" and it is unclear whether it is a stinted or a regulated pasture).

[64] Inclosure Act 1845, ss.113–120.

[65] See § 1.66.

[66] L.P.A. 1925, ss.1(6), 34(1), 39.

[67] L.P.A. 1925, Sched. 1, Pts. IV and V; see further § 7.87–8.

not subject to rights of common, any right to graze being derived from the ownership of the land, there is some doubt as to whether this land is registrable.[68] The Commons Forum has recommended that all regulated pastures should be removed from the commons registers.[69]

1.79   The characteristics of a regulated pasture are generally as described but, exceptionally, may also be subject to rights of common in addition to the rights of the owners.[70] In this event the pasture is of a hybrid nature being substantially subject to the rights to graze of the beneficial owners but also subject to subsidiary and collateral rights of common for other products of the land.

1.80   **(iii) Manorial wastes**   Manorial waste which has ceased to be subject to rights of common is self-evidently not common land. However, it has to be treated as part of the common lands because much of it (but, as will be seen, not all of it) is registrable as statutory common land.[71] Further, whether registered as statutory common land or not some manorial waste is subject to other legislation affecting common land.[72]

1.81   **(iv) Wastes subject to the rights of termors, tenants and licensees**   Attention has been drawn already to this class of land which is viewed neither as common land under the common law nor as statutory common land.[73] The acreage is substantial and includes land held under statute by water authorities.[74] The land and, the rights exercised over it, is very similar in nature to common land and in some cases at least is subject to a right of public access.[75]

1.82   **(v) Sheepheaves**   *Cooke's Inclosures* describes a class of land known as sheepheaves.[76] It is thought that Cooke was referring to a type of right, which is considered later,[77] and that he was mistaken in believing that land of this class ever existed as a form of common land.

---

[68] *cf.* §§ 2.27 *et seq.*

[69] Common Land Forum Report, Appendix C, § 113.

[70] See § 2.32 and n. 66.

[71] See § 2.36.

[72] Especially the L.P.A. 1925, s.193 for which see § 11.06.

[73] See § 1.56; see further § 3.11.

[74] *e.g.* 45,000 acres near Rhayader in mid-Wales held by the Welsh Water Authority by virtue of the Birmingham Corporation Water Act 1892.

[75] *e.g.* Birmingham Corporation Water Act 1892, s.53; Langfield Moor, West Yorkshire may be subject to a right of public access dependent upon the interpretation of s.193 of the L.P.A. 1925: *cf.* §§ 11.11–11.12.

[76] Cooke, p. 44.

[77] See § 3.119.

2. Common Land Registration

The Commons Registration Act 1965 ("C.R.A. 1965") requires that all common land and town or village greens, as defined in the Act, shall be registered, together with rights exercisable over the land and a record of its ownership. There was a period for registration between 1967 and 1970 which was mandatory to the extent that any land unregistered after the period, and capable of being registered, ceased to be common land or a town or village green. There is, nevertheless, a continuing requirement to register common land and town or village greens and the Act makes provision for land which becomes registrable land after the mandatory registration period. The two classes of land, common land and town or village greens, are not necessarily mutually exclusive as greens may be subject to rights of common and thus common land in the sight of the common law.[1] In this Chapter only common land, registrable as such, is considered with greens,[2] rights[3] and ownership[4] receiving separate treatment.

2.01

The registration procedure

(i) Registrable land   Section 1(1) of the C.R.A. 1965 provides: **2.02**

"There shall be registered, in accordance with the provisions of this Act and subject to the exceptions mentioned therein,—
(a) land in England or Wales which is common land or a town or village green; . . . "

Common land is defined in section 22(1):

"In this Act unless the context otherwise requires 'common land' means—
(a) land subject to rights of common (as defined in this Act) whether those rights are exercisable at all times or only during limited periods;

---

[1] ss.1(1)(b), 4(1) envisage rights of common being registered over a town or village green in spite of greens being excluded from the definition of common land: s.22(1). Thus, after registration, land which is conclusively not common land may be conclusively subject to rights of common.

[2] See §§ 13.18 *et seq.*

[3] See §§ 4.01 *et seq.*

[4] See §§ 7.33 *et seq.*

(b) waste land of a manor not subject to rights of common;
but does not include a town or village green or any land which forms
part of a highway; . . . "

The same sub-section includes the following further definitions:

" 'land' includes land covered with water; . . .
'rights of common' includes cattlegates or beastgates (by whatever
name known) and rights of sole or several vesture or herbage or of sole
or several pasture, but does not include rights held for a term of years or
from year to year; . . . "

2.03   **(ii) Exempted land**   The provisions for registration do not apply to the
New Forest, Epping Forest, the Forest of Dean[5] nor to any land exempted
from the provisions by order of the Minister.[6] The Minister was not empowered to make such an order unless the land was already regulated under the
Commons Acts 1876 and 1899, the Metropolitan Commons Acts 1866 to
1898 or a local Act, no rights of common had been exercised over the land
for at least 30 years and the owner of the land was known.[7] The power to
make exemption orders has now expired.[8] One application for exemption,
in respect of land regulated under the Metropolitan Commons Acts, was not
approved and the land also failed to achieve registration under the C.R.A.
1965.[9] All exempted land is required to be marked on the register maps.[10]

2.04   **(iii) Non-registration**   The effect of land not achieving registration is
described in section 1(2)(a) of the Act:

"After the end of such period, not being less than three years from the
commencement of this Act,[11] as the Minister may by order determine—
(a) no land capable of being registered under this Act shall be deemed
to be common land or a town or village green unless it is so registered; . . . "

2.05   **(iv) Registration periods**   Two separate periods for application for
registration were prescribed by Regulation and followed by periods allowing
for objection to provisional registrations:[12]

---

[5] The New Forest and Epping Forest are regulated under local statutes: see § 1.49
and n. 93 thereto. The Forest of Dean probably includes no common land: see
§ 1.21 and n. 57 thereto.
[6] s.11 of the C.R.A. 1965; for the list of 21 exemption orders made see Appendix 2.
[7] The Commons Registration (Exempted Land) Regulations 1965, (S.I. 1965
No. 2001).
[8] Expired October 1, 1966.
[9] See case cited at § 2.51 and n. 12 thereto.
[10] Commons Registration (General) Regulations 1966, (S.I. 1966 No. 1471),
reg. 16(5)(a).
[11] July 31, 1970: Commons Registration (Time Limits) Order 1966, (S.I. 1966
No. 1470), art. 2 as amended by the Commons Registration (Time Limits) (Amendment) Order 1970 (S.I. 1970 No. 383), art. 2.
[12] S.I. 1966 No. 1471, reg. 5; Commons Registration (Objections and Maps) Regulations 1968 (S.I. 1968 No. 989), reg. 4.

Application periods	Objection periods
(i) January 2, 1967—June 30, 1968	October 1, 1968—September 30, 1970
(ii) July 1, 1968—January 2, 1970	May 1, 1970—July 31, 1972

Registration authorities were required to register applications by July 31, 1970[13] and, as they were empowered to register on their own initiative,[14] it follows that registration of land without application, and after the closing date for applications, was possible between January 3, and July 31, 1970.

(v) Withdrawal of applications   Section 5(6) of the Act provides that **2.06** where an objection is made to a registration then, unless the objection is withdrawn or the registration cancelled before the end of such period as may be prescribed, the registration authority shall refer the matter to a Commons Commissioner for resolution.[15] The periods prescribed ended on December 17, 1971, and July 31, 1973 for first and second period objections respectively.[16]

(vi) Finality of registrations   Section 7 of the Act provides that, **2.07** where no objection to registration is made or, if all objections are withdrawn, at the end of the objection period or, at the date of withdrawal of an objection as the case may be, the registration shall become final. The earliest date for finality is, therefore, October 1, 1970. The effect of finality of registration of land is that there is conclusive evidence of the matters registered as at the date of registration.[17]

(vii) Land which becomes common land   Section 13(b) of the Act **2.08** makes provision for registration of any land which becomes common land or a town or village green after January 2, 1970.[18]

(viii) Registration authorities   The registration authorities for the **2.09** purposes of the Act were the councils of the county or county borough in which the land is situated or, in relation to any land in Greater London, the Greater London Council.[19] The duties under the Act were transferred to the new county councils following local government re-organisation in 1974[20] and, since the abolition of the metropolitan counties, the council of the metropolitan district or the council of the London borough in which the land is situated.[21] Where part of the land is in the area of one authority and

---

[13] See n. 11.

[14] s.4(2)(a) of the C.R.A. 1965.

[15] For referral procedure see the Commons Commissioners Regulations 1971, (S.I. 1971 No. 1727), regs. 8, 9.

[16] S.I. 1971 No. 1727, reg. 6; Commons Registration (Second Period References) Regulations 1973 (S.I. 1973 No. 815), reg. 2.

[17] s.10 of the C.R.A 1965.

[18] cf. § 2.56.

[19] s.2(1) of the C.R.A. 1965.

[20] Local Government Act 1972, Sched. 30.

[21] Local Government Act 1985, s.16; Sched. 8, para. 10(6).

part in another, the authorities may by agreement provide for one only to be the registration authority for the whole of the land.[22]

Duties of registration authorities

2.10   The primary duty of a registration authority is to maintain registers and related maps of (a) common land and, (b) town and village greens. The registers shall be open to inspection by the public at all reasonable times.[23]

1. Applications for registration

2.11   To effect the initial registration procedure the authorities were required to register any land as common land or a town or village green upon an application by any person, if accompanied by a declaration in a prescribed form.[24] The procedure to be followed by the authorities and the forms the registers must take, are prescribed primarily in the Commons Registration (General) Regulations 1966.[25] Upon receipt of an application for the registration of land, or one for rights over land, a registration authority was required to open a register for that unit of land (referred to as a C.L unit or a V.G unit as appropriate) divided into three parts: land, rights and ownership.[26] As the authorities were required to open a new register unit for each application, unless it related to land already registered and, remembering that any person could make an application, it is not surprising to find that, in the case of some registrations, the registered C.L units bear little relationship to the pre-existing common land areas. There are examples of amalgamation of commons and, more frequently, extensive fragmentation. The result is complexity and, in connection with rights, a not inconsiderable amount of confusion.[27]

2.12   Following commencement orders[28] and regulations relating to advance publicity about the Act,[29] the authorities were under a duty to give public notice through local newspapers at other stages in the procedure.[30] There

---

[22] s.2(2) of the Act; *cf.* Commons Registration (Publicity) Regulations 1966 (S.I. 1966 No. 972), reg. 4. This was not always done and there is at least one example of duplicated registrations in adjoining registration areas.

[23] s.3(2) of the C.R.A. 1965.

[24] s.4(2) of the C.R.A. 1965: note that any person could make an application based on a declaration that he believed the land to be common land. It was not necessary to have any legal interest in the land.

[25] S.I. 1966 No. 1471, Pts. II and III, Sched. 1 and 2.

[26] See reg. 4 and especially reg. 10(2).

[27] *cf.* §§ 4.26 *et seq.*

[28] The Commons Registration Act 1965 (Commencement No. 1) Order 1965 (S.I. 1965 No. 2000) (C. 22): ss.2(2) and 11; Commons Registration Act 1965 (Commencement No. 2) Order 1966 (S.I. 1966 No. 971) (C. 7): remainder.

[29] The Commons Registration (Publicity) Regulations 1966 (S.I. 1966 No. 972).

[30] The Commons Registration (Objections and Maps) Regulations 1968 (S.I. 1968 No. 989), reg. 3; Commons Registration (Objection and Maps) (Amendment) Regulations 1970 (S.I. 1970 No. 384); Commons Commissioners Regulations 1971 (S.I. 1971 No. 1727), reg. 11.

was however, no requirement to notify an owner or occupier of land directly that his land had been registered. The initial, mandatory, procedure has been long completed,[31] the final date for registration being July 31, 1970.

Where the procedure was not followed correctly the courts may intervene. **2.13** For example, under section 7 of the C.R.A. 1965, in the absence of any objection to a provisional registration, land became finally registered but only after public notice of the registration had been given.[32] For section 7 to take effect the registration authority must comply substantially with the regulations concerning notice. In *Smith* v. *East Sussex County Council* (1977)[33] the land concerned had been described inadequately in the required public notice. The plaintiff was awarded a declaration that the land had not become final. In *Pile* v. *Gwynnedd County Council* (1982)[34] the registration authority amended the register believing that the land was double-registered. The agent to the owners had objected to the deleted registration but not the one which remained substantive. The court awarded a declaration that the substantive registration had not become final for lack of objection and, ordered the registers to be amended.

If an authority has failed to conform with the procedural requirements in **2.14** the prescribed form it may be necessary to seek an amending Act to enable the reconstitution of the registers. This has happened on two occasions and involves several counties.[35]

The Commons Commissioners commenced hearing disputes in 1972 and in **2.15** the early years the registration authorities' main duty was to prepare and refer each dispute to the Commissioners.[36] Following a Commissioner's decision it is the duty of the authority to amend the registers in accordance with the decision.[37] It will be many years before all authorities have completed these two stages.[38]

2. Amendments to the registers

(a) Limited powers of amendment

Following the expiration of the objection and withdrawal periods,[39] the **2.16** duties of the authorities remain substantial but powers to amend the registers are strictly circumscribed. In particular, an authority may not amend to

[31] *cf.* §§ 2.05, 2.06.
[32] S.I. 1968 No. 989, reg. 3.
[33] (1977) 76 L.G.R. 332.
[34] (1982) Lexis, Enggen Library, Cases.
[35] Commons Registration (Cardiganshire) Act 1978, (c. viii); Commons Registration (Glamorgan) Act 1983, (c. ix).
[36] s.4(6) of the C.R.A. 1965; S.I. 1971 No. 1727, regs. 8, 9.
[37] s.6(2) of the C.R.A. 1965; S.I. 1971 No. 1727, reg. 32; Commons Registration (Disposal of Disputed Registrations) Regulations 1972 S.I. 1972 No. 437, regs. 3, 4.
[38] Aitchison, Hughes and Masters, *The Common Lands of England and Wales* (unpublished report to the Countryside Commission, 1984), p. 16: five years for the Devon authority to complete recording of Commissioners' decisions. West Glamorgan, by the beginning of 1987, had only its first hearing in progress.
[39] See §§ 2.05, 2.06.

correct clerical errors or omissions. Such a power did exist during the initial registration procedure but it expired once registrations became final or, fell to be referred to a Commons Commissioner.[40] An authority may amend a register or, open a new register, when land ceases to be or, becomes common land.[41] In addition the registers of rights may be amended when rights have been apportioned, extinguished, released, varied or transferred.[42]

(b) Notification by Chief Land Registrar

2.17 If the Chief Land Registrar notifies an authority that the title to the land has been registered under the Land Registration Acts 1925 and 1936 the authority is required to amend the ownership section of a register to show the event including, if there is an owner already registered, deletion of that owner's entry.[43]

(c) Order of the court

2.18 Under strictly limited circumstances an authority may be ordered by the court to rectify the register. Section 14 of the C.R.A. 1965 provides that—

"The High Court may order a register maintained under this Act to be amended if—
(a) the registration under this Act of any land or rights of common has become final and the court is satisfied that any person was induced by fraud to withdraw an objection to the registration or to refrain from making such an objection; or
(b) the register has been amended in pursuance of section 13 of this Act and it appears to the court that no amendment or a different amendment ought to have been made and that the error cannot be corrected in pursuance of regulations made under this Act[44];
and, in either case, the court deems it just to rectify the register."

(d) Amendment of addresses

2.19 The addresses of certain applicants for rights and ownership may be amended upon application to an authority.[45] The regulation applies to:
(a) any person registered as owner;
(b) where the registration of the land is provisional, any applicant for registration of the land or any person whose application has been noted under section 4(4) of the Act [second registration of the same land];
(c) where a right of common is registered, any person interested in the right, and, where the registration is provisional, the person on whose application the entry was made and any person whose appli-

[40] S.I. 1966 No. 1471, reg. 36.
[41] s.13(a), (b) of the C.R.A. 1965; see §§ 2.56 and 2.66.
[42] s.13(c) of the C.R.A. 1965; see § 4.79–4.86.
[43] s.12(b) of the C.R.A. 1965; see § 7.42–7.44.
[44] The only power to amend contained in Regulations has now expired: S.I. 1966 No. 1471, reg. 36.
[45] S.I. 1966 No. 1471, reg. 26.

cation is noted under regulation 9(5) [second application for the same right].

The Regulations are notable for their omissions. Where the ownership of land changes, other than upon sale, the ownership entry may not be changed. Similarly where a dominant tenement with appurtenant rights changes hands, whether by sale or otherwise, there is no provision for changing the name of the apparent rights owner.[46] It is otherwise in the case of an apportioned dominant tenement or the transfer of a right in gross, but the result of the omissions is that most ownership and rights sections of the registers now seem remarkably out of date.

3. Notes on the registers of matters affecting the public

Regulations provide for certain matters affecting the public to be entered as notes to the land sections of the registers.[47] The Regulations are permissive, the matters entered are not among those required to be registered, and an entry has no legal effect. **2.20**

The following matters may be entered as notes: **2.21**

(a) The registration authority, without application, or, the persons charged by law with the management or regulation of registered land, may apply for an entry to the effect that the land is regulated under Part I of the Commons Act 1899, the Metropolitan Commons Acts 1866–1898, a local Act regulating the land, or a provisional order confirmation Act made under the Commons Act 1876.[48]

(b) The owner of any part of the land, a person appearing to have a right of common, or, in the case of land any part of which belongs to a vacant ecclesiastical benefice, the Church Commissioners may apply for an entry noting the existence of an "Order of Limitations" made under the provisions in section 193 of the L.P.A. 1925.[49]

(c) Where any land is held for charitable purposes the owner of the land or trustees of the charity may apply for an entry noting that matter.[50]

(d) A person claiming to be entitled to certain rights or interests in the land may apply for his interest to be noted. The rights and interests concerned are easements, *profits à prendre* other than rights of common, franchises, rights of the lord of the manor other than ownership, mineral rights where severed from the ownership of the

---

[46] The apparent rights owner because an applicant for rights could be the owner or the tenant or both acting jointly or, where the right belongs to an ecclesiastical benefice of the Church of England which is vacant, the Church Commissioners or, any person otherwise entitled to make an application under the Act: S.I. 1966 No. 1471, reg. 7(2) as amended by the Commons Registration (General) (Amendment) Regulations 1968 (S.I. 1968 No. 658), Sched., reg. 7.

[47] S.I. 1966 No. 1471, regs. 22–24.

[48] *ibid.* regs. 22(2)(a), (b), (c), (3).

[49] *ibid.* reg. 22(2)(d), (3); for orders of limitation, see § 11.26.

[50] *ibid.* reg. 23.

surface and rights of lessees or licensees in any mineral lease or licence, and rights acquired by statutory undertakings.[51]

2.22 A registration authority may cancel an entry of a note if it is satisfied on reasonable grounds that the matter to which it refers is no longer subsisting.[52]

4. Searches and copies of the registers

2.23 A statutory search of the registers may be requisitioned by any person, or his solicitor. The official search certificate issued is conclusive as at the date of issue.[53] The requisition must be made in standard form, accompanied by an appropriate map and is subject to a statutory fee.[54] In addition any person may obtain, on the payment of a fee, a certified copy of, or extract from, the register or any part of it or, the maps of a register unit.[55]

The land registrable

2.24 The C.R.A. 1965 crossed the previously understood boundaries of the term common land in two respects: first, the expression rights of common was given an extended meaning and secondly, land not subject to any rights was included.

1. Land subject to rights of common

2.25 Under section 22(1) "common land means land subject to rights of common (as defined in this Act) whether those rights are exercisable at all times or only during limited periods." Ignoring the words in parenthesis the definition is one well understood by the common law and it is clear that waste land whether subject to rights of common at all times or for limited periods is included together with common fields which are subject to rights of common, *i.e.* rights exercisable by persons without land in the fields.[56]

2.26 However, in the Act the expression rights of common is given an extended meaning to include "cattlegates or beastgates (by whatever name known) and rights of sole or several vesture or herbage or of sole or several pasture, but does not include rights held for a term of years or from year to year." The definition it will be seen is inclusive, not exhaustive, leaving open considerations about land which is similar in nature to common land but is not

---

[51] S.I. 1966 No. 1471, reg. 24.

[52] *ibid.* reg. 25.

[53] *ibid.* reg. 32 as amended by the Commons Registration (General) (Amendment) Regulations 1980 (S.I. 1980 No. 1195), regs. 3, 4, 5.

[54] *ibid.* reg. 32(1)(2), Sched. 1, Form 21 and Sched. 3 as amended by S.I. 1980 No. 1195, regs. 4, 5.

[55] *ibid.* reg. 33, Sched. 3 as amended by S.I. 1980 No. 1195, reg. 5.

[56] *cf.* § 2.33.

strictly subject either to rights of common or the other classes of rights expressly included. It does seem clear that the stinted pastures are registrable both because the rights over them will be known as beastgates, cattlegates (or some other term) and they will also be sole pastures.[57] It is less self evident that rights exercisable between adjoining landowners, of the classes occurring on regulated pastures and common fields, can be brought into registration.

(a) Undivided shares in land

It can hardly be that all land held in undivided shares is registrable or many **2.27** farms held on a tenancy in common are brought into purview of the Act. Wherever the land is held by one title it is probably not registrable. The Chief Commons Commissioner also held that where the shares are derived from one title the land is not capable of registration. In *Re the Black Allotment, Muker, N. Yorks. (No. 1) (1977)*[58] an allottee under an inclosure award had anticipated the award and devised the land in three separate but undivided shares. The successors of the devisees were held not to be exercising rights of common but merely agreeing as to the use of the land. A similar decision was reached in the case of a moor where evidence was given that it had been held in three undivided shares by copyhold tenure.[59] The Commissioner agreed that the rights of grazing exercised were those of beneficial ownership in land and not rights of common. It followed that the land was not registrable.

A series of cases has come before the Commissioners dealing with the ques- **2.28** tion of ownership of regulated pastures.[60] The whole subject is dealt with at length in *Re Longton Out Marsh, Lancashire (1974)*[61] when the Commissioner held that a "combined grazing and soil ownership" can exist in law and can be distinguished from a tenancy in common of land, where the joint owners agree to graze in common, in which case the grazing derives its authority from the agreement and not from the ownership. It was concluded that in the case of the combined grazing/ownership "each cattlegate owner has a right of common over the entirety, not merely over the undivided share of which he is owner." That there is a right to graze over the whole cannot be denied but in the case of allotments thrown together to avoid fencing (which is the most usual origin of a regulated pasture) does not each allottee enter into an arrangement on the basis that there is, or will be, an agreement between all the allottees to allow grazing over the whole pending partition of the undivided shares? A satisfactory distinction between the two forms of agreement is difficult to discern.

A second factor influencing the Commissioners can be seen in the case of **2.29** *Re Newbiggin Moor, Newbiggin-by-the-Sea, Wansbeck D.C., Northumber-*

---

[57] See § 3.97.
[58] (1977) 268/D/84, 6 D.C.C. 342.
[59] *Re Accrington Moor, Accrington, Lancashire* (1972) 20/D/8, 9, 1 D.C.C. 62.
[60] For regulated pastures, see § 1.75.
[61] (1974) 20/U/81, 4 D.C.C. 464.

land (1977).[62] The register unit consisted of some 170 acres mainly used as a golf course. At the hearing evidence was given that in 1896 certain persons, known as the Freeholders of Newbiggin and being stated to be the beneficial and absolute owners in fee simple in gross of certain undivided shares commonly called "stints, freeholds and freeledges," conveyed the land to six of their number in fee simple as joint tenants upon the trusts there set out. The Commissioner in refusing registration of the land as a village green[63] noted that certain lands held in stints were registrable but—

> " . . . in my view the land is not properly so registered merely because it is beneficially vested in numerous persons as tenants in common, or because in the 1896 conveyance the parts or shares therein referred to are called 'stints'. The 1896 conveyance proceeds on the basis that the grantors could collectively deal with the freehold as they pleased, and provides some evidence that the land thereby conveyed is not within the said definition of 'common land' . . . "

As the holders of stints over regulated pastures are in the same position that they are beneficial owners who, ignoring for the moment the 1925 property legislation, can deal with the land as they wish, it is again difficult to see how the learned Commissioners distinguish one class of land from another.

2.30 The regulated pastures do not fit comfortably into the provisions of the C.R.A. 1965. Unlike other land a regulated pasture can hardly have lost any of its character by non-registration—ceasing to be common land in this context is meaningless. Similarly, in the event of non-registration of "rights" to graze they cannot cease to be exercisable when they are the product of an agreement between adjoining landowners. In the *Newbiggin* case the stintholder wishing to use his stint will merely say that he is exercising his proprietorial right in the land.

2.31 It is also arguable that the wording of the definition of rights of common in the Act is insufficient to include rights of an entirely different nature, particularly when the example of the clear distinction made in the Inclosure Act 1845[64] between stints where the land is and is not vested in the stintholders was available to the draftsman. Nevertheless, a considerable number of regulated pastures do appear on the commons registers. The Common Land Forum directed their attention to them and concluded that they should not be registered and recommended provision in the next stage of commons legislation for removal from the registers.[65] It should be noticed, however, that some of the pastures at least are subject to well used *de facto*, and possibly *de jure*, access by members of the public.[66]

---

[62] (1977) 27/D/41, 5 D.C.C. 425.
[63] The decision is entirely correct. There was no evidence that the land was, or ever had been, a village green which is how it had been provisionally registered. However, the Commissioner also considers the status of the land as common land.
[64] s.11: considered § 1.33.
[65] Commons Land Forum Report, Appendix C, paras. 108–113.
[66] An example is Langfield Common, West Yorkshire which consists of 605 ha. of open land. It is within an "urban" area for the purposes of the L.P.A. 1925, s.193 and, depending upon the interpretation placed upon that section, may be subject to a *de jure* right of public access. For further consideration of s.193 see § 11.06.

The exception of a regulated pasture, which in addition to the rights of the **2.32**
beneficial owners is also subject to rights of common, must be noted.[67] In
this type of case the land is clearly registrable, but the number of pastures in
this category is thought to be very small.

(b) Divided shares in land

Much fewer in number are the rights exercisable over common fields **2.33**
between adjoining landowners (rights of intercommonage) where there are
not also rights of common exercisable by persons without land in the fields.
Where intercommonage alone exists over land the same considerations as
apply to undivided shares in land are also relevant—perhaps with even
greater force when the power to terminate rights between adjoining landowners by enclosure has been preserved by statute.[68] Few cases of this
nature have been identified from study of the Commissioners' decisions but
in any consideration of amendment to the Act of 1965 they will also have to
be taken into account. Divided shares in meadow land known as "dales"[69]
and lot meadows[70] have both achieved registration.

(c) Charitable trusts

The definition of land and rights in the Act also seems insufficient to draw **2.34**
in land owned and held on trust for the benefit of classes of persons in a
community. There are no persons exercising rights over the land of another
person—the rights which are exercised are those of beneficiaries under a
trust and, if they are defeated, are actionable only against the trustees *qua*
trustees. This class of land is by no means unusual on the commons registers.[71] Within this class may be found fuel allotments under private inclosure awards, allotments for the labouring poor, and allotments made to
trustees to hold for freemen, burgesses, householders or inhabitants.[72]

(d) Sole rights to other products

The express inclusion of sole vesture, herbage and pasture in the definition **2.35**
of rights of common would seem to preclude the registration of land subject
only to sole rights for other products. The point does not always seem to
have been taken before the Commissioners. In *Re Roundhill, Threshfield,
Yorks. (No. 1)* (1973)[73] a quarry had been allotted under an inclosure award

---

[67] An example of land of this class is Thornham Common, Norfolk (CL unit 41)
where a regulated pasture is subject to largely unused stints and some 117 rights of
common vested, apparently, in local householders: *cf. Re Thornham Common,
Thornham, Norfolk* (1975) 25/D/79–95, 4 D.C.C. 198; § 3.76.

[68] By the Inclosure Act 1773, s.27 and the Inclosure Act 1857, s.1: § 1.71.

[69] *Re Tenants Meadow, Duddon, Cumbria* (1975) 262/D/4–7, 3 D.C.C. 214; *semble
Re East Stainmore Regulated Pasture, North Moor, Stainmore* (1986) 262/U/581,
17 D.C.C. 50.

[70] *Re Pixey Mead, Gosford and Water Eaton, and Yarnton or West Mead, Oxon.*
(1972) 29/D/5–13, 1 D.C.C. 91.

[71] Aitchison, Masters and Hughes, *The Common Lands of England and Wales*
(unpublished report to the Countryside Commission 1984), p. 9: see reference to
rights held by fluctuating bodies; *e.g.* Llantrisant Common, Mid Glamorgan.

[72] Inclosure Act 1845, ss.31, 87 and 108.

[73] (1973) 45/D/9, 2 D.C.C. 19.

to persons with rights over an adjoining stinted pasture for the extraction and burning of limestone for the pasture. The rights to take stone seemed to be sole rights. Nevertheless, the land was registered as common land.

2. Waste land of a manor not subject to rights of common

(a) Interpretation adopted

2.36   The second head of the definition of land which may be registered as statutory common land is "waste land of a manor not subject to rights of common."[74] It seems not unlikely that the intention of the legislators was to sweep up all land which had its origin in waste of a manor, was unoccupied and unused, and might be considered a prime candidate for amenity use.[75] If that was the intention, it is clear that it failed in its purpose largely due to the technical wording used in the Act.

2.37   In the next preceding legislation directly affecting common land the term used to describe similar land was manorial waste.[76] In the Commons Act 1876 waste land of a manor was defined to mean and include waste land of a manor on which the tenants have rights of common or, any land subject to any rights of common exercised *levant* and *couchant* or, to any rights of common exercised at all times of the year and unlimited by stints.[77] The effect is to draw in all land which is subject to rights of common whether the land still forms part of the waste of a manor or not. It was not unreasonable to deduce that the term waste land of a manor not subject to rights of common, as used in the C.R.A. 1965, was the same land, as described in the Act of 1876, which had ceased to be subject to rights.[78]

2.38   Waste land of a manor at law is a term of art. In *Attorney-General* v. *Hanmer* (1858)[79] Watson B. in giving an opinion, with which Stuart V.-C. concurred said:

> "The true meaning of 'wastes', or 'waste lands', or 'waste grounds of the manor', is the open, uncultivated and unoccupied lands parcel of the manor, or open lands parcel of the manor other than the demesne lands of the manor."[80]

It is the features of being open, uncultivated, unoccupied and parcel of the manor which have dominated consideration of registrability under the second head of the definition of common land. In particular, the interpret-

---

[74] § 2.02.

[75] A right of public access was granted over all manorial wastes in urban areas as long ago as the beginning of 1926: L.P.A. 1925, s.193.

[76] *cf.* L.P.A. 1925, s.193; see Appendix 3.

[77] s.37.

[78] This interpretation was circulating at the time of registration: see Campbell, *A Guide to Commons Registration* (Commons Society, 1966), p. 10. It was expressly rejected in *Re Britford Common* [1977] 1 W.L.R. 39 at 46 *per* Slade J.

[79] (1858) L.J. 27 Ch. 837.

[80] pp. 840 and 842.

ation of "parcel of the manor" has caused some difference of opinion both before the Commissioners and the courts.[81] Put shortly, the alternatives are that the expression refers to land which has its historical origin in the waste of a manor or, it must of necessity be that the land is still in the ownership of the lord of a manor. The Court of Appeal in *Re Box Hill Common* (1978)[82] held that—

> " . . . when one comes to paragraph (b) of the definition section, *i.e.* section 22(1), all the characteristics there specified must be satisfied at the time of registration and it would do violence to the language to hold it enough that the manor is presently waste land and now or formerly 'of a manor'."

It followed that waste land severed from the manor could not fall to registration under the second head of the definition in the Act. The decision of the Court came after many Commissioners' hearings had been concluded and decisions taken that the historical view was correct. There is no doubt that there is marked inconsistency in the registration of land which is not subject to rights. A large number of registrations do not apparently comply with the interpretation of the Court of Appeal.[83] However, where land has achieved finality and is not subject to rights, the effect of section 10 of the Act is that there is conclusive evidence that the land was waste land of a manor at the date of registration—even where all the parties concerned are agreed that the land is not, and never has been waste land of a manor.[84] **2.39**

(b) Elements of the definition

Although the definition of waste land of a manor is now sufficiently clear, the various features of the definition may advantageously be examined in more detail for the purposes of future hearings and, decisions as to whether land has ceased to be waste land of a manor and thus capable of removal from the commons registers.[85] **2.40**

(i) **"Parcel of the manor"** Upon severance of land from a manor it will clearly cease to be parcel of the manor and, where this has occurred before the date of a Commissioner's hearing, will provide evidence sufficient to uphold an objection to the registration of land under the second head of the definition. Such a severance will also be a sufficient act for the establishment of a claim that the land has ceased to be common land and a **2.41**

---

[81] For support for the historical interpretation see *Re Yateley Commons, Hants.* (1975) 214/D/9–13, 3 D.C.C. 153, *per* Cmr. Baden Fuller, [1977] 1 W.L.R. 840 at 853, *per* Foster J., *Re Chewton Common* [1977] 1 W.L.R. 1242 at 1249, *per* Slade J. The literal meaning is supported in *Re The Green, Woodford, Wilts. (No. 1)* (1975) 241/D/13–15, 3 D.C.C. 203, *per* Chief Cmr. Squibb (and in many other decisions), *Re Box Hill Common* [1980] 1 Ch. 109 at 115–118, *per* Stamp L.J., C.A.

[82] *ibid.* at 116, *per* Stamp L.J.

[83] Aitchison, Hughes and Masters, *The Common Lands of England and Wales* (1984), pp. 9 and 20.

[84] *Corpus Christi College* v. *Gloucs. C.C.* [1983] 1 Q.B. 360, considered at § 2.76.

[85] For de-registration of common land, see § 2.66.

successful application for the land to be removed from the registers should follow.[86]

2.42 **(ii) Severance** It may be that the severance must be complete so that independent control is established. In the *Box Hill* case it was noted that the so-called waste land had ceased to have any connection with the manor 50 years before the Act of 1965 and "it would be a misuse of language to describe it as waste land of the manor."[87] In *Re Cripplestyle, Cranborne Common and King Barrow Hill, Alderholt, Wimborne, Dorset* (1981)[88] it was found that after severance the persons entitled to control of land and manor were for all practical purposes the same after severance of land and lordship and the land was held still to be waste land of a manor.

2.43 **(iii) Burden of proof** In a hearing before a Commissioner it is the duty of a person claiming that land is common land to be prepared to prove that the land is as stated.[89] However, it is suggested that the burden of proof on the applicant is not absolute as the Commissioner is under a duty to inquire into the matter[90] and the hearing is not simply one *inter partes*.[91] In early hearings the Commissioners were prepared to accept evidence of sale of the lands[92] or an inclosure award[93] as sufficient evidence of severance, but not an unproved conveyance on sale.[94] Where the issue is not directly before a Commissioner it seems that probabilities are sufficient.[95]

2.44 **(iv) Reunification** If there has been a severance in the past, with a subsequent reunification, it seems that the earlier severance is not sufficient to take the land outside the definition. In *Re Chewton Common* (1977)[96] Slade J. in an *obiter dictum* approved the contention that land once severed might, after a period of time, be waste of the manor again by repu-

---

[86] In *Re Chewton Common*, above n. 81, Slade J. drew attention to this possibility at 1249 and the Court of Appeal in *Re Box Hill Common*, above, at 177 was not prepared to put any gloss on its words to avoid this result noticing that a lord only has to enclose and occupy land to avoid registration.

[87] *Re Box Hill Common* [1980] 1 Ch. 109 at 118 *per* Stamp L.J.

[88] (1981) 210/D/419–27, 464, 465, 11 D.C.C. 95.

[89] *Re Sutton Common* [1982] 1 W.L.R. 647 at 656–657, *per* Walton J.; *Bellord* v. *Colyer* [1983] Lexis, Enggen Library, Cases, *per* Nourse J. in respect of waste land of a manor; *Re West Anstey Common* [1985] Ch. 329 at 342–334, C.A., *per* Slade L.J. approving *Re Sutton Common*, above; *Corpus Christi College* v. *Gloucs. C.C.*, above, at 379, *per* Oliver L.J. *sed contra*, same case at 367, *per* Lord Denning M.R.

[90] s.6(1) of the C.R.A. 1965.

[91] For the reason that the public may have an interest in the registration of the land distinct from those of the parties legally interested in the land.

[92] *Re Church Green, Verwood, Dorset (No. 1)* (1972) 10/D/13, 1 D.C.C. 38; *Re The Old Ford, Holcombe, Oxon.* (1972) 29/D/4, 1 D.C.C. 77.

[93] *Re the Lord's Waste, Winterton-on-Sea, Norfolk* (1972) 25/D/12, 1 D.C.C. 112.

[94] *Re Hardown Hill, Whitechurch, Canonicorum and Chideock, Dorset (No. 1)* (1974) 10/D/45–55, 2 D.C.C. 230.

[95] *cf. Re Viscar Common, Wendron, Cornwall* (1975) 206/D/20–23, 3 D.C.C. 339; *Re The Cliffe, Ruyton-xi-Towns, Salop* (1975) 31/D/18–22, 3 D.C.C. 248; *Re The Green, Woodford, Wilts. (No. 1)* (1975) 241/D/13–15, 3 D.C.C. 203.

[96] [1977] 1 W.L.R. 1242 at 1250 approving *R.* v. *Duchess of Buccleugh* (1704) 6 Mod. 150, 87 E.R. 909; the judgment in *Re Chewton Common* was not overruled in *Re Box Hill Common* in spite of disapproval of the route adopted thus tacitly approving the doctrine of waste land by repute.

tation. Thus, detailed historical research is unnecessary—if the land and manor are currently in the same ownership the land may be considered to be parcel of the manor.

(v) Reputed manors In some hearings before Commissioners it has **2.45** been argued that there cannot be, in strictness, any manor since the abolition of copyhold and most manorial incidents at the beginning of 1926.[97] In his hearing of *Re Box Hill Common*[98] the Chief Commissioner sought to overcome this problem by holding that there could be waste land of a reputed manor. The Court of Appeal took special submissions on the point and noted that since the Conveyancing Act 1881[99] a conveyance of a manor included its reputed parts. This sufficed for the Court to take the view:

> " . . . that when 80 years later in 1965 the legislature used the simple phrase 'waste land of a manor not subject to rights of common' without further defining it, it was not drawing a distinction between manors and reputed manors, and was using the expression 'waste land of a manor' to comprehend waste land of the lord of a reputed manor."[1]

(vi) "Open, uncultivated and unoccupied lands" The other **2.46** features of the definition of waste land of a manor have attracted less attention but, are equally important in deciding the status of purported waste land before a Commissioner or, when considering whether the land has ceased to be within registrable status.

(vii) "Open" Open, in this context, means unenclosed. It does not **2.47** have the same meaning as in common open fields which were invariably enclosed to some extent. Thus, common fields can never be waste of a manor, although this has not prevented some common fields achieving this status as a result of the conclusive evidence provision in the C.R.A. 1965.[2]

If land, formerly waste, has been enclosed it may be that its status as **2.48** demesne, consequent upon the enclosure, can be lost as a result of abandonment. It is not unusual to find walls on waste land where some overoptimistic person imagined an advantage in enclosure but abandoned the attempt at conversion.[3] The matter was considered in one hearing before a Commissioner when three parcels of land, owned by the lord of the manor, were considered.[4] One had been partly cultivated and cropped since registration but not for the previous six years. It was held to have been taken into

---

[97] The question of whether a manor exists in its own right or merely as a reputed manor may hinge around whether a court baron can be held and this in turn depends upon the existence of at least two freeholders of the manor liable to suit of court; see *Scriven's Copyholds*, p. 3 and *Soane* v. *Ireland* (1808) 10 East. 259, 103 E.R. 773. It is noteworthy that fealty and suit of court were not amongst the incidents of the manor abolished in respect of freehold estates in the 1925 legislation: see L.P.A. 1922, ss.128(2), 138(1).
[98] (1977) 241/D/56–60, 5 D.C.C. 321.
[99] *cf.* L.P.A. 1925, s.205(1)(ix).
[1] [1980] 1 Ch. 109 at 118, *per* Stamp L.J.
[2] *cf. Corpus Christi College* v. *Gloucs. C.C.* [1983] 1 Q.B., considered at § 2.76.
[3] For example on Dartmoor and the Brecon Beacons.
[4] *Re Rush Green, Harleston, Suffolk* (1979) 234/D/84, 9 D.C.C. 20; *cf.* [1979] C.L.Y. 252, 129 New L.J. 810.

demesne by the acts of cultivation. The Commissioner went on to consider whether demesne could revert to waste. His provisional opinion was that it could not and at least he would want, in the absence of authority, to receive evidence of abandonment of demesne status. It is submitted that abandonment is possible in principle providing always that the conditions required for abandonment of rights over land are met.[5] There seems no reason why such land should not be treated as reputed waste land of a manor.[6]

2.49 Enclosure of waste is probably the most unequivocal act possible to indicate an intention to take the land into demesne. If waste land was not subject to rights of common on January 1, 1926, there is no statutory bar to enclosure.[7]

2.50 **(viii) "Uncultivated"** Whether land has been cultivated and taken into demesne status seems to be partly a question of degree of cultivation. Land taken into arable cultivation[8] or forestry[9] is unequivocally sufficient. The planting of a tree here and there is probably not enough.[10]

2.51 The purpose of the cultivation also seems to be relevant. Temporary enclosure, coupled with drainage works and reseeding the land, did not affect manorial status where the owner had declared his intention to leave the land as a public open space after completion of the works.[11] On the other hand, a regulated metropolitan common had been subject to a considerable amount of work by the conservators to keep down woodland, so that the public might enjoy the site. It was held that so much had been done that the land had ceased to be uncultivated waste.[12] Thus, an intention to maintain a site on a regular basis seems to destroy the waste land status.

2.52 **(ix) "Unoccupied"** It is quite clear that in describing waste land in the *Hanmer* case,[13] Watson B. did not mean that the land was not used for grazing purposes, for at the time, at the very least, the wastes were used by the tenants of the manor. Thus the land was used by persons, holding title under the lord, as copyholders exercising customary rights of common and, tenants or termors exercising contractual rights in common. It is possible to argue that the 1965 Act in providing for the registration of waste land not subject to rights of common ought to have included land which had ceased to be subject to copyhold rights and is subject now only to tenants' rights in common. It is argued elsewhere that the rights of tenants and termors have much greater strength since the 1925 property legislation than they appar-

---

[5] For abandonment, see § 5.38.

[6] See § 2.44.

[7] See L.P.A. 1925, s.194, considered at § 9.34.

[8] *Re The Drives, Puncknowle, Dorset* (1972) 10/D/7, 1 D.C.C. 14.

[9] *Re Norris Mill Moor etc., Puddletown, Dorset* (1973) 10/D/35–7, 1 D.C.C. 327.

[10] *Re (1) Huntsham Hill and (2) the Old Quarry both in Goodrich, Herefords.* (1973) 15/D/1–3, 6, 1 D.C.C. 410.

[11] *Re Knacker's Hole Common, Puncknowle, Dorset* (1972) 10/D/4, 1 D.C.C. 11.

[12] *Re Chislehurst and St. Pauls' Cray Commons, Bromley, Greater London* (1974) 59/D/9–10, 3 D.C.C. 17.

[13] See § 2.38.

ently did in the 19th century. It is somewhat anomalous to treat them today as though they are little more than rights *in personam*.[14] But in the event, the Act expressly excluded the rights of tenants and termors from registration.[15]

The question is considered at length in *Re Arden Great Moor, Arden with **2.53** Ardenside, N. Yorks.* (1977).[16] A moor was grazed by tenants of the manor holding agricultural tenancies with each tenant having a right to "stray" a fixed number of sheep on the moor. It was found that by 1900 there were no free or copyhold tenants of the manor and the whole manor had been taken by the lord *in propriis manibus* bringing it all into the lord's demesne. This was sufficient to take the land outside the *Hanmer* definition. The Commissioner went on to consider whether the land was also occupied and took the view that—

> " . . . to the extent to which the rents paid under the agreements are greater than the rents which could have been obtained for the farms without any right to graze on Arden Moor, the owner is in receipt of money from the Moor and is thereby enjoying benefit from it. The owner is using the land by taking in the sheep of other people to graze on it, it being immaterial that the owners of the sheep are also tenants of other land belonging to the same owner. In my view such a use of land is sufficient to make it occupied and thus to take it out of the category of 'waste lands'."

3. Tenanted and leased land

The Commissioners have consistently held that where land is let or leased **2.54** the land cannot be waste land of a manor. Thus, land let since 1897 must have been converted to demesne although still unenclosed,[17] land leased for a term of years is demesne[18] and the inclusion of land in a tenancy agreement without actual occupation is sufficient to destroy waste status.[19] In contradistinction, the existence of a sporting tenancy over a waste is not only not inconsistent with its character as parcel of the manor but may be supportive.[20]

---

[14] See § 3.14.

[15] s.22(1) of the C.R.A. 1965.

[16] (1977) 268/D/209, 6 D.C.C. 415.

[17] *Re Hardown Hill*, n. 94.

[18] *Re land to the north of Piper's Green, Brockley Hill, Stanmore, Greater London* (1974) 59/D/7, 2 D.C.C. 259.

[19] *Re Waste Land, Carperby, N. Yorks.* (1977) 268/D/96, 6 D.C.C. 344; *contra Re Twm Barlwm Common, Risca and Rogerstone* (1986) 273/D/106–7, 17 D.C.C. 200, *per* Chief Commissioner Langdon Davies: letting of land is a relevant but not conclusive consideration; a tenancy gives a right to occupy; "occupation" is a question of fact (*sed quaere* whether receipt of rent by the lord is not an indication that the land is of demesne status).

[20] *Re Burton Heath; Bellord* v. *Colyer* [1983], Lexis, Enggen Library, Cases, *per* Nourse J.

4. Protected land

2.55 There is no compelling reason why land which is regulated under the Metropolitan Commons Acts 1866–1878, the Commons Act 1876 or a local Act should be registered under the C.R.A. 1965. Such land was eligible for exemption from registration if no longer subject to rights of common.[21] However, whether registered or not the land remains regulated by the provisions in the relevant Act. Similarly, land which falls within the provisions of section 193 (public access to urban commons) and section 194 (development on land subject to rights of common on January 1, 1926, controlled)[22] of the L.P.A. 1925 was not necessarily registrable land under the 1965 Act. Again, lack of registration does not take the land outside the provisions of the Act of 1925 and such land remains "protected" by the two sections concerned.[23]

New common land

2.56 Any land which has acquired, or acquires, the essential features of either of the two statutory heads of common land, after the mandatory registration period, which ended on January 2, 1970,[24] is registrable. Section 1 of the C.R.A. 1965 provides that "there shall be registered . . . land in England or Wales which is common land" and "no land capable of being registered under this Act shall be deemed to be common land . . . unless it is so registered." Similar provisions apply to rights of common.[25] Section 13 of the C.R.A. 1965 provides for regulations to be made to enable the registers to be amended where "any land becomes common land." The Regulations giving effect to section 13 are the Commons Registration (New Land) Regulations 1969[26] which came into force on January 3, 1970. The notes to the model form for an application for the registration of new common land[27] provide four methods whereby land may become common land:

> "(1) By or under any Act of Parliament otherwise than as substituted land (as to substituted land, see category (4) below).
> (2) By a grant by the owner of the land of rights of common over it.
> (3) By rights of common being acquired over it by prescription.
> (4) By substitution or exchange for other land which has ceased to be common land under—
>   (a) sections 147 and 148 of the Inclosure Act 1845; or
>   (b) paragraph 11 of Schedule 1 to the Acquisition of Land (Authorisation) Procedure Act 1946[28] or

---

[21] See § 2.03.

[22] See §§ 9.34 and 11.06.

[23] See further discussion at §§ 9.42 and 11.18.

[24] For which, see § 2.05.

[25] Considered at § 4.01.

[26] S.I. 1969 No. 1843. For substituted land before January 3, 1970, see the Commons Registration (General) Regulations 1966 (S.I. 1966 No. 1471), reg. 28 as amended by S.I. 1969 No. 1843, reg. 9(2).

[27] *ibid.* Sched., Form 29, n. 5.

[28] Provisions now repealed and replaced in a slightly modified form by the Acquisition of Land Act 1981, s.19(1) and Sched. 3, para. 6(1).

(c) any other enactment providing, on the exchange of land, for the transfer of rights, trusts, or incidents attaching to the land given in exchange from that land to the land taken in exchange and vice versa."

Suggestions (1) and (4)(c) are self explanatory but the remainder justify some discussion. In addition, it will be noticed that it is not suggested that land might become new common land under the second head of the definition, *i.e.* waste land of a manor not subject to rights of common. It may be that this alternative, although not likely, is possible.

1. New common land subject to rights

(a) A grant of rights of common

Any grant of rights of common over land not registered under the section 4 **2.57** procedure (mandatory initial registration) will make both land and rights registrable under the provisions in section 1 of the Act. To create exercisable rights an application for registration of land and rights must be made under regulation 3 of the Regulations. The grant must be for a right as defined in the Act, *i.e.* for a right of common or a sole right of vesture, herbage or pasture for an interest equivalent to a fee simple. Conveyancers should be alert to the possibility that a grant, say, to shoot and take away game, or to fish, if not granted as a sole right may have created a registrable right of common which, in the absence of registration, is unexercisable.

(b) Acquisition of rights of common by prescription

Clearly, if rights of common may still be acquired on proof of long user, **2.58** then this alternative is a method whereby new common land may come into existence. It is suggested later, however, that there are now formidable obstacles in the way of proving rights by prescription and even that it may be impossible.[29]

(c) Exchange of land under the Inclosure Act 1845, ss.147, 148

Under section 147 exchanges of land may be effected by means of an order of **2.59** the Secretary of State. The provision is available for land whether subject to be inclosed or not. A similar provision in section 148 allows for exchanges of land "so intermixed or divided into parcels of inconvenient form or quantity that the same cannot be cultivated or occupied to the best advantage." Another provision, now probably obsolete, is also available in section 149 for the exchange of inconvenient allotments for the poor and public purposes. Exchanges under section 147 are not unusual and may be increasing in number: see Appendix 9.

The land received in exchange by each party is held under the same title and **2.60** subject to the same trusts and liabilities as the land given in exchange. This is of particular relevance in the case of land subject to rights of common as the order effectively annexes all rights exercisable over the land to the title

[29] See §§ 4.57 *et seq.*

during the exchange. The exchange is made between two titles, and not two applicants, so that a person holding parcels of land under different titles may apply for an order.[30] The Secretary of State must be satisfied that an exchange will be beneficial to the owners of the respective lands and that the value of the land to be received by each party will be no less than the value to him of the land given up.

2.61 An applicant must be a "person interested" in the land.[31] Where common land is involved the lord, or other owner of the soil, should make the application but if his interest is not equivalent to at least two-thirds in value of all the interests in the land a sufficient number of other persons interested, including commoners, will be required to join in the application.[32] An application must be accompanied by maps of the lands and an independent valuation of both parcels will be necessary. Once an application is found to be in order the proposal must be advertised in local newspapers indicating that an order will be made one month after the last notice appears.[33] If, before the period of one month expires, a notice of dissent is received from any person interested in any estate in the land, or charge on the land, the Secretary of State may not proceed until the dissent is withdrawn.[34] Where no notice of dissent is received or, if received is withdrawn and, the Secretary of State is otherwise of the opinion that the order should be made, a draft order will be prepared and, after approval and engrossment, will be made under seal.

2.62 An exchange may be made with mines and minerals, and/or easements over the land, excepted if they are not intended to pass with the land.[35] It seems that orders may be made in respect of fuel allotments for the poor made under private Inclosure Acts or, recreation grounds and allotments for the labouring poor (field gardens) allotted under the Inclosure Acts 1845–1868.[36]

(d) Exchange of lands under Acquisition of Land Act 1981, s.19 and Sched. 3.

2.63 Where land subject to rights of common is to be acquired by compulsory purchase the procedures in operation encourage the exchange of lands so as to provide the same amount of common land as existed before the purchase. This subject is dealt with later[37] and, at this point, it is only necessary to say that such exchanges are the rule rather than the exception: see Appendix 9. It also seems that where British Coal make a compulsory rights order, which allows for rights over land to be suspended while opencast coal operations are carried out, and offers land in exchange such land will become

[30] Inclosure Act 1849, s.11.
[31] Inclosure Act 1845, s.16 and *cf.* also s.19.
[32] Inclosure Act 1849, s.7.
[33] Inclosure Act 1845, s.150 as amended by Commons Act 1899, s.19.
[34] *ibid.*; note that a member of the public is not a person interested.
[35] Inclosure Act 1847, s.4.
[36] See further at § 13.48.
[37] See §§ 5.85 *et seq.*

temporarily common land subject to rights.[38] No special provision has been made in the Act of 1965 for such land.

2. New common land not subject to rights

It has been suggested that first, it may be possible for demesne land to be **2.64** abandoned to waste land of a manor[39] and secondly, that waste land may become reputedly of a manor by unified ownership of land and manor.[40] In both circumstances there seems no reason why land should not become statutory common land thereby.

There also seems no reason why registered waste land of a manor should not **2.65** be exchanged for other land under the provisions in section 147 of the Inclosure Act 1845[41] thus creating new common land. An exchange, however, does not seem to be required in the case of the compulsory purchase of waste land of a manor not subject to rights of common as it is not land "subject to be inclosed."[42]

De-registration of common land

The Act of 1965 purports to include within its purview only land "which is **2.66** common land in England or Wales."[43] For a number of reasons, associated largely with uncertainty about the definitions in the Act, this is patently incorrect so far as the registers are currently drawn, unless one takes the rather narrow view that, by registration, land is converted into common land irrespective of its previous status. If this view is adopted, no land can ever cease to be statutory common land whatever may happen to it subsequent to registration. However, section 13 allows for Regulations to be made to provide for the amendment of the registers where any land registered under the Act ceases to be common land or a town or village green. The Regulations are permissive and it is not obligatory for an owner to apply for removal. As a registration under the Act is only evidential of the matters registered as at the date of registration,[44] and not at any current date, there is no reason why an owner should not proceed to deal with the land in any way he chooses once it has ceased to be within the definition of statutory common land, subject always to any other statutory provisions which may affect the land. However, an entry on the registers is generally regarded as an incumbrance on the land because of the possible effect of future legislation, and most owners will seek to have the registers amended if it is possible. This section considers the classes of land which do not conform with the statutory definitions, examines whether each class is eligible

[38] See §§ 5.102 *et seq.*
[39] See § 2.48.
[40] See § 2.44.
[41] Expressly provided that exchanges of land not subject to be inclosed may be effected.
[42] Acquisition of Land Act 1981, s.19(4).
[43] s.1(1).
[44] s.10.

for an amendment application, describes the administrative procedures involved and records proposals for reform which have been promulgated.

2.67 There are three categories of land where an owner might feel justified in seeking to have the registers amended—

(a) where an event has occurred since registration to take land, which was correctly registered, outside the definition in the Act;

(b) where it is apparent from decisions by Commissioners, or the courts, that had an objection been made at the appropriate time it would have been successful; and within this category may be included the cases where the Commissioners, in the knowledge of subsequent decisions by the court, can now be seen to have made incorrect determinations;

(c) the not inconsiderable number of registrations where a totally mis-conceived registration of land has occurred without the knowledge of the owner; and within this grouping may be considered the substantial number of clerical errors occasioned by, for instance, the use of outdated maps.

In drafting the 1965 Act only the first class seems to be acknowledged. To the extent that some common land will be required for public purposes, it is essential that this provision for removal is included. The Act, however, allows de-registration for private purposes which may not have been foreseen by the draftsman. The second class has arisen in substantial numbers due to uncertainties in the definitions used in the Act. But, it must be the third class which is the greatest cause for concern. The drawing in of land which has not even a remote connection with common land, without notice to the owners that it is being registered, will approach confiscatory dimensions if a second stage of legislation makes no provision for rectification of the registers and the land becomes permanently incumbered.[45]

1. Land ceasing to be common land

2.68 The first class is concerned with land which was correctly registered under the initial registration procedure but which has ceased since to be within the statutory definition. It falls directly within section 13 of the Act:

"Regulations under this Act[46] shall provide for the amendment of the registers maintained under this Act where—
(a) any land registered under this Act ceases to be common land or a town or village green; . . . "

2.69 Although there are only two heads of common land expressed in the Act,[47] a third is implicit:

(a) waste land of a manor not subject to rights of common;
(b) waste land of a manor subject to rights of common; and
(c) other land, not waste land of a manor, subject to rights of common.

---

[45] For proposals for reform in a second stage of legislation, see § 2.82.
[46] Commons Registration (General) Regulations 1966 (S.I. 1966 No. 1471), reg. 27.
[47] *cf.* § 2.02.

If land has fallen to registration under (a) it seems reasonably clear that if **2.70** any of the facets of the *Hanmer* definition are changed the land will cease to be waste land of a manor and will be ripe for removal from the register. Thus, severance of the land from the manor, or enclosure, cultivation or occupation will create grounds for a successful application for de-registration.[48]

Where finally registered land is subject to rights and the land is also waste **2.71** land of a manor, extinguishment of the rights[49] will not provide grounds for de-registration. The land will remain within the statutory definition as waste land of a manor. In this event it will be necessary to prove also that the land has ceased to be waste of a manor.

In *Corpus Christi College* v. *Gloucestershire County Council* (1982)[50] the **2.72** third alternative was considered: where land was not waste land of a manor at the time of registration but subject to rights. Self evidently, in the event of the rights being extinguished it will not be possible to provide evidence that the land has also ceased to be waste land of a manor. In considering this event (hypothetically and *obiter dicta*) Oliver L.J. said:

"In order to make sense of section 13 at all in such a case, it must, as it seems to me, be open to the landowner to demonstrate by evidence which could have been brought before an inquiry if one had taken place that the land never was waste of the manor, for this is a critical part of the demonstration that it has indeed 'ceased' to be common land."[51]

In all events, it is clear that an applicant for de-registration may not merely **2.73** point to the absence of registered rights or non-compliance with the definition of waste land of a manor, for the effect of section 10, upon finality of registration, is to provide conclusive evidence of the matters registered as at the date of registration. It is, therefore, not open to an applicant to attempt to show that land has ceased to be common land "except by reference to some subsequent event or transaction."[52]

A successful application for de-registration does not necessarily mean that **2.74** the land will be free of all statutory control. In particular, the provisions of sections 193 and/or 194 of the L.P.A. 1925 may still apply. To free the land from these sections will require a resolution of the county council approved by a Secretary of State.[53]

2. Land registered without conforming to the definitions

There can be little doubt that there is a substantial number of registrations **2.75** of land which do not comply with the definitions of common land in the Act. They have arisen for a variety of reasons. In particular at the time of

[48] See §§ 2.36 *et seq.*
[49] For extinguishment generally, see Chap. 5.
[50] [1983] 1 Q.B. 360.
[51] p. 377.
[52] p. 381, *per* Kerr L.J.
[53] L.P.A. 1925, ss.193(1), proviso (*d*)(ii), 194(3), proviso (*b*).

registration there was some confusion about the meaning of waste land of a manor which was only finally resolved in 1978.[54] Until 1975, the Commissioners considered the status of the land at the time of its registration and were prepared to hold, sometimes on quite flimsy indications, that, although none had been registered, rights had existed at the date of registration and the land was registered on this account.[55] This approach was eventually held to be mistaken: the correct time for considering the status of the land is the date of the Commissioner's hearing.[56] The Commissioners have held differing views concerning the registrability of some classes of land.[57] Finally, there are classes of land registered which principle would suggest are incorrectly registered, but on which there has been no litigation to provide certainty.[58]

2.76 Once the land has achieved finality of registration it attracts the conclusive evidence provision in section 10 of the Act and, in the absence of rights registrations over it, is deemed to be waste land of a manor. For the land to be removed from the register it must be the subject of some event or transaction, which has occurred since the date of registration, to take the land outside the definition. This poses some difficulty in the case of land which is demonstrably not waste land of a manor but is deemed to be such. The point is well illustrated in the case of *Corpus Christi College* v. *Gloucestershire County Council* (1982).[59] Rights were provisionally registered by a local authority in respect of a meadow, formerly part of a common field, and the registration authority, as it was bound to do,[60] provisionally registered the meadow as common land. The owners objected to the rights registration but not the land registration. At the Commissioner's inquiry the local authority admitted that it had no title to the rights and the registration was refused. In the absence of objection the land registration became final. The owners applied, under section 13, for the land registration to be removed. The registration authority declined to amend the register. The parties agreed the facts and the owners sought a declaration that the meadow was not common land. The application was rejected and the owners appealed. The Court of Appeal were unanimous that the appeal failed and the land was held to be waste land of a manor. The agreed facts showed that the land

---

[54] *Re Box Hill Common* [1980] Ch. 109: disapproved by Lord Denning M.R. in *Corpus Christi College* v. *Gloucs C.C.* [1983] 1 Q.B. 360 at 369.

[55] cf. *Re Shottisham Poor's Common etc., E. Suffolk* (1973) 34/D/15 and 16, 1 D.C.C. 436: witness cut bracken for litter for a pig and gorse for a bread oven in the twenties and had seen bracken cut since—rights [sic] not abandoned; *Re Halling Common, Kent* (1973) 19/D/13 1 D.C.C. 348: right of sole vesture held vested in council without registration; *Re Dee Marsh Saltings, Flint* (1974) 52/D/3 and 4, 2 D.C.C. 183: stock from one small farm had been consistently grazed, intimation that rights had been extinguished but this, coupled with statements that other stock had grazed, held sufficient.

[56] *Central Electricity Generating Board* v. *Clwyd County Council* [1976] 1 W.L.R. 151 considered at § 14.42.

[57] See, *e.g.* the differences over waste land of a minor cited at § 14.38 and nn. 73 and 74 thereto.

[58] See §§ 2.27, 2.33 and 2.34: regulated pastures, common fields and land held for charitable purposes.

[59] [1983] 1 Q.B. 360.

[60] s.4(2)(*b*) of the C.R.A. 1965.

was not and never had been waste land of a manor. The land could only be removed from the registers by demonstrating that the land had ceased to be waste land of a manor and, not surprisingly, there is no authority as to the steps required in the case of deemed waste land.

3. Misconceived registrations

Of a similar nature, in that the land clearly does not conform with the defi- **2.77** nitions in the Act, is all the land which has been registered by mistake. The number of registrations in this class is unknown (and in some cases probably still unknown to the owners of the land concerned) but anecdotal accounts abound and such bizarre registrations as housing estates and churchyards can be seen in Commissioners' reports.[61] This type of registration has the added dimensions that the victims have been drawn into legislation with which they had no concern whatsoever and, their land was registered without any direct notification. Householders are unlikely to respond with alacrity to a newspaper advertisement calling attention to the registration of common land! There is also a substantial number of clerical errors occasioned by, for example, the use of obsolete maps—on occasions tithe maps, of an early nine- . teenth century vintage, were used for defining boundaries.

Again, this type of land registration is not directly remediable by an appli- **2.78** cation for removal from the registers unless it is possible to demonstrate some event or transaction whereby the land has ceased to be subject to rights and/or waste land of a manor. If the land is subject to registered rights, a deed of release of rights signed by all the commoners, coupled with evidence that the land had been severed from the manor at the date of regis- tration, should be sufficient. If the registration is not subject to rights and the land is thereby deemed, by finality of registration, to be waste land of a manor the problem is more difficult but in one or two cases has not proved insoluble. Some registration authorities have responded sympathetically where a deed of severance from the manor has been obtained releasing the owner of the land from all remaining manorial incidents, if any.[62]

4. Procedure for de-registration

The procedure for an application to amend the registers where any land has **2.79** ceased to be common land is prescribed in Regulations.[63] The application may be made in standard form by the owner, or the Church Commissioners in the case of a vacant ecclesiastical benefice of the Church of England, signed by the applicant or an authorised person of a body corporate. The application must be supported by a statutory declaration and such further evidence as the registration authority may reasonably require.[64] On receipt

---

[61] *Re Royden Fen (part), Royden, Norfolk* (1983) 225/U/247, 14 D.C.C. 50; *Re the tract of about three acres called Village Green, Llangyfelach* (1987) 278/U/1, 17 D.C.C. 273.

[62] *cf.* Gadsden, "De-Registration of Commons—An Alternative View" (1982) 126 S.J. 815; *semble Ladenbau (G. & K.) Ltd.* v. *Crawley & de Reya* [1978] 1 W.L.R. 266.

[63] Commons Registration (General) Regulations 1966 (S.I. 1966 No. 1471), reg. 27.

[64] See reg. 27(3).

of an application which, after preliminary consideration, the authority determines not to reject shall be displayed by the authority, and any other concerned authorities, in the form of a prescribed notice. Copies of the notice are required to be sent to any person, other than the applicant, who is registered as owner and, where a right of common is exercisable over the land, to any person appearing to be interested therein.[65] Upon expiry of 40 days from the date on which notices have been served and displayed the registration authority is required to further consider the application and, any written repr᾽ sentations which it has received, and, if it deems the application well founded, shall amend the register.[66]

2.80   The Regulations make no provision for appeal from the decision of the authority. The proper course of action by an applicant aggrieved by the decision of an authority not to amend a register is to apply for judicial review to the Divisional Court[67] or possibly, it seems, where the parties both agree, for a declaration through the County Court and thence to the Chancery Division of the High Court.[68]

2.81   Where an amendment has been made to the registers by the authority, under the provisions contained in section 13 of the Act (which includes an amendment to the land registers), the High Court may order rectification if it appears to the Court that no amendment ought to have been made, that the error cannot be corrected in pursuance of regulations made under the Act and, if the court deems it just to so act.[69]

5. Proposals for reform

2.82   The Common Land Forum in its report makes a series of recommendations which, if enacted, will materially affect the removal of land from the registers. First, the possible removal of land for private purposes by means of, for example, the owner of the land obtaining the release of all registered rights and then claiming an event or transaction whereby the land has ceased to be common land would be blocked by creating a new category of registered land:

> "We propose that from an appointed day land ceasing to be subject to rights of common by reason of unity of seisin shall become 'statutory common land' that is, it will retain all the other attributes of common land notwithstanding the absence of rights over it. It would be equivalent to manorial waste though not held under a manorial title."[70]

2.83   Similarly, it is proposed that, where land has fallen to registration as waste land of a manor not subject to rights, upon the land ceasing to be within the technical meaning of waste land of a manor it too should become "statutory common land."[71] What this recommendation perhaps does not do is to con-

---

[65] See reg. 27(5).
[66] See reg. 27(7).
[67] Under R.S.C., Ord. 53; *cf. Re Tillmire Common, Heslington* [1982] 2 All E.R. 615.
[68] *Corpus Christi College* v. *Gloucs. C.C.* [1983] 1 Q.B. 360.
[69] s.14 of the Act of 1965; *cf.* § 2.18
[70] Common Land Forum Report, Appendix C, para. 043.
[71] *ibid.* para. 046.

sider fully the position of land which has ostensibly fallen to registration as waste land but in fact is not, and perhaps never has been waste, *i.e.* the deemed waste land of a manor. Clearly, this class of land can never "cease" to be within the technical meaning of waste land.

The Forum also considers the problems of a miscellany of types of incorrect **2.84** registrations and concludes that it could not recommend a general re-opening of the registers to correct the mistakes. Instead a strictly limited extension of the removal categories is recommended:

> "We consider that land should be removed from the register only as a result of judicial process in which an applicant shows that the land was at the date of provisional registration neither waste land of a manor nor subject to rights of common and that the land is either occupied with a house or other building or is, and was, used for a purpose incompatible with its existence as a common."[72]

It is not entirely clear what is a purpose incompatible with existence as a common. For instance, is the registration of part of an enclosed agricultural holding incompatible because it is enclosed land or compatible because the primary use of the land is for grazing?

The judicial process suggested is a hearing before an Agricultural Land Tri- **2.85** bunal[73] with generally, parties meeting their own costs but, with a power in the Tribunal to award costs where a party has acted frivolously, vexatiously or oppressively and it is appropriate to do so having regard to all the circumstances.[74] The same procedure is recommended for the correction of administrative or clerical errors or where errors have arisen because of the use of obsolete or badly drawn maps.[75]

It is unclear, in the absence of a re-definition of rights of common, whether **2.86** the proposals of the Forum allow for the removal of doubtful categories of land such as common fields subject only to rights of intercommonage or, land held on charitable trusts.[76] The Forum does, however, make a separate recommendation that regulated pastures should be removed from the registers, presumably without application by the owners.[77]

[72] Common Land Forum Report, Appendix C, para. 011.
[73] *ibid.* paras. 114 *et seq.*
[74] *ibid.* paras. 068, 121.
[75] *ibid.* para. 014.
[76] *ibid.* para. 047: the Report seems to envisage an element of rough justice in the "public interest" which will entail certain classes of land, which were clearly never within the definition of common land, remaining on the registers.
[77] *ibid.* paras. 108 *et seq.; cf.* § 2.31 above.

3. Classification and Quantification of Common Rights

CLASSIFICATION

3.01 The principal characteristic of the common lands is that there is normally a commonality of use by a number of persons of the land of another person involving rights to take some part of the land or its produce. It is quite usual to refer to such rights as profits in common, rights of common or simply as commons. In respect of the most frequently encountered right, that of the right of common, this is an accurate representation but the grouping neither describes all the rights exercisable over the lands concerned nor sufficiently distinguishes the legal characteristics of the profit in common or the right of common.

This section commences with an analysis in legal terms of the various classes of rights over the lands, proceeds to a sub-classification of rights of common and other rights which for statutory purposes are treated as rights of common and concludes by considering certain rights which may now be considered obsolete.

Legal nature

1. Incorporeal hereditaments

3.02 For historical reasons, certain rights over property are treated as realty rather than, as might be expected in the case of a right, as personalty. The grouping, known as incorporeal hereditaments, consists of a disparate variety of interests the elements of which defy logical explanation. According to Blackstone, *profits à prendre* together with easements, advowsons, tithes, offices, dignities, franchises, corrodies, annuities and rents are all correctly viewed as incorporeal hereditaments.[1] The characteristics of an incorporeal hereditament are said to be first, that it will attract the formalities required for the creation and assignment of land and secondly, that, before 1926 upon a death intestate, it would devolve upon the heir as realty

[1] Bl.Comm., ii, 21.

56

rather than the next-of-kin as personalty.[2] The latter distinction has now been abolished,[3] but it must be doubted whether it could ever have applied to all so-called incorporeal hereditaments for appurtenant easements and profits annexed to a leasehold estate in land must have passed with the land.

All of the rights mentioned normally exist as rights in gross, with the excep- **3.03** tion of easements which may only be held as annexed to land[4] and *profits à prendre* which more usually exist as appurtenant to land but may be held in gross. Whether existing as appurtenant to land or in gross, the characteristic of incorporeity is an obvious attribute, but it is less than clear that a right perforce annexed to land may be properly viewed as a hereditament when it may not be separately devised, or otherwise dealt with, independently from the land to which it is annexed. A more appropriate description of ease- ments and profits annexed to land might be that they are benefits appurte- nant to corporeal hereditaments rather than separate incorporeal hereditaments.[5] In fact this distinction was always made when rating of land applied for poor law purposes. A *profit à prendre* in gross was treated as a separate tenement[6] whereas a profit annexed to land was not.[7]

In most circumstances the distinction drawn has little practical signifi- **3.04** cance. The formalities required for the creation of an easement or profit are those appropriate to corporealty.[8] After creation they will enure for the benefit of the land to which they are intended to be annexed[9] and will of necessity pass under the cover of the formalities for the disposal of the cor- poreal hereditament.[10] There is, however, one point in modern legislation where the two different types of incorporeal hereditament may be of signifi- cance. The Land Registry in its rules for the registration of title to land treats all "easements, rights and privileges" as required to be annexed to land and thereby prevents substantive registration of *profits à prendre* in gross with separate titles. This appears to be in spite of express provision for registration of incorporeal hereditaments as a form of land.[11]

2. *Profits à prendre* defined

A *profit à prendre* has been defined as a right to take from the land of **3.05** another person some part of the soil of the tenement or minerals under it, some of its natural produce or the animals *ferae naturae* upon it.[12] The

---

[2] Megarry and Wade, p. 813; *cf.* Co.Litt. 6a, 16a, 383a, b.
[3] *ibid.*
[4] But see *Gale's Easements*, pp. 43–44.
[5] *Re Brotherton* (1908) 77 L.J. Ch.D. 58 at 59, *per* Joyce J.; *cf.* Challis, *The Law of Real Property* (3rd ed., 1911), pp. 51, 52, 55.
[6] *R. v. Stoke (Inhabitants)* (1788) 2 T.R. 451, 100 E.R. 243; *R. v. Piddeltrenthide (Inhabitants)* (1790) 3 T.R. 772, 100 E.R. 851; *R. v. Tolpuddle (Inhabitants)* (1792) 4 T.R. 671, 100 E.R. 1237; *R. v. Hollington (Inhabitants)* (1802) 3 East. 113, 102 E.R. 540.
[7] *R. v. Churchill* (1825) 4 B. & C. 750 at 755, 107 E.R. 1240; *contra* Co.Litt. 6a.
[8] L.P.A. 1925, s.52; *cf.* § 4.35.
[9] *ibid.* s.187(1).
[10] *ibid.* s.62.
[11] Land Registration Rules 1925 (S.R. & O. 1925 No. 1093), r. 50; *cf.* §§ 4.14–4.17.
[12] *Alfred F. Beckett Ltd. v. Lyons* [1967] Ch. 449 at 482, *per* Winn L.J.

definition is wide and seems capable of including any part of the land or its natural products with the exception of water.[13] To constitute a profit the thing taken must at the time of the taking be susceptible to ownership and water has been held not to be owned by anyone nor is it part of the soil.[14] The margin between reducing a creature living on the land by killing it, or in the case of fish capturing it, into something capable of ownership and the same reduction of water by putting it into a container may seem narrow but it is clear that taking water, whether from a spring[15] or pump[16] or by cattle watering at a pond[17] may be an easement but not a *profit à prendre*. As the collateral right of *profit à rendre*[18] is now obsolete it is permissible to refer to a profit, albeit at the expense of the risk of confusion with the more vulgar use of the term.

3.06 Not all rights to take products, which are capable of being profits, necessarily include the intention of creating an interest in land. It is not unusual to find contracts to remove minerals or turf, purchase growing crops or exercise sporting rights. Where growing crops are concerned the position is clear as they are *fructus industriales* and a profit may only exist in respect of *fructus naturales*.[19] In the case of disposal of parts of the land it may be a question of intention as to whether a contract akin to one for the sale of goods, a *profit à prendre* or the grant of some strata of the land has been created. In *Lowe v. J. W. Ashmore Ltd.* (1970)[20] a taxpayer sought to establish that the sale of 12 acres of turf constituted a disposal of an equitable fee simple in the two inches of land concerned. Megarry J. thought that the taking was in the nature of an equitable profit but did not find it necessary to decide as it could certainly have no higher status. He inclined to the view that the informality of the transaction evinced no intention of creating an interest in land and that it was a contractual obligation and right to enter land, sever the turf and keep it, being thus a form of contract for the sale of goods.

3.07 A second area of difficulty can arise in connection with a sporting right which may fall to be considered as a licence, a contractual licence or, if removal of the game is included in the grant or contract, as a legal or equitable profit. If the transaction does create a profit, and the interest for which it is held is equivalent to a fee simple with the owner of the soil retaining an interest in the game, a registrable right of common has arisen.

3.08 Since 1925, a profit may only exist as a legal interest in land if held for an interest equivalent to a fee simple in possession or a term of years absol-

---

[13] For the purposes of the C.R.A. 1965 "land" includes land covered with water: s.22(1).

[14] *Ballard v. Tomlinson* (1885) 29 Ch.D. 115 at 121; nor, it seems, may ice be the subject matter of a grant of a profit: if the water is natural the taking may only be an easement, if contained and owned it is not a natural product: but *cf. Newby v. Harrison* (1861) 1 J. & H. 393, 70 E.R. 799, affirmed 4 L.T. 424.

[15] *Race v. Ward* (1855) 4 El. & Bl. 702, 119 E.R. 259.

[16] *Polden v. Bastard* (1865) L.R. 1 Q.B. 156.

[17] *Manning v. Wasdale* (1836) 5 Ad. & E. 758, 111 E.R. 1353.

[18] Co.Litt. 141b, 142a.

[19] For the distinctions between the two classes, see Megarry and Wade, p. 574.

[20] [1971] Ch. 545, especially at 557.

ute.[21] A profit created or conveyed other than in accordance with the formalities prescribed or for a term of different duration may only exist as an equitable profit.[22] As with corporealty demises and sub-demises may be carved out of the title to a legal or equitable profit.

3. The classes of profits

Profits may exist in one of two forms, as described by Coke: **3.09**

> "If a man claime by prescription any manner of common in another man's land, and that the owner of the land shall be excluded to have pasture, estovers, or the like, this is a prescription or custome against the law, to exclude the owner of the soyle; for it is against the nature of this word common, and it was implyed in the first grant, that the owner of the soyle should take his reasonable profit there, as it hath beene adjudged. But a man may prescribe or alledge a custome to have and enjoy *solam vesturam terrae*, from such a day till such a day, and hereby the owner of the soyle shall be excluded to pasture or feed there; and so he may prescribe to have *separalem pasturam*, and exclude the owner of the soyle from feeding there. *Nota diversitatem*. So a man may prescribe to have *separalem pischariam* in such a water, and the owner of the soyle shall not fish there; but if he claim to have *communiam pischariæ*, or *liberam pischariam*, the owner of the soyle shall fish there."[23]

Thus, a profit may exist as either a profit in common where the holder of the profit shares in the benefit of the product with the owner of the soil or, alternatively, as a sole or several profit where the owner of the soil is entirely excluded from benefit. While it may be more usual to find profits in common taken by a number of persons it will be noticed that Coke allows for prescription by one person. Whether it is a matter of necessity that more than one person be possessed of a profit in common has been a matter of some doubt,[24] but the position is now established that a right in common exists where one or more persons share the particular product with the owner of the soil.[25]

The second form in which a profit may exist is equally clear from Coke's **3.10** description. A sole or several profit will exist where a profit is granted away in its entirety so that the owner of the soil has no residual share left. The distinctive badge of the sole or several profit is the exclusion of the owner of the soil and not that a person holds the right solely. Sole and several in this context seem to be synonymous. While it is the case that a several fishery is

---

[21] L.P.A. 1925, s.1(1), (2).

[22] *ibid.* s.1(3).

[23] Co.Litt. 122a.

[24] *cf.* Elton, p. 2 and notes thereto; the doubts arise from a syntactic ambiguity in Bracton at folio 222.

[25] Authorities considered and reviewed by Chief Commons Commissioner G. D. Squibb in *Re Brookwood Lye, Woking, Surrey (No. 1)* (1977) 236/D/148, 6 D.C.C. 425.

frequently held by one person exclusively, it is also frequently found that sold pastures are held by a number of persons.[26]

4. A right of common distinguished

3.11   It is the usual practice in texts on profits or common rights to equate a profit in common with a right of common and, as lawyers would have it, a "common." But both common law and statute make the distinction that for a 3profit in common to be a right of common it must be held for an interest equivalent to a fee simple absolute in possession. The holding of a profit in common granted for the other legal interest, a term of years absolute, is not viewed as being a right of common. Prior to 1926, a right of common could also exist as a customary right annexed to a copyhold estate but upon the enfranchisement of copyhold estates this type of right became obsolete by conversion to rights of common annexed to freehold estates.[27]

3.12   As a result, a right granted to, say, graze animals over a parcel of land for a term of 999 years is neither the grant of a right of common nor a grant of statutory right of common attracting registrability under the Act of 1965.[28] This is not to say that a right of common may not be exercised by a termor or an agricultural tenant deriving title from the holder of a right of common, but that his derivative title is not a separate registrable right under the C.R.A. 1965. Some owners of former common land have avoided registration of the land under the C.R.A. 1965 by accepting the release of all rights of common and granting long terms in respect of the rights in their place.[29]

3.13   The modern formulation of the common law view may be seen in the judgment of Buckley J. in *White* v. *Taylor (No. 2)* (1969).[30] The court was asked to consider, *inter alia*, whether rights of common had been created or conveyed on the sale of tenements which had been in unified ownership with the alleged servient tenement until the time of the sale. Buckley J. said:

> "The subject-matter of these sales consisted of either freeholds belonging to the lord of the manor in respect of which no copyhold interests existed or of freeholds belonging to the lord of the manor subject to existing copyhold interests. In neither case could any rights of common have existed at the date of sale appertaining to the property sold,[31] for the lord of the manor could not have a right of common over the waste of the manor of which he himself was the owner. . . . If the vendor's leasehold tenants enjoyed grazing rights on the down, such rights would again be irrelevant to the sale: they would belong to the tenants

---

[26] *e.g. Potter* v. *North* (1669) 1 Wms.Saund. 346, 85 E.R. 503; *Rigg* v. *Earl of Lonsdale* (1857) 1 H. & N. 923, 156 E.R. 1475.

[27] L.P.A. 1922, s.188(6), Sched. 12.

[28] C.R.A. 1965, s.22(1) excludes rights held for a term of years from the definition of a right of common.

[29] *Re Trawden Moors, Pendle, Lancs (No. 1) and (No. 2)* (1982) 220/D/218–220, 217, 13 D.C.C. 114, 115.

[30] [1969] 1 Ch. 160.

[31] With respect, it is by no means clear that Buckley J. was entirely correct in this assertion as customary rights of common appurtenant to copyhold tenements were preserved upon enfranchisement.

under some express or inferred grant and would cease with the termination of their tenancies."[32]

This view seems to emanate from the case of *Baring* v. *Abingdon* (1892).[33] In considering a termor's right to graze over a manorial waste Kay L.J. stated that "in no sense was there any common belonging to this land, except that as between the lord and his tenants he had been accustomed to give his tenants permission to exercise rights of common such as he had himself in respect of this land when he let it."[34] This is to treat the termor's right as something akin to a personal licence which seems to be endorsed by Bowen L.J. in the same case when he said that a right enjoyed by a termor is "not a right created so as to be appurtenant to the lands at common law in the hands of any one to whom they might pass."[35]

The views expressed in *Baring* v. *Abingdon* clearly cannot survive the 1925 **3.14** legislation for section 187(1) of the L.P.A. 1925 provides that easements and rights created for a legal estate shall enure for the benefit of the land concerned. It would clearly be more logical now to recognise that a right of common may be created for either of the two legal estates. However, the common law has been reinforced by the C.R.A. 1965 which expressly excludes rights held from year to year or for a term of years from the definition of a right of common.[36]

A right of common, or any profit in common, may exist either as a right **3.15** annexed to land or as a right in gross.[37] The former is the most widespread in practice while the latter is but an occasional exception. Many apparent rights in gross and, especially statutory rights in gross, will be found on examination to be sole rights and not common law rights of common.

5. Sole profits

The feature which epitomises the sole or several profit and distinguishes it **3.16** from the profit in common is that, following the grant of a sole right, the owner of the soil of the servient tenement is excluded from any residual benefit in the product concerned.[38] It follows that there can only be one grant of a sole profit for a particular product as thereafter the owner has no remaining interest left. There is no reason, of course, why the grant should not be to a number of persons simultaneously and in the cases of sole pasture it is usual for the grant to have been shared by all the copyholders of a manor[39] or all the freeholders and copyholders.[40] Where a sole right is shared in this way it is usual for the individual share to be described as a

---

[32] *White* v. *Taylor (No. 2)* [1969] 1 Ch. 160 at 179.
[33] [1892] 2 Ch. 374.
[34] *ibid.* at 401.
[35] *ibid.* at 394.
[36] C.R.A. 1965, s.22(1).
[37] Capability of existence in the two forms does not mean that a profit granted as annexed to land may be converted into a right in gross: *cf.* §§ 6.01 to 6.22.
[38] *cf.* Coke, cited at § 3.09 *North* v. *Coe* (1668) Vaugh. 251 at 258, 124 E.R. 1060 at 1064.
[39] *Hoskins* v. *Robins* (1671) 2 Wms.Saund. 324, 85 E.R. 1123.
[40] *Potter* v. *North* (1669), above, n. 26.

stint, beastgate or cattlegate and there is nothing to prevent one person from holding, either as a result of the original grant, or by purchase, more than one stint or share.[41] It is also possible that one or more stints could have been reserved to the owner of the soil, although there does not seem to have been an example in practice.[42] Additionally, there is no reason why the owner should not recover a partial interest in the product by obtaining some of the stints by purchase or otherwise.[43]

3.17 The nature of a stint seems to be that it is a divided share in an incorporeal hereditament and as such may be disposed of as a separate hereditament. When such stints were held by copyhold they were subject to surrender and admittance in the customary court.[44] Unlike land subject to rights of common, where all residual benefit remains in the owner of the soil, there is no provision for any unused right to be taken up by the owner. It is, therefore, inappropriate to consider a sole profit as suitable to be attached as a benefit to land for if the land ceases to need the benefit there is no obvious recipient for the unused product.

In practice, with the exception remarked upon below, the general rule is that sole rights are held in gross, and may not be appurtenant to land.[45] Thus, in *Bailey* v. *Stephens* (1862),[46] when considering a grant to cut all the trees in a close, as a right attached to another close, Willes J. remarked that "the simple answer to that, is that it is not an incident which can be annexed by law to the ownership, much less to the occupation of land." Similarly, it was held in *Anderson* v. *Bostock* (1975)[47] that a sole and exclusive right to graze sheep could not be appurtenant to land. Being unlimited in quantum it is not possible to prescribe for a sole right appurtenant to land: one cannot prescribe in a *que* estate for a commercial profit à prendre in alieno solo; it must be for a *profit à prendre* measured by the nature, size and necessities of the estate.[48]

3.18 The exception to the general rule that sole rights may only be held in gross lies in omnipotent statutory enactment. Some inclosure awards allot sole rights as appurtenant to land. One such award is described in *Phillips* v.

---

[41] *cf. Earl of Lonsdale* v. *Rigg* (1856) 11 Ex. 654, 156 E.R. 992; see § 3.102.

[42] *Seymour* v. *Courteney* (1771) 5 Burr. 2814 at 2187, 98 E.R. 478 at 479 *per* Lord Mansfield C.J., referring to a liberty reserved upon alienation of a sole fishery.

[43] *Earl of Lonsdale* v. *Rigg*, above, n. 41: by forfeiture.

[44] *ibid.*

[45] See § 3.18. There are some other exceptions to this general rule, *e.g.* rights of common have been converted into sole rights following the exclusion of the lord from further benefit following a court decree: *Earl de la Warr* v. *Miles* (1881) L.R. 17 Ch.D. 535; *Duke of Portland* v. *Hill* (1866) L.R. 2 Eq. 765. It should also be noted that a sole right pleaded successfully in copyholders in *Hoskins* v. *Robins* (1671), above n. 39 and in copyholders and freeholders in *Potter* v. *North* (1669), above, n. 26, may or may not have been limited to use with tenements but in neither case did the court direct its attention to the nature of the right and was only concerned with deciding whether the sole right itself was capable of lawful existence.

[46] (1862) 12 C.B.(N.S.) 91 at 110, 142 E.R. 1077 at 1084.

[47] [1976] 1 Ch. 312.

[48] *Lord Chesterfield* v. *Harris* [1908] 2 Ch. 397 at 424, *per* Buckley L.J.; affirmed [1911] A.C. 623; *cf.* headnote.

Maile (1830)[49] where a sole pasture was allotted with rights to graze two cows each "to be used, stocked, and enjoyed by the owners and proprietors of commonable messuages and cottages and the respective tenants and occupiers of the said messuages and cottages only." It is hardly arguable other than that the rights awarded were annexed to the properties concerned. This produces an unsatisfactory result in theory, for if the cottages are pulled down where does the interest in the pasture vest? It may be that in practice no sole rights of this nature have remained to the present day.

6. Analogous rights

Some other rights existing over or in connection with the common lands **3.19** may bear a superficial resemblance to profits but nevertheless are not *profits à prendre* or statutory rights of common. It is clear, however, that many, but not all, of these rights have been registered and the commons registers under the C.R.A. 1965 are not entirely consistent.

(a) Common pur cause de vicinage[50]

The right of common *pur cause de vicinage* has recently been declared to be **3.20** properly classified as a right of common[51] but is distinctly anomalous within the class as it cannot be properly viewed as a *profit à prendre*. A common of vicinage can only exist as between contiguous unenclosed commons and it is the mutual right which holders of rights of common have, on each of the commons, not to be sued in trespass by their counterparts on the contiguous common if and when their animals stray from the home common to the other common. It can only apply in connection with, and annexed, to a right of common of pasturage and can have no independent existence. It is self evidently not a substantive right to take some part of the produce of the land of another person but is more in the nature of a quasi-contractual agreement for the avoidance of suits. It may not be granted by the owner of the soil, or prescribed for, as it is a matter of customary law. The right may be terminated at any time by the enclosure of one of the commons. The Commons Commissioners have consistently refused registration of vicinage as a right of common.[52]

(b) Intercommonage

Of a similar nature to the right of common of vicinage is the right of inter- **3.21** commonage which exists between owners of divided shares in a common field, considered above.[53] Each owner's entitlement to grazing is the amount supplied to the whole by his severalty portion and there is no

---

[49] [1830] 7 Bing. 133, 131 E.R. 51. See also *Place* v. *Jackson* (1824) Dow. & Ry. K.B. 318. For an example of copyhold allotments not exceeding three sheep to each house which "shall for ever thereafter remain, go along and be of the same tenure with such houses," see the Bourn Inclosure Act 1766 cited in *Pochin* v. *Duncombe* (1857) 1 H. & N. 842 at 844 n.(a), 156 E.R. 1440 at 1442.

[50] See further at § 3.46.

[51] *Newman* v. *Bennett* [1981] 1 Q.B. 726.

[52] See further at §§ 4.18–4.19.

[53] See further at § 1.65.

entitlement directly to take the profits from the land of another person. As with common of vicinage the purpose of the intercommonage is for the avoidance of suits. It is difficult to view intercommonage as any form of profit and, still less, a right of common.

(c) Quasi-rights

3.22 Rights of grazing exercised by the lord (or other owner of the soil of a common) over common land in association with demesne or purchased freeholds are clearly not rights of common for no person may have a *profit à prendre* over his own land. Nevertheless, rights exercised by the owner in respect of his land in hand will have all the characteristics associated with rights of common, such as limitation according to the acreage of the land concerned,[54] and the obligation to fence against the common will be accepted.[55] Such rights are only quasi-rights of common but they have frequently been accepted for compensation and allotment purposes[56] *pari passu* with true rights of common.

3.23 The quasi-rights of the owner would seem not to be registrable rights under the provisions in the C.R.A. 1965 and the Commissioners have so held consistently until about 1984 when we find one Commissioner taking the opposite view. The view of the present Chief Commissioner (1986) is that quasi-rights are unequivocally unregistrable. The commons registers can only be described as completely inconsistent in relation to this feature as many lords, and other owners, did register quasi-rights and some encouraged their tenants to do so. Many have become final through lack of objection.[57]

(d) Rights on regulated pastures

3.24 The rights exercised by owners of undivided shares in land to graze in common derive authority from the ownership of land and not from any recognisable form of *profit à prendre* or right of common. It might be anticipated that neither the land nor the rights are registrable under the C.R.A. 1965.[58] There is little doubt that a very high proportion of regulated pastures have been registered and a case against registration does not seem to have been fully argued before a Commons Commissioner.

(e) Rights under charitable trusts

3.25 It is not unknown for a corporation to hold land on a charitable trust for the benefit of classes of inhabitants of the locality.[59] It is difficult to identify any form of *profit à prendre* in such an arrangement as the right of the individual inhabitant is not a right against the owner of the soil but a right as a

---

[54] See § 7.13.

[55] In the present work fencing against a waste is considered as a customary duty which will apply to all persons adjoining a waste: see further at § 9.05.

[56] Land Clauses Consolidation Act 1845, s.99; Inclosure Act 1845, s.27 (now repealed).

[57] For which see § 4.10.

[58] See §§ 2.27–2.32.

[59] See § 2.34.

beneficiary under a trust. Nevertheless, it seems, that many such arrangements have been registered under the C.R.A. 1965.

Rights of common classified

Before 1926 both rights of common and sole rights could be distinguished   **3.26**
depending upon the form of tenure under which they were held. They could
have been annexed to freehold land as a private right or attached to a copyhold estate as a customary right. Since the abolition of copyhold tenure a
right of common may only exist as a freehold interest,[60] and any distinctions between the two classes of right have now ceased except in matters of
proving title.

Today, rights of common may be classified in several ways, of which the   **3.27**
two most important are by legal category and by the subject matter of the
grant. Thus, rights of common may be appendant, appurtenant, in gross and
pur cause de vicinage, i.e. of differing legal nature, or may be for pasturage,
turbary, estovers, pannage, piscary, rights in the soil and rights to animals,
fishes and birds, *i.e.* of differing subject matter. In this section the particular
law relating to the various classes of rights of common is considered and the
sole profit is dealt with separately.[61]

LEGAL CATEGORY

1. Appendant

Rights of common annexed to land may be sub-divided into those which are   **3.28**
appendant and those appurtenant. The older cases draw clear distinctions
between the two and in one important respect they are dealt with differently today.[62] The Royal Commission considered that the distinction "has
for many centuries been more tenuous in fact than in law, and is now without practical significance."[63] It was recommended that upon registration
appendant rights should become appurtenant.[64] The recommendation was
not adopted.

(a) Origin

It is not entirely clear that the modern distinctions were ever known to the   **3.29**
early commentators. In Glanvill, Bracton and Fleta *pertinere* and *pertinen-
tia* are used without distinction and in the Year Books *cum pertinentiis*.[65]
To Fitzherbert the distinction was that common appendant was the result
of a grant whereas an appurtenant right was one pleaded "out of tyme of

---

[60] See above, n. 27.
[61] § 3.90.
[62] § 3.42.
[63] Royal Commission Report (1958), para. 272.
[64] *ibid.*
[65] *cf.* Scrutton, *Commons and Common Fields* (1887), especially at pp. 42–55.

mynde."[66] Even in the time of Coke the distinction was not pleaded: the word *pertinens* must be "construed *subjecta materia*, the circumstance of the case directing the Court to judge the common to be appendant or appurtenant."[67] It is probable that the distinction is one promulgated by the Elizabethan lawyers as part of their manorial model. It is described by Coke in his report of *Tyrringham's Case* (1584)[68]:

> "The beginning of common appendant by the ancient law was in such manner; when a lord enfeoffed another of arable land to hold of him in socage . . . the feoffee should have common in the lord's wastes for his necessary cattle which plowed and manured his land, and that for two reasons, 1. Because it was, as it was then held, *tacite* implied in the feoffment, for the feoffee could not plough and manure his land without cattle, and they could not be kept without pasture . . . The 2d. reason was for the maintenance and advancement of tillage, which is much respected and favoured in law; so that such common appendant is of common right . . . and, therefore, it is not necessary to prescribe therein . . . but it is only appendant to ancient land arable hide and gain, and only for cattle, *sc.* horses and oxen to plough his land, and cows and sheep to manure his land . . . "

3.30 The legal thesis then is that, upon an enfeoffment of arable land, the law implied a right of common appendant which was of common right "and therefore a man need not prescribe for it."[69] It follows that, as the Statute of Quia Emptores 1290 abolished sub-infeudation, all appendant rights must pre-date the statute and that the class is closed and limited in number—common appendant cannot be created by a modern grant.[70] The right may be said to arise by privilege of law rather than grant although this has been denied to some extent when it was said that the right "belongs only to each grantee . . . by virtue of his individual grant, and as an incident thereto."[71] It followed that "it is not to be understood that every tenant of a manor has by common law such a right, but only that certain tenants have such a right, not by prescription, but as a right by common law, incident to the grant."[72] If within the privileged class, there is no need to support claim to an appendant right by evidence of actual user,[73] although long non-user may be some evidence of abandonment.[74] Clearly, evidence of being within the class of persons entitled will be difficult to find today. It is, of course, only the free-

---

[66] *Fitzherbert's Surveying,* folio vi.

[67] At 4 Co.Rep. 38a, 76 E.R. 980.

[68] (1584) 4 Co.Rep. 36a at 37a, 76 E.R. 973 at 977; *cf.* Inst. 85; 2 Inst. 96; Bl.Comm., ii, p. 33.

[69] Co.Litt. 122a, Bro.Abr. Common, pl. 23 cited Vin.Ab., Prescription Y 10.

[70] *Baring* v. *Abingdon* [1892] 2 Ch. 374 at 378, *per* Stirling J.; *cf.* 1 Ro.Ab. 396, citing 26 H8 4, 5 Ass. 9, *per* Herle.

[71] *Earl of Dunraven* v. *Llewellyn* (1850) 15 Q.B. 791 at 811, 117 E.R. 657 at 664, *per* Parke B.

[72] (1850) 15 Q.B. 791 at 810, 117 E.R. 657 at 664. It may be necessary to provide evidence of the individual grant and the right may belong to a class of tenants; *Chesterfield* v. *Fountaine* (1895), reported at [1908] 1 Ch. 243n. at 244, *per* Wills J.

[73] *Ughred* v. *C.* (1331) 5 Lib.Ass., folio 8, pl. 2; *Anon.* v. *T.* (1426) Y.B. 4 H. 6, folio 13, pl. 10; *Hayes* v. *Bridges and Guess* (1795) Ridg.L. & S. 390.

[74] For abandonment, see § 5.38.

hold tenants of the manor to whom it may apply and not the customary freehold or copyhold tenants[75] who were not enfeoffed.

From the theory of the origin of common appendant a number of conse- **3.31** quences flow. As the right attaches only to ancient arable feoffments, if it can be shown that the land was not arable at the time of the grant then the presumption of a right appendant does not arise.[76] On the other hand, it is not necessary for the land still to be arable so that if "of late time an house is built upon part, and some part is employed to pasture, and some for meadow . . . the common remains appendant."[77]

(b) Classes of animals limited

The classes of animals allowed with a common appendant are only those **3.32** required to plough and manure the land—horses, oxen, cows and sheep. The appendant classes of livestock are sometimes referred to as "commonable animals."[78] It may be better, henceforth, to use the term to describe the classes of animals which have achieved registration on any particular common under the C.R.A. 1965.

The number of animals which may be grazed is those which are *levant* and **3.33** *couchant* on the dominant tenement,[79] that is to say "for such and so many as he has occasion for to plough and manure his land in proportion to the quantity thereof."[80] It follows that there is no objection to division of the right *pro rata* upon division of the dominant land however small the parcels.[81] Rights *levant* and *couchant* may not be severed from the land nor allocated disproportionately on division of the dominant tenement.[82]

The legal theory of a right of common of pasture appendant, implied by law **3.34** for so many animals as are *levant* and *couchant* on the dominant land, seems to preclude the possibility of appendant rights ever being for fixed numbers. However, the practical reality must be that, in some cases at least, the numbers have been quantified.[83] They may have become "regulated by custom" or by agreement between the commoners.[84] It is argued below that

[75] For the distinctions, see *Scriven's Copyholds*, p. 14. The customary and other copyhold tenants of the manor held rights of common by custom and were never enfeoffed. Unified ownership of the manor and the tenement at any time will serve to extinguish a common appendant.

[76] *Warrick* v. *Queen's College, Oxford* (1871) 6 Ch.App. 716 at 730, *per* Hatherley L.C.

[77] *Tyrringham's Case* (1584) 4 Co.Rep. 36a at 37a, 76 E.R. 973 at 979; *cf. Carr* v. *Lambert* (1866) L.R. 1 Ex. 168.

[78] *Standred* v. *Shorditch* (1620) Cro.Jac. 580, 79 E.R. 496.

[79] Y.B.B., 17 E3 27; 37 H6 34; 10 E4 10b; 14 E4 32b.

[80] *Bennett* v. *Reeve* (1740) Willes 227 at 231, 125 E.R. 1144 at 1146, *per* Willes L.C.J.

[81] *ibid.*

[82] Chap. six, especially § 6.20.

[83] The early remedy for a commoner aggrieved by another surcharging the common with animals was by the writ of admeasurement, which had the result of defining entitlement to graze.

[84] *Follet* v. *Troake* (1705) 2 Ld.Raym. 1186, 92 E.R. 284; on many commons there are lists of recognised entitlements which, of course, were referred to at the time of registration under the C.R.A. 1965.

quantification for practical convenience must be distinguished from a grant for fixed numbers in considering severance of rights.[85]

(c) Purchase of part of the waste

3.35 If the owner of a right appendant purchases part of a waste, over which he exercises the right, the right is apportioned so that it is extinguished only in relation to the part purchased.[86] It is otherwise in the case of a common appurtenant.[87] If, on the other hand, an appendant right holder purchases the entire waste over which the right is exercisable the right is extinguished by unity of possession.[88]

2. Appurtenant

(a) General nature

3.36 A common appurtenant generally shares the feature with common appendant that it is a right annexed to land, being an incorporeal hereditament appurtenant (in the modern sense) to a corporeal hereditament.[89] There seems to be no reason in principle why an incorporeal hereditament may not be appurtenant to another incorporeal hereditament[90] in which case it may be correct to view rights annexed to, say, a manor or a corporation sole as appurtenant and not as rights in gross.[91] It can hardly be that a right granted to a church benefice, for example, may be granted away to any person which would be the result of treating them as rights in gross.

3.37 In contradistinction to a common appendant, a right appurtenant does not arise by privilege of law but by express, implied or presumed grant. It is said, again in contrast to the common appendant, to be "against common right."[92] While a common appurtenant may be granted at this day, the circumstances when a grant will be effective are limited by the provisions of the C.R.A. 1965. Briefly, it may be said that a grant, by any means, over land registered under the mandatory procedure contained in the Act, is ineffective.[93]

---

[85] See §§ 6.18–6.22.
[86] Co.Litt. 122a; *Wood* v. *Moreton* (1608) 1 Brownl. & Golds. 180, 123 E.R. 741; *Morse* v. *Well* (1608) 1 Brownl. & Goldo. 180, 123 E.R. 741; *contra* Brooke-Taylor, "Perdurable Estates" (1977) 41 Conv. 107 at 114.
[87] § 3.42.
[88] § 5.02.
[89] The corporeal and incorporeal hereditaments must agree in nature and quality: Co.Litt. 122a.
[90] *Contra* Co.Litt. 122a, but see Hargrave's note thereto and editor's note at 4 Co.Rep. 37a, 76 E.R. 975. *cf. Hanbury* v. *Jenkins* [1901] 2 Ch. 401 at 422 (several profit of piscary as dominant tenement); *White* v. *Taylor (No. 2)* [1969] 1 Ch. 160 at 198, 199 (common appurtenant as dominant tenement for an easement); *Mill* v. *Commissioners of New Forest* (1856) 18 C.B. 60, 139 E.R. 1286 (one right of common may not be appurtenant to another).
[91] See further at § 3.43.
[92] *Tyrringham's Case*, above, n. 77 at 37a, 978.
[93] See § 4.41.

(b) Subject matter

Free from the association with arable land, inherent in the appendant right, **3.38**
a right appurtenant may be annexed to any type of land, including buildings,
and in respect of any part of the land or product of the land which the court
will accept.[94]

In addition to bovine animals, sheep, and horses it is clear that appurtenant **3.39**
rights of pasturage may exist in respect of donkeys, swine, goats and geese.[95]
It is not entirely clear which categories of poultry, other than geese, may be
commonable. In 1312 it was said that *avers* included geese and chickens.[96]
In 1624 a case was adjourned on the grounds that turkeys were not *avers* as
they could fly.[97] The question might have been entirely resolved by registration under the C.R.A. 1965 but for inconsistent decisions. It was directly
considered in one hearing and the conclusion reached that geese were the
only commonable poultry largely, it seems, because the presence on a common of other poultry could be accounted for by difficulty in containment.[98]
In other decisions, however, chickens have been confirmed in registration
without comment.[99]

Occasionally one encounters rights of common for products other than pas- **3.40**
turage described as appendant.[1] In theory, there seems to be no compelling
reason why, say, turf to be burnt in a house should not be implied by law as
part of an enfeoffment, but there is no direct authority on the subject and it
seems possible to restrict the use of appendant to rights of pasturage and
treat all others as rights appurtenant. It is clear that appurtenant rights
other than pasturage must agree "in nature and quality" with the dominant
tenement.[2] Thus, a right of common to take peat for burning or, timber for
house repair, may only be appurtenant to a particular house.[3] The quantity
of such rights is usually related to the needs of the dominant tenement but
it is not unknown for it to be fixed.[4] There has been some comment
amongst text writers that where the quantity is fixed it may be severed from

[94] §§ 3.58 *et seq.*
[95] Co.Litt. 122a; *Smith* v. *Feverell* (1675) 2 Mod. 6, 86 E.R. 909 (hogs); *Earl of Dunraven* v. *Llewellyn* (1850) 15 Q.B. 791 at 811, 117 E.R. 657 at 665, *per* Parke B.: the
right, where by grant, has no limits and depends upon the will of the grantor.
[96] Y.B. 6 E2, 1 SS(34) 125; see also *Westley* v. *Fulewell* (1308/9) Y.B. 2 & 3 E2, SS(19)
149.
[97] *Fettyplace* v. *Bates* (1624) Benl. 143, 73 E.R. 999.
[98] *Re Bucklebury Common, Bucklebury, Berks.* (1978) 2/D/8, 8 D.C.C. 43; see also
Re Lodsworth Common, Lodsworth, W. Sussex (1976) 238/D/8–11, 5 D.C.C. 235
and *Re The Green, Elmstone Hardwick, Gloucs.* (1976) 213/D/54–55, 5 D.C.C.
251; *cf. Morley* v. *Clifford* (1882) 20 Ch.D. 753.
[99] *Re Mynydd Llangeinwyr and Braiach Yr Hydd, Llangeinor, Mid Glam.* (1977) 275/
D/196, 5 D.C.C. 378 and *Re Shucknall Hill Common etc.* (1978) 215/D/272–275,
277–279, 8 D.C.C. 92.
[1] *e.g.* Co.Litt. 121b; *Scriven's Copyholds*, p. 289.
[2] Co.Litt. 121b.
[3] *Loc. cit.*: "common of turbary or of estovers cannot be appendant or appurtenant to
land, but to a house to be spent there"; *cf. Tyrringham's Case*, above, n. 68.
[4] Y.B. 10 E4 3, Bro.Com., pl. 13 cited Woolrych (2nd ed.) p. 79; *Hayward* v. *Cunnington* (1667) 1 Lev. 231, 83 E.R. 383; *Att.-Gen.* v. *Reynolds* [1911] 2 K.B. 888.

the dominant tenement and converted into a gross.[5] The matter is considered in detail later and it is merely remarked at this point that there does not seem to be a single case in support of the proposition. In the only case where it was considered, the opinion was that the thesis was insurportable.[6]

3.41 While appendant rights of pasturage are always *levant* and *couchant*,[7] *i.e.* related to the needs of the dominant land, there is no reason why appurtenant rights should not be for a fixed number of animals. There is some rather elderly authority that where rights have been granted for a number certain they are more properly viewed as grants in gross. Thus for instance may be found: "If one grants to I.S. eight acres of land, *simul cum* so much common as belongs to his oxgang of land in a certain place, this is not common appurtenant, but in gross . . . "[8]

The significance of deciding whether or not a particular grant was in fact made as appurtenant to land lies in the current economic advantage which exists in treating the rights as severable from the land and separately saleable. The question of the severance of rights of pasturage is considered later.[9]

(c) Practical distinction from appendant rights

3.42 The main, and arguably the only, real practical difference today between an appendant and an appurtenant right of common lies in the differential treatment accorded to the owners of the rights upon a purchase or leasing of part of the land over which the right is exercised. The definitive expression of the law, effective to the present day, is that of Sir Edward Coke: "If a man purchase part of the land, wherein common appendant is to be had, the common shall be apportioned, because it is of common right; but not so of common appurtenant, or of any other common of what nature so-ever."[10]

The result of the rule is well illustrated in *Tyrringham's Case* (1584).[11] Rights attached to a farm were exercisable over two wastes. The lord, owner of one waste, purchased the farm. If the rights had been appendant the lord could have prescribed from the time of purchase "that he has put his cattle into the residue *pro rata portione*."[12] The court resolved that the right was appurtenant in which event "by the said purchase all the common was extinct."[13] In *Wyat Wyld's Case* (1609)[14] the principle was confirmed. If a commoner purchases part of a waste his whole right is extinguished and, if he leases part, the right over the whole waste is suspended but will revive at

---

[5] Elton, pp. 86, 87, 101; Cooke, p. 37; Joshua Williams, p. 199.
[6] *Att.-Gen.* v. *Reynolds*, above n. 4; see further § 6.32.
[7] § 3.33 and n. 79, above.
[8] Fitzherbert, *New Natura Brevium*, (8th ed., 1755), p. 420.
[9] §§ 6.01 *et seq.*
[10] Co.Litt. 122a; *Wood* v. *Moreton* (1608), above, n. 86; for a further discussion, see § 5.07.
[11] (1584) 4 Co.Rep. 36b, 76 E.R. 973.
[12] (1584) 4 Co.Rep. 36b at 38a, 76 E.R. 973 at 980.
[13] *Loc. cit.* The rule did not apply to copyhold tenements so that upon a regrant by copy of court roll following escheat or forfeiture the customary rights revived without more: *Worledg* v. *Kingswel* (1598) Cro.Eliz. 794, 78 E.R. 1024, *Badger* v. *Ford* (1819) 3 B. & Ald. 153, 106 E.R. 618.
[14] (1609) 8 Co.Rep. 78b, 77 E.R. 593; see also Co.Litt. 114b and *Anon.* (1581) Godb. 4, 78 E.R. 3.

the end of the lease. The rule has survived to modern times and was followed in the recent case of *White* v. *Taylor* (No. 1) (1969).[15]

3. In gross

The definitive explanation of a common in gross is usually to be considered **3.43**
that of Blackstone;

> "Common in gross or at large is such as is neither appendant nor appur-
> tenant to land but is annexed to a man's person; being granted to him
> and his heirs by deed; or it may be claimed by prescriptive right, as by a
> parson of a church, or the like corporation sole. This is a separate inher-
> itance, entirely distinct from any landed property, and may be vested in
> one who has not a foot of ground in the manor."[16]

The distinctive badge of a common in gross, it is said and Coke agrees, is
that it is "so called because it appertaineth to no land."[17] It is possible, however, within the description to discern two separate types of right: a right
annexed to a person and a right annexed to an incorporeal hereditament
such as a benefice, an office or a manor.[18] There is clearly a difference
between a right in gross granted to a man and his heirs, which it is now clear
may be alienated to another, and a right attached to an office which, it is
suggested, may not. It is perhaps better at the present day to consider a right
in gross only as a right which is not annexed to a hereditament, whether
corporeal or incorporeal, and classify all others as appurtenant. This is not,
as it might seem, to challenge the authority of Blackstone and Coke, whose
analyses were adequate at the time but have since been overriden by the
decision in the mid-nineteenth century that a common in gross might be
severed from the man and his descendants to whom it had been granted.[19] It
seems that it is only since then that a right in gross has finally assumed the
characteristic perceived today of being capable of free alienation.

The incidence of rights of common of pasturage in gross whether for grazing **3.44**
or any other product is extremely low. Studies of the commons registers
indicate that they are the very occasional exception. Statutory rights of
common in gross on the other hand are widely encountered in certain parts
of the country. Examination of most will, however, disclose that they are
usually derived from sole rights and not rights of common.

---

[15] [1969] 1 Ch. 150; approved *Central Electricity Generating Board* v. *Clwyd County
Council* [1976] 1 W.L.R. 151 at 157, *per* Goff J.
[16] Bl.Comm., ii, 34.
[17] Co.Litt. 122a.
[18] *Withers* v. *Iseham* (1552) 1 Dyer 70a, 73 E.R. 148: rights appurtenant to a park
keeper; *Miller* v. *Walker* (1670) 1 Sid. 462, 82 E.R. 1217: "burgagers in a burrow."
For whether customary rights which automatically revived on re-grant of a copyhold are appurtenant to a manor, see the cases cited above, n. 13; and see *Musgrave*
v. *Gave* (1742) Willes 319, 125 E.R. 1193 (copyhold incorporeal hereditaments said
to be appurtenant to the manor when in hands of lord).
[19] *Welcome* v. *Upton* (1840) 6 M. & W. 536 at 541, 151 E.R. 524 at 526 in argument
and at 543, 528, *per* Parke B.

3.45 A right in gross *ex hypothesi* is not related to the needs of a dominant corporeal hereditament and rights in gross for pasturage were usually granted for a fixed number, although some were said to be *sans nombre*.[20] Since registration under the C.R.A. 1965 requires quantification of all rights involving grazing animals the latter class is, in all events, now obsolete.

4. Pur cause de vicinage

3.46 The final category of right of common is the common *pur cause de vicinage, i.e.* by reason of neighbourhood. Unlike the first three categories it can have no independent existence always being ancillary to a primary common appendant, appurtenant or in gross.[21] Further, unlike the other rights, it is determinable at will by the person over whose land it is exercisable by the simple expedient of enclosure.[22] It is a customary right applicable to all the persons within the custom[23] and may not, therefore, be prescribed for in an individual estate.[24]

(a) General nature

3.47 The general nature of the right is described thus by Blackstone:

> "Common *because of vicinage*, or neighbourhood, is where the inhabitants of two townships, which lie contiguous to each other, have usually intercommoned with one another; the beasts of the one straying mutually into the other's fields, without any molestation from either. This is indeed only a permissive right, intended to excuse what in strictness is a trespass in both, and to prevent a multiplicity of suits: and therefore either township may inclose and bar out the other, though they have intercommoned time out of mind. Neither has any person of one town a right to put his beasts originally into the other's common; but if they escape, and stray thither of themselves, the law winks at the trespass."[25]

There is some confusion of terminology and in the present text vicinage is used only in the context of rights over contiguous wastes (or contiguous open fields which today will be most unusual) and as between neighbouring manors (or, as Blackstone would have it, townships). The similar right not

[20] See further at § 3.139.
[21] But see § 3.52.
[22] *Gullett* v. *Lopes* (1811) 13 East. 348, 104 E.R. 404, considered further at § 3.49.
[23] "A right of common appurtenant depends upon a grant from the lord and includes common of vicinage": *Minet* v. *Morgan* (1870) 11 L.R. Eq. 284 at 286, *per* Lord Romilly M.R. As a lord could not grant vicinage over the waste of another lord the conclusion is inescapable that vicinage of immemorial origin is a customary right of common and that access to a substantive right over a waste brings a person within the custom; *cf. Prichard* v. *Powell* (1845) 10 Q.B. 589 at 603, 116 E.R. 224 at 229, *per* Lord Denman C.J.
[24] § 3.54.
[25] Bl.Comm., ii, 33.

to be sued in trespass, found in common fields between holders of divided severalties, is referred to as intercommonage.[26]

(b) Conditions

There are a number of conditions required before a common of vicinage may **3.48** exist—

(i) The land must be contiguous and unenclosed If there are three commons, A, B and C, with B lying between A and C, the commoners of A and C may intergraze over common B and the commoners of B may intergraze with A and/or C, but the commoners of A may not intergraze with those of C.[27] The intergrazing must, it seems, be simultaneous and continuous and there is no room for a common contiguous to two others to be grazed for part of the year from one common and part from the other.[28]

(ii) The right is only exercisable from land where there is a lawful right for the animals to be Usually a holder of a right of vicinage will have a right appendant, appurtenant or in gross on his "home" common and may only turn out animals there whence they may stray to the contiguous common.[29] There are some indications that the lawful presence required may be derived otherwise than through a right of common.[30] There is no reason why a commoner may not have been granted a right of common over both wastes in which case the question of vicinage does not arise.[31]

(iii) The quantity of animals turned to the "home" common must not exceed the capacity of that common Thus, if "in the town of A there are 50 acres of common and in the town of B there are an hundred acres of common; in that case the inhabitants of the town of A cannot put more cattle into their common of 50 acres than their common will feed without any respect to the common within the town of B, *nec e converso.*"[32] It will be noticed that it is the capacity of the common and not the legally exercisable right over the common which is relevant although clearly the exercisable right also may not be exceeded or the animals will not be lawfully present on the home common.

---

[26] § 1.65.

[27] *Anon.* (1540) 1 Dyer 47b, 73 E.R. 104; *Bromfeild* v. *Kirber* (1706) 11 Mod. 72, 88 E.R. 897; *Commissioners of Sewers* v. *Glasse* (1874) L.R. 19 Eq. 134 at 160, *per* Jessel M.R.

[28] *ibid.*

[29] *Sir Miles Corbet's Case* (1585) 7 Co.Rep. 5a, 77 E.R. 417; *Anon.* (1573) 3 Dyer 316b, 73 E.R. 716, *per* Manwood J.; *Bromfeild* v. *Kirber,* above, n. 27.

[30] See § 3.52, for consideration of intergrazing between other lands.

[31] "There can be no doubt that a man may have two distinct substantial grants of rights of common over different wastes from different lords in respect of the same tenement.": *per* Ellenborough C.J. in *Hollinshead* v. *Walton* (1806) 7 East. 485 at 491, 103 E.R. 188 at 190; see also *Barwick* v. *Matthews* (1814) 5 Taunt. 365, 128 E.R. 730. However, where a farm lies on the boundary of two commons the rights are exercisable where a jury says they are even if there is a mistake as to the boundary: *Hetherington* v. *Vane* (1821) 4 B. & Ald. 428, 106 E.R. 993.

[32] *Sir Miles Corbet's Case* above, n. 29, *nota per* Coke; confirmed in *Commissioners of Sewers* v. *Glasse,* above, n. 27, at 161, *per* Jessel M.R. Overstocking may be fraudulent: *Prichard* v. *Powell* (1845) 10 Q.B. 589 at 603, 116 E.R. 224 at 229, *per* Lord Denman C.J.

(iv) There must always be, or at least have been, a mutuality of rights over and between the contiguous commons[33]

(c) Termination

3.49   The mutual interest may only be terminated unilaterally by the total enclosure of one of the commons. Partial enclosure will leave the unenclosed portion still subject to common of vicinage even if it was clearly the enclosing party's intention to terminate the mutual arrangement.[34] A partial enclosure will, however, have the effect of terminating the rights over and from the portion: over the land concerned because no beasts may escape from the home common and stray there; from the land because of the condition which limits the number of animals turned out to the capacity of the land which by partial enclosure has been reduced in area.

3.50   Although it cannot be said to be finally decided, the indications are that it is not possible for commoners on one common to decide unilaterally to terminate the mutual arrangement. In *Wells* v. *Pearcy* (1835)[35] there had been a private Inclosure Act extinguishing rights of common and it was contended that the resulting lack of reciprocity was sufficient to terminate the rights of vicinage. Tindal C.J. held that it was not, at least in the absence of notice. In *Clarke* v. *Tinker* (1845)[36] the question of notice was brought directly into issue. There had been statutory extinguishment of rights and allotment of the land into severalties. The allottees gave notice to a holder of rights in gross over contiguous unfenced land that they would distrain his straying sheep in future. The sheep did stray and an action in trespass was brought. It was open to the Court of Queen's Bench to decide the matter on the issue of notice if it in fact terminated the vicinage. Instead it took evidence about the practice over the lands and concluded that vicinage had never existed, as the regular practice was to drive the sheep back when they strayed. It seems, therefore, that a unilateral decision to withdraw from the arrangement is insufficient and that private allotment into severalty without enclosure is not enough. No doubt it would be otherwise if the extinguishment of rights was as the result of a general Act.[37]

3.51   The extinguishment of any or all the substantive rights of common will clearly also extinguish the ancillary right of vicinage if for no other reason than that the animals no longer have anywhere whence they may "escape and stray thither of themselves."

(d) Vicinage on other lands

3.52   Although strictly a right of common *pur cause de vicinage* can only apply as between contiguous commons the argument that it avoids a multiplicity of suits has equal application wherever there is intergrazing between unenclosed adjoining lands. There is some authority, without actual decision,

---

[33] *Heath* v. *Elliott* (1838) 4 Bing.N.C. 388, 132 E.R. 836; *Clarke* v. *Tinker* (1845) 10 Q.B. 604, 116 E.R. 230; *Bromfeild* v. *Kirber*, above, n. 27.

[34] *Gullett* v. *Lopes*, above, n. 22.

[35] (1835) 1 Bing.N.C. 556 at 568, 131 E.R. 1232 at 1236, *per* Tindal C.J.

[36] (1845) 10 Q.B. 604, 116 E.R. 230.

[37] Inclosure Act 1845, s.69: extinguishment of sheepwalk, common or other rights.

that it, or something of a similar nature, can apply to land which is not common land. It can certainly exist where the rights on one of the closes is that of sole pasture.[38] The proposition, however, seems to have been doubted in *Heath* v. *Elliott* (1838)[39] when it was held, in a case where the rights on one of the adjoining wastes were in the lord of the manor only, that vicinage could not exist "as there was but one common in the case."

Nevertheless, in *Jones* v. *Robin* (1845)[40] when a mutual right to intergraze **3.53** (to use a neutral term) between adjoining unfenced closes without risk of trespass was pleaded, it was thought for the first time, the principle was approved. The right was pleaded as one of custom and, in the absence of a precedent for a claim by custom, was held not to be valid. Error on the judgment was brought in the Exchequer Chamber and was heard by four barons and three justices. After consideration of all the authorities, the court concluded in a judgment by Parke B. as follows:

> "It must be considered to be established that a common . . . pur cause de vicinage, is not properly a right of common or profit à prendre, but rather an excuse for a trespass . . . The question then arises . . . whether it is essential, to support such a claim, that it should be between persons having rights of common properly so called, or at least that there should be commoners on both sides, or whether it may exist between two proprietors whose lands are not subject to common rights . . . If this had been the only question, we think, after a careful consideration of the arguments and of the authorities, we should probably have held that it might exist between two proprietors without commoners on either side. The reason of the law which sanctions a claim of this sort is either on account of its convenience, it being better to intercommon than that each should watch his own cattle; or to avoid multiplicity of suits . . . : and both these reasons apply to owners who interpasture as well as to commoners, though, as to the latter, not to the same degree. . . . On the whole the authorities appear to shew that there is no necessity for commoners on both sides in order to give validity to a claim for common pur cause de vicinage, though, where such common exists, most frequently there are commoners on both sides."[41]

In this particular case the matter did not end there and the court concurred with the decision in the lower court that a plea in custom could not be upheld for claims in private estates. It was remarked during the case that "no doubt it was competent to the owners of the respective farms to create such a usage by grant; and possibly it might be supported as a prescription."[42]

[38] *Whittier* v. *Stockman* (1613e) 2 Bulstr. 86, 80 E.R. 980.
[39] (1838) 7 L.J.C.P. 210 at 211, *per* Tindal C.J.
[40] (1845) 10 Q.B. 581, 116 E.R. 221; (1847) 10 Q.B. 620, 116 E.R. 235.
[41] At 10 Q.B. 632–635, 116 E.R. 240–241. Baron Parke later elevated to be a Lord of Appeal in Ordinary as Lord Wensleydale was considered to be the foremost judge of his day.
[42] *Per* Lord Denman C.J. at 10 Q.B. 587, 116 E.R. 224.

(e) Prescription

3.54 It has been said that common *pur cause de vicinage* may be claimed generally by prescription.[43] The case cited as authority is *Prichard* v. *Powell* (1845),[44] where prescription proved the right on the home common which then attracted the customary right of vicinage. In that case it was argued that as vicinage was of immemorial origin only an immemorial user of commoner appurtenant would suffice. The claim made before the court seems to have been altogether mistaken and it is clear that an express or presumed grant of a right of common will bring the right within the custom.[45] It is also clear that where the right of vicinage exists it precludes a claim to a substantive prescriptive right over the contiguous common. If it were otherwise, all claims to vicinage would be converted into substantive rights of common following the prescriptive period.[46]

(f) Limitations

3.55 Unlike the other substantive rights of common, vicinage arises through proof of a custom on the land, which requires immemorial user or, at least, what the courts will accept as equivalent to immemorial user. As it is a custom which is under consideration, unity of ownership in the past will not necessarily defeat a claim. On the other hand, evidence that it has been the practice to drive the straying animals back whence they came is supportive to a claim that the custom never existed.[47]

3.56 Once a claim to vicinage has been established, the right is classified as a right of common. Where a statute requires animals grazing, by a right of common, to be marked before turning out, those grazing by vicinage are within the requirements of the statute.[48] The main reason for the existence of the right has been repeatedly stated to be for the avoidance of multiplicities of actions in trespass.[49] It seems, therefore, that no actions may be brought under the Animals Act 1971 for damage caused or by way of detention.[50] For the purposes of actions between the commoners on the contiguous commons, the animals are lawfully present.

3.57 However, this is not to say that the animals are lawfully present for the purposes of action between the owner of the animals and third parties. In particular, it is difficult to see how the deemed agreement, implicit in vicinage between graziers on contiguous commons, can effect the liability of the owners of land within the entirely separate custom to fence against the

---

[43] Glanville Williams, p. 374.

[44] (1845) 10 Q.B. 589, 116 E.R. 224.

[45] *Minet* v. *Morgan* (1870) 11 L.R. Eq. 284; above, n. 23.

[46] Further, wherever vicinage exists the user can never be "as of right," the requirement for prescription, as it arises from a reciprocal condonence of trespass.

[47] *Heath* v. *Elliott* (1838) 7 L.J.C.P. 210 at 211, *per* Littledale J.; *Clarke* v. *Tinker* (1845) 10 Q.B. 604, 116 E.R. 230.

[48] *Newman* v. *Bennett* [1981] 1 Q.B. 726.

[49] Co.Litt. 122a; Bl.Comm., ii, 33; *Jones* v. *Robin* (1847), above, n. 40, at 587, and at 224, *per* Parke B.; *Cape* v. *Scott* (1874) L.R. 9 Q.B. 269 at 277, *per* Archibald J.; *cf. Commissioners of Sewers* v. *Glasse* (1874) L.R. 19 Eq. 134 at 161, *per* Jessel M.R. where the whole doctrine is approved.

[50] Animals Act 1971, ss.4, 7.

common,[51] who are third party to the agreement. It is submitted that the duty to fence against a common is owed to those with a substantive right to graze on the land and not to those with whom the commoners have a separate, albeit deemed and of long standing, agreement not to sue in trespass. As will be seen later, there is no reason why the animal owner using a right of vicinage may not rely upon the duty to fence in Animals Act 1971 actions,[52] but he may not be able to use the breach of a duty to fence to establish a claim for common law damages following on from the straying.[53]

SUBJECT MATTER

The classification of rights of common by subject matter has traditionally entailed six categories, namely, pasturage, pannage, estovers, turbary, piscary and common in the soil.[54] A seventh is also included here—the right to take animals *ferae naturae*. It must not be supposed that rights of common are limited to these categories, as there is no reason in principle why any natural product, part of the soil or animal *ferae naturae* may not form the subject matter of a grant of common. It is just that the categories described are those most frequently encountered. Further it should not be thought that the categories necessarily have a discrete content. They may overlap, rights within a category may be of differing nature, and some rights, of which the samphire rights of Norfolk are typical,[55] do not fit comfortably into any category. **3.58**

1. Pasturage

The right of pasturage or, as it is more usually known, a right of common of pasture is the most widespread and economically the most important common right in existence. It is the right to take grass by the mouths of cattle.[56] The commoner has no property in the grass until he takes it by grazing[57] and if a stranger cuts it the commoner may not take it away, nor does he have an action in trespass.[58] **3.59**

Although it is grass which is the primary product, pasturage includes anything which may be grazed or collected by the animals which may include mast, acorns, nuts, leaves and foliage of all sorts.[59] The right does not include a right to cut any herbage. Early authority was prepared to accept that a commoner might have a collateral right, in the form of a custom, to **3.60**

---

[51] For which see § 9.05.
[52] §§ 10.33 *et seq.*
[53] § 10.107.
[54] *cf.* Megarry and Wade, p. 909.
[55] § 3.76.
[56] *Fitzherbert's Surveying*, folio iiii; *Samborne* v. *Harilo* (1621) Bridgman J. 9 at 10, 123 E.R. 1162 at 1163, *per* Bridgman; *Earl de la Warr* v. *Miles* (1881) L.R. Ch.D. 535 at 577, *per* Bacon V.-C.
[57] § 8.02.
[58] § 8.21.
[59] *cf.* Bracton, folio 222.

cut rushes.[60] The position today is that any such collateral rights ought to be evidenced by an entry on the commons registers. In the absence of such a registration the grazier's rights are restricted to the taking of herbage by grazing. A right of pasturage will, however, carry with it a right to enter the land and any ancillary easements necessary for the proper exercise of the right.[61]

3.61 As has been demonstrated rights of grazing may exist as appendant, appurtenant, in gross or *pur cause de vicinage*.[62] In the case of appendant rights the classes of animals which may be grazed are limited.[63]

2. Pannage

3.62 Overlapping a right of pasturage is the right of pannage. It has been shown that an appurtenant right to graze animals may include the grazing of pigs.[64] Pannage, however, is a more limited right to graze pigs in woodlands or forests. There is little case law on the subject and the only case in modern times directly concerned is *Chilton* v. *Corporation of London* (1878)[65] where Sir George Jessel M.R. described the whole subject as obscure. He drew together all the definitions of which he was aware:

> "They all agree that the right of pannage is simply a right granted to an owner of pigs—the grant was usually to an owner of land of some kind who kept pigs—to go into the wood of the grantor of the right and to allow the pigs to eat the acorns or beech-mast which fell upon the ground. That is what the right has always been defined to be. The pigs have no right to take a single acorn or any beech-mast off the tree, either by themselves or by the hands of those who drive them. There is not even a right to shake the tree. It is only a right to eat what has fallen to the ground."[66]

3.63 It will be seen that the right is strictly limited and does not include the right to turn pigs to common land to graze. If any rights have been registered under the C.R.A. 1965, and the intention was to graze pigs, the right should have been registered as pasturage and not pannage.

3. Estovers

3.64 A common of estovers must be distinguished in consulting case authority from the same expression applied to the common law rights of a tenant for life,[67] a tenant for years[68] or the customary right of a copyhold tenant.[69] The various classes of rights may not be co-extensive.

[60] *Bean* v. *Bloom* (1773) 2 Wm.Bl. 926, 96 E.R. 547; right to cut rushes as a custom.
[61] See further at § 8.05.
[62] §§ 3.28 *et seq.*
[63] § 3.32.
[64] § 3.39.
[65] (1878) 7 Ch.D. 562.
[66] *ibid.* at 565.
[67] Co.Litt. 41b.
[68] Co.Litt. 53b.
[69] *Scriven's Copyholds*, p. 293; *cf. Heydon and Smith's Case* (1610) 13 Co.Rep. 67, 77 E.R. 1476.

(a) Classification

The traditional classification is by reference to estovers (Old French = **3.65**
"necessary") or botes (Old English = "useful"):

(a) *estoveria adificandi*, the greater house-bote, which is a liberty to
fell and take timber-trees, and either to repair ruinous houses, or to
rebuild such as are prostrate by tempest, enemies etc.;

(b) *estoveria ardendi*, the lesser house-bote or fire-bote, which is a like
liberty to cut and take tops and lops, or shrubs and underwoods, or
old decayed and dead trees, to burn in the house or tenement;

(c) *estovaria arandi*, plough bote, which is a like liberty to cut and
take proper timber, and other stuff, for mending the tenant's
ploughs, carts, wains and harrows, and for making rakes, forks etc.,
necessary for getting in his hay or corn;

(d) *estoveria claudendi*, hedge-bote or hay-bote, or estovers of inclosure, which is a liberty to take either proper timber for making
gates, stiles, etc., or boughs, shrubs, bushes etc. to repair hedges, or
to inclose open fields, where corn is sown etc.[70]

Bracton in considering estovers on broadly similar lines goes on to make it
clear that the list is not definitive by adding "and other necessary things,
much or little, according to the constitution of the servitude."[71]

A very substantial number of commons of estovers has been registered **3.66**
under the C.R.A. 1965. Most usually the term is refined no further. The Act
did not purport to provide additional rights and it follows that, in each case
of a registration of estovers, it is necessary to look behind the register to discover the scope of the right. It is unlikely that all the various classes will be
encompassed in most registrations. Occasionally, estovers are specifically
registered as a right to take, say, shrubs or loppings for fuel, a right to cut
timber for fencing, or a right to cut bracken for bedding, but this is the
exception rather than the rule.

(b) Annexation to a building

Not infrequently it will be found that a common of estovers, particularly for **3.67**
fuel or housebote, will be attached to a house or particular building. In these
cases the rights have long been held to be strictly annexed to the building:

"For if one grants estovers to another to be burnt in such a house, they
are appurtenant to the house . . . so that he who afterwards has the
house, by whatever title he comes to it, shall have the estovers . . . And
the estovers cannot be severed from the house . . . but by extinguishment; for if he who has the house will grant the estovers to another,
reserving the house to himself, or the house to another, reserving the
estovers to himself, the estovers shall not be severed from the house,
thereby, because they shall be spent in the same house."[72]

[70] Bird (1st ed., 1801), p. 2.
[71] Bracton, folio 187.
[72] *Sir Henry Nevil's Case* (1570) 1 Plowden 377 at 381, 75 E.R. 572 at 579.

Suggestions in the nineteenth century that estovers for a fixed quantity might be severed from a building[73] have received no support in the courts.[74] It follows that, in modern times, upon division of a tenement, it is not possible to divide the right to estovers to be used in a house between land and buildings. If the estovers are for, say, fencing the land or litter for animals, then apportionment on the division of the land is permissable but the total of the divided rights must not add any additional burden to the servient tenement. The Common Land Forum recommends a statutory prohibition on the apportionment of any right of common other than grazing.[75] With respect, it is suggested that this is inappropriate in respect of rights to estovers which are for the benefit of land, such as a right to take timber for fencing.

3.68 Where estovers have been annexed to a building the quantity is limited to that appropriate to the original premises,[76] even if substantially altered[77] or the same size of premises newly re-built whether on the existing site or nearby[78]: "it is enough if the right is to be exercised therein in continuance of the old right . . . and if there be no circumstances to inflict any additional burthen or injustice upon the lands over which the right is enjoyed."[79] In all events, unless limited to a fixed quantity the amount of estovers which may be taken is related to the reasonable needs of the dominant tenement.[80] There is some slight indication that a right to take timber for fencing is limited in quantity to that required for ancient fences.[81]

(c) Limitations on use

3.69 In some of the older cases it seems that a right of estovers may be limited spatially or temporally. In one case it is said that the rights existed between the feasts of St Michael and Christmas[82] and in another was not exercisable during the fawning month in a forest.[83] Control over the site where the

---

[73] For discussion, see § 6.31.
[74] *cf. Att.-Gen.* v. *Reynolds* [1911] 2 K.B. 888 at 904 and 919, *per* counsel in argument, and *per* Hamilton J. responding.
[75] Common Land Forum Report, Appendix C, para. 082.
[76] *Brown* v. *Tucker* (1610) 4 Leon. 241, 74 E.R. 847.
[77] *Luttrel's Case* (1601) 4 Co.Rep. 86a, 76 E.R. 1065.
[78] *Bryers* v. *Lake* (1655) Style 446, 82 E.R. 850; *cf. Countess of Arundel* v. *Steere* (1605) Cro.Jac. 25, 79 E.R. 19, which is probably explained as a right to erect a new bake house on a separate site and not an additional building.
[79] *Att.-Gen.* v. *Reynolds* (1911), above, n. 74, at 935, *per* Hamilton J.
[80] Bracton, folio 231; Co.Litt. 41B; Bl.Comm., ii, 35; *cf. Wilson* v. *Willes* (1806) 7 East. 121 at 127, 103 E.R. 46 at 49, *per* Lord Ellenborough C.J. It is sometimes suggested that, where there is a right to take firebote, timber may be felled if there is an insufficiency of underwood. It would be unwise to rely on the case cited, *Anon.* (1572) 3 Leon. 16, 74 E.R. 511, as it was concerned with the rights of a lessee for life.
[81] *Dowglas* v. *Kendall* (1610) 1 Bulstr. 93 at 94, 80 E.R. 792 at 793, *per* Croke in argument.
[82] Y.B. 10 E4 2b cited by Woolrych, p. 77.
[83] *Russel and Broker's Case* (1587) 2 Leon. 209, 74 E.R. 484.

estovers may be taken is sometimes exercised by a bailiff or steward of the manor.[84]

It is clear that the exercise of appurtenant rights of estovers is strictly **3.70** limited to use on the tenement. There is no right to use them in another tenement,[85] sell them,[86] or divert them to another use. The points are well illustrated in the report of *The Earl of Pembroke's Case* (1636)[87]:

> "A hath common of Estovers in wood of B, [scilicet] for houseboot, and he cuts down four trees to prepare this boots, and in the working, they prove unfit for that use, as for posts of a house, &c. In this Case it was holden by the Judge upon the evidence that this tenant cannot now convert this timber to any other use, &c. as to Cooper-ware, or the like, neither can he sell them and buy other fit wood with the mony, but note his intent to make provision to build or repair the house for which the bootes were &c. was not proved, as it seems he ought, and in this Case it was further held, that he cannot enlarge the house with this timber, nor board the sides of a Barn there, which had mudde walls, or the like before."

4. Turbary

A common of turbary is the right to take turf or peat for burning as fuel. It **3.71** was considered by Bracton to be a form of estovers[88] and to the extent that peat forms part of the soil it might be considered as a right in the soil, but it has long been recognised as a separate category of right of common. It seems to be of two classes: "*turba*, dry out of the body of the ground and *blestia*, pared from the surface."[89] The former class, as peat dug for fuel, is not unknown today,[90] while the latter right to strip turf for fuel is probably obsolete. It might be anticipated that a right to take turf could encompass a right to take for the making or repair of turf sided banks. However, in *Wilson v. Willes* (1806)[91] such a right, expressly pleaded, was held to be bad in law for being indefinite, uncertain and destructive of the common, as was taking turf for the making or repair of grass plots on customary tenements.

---

[84] Y.B. 8 E3 54, cited by Woolrych, p. 77; *cf. Clarkson* v. *Woodhouse* (1782) 5 T.R. 412, n. (*a*), 101 E.R. 231 and *Re Turnworth Down* [1978] Ch. 251: controlled by steward after private inclosure award.

[85] *Att.-Gen.* v. *Reynolds* (1911), above, n. 74, at 907, *per* Hamilton J.; *cf.* Woolrych, p. 81.

[86] *Valentine* v. *Penny* (1605) Noy 145, 74 E.R. 1107 (a case of turbary, but the principle is the same).

[87] (1636) Clayton 47.

[88] Bracton, folio 187: writ of novel disseisin where estovers are claimed in turbary or heath.

[89] Spelmanno, Henrico, *Glossarium Archaiologicum* (Londini: Apud Aliciam Warrn, 1664), pp. 547–548; Elton refers to *blestia* as "flags," p. 96.

[90] Aitchison and Hughes, *The Common Lands of Wales* (1983), Table 23: 4 per cent. of respondents claimed to be using rights of turbary.

[91] (1806) 7 East. 121, 103 E.R. 46.

This case, however, has nothing to say about the owner of the soil's right to strip turf for sale or otherwise.[92]

3.72   The law for turbary follows closely that for estovers and, where the right is annexed to a house or building, as it seems it must always be,[93] the same rules apply.[94] There cannot be a prescription in a *que* estate for a common of turbary without stint and it "must be limited by the number of chimneys or hearths in which the turf may be burnt."[95] If the right is fixed in quantity and is appurtenant to a house it "ought to be spent in the house, and not sold abroad."[96] It follows that it is not possible to sever the right from the house to which it is annexed or apportion it between parts of a divided tenement.

3.73   A right of turbary may extend over the whole or part of a waste depending upon the terms of the express or implied grant. At one time it was said that a right may exist over an entire waste even if it was not possible to enjoy the right where there were no turves.[97] Later it was held that the onus of proving such a general right lay on the claimant[98] and there could be no right where no turves had existed or could exist.[99] Occasionally the right may be exercised only on sites assigned by the owner of the soil or his agent and, even more occasionally, where such sites have been exhausted it may be possible for the owner to enclose them and use them in severalty.[1] Such practices are unusual today, although it is otherwise in Ireland where assignment of sites seems to be commonplace.

5. Piscary

3.74   Common of piscary, or the right to take fish from a pond, lake, stream or river belonging to another person is not unknown as a registered right of common and statutory common land includes land covered with water.[2] There is some nomenclative confusion over the terms applied to fisheries and it is sufficient for the present purposes to note the existence of free and several fisheries and public rights of fishing, which may be distinguished

---

[92] *Roberston* v. *Hartopp* (1889) 43 Ch.D. 484.

[93] *cf.* Co.Litt. 121b: common of turbary cannot be appendant to land but to a house to be spent there.

[94] §§ 3.67–3.68.

[95] *Lord Chesterfield* v. *Harris* [1908] 2 Ch. 397 at 421–422, *per* Buckley L.J.

[96] *Valentine* v. *Penny* (1605), above, n. 86 approved in *Lord Chesterfield* v. *Harris*, above, n. 95, at 422, *per* Buckley L.J.; *cf.* Common Land Forum Report, Appendix C, para. 082 recommends statutory enactment to prohibit severance or apportionment on division of the dominant tenement.

[97] *Fawcett* v. *Strickland* (1737) Willes 57 at 60, 125 E.R. 1054 at 1056, *per* Willes L.C.J.

[98] *Maxwell* v. *Martin* (1830) 6 Bing. 522 at 525, 130 E.R. 1382 at 1383, *per* Tindal C.J.

[99] *Peardon* v. *Underhill* (1850) 16 Q.B. 120 at 126–127, 117 E.R. 824 at 826, *per* Coleridge and Erle JJ.

[1] *Clarkson* v. *Woodhouse* (1782) 5 T.R. 412, n.(*a*), 101 E.R. 231.

[2] C.R.A. 1965, s.22(1).

from common of piscary.[3] Only common of piscary is capable of registration as a statutory right of common.

Although a common of piscary may exist as an appurtenant right or, as a **3.75** right in gross, the latter right will be very unusual. The former, as a right annexed to a tenement, will always be limited to the needs of the household[4] and is subject to the same rules regarding severance, apportionment and sale of the product as apply to estovers and turbary.[5] There is no reason in principle why a right of piscary in gross may not be granted, or claimed by prescription, (subject to the limitations now imposed by the C.R.A. 1965[6]) but there does not seem to have been a successful prescriptive claim, brought by a person in a private capacity, before the courts.[7] A claim made without stint and laid in a fluctuating class of persons such as inhabitants or freemen is not possible[8] unless an express or implied Crown grant incorporating the class of persons can be found to exist.[9]

One particular class of right which includes the right to take fish has been **3.76** noted in Norfolk. In a Commissioner's decision reported as *Re Thornham Common, Thornham, Norfolk* (1975)[10] "samphire rights" were claimed over an extensive area of saltings. The saltings had been allotted as a regulated pasture and there were five rights of grazing claimed, together with

---

[3] Co.Litt. 122a and see Hargrave's note thereto; *cf.* Bl.Comm., ii, 39; *Smith* v. *Kemp* (1693) 2 Salk. 637, 91 E.R. 537 and note thereto; for a more recent judicial consideration, see *Malcomson* v. *O'Dea* (1862–1863) 10 H.L.C. 593 at 618, 11 E.R. 1155 at 1166, *per* Willes J. A common of piscary may not exist in waters, such as the sea and tidal and navigable rivers, vested in possession in the Crown, for which see *Ward* v. *Creswell* (1741) Willes 265 at 268, 125 E.R. 1165 at 1166, *per* Willes L.C.J., and *Lord Fitzwalter's Case* (1674) 1 Mod. 105, 86 E.R. 766. But see *Lord Fitzhardinge* v. *Purcell* [1908] 2 Ch. 139 and *Edgar* v. *Special Commissioner for English Fisheries* (1871) 23 L.T. 732.

[4] Bl.Comm., ii, 35, applied in *Clayton* v. *Corby* (1843) 5 Q.B. 415 at 420, 114 E.R. 1306 at 1308, *per* Lord Denman C.J.; for two of the few cases concerned with common of piscary see *Benett* v. *Costar* (1818) 8 Taunt. 183, 129 E.R. 353 and *Rawlins* v. *Jenkins* (1843) 4 Q.B. 419, 114 E.R. 956; Common Land Forum Report, Appendix C, para. 082 recommends statutory prohibition on severance or apportionment on division of the dominant tenement.

[5] §§ 3.67–3.68.

[6] See § 4.41.

[7] " . . . it may be observed that the instances in which rights in gross have become before the courts are very rare . . . ": *Shuttleworth* v. *Le Fleming* (1865) 19 C.B.(N.S.) 687 at 710, 144 E.R. 956 at 965, *per* Montague Smith J.: 60 years enjoyment of a "free fishery" claimed in gross not within the provisions of the Prescription Act 1832. This was applied in *Warwick* v. *Gonville and Caius College* (1890) 6 T.L.R. 447, C.A.; *cf. Harris* v. *Earl of Chesterfield* [1911] A.C. 623, where *semble* a right in gross was rejected in the lower court: see Earl Loveburn L.C. at 630.

[8] *Harris* v. *Earl of Chesterfield,* above; *Tilbury* v. *Silva* (1890) 45 Ch.D. 98.

[9] *Goodman* v. *Mayor and Corporation of Saltash* (1882) 7 App.Cas. 633; *Re Company or Fraternity of Free Fishermen of Faversham* (1887) 36 Ch.D. 329: prescriptive company of fishermen recognised by statute.

[10] (1975) 25/D/79–95, 4 D.C.C. 198; see also *Re Low Common, Thornham, West Norfolk D., Norfolk* (1979) 25/D/112–125, 9 D.C.C. 172.

some 117 samphire rights recorded in the names of what appear to be local householders. The samphire rights were declared to be rights to take "samphire, sea lavender, seaweed, shell fish, bait, wildfowl, game, fish, sand, shingle and estovers." An agreement between counsel was confirmed, so that the rights were varied and all were converted into rights appurtenant to the addresses of the claimants. This type of right does not fall into any of the normal classes of rights but, as water related products are concerned, it may be possible to view them as an exceptional variant of the right to take fish.

6. Rights in the soil

(a) General nature

3.77 The right to take some part of the soil or minerals from the land of another person is well established as a *profit à prendre* and a right of common. In early times the right extended to metals, including gold and silver, but the inclusion of metals today is probably obsolete.[11] There has not been a reported case where they have been mentioned for several centuries.[12] The practices of tin bounding in Cornwall and, the taking of lead in Derbyshire and the Forest of Dean, have similar characteristics but separate local law applies and they do not need to be considered here.[13] Similarly, rights vested in persons "resident and dwelling" in the counties of Devon and Cornwall to take sea sand, granted by statute in 1609,[14] and rights for inhabitants in the Island of Portland to take stone, granted by Royal Warrant,[15] may be distinguished and disregarded for the present purposes.

3.78 As with other rights of common, rights in the soil may exist as appurtenant to a tenement or in gross. Most frequently they will be appurtenant but the commercial value of mineral and other rights is such that the taking of products in gross is sometimes encountered. It will be unusual, however, to find that a grant of rights in gross will have the effect of creating a profit and even less likely that a registrable right of common will result. Some of the difficulties in deciding the exact nature of a particular transaction have already been discussed.[16]

3.79 A profit, and a right of common, may only exist if the product is part of the soil and whether mineral substances deposited on the land form part of the land has been a matter of some doubt. It seems clear that, when "any thing

---

[11] Bracton, folio 231; Co.Litt. 122a; Bl.Comm., ii, 34.
[12] *e.g. Lord Mountjoy's Case* (1583) 1 And. 307, 123 E.R. 488; *cf.* Co.Litt. 164b.
[13] *cf. Halsbury's Laws* (4th ed.), Vol. 31, para. 819 *et seq.*; Elton, p. 111 *et seq.*
[14] Devon and Cornwall Sea-Shore Act 1609 (17 Ja. 1, c. 18) (part repealed by Statute Law Reform Act 1948), considered in *Re Gunwalloe Church Cove Beach, Cornwall (No. 2)* (1978) 206/D/480, 7 D.C.C. 16.
[15] *Re 655 acres of land, Portland, Dorset (No. 2)* (1977) 210/D/202, 5 D.C.C. 435.
[16] § 3.06.

in the nature of soil is lodged upon a man's close, it is part of the close."[17] Thus, wind borne sand or water borne mud will form part of the land. On the other hand, the court has proceeded upon the assumption that a colliery tip constituted chattels and had not become part of the realty[18] and the material of a spoil bank "partook very much of the character of a trade fixture."[19]

In theory at least any part of the soil may form the subject matter of a profit **3.80** and consequently a right of common. In reports of cases most frequently encountered are sand, gravel, stone, clay, marl and earth[20] with coal[21] occasionally mentioned. There does not appear to be a reported case of the recognition of brick earth. This may be for the reason given in one case that brick earth is to be distinguished from mines and minerals in that a claim to it is a claim to the whole of the soil, which is a right of ownership.[22] Occasionally a claim to a right of "quarre" has been made.[23] It is unclear whether this amounts to a claim to take stone or a claim to use a quarry.

(b) Limitations on use

In the case of appurtenant rights, unless the quantity is fixed by the grant, **3.81** the amount which may be taken is governed by the needs of the dominant tenement. As we have seen in connection with a right of estovers[24] the method of use is strictly circumscribed. In *Peppin* v. *Shakspear* (1796),[25] where a right to enter and take sand and gravel for repairs to a house was claimed, it was held necessary to allege not only that the house was out of repair and that the sand and gravel had been taken to effect the necessary repairs, but also that the material taken had been used for that purpose.

There seems to be no authority that an appurtenant right may exist for com- **3.82** mercial purposes such as taking clay for making pots[26] or use in a commercial brick kiln.[27] Nor does there seem to be any support for the propositions

---

[17] *Blewett* v. *Tregonning* (1835) 3 Ad. & E. 554 at 575, 111 E.R. 524 at 532, *per* Patteson J.

[18] *Ryan Industrial Fuels Ltd.* v. *Morgan (V.O.)* [1965] 1 W.L.R. 1347 but see a distinction made by Davies L.J. at 1354 where a tip is ancient and grassed over.

[19] *Robinson* v. *Milne* (1884) 53 L.J.Ch. 1070 at 1075, *per* North J.

[20] *e.g. Stile* v. *Butts* (1595) Cro.Eliz. 434, 78 E.R. 675 (clay) *Duberley* v. *Page* (1788) 2 T.R. 391, 100 E.R. 211 (sand and gravel); *Shakespear* v. *Peppin* (1706) 6 T.R. 741, 101 E.R. 802 (sand, gravel, loam); *Maxwell* v. *Martin* (1830) 6 Bing. 522, 130 E.R. 1382 (stone); *Heath* v. *Deane* [1905] 2 Ch. 86 (stone, gravel, clay, marl, soyle and earth)

[21] *Duke of Portland* v. *Hill* (1866) L.R. 2 Eq. 765; *cf.* Co.Litt. 122a.

[22] *Church* v. *Inclosure Commissioners* (1862) 11 C.B.(N.S.) 644, 142 E.R. 956.

[23] *Duke of Portland* v. *Hill*, above, n. 21; also noticed in the West Glamorgan rights register CL13.

[24] §§ 3.67–3.68.

[25] (1796) 6 T.R. 748, 101 E.R. 806, *cf. Duke of Portland* v. *Hill*, above: tenant's rights to coal limited to "propriis usis"; *Incledon* v. *Burges* (1689) Carth. 65, 90 E.R. 642: privilege to dig stones for necessary repairs of messuage.

[26] See the case cited in *Hayward* v. *Cunnington* (1668) 1 Lev. 231, 83 E.R. 383.

[27] *Clayton* v. *Corby* (1843) 5 Q.B. 415, 114 E.R. 1306.

that if the amount is certain any surplus may be sold[28] or the right converted into a right in gross.[29]

(c) Registered rights

3.83   As with other rights of common it will be necessary to look behind the registers, established under the C.R.A. 1965, to discover the nature and extent of rights in the soil. The registers only record the existence of a right and not its scope and nature. Whether a right extends over the whole of a waste or part only will depend upon the terms of the grant and the onus of proving that the right exists over the whole of the waste will lie upon the claimant.[30] It seems that there can be no general right where the product does not and cannot exist.[31]

3.84   Most rights to coal, were extinguished by the Coal Industry Nationalisation Act 1946[32] which vested all coal and rights extraction in the National Coal Board (now British Coal). Any right of common to take coal, claimed under the C.R.A. 1965, should have been notified to the Board before registration.[33] It seems that rights of common to take coal, if any have been registered, have been preserved as the Act of 1946 provided an exception in respect of coal dug other than in the course of colliery activities.[34]

(d) Removal of soil

3.85   Commoners, and indeed other persons, taking soil from a common should take account of the provisions of the Agricultural Land (Removal of Surface Soil) Act 1953 which creates an offence punishable on conviction by a fine, not exceeding level 3 on the standard scale, for removing more than five cubic yards of soil from agricultural land, in any three month period, without planning permission. Rights of turbary and turf removal are excepted.

7. Animals ferae naturae

3.86   The right to take and carry away animals *ferae naturae* has been long recognised as a *profit à prendre*[35] and the courts have accepted that it may exist as a right of common.[36] In modern times the distinction between a sporting

---

[28] *cf.* Cooke, p. 40; Elton, p. 109 (cases *contra* cited). The doubts seem to have arisen from comments by Lord Denman C.J. in *Clayton* v. *Corby* (1843) 5 Q.B. 415, at 422, 114 E.R. 1306 at 1309 drawing attention to the unlimited claim to take clay for a brick kiln. He notes the lack of quantification and concludes that an indefinite claim is a claim to the close. While no doubt an unlimited right may be granted in gross for purposes of sale this is not to say that an appurtenant right, which is of necessity limited to the needs of the tenement may, if more of the product exists than is necessary for the tenement, be sold or that all products granted for a fixed amount can be sold.

[29] For a discussion of severance, see § 6.31

[30] *Maxwell* v. *Martin* (1830) 6 Bing. 522, 130 E.R. 1382.

[31] *Peardon* v. *Underhill* (1850) 16 Q.B. 120, 117 E.R. 824.

[32] ss.1(1)(a), 5 and Sched. 1, Pt. 1.

[33] Commons Registration (General) Regulations (S.I. 1966 No. 1471), reg. 9(2).

[34] s.36(2).

[35] *Mason* v. *Clarke* [1955] A.C. 778.

[36] *Davies's Case* (1688) 3 Mod. 246, 87 E.R. 161; *Samford and Havel's Case* (1612) Godb. 184, 78 E.R. 112; *Duke of Portland* v. *Hill* (1866) L.R. 2 Eq. 765.

right which exists purely for pleasure purposes and an intended profit has become somewhat blurred. The Commons Commissioners in their hearings have grappled with this problem and generally seem to have concluded that sporting rights, even if the rights include the taking of the animals (which, of course, they usually do), are not correctly registrable as rights of common. The distinction does not seem to have been made with such force in the case of rights of piscary which have a similar duality of purpose. Nevertheless, the decisions of the Commissioners are not entirely consistent and some rights to take animals have achieved registration. The importance of deciding whether rights to take animals are registrable or not lies in the non-exercisability of unregistered rights.[37] If the rights are registrable, unregistered rights are no longer exercisable.

It cannot be doubted that the right to take animals may exist as a profit. The **3.87** definitive statement on the subject is that of Lord Campbell L.C. in *Ewart v. Graham* (1859)[38]:

> "The property in animals, *ferae naturae,* while they are on the soil, belongs to the owner of the soil, and he may grant a right to others to come and take them by a grant of hunting, shooting, fowling and so forth; that right may be granted by the owner of the fee simple, and such a grant is a licence of a *profit à prendre.*"

Lord Campbell followed the judgment by Parke B. in *Wickham v. Hawker* (1840),[39] where the older cases were reviewed[40] and the distinction made between "a mere personal licence of pleasure to be exercised by the individual licensee" and a grant by deed to persons, extending to heirs and assignees, which indicates that it is a *profit à prendre* which is intended to be granted.[41] Subsequent cases have never doubted that a right to shoot may be an incorporeal hereditament[42] and that, unless expressed as a personal licence, is an interest within the Statute of Frauds and may only be created by deed.[43] Of the animals recognised deer,[44] fowl,[45] conies,[46] wild duck,[47] and a "right to hunt, to take foxes, hares and birds and fish"[48] may be noticed. Prescriptions to take fowl[49] and conies,[50] as rights of common,

---

[37] C.R.A. 1965, s.1(2)(b).

[38] (1859) 7 H.L.C. 330 at 334, 11 E.R. 132 at 138.

[39] (1840) 7 M. & W. 63, 151 E.R. 679.

[40] *ibid.* at 76, 685 *et seq.* especially *Doe d. Douglas v. Lock* (1835) 2 Ad. & E. 705, 111 E.R. 271, *Duchess of Norfolk v. Wiseman* (1496–1497) Y.B. 12 H7 25 and 13 H7 13, pl.2, *Davies's Case,* above, n. 36, and Manwood, pp. 110 and 117.

[41] *Wickham v. Hawker,* above, n. 39.

[42] See *Musgrave v. Forster* (1871) L.R. 6 Q.B. 590; *Webber v. Lee* (1882) 9 Q.B.D. 315; *Lord Fitzhardinge v. Purcell* [1908] 2 Ch. 139.

[43] *Webber v. Lee* (1882) 9 Q.B.D. 315, at 318; but see *Mason v. Clarke* [1955] A.C. 778 for the creation of an equitable profit.

[44] *Duchess of Norfolk v. Wiseman,* above, n. 40.

[45] *Davies's Case,* above, n. 36.

[46] *Samford and Havel's Case,* above, n. 36.

[47] *Lord Fitzhardinge v. Purcell,* above, n. 42.

[48] *Duke of Portland v. Hill,* above, n. 36.

[49] *Davies's Case,* above, n. 36.

[50] *Samford and Havel's Case,* above, n. 36.

have been accepted but where appurtenant to a tenement are restricted in quantity to the needs of the household.[51]

3.88 It seems indisputable that a profit to take animals, if it also has the characteristics of a right of common, *i.e.* held for an interest equivalent to a fee simple and use shared with the owner of the soil, is a registrable right of common. In early cases before the Commissioners exclusive rights of fishing, fowling and sporting were correctly refused registration.[52] Later, the then Chief Commissioner allowed a right to take rabbits with snares and a right to shoot game as registrable rights, while at the same time noting that he doubted whether they were properly viewed as rights of common.[53] Fuller consideration was given to the subject in *Re Lustleigh Cleave, Lustleigh, Devon (No. 1)* (1978),[54] when the same Commissioner noted that a right to kill and carry away wild duck was a profit but distinguished a right of shooting or sporting, even when joined with a right to take game, as being exercised primarily for pleasure, the value of the game as food being a secondary consideration. In the decision concerned the rights had been claimed as appurtenant to land and the Commissioner stated that his decision not to allow registration did not affect enforceability of the right outside the provisions of the C.R.A. 1965. The various decisions are incapable of reconciliation.

3.89 Although this section is most usually concerned with rights of shooting there seems no reason in principle why other methods of taking, such as snaring,[55] netting, ferreting and falconry,[56] should not fall within the ambit of a right to take animals.

Sole profits

3.90 The legal nature of a sole profit has been considered above.[57] A sole profit may be distinguished from a profit in common by the single feature that, in the case of a sole profit, the owner of the soil over which it is exercised has no residual interest in the product concerned. Unlike a right of common, but as is the case with a profit in common, a sole profit may be held for either of the two legal interests appropriate to land, *i.e.* for an interest equivalent to a fee simple or for a term of years. Certain sole profits are registrable as statutory rights of common under the Act of 1965 but, as with

---

[51] *Samford and Havel's Case* (1612) Godb. 184, 78 E.R. 112.

[52] *Re Lumley Moor Reservoir, N. Yorks. (Nos. 1 and 2)* (1974) 45/D/12–13, 2 D.C.C. 253; *Re Florden Common, Norfolk* (1974) 25/D/142–146, 2 D.C.C. 310.

[53] *Re Eype Down, Symondsbury, Dorset (No. 2)* (1976) 210/D/115–118, 5 D.C.C. 74; *Re Cock Moor, Brompton-by-Sawdon, N. Yorks. (No. 2)* (1977) 268/D/171–175, 6 D.C.C. 232; non-registrability tacitly approved *Re Sutton Common* [1982] 1 W.L.R. 647 at 656, *per* Walton J.

[54] (1978) 209/D/114–130, 7 D.C.C. 320.

[55] See *Mason* v. *Clarke*, above, n. 35.

[56] "The liberty to hawk is one species of ancupium (Manwood, p. 117), the taking of birds by hawks and seems to follow the same rule" [a grant of a *profit à prendre*]: *Wickham* v. *Hawker*, above, n. 39, at 78, 686, *per* Parke B.

[57] § 3.16.

true rights of common, only if held for an interest equivalent to a fee simple. This section seeks to demonstrate the forms which a sole profit may take, with particular reference to those which are statutorily registrable.

The C.R.A. 1965 includes within the definition of registrable rights of com- **3.91** mon "cattlegates or beastgates (by whatever name known) and rights of sole or several vesture or herbage or sole or several pasture, but does not include rights held for a term of years or from year to year."[58] The definition is inclusive and not exhaustive but it seems likely that only those sole rights which fall four square within the definition are registrable. In particular, it is submitted that sole rights of shooting, or other methods of taking animals *ferae naturae* and, the well known right of the several fishery, are not included. There is a substantial number of sole rights which have achieved registration, most of which fall into the category of sole pasture with a smaller but not insignificant number which, although often not called by these names, are probably within the categories of sole vesture or herbage.

1. Vesture

The largest of the terms used is that of *vesturam* or sole vesture. It is des- **3.92** cribed thus by Coke[59]:

> "If a man hath 20 acres of land, and by deed granteth to another and his heires *vesturam terrae* and maketh livery of seisin *secundum formam chartae*, the land itselfe shall not passe, because he hath a particular right in the land: for thereby he shall not have the houses, timber-trees, mines and other reall things parcell of the inheritance, but he shall have the vesture of the land, (that is) the corne, grasse, underwood, swepage, and the like, and he shall have an action trespasse *quare clausum fregit.*"

It will be seen that vesture includes all the agricultural produce of the land excluding timber, but including "swepage," which is the right to cut by the sweep of a scythe, and underwood, which is the cropping of ground timber, usually by coppicing, for cordwood or mining props.[60] While the rights to the products are wide there is no right to dig in the soil.[61]

So extensive was the grant that, in early days, some judges considered that a **3.93** grant of vesture passed ownership of the land itself.[62] After Coke's time we

---

[58] C.R.A. 1965, s.22(1).

[59] Co.Litt. 4b; frequently, of course, there is only grass on the land and a right to vesture then overlaps with a right to herbage so that a right to cut hay is sometimes referred to as *vesturam terrae*: see *Re the Tenants of Owning* (1587) 4 Leon. 43, 74 E.R. 718.

[60] For a description of the management of underwood for commercial purposes see *Lord Fitzhardinge* v. *Pritchett* (1867) L.R. 2 Q.B. 135; *cf. Dickins* v. *Hampstead* (1729) Fitz-G. 87, 94 E.R. 666: lopping of pollards described as estovers.

[61] *Re the Tenants of Owning* (1587) 4 Leon. 43, 74 E.R. 718; *Anon.* (1588) Owen 38, 74 E.R. 883.

[62] Note at Keil 118, 72 E.R. 285; *cf. L'Evesque De Oxford's Case* (1621) Palm. 174, 81 E.R. 1032 where a difference is discerned between grants by King and subject, and *prima vestura* is held not to grant the land *aliter vesturae terrae*; the arguments of Sir Francis North in *Potter* v. *Sir Henry North* (1669), reported at 1 Vent. 383 at 393, 86 E.R. 245 at 251.

find the courts holding that, where there was no deed in evidence, the possession of the bulk of the produce in the year, carried with it the rebuttable presumption that the ownership of the land coincided with the right.[63] Another view was that evidence as a whole of the acts of ownership throughout the year was the main factor.[64] It cannot be doubted today that where there is evidence by way of deed of grant of sole vesture it does not serve to pass ownership. The matter is not so clear when the only evidence is that a person has a right to take all the product for part of a year and other persons have a right in common to graze for the remainder. This is not unknown in the case of common meadows, in which event one would expect the owner or owners of the land in severalty to take the hay crop, and either the owners jointly, or with other persons, to graze the land for the remainder of the year. During the hay season the right to cut one's own land for hay and a right of sole vesture for the same period of the year (in this case often referred to as *prima vestura* or *prima tonsura*) will look very similar in practice. The issue has been considered by the Commons Commissioners. On one common, "rights of forshear" (*prima tonsura*) were exercisable and were registered. A claim to ownership of the land by the owners of the rights of forshear was despatched by the simple expedient of holding that as rights of common and ownership were mutually exclusive the rights holders, having registered, could not be the owners.[65]

3.94 Coke also raises the possibility that where the use of land is divided temporally, in the way just described, the ownership of the land may vest in different persons at different times of the year or in different years.[66] The Commons commissioners have considered ownership of this nature and in some cases found it to exist.[67]

3.95 In practice today, right to cut hay with other persons grazing during the remainder of the year, the cutting being a product of the ownership of the land or, alternatively, through a right of vesture, is not wholly unknown. There seems little evidence of the full right of vesture including underwood having been registered although some claims have been made to entire dominion over the land for part of the year.[68]

2. Herbage

3.96 The right of *herbagium* or herbage is frequently mentioned but it does not seem to have been defined. It is possible to deduce that it probably includes a right to cut herbage and is to be distinguished thereby from a right of sole pasture which we shall see is limited to the taking of grass by grazing. In

[63] *Ward* v. *Petifer* (1634) Cro.Car. 362, 79 E.R. 916.
[64] *Stammers* v. *Dixon* (1806) 7 East. 200, 103 E.R. 77.
[65] *Re North Ham etc., Somerset (No. 1)* (1983) 232/D/294, 14 D.C.C. 265.
[66] Co.Litt. 4a, 165a.
[67] *Re the "open fields" in Chagford, West Devon D., Devon* (1985) 209/D/343–344, 16 D.C.C. 8. *Re The Holmes, the Pound and Broadheath, Shenstone, Staffs.* (1982) 233/D/15–19, 13 D.C.C. 46 .
[68] e.g. see the "raps" or *prima tonsura* registered in *Re Wick Moor, Stogursey, Somerset* (1976) 232/D/19–48, 5 D.C.C. 280, which, according to evidence given, were usually sold either as land or as a right to cut hay.

some cases a right of herbage and pasture is combined.[69] If the right is exclusive to one person this would be understandable for, if all the grass is vested in one person, there seems no reason why he should not have the choice of taking by cutting or grazing. Where the right is vested in several persons it seems that the right of *herbagium* is usually absent,[70] but it has to be admitted that sometimes the words herbage and pasture are used interchangeably. It is clearly less than the right of vesture as it does not include underwood. Perhaps it is best not to look restrictively at the terms used but examine the practices followed traditionally. There is some slight authority that the holder of a right of herbage in a forest had a right to enclose[71] but it is probable that this right, if it ever existed, is now obsolete. As with the right of vesture the owner of herbage may sue in trespass[72] but may not interfere with the soil.[73]

3. Pasture

(a) General nature

The least of the rights to herbage on land is that of sole or several pasture. **3.97** The distinction, if indeed there is one, between the use of the terms sole and several is unclear. In Coke's description of sole rights we find *solam vesturam terrae* but *separalem pasturam*.[74] In case reports it is usual to find, for instance, free and customary tenants prescribing that *habuerunt & habere consueverunt solam & separalem pasturam*.[75] In a deed granting a sole right to one person it is described as "the said sole and several herbage and pasturage of and in the said 217 acres. . . . "[76] It appears that the terms used are alternatives. In the present text the use of sole is preferred to avoid the syntactic ambiguity inherent in the word several.

The right of sole pasture is the sole right most frequently encountered in **3.98** practice and it is especially widespread in the midlands and north of England. It may be distinguished from rights of herbage and vesture by the single feature that the grass may only be taken through the mouths of cattle.[77] The legal nature of such a sole right has already been considered[78] and it only needs to be said at this point that it is most usually a right held in gross unattached to any land, with only the occasional exception occasioned by statutory award.[79] Unlike a right of common the owner of a sole

---

[69] *Earl de la Warr* v. *Miles* (1881) L.R. 17 Ch.D. 535.

[70] e.g. *Hoskins* v. *Robins* (1671) 2 Wms.Saund. 324, 85 E.R. 1123; *Rigg* v. *Earl of Lonsdale* (1857) 1 H. & N. 923, 156 E.R. 1475.

[71] (1569) 3 Dyer 285b, 73 E.R. 641; (1510) Keil, 159, 72 E.R. 334.

[72] Co.Litt. 4b: herbage is linked with vesture; it is obviously a lesser right and may be assumed to be similar but restricted to grass only.

[73] *cf.* above, n. 61.

[74] Cited at § 3.09.

[75] *North* v. *Coe* (1668) Vaughan 251, 124 E.R. 1060; in *Hopkins* v. *Robinson* (1671) 2 Lev. 2, 83 E.R. 424 it is *solam pasturam* alone which is described.

[76] *Welcome* v. *Upton* (1840) 6 M. & W. 536, 151 E.R. 524.

[77] *Cox* v. *Glue*, *Cox* v. *Mousley* (1848) 5 C.B. 533 at 548, 136 E.R. 987 at 993, *per* Wilde C.J.

[78] § 3.16.

[79] § 3.18.

right may sue in trespass to the herbage,[80] but his control of the land does not extend to interfering with the soil beneath the surface.[81]

3.99 There has been little discussion on sole pastures in texts[82] and few cases have come before the courts. In the earliest cases the issue was mainly whether a right, with the appearance of a right of common, could exist in a form which excluded the owner of the soil from the product.[83] Later there was not a little confusion between the sole right of pasture (referred to in the present text in the context of land as a stinted pasture) and the "regulated pasture."[84]

3.100 It is necessary to distinguish, as completely different, the term stinted common which is sometimes applied to true common land upon which the rights are fixed as a result of agreement, or otherwise, and the occasional use of the term to describe a common which is grazed for only part of the year.[85] The sole rights of pasture exercised over a stinted pasture are known by a variety of names such as stints, gates, gaits, beastgates, cattlegates, leazes, or cow pastures and it can only be stated with certainty that the name used is not definitive of the class of right.

(b) Modern characteristics

3.101 For modern illustrations of sole rights of pasture and stinted pastures one must rely largely upon two cases in the nineteenth century. In *Welcome* v. *Upton* (1840),[86] Lord Abinger C.B. found before him a right of sole or several pasturage which he held may be assigned as a valuable interest: "instances of sole pasturage are to be found in the South Downs in Sussex, and they are frequently transferred in gross: it is the same with the cattlegates in the north of England, although some have thought the owners of them are tenants in common of the soil." The facts of the case disclose that the sole right had been freely assigned and leased for many years.

3.102 The definitive case on stinted pastures, however, is that of *Earl of Lonsdale* v. *Rigg* (1856).[87] The case concerned an enclosed tract of land in Westmorland. Each owner of lands within the manor was entitled to rights of common on an adjoining common but the enclosed tract was depastured by the livestock of cattlegate owners only. There were 18 owners of the 80 cattlegates, each of which carried a right to graze one head of cattle from May 26, to April 14, every year together with an unlimited right to graze

---

[80] *Cox* v. *Glue*, above, n. 77, at 550, 994, *per* Wilde C.J.

[81] *cf.* the cases cited above, n. 61.

[82] Anon., *Commons* (1st and 2nd eds. s. 1698, 1702), Woolrych (1st and 2nd eds. 1824, 1850) do not discuss sole pastures and merely mention them in passing.

[83] *Potter* v. *North* (1669) 1 Wms.Saund. 346, 85 E.R. 503; *Hoskins* v. *Robins* (1671) 2 Wms.Saund. 324, 85 E.R. 1123.

[84] *Metcalf* v. *Roe* (1736) Cas.t.Hard. 167, 95 E.R. 107; *Barnes* v. *Peterson* (1736) 2 Strange 1063, 93 E.R. 1034; *Bennington* v. *Goodtitle* (1737) 2 Strange 1084, 93 E.R. 1047; *Gibson* v. *Smith* (1741) 2 Atk. 182, 26 E.R. 514; *R.* v. *Whixley (Inhabitants)* (1786) 1 T.R. 137, 99 E.R. 1016.

[85] *Cruise's Digest*, p. 80, citing Ro.Ab. 297.

[86] Above, n. 76, at 541, 527.

[87] (1856) 11 Ex. 654, 156 E.R. 992; subsequent proceedings *sub nom. Rigg* v. *Earl of Lonsdale* (1857) 1 H. & N. 923, 156 E.R. 1475.

sheep from October 10, to April 24. The cattlegate owners had repaired fences, appointed a frithman to supervise stinting, a herdsman to take care of the cattle, and without reference to the lord had altered the turnout dates. The owners were seised of the gates as customary estates of inheritance which passed by deed, with the alienee admitted by the lord's court. Some had been enfranchised following a private inclosure Act. The lord sought an opinion from the court of Exchequer as to whether he could bring an action in trespass against a cattlegate owner for taking game. The court was equally divided as to whether the property in the land remained in the lord or was that of the cattlegate owners in undivided shares. Upon a proceeding in error, the Exchequer Chamber was unanimous that the cattlegates were in the nature of copyhold tenements and that the owners were not in possession of the soil. From this case it is clear that stinted pastures may exist in the form of a divided sole right of pasture.

Each stint exercisable over a sole pasture is identical in size to any other **3.103** and represents a fixed proportion of the whole of the sole right. The stint usually has a recognized quantity of animals ascribed to it, but these are inherently variable by the agreement of the stintholders to take account of increased or decreased amounts of grazing.[88] It will be seen later[89] that not only are sole rights to pasture registrable under the provisions of the C.R.A. 1965 but, by consisting of a right to graze, must be quantified to a maximum exercisable number. This requirement of the Act is inherently inconsistent with the principle of a stint which is variable according to prevailing natural conditions.

The rights over a stinted pasture are clearly not rights to land itself. It fol- **3.104** lows that such rights granted *with* land are separate incorporeal hereditaments and do not fall within the provisions of the Agricultural Holdings Act 1986 for the purposes of security of tenure and right of succession.[90]

Sheepwalks

A sheepwalk (or some other local word) is the term used to describe the part **3.105** of a waste where an individual commoner has customarily grazed a flock of sheep, more or less to the exclusion of the flocks of other commoners. The flock so grazed is settled on, and acclimatised to, the restricted part of the waste and is known as a settled or hefted flock. The legal nature of rights of common used in this way is unchanged but the practices concerned are dealt with separately here because first, their nature seems sometimes to have been misunderstood and secondly, in parts of Wales the registration procedure under the Act of 1965 has resulted in an individual waste being split into a series of mini- or sub-commons each with only one rights holder.

---

[88] Which explains why the rights are defined as "stints" or shares rather than by reference to actual numbers of animals.

[89] C.R.A. 1965, ss.15, 22(1).

[90] *cf.* Act of 1986, Pt. IV, Sched. 6. See *Scott* v. *Bolton* (1982) ALT/2/881 for a precedent; *cf.* § 5.73.

1. The hefted flock

3.106 The practice of hefting or settling sheep flocks on a particular part of a waste is prevalent in the higher regions of the north of England. It is also a well known practice in Wales and Dartmoor. The terms used to describe it tend to be local. Thus, in Wales the land concerned is known as arosfa, cynefin, libert or sheepwalk, and on Dartmoor a hefted flock is described as leared. In case reports one tends to find the land described as a sheepwalk but it should be noted that none of the terms are definitive: for example in the Inclosure Act 1773, a sheepwalk is actually what is called in this text a fold-course.[91]

3.107 Settling, and acclimatising, a flock of sheep to a particular part of a waste has several advantages: the sheep become used to the weather conditions in the particular area and can seek shelter quickly when conditions are adverse; disease problems are specific to the area concerned; and the shepherd knows where his sheep should be and does not have to scour the entire waste looking for them. Quite often the sheepwalk is marked by stones and sometimes even partially fenced in. Almost invariably the boundaries of each walk are well known, and accepted, by all the users of the waste as being associated with a particular farm. If sheep stray from other sheepwalks it is not infrequently the practice to return them whence they came either on a regular basis or at gathering times. So important is this practice that, on a change of ownership of the associated inbye (enclosed) land, the settled flock is conveyed with the land and not sold separately. If the outgoer is a tenant he is entitled to and additional tenant right payment for each ewe in the settled flock.[92]

2. Legal nature of a sheepwalk

3.108 It is hardly surprising with the passage of time that flock owners often came to look upon the sheepwalk as part of their land in severalty and, if the owner of the waste was an absentee from the area, there was little to counteract this impression. Doubts over ownership seem to have been more prevalent in Wales than elsewhere, probably because some parts of Wales suffered absentee landowners for prolonged periods.[93] In Wales a substantial amount of the waste land was vested in the Crown through ownership of manors or as a result of inclosure awards. The position was complicated by continual disputes between large landowners and the Crown with the landowners apparently encouraging farmers to encroach on the wastes.[94] The practice of *ty-un-nos*, (literally a one night house), which tolerated a

---

[91] For which see § 3.116.
[92] Agricultural Holdings Act 1986, s.65, Sched. 8, Pt. II, para. 10, Sched. 12, paras. 6, 7.
[93] *cf.* Robinson, "The Litigation of Edward, Earl of Worcester concerning Gower 1590–1596" (1968) 22, *Bulletin of Board of Celtic Studies* 357 and (1969) 23 *Bulletin of Board of Celtic Studies* 60; Howell, *Land and People in Nineteenth Century Wales* (1978), pp. 88–90.
[94] Howell Land and People in Nineteenth Century Wales (1978); Jervis, *Report on the Crown Rights Merionethshire* (1840) (Reprint Caernarvon: W. Gwenlyn Evans, c. 1911).

farmer's younger son building a house on the waste in the night and, subject to smoke issuing from the chimney by sunrise, annexing some land to his own use seems to have survived down to the late nineteenth century.[95]

The nature of the problems created by sheepwalks in Wales may be dis- **3.109** cerned from two cases in the nineteenth century. In *Jones* v. *Richard* (1836–1837)[96] in an action in replevin two farmers claimed rights of common over land forming part of what was thought might be Crown waste.[97] The defendant abandoned his claim and in the alternate sought to claim an exclusive right of pasturage over the land as appurtenant to his farm. At assize, the jury found that the land was part of the defendant's farm and that the plaintiff had no right of common there. After appeal and two re-trials it was ultimately held that the defendant had only a right of common over the land and had exceeded his right by grazing it with sheep taken on tack. The lord, it was held, had reserved to himself all other modes of enjoying the pasture and was entitled to eat by the mouths of beasts or horses whatever the sheep did not take. It is evident that the jury thought that the land belonged to the farm concerned but the court was anxious to find otherwise, possibly because the Crown was reputed to be the owner.[98]

Later in the century the issue of a sheepwalk was brought directly before the **3.110** Court of Exchequer in the case of *Attorney-General* v. *Reveley* (1868–1869).[99] Evidence was given of 40 years uninterrupted user, coupled with partial enclosure, of a sheepwalk adjoining the defendant's farm. The court's decision was conclusively for Crown ownership in spite of the only evidence of ownership being acts over parts of the land adjoining.[1] In this case the sheepwalk was explained as the exercise of a right of common over a waste which by mutual consent or acquiescence was exercisable over that portion of the waste contiguous to, or conveniently depastured with, the enclosed land. This case, not having been challenged since, reflects the current state of the law.[2]

However, can it be said as a corollary that the user of a sheepwalk is in any **3.111** way estopped from using his rights of common over the remainder of the waste? In *Hall* v. *Byron* (1877)[3] a landowner sought to restrict the rights of a commoner by claiming that they were restricted to land adjoining his tenement or at the most to a second parcel of land connected with the first by a

---

[95] Everton, "Built in a Night . . . " (1971) 35 Conv.(N.S.) 249, (1972) 36 Conv.(N.S.) 241, (1975) 39 Conv.(N.S.) 246; Howell, *op.cit.*, p. 29.

[96] (1836) 5 Ad. & E. 413, 111 E.R. 1222; (1837) 6 Ad. & E. 530, 112 E.R. 203.

[97] *ibid.*, see the note at 416, 1223. Continuing doubts about Crown ownership in Wales can be seen in *White* v. *Williams* [1922] 1 K.B. 727 at 737, and *Davies* v. *Du Paver* [1953] 1 Q.B. 184 at 187, 208.

[98] *cf.* Lord Denman C.J., giving the judgment of the court at (1837) 6 Ad. & E. 530 at 533, 112 E.R. 203 at 204 (without an appearance by, or any evidence alluding to, an owner, his or her interests were remarkably well protected by the decision).

[99] Karslake's Special Report (Eyre and Spottiswoode for H.M.S.O., 1870).

[1] *cf. Tyrwhitt* v. *Wynne* (1819) 2 B. & Ald. 554, 106 E.R. 468.

[2] For a subsequent and similar case see *Ecclesiastical Commissioners for England* v. *Griffiths* (1876) 40 J.P. 84: shorthand notes of summing-up by Lord Chief Justice at the Cardiganshire Summer Assizes transcribed and published by Nichols & Sons, Westminster.

[3] (1877) 4 Ch.D. 667.

road. Hall V.-C. held that this contention failed: "There is evidence sufficient to establish here the ordinary rights of common of pasture; and the evidence to the contrary is all to be referred to arrangements made for mutual convenience, it not having the effect of permanently qualifying in the law the actual rights."[4]

Thus the defendant was entitled to rights over all the wastes of the manor.[5]

3. The sheepwalk today

3.112 In summary, it seems that, wherever arrangements are reached for more or less exclusive use of part of a waste by a commoner, it will not aid him in a claim to the possession of the land. Nor may the owner of the soil claim that, by this agreement, the commoner has forfeited his right to graze over the remainder. However, there seems no reason why a commoner, if he so wishes, should not abandon rights over part of the land on which in strict law he is entitled to graze. Abandonment requires that an intention never to use the right again be evinced.[6] This is what some commoners seem to have done at the time of registration under the C.R.A. 1965 by registering rights restricted to the area of their sheepwalk only. The effect is to create a series of sub-commons within what was previously one common, each with one rights holder only. Whether this was wise for them or not it seems that they have by this action given up rights over the remainder of the common land.[7] It is reiterated that the rights exercisable over a sheepwalk are ordinary rights of common, subject to the same rules as in other circumstances. There seems no reason why they may not be appendant[8] or appurtenant but the nature of the right seems to preclude a claim to a right in gross unless expressly granted.

Obsolete rights

3.113 It is not unknown to find completely obsolete rights discussed in both case reports and texts. This section is intended to identify certain rights which may now be considered only as historical curiosities, although in the case of the last one there just be some doubt as to whether it ever existed in the form described.

3.114 Two rights are often considered together usually in some form such as *libertatem faldagii* and *cursum ovium*, which may be translated as the privilege of free foldage and sheepcourse. Although frequently coupled, there are two distinct rights, of which foldage has disappeared without trace and foldcourse has been absorbed into a traditional right of common.

---

[4] *Hall* v. *Byron* (1977) 4 Ch.D. 667 at 673.
[5] See Joshua Williams, p. 186 (appeared for the plaintiffs).
[6] See § 5.38.
[7] Unregistered rights over statutory common land are unexercisable: C.R.A. 1965, s.1(2)(b).
[8] Although it is extremely unlikely in the case of remote hill land areas that they can have arisen as appendant to arable land; *cf.* § 3.29.

1. Foldage

Foldage was the reserved seignorial right to have all the sheep within a   **3.115**
manor, vill, town or other district folded on the lord's land at night.[9] It is a
right which seems to have been restricted to certain light soils in East
Anglia which required the treading and manuring of sheep to provide fertility for subsequent cereal crops. It would have been a peculiarly oppressive
right, for the corollary of the lord's land being improved would be a decrease
in fertility in the land of the tenants. In the sixteenth century the courts
were prepared to uphold an action against a tenant who erected a fold upon
his own land without licence from the lord.[10] At the end of the seventeenth
century strict pleading was needed for the right to be upheld.[11] The last
reported case on the subject seems to have been in 1793,[12] and the practice
seems not to be only of interest to historians. It is worth remarking that this
right was never one of common but was a reserved right of a landowner.

2. Foldcourse

The origin and nature of the foldcourse is well described in modern histori-   **3.116**
cal research.[13] In cases and legal texts the terms sheepcourse and sheepwalk
are sometimes used as synonyms. As with foldage, the practice seems to
have been restricted to the light infertile soils of East Anglia. It is best described as a reserved seignorial right to graze the only flock of sheep in the
manor. The manorial flock grazed, according to season, over the "shack"
lands, Lammas meadows, common pastures and wastes. Sometimes tenants
were entitled to place a number of sheep with the lord's flock in which
event the flock was known as a "cullet" flock. One unsuccessful claim to
rights for a cullet flock was made during registration under the Act of
1965.[14] It will be evident that the foldcourse, as land, was never common
land nor was a foldcourse, as a right, ever a right of common although sometimes treated as such by the courts.[15] As the system decayed, and as the
rights were divided and severed from the manor, they became rights exercisable over the land of other persons and thus *de facto* and *de jure* rights of
common.[16]

The final recognition of the right as a reserved right of the lord can be seen   **3.117**
in the case of *Ivatt* v. *Mann* (1842)[17] when a lord was unsuccessful in a

---

[9] *cf.* Joshua Williams, p. 275; *Sharpe* v. *Bechenowe* (1688) 2 Lut. 1249, 125 E.R. 692;
Punsany and Leader's Case (1583) 1 Leon. 11, 74 E.R. 10; *John of Sudford's Case*
(1329), cited at 2 Brownl. & Golds. 287, 123 E.R. 946; 8 Co.Rep. 125b, 77 E.R. 664.
[10] *Punsany and Leader's Case*, above, n. 9.
[11] *Dickman* v. *Allan* (1690) 2 Vent. 138, 86 E.R. 355.
[12] *Brook* v. *Willet* (1793) 2 H.Bl. 224, 126 E.R. 519.
[13] Allison, "The Sheep-Corn Husbandry of Norfolk in the Sixteenth and Seventeenth
Centuries" (1957) 5 Agric.Hist.Rev. 12.
[14] *Re Runton Half Year Lands, Runton, N. Norfolk* (1976) 25/D/34–78, 4 D.C.C. 366.
[15] *Fielding* v. *Wren* (1559) Cary 46, 21 E.R. 25; for severance from the manor see
Spooner v. *Day and Mason* (1636) Cro.Car. 432, 79 E.R. 975; no forfeiture for
enclosure against a foldcourse: see *Paston* v. *Utber* (1629) Hut. 102, 123 E.R. 1131.
[16] *Musgrave* v. *Gave* (1741–1742) Willes 319, 125 E.R. 1193.
[17] (1842) 3 Man. & G. 691, 133 E.R. 1318; *subsequent proceedings* 3 Man. & G. 702,
n. (a), 133 E.R. 1322.

claim for an allotment in respect of his foldcourse as the inclosure Act only compensated rights of common. By the time of *Robinson* v. *Duleep Singh* (1877–1879)[18] the courts were accepting the contention that "the mere use of the term 'fold-course' of itself imported that the right which was in question there was merely a right of common of pasture."[19] The foldcourse at this point in time seems to have made the transition from a seignorial right to a right of common.

3.118 There is no objection to the treatment of the foldcourse as a right of common in principle. Once severed from the manor, as was held at an early stage to be possible,[20] the right became one exercisable over the land of another person and, unless granted as a benefit attached to land, became a right of common in gross. It is not known whether traces of the foldcourse may still be discerned in practice but if they are then it is submitted they may be now considered as rights of common.

3. Sheepheaves

3.119 One right frequently mentioned in texts is that of the sheepheave. The source of the comments seems to be *Cookes' Inclosures*[21]:

> "There are also lands which in ordinary parlance are called common, although the right of pasture over them is in an individual. Such are the small plots of pasture often in the middle of a waste, called sheepheaves, the soil of which may or may not be in the lord, but the pasture is certainly a private property, and is leased and sold as such. These sheep-heaves obtain chiefly in the northern counties, and are possibly derived from that state of continual border warfare which was peculiarly favourable to the creation of rights of common in gross. In a country where a plunderer was every moment to be expected, it was absolutely necessary that there should be a perpetual staff of warders; and the most obvious and the least burdensome way of remunerating them was, to give them especial rights upon the commons which they watched . . . Now that the duties have ceased, the rights come down to us evidenced only by their immemorial enjoyment, and are held, and well held, by prescription."

3.120 In legal terms this is a peculiar mixture—a right of common in gross, which is a private property, but is well held by prescription. With respect, it is submitted that there is a confusion between two separate commons phenomena. On many commons may be found isolated islands of enclosed land. They may have their origin in some sort of public duty but an alternative explanation is that they were lands used by lords as a base for hunting.[22] Whatever their origin, if owned and occupied in severalty today, they have ceased to have any recognisable common land connection. A second possibility, and this is the explanation favoured by this writer, is that Cooke was

---

[18] (1877/8/9) 11 Ch.D. 798.

[19] *ibid.* at 817, *per* Brett L.J. approving a submission by Joshua Williams Q.C.

[20] *Spooner* v. *Day and Mason*, above, n. 15.

[21] Cooke, p. 44; repeated by Elton, p. 35.

[22] *cf.* Lloyd, *The Great Forest of Brecon* (1905), p. 144.

observing the heaf (pl. heaves) of the north of England.[23] These are the areas on a waste to which sheep are by custom and practice limited to the exclusion of other flocks, *i.e.* the flocks are hefted. They are identical with the sheepwalk (described above). It is suggested that Cook's category of sheep-heaves, if it ever existed, is completely obsolete and the term should now only be used in connection with hefted flocks.

QUANTIFICATION

The quantification of rights over the common lands depends to some extent **3.121** upon the class of land over which the rights are exercisable. For example, the stint or right exercisable over a sole pasture is a proportionate share of the entire grazing crop on the land. It is obviously inappropriate to consider it as being for certain numbers of animals as the quantity of grass available may vary from year to year. On the other hand, true rights of common exercisable over a waste usually have more relationship with land to which they are annexed than to the amount of the product available on the servient land. It is necessary, therefore, to consider quantification separately for each class of land.

1. Wastes

It is most usual to find that the rights of common of pasturage over wastes **3.122** are either appendant[24] or appurtenant[25] to dominant tenements. Without exception appendant rights of pasturage are described as being "levant and couchant."[26] Appurtenant rights are usually also referred to in this way but may sometimes be known as "*sans nombre.*"[27] Just occasionally, appurtenant rights have been granted for fixed numbers of animals or, as it is said, for a number certain.[28] Very infrequently rights are held in gross and, in the absence of a dominant tenement to which they might be related, are usually for a number certain. There are case reports and texts which indicate that at one time unlimited rights in gross were granted but they may have been only rights *in personam* and in all event may now be considered obsolete.[29]

The Act of 1965 requires that rights which consist of or include grazing by **3.123** animals shall be reduced to a maximum number of exercisable animals.[30] This has provided an element of certainty where there was none before, but common law principles still have relevance first, because the nature of *levancy* and *couchancy* may have more substance than merely being a

---

[23] *cf.* Royal Commission Report, Minutes of Evidence 12, p. 37: evidence by Friends of the Lake District and Earl Lonsdale.
[24] § 3.28.
[25] § 3.36.
[26] For which, see § 3.127.
[27] For which, see § 3.137.
[28] Where rights have been granted for a number certain it may be unclear as to whether the rights are appurtenant to land or are in gross: *cf.* § 3.41.
[29] § 3.139.
[30] C.R.A. 1965, s.15.

method of quantification[31] and secondly, because the registration of rights has provided, in some cases at least, a totality of rights which can only be described as nonsensical.[32] In certain circumstances, therefore, it is still necessary to look behind the registers and at the common law rules.

3.124   The most important right of common on the wastes is that of pasturage. Nevertheless, a variety of other rights are usually found to exist, of which estovers, turbary and piscary are numerous. Rights other than pasturage were not quantified under the registration provisions and although examples of fixed quantities for rights of this nature can be found in reports, they are wholly exceptional in practice. It follows that it is almost always necessary to consult common law principles to determine the size of rights other than those or pasturage. The principles were established early and seem unchanged by the passage of time. Bracton describes the amounts thus:

> " . . . where one ought to have the right of felling or cutting in another's forest or wood, or in other wastes, for his reasonable estovers, that is, for building, fencing, burning and other necessary things, much or little, according to the constitution of the servitude. In which taking due measure must be observed, that the estovers be reasonable according to the size of the wood or waste in which the servitude is constituted according as it is large or small. The size of the tenement to which the servitude is owed [must also be considered, that the estovers] neither exceed due measure nor are reduced below it, that everything remain in property proportion."[33]

The two principles involved are that the amount taken must be related to the needs of the dominant tenement and the total of the amounts taken by all the rights holders must have regard to the size of the servient tenement. In this connection the right of the owner of the soil in all events to have his share in the product must be remembered.[34]

3.125   The limitation of each right will depend upon its nature. A common of turbary will be limited by the number of chimney or hearths in the tenement[35]; plough-bote is restricted to the repairing requirements of the implements[36]; house-bote to repairing the timbers of the house[37]; and piscary, or the taking of rabbits, to the sustenance of the family.[38] There is some small indication that timber for fencing may be limited in quantity to the amount required to repair ancient fences.[39]

3.126   In the case of estovers, such as bracken for bedding, or rushes for thatching, the amount taken will be controlled by the number of animals which may be maintained on the dominant land and the number of stacks which may

---

[31] *cf.* §§ 3.135–3.136.
[32] *cf.* § 4.22.
[33] Bracton, folio 231.
[34] *cf.* Co.Litt. 122a, cited at § 3.09
[35] See § 3.72.
[36] *Chesterfield (Lord)* v. *Harris* [1908] 2 Ch. 397 at 421, *per* Buckley L.J.
[37] Bl.Comm., ii, 35.
[38] *ibid.; cf.* § 8.12.
[39] *cf.* § 3.68, and n. 81 thereto.

be made from the produce of the land. It is suggested that the grant may not be expanded beyond the level at which it was originally granted—for example animals bought in, and fed indoors, may exceed the number for which bracken may be cut for bedding.

(a) Levancy and couchancy

By far the greater number of grazing rights over wastes are thought to be qualified by *levancy* and *couchancy*. The literal meaning of the term is that the right extends to so many animals as get up and lie down on the land to which the right is annexed. The principle is used in determining how many animals are the subject of a presumed grant in claims to a prescriptive right. While the reduction of a grazing right to a known quantified number of animals is an important feature of the term it may be that *levancy* and *couchancy* has the additional effect of limiting the animals which are grazed to those which factually depend upon the dominant land.[40]   **3.127**

(i) **Numbers of animals**   From early days it has been understood that *levant* and *couchant* means "so many of the cattle that the land, to which the common is appurtenant, may maintain in the winter,"[41] that is to say "if my land to which I claim common belonging, can yield me stover [feed] to find a hundred cattell in winter, then I shall have common in summer for a hundred cattell."[42] This, however, begs the question as to whether modern farming techniques, which can influence fodder production, may be taken into account. The question was considered, but not decided, in *Robertson* v. *Hartopp* (1889).[43] In the absence of authority, it is submitted that the decision in *Mercer* v. *Denne* (1905)[44] is relevant. The case was concerned with a custom to dry fishing nets on private property and it was held that the adoption of new practices did not invalidate the custom, provided that an unreasonable burden was not cast on the servient landowner as a result. By analogy, it is submitted that, while new practices are unexceptionable, it is the stock carrying capacity of a farm at the time of the grant which is relevant and not necessarily the capacity as increased by new farming techniques. The question is of less importance today, since maximum numbers have been registered under the C.R.A. 1965 and landowners have had an opportunity to object to the rights owners' claims.   **3.128**

In connection with *levant* and *couchant* rights (and also those described as *sans nombre*[45]), notice must be taken of the essential feature of any right of common "that the owner of the soyle should take reasonable profit there."[46] Thus, there can be no certainty today that numbers established by the principle of *levancy* and *couchancy* provide an absolute right. In theory they ought to, but the practical reality is that most commons on which rights were originally granted have been subject to at least some, and in some cases extensive, inclosure and encroachment. On each occasion some   **3.129**

---

[40] §§ 3.135–3.136.
[41] *Cole* v. *Foxman* (1618) Noy 30, 74 E.R. 1000.
[42] *Smith* v. *Bensall* (1597) Goulds. 117, 75 E.R. 1034.
[43] (1889) 43 Ch.D. 484.
[44] (1905) 2 Ch. 538 at 581.
[45] § 3.137.
[46] Co.Litt. 122a.

part of the original *levant* and *couchant* right will have been expressly or impliedly released. The result is that it is now most frequently found that the totality of *levant* and *couchant* rights exceeds the grazing capacity of the common.[47] The position must be that *levancy* and *couchancy*, in many instances, can be no more than a means of assessing relative claims between rights holders and not the absolute right of any one individual.[48]

3.130 **(ii) Prescription** In the event of a claim to common of pasturage by prescriptive right the principle of *levancy* and *couchancy* will be applied. The judgment of Buckley L.J. in *Chesterfield (Lord) v. Harris* (1908)[49] is definitive:

> "But prescription in a que estate, being a prescriptive right in respect of particular land to a profit à prendre in alieno solo, is, I think necessarily measured by the size or nature or wants of the estate in respect of which the prescription is made. Thus if it be for common of pasture it must be for cattle levant and couchant; that is to say, it must be limited by the number of cattle capable of being supported during the winter upon the estate in respect of which the prescription is made."

3.131 **(iii) Without land** It was made clear in a case where actual *levancy* and *counchancy* was challenged that it is unnecessary for the land at any current date to be used for the production of winter fodder, provided that it is "in a state in which it might have been laid down for pasture, or for meadow, or cultivated so as to produce artificial plants and roots for the support of cattle." In the same case it was thought that it might be otherwise if the character of the dominant tenement is so altered that it could not be so converted—if, for example, a town of considerable extent had been built upon the land, or if it were turned into a reservoir. The use of the land for a garden or orchard is not sufficient to destroy the right.[50]

3.132 There are a number of cases where *levant* and *couchant* rights have been accepted in respect of a single building. Pleas of beasts *levant* and *couchant* have been held good after verdict in respect of a house,[51] a messuage[52] and a cottage[53] on the understanding that a cottage will always include a curtilage. These cases must be viewed with some reservation as from 1588 until 1775 it was unlawful to build a cottage without four acres of land being annexed thereto.[54] In 1792 a case came before the courts where the claim was for "common in right of a messuage for all commonable cattle levant and couchant," and it was proved that the house concerned had neither land, curtilage or stables. The claimant carried on his trade as a butcher from the house and kept four or five sheep overnight in a "sheephold" under

---

[47] § 4.22.
[48] The Common Land Forum recommends that all rights be amended to reflect the stock carrying capacity of registered commons: Report, Appendix C, para. 031.
[49] [1908] 2 Ch. 397 at 421; affirmed [1911] A.C. 623.
[50] *Carr* v. *Lambert* (1866) L.R. 1 Ex. 168 at 175, *per* Willes J.
[51] *Patrick* v. *Lowre* (1611) 2 Brownl. & Golds. 101, 123 E.R. 838.
[52] *Scambler* v. *Johnson* (1682) 2 Show. K.B. 248, 89 E.R. 919; see also *Hockley* v. *Lamb* (1698) 1 Ld.Raym. 726, 91 E.R. 1384.
[53] *Emerton* v. *Selby* (1704) 1 Salk. 169, 91 E.R. 156.
[54] *cf.* Erection of Cottages Act 1588: Erection of Cottages Act 1775.

the shop window. It was held that the claim failed and that there must be "land as will keep the cattle claimed to be commoned in the winter."[55]

The position of a claim to a right levant and couchant to a tenement with-   **3.133** out land is altogether different when the servient land is in a common field.[56]

(iv) Appendant and appurtenant distinctions In the case of an   **3.134** appendant right, which required no prescriptive plea, it was unnecessary to say "common for cattle *levant* and *couchant*" as it was an incident of appendancy.[57] The right of a commoner is for "horses and oxen to plough his land and cows and sheep to manure his land."[58] On division of the land it is not possible to claim that, however small a divided parcel, a right to keep sufficient animals to form a team for ploughing and cultivation must always be allowed,[59] nor does *levancy* and *couchancy* mean that the right is limited to animals actually used for manuring and cultivating.[60] Appurtenant and appendant rights seem to have the same *levancy* and *couchancy* characteristics with only the distinction that appendant rights are limited to commonable animals.[61]

(v) Use with dominant land While defining numbers of animals   **3.135** which may be grazed is obviously an important function of *levancy* and *couchancy*, it may be unwise to dismiss it as being the only one. In the older cases there was a general presumption that it also meant that the grazing animals must be directly connected with the dominant land. For instance, in *Hoskins* v. *Robins* (1671)[62] Saunders, in an answer accepted by the Court, stated that in claiming a common appurtenant

" . . . the commoner ought to say for his cattle *levant* and *couchant*, for *that* is the standard or metewand of the profit he is to have; that is to say, grass for all his cattle *levant* and *couchant* on his land and no others; and therefore if he puts in any cattle which are not *levant* and *couchant* he does a wrong to the lord and shall be punished as a trespasser for them."

Similarly, in *Patrick* v. *Lowre* (1611)[63] it was said that

" . . . it was agreed that (rising and lying down) shall be intended those beasts which are nourished and fed upon the land, and may there lie in summer and winter, and also beasts cannot be distrained if they be not rising and lying down upon the land, and receiving food there for some reasonable time . . . "

There is a general assumption in the older cases that animals *levant* and   **3.136** *couchant* were required to be actually grazed on the dominant tenement

[55] *Scholes* v. *Hargreaves* (1792) 5 T.R. 46 at 48, 101 E.R. 26 at 27, *per* Buller J.
[56] § 3.142.
[57] *Morse and Webb's Case* (1609) 13 Co.Rep. 65, 77 E.R. 1474.
[58] See § 3.29
[59] *Bennett* v. *Reeve* (1740) Willes 227 at 231, 125 E.R. 1144 at 1146, *per* Willes L.C.J.
[60] *Whitelock* v. *Hutchinson* (1839) 2 M. & Rob. 205 at 206, 174 E.R. 264 at 264, *per* Parke B.; see also *Robertson* v. *Hartopp* (1889) 43 Ch.D. 484 at 516, 517.
[61] *cf.* § 3.32.
[62] (1671) 2 Wms.Saund. 324 at 326, 85 E.R. 1123 at 1124.
[63] (1611) 2 Brownl. & Golds. 101, 123 E.R. 838.

and, if they were not, they were in breach of the grant made to the commoner. A later case makes it clear that it is not necessary for the land to be actually growing crops for the production of winter fodder so long as it can be easily converted to that purpose but, even in that case, the animals were housed on the land and grazed on such grass as was available.[64] It is submitted that a grant *levant* and *couchant* is to say that the grantee may graze animals which benefit the dominant tenement, in numbers related to the size of that tenement, and no others.

(b) Rights sans nombre

3.137 On occasions rights are described as *sans nombre*. It is not altogether clear in the case of rights annexed to land that the term was ever used other than in contradistinction to rights for a certain number; that is to say that *sans nombre* actually had the same meaning as *levant* and *couchant*. Certainly from a very early date the courts resisted any suggestion that it meant an unlimited right. In 1422 it was said that such a claim "cannot be a claim for feeding any number of beasts, but for a number certain."[65] In *Chichly's Case* (1658)[66] the court attempted to find an explanation for the term: " . . . common sans nomber cannot be appendant to any thing but lands, and that it is called sans nomber, because it is only for beasts levant and couchant; and it is incertain how many those are, there being more in some years than in other; but it is common certain in its nature; for id certum est quod certum reddit potest."

3.138 In 1705 the writ of admeasurement by reference to *levancy* and *couchancy* was held applicable to a common *sans nombre*[67] and in 1740 it was unequivocally declared that the term had no rational meaning other than in contradistinction to a right to common a particular number of animals.[68]

3.139 A right of "common sauns nomber in grosse" is referred to by Sir Edward Coke,[69] but by the time of Blackstone it was said that "such commons have not even a theoretical existence at the present day."[70] A right in gross *sans nombre* was clearly recognised in *Weekly* v. *Wildman* (1698)[71] when it was said that rights granted to inhabitants in gross and without number might be necessary to encourage, say, the population of the Fen country. The court was also careful to say that such rights could not be granted over, which per-

---

[64] *Carr* v. *Lambert* (1866), above, n. 50; *cf. Emerton* v. *Selby*, above, n. 53: foddering of cattle in a yard is evidence of *levancy* and *couchancy*.

[65] Y.B. 11 H6, 22B, pl. 19.

[66] *Chichley* v. ——— (1658) Hardres 117, 145 E.R. 409; in *Anon.* (1577) 4 Leon. 41, 74 E.R. 716, Dyer and Manwood JJ. agreed that *sans nombre* was "the number of the Cattle and the best and most substantial tenant of the said tenement at any time of memory had kept upon the said waste."

[67] *Follett* v. *Troake* (1705) 2 Ld.Raym. 1186 at 1187, 92 E.R. 284 at 285.

[68] *Bennett* v. *Reeve* (1740), above, n. 59, at 232, 1147, *per* Willes L.C.J.

[69] Co.Litt. 122a; *cf.* Bracton, folios 181, 183.

[70] Bl.Comm. ii, 34.

[71] (1698) 1 Ld.Raym. 405, 91 E.R. 1169; also *Stampe* v. *Burgesse* (1619) 2 Rolle 73, 81 E.R. 667; *cf. Leniel* v. *Harslop* (1669) 3 Keb. 66, 84 E.R. 597 (1000 sheep annexed to a cottage in Lincolnshire); distinguish the right of foldcourse which is a reserved seignorial right and is neither appurtenant nor limited: *Ivatt* v. *Mann* (1842) 2 Man. & G. 691, 133 E.R. 1318, especially n. (a) at 702, 1322.

haps indicates that they were only rights *in personam* granted for a particular and temporally limited purpose. They may now be considered to be completely obsolete not least because all rights had to be quantified under the C.R.A. 1965.

2. Stinted pastures

It has been demonstrated that the rights over stinted pastures are inherently incapable of direct quantification inasmuch as each right, or stint, is in legal theory simply a proportion of the whole of the grazing. However, it cannot be denied that each stint usually has a recognised quantum so that it might be, for example, one head of cattle, or half a horse or four to five sheep. Any variation of the stint clearly needs the agreement of all the participators which, if the pasture has been established by inclosure award, may be by means of a statutorily defined procedure. Another alternative seems to be that a stint can be, for instance, for one head of cattle throughout the year with an unlimited number of sheep to take up any surplus during the winter months.[72]   **3.140**

Levancy and *couchancy*, with consequent quantification by reference to a dominant tenement, clearly has no relevance in the case of a stinted pasture,[73] and the rights are held in gross. It is also self-evident that quantification of rights under the C.R.A. 1965 is inappropriate for a right which is inherently variable as each season requires.   **3.141**

3. Common fields

In connection with rights in and over common fields it is not unusual to find that the rights are described as *levant* and *couchant* but the meaning of the term in this context is somewhat different.   **3.142**

In *Cheesman* v. *Hardham* (1818)[74] a plaintiff claimed to be entitled to common of pasture for all his cattle *levant* and *couchant* in a common and open arable field of which he was part owner—the right called intercommonage in the present work. The court held that, in the case of "common of shack," grazing *levant* and *couchant* means the number of animals which the plaintiff's parcel of land in the field is capable of supporting. The "dominant" land was, in this case, also part of the "servient" land. This is similar to a regulated pasture in that the number of animals which can be grazed is the same proportion of all the animals which can be grazed as the area of the owner's land bears to all the land available.   **3.143**

Where the rights in common fields are exercisable by persons without land in the fields, *levancy* and *couchancy* may have yet another meaning. In *Mellor* v. *Spateman* (1669)[75] a burgess of the city of Derby claimed a right to   **3.144**

---

[72] *Earl of Lonsdale* v. *Rigg* (1856) 11 Ex. 654, 156 E.R. 992.

[73] *cf. Hoskins* v. *Robins* (1671) 2 Wms.Saund. 324 at 327, 85 E.R. 1123 at 1124, *per* Saunders and approved by the court.

[74] (1818) 1 B. & Ald. 706, 106 E.R. 260.

[75] (1669) 1 Wms.Saund. 343 at 345, 85 E.R. 495 at 502, *per* Kelynge C.J.; *cf.* 4 Vin.Ab. 585, 1 and 4.

graze his commonable cattle over an open arable field after harvest. The plea was held good only if the words "levant and couchant in the town" were added. It seems that here the words are added to limit the geographical location of the animals and says little about the numbers involved. Whether it is correct to view such rights as being appurtenant to a town is doubtful. In *Stables* v. *Mellon* (1679)[76] the *levant* and *couchant* rights of inhabitants in a town were said to be in gross.

---

[76] (1679) 2 Lev. 246, 83 E.R. 540.

4. Registration, Creation and Transfer of Common Rights

REGISTRATION

The C.R.A. 1965 requires the registration of land which is common land **4.01** and, additionally, rights of common over such land.[1] There is a continuing requirement to register both land and rights. As with common land, there was an initial registration period for rights following which "no rights of common shall be exercisable over any such land [land capable of being registered under the Act] unless they are registered either under this Act or under the Land Registration Acts 1925 and 1936."[2] The periods for application for registration of rights, objections thereto, and withdrawals of registrations or objections are the same as those applicable to the registration of land.[3]

In the case of a registered right which consists of or includes a right to graze **4.02** animals, or animals of a class, not limited by number, the Act further requires that it be treated, for the purposes of registration, as being exercisable by no more animals, or animals of that class than a definite number, and upon finality it shall be exercisable in relation to animals not exceeding that number or numbers.[4]

The effect of the C.R.A. 1965 on rights was to require the registration of all **4.03** rights (as defined in the Act) during a mandatory registration period following which any rights ceased to be exercisable. A possible exception to registration exists in respect of rights which had been registered prior to January 2, 1967, as a form of registered title to land or, possibly, as appurtenant to a registered title to land under the Land Registration Acts.[5] Any rights created over land, which did not achieve registration in the initial registration period, have the effect of creating new common land and in this event

[1] s.1(1)(a), (b).
[2] s.1(2)(b).
[3] §§ 2.5, 2.6.
[4] s.15.
[5] See §§ 4.13–4.17.

both land and rights are registrable.[6] However, it is not possible to create new exercisable rights over land which did achieve registration.[7]

1. Registration procedure

4.04   The procedure for registration of rights is prescribed in Regulations and results in a rights section as part of a register of common land.[8] Each rights section is divided into five parts showing: (1) the date of entry on the register, (2) the date of application for an entry, (3) the name and address of the applicant for registration, and the capacity in which he applied, (4) particulars of the right of common, and the land over which it is exercisable and, (5) particulars of the land, if any, to which the right is attached.

(a) Effect of final registration

4.05   Upon achieving finality of registration either, by lack of objection or, resolution or withdrawal of an objection or, following an inquiry and decision thereon by a Commons Commissioner, the registration shall be conclusive evidence of the matters registered as at the date of registration.[9] The matters required by the C.R.A. 1965 to be registered are the right of common and, where the right consists of or includes a right of grazing, the maximum number of animals for which the right is exercisable. It is clear that these matters and the date of registration (not let it be noted the date of application for registration) are affected by the conclusive evidence provision. Other matters recorded on the registers may not attract the same conclusivity.

4.06   In the third part of the section of the registers where rights, and in appropriate cases numbers of livestock, are recorded there is quite usually additional information qualifying the rights, for example, by stating the period of exercisability during the year. This additional information does not appear to form part of the matters which were required to be registered and consequently, it is suggested, does not come within the conclusive evidence provision. It is, for example, not unknown for land subject to *prima tonsura* to be subject to rights of grazing during an open period of the year some of which are expressed as being for part of the year and others for all the year.[10] The Act did not purport to increase rights, nor did it require the registration of the period of exercisability in each year, and it is suggested that the mistaken registration of grazing rights for the whole of the year cannot be used so as to affect adversely the right of *tonsura*. It will be otherwise where the section qualifies the right by limiting it to part only of the land of the register unit for the reason that the applicant will have made no claim to rights other than over the limited part.

---

[6] For the creation of new common land, see § 2.56.

[7] *cf.* § 4.41.

[8] Commons Registration (General) Regulations 1966 (S.I. 1966 No. 1471), especially Pts. II and III, as amended by Commons Registration (General) (Amendment) Regulations 1968 (S.I. 1968 No. 658).

[9] s.10.

[10] For *prima tonsura*, see § 3.93.

Similarly, the fifth section of the rights registers records the land, if any, to **4.07**
which the rights are attached. This information is again not amongst the
matters required to be registered and, it is submitted, does not attract the
conclusive evidence provision. The Commons Commissioners, in considering this section of the register have concluded that the attachment to land
has no more significance than that the right was used with the land at the
time of registration.[11] If this is correct, then the registers do not provide evidence that the rights are annexed to land.

(b) Applicants

An application for registration of a right could be made by, or on behalf of, **4.08**
the owner of the right or, where the right was attached to land comprised in
a tenancy, by the landlord, the tenant or both of them jointly or, in the case
of a vacant ecclesiastical benefice, by the Church Commissioners.[12] It follows that the person recorded as applicant was not necessarily the owner of
the right at the time of registration. Still less are the names of the applicants
necessarily indicative of current owners for there is no provision for amending the names of applicants when the ownership or occupation of land
changes, unless a right attached to land has been divided.[13]

2. Registrable rights

(a) In general

Under the Act land subject to rights of common is registrable "whether **4.09**
those rights are exercisable at all times or only during limited periods."[14]
Rights of common are given a special meaning so as to include— "cattlegates or beastgates (by whatever name known) and rights of sole or several
vesture or herbage or of sole or several pasture, but does not include rights
held for a term of years or from year to year."[15]

It is made clear by express mention that all common law rights of common whether exercisable for the whole year or part of the year are included,
so that all rights of common exercisable over wastes or common fields are
registrable.[15] It is also evident that rights over stinted pastures are registrable[16] as are sole rights to vesture or herbage.[17] It is less clear that rights of
intercommonage over common fields, *i.e.* rights between adjoining owners
of divided shares in land or, the rights between owners of undivided shares
in land as exist over the regulated pastures, are registrable. In the present
work the view has been advanced that the Act is insufficiently worded to
bring these two latter classes of land and right within the ambit of the Act.[18]

---

[11] See further § 4.83.
[12] Commons Registration (General) Regulations 1966 (S.I. 1966 No. 1471), regs. 7, 8,
as amended by the Commons Registration (General) (Amendment) Regulations
1968 (S.I. 1968 No. 658), Sched., paras. 1, 2.
[13] See further §§ 4.80–4.81.
[14] s.22(1).
[15] *ibid.*
[16] As sole or several pastures: *cf.* § 3.97.
[17] By express inclusion.
[18] See §§ 2.27, 2.33.

The Common Land Forum seems to accept this view in respect of regulated pastures and recommends that this class of land and rights be removed from registration but makes no mention of rights of intercommonage.[19]

(b) Quasi-rights

4.10 It is a well established common law rule that no rights of common can exist where the dominant and servient tenements are in unified ownership.[20] Thus the rights exercisable by the lord (or other owner of the soil) from any demesne land or purchased freehold land are but quasi-rights and are unregistrable. The express exclusion of rights held for a term of years or from year to year in the definition in the Act seems sufficient to establish also that all quasi-rights of the owner of the soil, when exercised by tenants or termors, are also unregistrable. Nevertheless, a very substantial number, possibly even the majority, of quasi-rights have been registered and a large number have achieved finality through lack of objection.[21] Some have come before the Commissioners for consideration and almost without exception in the early decisions registration has been refused.[22] More recently one Commissioner declared that such rights were registrable and probably allowed registrations to stand.[23] Simultaneously, the Chief Commissioner (at that time) was refusing registrations and even refusing a claim to ownership of land as "ownership and a right of common being mutually exclusive and the right of common attached to [the claimant's] land having become final, it is impossible fo him to be registered as the owner of the servient tenement."[24] The position of the current Chief Commissioner seems to be that quasi-rights are unequivocally unregistrable[25] but he has had no hesitation about the registration of finally registered commoners as owners with possessory title to the land.[26] It can only be stated with confidence that the registers demonstrate a marked degree of inconsistency in respect of this aspect of registration.

4.11 The Common Land Forum recommends that future legislation should provide for all entries of this class to be removed from the rights registers.[27] A further recommendation is made that quasi-rights be entered instead as

---

[19] Common Land Forum Report, Appendix C, paras. 108–113.

[20] See § 5.02.

[21] In regional meetings of commoners there has been some surprise, if not disbelief, when the proposition is advanced that rights registered by tenants of the owners of the soil are not correctly registered. Tenants have indicated that owners encouraged them to register. Certainly they are plain for all to see on some of the Powys commons registers: see *e.g.* Powys. C.L. 16.

[22] For early decisions see *Re Hedges Wood Common, Great Gaddesden. Herts. (No. 1)* (1973) 16/D/24, 1 D.C.C. 240; *Re Pen Braichmelyn, Bethesda, Caerns.* (1973) 50/D/7–8, 1 D.C.C. 289.

[23] *Re Yennadown Down, West Devon* (1984) 209/D/294–296, 15 D.C.C. 121; *Re Roborough Down, West Devon* (1984) 209/D/298, 15 D.C.C. 154; *Re Pasture End, Murton, Cumbria* (1981) 262/D/277–279, 11 D.C.C. 168; and especially *Re Trendlebere Down, Lustleigh, Devon* (1985) 209/D/430–432, 16 D.C.C. 87.

[24] *Re Roseacre Green (part), St. Gennys, Cornwall* (1985) 206/U/227, 16 D.C.C. 47.

[25] *cf. Re the tract of about 688 acres called Edlogan Common in the parishes of Panteg, Llanfechfa Upper and Abercarn* (1986) 273/D/104–105, 16 D.C.C. 437.

[26] *Re Plumstone Mountain, Camrose, Dyfed* (1986) 272/U/105, 16 D.C.C. 413.

[27] Common Land Forum Report, Appendix C, para. 029.

notes on the registers[28] (which at present do not attract compulsory registration) but be brought within the Act for purposes connected with
apportionment of rights.[29]

(c) Residual rights of the owner of the soil

The owner of the soil of a waste has a residual right to the benefit of all of **4.12**
the particular product remaining after the rights of common are satisfied.[30]
As a right arising directly from ownership of the land it is submitted that it
is not registrable under the Act. A Commons Commissioner has endorsed
this view[31] but some have been registered and were not subject to objection.[32]

(d) Rights registered under the Land Registration Acts

It has been mentioned that unregistered rights became unexercisable fol- **4.13**
lowing the expiry of the mandatory registration procedure but, an exception
was made in respect of rights registered under the Land Registration Acts
1925 and 1936.[33] It was further provided that upon the Act of 1965 coming
into force[34] "no rights of common over land which is capable of being registered under this Act shall be registered under the Land Registration
Acts . . . "[35] The intentions are fairly clear but the practice is somewhat
confused.

The Land Registration Acts allow for, and in certain circumstances **4.14**
require,[36] that estates in land be registered.[37] Land, for the purposes of the
Act, is defined to include, *inter alia*, incorporeal hereditaments, easements,
rights, privileges and benefits in, over or derived from land.[38] Thus, a right
of common held for a legal estate is prima facie registrable under the Acts.
There are, however, two rules, made under the Acts,[39] which seem to conflict. Rule 50 is concerned with the registration of incorporeal hereditaments:

> "Application for registration of manors, advowsons, rents, tithe rent-
> charges, or other incorporeal hereditaments [etc.] . . . shall be made
> according to the rules above prescribed . . . "

Rule 257 provides that—

[28] Common Land Forum Report, Appendix C, para. 030.
[29] *ibid.* paras. 030, 063–066.
[30] *Jones* v. *Richard* (1837) 6 Ad. & E. 530 at 533, 112 E.R. 203 at 204, *per* Lord Denman C.J.; *Arlett* v. *Ellis* (1827) 7 B. & C. 346 at 369, 108 E.R. 752 at 761, *per* Bayley
J.
[31] *Re Trendlebere Down, Lustleigh, Devon* (1985), above, n. 23.
[32] See the West Glamorgan Commons registers.
[33] C.R.A. 1965 s.1(2)(b); see also § 4.01.
[34] January 2, 1967: The Commons Registration Act 1965 (Commencement No. 2)
Order 1966 (S.I. 1966 No. 971) (C.7).
[35] s.1(1).
[36] In compulsory registration areas: see the Land Registration Act 1925, s.120; and on
the sale of statutory common land, the C.R.A. 1965, s.12. See also § 7.40.
[37] Land Registration Act 1925, s.2.
[38] *ibid.* s.3(viii).
[39] Land Registration Rules 1925 (S.R. & O. 1925 No. 1093).

"The benefit of an easement, right or privilege shall not be entered on the register except as appurtenant to a registered estate, and then only if capable of subsisting as a legal estate."

It might be anticipated that the effect of the two rules is to allow substantive registration of a right in gross, as a form of incorporeal hereditament and, where the right is of benefit to land, to allow registration only as appurtenant to land. However, it is understood that the view of the Land Registry is that no right of common whether appurtenant or in gross, is capable of substantive registration and before 1967 could only have achieved registration through appurtenancy to land.

4.15   The effect of the view taken by the Registry is that *profits à prendre* in gross were incapable of registration by any method before 1967 and it was not these rights, substantively registered, which were protected from the effects of non-registration under the C.R.A. 1965 but appurtenant rights, *i.e.* the only rights which could achieve registration. Thus, appurtenant rights, established to the satisfaction of the Registry before 1967, may have been preserved after 1967 and have not been tested by the provisions contained in the Act of 1965. There can, therefore, be no absolute certainty that all rights, capable of being exercised, can be identified from inspection of the commons registers.

4.16   A second consequence of the Land Registry view is that, although registrable rights of common in gross and many sole rights have now fallen to the public commons registers and are capable of protection thereby, there are sole rights which are not eligible for any form of registration. Typical examples are sole rights to a fishery, mining rights which do not subsist as a severed strata of land and sole rights to take game. The existence of these unregistrable rights is not incompatible with compulsory registration of title as incorporeal hereditaments are excluded from the effect of compulsory registration orders.[40]

4.17   The scale of rights registered under the Land Registration Acts before the enactment of the C.R.A. 1965 is likely to be quite small as most rural areas were not (and still are not) within compulsory registration areas. It should perhaps be remarked, however, that the writer has some empirical evidence that, since 1967, some rights of common, registrable under the Act of 1965, have been registered as appurtenant to a registered title, in spite of the ban on further registration imposed by the Act of 1965. Conveyancers should notice that such rights are not necessarily exercisable.

(e) Common pur cause de vicinage

4.18   Common of vicinage is the right of animals to stray from a waste over the boundary of an unenclosed contiguous waste without the owner being liable to be sued in trespass.[41] While the origin of the right undoubtedly lies, in theory, in an agreement between rights owners as a matter of practical convenience, it has long been recognised that it is a special form of right of

---

[40] Land Registration Act 1925, s.120(1), proviso.
[41] See § 3.46.

common and this view has recently been endorsed in the courts.[42] In all events it is clear that its nature is different from that of a substantive right which has been granted as it arises by custom, is determinable and may not attract all the attributes of a full right. Whether it is a registrable right of common has been a matter of some disagreement and the result is a substantial element of confusion in the rights registers.

It seems that the view of the Department sponsoring the Act was that a right of vicinage was registrable and advice to this effect was given.[43] There was, however, no provision for it to be distinguished during registration from other rights. It follows that where registration of this class of right has been achieved it appears in an identical form on the registers as does a substantive right. Applicants were in some difficulty. They might be able to prove their title to a substantive right but they could not claim a right of vicinage as appurtenant to their estate as it is matter of custom. It seems that some registered vicinage rights and some did not. The Commissioners when considering rights of vicinage, generally, held an opinion as expressed by Commissioner Settle: **4.19**

> "In my view a right of common a [sic] cause de vicinage is a contractual or quasi-contractual right in the sense that so long as one owner takes the benefit of the contract and allows his cattle to stray he must also accept the burden and permit his neighbours cattle to do likewise. The right is not in my view a right in rem and the Commons Registration Act is in my opinion only concerned with rights in rem; it does not in my opinion envisage the registration of a right against the land of B which B can terminate unilaterally at any time by enclosing the land."[44]

In hearings which took place in Dartmoor the Commissioners saw no good reason for departing from the long standing practice of refusing registration to rights of vicinage following the decision in *Newman* v. *Bennett* (1981)[45] which decided that a right of vicinage is the exercise of a right of common within the provisions of the New Forest byelaws. On Dartmoor a substantial number of registered rights included further rights "to stray" over other common land units. The expression is ambiguous and could be a synonym for a substantive right or a right of vicinage.[46] The Commissioners have amended some rights to stray to a right to graze and in other cases have

---

[42] See *Newman* v. *Bennett* (1981) 1 Q.B. 726; see also § 4.19.

[43] cf. *Common Land and Village Greens* (Ministry of Land and Natural Resources and Central Office of Information H.M.S.O., 1966), p. 16, question and answer no. 20.

[44] *Re Cheeswring Common, St. Clear etc., Cornwall* (1975) 206/D/4–13, 3 D.C.C. 347; also *Re Effingham Common etc., Effingham, Surrey (No. 1)* (1976) 236/D/24–24, 4 D.C.C. 386 *and Re St Breward Common etc., Cornwall* (1977) 206/D/211, 5 D.C.C. 329; *contra Re Colaton Raleigh Common, Colaton Raleigh, Devon* (1974) 9/D/11, 2 D.C.C. 264: rights registered over two C.L. units on one of which "the applicants have rights of common *per* [sic] *cause de vicinage.*"

[45] [1981] 1 Q.B. 726. For the Commissioners' views on the effect of this case see *Re Blackdown and West Blackdown etc., Devon* (1983) 209/D/310–312, 14 D.C.C. 238.

[46] cf. *Crow* v. *Wood* [1971] 1 Q.B. 77; a right of common described as a right to stray.

refused registration altogether.[47] In one hearing the Commissioner acceded to a request to refuse registration but noted that "15 registrations so expressed being undisputed have become final."[48] It follows that the registers are inconsistent in the registration of rights of vicinage and that their presence, unidentified in some cases, requires investigation behind the registers to ascertain the true nature of registered rights.

3. Quantification of rights

(a) The requirement in the Act

4.20   The C.R.A. 1965 does not require quantification of the rights registered except in the case of grazing animals—the most important right in numerical and economic terms. Section 15(1) of the Act provides that—

> "Where a right of common consists of or includes a right, not limited by number, to graze animals or animals of any class, it shall for the purposes of registration under this Act be treated as exercisable in relation to no more animals, or animals of that class, than a definite number."

Subsection 3 of the section goes on to provide that when a registration has become final the right shall be exercisable in relation to animals not exceeding the number or numbers registered or such other number or numbers as Parliament may hereafter determine.

(b) "a right, not limited by number"

4.21   The intention of the section seems reasonably clear. Before the Act a substantial number of grazing rights were known only as *levant* and *couchant* or *sans nombre*, *i.e.* they were related to the needs of dominant land.[49] If control of grazing over common land is to be incorporated into future legislation then animals not previously limited by number, except by reference to the land which they are exercisable, have, at some some, to be reduced to fixed numbers. The section is an attempt to commence that process and to move away from the uncertainty of *levancy* and *couchancy*. Following finality of registration, which attracts conclusive evidence of the matters registered, the question arises as to the effect of the Act in providing evidence that the numbers registered may lawfully be exercised. It is quite clear that to exercise a number exceeding the number registered is unlawful but is the converse also true that it is lawful, in all circumstances, to exercise the registered number? It is suggested that it would be unwise to make this assumption.

4.22   Establishing numbers of animals on a particular common by reference to the area and nature of the dominant land is entirely satisfactory as a method

---

[47] *cf. Re Blackdown etc.*, above, n. 45, and *Re The Forest of Dartmoor* (1983) 209/D/ 287–288, 14 D.C.C. 129 at p. 23 of the decision.

[48] *Re part of Hamel Down and part of Bonehill Down, Widecombe-in-the-Moor, Devon* (1985) 209/D/419–420, 16 D.C.C. 116; also *Re Buckfastleigh Moor, West Buckfastleigh, South Hams D., Devon* (1985) 209/D/406, 16 D.C.C. 201: 44 registrations expressed as "to stray" final before the Commissioner's hearing.

[49] For quantification, see § 3.121.

of comparison between the relative rights of the individual commoners. It, however, ignores the factor of the area of the servient land. The result, in practice, is that a large number, if not most, of the registered C.L. units of registered common land are now apparently burdened with an excessive number of registered rights—far more than the stock carrying capacity of the land.[50] Using *levancy* and *couchancy, i.e.* the stock carrying capacity of the dominant land almost inevitably produces this result. Consider a common which originally was, say, 1,000 acres in extent and 500 acres is enclosed. In modern times the commoners would have received compensation for loss of their rights which should have effectively been reduced by a half. To continue to use *levancy* and *couchancy* as a measure of quantum of rights is to revert to the position before the enclosure.

The wording of the Act is merely that where a right is not limited by **4.23** number it shall *for the purposes of the Act* be treated as exercisable in relation to no more than a definite number. It seems possible, therefore, in circumstances not concerned with the purposes of the Act, to revert to the common law position that while rights unlimited by number are primarily related to the needs of dominant land they are also limited by the capacity of the burdened land and the requirement "that the owner of the soyle should take his reasonable profit there."[51]

(c) The effect of quantification

As a general comment it can perhaps be stated that the Commissioners **4.24** have not concerned themselves overmuch with the livestock carrying capacity of the common land but have attempted to produce compatibility between the various right registered. One Commissioner has recorded his views on the subject at length and, *inter alia,* said:

"Section 15 uses the words "treated as exercisable in relation to no more animals . . . than a definite number"; this does not I think mean that when a number is inserted on the register pursuant to that section, the owner of the right thereafter has under section 10 the right in all circumstances to graze that number of animals. In my view section 15 does no more than provide an upper limit. If anybody wishes to claim that the number of animals grazed by anyone at any time is, notwithstanding that it is less than the upper limit, excessive, his right to take legal proceedings is unaffected by the 1965 Act, except to the extent that section 10 is applicable. It may be therefore that in this case and in many other cases the number put on the register pursuant to section 15 may be of little practical consequence."[52]

(d) Proposals for reform

The Common Land Forum recommends that one of the grounds for rectifi- **4.25** cation of the rights registers, to be incorporated into new legislation, shall be where registered rights exceed the stock carrying capacity of the common.[53] In view of the widespread existence of registered rights apparently in

[50] Aitchison and Hughes, *The Common Lands of Wales* (1983), p. 6.
[51] Co.Litt. 122a.
[52] *Re The Black Mountain, Dinefwr, Dyfed* (1985) 272/D/441–777, 16 D.C.C. 219 at p. 32 of the decision, *per* Commissioner Baden Fuller.
[53] Common Land Forum Report, Appendix C, para. 028.

this category this may be a very substantial task for the Agricultural Land Tribunal, which it is recommended should be the body entrusted to approve all such amendments.[54] It should perhaps be commented that the overstocking is more apparent than real as a substantial number of registered rights are, in practice, not exercised.

4. Multiple registrations

4.26 Any person was entitled to apply for registration of common land.[55] The result is that the boundaries of a substantial number of registered common land units registered do not correspond to those of the pre-existing commons. There has been both amalgamation and fragmentation of single commons. The position was compounded by the wording of regulations. There was no provision for additions to a unit of previously registered land—a registration authority was required to treat each application for land registration as a new and separate unit.[56] The result is that the rights registrations have, in many cases, achieved extraordinary complexity.[57]

4.27 To illustrate the predicament, consider a common registered as two separate units. A commoner wishes to register his right over the common upon which it is exercisable. Perhaps he should register over both, recording on each application that it is only one right which has been registered, *i.e.* cross referencing his registrations to two common land units. However, he may have decided to register his one right as exercisable over both of the two units without cross referencing. In this case the registers will apparently show that the commoner is entitled to double his pre-existing rights. Upon finality the registrations are conclusively evidential of the matters registered and it is arguable that the commoner now has evidence of twice his proper entitlement. This is a simple example—some of the registers show multiple registrations over dozens of individual units. On the face of the registers some commons units are subject to nonsensical stocking rates.[58]

4.28 Where commons have been amalgamated in registration other problems arise. Suppose that two contiguous unenclosed commons are registered as

[54] Common Land Forum Report, Appendix C, paras. 114–121.
[55] C.R.A. 1965 s.4(2). A substantial number of registrations was made by amenity bodies, their members or other persons with no legal interest in the land.
[56] Commons Registration (General) Regulations 1966 (S.I. 1966 No. 1471), reg. 10(2): "The registration authority shall, when registering any land, enter the particulars on a fresh register sheet . . . " Some authorities attempted to make sense of the registrations by making more than one entry. One of these authorities had to seek an amendment Act to redraw the registers: see the Commons Registration (Glamorgan) Act 1983 (c.ix).
[57] For example in the Black Mountains area of Powys where registrations are cross-referenced over many C.L. units, including some in an adjoining county. *cf.* Aitchison, Hughes and Masters, *The Common Lands of England and Wales* (1984), p. 10.
[58] In one study, a stocking rate on a heather moor in excess of 1.2 ewes per hectare resulted in a loss of weight of lamb weaned per hectare unless land improvement was carried out. Aitchison and Hughes, above, n. 50, p. 6 records a mean and median grazing intensity (as measured by registered rights) on grazing commons in the survey area of 26.6 and 9.4 sheep per hectare.

one. The commoners on each have substantive rights over one and rights of vicinage over the other. Some commoners, believing rights of vicinage to be unregistrable, register over their home common, relying on the custom of vicinage for grazing over the contiguous common. Others take a simple view of the matter and register rights over the common land unit as registered. If rights of vicinage are unregistrable then the rights registered over the whole are conclusive evidence of a substantive right over the whole, whereas if they are registrable the commoner who did not register seems to have a non-exercisable right of vicinage. If vicinage, quite apart from its determinability, has characteristics which set it apart from substantive rights[59] it becomes necessary to look behind the registers to discover the true nature of the rights involved.

The Common Land Forum recommends legislation to provide that upon an **4.29**
application by the owner of the soil, a commoner, or a registration authority, a tribunal should be empowered to remove registrations.[60] What is required, it is suggested, in the case of multiple registrations of land which is actually but one common, is a power to amend the registers not remove registrations.

5. Rights over sheepwalks

Rights exercisable over sheepwalks, or heaves, do not at law have the effect **4.30**
of limiting the rights to that sheepwalk.[61] They extend over the entire waste but as a matter of convenience or deemed agreement between the commoners are *de facto* exercised only over certain more or less defined areas of the waste. Some applicants for rights have registered only in respect of their defined sheepwalk with the result that the waste now has the appearance of a series of contiguous sub-commons each of which only has one rights holder. In this form of registration it appears that the commoner has abandoned all claim to rights over the entire waste and now has a sole right of common over the individual sheepwalk. The ramifications of this situation are unexplored. It seems, for instance, that there can be no question of a customary right of vicinage as between the contiguous sheepwalks and in the absence of agreement between the parties mutual actions for straying livestock will be possible. Some public concern has been expressed over this form of registration, for it is a comparatively simple matter for the owner of the soil to accept the release of rights over a sheepwalk and thus destroy the common land status.

CREATION

Historically, new rights of common could arise through statute, grant, pre- **4.31**
scription, privilege of law in connection with appendant rights, and by custom in the case of copyhold tenements. Of these, appendant rights can no

---

[59] It is suggested that it does: see § 3.57.
[60] Common Land Forum Report, Appendix C (Multiple rights registrations), para. 020–033.
[61] See § 3.111.

longer be created, as they arose upon sub-infeudation which was abolished following the Statute of Quia Emptores in 1290,[62] and copyhold tenure was abolished in the property legislation of 1925.[63] Any creation of entirely new rights in the future will be exceptional and the subject really only has significance in connection with the establishment of prescriptive claims in the inquiries still to be heard by the Commons Commissioners, the conversion of rights in common, at present exercised by tenants of the owner of the soil of common land, upon the sale of the freehold reversion of those tenements and upon the sale of a lord's quasi—dominant land in hand.

4.32   A *profit à prendre* may only exist as a legal interest in land if created: (a) by statute, grant under seal, or by prescription; and (b) held for an interest equivalent to a fee simple absolute in possession or a term of years absolute.

For a profit to be classed as a right of common it must also be created to allow the owner of the servient tenement to share in the benefit of the product and may only be held as an interest equivalent to a fee simple.[64] If the interest is for a term of years absolute, and the owner of the servient tenement shares in the product it will be a profit in common but not a right of common. Where the owner of the servient tenement has no share in the product the profit will be classed as sole whether held for a fee simple or a term of years.[65] All rights of common and certain sole profits are registrable as statutory rights of common.[66]

4.33   The conditions and formalities required to create a legal interest in land also apply to profits. It follows that a document not under seal will not be effective to create a legal profit but if made for value may bring into effect an equitable profit.[67] Similarly, a profit created for a term other than those prescribed can only result in an equitable profit so that, for example, a profit granted for life or lives can not be a legal profit. The significance in deciding whether a profit is legal or equitable lies largely in the requirements which exist to register certain equitable interests to protect them against purchasers of the burdened land.[68]

1. By statute

4.34   Although creation by statute is possible it is unlikely today. An inclosure award, for example, could include rights over regulated pastures or reserved rights of shooting over inclosed land. However, as inclosure is for all practical purposes obsolete the chances for this method of creation are slight. Rights over new common land are created when an exchange of land occurs to facilitate a compulsory purchase order but it is perhaps better to view this not so much as a creation of rights by statute but as a transfer of existing rights to new land.[69]

[62] 18 Edw. 1, c. 1–3.
[63] Law of Property Act 1922, s.128, Sched. 12.
[64] *cf.* §§ 3.9, 3.11.
[65] *cf.* § 3.10.
[66] C.R.A. 1965, s.22(1).
[67] § 4.36.
[68] See § 4.91.
[69] For compulsory purchase, see § 5.85.

2. By express grant and reservation

(a) Grant

For a legal profit to be created the document used should be under seal[70] and perhaps the most usual method will be to create an appurtenant profit incorporated into the conveyance of land on sale. Whether expressly granted or not the operation of section 62 of the L.P.A. 1925 may have the effect of implying the grant of a legal profit.[71] **4.35**

By analogy, it seems that the principle in the doctrine of *Walsh* v. *Lonsdale*[72] applies where the formalities for granting a legal profit have not been met, and the grant will be recognised in equity. Where a memorandum supported by consideration had been signed only by a plaintiff, the defendant was restrained by injunction from interfering with the plaintiff's right to a profit pending execution of the deed.[73] Thus, an agreement with consideration is sufficient to create an equitable profit[74] and the taking of possession of a profit is sufficient to enable the grantee to bring an action in trespass.[75] It seems that a contract for a profit may be protected as against the grantor by injunction and that an order for specific performance will be made for the granting of the legal interest providing that the transaction is not affected by fraud on the part of the plaintiff.[76] **4.36**

As for other interests in land a contract for a profit must comply with the requirements contained in section 40(1) of the L.P.A. 1925 that, in order to be enforceable, it must be evidenced in writing and signed by the person to be charged. The exception of part performance in lieu of writing contained in section 40(2) seems to apply to incorporeal hereditaments so that taking possession of a profit is sufficient to satisfy the section.[77] In *Duke of Devonshire* v. *Eglin* (1851)[78] on the strength of an oral agreement the plaintiff had constructed an underground water course under the defendant's land. The court granted an injunction preventing its obstruction. In fact in that case no final agreement had been reached about consideration and, it may, alternatively, be viewed as an early example of an estoppel arising where the plaintiff had acted to his detriment to the knowledge of the defendant. There is no authority on the point but there seems no reason in principle why the developing doctrines of estoppel licences and contractual licences binding successors in title who have notice[79] should not also apply to the taking of profits. **4.37**

---

[70] L.P.A. 1925, s.52.

[71] For which see § 4.48.

[72] (1882) 21 Ch.D. 9; *cf.* Megarry and Wade, p. 861.

[73] *Frogley* v. *Earl of Lovelace* (1859) Johns 333, 70 E.R. 450.

[74] *Mason* v. *Clarke* (1955) A.C. 778 at 787, *per* Lord Simonds.

[75] *Per* Lord Simonds at 794.

[76] *Mason* v. *Clarke* [1954] 1 Q.B. 460 at 469, 472 (C.A.); [1955] A.C. 778 at 794; *cf.* *Frogley* v. *Earl of Lovelace* (1859), n. 73, above.

[77] *McManus* v. *Cooke* (1887) 35 Ch.D. 681: easement of light.

[78] (1851) 14 Beav. 530, 51 E.R. 389; see also *Watson* v. *Gouldsborough* [1986] 1 E.G.L.R. 265; proprietary estoppel in absence of any legal interest in the land in either party; estoppel fed on acquisition of legal estate by purported grantor.

[79] *cf.* Megarry and Wade, p. 806.

4.38 The exception which allows the creation of parol legal leases of land, taking effect in possession for a term not exceeding three years, does not seem to apply to profits[80] although there is no direct authority on the point.

4.39 If the profit being created is sole it may not be granted as appurtenant to land. In *Anderson* v. *Bostock* (1976)[81] a plaintiff sought to establish that a sole and exclusive right of grazing had passed to him on conveyance of purported dominant land by virtue of the provisions contained in section 62 of the L.P.A. 1925. Blackett-Ord V.-C. held such a grant to be "unknown to the law."

(b) Reservation

4.40 An express reservation of a profit contained within a deed of conveyance is the converse of an express grant. The general rule for construing grants is *contra proferentem, i.e.* it will be construed against the grantor.[82] Prior to the 1925 property legislation a reservation operated as a grant of the land followed by the regrant of the profit by the grantee to the grantor. Section 65 of the L.P.A. 1925 provides that a reservation shall operate without a regrant. In spite of the express words it seems that the courts will still view a reservation as if it were a regrant and will construe the reservation against the grantee of the land.[83]

(c) Effect of the Act of 1965

4.41 The general principles covering express grant and reservation are stated above but the whole subject must be treated with some caution as the effect of the C.R.A. 1965 is to make most grants of rights of common unexercisable. Section 13 of the Act provides for the amendment of the commons registers and additions thereto:

> "Regulations under this Act shall provide for the amendment of the registers maintained under this Act where—
> ...
> (b) any land becomes common land or a town or village green; or
> (c) any rights registered under this Act are apportioned, extinguished or released, or are varied or transferred in such circumstances as may be prescribed . . . "

The section is effected through the Commons Registration (New Land) Regulations 1969.[84] Regulation 3 provides—

> "(1) Where, after 2nd January 1970, any land becomes common land or a

---

[80] L.P.A. 1925, s.54(2)(*d*): see *Mason* v. *Clarke* [1954] 1 Q.B. 460 at 468, 471.

[81] [1976] 1 Ch. 312; *cf. Bailey* v. *Stephens* (1862) 12 C.B.N.S. 91, 142 E.R. 1077 and § 3.17.

[82] *Williams* v. *James* (1867) L.R. 2 C.P. 577 at 581, *per* Willes J.; *Neill* v. *Duke of Devonshire* (1882) 8 App.Cas. 135 at 149, *per* Lord Selborne L.C. Notice, however, that a reserved right of fishing, in the absence of factors pointing the other way, will give rise to an exclusive right, but *aliter* other *profits à prendre: Lady Dunsany* v. *Bedworth* [1979] 38 P. & C.R. 546.

[83] *St. Edmundsbury and Ipswich Diocesan Board of Finance* v. *Clark* (No. 2) [1975] 1 W.L.R. 468; *Mason* v. *Clarke* [1954] 1 Q.B. 460 at 467, *per* Denning L.J., [1955] A.C. 778 at 786, *per* Lord Simonds. For a criticism of the present position, see Megarry and Wade, p. 858.

[84] S.I. 1969 No. 1843.

town or village green, application may be made subject to and in
accordance with the provisions of these Regulations for the inclusion of
that land in the appropriate register and for the registration of rights of
common thereover and of persons claiming to be the owners thereof.
(2) Where any land is for the time being registered under the Act, no
application shall be entertained for its registration under these Regulations, and, where any land is for the time being registered under section
4 of the Act (whether or not the registration has become final) no application shall be entertained for the registration of rights of common
over it.''

The effect is that section 13 by omission, and regulation 3 by express provision, prevents the registration of any rights exercisable over land registered under section 4 of the C.R.A. 1965, *i.e.* land which fell to the initial
registration procedure (hereafter section 4 land). Alternatively, rights
granted anew over land which is not section 4 land has the effect of creating
new common land with both rights and land registrable under the provisions in regulation 3 (hereafter regulation 3 land).

(i) Section 4 land The consequence of the provisions is that in the **4.42**
most likely circumstance for the creation of new rights of common, that is
to say the sale of the freehold reversion of a tenanted quasi-dominant tenement (or other demesne land) with existing rights in common over a quasi-
servient tenement registered as section 4 land, an express grant of a right of
common will result in an unregistrable and, therefore, unexercisable right.
Similarly on sale of the quasi-servient land an express reservation of rights
of common in favour of quasi-dominant land will be ineffective. At this
time the only practicable alternative is a grant, or reservation, of rights in
common for a term of years which is, as we have seen, unregistrable and
unaffected by the provisions in the C.R.A. 1965. It has been demonstrated
that many quasi-rights of the owners of the soil of registered commons have
been registered, albeit improperly.[85] It is submitted that a grantee would be
unwise to rely upon these registered but, by the terms of the Act unregistrable, rights as a foundation for exercisability.[86]

The Common Land Forum recommends that new legislation for common **4.43**
land should make provision for registration of new rights over section 4
land[87] with disputes arising therefrom to be resolved by hearings before a
Commons Commissioner or, if and when that office ceases to exist, an Agricultural Land Tribunal.[88] In this context, it is difficult to see any dispute
arising as the evidence which will be put forward will be a grant from the
owner of the soil.

(ii) Regulation 3 land A grant of a right of common (or any sole right **4.44**
which is capable of being a statutory right of common) over any land, which
is not section 4 land, will fall under the provision in section 1 of the Act
that "there shall be registered any land which is common land." For the
right to be exercisable it is required to be registered which will trigger the

[85] § 4.10.
[86] For further consideration, see § 4.96.
[87] Commons Land Forum Report, Appendix C, para. 085.
[88] *ibid.* para. 0.88.

registration of regulation 3 land. Unlike the provision applicable in the case of section 4 land there is no prohibition on the registration of further rights. The most likely factual circumstance for the creation of new statutory common land is where all the quasi-dominant and quasi-servient land was in unified ownership at the time of the initial registration. The grant of the first right of common over the land on the sale of a quasi-dominant tenement, or indeed the grant of a right in gross, will trigger the operation of the Act. Under these circumstances grants of rights in common for a term of years instead of an interest in fee simple will avoid the provisions of the Act.

3. By implied grant or reservation

4.45   The general rule is that a grant will be construed in favour of the grantee and must be given its widest possible meaning on the basis of the doctrine of non-derogation from grant.[89] Conversely, a grant will be construed against a grantor and, while easements and profits may be implied readily in favour of a grantee, there wil be a heavy burden of proof on the grantor to establish that any have been reserved without express mention. The rules for implied grant and reservation of easements are well developed but are less so for profits.

(a) Implied grant

4.46   **(i) Intended profits**   Although there is no authority on the point, there seems no reason why on the conveyance of a tenement for a particular purpose it should not be intended that the necessary profits for its use should pass. Where cellars were let to a tenant for use a restaurant, and use for that purpose was impossible without the construction of a ventilation system over the retained property, it was held that the tenant had an easement of necessity to construct and use the system.[90] Analogously, there seems no reason why a hill farm, which can have no ordinary use other than for sheep farming, conveyed for that purpose evidenced, say, by the contemporaneous sale of a hefted flock should not also, as a matter of necessity, be intended to enjoy rights of grazing over retained hill land.

4.47   **(ii) The rule in Wheeldon v. Burrows**   As a branch of the general rule that a grantor may not derogate from his grant the rule in *Wheeldon* v. *Burrows*[91] has developed to determine what rights (usually easements) are implied in favour of a grantee of part of a holding as against the vendor's retained part. Briefly, the rule lays down that all quasi-easements over the land retained will pass where they are continuous and apparent or (possibly and[92]), necessary to the reasonable enjoyment of the land granted and, in

---

[89] *cf.* § 4.40 and n. 82 thereto. For non-derogation from grant see Megarry and Wade, p. 848.

[90] *Wong* v. *Beaumont Property Trust Ltd.* [1965] 1 Q.B. 173.

[91] (1879) 12 Ch.D. 31; *cf.* Megarry and Wade, p. 861.

[92] Megarry and Wade, p. 862. These are alternatives; but there may have to be some *indicia* present for "in the absence of a continuous and apparent feature designed or appropriate for the exercise of the (easement) on the servient tenement, there is not a continuous and apparent (easement) within the requirements of *Wheeldon* v. *Burrows* . . .": *Ward* v. *Kirkland* [1967] Ch. 194 at 225, *per* Ungoed-Thomas J.; it is just possible that turbary might provide suitable *indicia*.

either case, are used at the time of the grant by the grantor for the benefit of the land granted. There seems no reason in principle why the rule should not apply to profits but it has been doubted whether it has any application. It is difficult to envisage circumstances when it might apply and the profit will not fall also to be considered as an intended profit.

(iii) Law of Property Act 1925, s.62 The rules of implied grants have **4.48** been considerably modified and extended by section 62 of the L.P.A. 1925, which repealed and replaced section 6 of the Conveyancing Act 1881. The section has the effect of automatically incorporating what are known as "general words" into many conveyances of land. As a result many easements, profits and other advantages, newly created by implication, may result through the conversion of what were formerly merely advantages enjoyed with, and of benefit to, the land conveyed. In spite of very clear words there has been some reticence in applying the section to profits which seems to have been compounded to some extent by an apparent reluctance to apply analogous easement cases. Selectively, section 62 states:

> "A conveyance of land shall be deemed to include and shall by virtue of this Act operate to convey . . . with the land . . . all liberties, privileges, easements, rights and advantages whatsoever, appertaining or reputed to appertain to the land . . . or enjoyed with . . . the land."

The section has application to a conveyance of land including a mortgage, **4.49** lease or assent[93] but not a mere contract whether for sale or the granting of a lease required to be granted under seal. There are a number of other limitations. The section cannot operate to create rights over the land of a third party so that A enjoying a precarious right over B's land cannot convert that enjoyment into a substantive right by conveying his land to a third party. Secondly, the right must be enjoyed at the time of the conveyance. A mere memory of past rights is not enough.[94] Thirdly, the right or advantage must be one which is capable of being granted at law so as to run with the land and bind successors in title.[95] Finally, there are highly persuasive statements emanating from the House of Lords which indicate that the section only operates where there has been a diversity of occupation of the two parcels of land prior to the conveyance. It has, however, been clearly established that the section applies to profits after direct challenge on the point in the Court of Appeal.[96]

(iv) The rule in *Long* v. *Gowlett* In terms of profits the section is **4.50** clearly of considerable importance on the conveyance of quasi-dominant tenements which have been in the occupation of the owner of a common or his tenants. In the case of unified ownership and occupation, the section has

---

[93] L.P.A. 1925, s.205(1)(ii).
[94] *Penn* v. *Wilkins* (1974) 236 E.G. 203, *per* Megarry J.; *Re Broxhead Common, Whitehill, Hampshire* (1977) 33 P. & C.R. 451 at 463: 21 years non-user of quasi-right, concluded not enjoyed at time of conveyance; *Re Yateley Common, Hampshire* [1977] 1 W.L.R. 840 at 851; user actually at the date of conveyance not required.
[95] *cf. Phipps* v. *Pears* [1965] 1 Q.B. 76 at 84, *per* Lord Denning M.R.; *e.g.* a sole profit not capable of running with the land: *Anderson* v. *Bostock* [1976] 2 Ch. 177.
[96] *White* v. *Williams* [1922] 1 K.B. 727.

no effect if there is an absolute rule that prior diversity of occupation of the sold and the retained land is necessary. The so-called rule can be said to be based on the judgment of Sargant J. in *Long* v. *Gowlett* (1923)[97]:

> " . . . in order that there may be a 'privilege easement or advantage' enjoyed with Whiteacre over Blackacre so as to pass under the statute, there must be something done on Blackacre not due to or comprehended within the general rights of an occupying owner of Blackacre, but of such a nature that it is attributable to a privilege, easement, right or advantage, however precarious, which arises out of the ownership or occupation of Whiteacre, altogether apart from the ownership or occupation of Blackacre. And it is difficult to see how, when there is common ownership of both Whiteacre and Blackacre, there can be any such relationship between the two closes as (apart from the case of continuous and apparent easements or that of a way of necessity) would be necessary to create a 'privilege, easement, right or advantage' within the words of s.6, sub-s. 2, of the statute."[98]

In *Sovmots Investments Ltd.* v. *Secretary of State for the Environment* (1977)[99] Lords Wilberforce, Edmund Davies and Keith expressly approved *Long* v. *Gowlett*. In general it seems that, in spite of the observations being strictly *obiter dicta*, they are binding on all courts of lower jurisdiction.[1] Unless that is, a factual situation occurs which overcomes the difficulty encountered by Sargant J.

4.51   Paradoxically it may be possible to find such a situation in the example used by him in reaching his conclusion. To make his point he exampled the, then, recent Court of Appeal case of *White* v. *Williams* (1922).[2] What if in that case, surmised Sargent J., a landowner who owned a farm and a "sheepwalk" had regularly turned sheep out on the sheepwalk from his own farm? If the owner came to sell his farm the purchaser could not obtain the right to graze his sheep on the retained sheepwalk as the result of section 6.[3] Strangely the point was directly considered in the earlier case by Atkin L.J. who reached the completely opposite opinion.[4] The sheepwalk in *White* v. *Williams* was in fact common land with several parties grazing from different farms.[5] If one of the farm owners also owned the sheepwalk he would have had no rights of common over the land but nor was he entitled to unrestricted grazing as the owner in fee simple of the servient land. His entitlement would be restricted, as were all the other graziers, to cattle *levant* and *couchant* on the quasi-dominant land.[6] In other words the situation exists, which Sargant J. found so difficult to envisage, of rights enjoyed over the quasi-servient Blackacre derived not from the ownership of that close but from the ownership of the quasi-dominant Whiteacre. It is submitted that

[97] [1923] 2 Ch. 177.
[98] *ibid.* at 200.
[99] [1979] A.C. 144, at 169, 176, 184 also approving *Bolton* v. *Bolton* (1879) 11 Ch.D. 968.
[1] *cf.* Jackson, *The Law of Easements and Profits* (1978) pp. 97–100.
[2] Above, n. 96.
[3] [1923] 2 Ch. 177 at 201.
[4] [1922] 1 K.B. 727 at 738.
[5] See the county court judgment at 732.
[6] See § 7.13.

in the case described there are rights enjoyed with a quasi-dominant tenement which are entirely appropriate for the operation of section 62 without the necessity for diversity of occupation.

(v) Land occupied by a tenant It might be anticipated that there   **4.52** would be no such problem where the lands were in separate occupation as, for instance, where the quasi-dominant land is occupied by a tenant. Rights enjoyed, however precariously, have been held to be within the meaning of the section, a tenant's use of a roadway over the landlord's land leading into a yard was converted by the section into an easement upon purchase of the reversion[7] and the use of a coal shed was affected by section 62 on the renewal of a lease.[8] The case of *White* v. *Taylor* (No. 2) (1969),[9] which was concerned with grazing rights over a moor, however, seems to have proceeded on the opposite assumption:

> "Enjoyment of grazing facilities on the down by tenants of the lord of the manor holding under leases or tenancy agreements could not, in my judgment, establish a reputation of rights appurtenant to the lands comprised in their holdings. The implication would be that they so grazed the down by the consent of the lord or possibly under contractual rights or grants limited in their operation at the most to the periods of their tenancies. This could found no reputation of any kind of right capable of surviving those tenancies."[10]

The view seems to be that to found a right of common one had to exist at the time of the conveyance and tenants' rights could not be in that category. If that was the law at that time (and with respect this is doubted as relevant easement cases were apparently not cited[11]) it can no longer stand with the Court of Appeal decision of *Graham* v. *Philcox* (1984)[12] when it was held that a right of way granted for a leasehold interest was sufficient to found an easement attached to the land on conveyance of the freehold reversion. In so doing the words of Farwell J. in *International Tea Stores* v. *Hobbs* (1903)[13] were cited with approval: " . . . the real truth is that you do not consider the question of title to use, but the question of fact of user; you have to inquire whether the way has in fact been used, not under what title it has been used . . . "

The law now appears to be that on the sale of a freehold reversion to a sit-   **4.53** ting tenant the rights in common enjoyed with the land at the time of the conveyance will pass as rights of common[14] providing that the general words of section 62 are implied.[15] This may also be the case when the rights

---

[7] *International Tea Stores Co.* v. *Hobbs* [1903] 2 Ch. 165.

[8] *Wright* v. *Macadam* [1949] 2 K.B. 744.

[9] [1969] 1 Ch. 160.

[10] *ibid.* at 185.

[11] In particular *International Tea Stores Co.* v. *Hobbs,* above, n. 7.

[12] [1984] Q.B. 747; *cf.* L.P.A. 1925, s.187(1), which seems to be of the same effect.

[13] [1903] 2 Ch. 165 at 172.

[14] See *Doidge* v. *Carpenter* (1817) 6 M. & S. 47, 105 E.R. 1160; approved in *Baring* v. *Abingdon* [1892] 2 Ch. 374 at 391, *per* Lindley L.J.; *Re Broxhead Common,* above n. 94, at 461, *per* Brightman J.; *Re Yateley Common, Hampshire,* above n. 94, at 851, *per* Foster J.; *cf.* also *Crow* v. *Wood* [1971] 1 Q.B. 77 (purported easement passing under s.62).

[15] The section may be excluded by a contrary intention: s.62(4).

are merely licensed but are exercisable with the land on a contract of tenancy whether the licence can be found to be part of the contract or not.[16] The position is less clear when the purchaser is taking land farmed by the lord although, it is suggested that, providing the general words of section 62 are incorporated, if the right of grazing the common is enjoyed by the lord at the time of the conveyance, rights of common ought to be impliedly granted.[17]

4.54 In connection with implied grants the same qualifications apply as with express grants that, where statutory rights of common are concerned, the C.R.A. 1965 does not allow registration and they are as a result unexercisable at present. Thus, conveyancers at the present time should always consider the express grant of rights in common for a term of years.

(b) Implied reservation

4.55 Normally there will be no implied reservations of profits in favour of the grantor of servient common land because of the *contra proferentem* rule. A grantor should be careful to reserve any rights to profits expressly. In the case of easements both those of necessity and intended easements may be impliedly reserved but it is difficult to envisage similar circumstances in relation to profits. However, there is no reason, in principle, why profits necessary to carry out the common intention of the parties should not be implied in favour of the grantor.

4. By prescription

4.56 Due to the ancient origin of many profits, and in particular the statutory rights of common, it is hardly surprising that the only mode of proof for many claimants is a presumed grant established by long user. This is sometimes described as acquisition by prescription but in most cases it is more accurate to think of it as proof by a prescriptive claim. It is still of considerable importance in establishing those statutory rights which are the subject of dispute and hearing before a Commons Commissioner.

(a) Prescription and the Commons Registration Act 1965

4.57 Special provisions affecting a prescriptive claim to registration of rights under the Act are contained in section 16:

> "(1) Where during any period a right of common claimed over any land was not exercised, but during the whole of part of that period either—
>> (a) the land was requisitioned; or
>> (b) where the right claimed is a right to graze animals, the right could not be or was not exercised for reasons of animal health;
>> that period or part shall be left out of account, both—
>>> (i) in determining for the purpose of the Prescription Act 1832, whether there was an interruption within the meaning of that Act of the actual enjoyment of the right; and

[16] *cf. Scott* v. *Bolton* (1982) A.L.T./2/881: a case of succession to a tenancy: considered further at § 5.73.

[17] *cf.* § 4.51, and see *Baring* v. *Abingdon*, above, n. 14.

>   (ii) in computing the period of 30 or 60 years mentioned in section
>   1 of that Act.
> (2) For the purposes of the said Act any objection under this Act to the
>   registration of a right of common shall be deemed to be such a suit
>   or action as is referred to in section 4 of that Act."

Subsection (3) defines the term requisitioned and provides a mode of proof
that the land has been within the scope of the term. Subsection (4) provides
a method of proof that rights could not be exercised or were not exercised
for reasons of animal health consequent upon restrictions imposed on the
land by Order. The wording of subsection (1)(b), however, does not seem to
preclude a voluntary withdrawal from exercising a right on the grounds of
animal health risks.[18]

The section is exclusively concerned with claims made under the Prescrip-   **4.58**
tion Act 1832. It is perhaps odd that an enforced interruption of user is "left
out of account" in computing the prescriptive periods rather than being
treated as intermission of user and not right.[19] However, it has not been
possible to detect among the Commissioners' decisions an example where
the result would have been different with any changed form of wording. The
Commissioners, it seems, have tended to rely more on the doctrine of lost
modern grant, as epitomised in *Tehidy Minerals Ltd.* v. *Norman* (1971),[20]
than the Prescription Act 1832, with a general inclination to accept user of
between 20 and 21 years as sufficient.

(b) Section 4 land

It has been demonstrated that it is not possible to register new rights over   **4.59**
land which achieved registration in the initial registration period. It follows
that it is also not possible to claim rights by prescription over that land if for
no other reason than that they may not be registered and are consequently
unexercisable.[21]

After the enactment of the C.R.A. 1965 the Law Reform Committee recom-   **4.60**
mended unanimously that prescription for profits should be abolished following a 12 year transition period.[22] It is now clear that some four years
after the Committee's report prescription was abolished over the major
class of land where prescription for profits might be expected.

(c) Regulation 3 land

In connection with the creation of new common land it was noticed that   **4.61**
one of the methods suggested was through the acquisition of rights by prescription.[23] There are, however, formidable theoretical difficulties to be

---

[18] As sometimes occurred just before the initial registration period in attempts to
control brucellosis among cattle.
[19] *Carr* v. *Foster* (1842) 3 Q.B. 581, 114 E.R. 629.
[20] [1971] 2 Q.B. 528: less than 20 years user nearly 30 years before date of action sufficient.
[21] See § 4.41.
[22] Law Reform Committee, Fourteenth Report (Acquisition of Easements and Profits
by Prescription, (Cmnd. 3100 (1966)), paras. 82, 98.
[23] *cf.* § 2.56.

overcome. Prescription for any statutory right of common is probably impossible. That is not necessarily to say that a claim to a prescriptive right might not achieve registration for the procedures established under the C.R.A. 1965 are less than might be expected in the case of a person claiming right to an incumbrence over the land of another person.

4.62   The notes to the application form for registration of rights over new common land[24] require the production of supporting evidence:

> "Where the right is stated to have become exercisable by prescription, and there is a declaration by a court of competent jurisdiction to that effect, an office copy of the order embodying that declaration. (In the absence of such a declaration, a claim based solely on the Prescription Act 1832 cannot be admitted, and a claim based on prescription otherwise than under that Act is unlikely to be admitted if any objection is received by the registration authority)."

It seems that a registration authority may accept as valid, without further enquiry, an application which is not disputed by objection and also is able to dispose of an application by registration even if an objection is received. It is said that such an application "is unlikely to be admitted" but there is no provision for proper hearing and appeal as would have occurred in the case of a disputed application on section 4 land. A quasi-judicial role for registration authorities seems inappropriate.

4.63   Assuming, however, that most cases will be subject to a proper judicial inquiry we can proceed to consider the methods of claiming by prescription. It has been said that "every prescription presumes a grant to have existed."[25] The methods available may be stated, shortly, as prescription in the true sense of the word, *i.e.* a claim that user has existed since before the beginning of legal memory, the doctrine of a lost modern grant and under the Prescription Act 1832.[26]

4.64   *Common law prescription* A prescriptive claim, or as it is sometimes known common law prescription, seems, by the terms of the C.R.A. 1965, to be doomed to failure. It is impossible to claim that the right has existed for the time of legal memory without admitting that it existed at the time of the initial registration period under the Act of 1965. The Act provides that at the end of such period as the Minister may determine "no rights of common shall be exercisable . . . unless they are registered." It can hardly be the intention of Parliament that the rights were merely suspended thereby, awaiting revival at a later date by registration. The effect must be that they are extinguished, *i.e.* permanent non-exercisability resulted.[27] The relevant section should be read perhaps as though the wording was "after the period of three years no rights of common shall be exercisable again unless they have been registered during that period."

---

[24] Commons Registration (New Land) Regulations) 1969 (S.I. 1969 No. 1843), Sched., Form 31, n. 11.

[25] Bl.Comm., ii, 265.

[26] For fuller discussion see Megarry and Wade, p. 869.

[27] Cease to be exercisable is synonomous with extinguished: *Central Electricity Generating Board* v. *Clwyd C.C.* [1976] 1 W.L.R. 151 at 155–156, *per* Goff J.

Lost modern grant   Equally formidable are the difficulties confront- **4.65**
ing an applicant under the doctrine of lost modern grant. In this circumstance an applicant is claiming that he has benefited from a grant which has
been lost and, it seems, it is necessary in pleading to allege the date before or
after which the grant commenced.[28] This is, it is suggested, to place him in
a quandary from which he cannot escape. To allege a grant is to admit the
grant of a right which, by the terms of the Act, is registrable—"there shall
be registered . . . rights of common."[29] Failure to register the right granted
results in non-exercisability.[30] If there has been any use of the alleged grant
it was, at the time of the use, unlawful. An indication that the courts are
unlikely to give any form of recognition to rights unlawfully exercised may
be seen in connection with another statute concerned with the control of
natural resources. The general aim of the Water Resources Act 1963 is to
make water extraction illegal without licensing. In *Cargill* v. *Gotts* (1981)[31]
the Court of Appeal was asked to consider a prescriptive claim to a right to
take water which included a period of unlicensed extraction. It was held
that the court "will not recognise an easement established by illegal
activity."[32] The situation is analogous to rights of common only in that in
order to allow a prescriptive claim based on user since 1970 a court would
have to recognise a period of unlawful activity, it being the purpose of the
C.R.A. 1965 to require the registration of all lawful rights.[32a]

Prescription Act 1832   Finally, a claim under the Prescription Act **4.66**
1832 is one of existence since the time of legal memory which may not "be
defeated or destroyed by showing only that such right, profit or benefit was
first taken or enjoyed at any time prior to [the prescriptive periods]."[33]
Again it is a claim to existence of the right during the initial registration
period under the C.R.A. 1965 and seems to suffer from the same difficulty as
an ordinary common law prescription that the Act clearly intended to
extinguish any right, which existed at the time of the initial registration
period, if not registered.

In summary it can be stated that prescription has been probably abolished in **4.67**
respect of all statutory rights of common. This is much as might be
expected from the intention of the C.R.A. 1965. It was clearly intended that
a period should be allowed for the registration of all common land and rights
existing at the time of enactment, following which no unregistered land or
rights were to be considered as within the categories. The intention not to
allow new rights to arise on registered common land is underlined by the
lack of provision for registration thereof. If in 'a once and for all' process all
the last remaining vestiges of common land and rights were to be recorded it

---

[28] *Tremayne* v. *English Clays Lovering Pochin & Co. Ltd.* [1972] 1 W.L.R. 657, *cf.*
Palmer v. *Guadagni* [1906] 2 Ch. 494.
[29] C.R.A. 1965, s.1(1).
[30] s.1(2)(*b*).
[31] [1981] 1 All E.R. 682.
[32] At 686, *per* Templeman L.J.
[32a] See also *Neaverson* v. *Peterborough R.D.C.* [1902] 1 Ch. 557, C.A., (an attempt to
set up a lost grant contrary to the provisions of an inclosure award); *Att.-Gen.* v.
Mathias (1858) 4 K. & J. 579 at 590, *per* Byles J.: reasons against a claim to a right
unlawful in itself.
[33] Prescription Act 1832, s.1.

hardly seems possible that new common land would be allowed to come into existence by a method of creation which had been abolished over existing common land.

(d) Rights other than statutory rights of common

4.68 Sole profits for products other than vesture, herbage and pasture, and profits in common and sole profits held for an interest less than a fee simple are not registrable under the C.R.A. 1965.[34] It follows that prescription has not been abolished in respect of these rights if otherwise possible.

(e) Prescription where there is unity of ownership

4.69 It is usually said that, under English law, and in contradistinction to Irish law,[35] the necessary enjoyment for a prescriptive claim has to be claimed by a fee simple owner against a fee simple owner,[36] that any prescriptive enjoyment by a tenant is on behalf of and in the name of the fee simple owner and where this occurs a profit in fee simple results.[37] It follows that a tenant of a quasi-dominant tenement cannot prescribe against his landlord owner of the quasi-servient land. While there seems to be general agreement that this is correct in respect of a prescriptive claim beyond the time of legal memory it has sometimes been questioned as to whether it is necessarily applicable in the case of the doctrine of lost grant.[38] If a profit can be granted for a term of years, which it can be,[39] there seems no reason why, in suitable circumstances, it should not be possible to prove to the satisfaction of a court that a grant for a limited period was made and has been lost. Certainly it seems to have been possible before the Prescription Act 1832 was passed.[40] In *Cowlam* v. *Slack* (1812)[41] a plaintiff commoner brought an action against another for surcharging. The plaintiff was non-suited at trial when it became apparent that he, his father and grandfather had occupied the manor house and farm for 50 years past as tenants of the lord of the manor, owner of the common. The objection was taken that the plaintiff could not have a right of common and therefore could not bring an action for surcharging. On a motion to set aside the non-suit the court held that "common appurtenant" could be claimed by grant as well as by prescription and that evidence of 50 years use is evidence for a jury to presume a grant of common to support an action for surcharging. It will be noticed that in this case the prescriptive claim was not adverse to the owner of the burdened tenement but was necessary to allow an action against a third party. It may be that in

---

[34] s.22(1).

[35] For which, see *Deeble* v. *Linehan* (1860) 12 I.C.L.R. 1; *Fahey* v. *Dwyer* (1879) 4 L.R.Ir. 271; *Timmons* v. *Hewitt* (1888) 22 L.R.Ir. 627; *Hanna* v. *Pollock* [1900] 2 I.R. 664; *Flynn* v. *Harte* [1913] 2 I.R. 322; *Tallon* v. *Ennis* [1937] I.R. 549.

[36] *Bright* v. *Walker* (1834) 1 C.M. & R. 211, 149 E.R. 1057, *per* Parke B.; *Kilgour* v. *Gaddes* [1904] 1 K.B. 457; for the various possibilities where lessees are in possession see Kiralfy, "The Position of the Leaseholder in the Law of Easements" (1948) 13 Conv.(N.S.) 104.

[37] *Wheaton* v. *Maple & Co.* (1893) 3 Ch. 48; *Pugh* v. *Savage* [1907] 2 Q.B. 373.

[38] Delany, "Lessees and the Doctrine of Lost Grant" (1958) 74 L.Q.R. 82.

[39] L.P.A. 1925, s.1(2)(a); *Booth* v. *Alcock* (1873) 8 Ch.App. 663.

[40] *Bright* v. *Walker*, above n. 36, at 221, 1061, *per* Parke B.

[41] (1812) 15 East. 108, 104 E.R. 785.

similar circumstances today, and in the absence of an express grant of rights in common to a tenant, the question of a lost grant could be reopened.

(f) Prescription for certain rights in gross

The second remaining possibility for a prescriptive claim is in relation to **4.70** products other than vesture, herbage and pasture. The claim can only be in gross for, if appurtenant to land, it will be limited to the needs of the dominant tenement.[42] Limitation to part of the total product implies a remainder in the owner of the soil and the claim is to a right of common which in all cases is a registrable right under the C.R.A. 1965. First, it should be noticed that a claim to a right in gross has been held not to be within the terms of the Prescription Act 1832.[43] Secondly, there are several authorities that a prescriptive right in gross may be claimed.[44] However, there are very few cases of claims to a right in gross which have come before the courts in modern times and succeeded. In all there seems to have been strong supporting evidence. In *Welcome* v. *Upton* (1840),[45] there had been dealings in the right for nearly 100 years. Similarly, in *Johnson* v. *Barnes* (1873)[46] there was evidence of deeds of release back to the time of Henry VIII. It seems that it may be possible to prescribe where there is evidence of the fact of a grant but that it may be much more difficult to ask the court to presume the fact based on user of a right alone. Apart from anything else, without a dominant tenement to provide measurement of the quantity of the right, the court is in some difficulty in deciding the size of the grant. Nevertheless, in suitable circumstances there seems no reason in principle why a prescriptive claim to a right in gross for any product of the land, other than vesture, herbage and pasture, may not be made today.

5. Of ancillary rights

Upon the creation of a profit, whether express, implied or presumed, the **4.71** grantee will be entitled to all ancillary easements necessary for its proper enjoyment[47] and in appropriate circumstances will come within the custom of common *pur cause de vicinage*.[48]

---

[42] *Lord Chesterfield* v. *Harris* [1908] 2 Ch. 397 at 421, *per* Buckley L.J.

[43] *Shuttleworth* v. *Le Fleming* (1865) 19 C.B.(N.S.) 687, 144 E.R. 956; *cf. Mercer* v. *Denne* [1905] 2 Ch. 538 at 586 (refusal by Cozens-Hardy L.J. to reconsider).

[44] Co.Litt. 122a. This has been confirmed by a series of cases: *North* v. *Coe* (1668) Vaughan 251, 124 E.R. 1060; *Potter* v. *North* (1669) 1 Wms.Saund. 346, 85 E.R. 503 at 353, 512, *per curiam*; *Hoskins* v. *Robins* (1671–1672) 2 Wms.Saund. 324, 85 E.R. 1123.

[45] (1840) 6 M. & W. 536, 151 E.R. 524.

[46] (1873) L.R. 8 C.P. 527.

[47] *cf.* § 8.05.

[48] "A right of common appurtenant depends upon a grant from the lord and includes common of vicinage": *Minet* v. *Morgan* (1870) 11 L.R. Eq. 284 at 286, *per* Lord Romilly M.R.

TRANSFER

1. Formalities

(a) Rights of common

4.72 Rights of common annexed to land whether by appendancy or appurtenancy pass on conveyance of the land without express mention.[49] When land comprising a dominant tenement is divided an apportionment of rights will occur and for the avoidance of doubt the particulars ought to be expressed in the conveyance. Nevertheless, if not stated, an apportionment in accordance with common law rules will probably still apply.[50] If a right annexed to land is expressly excluded on conveyance of dominant land it seems that the result will usually be the extinguishment of the right.[51]

4.73 Rights of common in gross are separate incorporeal hereditaments and at law may only be conveyed to deed.[52] In the absence of the required formality there may still be a contract for sale which to be enforceable must be evidenced by either writing or part performance.[53] To be protected against a subsequent purchaser of the servient land it should be registered as an estate contract.[54]

(b) Stints

4.74 Rights over stinted pastures, *i.e.* sole rights, are shares in an incorporeal hereditament, are always held in gross and on transfer follow the same rules as rights of common in gross. At law they may only be conveyed by deed. With this class of statutory right there may be some difficulty in obtaining an amendment to the commons registers, referred to below,[55] as some have been registered as though annexed to land.

4.75 The nature of a stinted pasture is such that there can, in theory, have been only one grant at its inception. A subsequent grant of a sole right is absurd. It is tempting therefore to consider the individual stints as but part of one hereditament held jointly. However, in practice the point seems not to have been taken and each stint is treated as a separate hereditament held for a legal interest. There seems to be some support for this in the L.P.A. 1925, s.187(2) which allows the holding of separate rights for a legal estate over the same land with exercisability in common.

---

[49] *Godwin* v. *Schweppes* [1902] 1 Ch. 926 at 932, *per* Joyce J.; *cf.* L.P.A. 1925, s.187(1). For registered land, see *Hesketh* v. *Willis Cruisers Ltd.* (1968) 19 P. & C.R. 573 at 580, *per* Diplock L.J.; Land Registration Act 1925, ss.3(xxiv), 5, 6, 7, 9, 11, 12, 20(1), 23(1) and 72 and Land Registration Rules 1925, r. 251.

[50] For apportionment, see § 6.47.

[51] *cf.* § 6.37 *et seq.*

[52] L.P.A. 1925, s.52: for a precedent for conveyance of fixed rights see 7 Forms & Precedents (4th ed.) 124.

[53] *ibid.* s.40.

[54] See § 4.91.

[55] § 4.82.

(c) Divided shares in land

Whatever form divided shares in land may have achieved in registration **4.76** under the C.R.A. 1965 this form of common land is clearly corporeal and follows the normal rules for the conveyance of land.

(d) Undivided shares in land

The regulated pastures[56] are owned in equity in undivided shares with the **4.77** legal estate, usually, vested in the Public Trustee.[57] There are some marginal doubts about the mode of vesting but in general the stintholders may not deal with the legal estate to the land without the consent of the court.[58] The conveyance of the equitable interest in a stint is not required to be by deed but must be in writing signed by the person conveying the same.[59] In spite of the express exclusion of undivided shares in land from the definition of land in the L.P.A. 1925, it also seems that any contract for the sale of a stint must be evidenced in writing to satisfy section 40 of that Act.[60] Protection of the transaction or a mortgage of the interest may be afforded by serving notice on the trustees of the legal estate.[61] It seems however, that where the legal estate is vested in the Public Trustee prior appointment for the purpose is required as he is a corporation sole.[62]

(e) Leased interests

Where a right of common is appurtenant to land and the land is leased or, as **4.78** is more usually the case, let from year to year the right passes as appurtenant to the land. Under these circumstances a deed for the conveyance of the land and the right is sometimes unnecessary. In the case of land leased or let, and taking effect in possession, for a term not exceeding three years (whether or not the lessee is given power to extend the term) at the best rent which can be reasonably obtained without taking a fine, the lease may be created by parol.[63]

2. Amendment of the commons registers

The registers, including the rights sections, upon finality are conclusively **4.79** evidential of the matters registered as at the date of registration.[64] It follows that they are not evidential of any matters at any current date. There is

---

[56] The term covers all land held in undivided shares whether granted or awarded under private Act or general inclosure statute providing that it was intended thereby to create a joint land ownership/grazing system. It does not usually include land held on a tenancy in common under one title, but may where the intention was to grant land to a number of person for grazing in common.

[57] For vesting, see § 7.81.

[58] L.P.A. 1925, Sched. 1, Pt. V, para. 2,3.

[59] *ibid.* s.53(1)(c).

[60] *ibid.* s.205(1)(ix); *Cooper* v. *Critchley* [1955] Ch. 431; *cf. Elias* v. *Mitchell* [1972] Ch. 652.

[61] *ibid.* s.137(2)(ii); or endorsed on the instrument under which the equitable interest is acquired: s.137(4), (6).

[62] *ibid.* s.138.

[63] *ibid.* s.54(2).

[64] C.R.A. 1965, s.10; and see the definition of registration in s.22(1).

provision, but no requirement, for the registers to be amended to reflect certain changes in rights registrations. The lack of current conclusivity suggests that purchasers of rights should pay due regard to the original registrations and be prepared to trace the disposition of rights since the date of registration in accordance with the general law governing transfer and disposition of rights and not rely on current entries in the commons register. The practice of registration authorities in allowing amendments seems to vary from one authority to another—from amendment on request to proof that the amendment can be substantiated by reference to the relevant legal rules.[65] Reference was made earlier to the possibility that not all the matters recorded on the registers are necessarily within the conclusive evidence provision.[66] The only matters required by the C.R.A. 1965 to be registered are the fact of a right of common and, where the right consists of or includes a right to graze animals, a maximum number of animals for which the right is exercisable.

4.80   Section 13 of the Act allows for regulations to provide for the amendment of the registers where "any rights registered under this Act are apportioned, extinguished or released, or are varied or transferred in such circumstances as may be prescribed." The Commons Registration (General) Regulations 1966[67] consequently provides that:

> "Where a right of common registered under the Act has been apportioned, varied, extinguished or released or, being or having become a right in gross, has been transferred, application may be made to the registration authority . . . for the amendment of the register."[68]

An application may be made by or on behalf of any person having an interest under the apportionment, variation, extinguishment, release or transfer.[69] In the case of extinguishment or release the owner of the common land may apply for the registers to be amended.[70]

4.81   The regulation is permissive not mandatory. There is no provision for the amendment of the name of an applicant for rights appurtenant to land unless there has been an apportionment. It follows that the majority of rights are now recorded against the names of the original applicants, as tenants or, owners in fee simple or landlords and tenants jointly, of the dominant land at the date of registration. There is, however, provision for a change of address of the original applicant.[71] The result overall is that as a record of persons entitled to exercise rights the registers are woefully out of date.

---

[65] Not that it can be said with any great confidence exactly what the rules are; *cf.* §§ 6.38 and 6.47 *et seq.* for apportionment and severance.

[66] § 4.05.

[67] S.I. 1966 No. 1471, as amended by the Commons Registration (General) (Amendment) Regulations 1968 (S.I. 1968 No. 658).

[68] *ibid.* regs. 29(1), 31A (as added by the Commons Registration (General) (Amendment) Regulations 1968, reg. 5).

[69] *ibid.* reg. 29(2) as substituted by the Commons Registration (General) (Amendment) Regulations 1968, reg. 4.

[70] *ibid.* reg. 29(2)(*b*)(ii).

[71] *ibid.* reg. 26(1), (2)(*b*).

(a) Rights in gross

Where a right in gross is transferred, an application may be made for the   **4.82**
new owner's name to be entered on the register. This provision has equal
application to rights held over sole pastures as they are, with an occasional
exception,[72] inherently rights in gross. However, it appears that on
occasions sole rights have been registered with an entry in column 5 of the
rights registers under the heading "particulars of the land (if any) to which
the right is attached." The view has been advanced that, by the terms of the
Act, this column is not a part of the matters which are conclusively evidential.[73] For this reason, it is submitted, that the owner of the right in gross is
not bound by an entry indicating an attachment to land to treat it henceforth as an appurtenant right. It follows that, where the right is one in gross,
such an entry should be no barrier to an amendment of the register in favour
of a transferee, although there are some indications of resistance to this line
of action by certain registration authorities. The doubtful nature of some of
these entries is supported by anecdotal suggestions that some registration
authorities returned application forms for the completion of the relevant
section about attachment to land where the applicant was self-evidently a
farmer.

The question of column 5 of the rights registers has been considered by the   **4.83**
Commissioners and the following comment is relevant:

> "The circumstances that the right registered by [the applicant] is
> expressed to be 'attached' to his stock rearing farm does not I think
> oblige me to treat him as claiming only a right 'appurtenant' to such
> land within the technical meaning of the word 'appurtenant.' In my
> opinion the word 'attached' as used in the printed part of the Rights
> Section Register is sufficiently satisfied if the right is at the time of the
> registration reputed to belong to and to be exercisable by the owner of
> the attached land."[74]

It follows that the Commissioners have not generally directed their attention to consideration of whether rights may be rights in gross when
expressed as attached to land. On the other hand, there are indications that
where rights have been expressed as in gross the Commissioners have been
anxious, where appropriate, to amend them so as to indicate that they are
attached to land.[75]

(b) Regulated pastures

The rights over regulated pastures being a form of undivided share in land   **4.84**
can never be appurtenant to land for "a thing corporeall cannot properly be
appendant to a thing corporeall."[76] The view has been advanced that this
class of land is not properly registrable and the Common Land Forum has

---

[72] *i.e.* where statute has annexed sole rights to land: see § 3.18.

[73] § 4.07.

[74] *Re the Salt Marsh, Thurnham, Lancaster City, Lancs.* (1977) 220/D/69, 6 D.C.C.
260, *per* Commissioner Baden Fuller.

[75] *cf. Re The Black Mountain, Dinefwr, Dyfed* (1985) 272/D/441–777, 16 D.C.C. 219
at p. 22 of the report, *per* Commissioner Baden Fuller.

[76] Co.Litt. 121b.

recommended that all such pastures should be removed from the registers.[77] While they are registered there is, however, little alternative but to view them as being a form of right in gross and they may, of course, be freely transferred without reference to other land. An amendment to reflect the result of a transfer ought always to be obtainable.

(c) Apportionment

4.85   Where rights are annexed to land and the land is divided the rights should be apportioned according to common law rules.[78] Where an apportioned right now appears on the registers notice should be taken that if the apportionment has been incorrectly carried out it may not necessarily attract the conclusive evidence provision.[78a] Conveyancers should, therefore, satisfy themselves that, upon a further apportionment or upon the purchase of a right which has already been apportioned, the current registration is supported by the general law.

4.86   The Common Land Forum recommends that legislation should provide for approval of apportionments by an Agricultural Land Tribunal with all rights unexercisable between the dates of the purported transfer of the apportioned parts and the approval.[79]

3. Protection of purchasers

(a) Pre-contract enquiries

4.87   It is normal conveyancing practice in land purchases, following the judgment of Mocatta J. in *Ladenbau (G. & K.) Ltd.* v. *Crawley & de Reya* (1978),[80] for a statutory search of the common registers to be made wherever land has not been built upon.[81] There is now enough empirical evidence to suggest a substantial number of incorrect common land registrations which are no respecters of whether the land has been developed. The prudent conveyancer might now consider a commons search wherever there is any open land in the vicinity. The *Ladenbau* case indicates that to follow normal practice in searching technique is not necessarily a defence to a negligence claim.

4.88   Where rights of common are included in a proposed purchase, a Local Land Charges Act 1975 search of the burdened land should be undertaken. A purchaser of a right of common will be effected, for instance by the existence of a Site of Special Scientific Interest (S.S.S.I.) on the common land, which may

---

[77] cf. §§ 2.27 et seq.

[78] For which see §§ 6.47 et seq.

[78a] By virtue of the C.R.A. 1965, s.22(1) an amended registration attracts conclusivity under s.10 but, any amendment made under the provisions of s.13 may be challenged in the High Court under s.14(b).

[79] Common Land Forum Report, Appendix C., para. 067–070.

[80] [1978] 1 W.L.R. 266; Commons Registration (General) (Amendment) Regulations 1980 (S.I. 1980 No. 1195), reg. 4, Sched., substituted Form 21.

[81] Brown, "Purchasers Search of the Registers of Commons" (1977) 121 S.J. 718; cf. (1977) 74 L.S.Gaz. 587.

be highly restrictive of the proposed use of the right and notification of an S.S.S.I. is a registrable land charge.[82]

Similarly, a search of the common registers in respect of the burdened land **4.89** will disclose the extent of the land and the rights exercisable thereover including the registered rights of the intending purchaser. The conveyancer should, however, be aware that the conclusive evidence provision does not apply to entries of names on the commons registers at any current date and a search does not obviate the need for other enquiries and the investigation of title to the rights.

(b) Unregistered titles

A high proportion of the common lands and associated dominant land are **4.90** outside areas of compulsory registration of title under the Land Registration Acts. Registered common land is an exception to the general rules about compulsory registration. The C.R.A. 1965 makes provision for registration of title to common land on sale whether the land is situated in a compulsory area or not.[83]

In the case of a right appurtenant to an unregistered title held for a legal **4.91** estate the right passes without any express reference on conveyance of the land.[84] On conveyance, with proper formality, a right in gross held for an interest equivalent to a fee simple is protected without more. It is otherwise in the case of an equitable interest in the land or right as the case may be. A contract to grant land, if specifically enforceable in equity, creates an equitable interest in the land[85] and may be protected by the registration of a Class C(iv) estate contract under the Land Charges Act 1972.[86] In the same way a contract to grant a right of common will bind the original grantor of the burdened land and, if registered, subsequent purchasers.[87] Such contracts can, and should if there is any delay in proceeding to conveyance, be registered as C(iv) estate charges. It seems that it is also possible to protect an equitable profit as a Class D(iii) charge but this section is perhaps more appropriate for the registration of a profit created for an estate which can no longer exist as a legal estate, such as a profit for life.

(c) Titles registered under the Land Registration Acts

Although, as has been shown,[88] the benefit of an appurtenant right of com **4.92** mon may no longer be registered as appurtenant to a registered title to land it is, nevertheless, clearly comprised in the legal title whether entered on the register or not.[89] It may be protected by a note on the register against the burdened land if the title to that land is registered.[90] Indeed, it seems that on

---

[82] Wildlife and Countryside Act 1981, s.28(1).
[83] For which see § 7.42.
[84] *cf.* above, n. 49.
[85] *Mason* v. *Clarke* [1955] A.C. 778 at 798–799.
[86] Land Charges Act 1972, s.2.
[87] Without registration, an estate contract is void as against a purchaser for money or money's worth: Land Charges Act 1972, s.4(6).
[88] § 4.13.
[89] Land Registration Act 1925, s.20(1).
[90] *ibid.* s.70(3).

first registration the Registrar shall note on the register against burdened land any right "created by an instrument and appearing on the title."[91] If, however, the title to the servient tenement is not so affected purchasers will take subject to rights of common, *profits à prendre* and rights of sheepwalk as overriding interests.[92] This seems to apply whether the rights are legal or equitable.[93]

4.93   It has been demonstrated that, on the view of the Land Registry, it may be that certain rights appurtenant to a registered title, in existence prior to the initial registration procedure under the C.R.A. 1965, may have survived as exercisable rights in spite of non-registration under that Act.[94] It was also concluded that profits held in gross which are unregistrable under the Act of 1965 are also not registrable as incorporeal hereditaments under the Land Registration Acts.[95] They will, however, be protected as overriding interests on registered servient land.

4.94   The position is altogether different in the case of rights in common held as appurtenant to land for a term of years. These rights are unaffected by the C.R.A. 1965. It follows that, where dominant land held for a term is registered with a leasehold title, a legal interest to a right appurtenant may be registered in accordance with rules 252 and 254 of the Land Registration Rules 1925.[96] The odd result ensues that, whereas the owner in fee simple may not have a right of common entered as a right appurtenant to the land, a person deriving title under him may have his leasehold interest in the same rights entered.

(d) Regulated pastures

4.95   It is necessary to draw attention to the unsatisfactory nature of some of the C.R.A. 1965 registrations of regulated pastures. From the evidence of empirical investigations, some can only be described as extraordinary. In one case the number of stints, *i.e.* undivided shares in land, appears from the entries on the registers to have increased substantially since registration. In the same case some stints were not registered (which may be the correct view to take of the provisions in the Act) and are still being dealt with outside the commons registers, but are also recorded as appurtenant to land on titles registered under the Land Registration Acts. Attention has already been drawn to the difficulty there is in considering rights to land as though they were rights over land—for example, non-registration can hardly make such rights unexercisable whatever the C.R.A. 1965 provides.[97] It is evident that if the recommendation of the Common Land Forum to remove this class of land from the registers[98] is not taken up, new legislation will have to regu-

---

[91] Land Registration Act 1925, s.70(2).

[92] *ibid.* s.70(1).

[93] *cf. Celsteel Ltd.* v. *Alton House Holdings Ltd.* [1985] 1 W.L.R. 204 at 219–221, *per* Scott J.

[94] C.R.A. 1965 s.1(2)(*b*), and § 4.15.

[95] § 4.16.

[96] S.R. & O. 1925 No. 1093.

[97] The Act did not purport to affect rights of land ownership but only rights of common.

[98] For which, see § 4.09.

larise the registrations in some way. Thus, the future almost certainly holds some return to the position prior to the enactment of the 1965 commons legislation. In the meantime it is suggested that conveyancers should be aware that they cannot necessarily rely either on the entries in the commons registers or on dealings, whether in connection with registered or unregistered land titles, outside the registers.

(e) Quasi-rights

In discussing the effect of the C.R.A. 1965 on the creation of new rights of **4.96** common over land which has achieved registration as statutory common land, attention was drawn to the difficult position which a purchaser might have in attracting exercisable rights of common to former demesne or other quasi-dominant land.[99] It is reiterated that it would be unwise for a purchaser to rely on wrongly registered quasi-rights as a foundation for new exercisable rights of common. In spite of the conclusive evidence provision in the Act it seems that this cannot apply to matters registered in contravention of the provisions in the Act. The better view must be that quasi-rights were unregistrable with the result that any such registration is of doubtful validity. Even if this view is incorrect, notice should be taken of the recommendation of the Common Land Forum that all quasi-rights should be removed from the registers and converted into notes on the registers.[1] If this occurs the purchaser will have no right on the register as it will have been removed nor will he be able to lay claim to the right of a tenant exercising a quasi-right any longer as he will be outside this category. It may be that in any new legislation special provision will be made for the situation. It is, nevertheless, one fraught with uncertainty and probably the only safe alternative is to consider seeking a grant from the vendor of an unregistrable term of years to a right in common with an option to purchase the freehold reversion to the right.

[99] § 4.42.
[1] Common Land Forum Report, Appendix C, para. 030.

5. Extinguishment of Common Rights

BY ACTS OF THE PARTIES

5.01 Rights of common may be extinguished in a variety of ways, as a result of the acts of the rights holders and the owner of the soil, because of alterations made to the dominant and servient tenements, or by statutory intervention. The consequence in all cases is that the rights revert to the owner of the soil—he may use any resulting surplus of the product as he wishes, and is entitled to inclose any surplus land by the process known as approvement.[1] If all the rights are extinguished the land ceases to be common land and, in certain circumstances, will also cease to be statutory common land. This section is concerned with extinguishment by the acts of the parties but does not include approvement as that process does not affect directly the quantum of grazing or other rights over the land.[2]

Unity of ownership

5.02 The general rule is that unity of ownership of common land and a right of common will extinguish the right[3] as no man may hold a *profit à prendre* over his own land. The rule is, however, subject to some qualifications and exceptions.

(a) The quality of ownership required

5.03 It is necessary for the combined ownership to be of the most durable estate *i.e.* a fee simple absolute in possession. In *R. v. Inhabitants of Hermitage* (1692)[4] King Henry VIII held a manor in fee simple and the commons in pos-

---

[1] *Arlett* v. *Ellis* (1827) 7 B. & C. 346 at 369, 108 E.R. 752 at 761, *per* Bayley J. See also § 6.14.

[2] For approvement, see § 7.47.

[3] The primary authority for the proposition is *Tyrringham's Case* (1584) 4 Co.Rep. 36b, 76 E.R. 973. See also *Nelson's Case* (1585) Gouldsb. 3, 75 E.R. 957; *The Case of Proxies* (1604) Davies 1 at 5, 80 E.R. 491 at 495; *Sawyer's Case* (1632) W. Jones 284, 82 E.R. 150; *Reynolds* v. *Clarke* (1725) 2 Ld.Raym. 1399 at 1400, 92 E.R. 410 at 411; *Warburton* v. *Parke* (1857) 2 H. & N. 64 at 69, 157 E.R. 26 at 29; *Musgrave* v. *Inclosure Commissioners* (1874) L.R. 9 Q.B. 162 at 174.

[4] (1692) Carth. 239, 90 E.R. 743; also *Anon.* (1581) Godb. 4, 78 E.R. 3.

session, determinable upon the birth of a Duke of Cornwall. The rights of common were held not to be extinguished. In *James* v. *Plant* (1836)[5] the unity of ownership was of two sisters holding as co-parceners as to the dominant tenement and as tenants in common in tail general as to the servient land. There was thus unity of seisin but the right (in this case a disputed way) was held to be in suspense pending the determination of the estate tail.

It must not be supposed that where dominant and servient tenements are **5.04** held for different estates that it is necessarily possible to prescribe for a right of common. In *Warburton* v. *Parke* (1857)[6] an owner in fee simple also held an estate for life in a moor. His separate successors to the farm and the moor came into dispute over alleged prescriptive rights to graze the moor. The court held that the tenants of the farm during the original ownership could not have prescribed for rights of common for an owner in fee simple would have been prescribing against himself as life tenant.

(b) Unity of possession without sufficient unity of estate

Where unity of possession of the dominant and servient tenements occurs, **5.05** without the necessary unity of estate to effect extinguishment, a suspension of right results. Thus Coke comments[7]:

> " . . . if a man hath a common by prescription, and taketh a lease of the land for twenty yeares, whereby common is suspended, after the yeares ended, he may claime the common generally by prescription, for that the suspension was but to the possession and not to the right, and the inheritance of the common did always remain."

The suspension of right during unity of possession makes little difference to the use of the right for the lessee, or other possessor, is able to exercise the quasi-rights of land ownership.

However, in certain circumstances, the doctrine of suspension during unity **5.06** of possession applies not only to the land concerned, but also to the remainder of the land over which the rights are exercisable so that "if a commoner takes a lease of any part of the land, in which &c., the whole common is suspended."[8] The reason for this apparently harsh decision is given in *Wyat Wyld's Case* (1609)[9] when it was said that "if he who has common appurtenant . . . takes a lease of parcel of the land, all is suspended, because it is the folly of the commoner to intermeddle with part of the land in which &c. belongs not to him."[10] The reason given is less than convincing in terms of legal principle when the intermeddling was self-evidently with the connivance of the owner of the land. The decision is, nevertheless, inevitable in the light of the equally unconvincing posture taken up by the courts at the time on the question of purchase of part of a common, (considered below).

---

[5] (1836) 4 Ad. & E. 749 at 761, 111 E.R. 967 at 972.
[6] (1857) 2 H. & N. 64, 157 E.R. 26.
[7] Co.Litt.114b; *cf. Anon.* (1581) Godb. 4, 78 E.R. 3.
[8] *Ascough's Case* (1603) 9 Co.Rep. 134a, 77 E.R. 922.
[9] (1609) 8 Co.Rep. 78b, 77 E.R. 593.
[10] *ibid.* at 79a, 594.

(c) Unity by purchase

5.07 Unity of servient and dominant land by purchase, so that both parcels are held in fee simple, will result in extinguishment of all rights of common formerly exercised from the dominant land. Nevertheless, although technically rights of common have ceased to exist, something similar remains in the owner of the, now quasi-dominant, land and those persons deriving title from him: in *Bradshaw* v. *Eyre* (1597) it was said that "it is *quasi* common used therewith; and although it be not the same common it was before, yet it is the like common."[11]

5.08 **(i) Extinguishment without unity of possession** It is sometimes said that, for an extinguishment of an easement or profit to occur, unity of ownership and possession in terms of actual occupation is necessary.[12] This is accurate in relation to easements and profits as such but cannot be taken to mean that a right of common will survive unity of ownership without actual occupation of the dominant land. The proposition has particular relevance to easements and was expressed by MacDonald C.B. in *Buckby* v. *Coles* (1814)[13] and the Court of Appeal in *Richardson* v. *Graham* (1908).[14] The latter case serves to illustrate the point: a leaseholder had acquired a right to light against a neighbouring developer who obstructed the light; the developer purchased the freehold reversion of the lease and claimed the extinguishment of the right by unity of ownership of the freeholds. The Court held that the freeholder who had granted the lease could not derogate from his grant or, as Kennedy L.J. put it, "having given by legal act the right to light to the plaintiffs, cannot give by legal act to another person something which is absolutely inconsistent with that right which he has already granted to the plaintiffs."[15] Thus the right endured during the time of the lease.

5.09 Rights of common have been treated differently, although the practical result may be the same. Upon unity of ownership, the right of common ceases but something similar—the "like common" of *Bradshaw* v. *Eyre*—remains. In other words the tenant's exercise of the landlord's right of common ceases and is replaced by a right in common enduring to the end of the term. This is merely a reflection of the different development of easements and profits in that an easement may be granted for a term of years whereas a right of common may not. The subject has relevance in a modern context in that the purchase of dominant tenements by the owner of a common, without taking up occupation of them, will suffice to extinguish rights of common so that the land will cease to be common land and, possibly also, statutory common land.

5.10 **(ii) Unity of ownership on part of the servient land** If a dominant tenement and part of the waste land are unified by purchase the result is different depending upon whether the right of common attached to the dominant land is appendant or appurtenant. The definitive statement, apparently still good law today, is that of Coke:

[11] (1597) Cro.Eliz. 570, 78 E.R. 814, *per* Gawdy and Fenner JJ.
[12] *cf.* Megarry and Wade, p. 899.
[13] (1814) 5 Taunt. 311 at 315, 128 E.R. 709 at 711.
[14] (1908) 1 K.B. 39.
[15] *ibid.* at 46.

"If a man purchase part of the land, wherein common appendant is to be had, the common shall be apportioned, because it is of common right; but not so of a common appurtenant, or of any other common of what nature so-ever."[16]

Tyrringham's Case (1584)[17] illustrates the rule. Rights attached to a farm were exercisable over two separate wastes. The lord, owner of one waste, purchased the farm. If the right had been appendant it was held that the lord ought "to prescribe to have common in the whole till such a day, then to shew the purchase of part, and from that time that he has put in his cattle into the residue *pro rata portione*." The court resolved, however, that the right was appurtenant in which event "by the said purchase all the common was extinct." The practical result was that the owner of one waste was relieved of the burden of the rights he had granted over it as a result of the act of the owner of the other waste. This seems a particularly unmeritorious result, to say nothing of the predicament of the tenant of the farm.

The decision was followed by *Wyat Wyld's Case* (1609)[18] where "it was **5.11** well agreed that common appendant was of common right, and severable; and although the commoner in such case purchase parcel of the land in which &c. yet the common shall be apportioned" but "if he who has common appurtenant purchases part of the land in which &c. all the common is extinct." The reason given for the differential treatment accorded to appurtenant rights was, as in the case of suspension of rights, that it is the folly of the commoner to intermeddle with part of the land which does not belong to him. Why it is intermeddling in the case of appurtenant but not appendant rights is unexplained. Possibly the explanation of differential treatment for appurtenant rights lies in the support which it seems the courts were displaying towards arable as opposed to pastoral farming at the time. In a note to *Tyrringham's Case*, Coke lists six "inconveniences" and two "deplorable consequences" of converting arable land to pasture—one of the consequences is that it tends "to the great displeasure of God."[19] Appendant rights are associated only with arable land.

The logical rule would be that, if the owner of a dominant tenement pur- **5.12** chases part of the waste his right appurtenant will be extinguished over that part, but that an apportioned part will continue over the remainder, *i.e.* the rule in respect of appendant rights. For there to be a distinction depending upon the basis of the original grant of rights was, it is suggested, legally inconsistent. Nevertheless, it has been followed in modern times. In *White* v. *Taylor (No.1)* (1969)[20] Buckley J. accepted *Wyat Wyld's Case*, by then over three and a half centuries old, as good law and held that the purchase of part of the land extinguished the whole right of common.

[16] Co.Litt. 122a; also *Wood* v. *Moreton* (1608) 1 Brownl. & Golds.180, 123 E.R. 741; *contra* Brooke-Taylor, "Perdurable Estates" (1977) 41 Conv. 107 at 114, citing *Sury* v. *Pigot* (1626) Pop. 166, 79 E.R. 1263, *dictum per* Doddridge J. For consideration of the nature of appendant and appurtenant rights, see §§ 3.28 and 3.36.
[17] (1584) 4 Co.Rep. 36b at 38a, 76 E.R. 973 at 980.
[18] (1609) 8 Co.Rep. 78b at 79a, 77 E.R. 593 at 594.
[19] *ibid*. at 39a, 982.
[20] [1969] 1 Ch. 150. *cf. Re West Anstey Common* (1986) 209/D/234–243, 17 D.C.C. 100: principles of equity applicable: prescriptive reacquisition of rights considered.

5.13   **(iii) Common rights in gross**   Commons in gross are by their nature neither appendant nor appurtenant but by the authority of Coke[21] and the case of *Jordan* v. *Atwood* (1605)[22] the principle that unity with part of the servient tenement will extinguish the entire right applies. If the whole of the servient tenement comes into unity with the right in gross the right merely merges with the residual right of the owner of the waste which passes to the purchaser.[23]

(d) Unity resulting from act of law

5.14   There is some small amount of authority, unsupported by litigation, that where unity occurs by result of an act of law no extinguishment results. It has its origin in Coke[24]:

> "A hath common of pasture *sauns nombre* in twenty acres of land, and ten of those acres descend to A: the common *sauns nombre* is entire and incertaine and cannot be apportioned, but shall remaine. But if it had been a common certaine (as for ten beasts), in that case the common should be apportioned."

The principle seems to be that of *actus legis nulli facit injuriam*[25] and prevails over the doctrine of extinguishment following purchase. At the worst, it seems, the right will be apportioned.

(e) Stinted pastures

5.15   The rule of extinguishment by unity of ownership has no application in the case of stints over stinted pastures. Thus, the owner of a stinted pasture may purchase, or otherwise acquire, stints and they are exercisable or alienable as before.[26]

(f) Common fields

5.16   Intercommonage between adjoining owners in a field clearly does not suffer from extinguishment by unity of ownership and right, for the right is dependent upon the ownership. Nor, if a tenant of land in a common field purchases the land from which his right is exercisable, is there an extinguishment; this is expressly dealt with in *Bradshawe's Case* (1597)[27] and the *Bishop of London's Case* (1614).[28] However, this seems to be denied by *Kimpton's Case* (1587).[29] The facts seem to have been that there was a common appurtenant to 140 acres exercisable in a common field of 46 acres, of which two acres were in the same possession as the 140 acres. The two

---

[21] Co.Litt.122a, cited at § 5.10.

[22] (1605) Owen 121 at 122, 74 E.R. 945 at 946.

[23] *cf.* 1 Ro.Ab.396, B, 1, 2. See also § 6.43.

[24] Co.Litt. 149a.

[25] *cf.*Co.Litt. 148a.

[26] *Lonsdale (Earl)* v. *Rigg* (1856) 11 Ex. 654, 156 E.R. 992.

[27] (1597) Moore (K.B.) 462, 72 E.R. 697: "Prescription pur common appendant unity extinct ceo, nemy common pur arable terre, &c."

[28] 1 Ro.Ab. 935: "Shack common ou mutuall common en regard que jeo ay common en votre ground que vous averes en mon terre, ne ferra extinguish per unitie de possession, pur le necessitie del bien publique d'user sans closure."

[29] (1587) Gouldb. 53, 75 E.R. 990; s.c. 1 Leon. 43, 74 E.R. 40; 1 And. 59, 123 E.R. 407.

acres were purchased and the entire common in the 46 acres was held to be extinguished. The explanation may be that, although the right was pleaded as appurtenant to the 140 acres, it was actually a right of intercommonage from and over the two acres and what the purchaser did was to enclose the two acres while seeking to continue using his purported appurtenant right. The result of an enclosure of the two acres should have been extinguishment of all rights in the common field[30] and this was the decision of the court. That there was an enclosure of the two acres can be judged from a marginal note to a case in 1597, referring to the case of *Kempson* heard in 1587 that the "reason for this case was because the land *improved* is utterly discharged of common."[31]

(g) Inclosure and encroachment

The doctrine of extinguishment never seems to have been applied in the cases of approvement,[32] customary inclosure[33] or licensed encroachment. In particular manorial court rolls abound with examples of encroachments being confirmed upon payment of a fine and there has been no suggestion that this was a purchase of part of the waste resulting in extinguishment of rights. It seems that the Crown Estate Commissioners in modern times have sold land which has been enclosed from a common. Where such a case came before a Commons Commissioner, on an objection to rights, it was held that the purchase of land enclosed extinguished the rights over the remainder of the common.[34] **5.17**

Express release

It has long been held that rights over the land of another person may be expressly released as well as they may be expressly granted.[35] Similarly, as rights may be implied so they may be impliedly released.[36] The effect of a release is to extinguish the right by merger with the rights of the owner of the soil. To effect an express release at law the document must be under seal.[37] The law is clear where the release relates to the totality of an individual right but has been thought to be less clear in the case of a partial release of rights. It has been said to be an open question whether the release of rights over part of the servient tenement serves not to extinguish right over that part but extinguishes the whole right.[38] As releases of this type have been, and are, exceedingly common the matter deserves careful attention. **5.18**

---

[30] See § 1.70.

[31] (1587) 3 Dyer 339a, 73 E.R. 764.

[32] *ibid.* lord approving land and enfeoffing tenant does not extinguish tenant's preexisting rights.

[33] *cf.* § 7.63.

[34] *Re The Beacon, Black Mountain etc., Radnor D.* (1977) 276/D/1–4, 6 D.C.C. 222: encroachment in 1932 conveyed by the Crown Estate Commissioners in 1962.

[35] *cf.* Bracton, folio 223; Fleta Book iv, Chap. 20, (1972) 89 S.S. 97.

[36] Bracton, folio 223.

[37] Co.Litt. 264b; for precedents for registered and unregistered land see 7 Forms and Precedents, (4th ed.), pp. 122–123.

[38] Harris and Ryan, para. 2.84.

(a) A collective release of all rights

5.19   Where a collective release of the totality of rights of common is obtained by the owner of the soil from persons with rights over the servient land , the land will cease to be common land and, in suitable circumstances, may also cease to be statutory common land.[39] In some cases which have come before the Commons Commissioners it is evident that owners have taken advantage of this common law position. At one series of hearings the applicants for rights registrations withdrew following a surrender of rights of common to the owner of the soil coupled with the granting of 999 year leases of grazing rights in common. The rights registrations were refused and at a subsequent hearing the registration of the land as common land likewise.[40]

5.20   In the event that not all the commoners join in the collective release the land will remain common land subject to the unreleased rights. At one time the courts were, it seems, prepared to have an objecting minority overridden but later this was disapproved.[41]

(b) An individual release of a right

5.21   An express release by deed of rights of common by an individual commoner will extinguish those rights alone. The practice seems to have been not unusual in the nineteenth century and an illustration can be seen in the case of *Robertson* v. *Hartopp* (1889),[42] where an owner obtained the release of rights in order to reduce the totality of rights exercisable and thus defeat claims that he had allowed an insufficiency of grazing following inclosure and removal of turf and loam. There are indications that there is some current interest in the practice particularly on moors where the rights exercisable are seen as detrimental to a grouse population. There are practical difficulties where the flocks on the moors are hefted as the removal of rights on one of the sheepwalks merely leads to adjoining flocks straying over the ungrazed land and unless numbers are increased there may be under-grazing instead of over-grazing. A more effective method of reducing grazing intensity would be the partial release of all the rights, *i.e.* for a proportionate decrease of all exercisable rights (for which see below).[43]

(c) A collective release over part of the common land

5.22   The most frequent occurrence, and the one in most danger unless the law is clear, is where all the rights holders agree to a release of rights over part of the land. It occurs wherever part of a common is about to be converted to another use. It has been said that a release of a portion of a common appurtenant extinguishes the whole common[44] and indeed the case cited in sup-

[39] §§ 2.68 *et seq.*
[40] *Re Trawden Moors, Lancs. (No.1) and (No.2)* (1982) 220/D/218–220, 217, 13 D.C.C. 14, 15.
[41] See Woolrych (2nd ed., 1850), pp. 440–445 and cases there cited.
[42] (1889) 43 Ch.D. 484.
[43] § 5.36.
[44] Megarry and Wade, p. 897; Hall, p. 334; Bird, p. 62; *cf. Cooke's Inclosures*, p. 57, where the doctrine is described as discredited.

port, *Miles* v. *Etteridge* (1692), endorses this by saying "a release of common in one acre is an extinguishment of the whole common."[45]

Although there can be no absolute certainty that the argument about to be expounded is necessarily correct, it is more likely than not that it is for the one simple reason that, if the law is that a partial release of rights extinguishes the whole right of common, there can hardly be a common in the country which has been unaffected. The argument has to be to some extent speculative because of the poor quality of the reports but, nevertheless, it is believed that there are sufficient indications that the land with which they are all concerned is in common fields and not wastes. The rules of law in common fields are inevitably different. **5.23**

(i) The supposed rule in Rotherham v. Green The earliest and most frequently cited case is *Rotherham* v. *Green* (1597).[46] It is regarded as the foundation for the doctrine of partial release. Green, a defendant in a case of trespass, was seised of a tenement for which he pleaded a right of common in the *locus in quo*. Evidence was given that Green's grandfather had released "all his right and his common in part of the land where he had common" to the plaintiff's ancestor. It is immediately relevant to consider the circumstances when a commoner would release his right over, say, five acres, in a 500 acre waste. They are difficult to imagine. What would be not unlikely, on the other hand, is the release of all the right to five acres in a common field with which he would automatically release his right of intercommonage therefrom. If this is what was happening, then all the case illustrates is a defendant attempting to exercise a right of common from dominant land outside a common field on the strength of his ancestor's rights in the past which were really related to land in the field. This is similar to *Kimpton's Case* (1587), considered above,[47] which, it seems, is how it was described by Anderson in argument: "this is like to *Rampton's Case* [sic]." In a dissenting judgment Walmesley remarks that "this release went to the benefit of the ter-tenant, and it was an *improvement* by him." The case makes sense if it relates to a common field, where the rule is that an enclosure of a part into permanent severalty destroys the right of intercommonage exercisable from and over the enclosed land.[48] **5.24**

The next case supposedly supportive of the doctrine is *Morse* v. *Well* (1609),[49] which states quite baldly "a release of common in one acre, is a release of all." A better report is found in *Morse and Webb's Case* (1609),[50] by Sir Edward Coke, who sat on the case. Morse was seised of two yard lands with appurtenant rights of grazing in a place called Downfield. He demised parcels of the land, namely "the four buts of arable with the common and inter-common to the same belonging" for a term of 400 years. The freehold possession and reversion of the two yard lands descended to his son John who proceeded to graze two oxen in the field. The animals were **5.25**

---

[45] (1692) 1 Show. K.B. 349, 89 E.R. 618.
[46] (1597) Cro.Eliz. 593, 78 E.R. 836.
[47] § 5.16.
[48] See further § 1.70.
[49] (1609) 1 Brownl. & Golds. 180, 123 E.R. 741.
[50] (1609) 13 Co.Rep. 65, 77 E.R. 1474; s.c. *Mors* v. *Webbe* (1609) 2 Brownl. & Golds. 297, 123 E.R. 952.

distrained and John prescribed for rights of common in his freehold, which he undoubtedly had; the distrainor mistakenly traversed the prescription instead of pleading the demise. The court resolved that "if the said lease had been pleaded, that the common during the lease for years is not suspended or discharged; for each of them shall have common rateable, and in such a manner, that the land in which &c. shall not be surcharged." The case clearly has nothing to say about the release of rights over a waste being entirely concerned with arable land in an open field.

5.26 Finally consideration must be given to the case of *Miles* v. *Etteridge* (1692),[51] which, as seen above, provides the saying that a "release of common in one acre is an extinguishment of the whole common." This case too was, it seems, concerned with land in a common field. A plaintiff claimed a licence from the defendant's father to inclose the land concerned. The court stated that the reply was ill by way of licence but good by way of release of common continuing with the comment already cited. The case is completely coherent if the facts were that the defendant's father had granted a licence to the plaintiff to enclose part of a common field which, on a reciprocal basis, destroyed the rights of common issuing from, and exercisable over, the enclosed part. It was ill to plead the licence, as this would have expired with the death of the father, but good by way of release of his right of common on enclosure which would have extinguished the "whole common," *i.e.* the right of the defendant's father or his successors to graze over the enclosed part. This case again only seems relevant to land in common fields.

5.27 **(ii) The supposed rule doubted** In the next case to be noticed the issue of a partial release was directly considered. In *Benson* v. *Chester* (1799),[52] a court decree had endorsed an agreement whereby the commoners had released rights over a waste, an "adventurer" had drained the whole and received one-third alloted in severalty as a reward, the remainder being awarded to trustees to hold in severalty for the commoners to enjoy their pre-existing rights. A question arose as to the nature of the new rights and counsel in argument submitted that "by a release of part of the right of common the whole is gone." Lord Kenyon C.J., characteristically without reviewing the cases, seized upon the crucial issue:

> "To one argument urged on behalf of the defendant I cannot give my assent. It is said that a release of a right of common over part of the common, is an extinguishment of the whole right of common; and cases have been cited to that effect: but I should wish to examine those cases thoroughly before I subscribed to such a position, especially where all the commoners join in the release. A release by one commoner of his right over part of the common, may possibly operate as a release of his right over the whole; but if that were the consequence of a release by all the commoners, there would long ago have been an end of almost all the rights of common throughout the kingdom."[53]

The force of Lord Kenyon's argument, which required no consideration of

---

[51] Above, n. 45.

[52] (1799) 8 T.R. 396, 101 E.R. 1453.

[53] *ibid.* at 401, 1456; as a landowner's son from Flintshire Lord Kenyon was well versed in the practice of agriculture.

case authority, has gathered even greater strength with time, and it is submitted that self-evidently a collective release by all over part of the common cannot effect an extinguishment. In practice the question is never raised. If it ever were held to be good law no commoner could agree to a release. Every changed use would have to proceed through statutory extinguishment or compulsory purchase with exactly the same ultimate result but a good deal of inconvenience. It is suggested that, for Lord Kenyon's reason alone, the law must be that a collective release of part of the common does not extinguish the whole right. The cases usually cited as authority for the doctrine of partial release are probably relevant only to common field lands and have no application to wastes.

(iii) The supposed rule avoided Before leaving the matter some   **5.28**
notice must be taken of a case where the matter was discussed albeit, as it turned out, that the discussion was *obiter dicta*. In *Johnson* v. *Barnes* (1872),[54] a town corporation had an exclusive right of pasturage over the arable fields round the town when the land was not sown to corn. On numerous occasions over the previous 300 years grazing rights had been granted to third parties and rights released to the owners of some of the arable land. The effect of the releases came under challenge and it was argued that a release of part of the rights had extinguished all. In the lower court the argument was accepted on the grounds, it seems, that otherwise the land remaining would be surcharged.[55] In the Court of Exchequer Chamber it was accepted, as argued, that "according to the old rule which was law as early as the time of Littleton, the release of part of the land over which the right was exercisable would extinguish the right."[56] The argument was that a common was similar to a rent charge which "is entire and against common right, and issuing out of every part of the land and therefore by purchase of part it is extinct in the whole." Yet similar arguments had been brought in *Wyat Wyld's Case* (1609)[57] in an attempt to show that a common was entire and could not be divided: "common appurtenant is a thing against common right, and therefore by the act of the party shall be no more severed or divided than a condition or nomine poenae, or any other thing against common right." However, alienation of an apportioned right was there upheld on policy grounds for if the law was otherwise "all common appurtenants in England would be destroyed (which would be against the commonwealth) for no land continues in so entire a manner, every acre together with another, as it has been *ab initio*."

To have followed the argument in the case before the court would have had   **5.29**
the most awkward consequences—some 300 years of grants and releases would have been held unlawful. In the event, in the lower court it was held that the corporation had been granted a right of common in gross with powers to grant or release parts of the right, and in the Exchequer Chamber it was found that the right was of sole pasture which was not governed by the same rules as rights of common. The case, therefore, is authority that a sole right of pasture may be released over part of the land over which it is exercisable. It is, of course, no authority with regard to the release of rights

[54] (1872) L.R. 7 C.P. 592; *sub. proc.* (1873) L.R. 8 C.P. 527.
[55] L.R. 7 C.P. 599.
[56] L.R. 8 C.P. 531.
[57] (1609) 8 Co.Rep. 78b, 77 E.R. 593.

of common although the opinions expressed are persuasive. However, in view of the lack of authority for the arguments accepted by the court it is suggested that they must be considered *per incuriam*.

5.30   One argument in *Johnson* v. *Barnes* merits further consideration. It was remarked by Willes J. that a release of rights over part of a common would lead to surcharging.[58] This must be correct if the release is not also accompanied by a proportionate reduction in the quantum of the right. This question has already been considered, in connection with both the theory of levancy and couchancy and the practicalities of rights registrations under the Act of 1965.[59] It merely needs to be stated at this point that, where rights were granted levant and couchant, the description remains as the method of assessing numbers but following enclosure, encroachment or any other method, whether express or implied, of releasing some part of the rights over the land, the rights have been proportionately reduced. Today *levancy* and *couchancy* can probably be no more than a method of assessing the proportionate right of each commoner to the totality of rights and not his absolute entitlement. Willes J.'s difficulty is only relevant if *levancy* and *couchancy* is viewed as an absolute measurement which is unalterable, whereas it has been shown the meaning of the term is much wider than that and varies according to the context in which it is used.[60]

5.31   In summary it is suggested that the whole doctrine of a collective release of rights over part of the land leading to extinguishment of all of the right has no sound base in case law authority. Thus, the endorsement of it in *Johnson* v. *Barnes* was mistaken and, for the reasons given in *Benson* v. *Chester* by Lord Kenyon, a collective release cannot result in extinguishment.

5.32   **(iv) Treatment by the Commons Commissioners**   The subject appears to have been considered by the Commons Commissioners on but few occasions. They have, however, endorsed the principle of the doctrine. In *Re Aylesbeare Common, Aylesbeare, Devon* (1974)[61] rights were claimed by three persons over finally registered land which had consisted of some 682 acres until 1960. In February of that year some 200 acres were acquired by the Ministry of Agriculture, Fisheries and Food under a compulsory purchase order. Two of the applicants were unable to adduce evidence of title to rights, but the third satisfied the Commissioner that he had a prescriptive title down to 1960. However, in June 1960 he released his rights over the 200 acres acquired by compulsory purchase the previous February. The Commissioner felt bound by the authority of *Rotherham* v. *Green*, and its approval by Willes J. in *Johnson* v. *Barnes*, and held that the partial release had extinguished the prescriptive right.

5.33   Another Commissioner seems to have given tacit approval to the doctrine while distinguishing it on the facts. In *Re Yateley Common, Hampshire* (1975)[62] an objector claimed that the release of rights by all the commoners over land used for a cemetery, by informal agreement at a parish meeting,

[58] L.R. 7 C.P. 599.
[59] §§ 3.129, 4.21.
[60] *cf.* §§ 3.127 and 3.142 *et seq.*
[61] (1974) 9/D/20, 2 D.C.C. 274.
[62] (1975) 214/D/9–13, 3 D.C.C. 153.

had extinguished all the rights. The Commissioner refused the objection on the grounds that there is a difference between a formal release of rights and an agreement or declaration of intention not to sue.

(d) An individual release over part of the land

As a matter of general practice a release by an individual over part of a common is unlikely, as the land remains subject to any unreleased rights and there are obvious practical difficulties in preventing the exercise of the released right. However, it might arise as a gradual progression towards a collective release. If the owner of the soil is prepared to accept a release in this way there seems no reason in principle why the law for an individual release does not follow what is now suggested is the law for a collective release. That is to say there is a reduction in the exercisable right but no extinguishment of the whole right.   **5.34**

One circumstance where a release of rights over part of the land may be said to have occurred is where rights of common have been registered under the C.R.A. 1965 over a "sheepwalk" instead of, as might have been the case, over an entire waste.[63] This limitation of a right, by release over the remainder of the waste probably has no extinguishing effect on the exercisability of the right registered.   **5.35**

(e) A release of a proportion of a right

There seems no reason in principle why a rights holder should not agree to the release of a proportion of his right to the owner of the soil. This is now much easier to effect since the enactment of the maximum quantification provisions contained in the C.R.A. 1965. In some circumstances this might appeal to an owner of a common where the land is currently overstocked, but note should be taken of the comments made on registered numbers of livestock where it is suggested that they may not be definitive and that, in spite of the numbers registered, the exercisable rights may be for a lesser number.[64]   **5.36**

Implied release

Implied release is frequently referred to as abandonment but it is suggested that it is convenient to separate the two terms as different considerations may apply to each. "Abandonment" is here the term applied to an individual release where the entitled party has turned his back on his rights without necessarily anticipating any particular consequences. As will be shown, the courts now require some external manifestation of a subjective intention not to resume use of the rights before abandonment will be presumed. Distinguishable is the use of the term "implied release," which is reserved in the present text for the occasions when an implied collective release may be presumed over a particular piece of land. It seems that an implied release   **5.37**

---

[63] For sheepwalks, see § 3.105.
[64] *cf.* §§ 4.20 *et seq.*

may be presumed as a consequence of reliance by third parties that the rights will not be enforced.

(a) Abandonment

5.38 Loss of right by neglect was recognised from very early times and may be encapsulated in the view that "common is obtained by long sufferance; and also it may be lost by long negligence."[65] At one time it was necessary to resort to forceful use in order to maintain a right.[66] This could be anticipated at a time when seisin was all important and actual possession and the right to possession had not been entirely separated. However, in the late eighteenth and nineteenth centuries the courts seemed to be re-adopting the view that in order to maintain a right it had to be used. At this time the law of prescription was developing to allow a comparatively short period of use to establish a right and, as a parallel development, a short period of non-use to imply abandonment.

5.39 **(i) The nineteenth century view** As late as 1848 we find a judge at assize proceeding "on the ground, that, as twenty years' user in the absence of an express grant would have been necessary for the acquiescence of the right [an easement of way], so twenty years' cessor of the use in the absence of any express release was necessary for its loss."[67] However, it cannot be said that any doctrine of presumed abandonment from non-user was fully developed or properly expressed. There was some reluctance to interfere with express rights on the grounds of non-user. In *Seaman* v. *Vawdrey* (1810)[68] a reservation in a deed of mining rights, unused for 104 years, was held good as the right had not been interfered with in that time. Rights of common were directly considered in *Hawke* v. *Bacon* (1809)[69] when a note of *Creach* v. *Wilmot* (1752)[70] at assizes was approved as good law. In that case it was pleaded that the recovery of a right of common was not covered by the, then, statute of limitations. Lee C.J. held that:

> "A possession of above 40 years has been proved, and there is no difference between the lord of a manor and a commoner. The lord could not have brought an ejectment after twenty years possession. Here the commoner, if he had any right, should have brought an assize of common, and not made an entry."

Thus, while entry was barred, the right of recovery by an assize (of novel disseisin) was upheld following 40 years of non-user. Perhaps the correct view of the law at the time was that of Lord Denman in *R.* v. *Chorley* (1848) when he held that "the period of time is only material as one element from which the grantee's intention to retain or abandon his easement may be inferred

---

[65] *Anon.* (1588) 3 Leon. 202, 74 E.R. 632; *cf.* Bracton, folio 223; Fleta Book iv, Chap. 20, (1972) 89 S.S. 97.

[66] Fleta Book, *loc. cit.*, (1972) 89 S.S. 98.

[67] *R.* v. *Chorley* (1848) 12 Q.B. 515 at 518, 116 E.R. 960 at 962 *per* Platt B.; *cf. Scrutton* v. *Stone* (1893) 9 T.L.R.478 *per* Charles J., affirmed on other grounds (1894) 10 T.L.R.157.

[68] (1810) 16 Ves.Jun. 390, 33 E.R. 1032.

[69] (1809) 2 Taunt. 156, 127 E.R. 1036; *semble* adopted by Denman C.J. in *Tapley* v. *Wainwright* (1833) 5 B. & Ad. 395 at 398, 110 E.R. 836 at 837.

[70] (1752) 2 Taunt. 160, 127 E.R. 1038.

against him; and what period may be sufficient in any particular case must depend on all the accompanying circumstances."[71]

(ii) The definitive modern rule Recent cases have dealt directly with **5.40** subject of abandonment. In *Tehidy Minerals Ltd.* v. *Norman* (1970)[72] Buckley L.J. gave the judgment of the Court of Appeal in a case where abandonment of rights was directly considered, although, it seems, with less than complete argument on the subject. The Court held that:

> "Abandonment of an easement or of a profit à prendre can only, we think, be treated as having taken place where the person entitled to it has demonstrated a fixed intention never at any time thereafter to assert the right himself or to attempt to transmit it to anyone else."[73]

A few days later the same judge referred obliquely to the burden of proof:

> "To establish abandonment of an easement the conduct of the dominant owner must, in our judgment, have been such as to make it clear that he had at the relevant time a firm intention that neither he nor any successor in title of his should thereafter make use of the easement."[74]

The two statements were to be brought together by Foster J. in another case where abandonment of rights of common were directly at issue, *Re Yateley Common, Hampshire* (1976)[75]:

> "A right of common is a legal right, and it is exceedingly difficult to prove that a person having such a legal right has abandoned it. Non-user, if the owner of the right has no reason to exercise it, requires something more than an immense length of time of non-user. It is essential that it be proved to the court's satisfaction that the owner of the legal right has abandoned the right—in the sense that he not only has not used it but intends never to use it again. The onus lies fairly and squarely on those who assert that the right has been abandoned."

(iii) The Commons Commissioners' hearings It seems that, **5.41** henceforth, it will be difficult to establish that there has been an abandonment of rights in the absence of an express declaration or other unequivocal act on the part of the owner. The weight given to non-user seems to have lessened since the nineteenth century. The Commons Commissioners have been bound in their dispute hearings by *Tehidy Minerals Ltd.* v. *Norman*. In most hearings non-user has figured more in providing evidence that a right never existed rather than that a right had been abandoned. Where the right could be established in the past considerable periods of non-user have been disregarded. In one hearing evidence was given of an Inclosure Award of 1783 which had allotted rights to take stone from a quarry to "proprietors, owners and occupiers of land and tenements." There was no evidence of user in living memory but tenements existed in the vicinity which at some time in the future might require the use of stone. The right to take stone was confirmed and the suggestion of abandonment rejected.[76] At another

---

[71] Above, n. 67, at 519, 962.
[72] [1971] 2 Q.B. 528.
[73] *ibid.* at 533.
[74] *Gotobed* v. *Pridmore* [1970] Bar Library Transcript No. 498A; (1971) 115 S.J. 78.
[75] [1977] 1 W.L.R. 840 at 845.
[76] *Re Land Northeast of Screetham Lane, Ashover* (1974) 8/D/16; 2 D.C.C. 109.

hearing an established right of pasturage was found which had been unused for 40 years for reasons of animal disease control. Non-user was held to be insufficient to infer abandonment.[77] Non-user coupled with near impossibility of user, on the other hand, was sufficient in a case where a right to take stone was established but the site had been filled in and grassed over.[78] Similarly, non-user, coupled with impossibility of user for 40 years occasioned by enclosure, was sufficient to warrant a finding of abandonment.[79]

5.42   Impossibility of user over part of the land will not necessarily lead to a conclusion that the right over that part has been abandoned. Where part of a common had been covered with tarmac leaving no pasturage it was held that rights had not ceased over that part if for no other reason than that livestock would travel over it to reach other parts of the common.[80]

(b) Implied release

5.43   An implied release is the situation which arises when an intention not to use rights again can be imputed to all the commoners so that all the rights over part or the whole of a common can be implied to have been released. This circumstance is directly analogous to the abandonment of an easement inasmuch as in both examples the servient land ceases to be burdened.

5.44   The most obvious example when an implied release will be considered is when land has been enclosed or otherwise rendered incapable of use as common land. As has been seen, in *Creach* v. *Wilmot* (1752) an enclosure for upwards of 40 years was insufficient to bar an action through an assize.[81] It cannot be, however, that such a period will be allowed in all circumstances. The absurdity of such a proposition can be seen in the example of a release, by tacit acceptance in an advertised parish meeting, of a proposal to use land as a cemetery.[82] It can hardly be that any commoner is free, under such circumstances, to maintain his right beyond, say, the first burial. Clearly in these circumstances factors other than, or perhaps in addition to, a lapse of time will be taken into account. What these factors might be may be apparent from analogous easement cases.

5.45   **(i) Analogous easement cases**   A leading case is *Moore* v. *Rawson* (1824).[83] The facts were that a house in which there had been ancient windows was demolished and another with a blank wall erected. Fourteen years later the adjoining owner erected a new building. Three years afterwards the plaintiff opened a new window on the site of the old one and claimed his ancient right of light. The court held that the plaintiff by pulling down the

---

[77] *Re Florden Common, Florden, Norfolk* (1974) 25/D/ 142–146, 2 D.C.C. 310.

[78] *Re Lannock Hill Chalk Pit, Weston, Herts* (1973) 16/D/11, 1 D.C.C. 235; the same confluence was required for a finding of abandonment in *Scrutton* v. *Stone*, above, n. 67.

[79] *Re Bridgend Common, Donnington* (1972) 22/D/1, 1 D.C.C. 10.

[80] *Re Flaxton Village Green and Common Land, Flaxton, Yorks (No.1)* (1975) 268/D/ 12, 3 D.C.C. 111, following *Peardon* v. *Underhill* (1850) 16 Q.B. 120 at 125, 117 E.R. 824 at 826, *per* Patteson J. (*obiter*).

[81] § 5.39.

[82] *cf.* § 5.33.

[83] (1824) 3 B. & C. 332, 107 E.R. 756.

original building lost his right to light unless he had evinced an intention to erect a similar one in its place, which in this case he had not. Littledale J. held that:

" . . . if a party does any act to shew that he abandons his right to the benefit of that light and air which he once had, he may lose his right in a much less period than twenty years."[84]

In *Stokoe* v. *Singers* (1857).[85] where there was some doubt, best left to a jury, as to whether the blocking up of ancient windows had induced another party to believe that a right to light had been abandoned, Campbell C.J. felt certain that an intention to abandon, communicated to the owner of the servient tenement and acted upon, would destroy the right but left in doubt the question as to whether communication alone was sufficient. The communication in this case was not direct but to be inferred from the acts of the dominant owners.   **5.46**

The principles involved can best be expressed by adopting the words of Lord Denman C.J. in *R.* v. *Chorley* (1848):[86]   **5.47**

" . . . we apprehend that, as an express release of the easement would destroy it at any moment, so the cesser of use coupled with any act clearly indicative of an intention to abandon the right would have the same effect without any reference to time . . . It is not so much the duration of the cesser as the nature of the act done by the grantee of the easement, or of the adverse act acquiesced in by him, and the intention in him which either the one or the other indicates, which are material for the consideration of the jury. The period of time is only material as one element from which the grantee's intention to retain or abandon may be inferred against him; and what period may be sufficient in any particular case must depend upon all the accompanying circumstances."

(ii) Application to commons cases   Applying the principle to rights of common it seems that, where owners of rights of common have stood by and watched the owner of the servient tenement act to his detriment, a quite short period of non-user may result in an implied release of rights. Although not expressly stated in these terms, the courts have refused to uphold rights of common in this type of situation. In a case in 1726, a building had been erected on Hampstead Heath without the consent of the homage: the court refused to order the removal of the building as "on laying of the first stone the commoners ought to have objected to it."[87] Similarly, in *Wimbledon and Putney Commons Conservators* v. *Nicol* (1894)[88] the court was not prepared to order the removal of buildings where the   **5.48**

---

[84] *Moore* v. *Rawson* (1824) 3 B. & C. 332, 107 E.R. 756 at 341, 760; but *cf. Ward* v. *Ward* (1852) 7 Ex. 838 at 839, 155 E.R. 1189 at 1190: mere non-user of easement, if more convenient way used, is not sufficient, *per* Alderson B.
[85] (1857) 8 El. & Bl. 31, 120 E.R. 12.
[86] (1848) 12 Q.B. 515 at 519, 116 E.R. 960 at 962.
[87] *Anon.* (1726) 6 Vin.Ab. 182; also *The East India Company* v. *Vincent* (1740) 2 Atk. 83, 26 E.R. 451, *per* Lord Hardwicke L.C.; *Harvey* v. *Reynolds* (1823) 1 Car. & P. 141, 171 E.R. 1137.
[88] (1894) 10 T.L.R. 247.

commoners had delayed in making an application for declaration as to rights and had stood by while construction work took place. In more recent times a discretionary power available to the court to order restoration, where works have been carried out on common land without the consent of a Minister, has been refused as an aggrieved party failed to make his grievance known but stood by and allowed the work to go ahead.[89]

5.49   **(iii) No application following acts of the servient owner**   From analogous easement cases, it seems that an implied release will not be inferred where the dominant owner has relied upon the acts or representations of the servient owner. Where an immemorial right to the overflow from a well into a pond was interrupted by the owner of the well diverting it into another course, and the dominant owners of the right relied upon it in excess of twenty years, it was not open to the servient owner to claim that the original course had been abandoned.[90] Similarly, where an established right of way was diverted to a more convenient route, by parol agreement, the owners of the servient land were not able to claim abandonment of the original route.[91]

(c) Abandonment by severance

5.50   If appurtenant rights are excepted on conveyance of the dominant land to which they are attached, in circumstances in which the law will not allow such a severance, the result is an extinguishment of the right. This might be viewed as a form of abandonment as the vendor has indicated his intention not to use the right again nor to transfer it to anyone else.[92] The subject is considered in more detail below.[93]

BY ALTERATION TO TENEMENTS AND ESTATES

5.51   This section is concerned with physical alteration to both servient and dominant tenements, alterations to the quality of the dominant estate and finally the effect of a transmission of tenancy on the death of a tenant of an agricultural holding.

Alterations to the servient tenement

5.52   On principle it seems inevitable that the exhaustion or destruction of the product with which a right of common is concerned will lead to the extinguishment of the right to take it. A distinction, however, must be made between the temporary exhaustion of a renewable product, such as herbage, and the permanent exhaustion of a non-renewable product, such as stone. The former will lead to a suspension of rights while the latter will result in

---

[89] *Symonds* v. *Malvern Hills D.C.* (1978) 248 E.G. 238, considered at § 8.32.
[90] *Hale* v. *Oldroyd* (1845) 14 M. & W. 789, 153 E.R. 694.
[91] *Lovell* v. *Smith* (1857) 3 C.B.(N.S.) 120, 140 E.R. 685.
[92] The requirements for abandonment: see § 5.40.
[93] At § 6.39.

extinguishment. A second distinction may be found as between classes of rights. A right of grazing may extend over the whole of a common, whether grazing is possible over all the land or not, whereas the right to take a non-renewable product may extend only to the areas where it can be taken

.(a) Rights to renewable products

Activities such as turf removal, loam removal, gravel extraction, or brick   **5.53** clay digging which result in the destruction of pasture merely suspend use pending re-growth of the grass and the rights to graze are not prejudiced.[94] Nor is a right of pasture necessarily extinguished where destruction of the herbage is permanent, as might occur in the cases of, say, sea-deposited shingle, or even the application of tarmac, over the surface: "common of pasture in a waste extends to every spot on which there is food for the cattle, and also to every spot across which the cattle may wander in search of food, though there be none on the spot itself . . . "[95] This may apply even in the case of building operations. In a case where rights were proved to exist over land which had been built upon, Lord Hatherley L.C. said:

> "I do not think . . . that I ought to say that any portion of these rights which are proved by the evidence before me to have been granted, have been destroyed by the circumstance of the buildings having been erected."[96]

However, destruction accompanied by non-user of the land may result in the presumption that the right has been abandoned and, as has been shewn, inactivity in pursuing rights may lead to a presumption of implied release of rights.[97] The total and permanent destruction of all the products which will occur if the land is completely developed must surely lead to an extinguishment of rights if for no other reason than the unrealistic nature of a right to take something which does not exist. There does not, however, seem to be any direct authority on the subject.

A total removal of a particular product, so that there is no immediate pros-   **5.54** pect of taking a right of common, will not necessarily result in an extinguishment for it has been held that a right, for instance, to future estovers may be maintained.[98]

(b) Rights to non-renewable products

If the particular product is non-renewable, such as stone, sand, gravel or   **5.55** peat, it seems clear that the exhaustion of the subject matter will extinguish a right to take it as there can be no right to take something which does not

---

[94] cf. *Hall* v. *Byron* (1877) 4 Ch.D. 667 at 675, *per* Hall V.-C.

[95] *Peardon* v. *Underhill* (1850) 16 Q.B. 120 at 125, 117 E.R. 824 at 826, *per* Patterson J. (obiter); cf. *Farmer* v. *Hunt* (1611) Yelv. 201, 80 E.R. 132; *Scrutton* v. *Stone* (1893) 9 T.L.R. 478 (impossibility of user coupled with "practically no-user" to infer abandonment).

[96] *Warrick* v. *Queens College, Oxford* (1871) L.R. 6 Ch.App. 716 at 731, *per* Lord Hatherley L.C.

[97] § 5.43.

[98] *Cowper* v. *Andrews* (1612) Hob. 39 at 43, 80 E.R. 189 at 193, *per* Hobart L.C.J.; cf. *Stanley* v. *White* (1811) 14 East. 332 at 339, 104 E.R. 630 at 632, *per* Ellenborough C.J. (right to future trees).

exist.[99] In one case the exhaustion of a right to take peat was accompanied by a right for the owner to enclose and convert into severalty with a consequent extinguishment of all rights of common over the land.[1] The owners had been in the habit of allotting "moss dales," for digging peat, to the owners and occupiers of ancient messuages and after removal of the peat the land was, by custom, "freed from all common pasture and turbary thereon." This example was dependent upon proof of the custom and has no general application.

5.56 The difficulty associated with the exhaustion of non-renewable products is that in the case of many they have been taken only at a particular site which becomes exhausted. It may be unclear whether a right of common extends only to that site or to any part of the common land where the product can be found to occur. The burden of proof in this circumstance can be discerned from the case of *Maxwell* v. *Martin* (1830),[2] where there was no evidence one way or the other as to the extent of rights to take stone on a common. There was dispute about the rights to take stone from a certain unseparated part of the common. There might have been a general right to dig stone over the whole of the common or, a grant to dig stone over the whole with the exception of the part in question. The court held that "if the original grant cannot be produced and the evidence as to the prescriptive rights over the part [called the Lord's Leys] hangs in even scales . . . the burden of making the scale preponderate is cast upon the claimant."[3] A general right, it seems, cannot be established over land where the particular product never has been found or, could ever be expected to be found.[4]

5.57 Today it seems that rights to take non-renewable products which have been registered under the C.R.A. 1965 are maintainable over the sites from which extraction was occurring at the time of registration and, upon exhaustion at those sites, may only be maintainable elsewhere if the claimant is in a position to establish a general right.

Alterations to the dominant tenement

5.58 Rights appurtenant to a dominant tenement are granted for the benefit of that tenement and it might be considered self-evident that, once the tenement can no longer take advantage of the benefit, the right is extinguished. There is some case law authority to this effect in respect of houses but almost none in relation to land. To some extent, therefore, it is necessary to deduce principle rather than point to authoritative sources. It is clear that

[99] There does not seem to be an example of exhaustion in case reports. Many texts cite the *Dean and Chapter of Ely* v. *Warren* (1741) 2 Atk. 189, 26 E.R. 518, but the case is concerned with the mistaken belief of occupiers in the Fens that their rights of turbary had survived the inclosure and conversion into severalty of much of the land. Rights were extinguished but by inclosure not exhaustion and the use of turf as the favourite fuel in the Isle of Ely lasted well into the 19th century.

[1] *Clarkson* v. *Woodhouse* (1782) 5 T.R. 412, n. (a); 101 E.R. 231.

[2] (1830) 6 Bing. 522, 130 E.R. 1382.

[3] *ibid. per* Tindal C.J. at 526, 1383.

[4] *Peardon* v. *Underhill* (1850), above, n. 95, at 126, 826, *per* Erle J.

where the dominant tenement is land, and is altered in extent by division, an apportionment of rights results.[5] On the other hand, there is also authority that where the dominant tenement is a house or other building no apportionment on division of any land contained in the holding is possible.

(a) Where the dominant tenement is a building

It has been said that "an ancient right of turbary can only exist as being a right in respect of an ancient dwelling house or building, or, at the most, for the house which supplies the place of that house."[6] In this context the right of estovers of fire-bote and house-bote may be considered in all respects subject to the same rules as turbary, *i.e.* they are strictly annexed to a particular house or other building of ancient origin. The quantity of the right is limited to the needs of the original building and cannot be increased:

5.59

> "If a man have estovers to such a house, and he enlargeth his house, or buildeth more houses or chimneys, the estovers remain to all the houses and chimneys which were there before, and not to those added or new builded, as it was adjudged."[7]

It does not follow that it has to be the original edifice for the right to continue for:

> "if an antient cottage which had common [for estovers] be fallen down, and another cottage is erected in the place where the old cottage stood; this is no new cottage, but it may claim common as antient cottage by prescription."[8]

Nor will substantial alteration affect the original right:

> "so if a man has estovers either by grant or prescription to his house, although he alters the rooms and chambers of this house, as to make a parlour where it was the hall, or the hall where the parlour was . . . and although he builds new chimney, or makes a new addition to his old house, by that he shall not lose his prescription, but he cannot employ or spend any of his estovers in the new chimneys, or in the part newly added."[9]

The principle is clearly that the right survives changes on the original site but the quantum is limited to the original amount. What was less clear was whether the right could be transferred to a new site.

On one occasion arguments on the point were put by the Attorney-General but the court found it unnecessary to decide them.[10] The point was further considered in a case concerned with a right of turbary and fuel wood in the

5.60

---

[5] For apportionment, see § 6.47.

[6] *Warrick* v. *Queens College, Oxford* (1871) 6 Ch. App. 716 at 730, *per* Lord Hatherley L.C.

[7] *Brown* v. *Tucker* (1610) 4 Leon. 241, 74 E.R. 847.

[8] *Bryers* v. *Lake* (1655) Style 446, 82 E.R. 850; *Costard and Wingfield's Case* (1588) 2 Leon. 44, 74 E.R. 344.

[9] *Luttrel's Case* (1601) 4 Co.Rep. 86a at 87a, 76 E.R. 1065 at 1067.

[10] *Arlett* v. *Ellis* (1829) 9 B. & C. 671, 109 E.R. 249: the original house had been destroyed but the claim was to the right not the use of the turbary and it was, therefore, unnecessary to decide whether the right had been annexed to a new house.

New Forest.[11] Rights were proved in respect of an ancient messuage consisting of a dwelling house and a little over an acre of land. The dwelling was dilapidated and unoccupied from 1882. It was pulled down in 1905 and another was erected within the curtilage of the messuage but away from the original site. After a review of all the authorities Hamilton J. concluded:

> "However the right might be expressed in the grant, I think it is reasonable to assume that the grant should be read in favour of the grantee of a right appurtenant to a house then existing or to a new house in continuance of the same. What continuity may be is another matter; that is a question of fact . . . It is enough if the right is to be exercised therein in continuance of the old right, as this was certainly intended to be, and if there be no circumstances to inflict any additional burthen or injustice upon the lands over which the right is enjoyed."[12]

5.61 If the old tenement is out of use there is no right to divert the estovers to an alternative tenement[13] nor is there any authority that they may be sold.[14] The rights are suspended until a new building is erected,[15] unless an intention to abandon can be inferred in which case the right will be extinguished.

(b) Where the dominant tenement is land

5.62 The most extensive right attached to land is pasturage and the most usual condition for grazing animals is that they shall be levant and couchant on the dominant tenement. In principle, therefore, the animals should be kept on, and fed from, the dominant land. Nevertheless, it is not necessary that the animals should actually be fed from the produce of the land and a changed use rendering the land incapable of currently providing winter food will not necessarily suspend or extinguish a right of pasturage. In *Carr* v. *Lambert* (1866)[16] no livestock were maintained in the winter on the produce of the land as the majority of the land had been planted to an orchard some 50 years previously. Willes J. gave the judgment of the court, which held that a changed use of the land is not sufficient to extinguish or suspend the right providing the tenement is still in such a state that it might easily be turned to the purpose of feeding cattle. Some limitations on the principle in this case may be noticed: the cattle were in fact grazed in the orchard, housed on the land[17] and, in the words of Willes J., the tenement "had land in a state in which it might have been laid down for pasture, or for meadow, or cultivated so as to produce artificial plants and roots for the support of cattle."[18]

---

[11] *Att.-Gen.* v. *Reynolds* [1911] 2 K.B. 888.

[12] *ibid.* at 934.

[13] *Per* Hamilton J. at 907. See also § 6.34.

[14] *Earl of Pembroke's Case* (1636) Clayton 47, cited at § 3.70; *Valentine* v. *Penny* (1605) Noy 145, 74 E.R. 1107 approved in *Lord Chesterfield* v. *Harris* [1908] 2 Ch.397 at 421–422, *per* Buckley L.J.

[15] *Cowper* v. *Andrews* (1612) Hob. 39 at 40, 80 E.R. 189 at 190 *per* Hobart L.C.J.

[16] (1866) L.R. 1 Ex. 168.

[17] Earlier proceedings, reported at (1865) 3 H. & C. 499, 159 E.R. 626: see the statement of proven facts.

[18] At L.R.1 Ex. 175.

In the light of these factors, it may be unwise to assume that the principle of   5.63
a sufficiency of land to convert to winter fodder being adequate to protect a
right from extinguishment will necessarily apply in other circumstances
such as the planting of land to commercial forestry.

In the same case a suggestion was made that a total and permanent change   5.64
in the use of the land would serve to extinguish rights. The examples given
were where the land is totally built over or turned into a reservoir. The
court, in giving a considered decision, did not dismiss the suggestion but
found it unnecessary to decide on the particular facts.[19] However, a right
granted for the benefit of land, as is any appurtenant right, can probably
never survive the incapability of the land to use that benefit and, consequently, a permanent change of use extinguishes rights. There is certainly
an assumption in other cases that when rights are no longer needed the use
of the land reverts to the lord.[20]

Some of the more difficult problems associated with alterations in the   5.65
dominant tenement are concerned with division of the tenement and
apportionment of rights particularly where the division is into very small
units. In this context it is appropriate to consider the comment of Lord
Kenyon C.J. in *Scholes* v. *Hargreaves* (1792),[21] in dismissing a claim to
rights to graze sheep from a shop: "I have always understood that levancy
and couchancy must be proved by shewing that the party claiming the right
was in possession of some land, whereon the cattle might be levant and couchant."

Alterations to the dominant estate

(a) Destruction of the estate

The destruction or termination of the dominant estate is sometimes given   5.66
as a ground for the extinguishment of rights of common, with *Bruster's
Case* (1600)[22] cited as an example. The case was concerned with the dissolution of church estates under statute. In similar circumstances today Parliament can be expected to make provision for all property to be vested[23] and,
in the case of involuntary dissolution of a corporation, statute provides for
property to be vested in the Crown or Duchy of Cornwall as *bona vacan-
tia.*[24] As a method of extinguishment, destruction of the estate may now be
considered obsolete.

---

[19] See at 171, 173 and 175
[20] *Arlett* v. *Ellis* (1827) 7 B. & C. 346 at 369, 108 E.R. 752 at 761, *per* Bayley J. See also
    § 6.14.
[21] (1792) 5 T.R. 46 at 47, 101 E.R. 26 at 27.
[22] (1600) cited at 2 Ro.Rep.251, 81 E.R. 780.
[23] *e.g.* Welsh Church Act 1914.
[24] Companies Act 1985, ss.652, 654.

(b) Copyhold enfranchisement

5.67   As copyhold tenure was abolished in the 1925 property legislation any extinguishment of rights which may have occurred upon enfranchisement now only has relevance in the settlement of those disputes still to be resolved before the Commons Commissioners. Where enfranchisement occurred under statutory authority the customary rights continued without change[25]:

> " . . . nothing herein contained shall operate to deprive any tenant of any commonable right to which he may be entitled in respect of such lands [enfranchised lands], but such right shall continue attached thereto notwithstanding the same shall become freehold."

5.68   Where enfranchisement took place outside the statutory provisions the rule at law was that rights were extinguished. The reason was "for the common first used was gained by custom and annexed to the customary estate, and is lost with it, the common not being of its proper nature incident to the copyhold estate but a collateral interest gained by usage."[26] Clear words such as *cum pertinentiis* indicating a new grant were required for the rights to continue.[27]

5.69   There were some indications that the rule at law would not be followed by the Court of Chancery. In *Styant* v. *Staker* (1691)[28] a person was permanently restrained by injunction from taking advantage of the rule so that rights were created in equity. It seems that equity would not allow a person to lose any rights he had before, enfranchisement being intended to provide the freehold in addition. In any event, extinguishment could not apply to rights of common exercisable over land outside the manor of which the copyhold estate was held.[29]

5.70   The matter has been considered by the Commons Commissioners only infrequently. In *Re Yateley Common* (1975)[30] it was held that upon a voluntary enfranchisement, without clear words of grant, rights in equity arose and were converted into rights at law by the transitional provisions contained in the L.P.A. 1925. Further, it was held that the rights of common required to be registered under the C.R.A. 1965 included rights which subsist in equity.

---

[25] Enfranchisement of Copyholds Act 1841, s.81; Copyhold Act 1894, s.22; Law of Property Act 1922, Sched. 12, para. 4.

[26] *Massam* v. *Hunter* (1610) Yelv. 189, 80 E.R. 125, cited with approval in *Baring* v. *Abingdon* [1892] 2 Ch. 374 at 383, *per* Stirling J.; *Lee* v. *Edwards* (1621) 1 Brownl. & Golds. 173, 123 E.R. 736; *Darson* v. *Hunter* (1610) Noy 136, 74 E.R. 1099.

[27] *Baring* v. *Abingdon*, above, n. 26, at 390, *per* Stirling J., approving *Gale's Easements* (3rd ed., 1862), p. 77.

[28] (1691) 2 Vern. 250, 23 E.R. 761.

[29] *Field* v. *Boothsby* (1658) 2 Sid. 81, 82 E.R. 1269; *Crowder* v. *Oldfield* (1706) 6 Mod. 19, 87 E.R. 783; *Barwick* v. *Matthews* (1814) 5 Taunt. 365, 128 E.R. 730.

[30] (1975) 214/D/9–13, 3 D.C.C. 153 at 166 *et seq.*; affirmed on appeal, [1977] 1 W.L.R. 840 at 850, *per* Foster J.: sufficient to show that the deed did not show an intention to terminate pre-existing rights.

(c) Leasehold enfranchisement

It is a general rule that, providing there are general words indicating the **5.71** intention in the document of conveyance, the purchase of of a freehold reversion by a lessee includes rights of common which had been enjoyed with the lease.[31]

Provisions for statutory enfranchisement of leasehold tenure are contained **5.72** in the Leasehold Reform Act 1967.[32] Few tenements with rights of common will be affected by its provisions as houses which are occupied with land and those comprised in agricultural holdings are excluded by the Act.[33] Some registered rights, however, particularly for estovers and turbary, are annexed simply to a house. When this is the case it seems that section 10 of the Leasehold Reform Act 1967 will have effect "to grant all such easements and rights over other property, so far as the landlord is capable of granting them, as are necessary to secure to the tenant as nearly as may be the same rights as at the relevant time were available to him under or by virtue of the tenancy . . . "

(d) The deceased agricultural tenant

In a substantial number of cases certain successors to deceased tenants of **5.73** agricultural holdings have a right to require the contract of tenancy to be transferred to them.[34] There seems little doubt that, where rights of common are appurtenant to the land of the agricultural holding in question, they will pass automatically upon the transfer of the contract.

The situation may not be so straightforward in the case of stints or gaits **5.74** which are in the nature of rights of common in gross. The Agricultural Holdings Act 1986 refers to a contract of tenancy of an agricultural holding[35] which means the aggregate of the land comprised in a contract of agricultural tenancy.[36] If the stint or other right is merely an additional right to graze land, it cannot be properly described as land comprised in a contract of tenancy and may be a separate hereditament. It seems, therefore, that a successful applicant for the right to succession to an agricultural tenancy will not, necessarily, also succeed to the stints. In one hearing before an Agricultural Land Tribunal[37] a holding had been defined by reference to acreage and named fields. The Tribunal held that the stints licensed to the deceased tenant did not form part of the agricultural holding. However, the matter did not end there as the schedule to the fields in the contract also included express reference to the licensed stints. The Tribunal held that this had the effect of incorporating the rights into the contract to which the applicant for the tenancy of the land was entitled to succeed. It follows that stinted rights which have not been incorporated into a tenancy agreement, and *a fortiori*

---

[31] *Doidge* v. *Carpenter* (1817) 6 M. & S. 47, 105 E.R. 1160; affirmed in *Baring* v. *Abingdon* (1892), above, n. 26; and *cf.* §§ 4.46 *et seq.* for implied grants.
[32] As subsequently amended.
[33] s.1.
[34] Agricultural Holdings Act 1986, Pt. IV.
[35] *ibid.* ss. 34, 35.
[36] *ibid.* s.1.
[37] *Scott* v. *Bolton* [1982] A.L.T./2/881.

any held under a separate contract, will revert to the owner of the rights irrespective of whether there is a successful application for succession to the tenancy of an agricultural holding.

BY STATUTE

5.75 Extinguishment of rights by statutory enactment was an important and widespread procedure until the beginning of the present century. The process of inclosure of common fields and wastes into land held in severalty resulted in millions of acres being taken out of common use. Inclosure is now little more than an historical curiosity and extinguishment by statute is largely confined to the occasions when there is a perceived public need to change the use of the land. There is a steady and continuing requirement for parcels, large and small, to be converted to other uses but in terms of extinguishment of rights the effect is somewhat mollified by incentives directed towards an exchange of land so that the taken land is replaced by other land which is subject to rights.

5.76 Temporary extinguishment, or suspension, for short or longer periods under statutory authority, or by agreement, is also possible, again in circumstances where there is a local or national need for the land to be diverted to a different use. The most notable national example of temporary use is in connection with opencast coal mining, and it is not altogether unknown to find common land used for such purposes as local authority tipping.

5.77 Where rights are extinguished by statute, whether permanently or temporarily, there is usually provision for compensation to be made available. There are statutory provisions to assist disbursement of moneys received as the result of extinguishment but none where the payment is for suspension of rights.

General Inclosure Acts

5.78 Between 1700 and 1836 it has been estimated that there were about 4,000 private inclosure Acts.[38] Apart from extinguishment of rights the Acts also had the function of creating new forms of rights. Some of these still affect the common lands today. For example, a number of the Acts established stinted or regulated pastures each with its own particular set of rules.

5.79 The final instrument intended to facilitate general inclosure of the remaining wastes and common fields was the Inclosure Act 1845. Under its provisions somewhere in the order of half a million acres were inclosed through the means of nearly 1,000 awards.[39] This was in spite of a reduction in the powers of the Inclosure Commissioners in 1852 and a complete

---

[38] Royal Commission Report, Minutes of Evidence, Vol.1, Appendix 1, p. 13, para. 2.
[39] See Table 1 at § 1.08.

change of emphasis occasioned by the Commons Act 1876. The general scheme of the Act was for appointed Commissioners to be empowered to approve schemes, subject to the approval of Parliament of an annual report, without the necessity of an individual Act for each inclosure.

The Inclosure Act 1845, as amended by subsequent Acts, was applied to a wide range of lands used in common under the definition of "land subject to be inclosed," including wastes and most types of common fields and stinted pastures. Waste lands and land in the vicinity of London and other towns could not be inclosed without the direction of Parliament.[40] Where two-thirds of the interests in the land agreed to the planned inclosure, and the land was outside the classes requiring the direction of Parliament, the Commissioners were empowered to proceed directly.[41] Where the direction of Parliament was required the Commissioners certified in their next annual report that it was expedient to carry out the proposed scheme, and the required direction was given through an annual Inclosure Act.[42] The power of the Commissioners to proceed without direction was repealed in 1852.[43]

5.80

The Commons Act 1876 provided a change in emphasis which was intended to, and in fact did, effectively prevent any further major inclosure. Henceforth "inclosure in severalty as opposed to regulation of commons should not be hereinafter made unless it can be proved to the satisfaction of the said Commissioners and of Parliament that such inclosure will be of benefit to the neighbourhood as well as to private interests, and to those who are legally interested in any such commons."[44] In the words of the Ministry of Agriculture, Fisheries and Food evidence to the Royal Commission "it is easy to see how regulation can be of benefit to the neighbourhood as well as to the private interests but more difficult in respect of inclosure."[45] So difficult was it that, in 1913, a Select Committee of the House of Commons commented:

5.81

> "Except as to inclosure of common field land which is now of rare occurrence, inclosure under the Inclosure Act 1845, and amending Acts, including the Commons Act of 1876, may be said to be practically obsolete."[46]

In spite of the Inclosure Act 1845 and its amending Acts still being on the statute book, the process of inclosure as a means of extinguishment of rights of common inevitably seems even more obsolete today than it did in 1913. Unused since the first few years of the century there must be great doubt as to whether the legislation will ever be used again to effect inclosure.

---

[40] Inclosure Act 1845, ss.12, 14.

[41] *ibid.* s.27.

[42] *e.g.* Local and Personal Inclosures Act 1846.

[43] Inclosure Act 1852, s.1.

[44] Commons Act 1876, preamble.

[45] Royal Commission Report, Minutes of Evidence, Vol. 1, Appendix 1, p. 19.

[46] Report of a Select Committee, *Commons (Inclosure and Regulation)* (H.M.S.O., 1913), p. v, para. 8.

Metropolitan Commons and Commons Acts

(a) Metropolitan Commons Acts 1866–1878[47]

5.82 The Acts provide for regulation of commons in the Metropolitan Police District. Inclosure of any such common is effectively prohibited by providing that the Inclosure Commissioners shall not entertain an application for the inclosure of a metropolitan common, or any part thereof.[48] The Acts may still, it seems, be used as instruments for the extinguishment of rights of common for it is also provided that "no estate, interest, or right of a profitable or beneficial nature in, over, or affecting a common shall, except with the consent of the person entitled thereto, be taken away or injuriously affected by any scheme, without compensation being made or provided for the same."[49] Schemes of regulation under these Acts are effected through a Metropolitan Commons Supplemental Act for each scheme. Reference to the particular Act is necessary to discover the powers granted in respect of any individual common.

(b) Commons Act 1876[50]

5.83 A scheme for the regulation of a common, effected through a provisional order confirmation Act, may include an "adjustment of rights." By adjustment is meant the determination of persons entitled to rights of common, the mode and places of taking the rights and, in certain circumstances, the restriction, modification or abolition of rights.[51] Thus, the Commons Act 1876 may have the effect of extinguishing rights. It should perhaps be noticed that a draft provisional order shall not be certified as expedient unless two-thirds in value of the interests in the common consent,[52] and in all cases, where rights are affected, monetary compensation is available.[53]

(c) Commons Act 1899[54]

5.84 Under this Act a district council is empowered to adopt a model management scheme prescribed in Regulations. The Act contains provision for compensation if rights are taken away or injuriously affected.[55] There is, therefore, a possibility under the Act of extinguishing rights. However, the combined effects of sections 1, 2 and 15 of the Commons Act 1899 is that a scheme of regulation may only be adopted in the form prescribed by Regulations. The current Regulations provide that "nothing in this Scheme or any byelaw made under it shall . . . prejudice or affect any right of the commoners in or over the common."[56] It seems that the potential for extinguishment, inherent in the Act, is at present negatived by the form of the current Regulations.

---

[47] See further § 12.34.
[48] Metropolitan Commons Act 1866, s.5.
[49] *ibid.* s.15.
[50] See further § 12.43.
[51] s.4.
[52] s.12(5).
[53] s.4(2)–(4).
[54] See further § 12.64.
[55] s.6.
[56] Commons (Schemes) Regulations 1982 (S.I. 1982 No. 209), para. 10.

Compulsory Purchase

Arguably the most important form of inclosure, accompanied by a statutory   **5.85**
extinguishment of rights, is where land is acquired compulsorily for public
development purposes. A substantial number of statutory bodies[57] and local
authorities[58] have powers of compulsory purchase of land, including common land, under the provisions contained in the Acquisition of Land Act
1981. Provisions for compensation contained in the Compulsory Purchase
Act 1965 apply in such cases. In addition a considerable number of private
and public Acts, authorising compulsory purchase of land, incorporated the
provisions of the Land Clauses Consolidation Act 1845 which includes
methods of compensation broadly the same as those contained in the Act of
1965. Most current purchases, however, will now fall under the provisions
in the Acts of 1965 and 1981.

The first provision affecting the compulsory purchase of common land to be   **5.86**
noticed is section 19 of the Acquisition of Land Act 1981. It provides that
where a compulsory purchase order authorises the purchase of any land
forming part of a common,[59] open space or fuel garden allotment the order
shall be subject to special parliamentary procedure[60] unless it is preceded by
a certificate given by the Secretary of State. Before giving such a certificate
the Secretary of State must be satisfied:

"(a) that there has been or will be given in exchange for such land, other
land, not being less in area and being equally advantageous to the
persons, if any, entitled to rights of common or other rights, and to
the public, and that the land given in exchange has been or will be
vested in the persons in whom the land purchased was vested, and
subject to the like rights, trusts and incidents as attach to the land
purchased, or
(b) that the land does not exceed 250 square yards in extent or is
required for the widening or drainage of an existing highway or
partly for the widening and partly for the drainage of such a highway and that the giving in exchange of other land is unnecessary,
whether in the interests of the persons, if any, entitled to rights of
common or other rights or in the interests of the public . . ."[61]

If it is proposed to issue a certificate, a public notice of intention to do so has
to be given affording an opportunity for all persons interested to make representations. A public enquiry may be held if it seems expedient to do so.[62]

---

[57] Acquisition of Land Act 1981, Sched. 4.
[58] Town and Country Planning Act 1971, s.112.
[59] Acquisition of Land Act 1981, s.19(4): common land defined as land subject to be
inclosed. It is not necessarily the case that all statutory common land will fall
under the provisions. The same procedures also apply when any local authority
proposes to "appropriate" land forming part of a common, open space, fuel or field
garden which is for the time being held by them: Town and Country Planning Act
1971, s.121.
[60] Under the Statutory Orders (Special Procedure) Acts 1945 and 1965.
[61] s.19(1).
[62] s.19(2).

5.87 The effect of section 19 is to encourage an exchange of land so that while rights are extinguished over the taken land, new and equivalent rights are created over the substituted land. The substituted land is registrable as new common land where the taken land is registered under the C.R.A. 1965.[63] Excepting the small acquisitions of land for highway purposes, the taking of common land by compulsory purchase requires either an exchange of land or the special parliamentary procedure.

5.88 The Compulsory Purchase Act 1965 is applied to any compulsory purchase to which Part II (purchase by local and other authorities) or Schedule 1 (purchases by Ministers) to the Acquisition of Land Act 1981 applies. Section 21 applies Schedule 4 to the Act (compensation procedures) to all compulsory purchases of common land and provides that the procedures of the Act are subject to section 22 of the Commons Act 1899.[64] Section 22 makes any grant or inclosure of common land subject to the consent of a Secretary of State unless the order is specially authorised by an Act of Parliament or, the order is made to or by a government department. Thus, any order proposed by a local or other authority is subject to a section 22 consent and in this case the Secretary of State is required to take into account the benefit of the neighbourhood.

5.89 The number of occasions when a compulsory purchase order has been made for common land is clearly substantial. The Department of the Environment reports 469 applications decided under section 19 of the Acquisition of Land Act 1981 (or its predecessor) and 219 under section 22 of the Commons Act 1899 between 1956 and 1986. The figures for Wales for the period 1964–1986 are 17 and 20 respectively.[65]

Compensation for extinguishment

5.90 The procedure for the acquisition of common land and "commonable and other rights" is contained in Schedule 4 to the Compulsory Purchase Act 1965. Common land is not defined but it is clear that the provisions in the Schedule have application whether the land is owned by a person other than the rights holders or is vested in the persons exercising the rights. Commonable rights, it has been suggested, is a term wide enough to encompass not only rights of common but also analogous rights exercised in common.[66] There are separate provisions where land is vested in a person other than the rights holders,[67] and secondly where land and rights are owned by the same persons.[68] In the former event the acquiring authority treats separately with the owner of the land and the owners of commonable rights and the purchase of the land does not, in itself, extinguish rights. In the latter circum-

---

[63] For new statutory common land, see §§ 2.59, 2.63.
[64] For which see § 7.58; in Wales it should be noted that both compulsory and voluntary acquisitions by the Land Authority for Wales are subject to the s.22 procedure: Local Government Planning and Land Act 1980, Sched. 20, Pt. II.
[65] *cf.* Appendix 9.
[66] *cf.* § 1.44.
[67] Sched. 4, para. 1.
[68] *ibid.* para. 3.

stance ownership and rights are dealt with in only one negotiation following the procedure described hereafter applicable to the extinguishment of rights.

The Schedule empowers an acquiring authority to convene a meeting of the **5.91** persons entitled to commonable rights over the land subject to the purchase order. The meeting may appoint a committee with power to bind minorities, negotiate and receive the agreed compensation.[69] In the event of failure to establish a committee, the authority may proceed to acquire and extinguish rights by deed poll with compensation paid into court.[70] When the compensation is paid to a committee the money shall be apportioned among the several parties interested.[71] There are statutory provisions which may be invoked by the committee in dealing with the compensation moneys and the Act saves these provisions.[72]

It seems that it is not essential for the formation of the committee of com- **5.92** moners that the acquiring authority should call a meeting of the persons interested. They may deal with any authorised committee of commoners. In *Bee* v. *Stafford and Uttoxeter Railway* (1875)[73] an acquiring company agreed compensation with a committee of rights owners and then refused to proceed on the basis that the formalities contained in the Land Clauses Consolidation Act 1845[74] had not been complied with. Hall V.-C. held that the sections of the Act were "not imperative so as to exclude agreements entered into otherwise than mentioned in those sections."

Following the appointment of a committee by those persons prima facie **5.93** entitled to attend a meeting,[75] or establishing that a committee is authorised to act, the acquiring authority treats with the committee to establish a global sum appropriate for the extinction of commonable and other rights. Even if the authority has acquired the land, until compensation has been paid to the committee, any rights holder may maintain an action for disturbance of his rights if the authority enters the land.[76] On payment or tender to the committee of the compensation due, the authority may execute a deed poll vesting the land in themselves free of all rights.[77] The authority is under no duty to see to the apportionment of the compensation nor is it liable for non-application or misapplication of the compensation.[78]

The committee is required to apportion the moneys among the persons **5.94** entitled and, together with the Secretary of State if one of the statutes

[69] Compulsory Purchase Act 1965, Sched. 4, paras. 4, 5.
[70] *ibid.* paras. 6, 7.
[71] *ibid.* para. 5(3).
[72] Compulsory Purchase Act 1965, s.21(2)(a). See §§ 5.95–5.98.
[73] (1875) 23 W.R. 868.
[74] ss.99–107 (substantially re-enacted in the Compulsory Purchase Act 1965, Sched. 4).
[75] *Salmon* v. *Edwards* [1910] 1 Ch. 552. It seems that the Secretary of State, if asked to act under the statutory provisions in the Inclosure Acts 1852 and 1854 and the Commonable Rights Compensation Act 1882, need not inquire into the appointment or constitution of the committee if there is a *de facto* committee.
[76] *Stoneham* v. *L.B. & S.C. Railway* (1871) L.R. 7 Q.B. 1.
[77] Compulsory Purchase Act 1965, s.9(3), Sched. 4, para. 7(1),(2).
[78] *ibid.* Sched. 4, para. 5(3).

referred to below is invoked, is a competent tribunal to determine the apportionment.[79] It should be noted that the costs of apportionment, including those of the Secretary of State, if any, are a charge on the global compensation amount.[80]

(a) Inclosure Act 1852, s.22

5.95 Where the committee is of the opinion that the provisions for apportionment of the compensation cannot be carried into effect, section 22 of the Inclosure Act 1852 may be invoked. Under its provisions the committee may request the Secretary of State to, and he may, call a meeting of the persons interested in the compensation moneys to appoint trustees, and to authorise the moneys to be invested. The interest received on the invested money may be applied as the Secretary of State may approve. In the absence of agreement he may make an order under seal as seems to him appropriate. The effect of the section is to remove from the committee the requirement to apportion the money immediately. It may also be appropriate to invoke the section in the event that compensation is apportionable among a fluctuating body of persons such as freemen of a borough.[81]

(b) Inclosure Act 1854, ss.15–20

5.96 Alternatively, where the committee is of the opinion that the provisions for apportionment under the Act authorising payment cannot be carried out satisfactorily, a majority of the committee may apply to the Secretary of State to call a meeting of persons interested to determine whether or not the compensation money shall be apportioned under provisions contained in the Inclosure Act 1854.[82] If the majority in number and interest of such persons shall resolve that the compensation money be apportioned, the money shall be paid into an account with the Bank of England forthwith and the committee are absolutely discharged from all liability in respect of the money.[83]

5.97 As soon as the money is paid into the Bank the Secretary of State shall proceed to determine the rights and interests, and the value of the apportionment thereof, making an award under seal which shall be binding on all the parties.[84] Where any of the parties entitled are only entitled to a limited interest, and the sum payable exceeds £20, it shall be lawful for them, or the

---

[79] *Richards v. De Winton* [1901] 2 Ch. 566; *Salmon v. Edwards*, above, n. 75; *Evans v. Merthyr Tydfil U.D.C.* [1898] 1 Ch. 241. Nevertheless, the High Court has power to make an order as it thinks fit in respect of money paid into court: Compulsory Purchase Act 1965, Sched. 4, para. 3, and has accepted jurisdiction where no objection has been raised: *Nash v. Coombs* (1868) L.R. 6 Eq. 51; *Austin v. Amherst* (1877) 7 Ch.D. 689; *Weatherley v. Layton* [1892] W.N. 165; *Att.-Gen. v. Meyrick* [1893] A.C. 1.

[80] Inclosure Act 1852, s.22; Inclosure Act 1854, s.18; Commonable Rights Compensation Act 1882, s.2(1).

[81] *Nash v. Coombs*, above, n. 79; for a precedent for the use of this section see The Great Forest of Brecknock (Application of Compensation) Order 1952 (not published) made under the seal of the Minister of Agriculture and Fisheries.

[82] s.15; for a precedent for an application see 7 Forms and Precedents (4th ed.) 110.

[83] s.16.

[84] s.17.

Secretary of State to direct that the money is paid to trustees acting under a will, conveyance or settlement or, where there are none, to trustees appointed by the Secretary of State.[85] If the sum is under £20 and the person entitled is under any disability, it may be paid directly to a guardian, committee or husband of such person.[86]

(c) Commonable Rights Compensation Act 1882

This Act makes provision "for the better application of moneys paid by way of compensation."[87] A committee in receipt of compensation money may apply to the Secretary of State to call a meeeting of the interested parties at which a majority in number and interest may resolve to lay the money out on one or more of the following alternatives:

   (i) improvement of the remaining common land;
   (ii) in defraying expenses incurred in statutory, or other, schemes of regulation, management or preservation of the remaining land;
  (iii) in defraying expenses of legal proceedings for the protection of land or other rights over it;
  (iv) in the purchase of additional land to be used as common land; or
   (v) in the purchase of land to be used as a recreation ground for the neighbourhood.[88]

5.98

The resolution may encompass moneys which have already been applied towards any of the prescribed purposes, and the Secretary of State is empowered to make an award under seal to effect the purposes of the resolution.[89]

Suspension of rights

A suspension of rights while the land is used for an alternative purpose is not altogether unusual whether it be for some local purpose, such as tipping, or for a national purpose connected, say, with defence needs. In such circumstances compensation may be paid. Unlike the position where compensation is paid for extinguishment of rights there is little, if any, assistance given to aid a committee in disbursement. This may place a commoners' association in a difficult position as such an association has no power to bind a dissenting minority of its members. There are two statutes which make express provision for suspension of rights for prolonged periods.

5.99

(a) Inclosure Act 1773

The Act provides a number of measures, considered in more detail below,[90] "for the better Cultivation, Improvement and Regulation of the Common Arable Fields, Wastes and Commons of Pasture in this Kingdom." It is

5.100

---

[85] s.19.
[86] s.20.
[87] Preamble.
[88] s.2; for a precedent for an application see 7 Forms and Precedents (4th ed.) 112.
[89] s.4.
[90] At § 12.03.

sufficient to say at this point that there are provisions in the Act for the suspension of rights in common fields for periods of six years or two rotations of crops and, for parts of wastes to be enclosed and leased for four years. It is thought that no current use is made of this statute.

(b) Opencast Coal Act 1958

5.101   British Coal (formerly the National Coal Board) has powers to compulsorily acquire land and suspend rights over it for a period of up to two decades. The provisions for compensation are different from those for extinguishment of rights in the way in which it is paid and the persons to whom it is due.

5.102   The powers of the authority largely emanate from the provisions of the Opencast Coal Act 1958 as amended by the Coal Industry Act 1975. Section 4 of the Opencast Coal Act 1958 allows the authority to acquire land to facilitate the working of opencast coal by means of an order known as a "compulsory rights order." Such an order allows for temporary rights of occupation and use of the land during the period for which it has effect, not exceeding 20 years. Section 4A of the Act provides that Parts II, III and IV of the Acquisition of Land Act 1981 shall apply to such an order subject to section 29 of the 1981 Act, which provides that reference in the Act to compulsory purchase orders shall be read as referring to compulsory rights orders. Thus the procedure, in relation to common land (in this context with an enlarged definition[91]) which flows from section 19 of the Acquisition of Land Act 1981 in relation to compulsory purchase orders also applies to compulsory rights orders. Briefly, this requires that an order is subject to special parliamentary procedure unless a certificate is given by the Secretary of State; a certificate may only be given if land is made available in exchange for the land acquired.[92] The exchange of land required in respect of a compulsory rights order is not, however, a permanent exchange but is "construed as a reference to making other land available during the period for which the compulsory rights order is to have effect."[93] There seems to be no provision in the C.R.A. 1965 for this "temporary" common land to be registered.

5.103   Section 4(7) of the Opencast Coal Act 1958 expressly excludes the operation of the Land Clauses Acts and the Compulsory Purchase Act 1965. A special procedure for compensation, relating only to compulsory rights orders, is contained in section 31 of the Act of 1958 having effect where "the exercise of any easement or similar right over any land comprised in the order . . . is prevented or injuriously affected." For each year that the right is prevented or injuriously affected the person for the time being entitled to the right "shall be entitled to compensation from the Board [British Coal] of an amount equal to the loss (if any) suffered by him."

5.104   There are differences between the compensation paid for extinguishment of rights and the payments for suspension under a compulsory rights order.

---

[91] A compulsory rights order has application to easements or similar rights thus land other than statutory common land may be encompassed: Opencast Coal Act 1958, s.31(1).

[92] *cf.* § 5.86.

[93] Opencast Coal Act 1958, Sched. 2, para. 7.

Extinguishment payments are capital in nature and are due to the fee simple owner of the common rights whereas compensation for suspension is of an income nature and is due to the person entitled and suffering loss in any year, *i.e.* the person exercising the right, who may well be a tenant. Where rights are extinguished the tenant is entitled to no payment and is reimbursed for his loss of right by a reduction in rent. Where rights are suspended the tenant is entitled to compensation and the out-of-occupation owner receives nothing unless, after the period of the rights order has elapsed, and then only to the extent that the value of the land to him has been diminished or, in the case of a common right in gross, the market value of the right has diminished.[94]

Another major difference between the two types of order is that there is no **5.105** direct power to assess a global sum of compensation moneys and pay it directly to a committee of commoners. The Act does provide a power to a Minister to make regulations modifying the operation of the method of compensation so that it may be assessed globally and apportioned as the Minister considers appropriate.[95] This clearly envisages a procedure similar to that in operation for extinguishment of rights but, at the time of writing, no such regulations have been made. The duty of British Coal, therefore, is to deal individually with each commoner.

(i) The practice of British Coal   Observation suggests that it is the **5.106** practice of British Coal not to proceed to a compulsory rights order over common land but to negotiate on a commercial basis directly with commoners or, more usually, a committee of commoners. It is not unknown for a commoners' association to accept very substantial annual payments on behalf of its members. Without adequate authority the association can find itself in a somewhat precarious position over disbursement, particularly in cases where registration of rights has not been finalised under the C.R.A. 1965, as it can be unclear who is entitled to receive the compensation.

(ii) Disbursement of compensation   It has been demonstrated that **5.107** there are provisions in three statutes which may assist a committee of commoners in disbursement of moneys received in compensation for extinguishment of rights. It is relevant to consider which of these, if any, may be used to assist a committee receiving money for disturbance or suspension of rights.

Where the arrangement for compensation is voluntary, including the compensation paid by British Coal in the absence of a compulsory rights order, none of the Acts has any application. Assuming that the word extinguishment can be given a wide meaning to encompass prolonged suspension (and it is by no means clear that it can be), nevertheless in each case the sections in these Acts are worded so that they apply only where money has been paid under an Act of Parliament to a committee of commoners. Thus, although the acquiring authority is established under statute, payments made in pursuance of a commercial transaction surely cannot be said to be payment under the provisions of an Act.

[94] s.31.
[95] s.31(5).

5.108   If a compulsory rights order is in operation under the provisions of the Opencast Coal Act 1958 the position may be different. The provisions in the Inclosure Acts 1852 and 1854 will still not apply, for the sections concerned make it clear that the compensation must have been directed to be paid to a committee by the statute under which the payment is made and the Opencast Coal Act 1958 contains no such provision. The Commonable Rights Compensation Act 1882 is worded differently and merely requires that payment shall have been made by a corporate body under the provisions of an Act to a committee of commoners. If the Secretary of State is prepared to accept that extinguishment of rights includes prolonged suspension prima facie it seems that the Commonable Rights Compensation Act 1882 could be invoked. However, it is submitted that use of the Act is inappropriate in the case of compensation for suspension, assessable on an annual basis, when the purposes to which money may be applied under the Act are primarily of a capital nature. No tenant, for instance, should be forced by a majority vote to contribute to works of benefit only to his landlord.

Commons Registration Act 1965

5.109   Following the initial registration procedure under the C.R.A. 1965 any rights not registered "shall not be exercisable."[96] The expression has been held to be synonomous with extinguishment.[97] It is arguable that the Act must have had a dramatic effect in extinguishing rights. However, it should be noticed that rights were not expressly extinguished and there may be circumstances when they could revive. Suppose that the land with which the rights are concerned was not registered under the Act of 1965 but becomes subject to a newly granted right at some time in the future. It will become "new" common land and there seems no reason why a right unregistered in the initial procedure, and thereby rendered unexercisable, should not be registrable over the new common land.

5.110   That some rights which existed before the C.R.A. 1965 came into force have been rendered unexercisable, and in practical terms extinguished, can hardly be disputed. But as an instrument of extinguishment the Act may have had little overall effect. In the face of what was, in effect, a mandatory registration procedure, non-registration may carry with it an implication of abandonment. There can be little doubt that many unregistered claims to rights were stale or even spurious and these have been effectively disposed of. On the other hand, most observers would accept that not only have many unused rights been registered, and consequently been given a fresh lease of life, but many claims to rights which would not have borne close legal examination have slipped into registration through lack of objection. The overall result of the Act of 1965 may well have been to create more rights than it extinguished.

---

[96] s.1(2).
[97] *Central Electricity Generating Board* v. *Clwyd C.C.* [1976] 1 W.L.R. 151 at 155–156, *per* Goff J.

6. Severance and Apportionment of Common Rights

SEVERANCE

Severance of appurtenant grazing rights

There are numerous comments in both texts and case reports that, where **6.01** the number of animals is certain, rights attached to land may be severed and converted into rights in gross. The majority of rights of common are appurtenant to land and expressed as attached to land in registration under the C.R.A. 1965. Registration under the Act also required grazing rights to be reduced to a fixed number of animals. Since registration it has become a question of major importance to discover whether one of the results of the C.R.A. 1965 is that all appurtenant grazing rights may now be severed, having become fixed in number. If this is the case, there has been a radical departure from the law as it stood before the Act, carrying with it the possibility of almost revolutionary change in the way that rights are held and exercised.

To lawyers unversed in the intricacies of the law of common lands, it might **6.02** seem little short of heretical to suggest that any right which is appurtenant to land may be severed from the land. As Sir George Jessel M.R. once said, in commenting about appurtenant grazing rights for fixed numbers of animals, "used in some way on the land, I think the beasts must be, to make the right appurtenant; otherwise I do not see what the meaning of the word 'appurtenant' is. It is a right appurtenant to the land."[1] There must be more than a suspicion that he would have required some convincing that rights might be severed at the will of the commoner and disposed of as a separate hereditament. Considered in the context of easements instead of profits, it is difficult to imagine a court accepting that a right granted to, say, take a vehicle from Blackacre once a day over Whiteacre might immediately be sold as a separate hereditament to the owner of Greenacre. Of course, easements can be distinguished from profits in that a profit may be held in gross, whereas it

---

[1] *Baylis* v. *Tyssen-Amhurst* (1877) L.R.6 Ch.D. 500 at 508; see also *Att.-Gen.* v. *Reynolds* [1911] 2 K.B. 888 at 918, *per* Hamilton J., cited at § 6.35.

is usually considered that an easement may not.[2] But, suppose the courts did decide to hold valid an easement in gross to, say, the use of a helicopter pad; would this bring all easements into conformity with profits so that quantified appurtenant easements were severable?

6.03   This section is devoted to consideration of the cases and other authorities concerned with severance of fixed grazing rights. It is argued that many of the statements do not necessarily support the suggestion that any rights which have become quantified may be severed but only those which were granted for a certain number. As with so many aspects of the law relating to common land there can be no absolute certainty, for the issue now under consideration was of no importance until the advent of the C.R.A. 1965— most rights were not quantified—and there has been no reported litigation directly on the point.

(a) Case authority

6.04   The primary authority on severance of rights usually cited is *Drury* v. *Kent* (1603).[3] The full report is as follows:

> "Replevin. Upon a special verdict, the case was, a man prescribes to have common appurtenant to the manor of B. for all his beasts levant & couchant upon it: he grants this common to A. Whether this grant be good or no? was the question.—And adjudged, that he could not grant it over, for he hath it *quasi sub modo*, viz. for the beasts levant & couchant; no more than estovers to be burnt in a house certain; but common appurtenant for beasts certain may be granted over. Wherefore it was adjudged *ut supra.*"

It is a somewhat meagre report upon which to erect an important proposition of law and, of course, it does not deal directly with the point at issue, the case being authority that *levant* and *couchant* rights may not be severed. The earliest book, *Commons*, merely treats it as an authority that no rights *levant* and *couchant*, whether appendant or appurtenant, can be severed without extinguishment.[4]

6.05   A second frequently cited case is *Daniel* v. *Hanslip* (1672):[5]

> "In this case Hale C.J. said, that if a man hath common appurtenant to a messuage and land for certain number of beasts he may alien the same; *aliter* if it be for all his beasts levant and couchant upon the land, he cannot by his alienation sever that from the land."

Again the non-alienability of *levant* and *couchant* rights is remarked upon but the decision in this case was that fixed rights could be severed. It is as well to examine the nature of the rights concerned by considering another report of the case *sub nom. Leniel* v. *Harslop* (1672).[6] The question before

---

[2] *cf.* Sturley, "Easements in Gross" (1980) 96 L.Q.R. 557; *Gale's Easements*, pp. 7–8, 43–44.

[3] (1603) Cro.Jac. 14, 79 E.R. 13.

[4] Anon., *Commons*, p. 39; *cf. Sir Henry Nevil's Case* (1570) Plowd. 377 at 381, 75 E.R. 572 at 579; *Musgrave* v. *Gave* (1741–1742) Willes 319 at 322, 125 E.R. 1193 at 1195, *per* Willes L.C.J.

[5] (1672) 2 Lev. 67, 83 E.R. 452 (the entire report is cited in the text).

[6] (1672) 3 Keb. 66, 84 E.R. 597.

the court was whether on division of the land a disproportionate quantum of rights could be attached to a severed parcel. The number of livestock concerned was "four beasts levant and couchant on two yard lands," which is perhaps 108 acres. The court held that a disproportionate allocation was good in the particular case. However, it should be noticed that the rights are not *levant* and *couchant* as normally understood, *i.e.* rights granted to benefit the whole of the dominant land, but rights granted for a small number of beasts which were kept on the dominant land.

In *Leniel* v. *Harslop*, cases are cited in support of the proposition that rights may be severed. First, there is the anecdotal, or possibly hypothetical, example of 1,000 sheep prescribed for, and appurtenant to, a cottage in Lincolnshire. Again this type of right is clearly not of the normal *levant* and *couchant* type. Then the case of *Spooner* v. *Day and Mason* (1636)[7] is considered. It had been held that a foldcourse belonging to a manor could be severed and granted with parcel of the manor. A foldcourse, however, was not a right of common exercisable over the lord's land but a reserved seignorial right for the lord to graze over the land of his tenants.[8] Once severed and granted away from the manor it became perceived as being a right of common,[9] and once exercisable by tenants over the land of other tenants this is undoubtedly a correct view. But at the time of the *Spooner* case it was a seignorial right which was under consideration.   **6.06**

In other cases it has been ruled that in prescribing for a certain number of cattle there is no need to add *levant* and *couchant* "because it is no prejudice to the owner of the soil, for that the number is ascertained."[10] There are, it seems, two classes of rights: those which are *levant* and *couchant*, *i.e.* the number of cattle is that which the land is capable of supporting in the winter, and those where *levancy* and *couchancy* is unnecessary because they are for a fixed number and are not related to the acreage of land. Both are described as appurtenant to land but it may be that the rights for fixed numbers were not granted in that way. Thus in *Fitzherbert's New Natura Brevium* can be found[11]:   **6.07**

> "If one grants to I.S. eight Acres of Land, *simul cum* so much Common as belongs to his Oxgang of Land in a certain place, this is not Common appurtenant, but in gross; *per Herle*; but see there it is adjudged, if one grants an Assart *simul cum tota Communia quant' pertinet ad unam Bovatam Terrae*, adjudged this is Common in Gross, and he shall take as much as another takes for two Bovates or Oxgangs in gross, and when he pleases. Ratio for such Common cannot be appendant to Land."

This is expressed similarly by Woolrych: "Thus, if one grant so many acres

---

[7] (1636) Cro. Car. 432, 79 E.R. 975; s.c. *Day* v. *Spoone* (1636) Jones W. 375, 82 E.R. 196.

[8] For foldcourses, see § 3.116.

[9] *Robinson* v. *Duleep Singh* (1877–1879) 11 Ch.D. 798.

[10] *Richards* v. *Squibb* (1698) 1 Ld.Raym. 726, 91 E.R. 1384, *per* Holt C.J.; *Stevens* v. *Austin* (1677–1678) 2 Mod. 185, 86 E.R. 1015; *Sir John Thornel* v. *Lassels* (1604) Cro.Jac. 26, 79 E.R. 21; *Earl of Manchester* v. *Vale* (1666) 1 Saund. 27, 85 E.R. 28.

[11] At p. 420; *cf. contra*, *Stamford* v. *Burges* (1675) Shepp. Ab. 381: grant of common for all animals is a common in gross but a grant for a certain number is a right appurtenant.

of land, with as much common as belongs to his ox-gang of land in a certain place, or grants an assart with all the common that pertains to one bovate of land, or grants common to a corporation for all manner of cattle: these are all grants of common in gross."[12] It seems that where the grant is not related to the land with which it is granted, but is measured in some other way, by reference to some fixed number, the right is held to be in gross and not appurtenant to land. Such rights would clearly be capable of severance as they never were, strictly, rights appurtenant.

6.08 But, it seems, many of these rights for fixed numbers were pleaded as being appurtenant to land. Why were they not always pleaded by reference to their true nature as rights in gross? In *Commons*, two methods of pleading a right of common are described: for a right in gross as one "which he and his ancestors of whom he is heir, from time whereof, etc." and an appurtenant right as one "which he and all those whose estate he has in the same land, from time whereof etc."[13] The owner of a purchased right in gross, however, was unable to support the plea that his ancestors had enjoyed the right from time immemorial. Further, whether a right in gross could be assigned or whether it perforce descended to a man's heirs was a question not finally settled, it seems, until the case of *Welcome* v. *Upton* (1840).[14] The dangers for the purchaser of a right in gross are obvious if he pleads it as such. The viable alternative is to plead that the right has been immemorially enjoyed as appurtenant to the land which he purchased with the right in gross. This is unassailable if the right had in fact been enjoyed with the land. It is entirely possible to speculate that certain rights, although pleaded as rights appurtenant were, from the outset, rights in gross and are distinguishable from true rights appurtenant which were granted as a benefit to land.

(b) The nineteenth century treatises

6.09 The treatise writers do not examine the proposition at any great length and some of the statements seem to be at variance. At the time, as will be shown,[15] there was a general acceptance in agricultural practice that rights appurtenant to land could not be severed, so in legal circles the matter was not one of much significance. Typical are the remarks of Woolrych who states in connection with extinguishment:

> "Another mode of destroying commons is, by severing them from the tenements to which they are appendant or appurtenant; as where one aliens his messuage or tenement, and excepts the right attached to it. So, a common of estovers appendant or appurtenant will be utterly gone, if the owner destroys the house, *i.e.* alters the nature of the tenement to which either belong, for they will thereby be severed from the thing to which they are appendant. If this were to take effect otherwise than by severance, the common would become in gross, which the law will not allow in cases where the right belongs to the land.[16]

And in connection with rights in gross he comments: "But a common

[12] (2nd ed., 1850), at p. 60.
[13] *Anon., Commons* (1st ed., 1698), at p. 119.
[14] (1840) 6 M. & W. 536 at 541, 151 E.R. 524 at 527, *per* Lord Abinger C.B.; *cf.* Bl.Comm., ii, 258: a prescription in ancestors descends only to heirs of line.
[15] See Blamire, cited at § 6.12.
[16] Woolrych, at p. 133.

appurtenant for beasts certain may be granted over for such a grant has no reference to connexion of tenure.[17]

The statements seem incompatible, but are not if the general rule is that appendant and appurtenant rights are not severable while fixed rights which have been granted without connection with (not annexed to) land may be severed.

Joshua Williams does not discuss the matter but states quite baldly: **6.10**

> "*Common in gross* is common which a man has, irrespective of the ownership or occupation of any tenement. It may be created by the owner of a common appurtenant, for a fixed number of cattle, alienating his common appurtenant, without the tenement to which it belongs. It is held to be immaterial to the owner of a waste, when the right is fixed and stinted to a certain given number of cattle, whether those cattle are put on in respect of a tenement, or by a person who owns no land. Common appendant, however, for cattle levant and couchant upon a tenement and common appurtenant in like manner for cattle levant and couchant upon a tenement, cannot be severed from the tenement, and aliened so as to become a common in gross."[18]

If one word is added to the statement so that it reads "common in gross . . . may be created by the owner of a common appurtenant, *granted* for a fixed number of cattle . . . ," it is entirely consistent with the argument presently advanced. The passage does, however, introduce a reason why any right for a certain number may be severed—it matters not to the owner of the soil who exercises the right. As is shown later, this view may be misleading if applied to any rights which have become quantified as distinguished from those granted for a fixed number.[19] It seems, although not acknowledged as such, to owe something to arguments by Saunders in *Hoskins* v. *Robins* (1671)[20] although he was actually concerned with a right of sole pasture. No attempt is now being made to argue that rights over a sole pasture are not properly viewed as rights in gross and are freely alienable without land.

Various other cases are introduced by the treatise writers in support of **6.11** severance for fixed rights, notably the early nineteenth century cases of *Bunn* v. *Channen* (1813)[21] and *Lathbury* v. *Arnold* (1823).[22] Both are concerned with the demise of cottagers' rights to graze two and one cows respectively and it was said in the cases that it was the practice or custom to allow the right to be demised. Whatever the rules may be about leasing or licensing rights attached to land, there can be little doubt that the owner of the soil of a common may expressly or impliedly allow rights to be used in

[17] Woolrych, at p. 61.
[18] Joshua Williams, p. 184; repeated almost *verbatim* in *Scriven's Copyholds*, p. 378.
[19] *cf.* § 6.14.
[20] (1671) 2 Wms.Saund. 324 at 327, 85 E.R. 1123 at 1124.
[21] (1813) 5 Taunt. 244, 128 E.R. 683.
[22] (1823) 1 Bing. 217, 130 E.R. 88. Two other cases are sometimes cited as authority that rights may be severed but neither has anything to say on the subject: *The Earl of Pembroke's Case* (1636) Clayt. 47 (cited at § 3.70) and *Stamford* v. *Burges* (1675) Shepp. Ab. 381, which merely states that a grant by a lord for "common within the wastes of a manor" is a right in gross but if the number is laid down and attached to land it is a common appurtenant.

this way if he wishes and a practice or custom would suggest such agreement. Neither case has anything to say about the permanent severance of appurtenant rights.[23]

(c) Select Committee on Commons Inclosure

6.12 In 1844 a Select Committee of the House of Commons was preparing a report upon which the Inclosure Act 1845 was eventually based.[24] The Committee took evidence from a number of sources; the principal witness on agricultural practice was William Blamire, the first Chief Tithes Commissioner. His evidence to the Committee provides some insight into practice at that time. He was asked whether rights of cottagers and smallholders were appurtenant to tenements and he replied:

> "No doubt they are; and the use of the common right cannot be severed from the tenement to which the right is attached; the renter of the tenement has the power of turning his own stock upon the waste of the manor, but he has not the power of transferring that right of turning stock to anybody else; he must either exercise it himself, or it is lapsed and cannot be exercised at all."[25]

He was then asked about fixed rights and whether rights for 20 sheep attached to a tenement could be let separately. His reply is enlightening:

> "Certainly not; the common right is inseparably attached, indissolubly attached, to the tenement, and the person renting from the owner of the tenements the land and house must of necessity rent the common right; there are within my knowledge a great many cases where the right of pasturage under these circumstances is of more monied value than the tenement and the ancient land attached to it, and a larger consideration is given for the common right than for the tenement and the ancient land."[26]

It is quite apparent that expectations among landowners at the time did not include that of severing rights from the land to which they were attached. Victorian landowners were not exactly renowned for being unaware of their legal rights. The odd remark in the books of London lawyers obviously had little effect in the Shires, as is self evident when one comes to examine the commons registers today. A right in gross over a waste is the remarkable exception requiring speculation as to the reason for its presence.

6.13 Some 20 years after the passing of the Inclosure Act 1845 the whole emphasis towards the common lands began to change and a protection society for commons was established. There was considerable interest in purchasing rights of common to prevent further inclosure. It is interesting to note that the first secretary of the Commons Preservation Society opined that the only rights which could safely be purchased, severed from any land, were those exercised over stinted and gated pastures.[27]

---

[23] For severance of use of rights, see § 6.23.

[24] Commons Inclosures, Reports from Committees (1844), First Volume, ordered by the House of Commons to be printed August 5, 1844.

[25] *ibid.* at p. 33, question 345.

[26] *ibid.* question 346.

[27] Sir Robert Hunter, *Open Spaces, Foot-paths, and Rights of Way* (1896), pp. 83–84.

(d) The rights of the owner of the soil

Joshua Williams, as seen above, thought that once rights were fixed it was **6.14** immaterial to the owner of the soil who exercised the rights. To a certain extent this is true. If the owner grants a person a right to graze a fixed number of cattle in gross then unless this is personal to the grantee it makes no difference whether it is A or B who turns out the cattle. A fixed proportion of the total of the grazing has been granted away permanently. A right truly appurtenant to land, however, seems to be of an altogether different nature. The owner of the soil, in this case, has granted land together with the benefit of grazing over the waste to the extent that the land can benefit from it at any particular time. The grant is probably conditional, so that if the grantee does not require or use the right at any time the owner may take advantage of the residual grazing, and if the rights cease to be of use to the land, they revert to the owner. That this was the view of the courts may be assessed from the judgment of Bayley J. in *Arlett* v. *Ellis* (1827)[28]:

> "The lord has rights of his own reserved upon the waste . . . He has a right to stock the common . . . And when it is ascertained that there is more common than is necessary for the cattle of the commoners, the lord, as it seems to me, is entitled to take that for his own purposes . . . The common may have been originally destined for a definite number of cattle, or for all cattle levant and couchant upon certain lands. Many of these rights may be extinguished, or the common itself may produce so much more herbage, that a smaller proportion of that common may be sufficient for depasturing the cattle of the persons entitled, than when it was originally destined to that purpose. Now, whenever that is the case, I think the lord has the right to inclose . . . "

It is clear that whenever a right is reduced or extinguished, on principle the **6.15** surplus grazing should, and in practice does, revert to the owner of the soil. This is clearly a valuable residual right which should not be usurped lightly. Thus where rights are appurtenant, whether or not they are for a certain number, on principle the grantee should not be free to usurp the rights of the owner unless statute or common law has unequivocally made an exception. It has been suggested that the common law by no means indicates that an exception has been made and that the relevant cases are susceptible to alternative explanation.[28a]

Nor does statutory enactment provide much support for the view that the **6.16** 1925 property legislation did other than envisage that rights appurtenant are firmly attached to land. Section 187(1) of the L.P.A. 1925 provides that: "Where an easement, right or privilege for a legal estate is created, it shall enure for the land to which it is intended to be annexed."

The C.R.A. 1965 too does not appear to have wrought any change by requir- **6.17** ing quantification of rights. Section 15 merely requires that a right not limited by number shall for the purposes of registration under the Act be treated as exercisable in relation to no more than a definite number. Inclusion of the expression "for the purposes of registration under the Act"

[28] (1827) 7 B. & C. 346 at 369, 108 E.R. 752 at 761.
[28a] See §§ 6.04–6.08 and 6.11.

seems to carry with it the connotation that rights unlimited by number before the Act retain all their pre-existing qualities. The wording seems to evince an intention not to interfere with the common law any more than was necessary to effect the purposes of the Act.

(e) Summary

6.18   For a matter which has achieved the status of perhaps the most important single issue currently connected with the common lands, it is surprising to have to admit that there can be no certainty as to the present law. The matter seems never to have been the subject of direct litigation during several centuries and the only time it seems to have been considered in modern times is in the case *White* v. *Taylor (No.2)* (1969).[29] In that case Buckley J. approved the view that rights certain can be severed but the actual decision endorsed an apportionment *pro rata* on division of the land.

6.19   It has been argued here that appurtenant rights may not be severed for the simple reason of principle that to allow such rights to be severed would enable a grantee to defeat the residual right of the owner of the soil to any surplus which remains when rights of common are satisfied. This view pertains whether the severance is by lease or licence for a limited period and *a fortiori* when the proposed severance is in fee simple attempting to create a right in gross. The cases cited in support of severance are susceptible to the alternative explanation that rights which have been granted, without the necessary nexus between the right and the land with which they are exercised, are severable. To accept that it is only this class of fixed right which is severable is consistent not only with case decisions and textual commentary but also avoids the awkward consequence, if the law were otherwise, that mere grantees of profits can defeat some of the owners' rights at will and, perhaps more fundamentally, is consistent with the meaning of appurtenancy as it seems to have been understood by all authority.

6.20   The recognition in practice of the two separate classes of rights should not cause too much difficulty. A large majority of rights registered over wastes under the C.R.A. 1965 were proved, or are only capable of proof, by prescription which automatically implies a nexus with the dominant land. The hallmark of the severable right will be that it was granted for a fixed number of animals without regard to the acreage of land with which it is used. Rights which have become fixed, by whatever means, as a matter of practical management convenience, must be distinguished. The number of occasions when a severable right will be encountered on a waste is very small. In a study of a sample of commons registers the writer has not observed an obvious example. Where rights have been granted for fixed numbers in modern times, it will be a matter of construction of the grant as to whether it was made appurtenant to land or was collateral to the grant of land.

6.21   On policy grounds most observers seem to view the possibility of severance of appurtenant rights with disfavour. The Royal Commission recommended that "rights appurtenant should not be severable from land to which they appertain, unless extinguished or transferred within an approved scheme of

---

[29] [1969] 1 Ch. 160 at 190.

management and improvement."[30] The Dartmoor Commons Act 1985 contains a section expressly barring any severance of rights held with land or a tenement at the time of the passing of the Act[31] and the Common Land Forum makes a similar recommendation for inclusion in future legislation.[32] The Forum seems to go somewhat further than preventing severance of appurtenant rights for it is attached rights which are mentioned. This seems to indicate an intention to prevent the severance of any rights recorded on the common registers as attached to land and, as has been shown, some rights presently held in gross are registered in this manner.[33]

It seems possible that the only way in which the question of the effect of severance can be satisfactorily resolved is through statutory enactment. This does not mean that owners of rights would be wise to sever before statute finally makes the matter clear because, if the common law is as has been suggested in the present text, the effect of a severance is not to create a right in gross but to effect a total extinguishment.[34]   **6.22**

Leasing and licensing appurtenant grazing rights

One popular text dealing with common land states that a commoner may license another to exercise his registered grazing rights so long as the rightful numbers are not exceeded.[35] This statement flies in the face of a substantial amount of case authority to the contrary and appears to breach the principle that the owner of the soil is entitled to any surplus of grass after the commoners' grazing is satisfied. If the statement is inaccurate then any persons exercising unlawful rights will obviously be in a different legal position from the commoners. For example, in the case of a road traffic accident if the rights are not lawfully exercised a defence which justifies animals straying on a highway across a common may be unavailable.[36] While due to a quirk in the Animals Act 1971 the unlawful licensee may be able to take advantage of a breach of a duty to fence causing animals to stray as a defence in an Animals Act action,[37] he may not be able to claim for damage done to his animals consequent upon the straying.[38] If the licensed rights are in respect of a hefted flock a tenant might have some difficulty in establishing a claim to tenant right compensation on termination of the tenancy.[39]   **6.23**

It is a matter of some importance for the position to be clarified and yet again it has to be said that the position is not entirely clear. A cautious   **6.24**

---

[30] Royal Commission Report, p. 129, recommendation 5.
[31] s.8.
[32] Appendix C, para. 051.
[33] *cf.* § 4.82; the Common Land Forum Report seems to proceed on the assumption that all rights of common ought, in legal theory, to be rights annexed to land, which takes no account of the disparate variety of rights registrable under the Acts, and ignores the presence of sole rights: *cf.* Appendix C, para. 048.
[34] See § 6.37 *et seq.*
[35] Clayden, *Our Common Land* (1985), p. 37.
[36] Animals Act 1971, s.8(2).
[37] *ibid.* s.4(6). See further at § 10.43.
[38] *cf.* § 10.102.
[39] For hefted flocks, see § 3.105.

stance is tended towards here, on the basis that there is no express authority that rights may be leased or licensed away from the land to which they are appurtenant.

6.25 The view has already been advanced that any residual grazing accrues to the owner of the soil and the implication is that, as a matter of principle, a commoner may not attempt to defeat that right by leasing or licensing rights away from the dominant land.[39a] This is not to say that where rights of common are appurtenant to land and held in fee simple that demises, subdemises and licensed use of the land together with the right is inadmissable. It is also, it is suggested, within the power of the owner expressly or impliedly to release his right to residual grazing to the commoners so that they may deal with their rights as they wish. No doubt this can be seen to have occurred in the case of some commons regulated under statute. In a recent survey of regulated commons it was found that on nearly one-third of them commoners were leasing their rights, but on two-thirds of the management committees (Boards of Conservators) the owners of the soil were represented.[40] It seems possible that where rights are leased on these commons it is, on some of them at least, with the implied consent of the owner. Thus, there may be circumstances where leasing or licensing is lawful and on some commons it is, of course, positively welcomed by the owners in order to have the land properly grazed. It follows that this section is not concerned with rights which may be lawfully let with the approval of the owner, but only those cases where there is no indication one way or the other of his attitude or, he expressly objects.

6.26 The rights of the commoner in using the common were in early days very strictly circumscribed and there does not appear to be any old case authority that the rights might be licensed or leased to a stranger. All the cases point in the other direction. The right of pasturage is not his own "until his cattel have fed there"[41]; he must have sufficient property in the animals[42]; he may only use borrowed animals if they are to compester the dominant land[43]; he may not agist animals[44] nor may he graze his own animals *levant* and *couchant* on land other than the dominant land.[45] In *Rumsey* v. *Rawson* (1669)[46] a plaintiff in replevin replied in answer to an avowry damage feasant that his beasts were *levant* and *couchant* on glebe land owned by a parson. It was moved that judgment in favour of the plaintiff be arrested on the grounds that only the tenant, the parson, could use the right for his own beasts or beasts which he had taken to compester the land. It was held that the defendant might have objected on these grounds but that after verdict the court would accept that the beasts had been used for compestering. This

---

[39a] See § 6.14.
[40] *Land Use Consultants, Management Schemes for Commons* (1985), Table 8.
[41] *Samborne* v. *Harilo* (1621) Bridgman J. 9 at 10, 123 E.R. 1162 at 1163, *per* Bridgman.
[42] *Manneton* v. *Trevilian* (1683) 2 Show. K.B. 328, 89 E.R. 969.
[43] *Molliton* v. *Trevilian* (1683) Skin. 137, 90 E.R. 64; 1 Ro.Ab. 401, 402; 4 Vin.Ab. 585 at 593.
[44] *Cooper's Case* (1586) at 2 Leon. 202, 74 E.R. 478 in argument; *ibid.* 4 Vin.Ab. 585 at 593; *Jones* v. *Richard* (1837) 6 Ad. & E. 530, 112 E.R. 203, *per* Lord Denman C.J.
[45] *Molliton* v. *Trevilian*, above, n. 43.
[46] (1669) 1 Vent. 18, 86 E.R. 13.

case seems to be authority that licensing is only lawful if the animals are compestering the dominant land.

The case usually cited today as authority that rights may be licensed is one **6.27** concerned with a road traffic accident. The issue in *Davies* v. *Davies* (1974)[47] was that the right of the owner of the animals to graze common land was challenged following a road traffic accident. Mrs. Davies owned a farm to which registered rights of grazing were attached. The commons register showed that the rights applicants were Mrs. Davies and her brother.[48] The straying animals were owned by Mrs. Davies' son who lived with his mother and worked on the farm. Counsel for the plaintiff drew the attention of the court to the applicants for rights registration and claimed that as the son had no right to graze he was not protected by the section of the statute upon which he relied for his defence.[49] Lord Denning M.R. dismissed the argument and declared that:

> " . . . when the owner of land has a right of pasture on a common for a certain number of cattle or sheep he can exercise it, not only by putting his own animals on the common, but also licensing others to put their animals on it, so long as the appropriate number is not exceeded."[50]

Cairns L.J. seemed to hold a similar view when he said:

> " . . . once it appears that the number of animals that can be pastured there is limited, as it now is under the Commons Registration Act 1965, it is clear law that the person who has the right can license another person to have his cattle there."[51]

But he seems to qualify this statement when he said a little later:

> "I think it ought to be held that where there is a right of pasturing, it allows the commoner to permit certainly another member of the family, and a person with whom he or she has a business association in connection with a farm, to have his animals there."[52]

Ormrod L.J. did not find it necessary to go back into the "fascinating manorial customs" and was prepared to construe the relevant statute in "a sensible contemporary fashion":

> " . . . was the man who placed the animals on the common entitled to do so? I am quite satisfied that he and his mother are farming together to all intents and purposes and he has some sheep. So it would be ludicrous in 1974 to hold that he had no right to use his mother's commons rights within the meaning of the Animals Act 1971, no matter whether the conclusion might have been different if we were sitting in a manorial court in Glamorgan in 1270."[53]

---

[47] [1975] Q.B. 172.
[48] In fact as we have seen the applicants for registration are not necessarily the fee simple owners of the rights: see § 4.08.
[49] Animals Act 1971, s.8(2).
[50] *Davies* v. *Davies*, above, n. 47, at 177.
[51] *ibid.* at 178.
[52] *ibid.*
[53] *ibid.* at 179.

6.28 The cases relied upon by Lord Denning and Cairns L.J. were *Rumsey* v. *Rawson*, cited at § 6.26, and *Hoskins* v. *Robins* (1671).[54] As has been shown, *Rumsey* v. *Rawson* is an authority that rights may only be licensed with the dominant land and it was an express finding of the court that the rights had been used in that way. In *Hoskins* v. *Robins* an extract from the argument of Saunders, which was accepted as good law by the court, is the authority cited: "where one claims all . . . the pasture for a certain number of cattle, he may license a stranger to put in his cattle for it is no wrong to the land or owner of the soil, because it cannot be a surcharging."[55]

The difficulty with the extract is that the "pasture" referred to is a right of sole pasture and not a right of "pasturage," *i.e.* a right of common. All that Saunders was saying at that point was that a right of sole pasture can be distinguished from a right of common in that it may be used without reference to dominant land.

6.29 As an authority that rights may be severed, and leased or licensed separately from the land (and it is not necessarily clear that any of their lordships were saying this), *Davies* v. *Davies* is substantially flawed. First, the case was concerned with rights which were used with land probably, in technical terms, on licence. Secondly, the cases relied upon by both Lord Denning M.R. and Cairns L.J. have nothing to say about rights severed from the land. Thus, any inference from the words used, that rights may be used separately from the land, is *obiter* and may be readily distinguished in any subsequent case. The case is clear authority that, to use the words of Ormrod L.J., where members of a family are to all intents and purposes farming together, the court will not enquire closely as to where the fee simple ownership of the rights lies. This is to say, in effect, that a licence without deed is acceptable where members of the same family are concerned. It is not to say that an informal licence will suffice to pass an interest in the rights in all circumstances.

6.30 It is safe to say that land together with appurtenant rights may be let or licensed away from the fee simple ownership, providing that any necessary formalities for the proper conveyance of an interest in land are observed. It may be less than wise to rely upon selected extracts from the judgments in *Davies* v. *Davies*, unsupported by the actual decision in the case, to assert that appurtenant grazing rights may be let or licensed without the dominant land.

Severance of estovers

6.31 There is a a not inconsiderable amount of comment that estovers for a fixed quantity may be severed from the dominant tenement.[56] Why this should be so is unclear for no authority can be cited for the proposition and all the

---

[54] (1671) 2 Wms.Saund. 324, 85 E.R. 1123; *cf.* s.c. 2 Lev. 2, 83 E.R. 424.

[55] At 327, 1125. This is put somewhat differently at 2 Lev. 2, 83 E.R. 424: "This being a right of pasture and not of common the herbage may be eaten by the beasts of strangers, though otherwise perhaps if it were common."

[56] Elton, pp. 87, 101 citing Cooke; *Cooke's Inclosures*, p. 37 without citing authority; Woolrych (1st ed., 1824) p. 94, and (2nd ed., 1850), p. 83, in added footnotes without authority.

cases proceed on the opposite assumption. From a very early date it was clearly the view that estovers were strictly annexed to the dominant tenement:

> " . . . if he who has the house will grant the stovers to another, reserving the house to himself, or the house to another, reserving the estovers to himself, the estovers shall not be severed from the house thereby, because they shall be spent in the same house."[57]

It has been demonstrated that the rules governing the use of estovers are strict[58] and, where a right of turbary is for a fixed amount, a surplus may not be sold.[59] It would be extraordinary if, on the other hand, it is possible to sever a fixed right at will and convert it into a right in gross.

The use of estovers and turbary was considered at length in the case of *Att.-Gen.* v. *Reynolds* (1911).[60] It came before the Kings Bench Division and may be considered of some significance as the Attorney-General, Sir Rufus Isaacs, appeared personally and the judgment was considered and detailed. The case was concerned with the New Forest, and an Act of 1854[61] which provided for the settlement of all claims to turbary and fuel in the Forest. In the settlement, an identified messuage was allocated common of turbary and one load of fuel wood. An information was laid that the messuage had been pulled down and a declaration was sought, *inter alia*, that the soil of the open and unenclosed parts of the Forest was discharged from the claim for fuel and turbary.

6.32

It was argued by counsel for the defendants that estovers normally cannot exist in gross, because they are necessarily attached to a particular house and tenement and must be expended there, but "when the amount of wood to be taken is already ascertained so that neither the commoner nor his grantee could take more than a certain number of trees, faggots or cartloads of wood, there is no reason why the common should not become a right in gross."[62] In support Elton, *Cooke's Inclosures*, Joshua Williams and *Daniel* v. *Hanslip* (1673) were cited and an extract from Woolrych quoted. Austen-Cartmell, counsel for the Crown, replied pungently to the formidable list: "There is in fact no instance of estovers originally appurtenant to a house having become a right in gross.[63]

6.33

Hamilton J. was equally sceptical:

> "Whether it be possible to convert a right appurtenant, such as this, into a right in gross is a question which, though much discussed, I need not decide. There are passages in Cooke on Inclosures, Elton on Commons and Woolrych on Commons which seem to keep the matter open. There seems to be a clear preponderance of opinion to the contrary . . . "[64]

---

[57] *Sir Henry Nevil's Case* (1570) Plowd. 377 at 381, 75 E.R. 572 at 579.
[58] *cf.* §§ 3.67 *et seq.*
[59] *Valentine* v. *Penny* (1605) Noy 145, 74 E.R. 1107.
[60] [1911] 2 K.B. 888.
[61] New Forest Act 1854.
[62] Above, n. 60, at 903, *per* Danckwerts K.C. and Gurdon.
[63] *ibid.* at 904.
[64] *ibid.* at 919.

6.34 The facts showed that the defendant's predecessor in title had used the fuel wood between 1882 and 1883, until the time when the messuage was sold, in another premises where he lived. This, in the view of Hamilton J. was clearly impermissible:

> "In doing that he was unquestionably doing what was wrong, because it is laid down in Manwood's Law of the Forest, 4th. ed., p. 133 that 'a man may have stovers . . . as appurtenant to a house . . . and in such case if the stovers are spent in any other house, 'tis a good cause of seizure.' "[65]

6.35 Appurtenancy was much at issue and, having been faced with the argument that it was no more than a method of quantification, and although it was unnecessary to decide the point, Hamilton J. also gave his views on this subject:

> "It is said that the old house is really immaterial; that it was never anything but a measure of the right to be enjoyed; that the only reason for insisting on the old house is to prevent an undue burden on the owner of the soil; and that as soon as the Commissioners fixed the allowance at one load all need for measurement ceased . . . I do not think, when the right is clearly appurtenant to a house, that the identity of the house can be treated as a mere formality or irrelevancy. The appurtenancy to a house is much more than a question of measure. The needs of the house or its inhabitants no doubt served as a measure before the quantity was fixed, just as levancy and couchancy are the measure of rights of pasture in respect of land. But to give no further force to the term "appurtenant" would almost reduce the term to insignificance, and would be contrary to all the authorities."[66]

6.36 As with appurtenant rights of pasture, there seems to be no authority that rights for other products, when reduced to a certain amount, may be severed and converted into rights in gross. The law in respect of the severance of all appurtenant rights is, it is submitted, entirely consistent. The Common Land Forum recommends that future legislation shall provide that no rights currently attached to land shall be severable including rights of common other than pasturage.[67]

Extinguishment by severance

6.37 It has been suggested that the circumstances when rights attached to land may be lawfully severed from the land are strictly circumscribed.[68] It is necessary, therefore, to consider the consequences if a purported severance is attempted. Although there is ample authority that rights may not be severed in most circumstances the case authority dealing with results of severance is meagre. It may today, therefore, be more pertinent to consider the matter in principle than to rely entirely on rather ancient cases.

---

[65] *Att.-Gen.* v. *Reynolds* [1911] 2 K.B. 888 at 907.
[66] *ibid.* at 918.
[67] Common Land Forum Report, Appendix C, paras. 051, 077.
[68] *cf.* § 6.19.

(a) Principles

Considering only circumstances where a severance is not permissible, there **6.38** are two events which might indicate a purported severance: a conveyance of the right without the land, and a conveyance of the dominant land with an express reservation of the right. If a conveyance of a right without the land is unlawful then it is suggested that an attempt to convey the right in gross is ineffective and void. The indication is that in this event no conveyance has taken place and the result can only be that the right remains with the land.

On the other hand, if the transaction is a conveyance of the land without **6.39** the right, there is no reason in principle why the vendor should not contract to convey some of his property retaining part, and the transaction itself is not unlawful. The result, however, is that the part retained, *i.e* the excepted appurtenant right, is not lawfully exercisable without the land and is thereby extinguished. An express exception of rights may be viewed as an abandonment with the rights holder evincing an intention not to use the right again or to transfer it to anybody else.[69]

The only case where the question of severance seems to have been directly **6.40** considered by the Commons Commissioners is one where a parish council put in evidence an indenture of 1922 purporting to grant the council a right in gross to pasture two horses which right was "heretofore appendant and appurtenant" to two messuages. The (then) Chief Commissioner held that the correct view was that such a conveyance was entirely ineffective, so that the right remained attached to the land.[70]

In other Commissioners' decisions there is an obvious reluctance to accept **6.41** severed rights although the reasons for the decisions are not always clearly enunciated. In one case, evidence was given that an applicant for rights had purchased a hefted flock together with the right to graze it in 1955—some 20 years before the hearing. The Commissioner held the claim to be bad in law since "grazing rights are appurtenant to land on which the sheep are based."[71] In another case the applicant had, similarly, purchased a flock of ewes formerly grazed from another farm. The Commissioner refused the registration saying that the agreement was not effective to sever the rights from the farm.[72]

The little direct authority on the effect of severance is not entirely clear **6.42** except to the extent that severance has the effect of extinguishment. In Rolles Abridgment can be found:

> "Common appendant ne poet etre fait common en grosse car ceo est pur avers levant sur le terre a que, &c., & pur ceo ne poet estre sever

---

[69] The principle requirement for abandonment: *cf.* § 5.40.

[70] *Re Baddesley Common, Baddesley Ensor, Warwickshire (No.2)* (1983) 239/D/ 28–31, 14 D.C.C. 317.

[71] *Re Moel Faen, Llantysilio and Bryneglwys* (1976) 51/D/143–144, 4 D.C.C. 442.

[72] *Re Arenig Fawr, Mynydd Nodol, Cefn Llwyn Bugail Y Castell, Meirionnydd D.* (1977) 54/D/32–49, 6 D.C.C. 149.

sans extinguishment. Sic Common appurtenant per avers levant & couchant sur le terre ne poet etre fait en grosse pur cause avandit."[73]

Thus, the indication is that any severance whether by sale without the land or by exception on sale of the land will result in extinguishment, but it may be preferable to rely on the analysis already given above.

(b) Owners' rights distinguished

6.43   The owner of the soil's residual right in a waste is in an altogether different category. It is not a right of common but a reserved right arising as an incident of the ownership of the land. Nevertheless, this right and other seignorial rights may become profits over the land of another person if the land is alienated and the right excepted. Rolle expressly refers to the subject:

"Si le seigneur alien en fee le soil lou le Common est detre prise savant son power de paster come seigneur, il auera Common la comme seigneur . . . " Si le seigneur alien le soile lou le Common est detre prise sans ascun savant, son Common come seigneur est ale per le feffment; mes l'alinée del soile poet ceo paster come le seigneur puissoit devant, pur ceo que cest Common est done pur ceo quo est en son soile, lou le seigneur ceo ad, & nemy pur ceo que il est seigneur, & cest reson tient ity, car semble que ils voilent ceo prover."[74]

The effect seems to be that on disposal of a common the lord may except his rights to pasture, in which event they will clearly be rights of common thenceforth, but in the absence of an exception the alienee will have the residual right to the grazing which the lord formerly had "for this common is in the soil" and not exclusively a seignorial right. It will be seen that in the event of an exception the lord will have created a right in gross.

6.44   Of similar effect is the alienation of a right of foldcourse away from the manor which may be granted in gross or annexed to a parcel of the manor.[75]

6.45   As the residual right of the owner may be severed by exception on sale of the land there seems no reason in principle why it should not be severed by alienation away from the land. There seems to be no authority on the point and today there would be practical difficulties as the right would become a

---

[73] 1 Ro.Ab. 401, 0, 1, [Translated as: Common appendant cannot be made common in gross for this for cattle levant on the ground to which &c., and for this reason cannot be severed without extinguishment] citing Y.B.B. 9 E4, 39, 26 H8, 3; 1 Ro.Ab. 402, 0, 2, [Translated as: Thus common appurtenant for cattle *levant* and *couchant* on the land cannot be made common in gross for the reason aforesaid] citing *Nevill's Case* (1570) 1 Plowd. 377 at 384, and Y.B. 19 H6, 33b.

[74] 1 Ro.Ab. 396, B, 1, 2, [Translated as: If the lord aliens in fee the soil where the common is to be taken saving his power of pasture as lord, he will have common there as lord. If the lord aliens the soil where the common is to be taken without such saving, his common is gone by the feoffment; but the alienee of the soil will be able to have such pasture as the lord might have before, for this common is given for it is in his soil, where the lord had it, and not for that which is in the lord and thus it is for such a reason, for it seems they may approve this] citing Y.B. 18 E3, 30, b43, 44, 18 Ass., pl4.

[75] *Spooner* v. *Day and Mason* (1636) Cro.Car. 432, 79 E.R. 975; for foldcourses, see § 3.116.

right of common in gross without number which, in order to be exercisable, would have to achieve registration under the C.R.A. 1965.

(c) Demised rights

Exception of rights on demise of the land does not appear to result in extinguishment. That, in principle, the owner of an appurtenant right may except the right on demise of the land seems indisputable for the reason that no person can be forced to convey all of his property. In *Smith d. Jerdon* v. *Milward* (1782) it was held that, on demise of a copyhold estate of inheritance, the right could not be severed as nobody but the tenant could enjoy the common belonging to the farm.[76] Similarly in a case of demise of land with rights to graze (which were not rights of common because of unified ownership), the lessor was not able to plead the exception.[77] Thus there are some indications that rights pass on demise irrespective of purported exception, but for the reason already given it is considered that, on principle, this must be incorrect. This is not to say that the lessor is entitled to use the rights but there seems no reason why they should not be put into suspense during the term of the lease. Unlike an exception upon a grant in fee, the estates to the land and the right will, at the end of the term, re-unite.

6.46

APPORTIONMENT

Where a dominant tenement, to which an appurtenant right is attached, is divided the C.R.A. 1965 allows an application to amend the registers accordingly.[78] The procedure is to cancel the original registration and make new entries for the apportioned right which, in relation to grazing rights, do not total more than the quantity of the original registration. An apportionment of rights for products other than grazing is less likely but where it is necessary follows the same common law rules.

6.47

(a) Apportionment of grazing rights

It has been clearly established since *Wyat Wyld's Case* (1609)[79] that, where a dominant tenement with appendant or appurtenant *levant* and *couchant* rights is divided, (whether on alienation in fee or on demise) each divided portion will continue to enjoy rights based on *levancy* and *couchancy* apportioned rateably to the separate parts. There is some authority that deviation from strict rateable apportionment is possible to take account of the quality of the land.[80]

6.48

The position is not so clear when the rights are for fixed numbers of animals. In *White* v. *Taylor (No.2)* (1969) Buckley J. opined that, where nothing

6.49

---

[76] (1782) 3 Doug. 70, 99 E.R. 543.

[77] *Gargrave* v. *Gargrave* ((1610) 2 Brownl. & Golds. 52, 123 E.R. 810.

[78] *cf.* § 4.79.

[79] (1609) 8 Co.Rep. 78b, 77 E.R. 593; see also *Mors* v. *Webbe* (1609) 2 Brownl. & Golds. 297, 123 E.R. 952; *Sacheverill* v. *Porter* (1657) Cro. Car. 482, 79 E.R. 1016; *Smith* v. *Bensall* (1597) Gouldsb.117, 75 E.R. 1034.

[80] *Smith* v. *Bensall*, above, n. 79, at 117, 1035, *per* Walmisley; also *cf.*Y.B. 37 H6, 34.

is said specifically about reserving, assigning or apportioning a fixed right that apportionment rateably to area is both equitable and convenient.[81] The judgment proceeded on the basis that fixed rights could be severed, and that apportionment as the parties agreed was possible. The cases cited are those which have been considered above in connection with severance of fixed rights.[82] It has been argued that these cases do not result in the law being that any fixed rights may be severed but only those which were granted without a sufficient nexus with the land so as to make them appurtenant. It follows that the views of Buckley J. on disproportionate apportionment on division of dominant land are, with the greatest respect, considered to be mistaken.

6.50   When rights are to be apportioned upon division of a tenement it seems that it is currently a simple matter to allocate them to the divided parts as registration under the C.R.A. 1965 required that grazing rights attached to land should be accompanied by a map or list of field numbers showing which parcels had rights attached to them.[83] Although it has been suggested that the details of the land to which the rights are attached may not be conclusively evidential,[84] the declaration that the rights were attached to land at the time of registration seem sufficient to place a duty firmly on an applicant for amendment to provide evidence to the registration authority that the entry is misconceived, or that apportionment should be other than in relation to the parcels concerned.

6.51   Where the division of the land and rights *pro rata* results in fractional animals, there is some authority that to plead a right in that form will be "unintelligible and bad."[85] However, it will not in itself make the whole claim bad where, for example, the plea is for four-and-a-half cows and it is only one cow for which the plaintiff seeks to justify right.[86] If the division of the land on demise is such that a grantee is entitled to only part of an animal it has been held that the part remains with the grantor.[87] Where the division of a stint or gate over a sole pasture results in fractional animals, it seems that there can be no objection for the nature of the right, in this case, is that it is actually a proportion of the total of the grazing and is not strictly in respect of numbers of animals.

6.52   If the division of the land is into very small portions, or includes one or more small portions, notice should be taken of the case of *Scholes* v. *Hargreaves* (1792) where it was said that there must be "land as will keep the cattle claimed to be commoned in the winter."[88]

[81] [1969] 1 Ch. 160 at 190.
[82] Namely *Daniel* v. *Hanslip, Leniel* v. *Harslop, Drury* v. *Kent, Bunn* v. *Channen*: considered at §§ 6.04 *et seq.*
[83] Commons Registration (General) Regulations 1966 (S.I. 1966 No. 1471), reg. 31.
[84] *cf.* § 4.7.
[85] *Nichols* v. *Chapman* (1860) 5 H. & N. 643, 157 E.R. 1337.
[86] *Hill* v. *Ellard* (1664) 1 Lev. 141, 83 E.R. 338; see also s.c. *sub nom. Ellard* v. *Hill* (1664) 1 Sid. 226, 82 E.R. 1072: *semble* half a cow may be taken as one cow for half a year.
[87] *Morse and Webb's Case* (1609) 13 Co.Rep. 65, 77 E.R. 1474.
[88] (1792) 5 T.R. 46 at 48, 101 E.R. 26 at 27, *per* Buller J.

(b) Apportionment of other rights

Rights for products which are annexed by appendancy or appurtenancy to a
house or other building clearly may never be apportioned on division of land
but remain with the building or some other building which, as a matter of
fact, replaces the old building.[89] An alienor of land has no choice in the matter so far as the disposition of the rights are concerned. Rights expressly
excepted on sale of a building may lead to the presumption of abandonment
with consequent extinguishment.[90] Rights which are self evidently
annexed to buildings (usually houses) are turbary, piscary and estovers of firebote and house bote.

6.53

The position will be different in the case of estovers of haybote or hedgebote
which are rights to take timber for the repair of implements or fences. There
seems no reason, in principle, why rights relating to land, or implements
used on land, may not be apportioned to divided parts of the land subject
only to the burden on the servient land not being increased.

6.54

(c) Proposals for change

The Common Land Forum recommends detailed control of all apportionment including the following matters:

6.55

(1) If land is remaining in agricultural use the grazing rights to be
apportioned to the divided land "according to what would be the
reasonable agricultural requirement of those holdings, judged
objectively. In some cases the appropriate method of apportionment would be by reference to the extent of the registered parcels of
the dominant tenement which is being divided."[91]

(2) If the right is for one animal only the right to be assigned to one
divided part only.[92]

(3) If the land is developed for purposes other than agriculture the right
to be extinguished.[93]

(4) If the right is one attached to a building, or is a right of estovers,
pannage, piscary, turbary or a right to dig stone, and the dominant
tenement is split into two plots, the right is to be attached to one
plot with no apportionment permitted for any right other than grazing.[94]

(5) All apportionments of grazing rights are to be submitted to an Agricultural Land Tribunal, with approval as a formality if certain cri-
teria are met but, if otherwise, following a hearing.[95] The
apportioned rights, it is proposed, shall be unexercisable until

[89] See further at § 5.59.
[90] cf. § 6.39.
[91] Common Land Forum Report, Appendix C, para. 064.
[92] ibid. para. 066.
[93] ibid. para. 071
[94] ibid. para. 082.
[95] ibid. para. 067.

approved by the Tribunal.[96] In the event that the existence of a right is not disclosed by a vendor it is to be the duty of any management committee, and the right of a commoner, to propose a suitable apportionment to the Tribunal.[97]

---

[96] Common Land Forum Report, Appendix C, para. 069.
[97] *ibid.* para. 070.

7. The Ownership of Common Land

Rights to use the land

1. Land subject to rights of common

(a) *General principles*

The modern view of the ownership of common land is that it may be con- **7.01**
sidered as equivalent to an ordinary freehold, subject only to the rights of
common granted expressly or impliedly by the owner or his predecessors,
and, statutory enactments which affect the land. In the words of the judges
the owner has "the entire dominion over the soil subject to the tenants'
rights of common"[1] and "all that the lord has not granted remains in him."[2]
The same remarks apply even in the case of sole pastures where the entire
benefit in the grazing has been granted away "for the soil is the lord's and he
has the mines, trees, bushes etc. and he may dig for turfs."[3]

Traditionally ownership of most of the common lands was vested in the **7.02**
lord of the manor and indeed over many of the wastes this is still so today.
On many others, however, a variety of persons, corporations, institutions
and trusts are encountered as current owners. In the case of regulated pastures the Public Trustee has a special role defined by statute.[4] The land may
be owned by any person capable of land ownership and in general it makes
no difference whether the land is still owned by the lord of the manor,
except in certain statutory provisions where the lord appears to have a role
denied to other owners.[5] For the purposes of this chapter "the lord" and
"the owner of the soil" may be treated as synonyms except where particularly noted. In the older cases it was almost universal practice to describe
the owner as lord and in statutes it is only recently that the alternative of

---

[1] *Doe d. Lowes* v. *Davidson* (1813) 2 M. & S. 175 at 184, 105 E.R. 348 at 352, *per*
Ellenborough C.J.
[2] *Arlett* v. *Ellis* (1827) 7 B. & C. 346 at 362, 108 E.R. 752 at 759, *per* Bayley J.
[3] *Hopkins* v. *Robinson* (1671) 1 Mod. 74 at 74, 86 E.R. 742 at 743, *per* Hale C.J.
[4] See § 7.85.
[5] For the rights of lords and other owners, see *Glover* v. *Lane* (1789) 3 T.R. 445, 100
E.R. 669; for the special role of the lord in statutes, see §§ 7.72 *et seq.*

lords and owners of the soil are mentioned. It follows that in considering earlier cases and statutes it is necessary to decide whether it is only lords of manors to whom reference is intended.

7.03 A frequently quoted statement on the rights of the owner of the soil, and one which is crucial to the principles of current use, is that of Bayley J. in *Arlett v. Ellis* (1827)[6]:

> "The lord has rights of his own reserved upon the waste; I do not say subservient to, but concurrent with, the rights of the commoners. And when it is ascertained that there is more common than is necessary for the cattle of the commoners, the lord, as it seems to me, is entitled to take that for his own purposes."

The way in which the surplus may be taken depends upon whether it is seasonal or permanent. If seasonal, it may be taken by the lord, or his licensee, at the time when it occurs; if permanent, by the procedure known as "approvement," *i.e.* by enclosure of the surplus land with extinguishment of rights over that land.[7] The right to take a seasonal surplus survives today but the right of approvement, although still theoretically extant, is so circumscribed by statute as to be all but obsolete.

7.04 The general principle governing the rights of the lord to use the land is that prima facie he is entitled to use the land or take its products subject only, based on the doctrine of non-derogation from grant, to not using the land unnecessarily or wantonly[8] and leaving a sufficiency of the products to satisfy whatever has been expressly or impliedly granted away. It will be seen that exceptionally it is possible to establish that the lord has reserved rights enabling him to encroach on the grants.[9] The exceptions are unusual and the burden of proof on the lord in establishing their existence is heavy.

7.05 In considering whether a sufficiency to satisfy the rights of the commoners has been left, following an act by the lord, the burden of proof is different, depending upon whether rights have been extinguished by approvement. Upon an approvement, the onus of proof lies on the lord to satisfy the court that a sufficiency has been left to satisfy the totality of the rights whether currently used or not.[10] It is otherwise if the lord acts say, to, take a seasonal surplus of a product, to remove a renewable product such as turf, or to remove part of the soil. Under these circumstances the plaintiff commoner will have to declare that the lord has put in his cattle (or done some other act) so that he, the commoner, was not able to enjoy his common so fully as before.[11] In other words, the commoner can only complain if he has suffered damage by the act of the lord.

---

[6] *Arlett v. Ellis* (1827) 7 B. & C. 346 at 369, 108 E.R. 752 at 761; see also *Kirby v. Sadgrove* (1797) 1 Bos. & Pul. 13 at 17, 126 E.R. 751 at 753, *per* Eyre C.J.

[7] For which see § 7.47.

[8] *Place v. Jackson* (1824) Dow. & Ry. K.B. 318,; see also *Trulock v. Rigsby* (1610) Yelv. 185, 80 E.R. 122; *Cronin v. Connor* (1913) 2 I.R. 119.

[9] See *Bateson v. Green* (1793) 5 T.R. 411, 101 E.R. 230, considered at § 7.22.

[10] *Robertson v. Hartopp* (1889) 43 Ch.D. 484.

[11] See *Smith v. Feverell* (1675) 2 Mod. 6, 86 E.R. 909; *Greenhow v. Ilsley* (1746) Willes 619, 125 E.R. 1351.

A second feature governing the relationship between lord and commoner is **7.06**
that the self help remedy of abatement is not available to the commoner in
respect of any prima facie lawful use of the common by the lord although
there is, of course, no inhibition on taking an action before the courts. This
matter is considered more fully in connection with the rights of commoners,[12] when it will be seen that their substantive rights over a common
are strictly circumscribed. At one time it was held in an action for trespass
that a commoner could not justify coming to the common with an intent to
put in his cattle unless he did put them in, but he might justify in coming to
see if the pasture is fit to receive his cattle.[13]

It hardly needs to be said that strangers will have even greater difficulty in **7.07**
justifying presence on a common. A lord is entitled, if he wishes, to take an
action against a stranger who walks, rides or "takes his carriage" upon a
common.[14] It will be otherwise in the case of commons subject to sole
rights when the lord will have an action for injury to the soil but not to the
herbage growing thereon.[15]

The rights of the owner of a common, as described in this chapter, may **7.08**
seem quite extensive. The practical reality, however, is that their scope
today is strictly circumscribed by a number of statutory measures and on
the majority of the commons the owner is a passive bystander. Prior to
registration under the C.R.A. 1965 the difficulties of the owner were compounded by uncertainty about the existence and quantum of rights exercisable over the land. Many of these uncertainties have been removed by
registration and there is anecdotal evidence of an increase in interest on the
part of owners. For some, however, the new certainty has come too late and
many have severed their connection with the land and are untraceable. The
C.R.A. 1965 sought, as indicated below not entirely successfully, to establish a public record of all owners.[16]

(b) *Grazing rights*

(i) Residual rights   The residual right to graze common land vested in **7.09**
the owner is an incident of the ownership of the land and is a direct consequence of the concept underlying rights of common, *i.e.* common land is
land where rights are shared by owner and commoners. It was put by Sir
Edward Coke thus:

"If a man claime by prescription any manner of common in another
man's land, and that the owner of the land shall be excluded to have
pasture, estovers, or the like, this is a prescription or custome against
the law, to exclude the owner of the soyle; for it is against the nature of
this word common, and it was implyed in the first grant, that the owner
of the soyle should take his reasonable profit there, as it hath beene
adjudged."[17]

---

[12] At § 8.15.
[13] *Spilman* v. *Hermitage* (1619) 5 Vin.Ab. 35.
[14] *Blundell* v. *Catterall* (1821) 5 B. & A. 268 at 315, 106 E.R. 1190 at 1207, *per* Abbott
C.J.
[15] *Cox* v. *Glue, Cox* v. *Moulsley* (1848) 5 C.B. 533, 136 E.R. 987.
[16] § 7.33.
[17] Co.Litt. 122a.

7.10   The owner may take a surplus of grazing in any year by means of his own cattle[18] or by licence to a stranger,[19] but "cannot let out to pasture so much as not to leave sufficient for the commoners."[20] It is not altogether unknown for owners to license strangers to graze[21] and there is some anecdotal indication of growing interest in the subject now that rights of common of pasture have been quantified under the provisions in the C.R.A. 1965. A licence for a period of one grazing season is, it is suggested, not necessarily an interest in land but more in the nature of a contract for the removal of a crop and does not need to be under seal.[22] A term of years absolute on the other hand, whether known as a licence or not, is actually the grant of an incorporeal hereditament and should be by deed.[23] The possibility of licensed rights deriving title from the unregistrable right of the owner raises potential difficulties for any management proposals which include the regulation of grazing.[24]

7.11   Where there is a permanent surplus occasioned by, say, former dominant tenements being taken out of agriculture, or the release of rights, there seems no reason in principle why the owner should not make new grants of rights for interests equivalent to a fee simple or for a term of years (but see the current restrictions on registration and exercisability of fee simple interests described earlier[25]).

7.12   In some early cases it was said that the lord may not agist cattle, *i.e.* allow strangers to graze the common subsuming the animals to his own control, unless there is a custom which allows the practice.[26] The reason for the distinction between lawful licensing and unlawful agistment is unclear but may be concerned with property in the animals and the law of distress damage feasant. Under the old law the animals of the owner of the soil were not generally subject to distraint[27] unless the owner was restricted to a certain number[28] or he unlawfully agisted[29] or he grazed at a time when the land was customarily depastured.[30] Following the abolition of distress damage feasant and the instigation of new actions under the Animals Act

---

[18] *Jones* v. *Richard* (1837) 6 Ad. & E. 530 at 533, 112 E.R. 203 at 204, *per* Lord Denman C.J.; *Arlett* v. *Ellis* (1827) 7 B. & C. 346 at 369, 108 E.R. 752 at 761, *per* Bayley J.

[19] *Smith* v. *Feverell* (1675), above, n. 11; accepted *Atkinson* v. *Teasdale* (1772) 3 Wils. K.B. 278 at 289, 95 E.R. 1054 at 1060, *per* de Grey L.C.J.

[20] *ibid.*; *contra* but doubted *Halsbury's Laws*, Vol. 4, para. 640, citing Co.Litt. 122a.

[21] *e.g.* Merthyr and Gelligaer Commons, Mid Glamorgan where, it seems, a licence to graze 100 ponies has been granted by the owner.

[22] *Monk* v. *Butler* (1619) Cro.Jac. 574, 79 E.R. 491; *Rumsey* v. *Rawson* (1669) 1 Vent. 18, 86 E.R. 13.

[23] L.P.A. 1925, s.52.

[24] The Common Land Forum Report recommends new legislation to establish statutory management associations with powers to regulate numbers of grazing animals: Report, para. 4.12.

[25] *cf.* § 4.41.

[26] Y.B. (1356) M. 30 E3, 27a.

[27] *Carril* v. *Pack and Baker* (1613) 2 Bulstr. 115, 80 E.R. 996.

[28] *Kenrick* v. *Pargiter* (1608) Yelv. 129, 80 E.R. 87.

[29] See above, n. 24.

[30] *Trulock* v. *White* (1638) 5 Vin.Ab. 33.

1971, which make the person in possession of animals liable for surcharging, it may be that the distinction is now obsolete.[31]

(ii) Quasi-rights to graze   The lord of a waste is entitled to quasi-   **7.13**
rights of common, in respect of his demesne land and purchased freeholds,
which attract the same characteristics and obligations as true rights of common. They provided an identical entitlement to an allotment, upon inclosure of the waste.[32] The quantum is based on the needs of the quasi-dominant tenement: the lord "has a right to turn his cattle on the common in respect of the land as any other commoner may, observing not to overstock."[33] In *Musgrave* v. *Inclosure Commissioners* (1874)[34] Blackburn J. referred to "rights of pasturage and common which have been enjoyed by the lord and tenants in such manner as, if it were not for the technical rule—that the lord being freeholder of the dominant tenements and the soil of the waste too, cannot have a right of common—would prove an established right beyond the memory of man to common over the waste in question." Similarly, in *Lloyd* v. *Earl of Powys* (1853)[35] the court accepted the principle laid down in *Bradshaw* v. *Eyre* (1597)[36] that upon unity of ownership of dominant and servient land a right of common is extinguished but something similar remains in favour of those deriving title from the owner: "it is *quasi* common used therewith; and although it be not the same common it was before, yet it is the like common." In *Birch* v. *Wilson* (1677)[37] the court seems to go even further in declaring that tenants of a lord enjoy common and not merely a licence. Certainly the quasi-right exercisable by a tenant is of sufficient substance to support an action by a commoner against another commoner.[38]

In practice, it seems that the obligation to fence against a common is   **7.14**
accepted by the lord, and his tenants, where the dominant land adjoins a
waste. This is much as might be expected if the obligation lies in custom.[39]

Unfortunately the C.R.A. 1965 did not require the registration and quantifi-   **7.15**
cation of quasi-rights (although this has been denied by one Commissioner),
with the result that the commons registers are not only incomplete as a
record of all lawful rights over the land but also inconsistent as a result of
differing treatment.[40]

---

[31] See § 10.19.
[32] Inclosure Act 1845, s.27 (repealed by the Commons Act 1876, s.34); *Musgrave* v. *Inclosure Commissioners* (1874) L.R. 9 Q.B. 162; *Arundell* v. *Lord Falmouth* (1814) 2 M. & S. 440, 105 E.R. 444; *Lloyd* v. *Earl of Powys* (1855) 4 El. & Bl. 485, 119 E.R. 177, 24 L.J.Q.B. 145.
[33] *Arundell* v. *Lord Falmouth* (1814), above, n. 32, at 443, 446, *per* Dampier J.
[34] Above, n. 32, at 175.
[35] Above, n. 32.
[36] (1597) Cro.Eliz. 570, 78 E.R. 814, *per* Gawdy and Fenner JJ.
[37] (1677) 2 Mod. 274 at 277, 86 E.R. 1068 at 1070, *per* Chief Justice and Wyndham J.
[38] *Cowlam* v. *Slack* (1812) 15 East. 108, 104 E.R. 785.
[39] See § 9.05.
[40] See § 4.10.

(c) *Rights to other products*

7.16 The general right to the residue, after satisfaction of rights of common granted away, applies as much to any other product of the land as it does to grass. In addition the owner *qua* owner has rights to take other products and parts of the soil together with the right to take animals *ferae naturae*.

7.17 **(i) Timber and woodland** A very high proportion of the common lands are physically suited to the production of timber. The owner of the soil may plant trees—"the right here exercised by the lord is an original right in the soil, prior to that of common, which is only concurrent with it."[41] As with other rights over the land, and in compliance with the doctrine of non-derogation from grant, it may not be used in such a way as to injure the rights of commoners, *i.e.* a sufficiency of grazing or any other product must be left. Similarly, whether the trees are planted, or are re-generated and natural, the owner is entitled to cut them down and convert them to his own use as one of the natural fruits of the soil. The only restriction once again is that a sufficiency of timber must be left to satisfy the rights to timber (if any) of the commoners. It is submitted that it is unnecessary to leave trees to satisfy estovers of, say, dead and fallen boughs as it has been held that there is a right to future estovers in similar circumstances.[42] If the commoner is injured by the planting of trees he may bring an action against the owner but may not abate the nuisance by, say, cutting down the trees[43] unless, possibly, all the grazing is destroyed.[44]

7.18 In practice there are considerable difficulties in the way of the owner seeking to use land for forestry. It is usually necessary to protect young trees from grazing animals by fencing, which will normally require the consent of the Secretary of State under the provisions contained in section 194 of the L.P.A. 1925.[45] Before giving his consent the Secretary of State will have to be satisfied that the proposal will not detract from the "benefit of the neighbourhood."[46] It should also be noticed that the granting of consent only makes the fencing lawful to the extent that it would be unlawful without consent. It has nothing to say about rights between owner and commoner. It follows that rights of common remain unaffected by a consent and any course of action open to a commoner under the common law remains. Prima facie a commoner may remove the fence or make openings in it if his ingress and egress to the common is obstructed.[47] The position is entirely different if the owner purports to be carrying out an "approvement" in which event rights of common are extinguished by the enclosure. However, approvement also requires the consent of the Secretary of State and there appears to be no modern example of a successful private inclosure to effect a commercial purpose.[48]

---

[41] *Kirby* v. *Sadgrove* (1797) 1 Bos. & Pul. 13 at 17, 126 E.R. 751 at 753, *per* Eyre C.J.
[42] *ibid.*
[43] *ibid.*; *Hope* v. *Osborne* [1913] 2 Ch. 349.
[44] *Hope* v. *Osborne*, above, n. 43.
[45] See further at § 9.34.
[46] For which see further at §§ 9.44–9.46.
[47] *cf.* § 8.16.
[48] For approvement, see § 7.47. See the Law of Commons Amendment Act 1893, cited at § 7.55, and *cf.* Table 2 at § 1.09.

(ii) Rights in the soil   There is a reserved right in the owner of the soil   **7.19**
to take part of the soil for any purpose including sale. The principles were
outlined by Hall V.-C. in *Hall* v. *Byron* (1877)[49]:

> "The law I consider to be that the lord may take gravel, marl, loam, and
> the like, in the waste, so long as he does not infringe upon the com-
> moners' rights, his right so to do being quite independent of the right of
> approvement under the Statute of Merton or at Common Law, and
> existing by reason of his ownership of the soil, subject only to the inter-
> ests of the commoners."

In the case concerned the lord had removed quantities of gravel, loam and
similar substances and had stripped off large portions of the turf. The type of
substance did not seem material to Hall V.-C., except that "the right to get
gravel so as to permanently destroy the herbage would ordinarily be less
admissable than that of getting loam, turf, and subsoil, which is only temporarily detrimental to the tenements."[50] It seems that the temporary
nature of the effects of some types of extraction will be taken into account
in considering a claim that sufficiency of herbage has or has not been left. In
the event, an injunction restrained the lord from any further works which
interfered with the rights of the complainant commoner. In the case of quarrying for gravel, sand and minerals the lord has a right to carry out any
necessary works so long as "he does not materially deprive commoners of
their rights of common."[51]

Among the products which the courts have recognised the owner may take   **7.20**
are turf and peat,[52] potting clay,[53] brick earth,[54] stone,[55] and coal.[56] Excava-
tion into the surface of the soil is permitted[57] and it seems that the commoner has no right of abatement even if the pits created are dangerous to his
animals.[58] However, the work must not be wantonly carried out and at least
some regard must be had to the safety of grazing animals[59]: "if the lord were
to exercise the right of taking stone wantonly, so as to unnecessarily interfere with the commoners' rights of pasture he would be liable to an
action."[60]

If the extraction of minerals causes collateral damage, as may occur where   **7.21**
spoil is spread, the owner is able to justify his actions in the case of ancient
mines if the damage is kept to a minimum.[61] Thus, a customary practice,

---

[49] (1877) 4 Ch.D. 667 at 675.
[50] *ibid.*
[51] *Malvern Hills Conservators* v. *Whitmore* (1909) 100 L.T. 841 at 845.
[52] *Greenhow* v. *Ilsley* (1746) Willes 619, 125 E.R. 1351.
[53] *Bateson* v. *Green* (1793) 5 T.R. 411, 101 E.R. 230.
[54] ——— v. *Palmer* (1729) 5 Vin.Ab. 7, 33.
[55] *Place* v. *Jackson* (1824) Dow. & Ry. K.B. 318.
[56] *Geo* v. *Cother* (1663) 1 Sid. 106, 82 E.R. 999.
[57] *Robinson* v. *Duleep Singh* (1878) 11 Ch.D. 798, at 832, *per* Fry J.
[58] cf. *Carril* v. *Pack and Baker* (1613) 2 Bulstr. 115, 80 E.R. 996.
[59] *Geo* v. *Cother*, above, n. 56.
[60] *Place* v. *Jackson*, above, n. 55, *per* Bayley J.; cf. *Malvern Hills Conservators* v.
Whitmore, above, n. 51.
[61] *Coo* v. *Cauthorn* (1662) 1 Keb. 390, 83 E.R. 1012.

proved by use, may enlarge the rights of the owner at the expense of the abridgment of the commoners' rights. To provide validity to a custom which does abridge rights it is necessary to prove certainty, reasonableness and immemorial origin.[62] A right to mine and let down the surface under buildings without paying compensation is unreasonable,[63] but a similar custom confined to wastes might be good,[64] although there is some authority to the contrary.[65] The rights of the owner in this context are not altogether clear and perhaps the correct legal principle is that enunciated by Hall V.-C. in *Hall* v. *Byron* (1877)[66]:

> " . . . assuredly whatever the lord can reasonably be supposed to have reserved out of his grant the usage may adequately prove that he did reserve. But a claim destructive of the subject-matter of the grant cannot be set up by any usage."

7.22 It is not possible to reconcile all the cases. One, which at first glance seems to be at variance with principle, is *Bateson* v. *Green* (1793).[67] A plaintiff, with a right of common of pasture over 10 acres, complained that the lessee defendant, claiming under the lord, had dug potting clay so that four acres were destroyed. Even without the digging there was insufficient grazing for the commoners. Evidence was adduced of licensees and lessees under the lord taking clay for pipe making for the past 70 years, and one of the licensees, 12 years previously, had been the plaintiff himself. The court found for the defendant, it being noticed that in this case the right was not claimed for his sole benefit, in which case the digging would have been an excess of right. It was instead a general right.[68] The custom showed the right of commoners in this case to be subservient to the right of the lord to take clay.[69] The case provides precedent for little other than saying that there may be land where the primary use is extraction for minerals with subsidiary and subservient rights of common.

7.23 It is not necessary to apply for a consent under section 194 of the L.P.A. 1925 for buildings, fences and other works of construction in connexion with the taking or working of minerals in or under a common.[70] It is necessary, however, to take account of the provisions contained in the Agricultural Land (Removal of Surface Soil) Act 1953.[71]

---

[62] *Wolstanton Ltd.* v. *Newcastle-under-Lyme Corporation* [1940] A.C. 860 at 876, *per* Viscount Maugham.
[63] *ibid.*; affirming the decision in *Hilton* v. *Granville (Earl)* (1845) 5 Q.B. 701, 114 E.R. 1414.
[64] *Gill* v. *Dickinson* (1880) 5 Q.B.D. 159.
[65] *Blackett* v. *Bradley* (1862) 1 B. & S. 940, 121 E.R. 963 (*Quaere per incuriam* as submission accepted that facts were indistinguishable from the *Hilton Case*, whereas that case was concerned with copyhold buidings).
[66] (1877) 4 Ch.D. 667 at 677.
[67] (1793) 5 T.R. 411, 101 E.R. 230.
[68] *ibid. per* Lord Kenyon C.J. at 416, 234.
[69] *ibid. per* Grose J. at 417, 234.
[70] s.194(4).
[71] See further at § 3.85.

(iii) Sporting rights In all cases, the right to take animals *ferae* **7.24**
naturae is an incident of the ownership of the soil of a common.[72] It is a
right which may be assigned as an incorporeal hereditament in gross.[73] The
commoner has no right to game or ground game,[74] simply in his capacity as
a commoner, but may, nevertheless, hold rights of common to take animals
or fish. A right of piscary is not altogether unusual and a right to take rabbits
not unknown.[75] Where a right of common appurtenant exists, the quantum
which may be taken will normally be limited to the needs of the dominant
tenement.[76] In all cases the owner of the soil will be required to leave a sufficiency of animals to satisfy the rights granted away.

In some cases, particularly on heather moors, the sporting rights can be of **7.25**
extraordinary value. While there may be an identity of interest between
owner and commoner in maintaining the heather at an appropriate growth
stage suitable for sheep and, say, grouse it seems that sometimes over-
grazing may affect the herbage to the disadvantage of the sportsman. In the
absence of a statutory management scheme there is no effective method of
reconciling the conflicting interests other than by agreement and the application of the ordinary common law rules. These are that the commoner
may only take the herbage through the mouths of his animals,[77] may not
interfere with the herbage[78] and may not exceed his quantum of right.[79] The
owner of the soil may not act in such a way as to deprive a commoner of his
sufficiency of grazing.

(c) *Other uses of the common*

(i) Coney-burrows Many of the early cases concerned with the rights **7.26**
of owners involved the use of the land for commercial rabbit keeping and
the maintenance of, what were known at the time as, coney-burrows. The
whole practice is now completely obsolete but the cases concerned may be
relevant for analogous application to future practices and they also indicate
limitations on the rights of commoners. It seems that establishing conies *de
novo* on a common was justifiable as they were beasts of warren, much as
deer, and were to be distinguished from animals such as foxes and other ver-
min,[80] but the usual principle of sufficiency of grazing being left for commoners applied.[81] Further, once established the conies could not be allowed
to increase so as to impinge upon the sufficiency.[82] As the use of the land in
this way was a lawful use by the lord there was no right of abatement available to the commoner by killing the conies[83] or, it seems, levelling and

---

[72] *Blades* v. *Higgs* (1865) 11 H.L.C. 621 at 631, 11 E.R. 1474 at 1479, *per* Lord
Westbury L.C.
[73] *Mason* v. *Clarke* [1955] A.C. 778.
[74] See § 8.12.
[75] *Samford and Havel's Case* (1612) Godb. 184, 78 E.R. 112; *Duke of Portland* v. *Hill*
(1866) L.R. 2 Eq. 765.
[76] *cf.* §§ 3.124–3.126.
[77] § 8.02.
[78] *ibid.*
[79] C.R.A. 1965, s.15.
[80] *Pelling* v. *Langden* (1601) Owen 114, 74 E.R. 940.
[81] *Gresill* v. *Hoddesden* (1608) Yelv. 143, 80 E.R. 96.
[82] *ibid.*
[83] *Hadesden* v. *Gryssel* (1607) Cro.Jac. 195, 79 E.R. 170.

destroying the burrows even if they were of such a nature as to be dangerous to commonable animals.[84] The last point must be balanced against another decision where it was said that the lord may not dig holes so as to endanger animals on the common.[85]

7.27 **(ii) Fish ponds**   A use for which there seems to be no modern precedent but which may, nevertheless, be of current interest to some owners is the construction of fish ponds. There seems no reason in principle why the land should not be used for this purpose providing a sufficiency of grazing is left for the commoners. The courts have mentioned such a use with approval.[86] Although, for the purposes of the C.R.A. 1965, common land includes land covered with water,[87] and its status is unchanged under that Act by inundation, it seems that, for the purposes of section 194 of the L.P.A. 1925, land probably means land in the sense of soil. It follows that the construction of fish ponds falls within the class of works requiring the consent of the Secretary of State.[88]

7.28 **(iii) Cultivation**   In principle there seems no reason why the owner of the soil should not plough or otherwise cultivate the surface of a common although there seems to be no authority on the point. Clearly, in the case of land which is subject to ownership and occupation for part of the year in severalty, there can be no objection. Indeed, in common arable fields that is the historical use of the land. On wastes there is no doubt that the erection of any associated fencing normally requires the consent of the Secretary of State under section 194 of the L.P.A. 1925,[89] but in common fields there may be a common law or statutory right to enclose.[90]

7.29 **(iv) Recreational use**   It is not unknown for sporting and recreational events to be licensed over, or more permanently authorised, on commons. Perhaps the most complete use of this nature is the granting of land for use as a golf course of which there are a substantial number on commons.[91] In one survey of statutorily managed commons, eight of the 25 considered had one or more golf courses on them.[92] Once again any fencing or other works will normally attract the requirement of the consent of the Secretary of State under section 194 of the L.P.A. 1925.[93] It is suggested that, where greens are enclosed and fairways mown, a golf course can only be lawful if a sufficiency of grazing is left for the commoners.

---

[84] *Carril* v. *Pack and Baker* (1613) 2 Bulstr. 115, 80 E.R. 996.

[85] *Geo* v. *Cother* (1663) 1 Sid. 106, 82 E.R. 999.

[86] *Pelling* v. *Langden*, above, n. 80; *cf. Boulston's Case* (1596) 5 Co.Rep. 104b, 77 E.R. 216: dovecote.

[87] C.R.A.1965, s.22(1).

[88] For s.194 consent, see further at § 9.31.

[89] *ibid.*

[90] *cf.* §§ 1.71–1.72.

[91] *e.g.* see *Pennard Golf Club* v. *Richards (V.O.)* (1976) 20 R.R.C. 225; *R.* v. *Doncaster Metropolitan Borough Council, ex p. Braim* (1987) 85 L.G.R. 233.

[92] *Land Use Consultants, Management Schemes for Commons*, (1985), p. 20, Table 6.

[93] *cf.* § 9.34. See also the case cited at § 9.27 and n. 49 thereto for the restriction of public access authorised under s.193 of the L.P.A. 1925.

2. Land subject to sole rights

The rights of the owner of the soil of land which is subject to sole rights of   **7.30**
vesture, herbage or pasture are much more restricted than those over true
common land. The essence of the sole right is that the owner has granted
away his entire interest in the product concerned. In contradistinction to
land subject to rights of common the holders of sole rights may bring an
action in trespass against strangers to the common and the owner may not
unless there is trespass against the parts of the land retained. A trespass will
be actionable by the owner for driving stakes into the ground but not for riding over the surface.[94]

There is little authority on the substantive rights of the owner of land sub-   **7.31**
ject to sole rights, although it seems clear that he may take trees and
bushes,[95] parts of the soil such as stone[96] and may exercise gaming and
sporting rights.[97] The holders of sole rights have no right to take game[98] but
may take ground game.[99] Where there is neither statutory authority nor
past practice to support a particular type of act the owner should proceed
with caution as any interference with the products granted away may be a
trespass.[1]

Although all the sole rights have been granted away there is no reason why   **7.32**
the owner of the soil should not acquire a share in those rights by purchase
and take his place alongside other stint holders,[2] but there is no question of
an entitlement to residual grazing as there is with true rights of common.
Any surplus or residue accrues to the entirety of the stint holders.

Registration

(a) *The registration of owners*

Unlike the registration of land and rights the registration of ownership   **7.33**
under the C.R.A. 1965 does not purport to be definitive or conclusive. Section 1 of the Act requires that:

> "There shall be registered . . .
> (a) land in England or Wales which is common land or a town or village
>   green;
> (b) rights of common over such land; and
> (c) persons claiming to be or found to be owners of such land or becom-
>   ing owners thereof by virtue of this Act . . . "

---

[94] 3 Dyer 285b, 73 E.R. 641; Co.Litt. 4b; *Welden* v. *Bridgwater* (1592) Moore (K.B.)
453, 72 E.R. 594; *Cox* v. *Glue* (1848) 5 C.B. 533, 136 E.R. 987; *Walker* v. *Murphy*
[1915] 1 Ch. 71.
[95] *Hopkins* v. *Robinson* (1671) 1 Mod. 74, 86 E.R. 742, *per* Hale C.J.
[96] *Place* v. *Jackson* (1824) Dow. & Ry. K.B. 318.
[97] *Lonsdale (Earl of)* v. *Rigg* (1856) 11 Ex. 654, 156 E.R. 992.
[98] Game Act 1831, s.10.
[99] Ground Game Act 1880, s.1; see further at § 8.12.
[1] As with all sole rights the owner of the soil has granted a separate incorporeal hereditament which is protected by an action in trespass; *cf.* § 8.30.
[2] *e.g. Lonsdale (Earl of)* v. *Rigg*, above, n. 97.

But, section 10 of the Act, which provides that a final registration shall be conclusive evidence of the matters registered as at the date of registration, has no application to the ownership section of the registers.

(b) *The categories of owners*

7.34 The wording of the section provides for three separate categories of owner, one of which consists of a form of vesting of ownership by a Commons Commissioner, but no class of recorded owner may point to the registers as conclusive evidence of the matters recorded there.

7.35 **(i) "persons claiming to be owners"** Under the inital registration procedure any person with a claim to the fee simple was able to register his ownership of any land on the commons registers.[3] No evidence to support the claim was required other than a statutory declaration stating that the applicant believed in his claim. The periods for objection having elapsed, and in the absence of objection, a claim became final.[4] A finalised entry of ownership in the commons registers does not, however, provide conclusive evidence of the matters registered and it seems that a person claiming ownership in this way may be displaced, without more, by the registration of title under the Land Registration Acts.[5] The Common Land Forum recommends that future legislation shall provide an "unequivocal power," to a court or other judicial body, to order rectification of the commons register upon proof that the registered owner has no justifiable title.[6]

7.36 **(ii) "persons found to be owners"** Failure to register land or rights under the C.R.A. resulted in loss of status as common land and non-exercisability respectively.[7] There was no corresponding sanction for non-registration of a claim to ownership. It is hardly surprising, therefore, to find that of the original 16,250 claims for land registration only about 6,000 were matched to claims for ownership.[8] Where no person claimed ownership under the initial registration procedure, a registration authority is required to refer the matter to a Commons Commissioner for an inquiry.[9] After the registration authority has given notices, as prescribed under regulations, a Commissioner holds an unclaimed ownership hearing at which claimants and others with information as to ownership may be heard.[10] Where, following an inquiry, the Commissioner is satisfied that a person is the owner

---

[3] Commons Registration (General) Regulations 1966 (S.I. 1966 No. 1471), reg. 7(3), Sched., Form 10.

[4] C.R.A. 1965, ss.7(1), 10.

[5] See § 7.42.

[6] Common Land Forum Report, Appendix C, paras. 124, (4), (5).

[7] C.R.A. 1965, s.1(2)(a), (b).

[8] *Common Land. Preparations for Comprehensive Legislation. Report of an Interdepartmental Working Party 1975–1977* Department of the Environment (1978), para. 4.5.

[9] C.R.A. 1965, s.8(1).

[10] Commons Commissioners Regulations 1971 (S.I. 1971 No. 1727), regs. 11, 15, 19(4).

of the land he shall direct the registration authority to register that person accordingly.[11] Under this circumstance a person may be said to have been found to be the owner. The conclusive evidence provision in section 10 of the Act does not apply and it seems that registration of title may still override a commons registration.

(iii) "persons becoming owners" If the Commissioner holding an **7.37** unclaimed ownership inquiry is not satisfied that any person is the owner of the land, *and* the land has been registered as a town or village green, the Commissioner shall direct the registration authority to register a local authority as owner.[12] Local authorities appear to be the persons becoming owners under the C.R.A. 1965. It is further provided that upon such a registration the land shall vest in the local authority but yet again the conclusive evidence provision has no application.[13] While it seems likely that the intention of the Act was to vest unclaimed greens in a local authority conclusively, the wording of the Act seems somewhat sparse to divest another previous owner. However, as the effect of the Act is to vest the land in possession the Limitation Act 1980 will probably apply to prevent recovery of the land by a previous owner once the statutory limitation period has elapsed. The Common Land Forum recommends that future legislation shall allow "aggrieved claimants" to the ownership of a village green to apply to the county court for the registers to be amended.[14]

Where vesting in a local authority has taken place, and providing that the **7.38** land is not regulated by a scheme under the Commons Act 1899, sections 10 and 15 of the Open Spaces Act 1906 (power to manage and make byelaws)[15] shall apply to the land as if the local authority had acquired ownership under that Act.[16]

The local authority in which land is vested is the parish or community **7.39** council, where there is one,[17] unless the common is regulated under the Commons Act 1899,[18] in which case the vesting will only take place if the powers of management are already vested in the parish or community council; if the land is in a London borough, the council of that borough; and in any other case the district council.[19]

---

[11] C.R.A. 1965, s.8(2).

[12] ss.1(3), 8(3).

[13] *cf.* C.R.A. 1965, s.10. The Common Land Forum recommends that new legislation shall provide that where land has been vested in a local authority "an aggrieved claimant" to the ownership of the land shall be able to apply to a county court for a divesting and re-vesting order: Common Land Forum Report, Appendix C, paras. S16, S20, and *cf.* para. 019.

[14] Common Land Forum Report, Appendix D, para. S20.

[15] For which see further at § 12.133.

[16] C.R.A. 1965, s.8(4).

[17] Where a parish or community council comes into existence after vesting it may require the registration authority to vest the land in it: s.8(6).

[18] For which see § 12.64.

[19] C.R.A. 1965, s.8(5).

(c) *Protection of unclaimed common land*

7.40   Where any *land* has become finally registered whether as common land or a town or village green and no owner is registered either under the C.R.A. 1965, or the Land Registration Acts, section 9 provides that "any local authority in whose area the land or part of the land is situated may take such steps for the protection of the land against unlawful interference as could be taken by an owner in possession of the land, and may . . . institute proceedings for any offence committed in respect of the land."[20] The power is available before an unclaimed ownership hearing and, in respect of common land, afterwards if no person is found to be the owner. It should be noticed that there is no duty imposed upon an authority to act under section 9 and the incentive to do so is limited when the land is currently vested in some other person, albeit at present unknown. If an authority does decide to act it seems that the section is drawn widely enough to allow both civil and criminal proceedings.

7.41   The Act provides that unclaimed common land land shall "be vested as Parliament may hereafter determine."[21] It has been estimated that some 10,000 acres of land will attract statutory vesting[22] presumably when, and in the way that, Parliament determines in a second stage of legislation.

(d) *Provisions on sale and purchase*

7.42   The Act precluded the registration under the initial registration procedure of any person as owner if the title to land was registered under the Land Registration Acts.[23] Further, where an owner has been registered under the C.R.A. 1965, either provisionally or finally, section 12 of the Act comes into effect. The section provides that, if the land is finally registered, section 123 of the Land Registration Act 1925 (compulsory registration of title on sale) applies to the land whether the land is in a compulsory registration area or not.[24] If, however, the common land registration is provisional, *i.e.* there is an unresolved dispute, compulsory registration of title is not required unless , of course, the land is in an area of compulsory registration.

7.43   Where title is registered under the Land Registration Acts, and a commons registration authority is notified of the fact by the Chief Land Registrar, the authority is required to delete the previous ownership entry from the commons registers and indicate merely that the land is registered under the Land Registration Acts.[25] Registered title supercedes and seems to override any ownership registration on the commons registers.

---

[20] See further at § 11.30 for a power of county and district councils in connection with urban commons.

[21] C.R.A. 1965, s.1(3).

[22] *Common Land. Preparations for Comprehensive Legislation. Report of an Interdepartmental Working Party 1975–77*, Department of the Environment (1978), para. 5.5.

[23] C.R.A. 1965, s.4(3).

[24] For compulsory registration see the Land Registration Act 1925, s.120.

[25] C.R.A. 1965, s.12(*b*); *cf.* Commons Registration (General) Regulations 1966 (S.I. 1966 No. 1471), reg. 21.

Once the title to common land is registered under the Land Registration **7.44**
Acts the public registers of common land cease to be public so far as this
feature of registration is concerned. The names of proprietors of registered
titles are hidden by the secrecy provisions of the Land Registration Act
1925,[26] but local authorities have powers to breach these provisions.[27] The
Common Land Forum recommends that regulations made under the Land
Registration Acts shall provide that when a commons registration authority
certifies that a piece of land is registered as common land any person may
carry out an official search to discover the name(s) and address(es) of the
owner(s) of the land.[28]

(e) *Registration of residual and quasi-rights*

It has been demonstrated that the owner of common land may have two dis- **7.45**
tinct classes of rights over the land which are analogous to rights of common: a residual right to any surplus of a particular product after the rights of
common are satisfied and quasi-rights in respect of demesne land and purchased freeholds.[29] The C.R.A. 1965 set out to provide for the registration of
rights of common, the definition of which was not exhaustive but included
sole rights of pasture, herbage and vesture, while expressly excluding rights
held for a term of years or from year to year.[30] Thus, prima facie, the owners'
quasi-rights were not intended to be registrable. However, the Commons
Commissioners have not taken this view consistently and a substantial
number of quasi-rights, in the possession of owners and tenants, have
achieved registration.[31] Occasionally residual rights have also been registered.[32]

Land ceasing to be common land

Probably the most prolific source of removal of land from common land **7.46**
status today is compulsory purchase for public purposes. *Ex hypothesi* compulsory purchase is outside the control of the owner of common land and, as
it is the rights and obligations of the owner which are under consideration
in this chapter it is considered elsewhere.[33] It is only those procedures
which are within the direct influence of the owner of the land which are
dealt with in this section—approvement, customary inclosure, release of
rights, change of use following planning permission and the removal of land
from statutory common land status.

---

[26] s.112.
[27] *ibid.* s.129; Local Government (Miscellaneous Provisions) Act 1976, s.16.
[28] Common Land Forum Report, Appendix C, paras. 097–099.
[29] *cf.* §§ 7.09, 7.13.
[30] C.R.A. 1965, s.22(1).
[31] See further at § 4.10.
[32] Noticed on the West Glamorgan registers.
[33] § 5.85.

1. Approvement

7.47 Approvement is the right of the lord of a manor or other owner of the soil[34] to take in hand land which is surplus to the total amount necessary to satisfy all the rights of common over a waste.[35] It was described by Bayley J. in *Arlett* v. *Ellis* (1827)[36] in this way:

> "When it is ascertained that there is more common than is necessary for the cattle of the commoners, the lord, as it seems to me, is entitled to take that for his own purposes. . . . It seems to me that the lords right is this: he may approve provided he leave sufficiency of common of pasturage for all the cattle which are entitled to feed upon it."

The process of approvement involves unilateral action by the owner whereby the surplus land is enclosed[37] and converted into unincumbered freehold. The approved land is relieved of all rights of common but attracts no right of common to itself.[38]

7.48 In the nineteenth century there was much debate on the scope of the owners' right to approve. It is a procedure of little practical importance today due to several statutory control provisions and is dealt with here only in outline to provide guidance for the small number of occasions when it might prove of relevance.

(a) History

7.49 The Statute of Merton 1235[39] enacted that, whenever an assize of novel disseisin was brought for a common by the feoffees of the lord of a manor and it appeared that they had sufficient pasture on the wastes for their tenements, and free egress and regress therefrom, the enclosing lord should go quit of the charge. The Statute of Westminster II 1285[40] applied the same principle between neighbours as between lords and tenants, and also permitted enclosure for certain buildings and enlarged curtilages. Both statutes were confirmed by a further Act in 1549.[41] It has been argued that in the thirteenth century statutes were only declaratory of the common law, with the

---

[34] *Glover* v. *Lane* (1789) 3 T.R. 445, 100 E.R. 669 (alienee of the lord); *Patrick* v. *Stubbs* (1842) 9 M. & W. 830, 152 E.R. 351 (tenant *pur autre vie*); *Hamerton* v. *Eastoff* (1635) Clayt. 38 (lord in by wrong); 18 Ass., pl. 4 (tenant of soil against own lord).

[35] *Robertson* v. *Hartopp* (1889) 43 Ch.D. 484 at 517, *per* Fry L.J. disapproving *Lascelles* v. *Lord Onslow* (1877) 2 Q.B.D. 433, which proceeded on the basis of sufficiency assessed by the last 10 years user, unless user had been taken in lieu of other unavailable evidence.

[36] (1827) 7 B. & C. 346 at 369, 108 E.R. 752 at 761.

[37] An approvement must be fenced: 2 Inst. 87; gaps in the fence will not prevent a parcel from being considered as enclosed: *Paston* v. *Utbert* (1629) Litt. 264 at 267, 124 E.R. 238 at 240.

[38] *Costard and Wingfield's Case* (1588) Godb. 96, 78 E.R. 59; *Bradshaw* v. *Bokingham* (1603) Noy 106, 74 E.R. 1072; an enfeoffment of the approved land by the lord does not affect the feoffee's rights over the remainder of the waste: *Anon.* (1574) 3 Dyer 339a, 73 E.R. 744.

[39] Repealed by the Statute Law Reform Act 1953.

[40] Commons Act 1285.

[41] Improvement of Commons Act (repealed by the Civil Procedure Acts Repeal Act 1879).

conclusion reached that approvement has an existence independent of the statutes.[42] It seems unlikely that this argument would hold much appeal for a court today.

The existence of the Statutes 1235 and 1285 indicates that, at the time,   **7.50** approvement by the unilateral act of the lord was a live issue. As the centuries went by, however, enclosure and engrossment of holdings proceeded initially by means of a court decree to legitimise enclosure, and later by private Act.[43] By the end of the eighteenth century approvement seems to have fallen into almost total disuse.[44]

During the nineteenth century the emphasis was on inclosure by private   **7.51** Act, facilitated by the Inclosure Consolidation Act 1801 and later the Inclosure Act 1845. This seems not to have been enough for some owners and attention turned towards unilateral action by approvement. The conflicting interests of commoners, lords and the growing commons preservation faction met head on in the courts in a series of legal confrontations.[45] The outcome was a series of stinging defeats for the lords but, more importantly perhaps, public attention was focussed on the rapid progress towards total inclosure. From 1866 onwards statutory changes were introduced to protect wastes from inclosure and in 1893 further approvement was forbidden without the consent of the Inclosure Commissioners. There has been no large scale approvement since.

(b) Legislative control

(i) Commons Act 1876, s.31   The section provides that any person   **7.52** intending to inclose or approve a common shall give notice to all persons claiming any legal right in such a common by publishing a notice of his intention at least three months beforehand.

This is more widely drawn than is necessary to effect approvement, which   **7.53** applies only to wastes, and encompasses any form of inclosure of a common or part of a common, defined in the Act to mean "any land subject to be inclosed under the Inclosure Acts 1845 to 1868."[46] Thus, most land used in common for agriculture is included but a proviso excepts "any commons or wastes whereon the rights of common are vested solely in the lord of the manor." The exception seems to have no application to land not owned by a lord of a manor.

Inclosure of metropolitan commons by means of an award under the Inclosure Act 1845 is prohibited.[47] Nevertheless, section 31 is expressly applied   **7.54** to this class of land,[48] presumably to cover approvements.

---

[42] Elton, pp. 177 *et seq.*; Joshua Williams, *contra*, pp. 103 *et seq.*

[43] *cf.* Hoskins, "History of Common Land and Common Rights" in Royal Commission Report, Appendix II, especially at p. 162.

[44] *The Cultivation etc. of Waste Lands*, Reports from Committees of the House of Commons, (1774–1802) Vol. ix: printed by order of the House, (1803), p. 208, Appendix B.

[45] For a full description see Eversley, *Commons, Forests and Footpaths* (1910).

[46] Commons Act 1876, s.37; Inclosure Act 1845, s.11.

[47] Metropolitan Commons Act 1866, s.5.

[48] Metropolitan Commons Act 1878, s.3.

7.55 **(ii) Law of Commons Amendment Act 1893**   Section 1 provides:

> "An inclosure or approvement of any part of a common purporting to be made under the statute of Merton and the statute of Westminster the second, or either of such statutes, shall not be valid unless it is made with the consent of the Secretary of State."

The effect of the section is not to provide validation for an approvement but merely makes an approvement unlawful without a consent. It, therefore, has nothing to say about the lawful nature of the approvement as between the parties interested in the common. Section 4 expressly preserves the right of any person affected to take proceedings by way of information, action or otherwise. The lawfulness of a proposed or purported approvement may be challenged in a county court through an action under section 30 of the Commons Act 1876.[49]

7.56   In giving or withholding his consent the Secretary of State is required to have regard to the same considerations and hold the same enquiries as are directed by the Commons Act 1876 to be taken into consideration before forming an opinion whether an application for inclosure shall be acceded to or not.[50] The nature of the considerations and enquiries are considered more fully later[51] but for the present purposes it can be said that "the benefit of the neighbourhood" test is applied, requiring that the works be expedient having regard to the health, comfort and convenience of the inhabitants of the neighbourhood. It will clearly be difficult in most cases to establish that an approvement is of benefit to anyone other than the owner. Since the Act was passed there have been 45 inclosures and the average area involved has been under one and a half acres.[52]

7.57   The scope for an approvement is strictly limited by the Act, but it may be possible to invoke the procedure in order to effect some public purpose where there is difficulty in obtaining a release of rights from all holders of rights of common.

7.58   **(iii) Commons Act 1899, s.22**   A form of approvement was, and in a few cases still is, allowed under certain statutory provisions.[53] The owner of a common[54] may grant land for a number of public purposes, which will have the effect of extinguishing the rights and interests of all other persons in the land. For example, upon conveyance of land for the purposes of a site under the School Sites Act 1841, if gratuitously made, "the rights and inter-

---

[49] For which see § 8.31.

[50] Law of Commons Amendment Act 1893, s.3.

[51] See § 9.40, as applied to s.194 of the L.P.A. 1925.

[52] See Table 1 at § 1.09.

[53] Commons Act 1899, Sched. 1: Poor Relief Act 1601 (repealed in 1967); Clergy Residences Repair Act 1776 (repealed in 1978); Gifts for Churches Act 1811; Church Building Act 1818 (repealed in 1974); Poor Relief Act 1831 (repealed in 1927); Crown Land Allotments Act 1831 (repealed in 1927); Union and Parish Property Act 1835 (repealed in 1929); School Sites Act 1841; Land Clauses Consolidation Act 1845; Literary and Scientific Institutions Act 1854; Compulsory Purchase Act 1965, Pt. I.

[54] Any grant or inclosure is affected by the section irrespective of the nature of the grantor's title.

ests of all persons in the said land shall be barred and divested by such conveyance."[55]

Where such a conveyance is made section 22 of the Commons Act 1899 is **7.59** brought into operation. It provides that the grant shall not be valid unless specially authorised by Act of Parliament, made to or by a Government Department or made with the consent of the Secretary of State. In giving or witholding his consent the Secretary of State shall have regard to the same considerations and make the same enquiries as are required for an application for inclosure.[56] The procedure under this Act is not correctly viewed as an ordinary approvement but the result is much the same. The section also applies to compulsory purchase orders made under Part I of the Compulsory Purchase Act 1965.[57]

(c) *Limitations on approvement*

There are obvious difficulties in claiming, at this date, that an approvement **7.60** is being carried out under the common law as it existed prior to the passing of the thirteenth century statutes, but there may still be some very limited scope for approvement under those statutes.[58] It is necessary, therefore, to mention some supposed limitations on its use.

An issue which caused much discussion and extensive consideration in the **7.61** courts was whether the owner of a waste might approve against rights of common other than pasturage, for the statutes do indeed only mention grazing rights.[59] The law today must be as stated by Willes L.C.J. in *Fawcett* v. *Strickland* (1737),[60] when he said that "it would be absurd to say that a lord cannot enclose against common of pasture, because his tenants or some other person have common of piscary or common of estovers in the same waste." However, if the enclosure did effect prejudicially the piscary or estovers the lord would not be able to justify his action.[61]

There were also doubts about the validity of approving against rights of **7.62** common sans nombre or in any way which derogated from grant.[62] As has been shown, rights sans nombre are now obsolete, not least as the result of the C.R.A. 1965, and may be disregarded.[63] It is probably still the case, as a matter of general legal principle, that an approvement which infringes the terms on which the original grant of rights of common was made is unlawful, but it is very unusual today for evidence of the original grants to be available.

[55] School Sites Act 1841, s.2.
[56] s.22(2); *cf.* § 9.44.
[57] For compulsory purchase of common land, see § 5.85.
[58] There does not appear to have been a successful claim, at least in modern times, to an approvement outside the statutes. There seems no reason in principle why the procedure under the statutes should not be invoked to facilitate an alternative and limited public use of land in circumstances where it has proved impossible to obtain a release of rights from all the rights holders.
[59] See the Commons Act 1285.
[60] (1737) Willes 57 at 61, 125 E.R. 1054 at 1056; similarly, *Arlett* v. *Ellis* (1827) 7 B. & C. 346 at 371, 108 E.R. 752 at 762, *per* Bayley J.
[61] *ibid.*
[62] See Elton, pp. 194 and 200; Joshua Williams, p. 113.
[63] § 3.137.

2. Customary inclosure

7.63 Similar to approvement, but to be distinguished therefrom, is inclosure by the lord of the manor with the consent of the homage.[64] This had the effect of creating new customary copyhold tenements and in some manors was extensively practised. The process is now obsolete for the obvious reason that copyhold tenements may no longer be created.[65] The subject is only mentioned now as it may be necessary to be aware of it in matters of title investigation.

7.64 The nature, procedure and extent of the practice depended upon the custom of the manor. It can be distinguished from approvement in that it was copyhold tenure which resulted and the new estate attracted customary rights of common.[66] The legal theory justifying the creation of new copyhold estates and encroachment on the commons is explained in *Lord Northwick* v. *Stanway* (1803)[67] as a reservation by the lord to hold the waste as potentially demisable by copy of the court rolls.

7.65 The procedure became controlled by the Copyhold Act 1887, s.6 (substantially repeated in the Copyhold Act 1894, s.8), which provided that any new grants of land not previously of copyhold tenure required the consent of the Inclosure Commissioners. In giving or witholding their consent the Commissioners were required to have regard to the same considerations as were to be taken into account by them when considering inclosure of commons.[68]

3. Release of rights

7.66 The release of all rights exercisable over a common to the owner of the soil, whether express or implied,[69] will result in the land ceasing to be common land. An express release of rights to be effective at law should be by deed.[70] Such a release will not necessarily, however, have the effect of taking the land outside legislation affecting common land.

---

[64] *Lady Wentworth* v. *Clay* (1676) Rep.Temp.Finch 263, 23 E.R. 144; *Hughes* v. *Games* (1726) Sel.Cas.Temp.King 62, 25 E.R. 224; *R.* v. *Warblington (Inhabitants)* (1796) 1 T.R. 241, 99 E.R. 1073; *Folkard* v. *Hemmett* (1776) 5 T.R. 417n., 101 E.R. 234; *Lord Northwick* v. *Stanway* (1803) 3 Bos. & Pul. 346, 127 E.R. 189; *Boulcott* v. *Winmill* (1809) 2 Camp. 261, 170 E.R. 1149; *Earl Cowley* v. *Wellesley* (1866) 35 Beav. 635, 55 E.R. 1043.

[65] L.P.A. 1922, s.188, Sched. 12.

[66] *Lord Northwick* v. *Stanway*, above, n. 64; see also *Swayne's Case* (1608) 8 Co.Rep. 63a, 77 E.R. 568.

[67] (1803) 3 Bos. & Pul. 346, 127 E.R. 189.

[68] *i.e.* the conditions in the Commons Act 1876, s.7, for which see § 9.44.

[69] For implied release of rights, see § 5.43.

[70] Co.Litt. 264b; *Lovell* v. *Smith* (1857) 3 C.B.(N.S.) 120 at 127, 140 E.R. 685 at 687, *per* Willes L.C.J.

(a) *Law of Property Act 1925*

Section 193[71] provides a statutory right of public access to metropolitan **7.67**
commons, and wastes and commons in certain urban areas and, additionally, may have been applied to rural commons by a revocable or irrevocable
deed executed by the owner of the soil. The right will survive a release of
common rights over the land but not a statutory extinguishment of rights[72]
or, a resolution of a county council approved by the Secretary of State.[73] In
the case of rural commons it will cease upon revocation of the deed of dedication by the owner.

Section 194[74] makes unlawful the erection of any building or fence, or the **7.68**
construction of any other work whereby access to land, which was subject
to rights of common on January 1, 1926, is prevented or impeded, without
the consent of the Secretary of State. The section does not apply to all statutory common land[75] but has continuing application to any land subject to
rights of common on January 1, 1926, irrespective of its later status. As with
section 193 the provision ceases to apply if rights of common are
extinguished by statute[76] and as was noticed earlier has no application in
respect of the otherwise lawful works carried out by the owner of the soil in
connection with the taking or working of minerals in or under the land.[77]
As for section 193, the county council may by resolution assent to, and the
Secretary of State may approve, the land being excluded from the section.
Thus where a change of use is to be effected and a release of rights has been
obtained it is possible, and not entirely unusual, for a county council to
assent to the exclusion of the land from the scope of section 194.[78]

(b) *Commons Registration Act 1965*

An express release of rights, with the consequence that in the sight of the **7.69**
common law the land has ceased to be common land, will not necessarily
result in a successful application for removal of land from the commons
registers. It will also be necessary to prove that at the time of registration
the land did not also fall under the second head of the definition of common
land in the Act, *i.e.* waste land of a manor not subject to rights of common,
or that it has since registration ceased to fall under that head.[79] Strictly
there is no need to apply for removal of the land from the registers when
land ceases to be statutory common land as the registers are evidential only
as at the date of registration but most would prefer to apply for removal.
Where an act or event can be proved, which takes the land outside the statutory definition, the registration authority has no alternative but to accede to
the application for removal. The removal of the land from the commons

---

[71] For which see further at § 11.06.
[72] s.193(1)(*d*)(i); This provision does not however apply to "extinguishment" due to
non-registration of rights under the C.R.A. 1965: see s.21(1).
[73] s.193(1)(*d*)(ii).
[74] For which see further at § 9.34.
[75] For exceptions, see § 9.40.
[76] s.194(3)(*a*).
[77] s.194(4); *cf.* §§ 7.19 *et seq.*
[78] *cf.* Appendix 9.
[79] See further at § 2.68.

registers does not, of course, exempt the land from the provisions in sections 193 and 194 of the L.P.A. 1925 which have continuing effect until the procedures described above are put into effect.[80]

7.70 In some cases where land was still provisionally registered under the C.R.A. 1965 owners have been able to avoid registration by the simple device of obtaining a release of all rights and re-granting unregistrable rights for a term of years, thereby enabling evidence to be given at a Commons Commissioner's inquiry that the land was no longer statutory common land at the time of the hearing of the dispute.[81]

4. Waste land of a manor

7.71 Waste land of a manor not subject to rights of common is self evidently not common land but is statutory common land and registrable under the provisions of the C.R.A. 1965. Irrespective of whether the land is statutory and registered common land or not, waste land of a manor in an urban area is subject to section 193 of the L.P.A. 1925 and if it was subject to rights of common on January 1, 1926, is subject to section 194 of the same Act.

7.72 As we have seen, for the purposes of the C.R.A. 1965, the interpretation which waste land of a manor bears is that it is open, uncultivated and unoccupied land parcel of a manor.[82] This somewhat delicate structure can be destroyed by enclosure, cultivation, occupation or alienation from the manor. It follows that in any of these events an application for removal of the land from the commons registers should be successful. It will not be sufficient merely to point to the fact that the land does not comply with the definition as an act or event must have occurred since registration to take the land out of the definition.[83]

Management

7.73 It has been demonstrated that the owner of common land is able to use the land in a number of ways, providing that he does not infringe the rights of the commoners, and subject to the restrictions contained in statutes. The opportunity for management of the land as a whole, *i.e.* influencing and controlling all the activities on the land, is limited compared with ordinary unincumbered freehold land. Nevertheless there are a number of statutory provisions for management which enable the owner to manage to a limited extent, influence management and in some cases prevent management. The special role of the owner of the land is considered at this point while the general management of commons is dealt with later.[84]

---

[80] *i.e.* a resolution by a county council approved by a Secretary of State.
[81] *Re Trawden Moors, Pendle, Lancs. (No. 1), (No. 2)* 220/D/218–220, 220/D/217, 13 D.C.C. 14, 15.
[82] See further at § 2.36.
[83] *Corpus Christi College* v. *Gloucs.C.C.* [1983] 1 Q.B. 360: *cf.* §§ 2.72, 2.73.
[84] Chapter 11.

In the absence of statutory powers the only direct power of management **7.74**
available to the owner affecting rights of common is the right to drive the
common.[85] Few owners take advantage of this right today.

(a) *Inclosure Act 1773*[86]

The most elderly management statute still in force is the Inclosure Act **7.75**
1773. It must be doubted whether it is used today. It should be noted that, in
this Act, it is only the lord or lady of a manor who is empowered to act and
not any other owner of the soil.

The main part of the Act is directed towards ordering, fencing, cultivation **7.76**
and improvement of common fields.[87] With the consent of the lord or lady
balks, meers and slades may be ploughed.[88]

A power is given under this Act for a lord to lease a twelfth part of a waste or **7.77**
common, for a term not exceeding four years, subject to the consent of
three-fourths of the commoners. The net rents so obtained shall be applied
to draining, fencing or otherwise improving the residue of the wastes or
commons.[89] An alternative is available to the lord where the manor
includes stinted pastures: providing that both the lord and the majority in
number and value of the owners or occupiers agree, an assessment may be
levied on the stint holders for the purposes of improving the stinted pastures.[90]

On stinted pastures, which are shut for periods of the year, the major part in **7.78**
value and number of the owners and occupiers of the stints may resolve to
postpone the opening of the pasture for up to 21 days. The consent of the
lord is required for the resolution to be put into effect.[91] Similarly, where a
stinted or limited right pasture is normally open for the whole year, two-
thirds in number and value of the commoners may direct, again with the
consent of the lord or his steward or agent, times when the land shall be
closed for grazing.[92]

(b) *Inclosure Act 1845*[93]

A lord has the power to veto any application for inclosure under this Act if it **7.79**
includes land which is waste land of the manor or any land in the manor to
the soil of which the lord is entitled in right of his manor. Thus, the Inclosure Commissioners shall not proceed to an inclosure or certify that an
inclosure is expedient without his consent.[94] An owner other than a lord is
not so empowered.

---

[85] See at §§ 10.87 *et seq.*
[86] See further at § 12.03.
[87] ss.1–10.
[88] s.1.
[89] s.15.
[90] s.16.
[91] s.17.
[92] s.18.
[93] See further at § 5.78.
[94] s.29.

(c) *Metropolitan Commons Act 1866*[95]

7.80 The lord of a manor is one of the parties who may initiate a scheme of local management under the Act, the others being the commoners, the local authority[96] and 12 inhabitants of the parish or parishes in which the common is situated.[97] The lord has no power under this Act to veto a scheme but there is provision for objection to a proposal[98] and a right to petition Parliament against a Bill to effect the management scheme.[99]

(d) *Commons Act 1876*[1]

7.81 The power to veto a proposal to inclose, available to a lord under the Inclosure Act 1845,[2] is extended so that the same power is available over any scheme of proposed regulation.[3] Again it is a lord and not any other owner who is so entitled. An owner other than a lord seems to merely take his place alongside the commoners, as one of the persons representing two thirds in value of affected interests, who must consent before an order is certified as expedient by the Inclosure Commissioners.[4]

(e) *Commons Act 1899*[5]

7.82 Where a council proposes to make a scheme for the regulation and management of a common under this Act the council may proceed no further if, at any time before approval of the scheme, it receives a written notice of dissent from the person entitled as lord of the manor, or otherwise, to the ownership of the soil.[6]

(f) *Law of Property Act 1925, s.193*[7]

7.83 The section provides a right of public access over "urban" commons. The lord of the manor, or any other owner of the soil, may by revocable or irrevocable deed declare that the section shall apply to any other land which was subject to rights of common on January 1, 1927.[8] On land within, or brought within, section 193 the lord or other owner of the soil may apply to the Secretary of State for an order of limitations.[9]

---

[95] See further at § 12.34.
[96] s.6.
[97] Metropolitan Commons Amendment Act 1869, s.3.
[98] s.10.
[99] s.23.
[1] See further at § 12.43.
[2] Inclosure Act 1845, s.29.
[3] s.12(5).
[4] *ibid.*
[5] See further at § 12.64.
[6] s.2(4)(*a*).
[7] See further at § 11.06.
[8] s.193(2).
[9] s.193(1), proviso (*b*); see further at § 11.26.

(g) *National Parks and Access to the Countryside Act 1949*[10]

Under the provisions contained in section 64 of the Act an owner of any   **7.84**
class of common land may enter into an access agreement with a local planning authority providing that the land is "open country." The purpose of
such an agreement is to enable the public to have access for open air
recreation. "Open country" means any area appearing to the authority to
consist wholly or predominately of mountain, moor, heath, down, cliff or
foreshore (including any bank, barrier, dune, beach, flat or other land adjacent to the foreshore).[11] Unlike the statutory access provided by section 193
of the L.P.A. 1925, an access agreement made under the National Parks and
Access to the Countryside Act 1949 may provide for the making of payments by the local authority by way of consideration for the agreement or as
a contribution towards consequential expenditure.[12]

Regulated pastures

It has been suggested that regulated pastures may not be correctly registered   **7.85**
under the C.R.A. 1965.[13] Nevertheless, a very substantial number have
been registered and must be considered at the moment as a form of statutory common land. It is unclear whether in a second stage of legislation they
will be confirmed in registration or removed from the registers.[14]

(a) *Origin and general nature*

They may have originated in express grant by a lord of the manor, as a result   **7.86**
of a private inclosure Act or under the provisions contained in the general
Inclosure Act 1845. The term used here to describe those arising under the
Act of 1845 is "statutory regulated pastures" as they attract special comprehensive management provisions.[15] In all cases the nature of the land is that
it is owned in undivided shares by the persons having grazing "rights" over
the land in the proportion that each person's grazing right bears to the totality of rights. For many graziers the actual ownership of the land had no
great importance as it was the grazing which was of primary importance.
The C.R.A. 1965, which required the registration of ownership, directed
attention to the issue and the rights holders, for the first time in many
cases, had to consider ownership.

(b) *Legal nature*

The legal characteristics of this class of land and right, although quite fre-   **7.87**
quently not understood by the graziers, may now be considered well settled.
Until 1925, the graziers were seised of the land in undivided shares as legal
and beneficial tenants in common. As a result of the provisions in the L.P.A.

---

[10] See further at § 11.34.
[11] s.59(2).
[12] ss.64(2), 70.
[13] See §§ 2.27 *et seq.*
[14] *cf.* § 2.31.
[15] See § 12.18.

1925, from January 1, 1926 the legal estate could no longer be held on a tenancy in common.[16] Transitional provisions in Parts IV and V of Schedule 1 to the Act converted the pre-existing legal estate in the undivided shares into equitable interests with, most usually, an automatic vesting of the legal estate in the Public Trustee. It follows that, henceforth, the graziers were unable to deal in the legal estate to the land. This has escaped the notice of some of the graziers and land has been purportedly sold by them in fee simple, or leased.

7.88 The transitional provisions did not affect land which was already vested in trustees and the arrangement continued undisturbed.[17] In most cases, however, the provisions in Schedule 1 took over. Part IV dealt with the generality of cases by providing default vesting in the Public Trustee, and Part V made special provision for a particular class of land:

> "2. Where, immediately before the commencement of this Act, an open space of land (with or without any building used in common for the purposes of any adjoining land) is held in undivided shares, in right whereof each owner has rights of access and user over the open space, the ownership thereof shall vest in the Public Trustee on the statutory trusts which shall be executed only with the leave of the court, and subject to any order of the court to the contrary, each person who would have been a tenant in common shall, until the open space is conveyed to a purchaser, have rights of access and user over the open space corresponding to those which would have subsisted if the tenancy in common had remained subsisting.
> 3. Any person interested may apply to the court for an order declaring the rights and interests under this Part of this Schedule, of the persons interested in any such [party structure or] open space, or generally may apply in relation to the provisions of this Part of this Schedule, and the court may make such order as it thinks fit."

Under Part IV of the Schedule there is provision for the re-vesting of the legal estate in duly appointed trustees instead of the Public Trustee while Part V makes no such provision and, additionally, requires the consent of the court before the trust is executed. It is clearly a matter of some importance to decide under which Part regulated pastures vested.

7.89 From the wording of Part V it seems inescapably conclusive that regulated pastures have vested under it and not under Part IV. This indeed was the decision in two incompletely reported cases where the Public Trustee took out an originating summons to discover whether "gated" pastures had vested under Part IV or Part V. In *Re Cotherstone Moor* (1961)[18] Pennycuick J. held that the land, which was a statutory regulated pasture, "was precisely the type of case to which the authors of [Part V of the Schedule to] the [1925] Act intended it to apply." In *Re Brotherton Marsh Pasture, West Rid-*

---

[16] L.P.A. 1925, ss.1(6), 34, 39.

[17] *e.g. Re Newbiggin Moor, Newbiggin-by-the-Sea, Northumberland* (1977) 27/D/41, 5 D.C.C. 425, considered at § 2.29.

[18] (1961) 179 E.G. 11.

ing of Yorks. (1965)[19] Ungoed-Thomas J. reached the same conclusion about land awarded under a private inclosure Act of 1793.

7.90 There has been, however, some doubt cast upon the intention of the drafts-man in regard to Part V. In *Re Bradford City Premises* (1928)[20] consideration was given to whether a small backyard was an open space for the purposes of Part V. It was suggested by King, as *amicus curiae*, that the history of paragraph 2 of Part V was that the closing of the bracket had accidentally been shifted from after "building" to its present position. Tomlin J. felt himself unable to look behind the actual wording and held that paragraph 2 of Part V applied to any unbuilt upon open space held in undivided shares with or without a building on the open space. The decision was implicitly followed in *Re Townsend* (1930),[21] although the decision was different.

7.91 If the submission by King is correct, only an open space held in undivided shares and used in common for the purposes of adjoining land should be encompassed, *i.e.* typically, the small backyards of the *Re Bradford City* case. In this event the regulated pastures which are necessarily not used for the purpose of adjoining land, having their own individual identity as land without attachment to other land, would have fallen to vesting under Part IV with the capability of re-vesting the land in local trustees. However, the wording has to be accepted as it is and it is submitted that all regulated pastures which were held absolutely and beneficially in undivided shares at the end of 1925 forthwith vested in the Public Trustee under Part V.

(c) *Vesting following decision by the Commons Commissioners*

7.92 There the matter might well rest but for the fact that in a number of decisions the Commons Commissioners have, in considering unknown ownership, declared that vesting has taken place under Part IV and not Part V. The Public Trustee is informed by the Commissioners whenever he is directed to be registered as owner of statutory common land and is aware of a number of decisions where vesting is said to have been under Part IV.[22] The Trustee has no information as to why this has occurred. In *Re Burgh Marsh, Burgh by Sands, Cumbria* (1983)[23] it appears that the Commons Commissioner adjourned the hearing to allow for a deed of appointment of new trustees to be executed under paragraph 1(4)(iii) of Part IV of the Schedule. This was done, the Public Trustee was informed and raised no objection, and the Commissioner confirmed the new trustees as owners for the purposes of the C.R.A. 1965. Since that decision other Commissioners have continued to declare regulated pastures to have vested under Part V of the Schedule.[24]

---

[19] (1965) 112 S.J. 48; see also a similar decision in *Re Forebridge Green Common* (1957) (unreported).
[20] [1928] 1 Ch. 138.
[21] [1930] 2 Ch. 338.
[22] Six notified to the Public Trustee between June 1975 and November 1980.
[23] (1983) 262/U/547.
[24] *e.g. Re The Moor, Luton, Beds.* (1984) 201/U/8, 15 D.C.C. 115; *Re Bowes Moor, Bowes, Co. Durham* (1985) 211/U/86, 16 D.C.C. 134. For early decisions see *Re Longton Out Marsh, Little Hoole and Longton, Lancs.* (1974) 20/U/81, 4 D.C.C. 464; *Re Ireshope Moor, Stanhope, Durham* (1974) 11/U/19, 4 D.C.C. 478; *Re Bethecar Moor, Colton, Cumbria* (1975) 20/U/94, 4 D.C.C. 492.

(d) *Dealing with the legal estate*

7.93 Where a regulated vesture has vested under Part V it is clear that the legal estate may only be dealt with by the Public Trustee after an application has been made to the court for an order to execute the trust.[25] As the court has discretion to order as it thinks fit the appropriate step for the stintholder seeking an order must to be go there supported by a majority in number and value of all the interests in the land.

[25] L.P.A. 1925, Sched. 1, Pt. V, para. 3.

8. The Rights and Obligations of the Commoner

Substantive Rights

(a) *Restrictions on use*

(i) The right to graze   The substantive rights of a commoner over **8.01** common land are few. So restricted were they at one time that it was held that he had no right to even go to the common unless intending to put in his cattle and actually did so or he was, alternatively, going to the common to see if it was fit to graze.[1]

The right of pasturage may be taken by "onely bytte of mouth with their **8.02** catell"[2] or, as it was put in argument the commoner: "hath nothing at all to do with the land more than a meer stranger, but only to put therein his cattel, and to let them feed with their mouths, and it is not his own common until his cattel have fed there."[3]

There are no rights to the grass itself until it is grazed. Similarly, in the case of any other product, the commoner can lay no claim to property in it until he severs or takes it. It follows that he may not take a product severed, rightly or wrongly, by another person.[4] The position is altogether different in the case of sole rights.[5]

(ii) Interference with the soil   It seems that the grazier commoner **8.03** may not interfere with the soil or its products, even if the intention is to improve the quality of the common. The lack of rights was summarised thus:

" . . . neither can a commoner do any thing upon the soile which tends

---

[1] *Spilman* v. *Hermitage* (1619) 5 Vin.Ab. 35.

[2] *Fitzherbert's Surveying*, folio iiii.

[3] *Samborne* v.*Harilo* (1621) Bridgman J. 9 at 10, 123 E.R. 1162 at 1163, *per* Bridgman.

[4] *Spilman* v. *Hermitage* (1619), above, n. 1; *Dewclas* v. *Kendall* (1610) Yelv. 187, 80 E.R. 124; *Stiles* v. *Buts* (1595) Moore (K.B.) 411, 72 E.R. 662 (commoner may not take clay dug by another); *Woadson* v. *Nawton* (1722) 2 Str. 777, 93 E.R. 842 (commoner may not spread ashes of fern burnt by another); *Rackham* v. *Jesup and Thompson* (1772) 3 Wils. 332, 95 E.R. 1084 (cut rushes belong to the cutter).

[5] See § 8.30.

to the melioration or improving of the common, as to cut bushes, ferne or such things which do much impaire the common, neither can he make a fence or ditch to let out the water which spoiles the common. . . . And as the commoner may not meddle with the soile, so cannot he meddle with anything arising out of the land, or that doth grow or is nourished by the same."[6]

8.04 It has been argued that the true rule is that "if a commoner does anything *de novo* in the land he is a trespasser but if he amends and reforms a thing abused it is no trespass."[7] In the case concerned it was said that if the common was full of mole hills the commoner may level them, and also that if the lord made a pond on the land the commoners may dig trenches to let the water out. As will be seen, the suggestion that the commoner may abate the *lawful* act of the lord is against later authority.[8] The modern rule probably is that the commoner may take limited forms of action such as the prevention of the spread of pests, like moles,[9] and noxious weeds, such as bracken, but any other interference with the soil is trespass unless the commoner can prescribe or prove a custom for the particular act. An example of such a prescription or custom might be an immemorial right to scour ditches to let out water,[10] or to burn heather or grass.[11]

8.05 **(iii) Ancillary easements** However, before it is thought that the commoner is too severely restricted in his rights it should be noted that a right of common also includes all easements which are "reasonably necessary for the reasonable enjoyment of the principle or primary right."[12] Thus, a commoner may take vehicles on the land to place troughs there and carry water to them either himself or through his servants or agents,[13] and an easement to reach a river bank to exercise a right of piscary will be implied.[14] The additional rights may not be exercised independently of the right of common so that, for example, the use of a vehicle over a common for personal convenience is barred.[15] It is probably correct to view such ancillary benefits as easements appurtenant to an incorporeal hereditament rather than as appurtenant to land for it is clear that in the case of rights in

---

[6] *Samborne* v. *Harilo*, above, n. 3, at 10, 1163; see also *Cooper's Case* (1586) 2 Leon. 202, 74 E.R. 478, *per* Coke in argument; *Sir Simon de Harcourt's Case* (1520) YB 12 H8, 2a, 1 Ro.Ab. 406, pl. 10.

[7] *Carril* v. *Baker* (1613) 1 Brownl. & Golds. 227, 123 E.R. 770.

[8] For which see § 8.16; and *cf. contra*, *Pelling* v. *Langden* (1601) Owen 114, 74 E.R. 940.

[9] *Contra*, *Howard* v. *Spencer* (1640) 1 Sid. 251, 82 E.R. 1088.

[10] *ibid.*; *Anon.* (1611) Godb. 182, 78 E.R. 110; *cf. Sir Simon de Harcourt's Case*, above, n. 6.

[11] For regulations controlling burning, see § 8.44.

[12] *White* v. *Taylor* (*No. 2*) [1969] 1 Ch. 160 at 196, *per* Buckley J.; *cf. Pomfret* v. *Ricroft* (1669) 1 Wms. Saund. 321 at 323, 85 E.R. 454 at 459; *Liford's Case* (1614) 11 Co. Rep. 46b at 52a, 77 E.R. 1206 at 1217; *Pwllbach Colliery* v. *Woodman* [1915] A.C. 634 at 642–643, 646.

[13] *White* v. *Taylor* (*No. 2*), above, n. 12, at 199.

[14] *Hanbury* v. *Jenkins* [1901] 2 Ch. 401: Co.Litt. 121b explained.

[15] *White* v. *Taylor* (*No. 2*), above, n. 12, at 199.

gross no corporeal dominant tenement is required.[16] However, an alternative view is that they are irrevocable licences.[16a]

If the correct view of benefits ancillary to a right of common is that they are **8.06** easements, there seems no reason in principle why they should not be acquired by prescription. Thus, where practices in husbandry change, a sufficient period of user may establish a right to exercise by the new methods. An example might be a right to feed animals on a common.

Conversely, it seems that there is no method available to the owner of the **8.07** soil whereby he may insist that rights be used in a certain way or, indeed, that they are used at all. He cannot acquire a prescriptive right to this end nor should he rely on a changed method of use continuing: "an [easement] exists for the benefit of the dominant owner alone and . . . the servient owner acquires no right to insist on its continuance or to ask for damages on its abandonment."[17]

(iv) Animals to be grazed In using a right of pasturage a commoner **8.08** must have a sufficient property in the animals,[18] although borrowed animals will be considered in his possession if they are used to compester the dominant land.[19] It follows that he may not agist animals for payment on the common.[20] Nor may he graze his own animals *levant* and *couchant* on land other than the dominant tenement to which his right is annexed.[21] Probably, he may not license the use of the right to graze to strangers without the dominant land to which the right is appurtenant.[22] *A fortiori,* severance by grant of the right separately from the land is is not permitted and indeed such a grant may result in the extinguishment of the right.[23] Where, however, the right to graze is a right in gross or a sole right there are no such restrictions, but any licence or grant to a third party should be under seal.[24]

(v) Rights appurtenant to buildings In the case of any other pro- **8.09** ducts, if the right is appurtenant to land or a building it may only be used in, or in connection with, the dominant tenement. A right to take firewood or a right of turbary, for instance, only allows use in the house to which the right is annexed and not any other.[25] The product also may only be used for the

---

[16] *Hanbury* v. *Jenkins,* above, n. 14.

[16a] For which see Megarry and Wade, p. 800. An irrevocable licence to enter land to take a profit has always been recognised by the common law. However, this generally right of entry is probably distinguishable from specific ancillary rights which seem more closely akin to defined easements.

[17] *Mason* v. *Shrewsbury and Hereford Railway Co.* (1871) L.R. 6 Q.B. 578, *per* Cockburn C.J.; *cf. National Guaranteed Manure Co.* v. *Donald* (1859) 4 H. & N. 8, 157 E.R. 737.

[18] *Manneton* v. *Trevilian* (1683) 2 Show. K.B. 328, 89 E.R. 969.

[19] s.c. *Molliton* v. *Trevilian* (1683) Skin. 137, 90 E.R. 64; 1 Ro.Ab. 401, 402; 2 Assiz. 84; Y.B. 14 H6, 6B.

[20] *Jones* v. *Richard* (1837) 6 Ad. & E. 530, 112 E.R. 203, *per* Lord Denman C.J.; *Cooper's Case* (1586) at 2 Leon. 202, 74 E.R. 478 in argument; 4 Vin.Ab. 585, 593.

[21] *Molliton* v. *Trevilian,* above, n. 19.

[22] See §§ 6.23 *et seq.*

[23] See §§ 6.37 *et seq.*

[24] See § 4.74.

[25] See § 3.70.

purpose for which it was granted. A right to take timber for house repair may not, even if the timber proves unfit for the purpose after cutting, be diverted to an alternative use nor may defective wood be sold and replaced with other timber.[26] Similarly the quantum is strictly limited to the needs of the tenement. In one case where a right to take sand and gravel for repairs to a house was claimed, it was held necessary to allege not only that the house was out of repair and that the sand and gravel had been taken to effect necessary repairs, but also that the material taken had been used for that purpose.[27] There seems to be no authority that an appurtenant right may exist for commercial purposes such as taking clay for making pots[28] or use in a commercial brick kiln.[29] Nor does there seem to be any support for suggestions that if the amount is certain any surplus may be sold or the right converted into a right in gross.[30]

8.10   **(vi) Quantification of rights**   For rights other than pasturage there was no requirement for registration of quantity under the provisions in the C.R.A. 1965.[31] However, all such rights are subject to some form of limitation, usually by reference to the needs of the dominant tenement,[32] and it follows that recourse to the status of the rights before registration is necessary. It should also be noticed that some registered rights are less than definitive in their registration—a right of estovers, for example, can take many forms. Registration does not in itself provide any additional right, and again it is necessary to consider the status of the rights before registration and not just assume that a right of estovers includes any form the right may take—from collecting firewood to felling trees. Finally, registered rights of estovers in the form of a right to cut timber for fence repairs are occasionally encountered.[33] There is some slight authority that rights of this nature may only be used in connection with ancient fences.[34]

8.11   **(vii) Sole rights appurtenant**   It has been remarked that sole rights and rights in gross are not usually subject to the same rules and that generally there is no limitation by reference to a dominant tenement or inhibition on use by strangers. The position is not entirely clear in those few cases which exist of sole rights created by statute as appurtenant to land.[35] If any still exist in practice it seems that in all probability they are as much appur-

---

[26] *Earl of Pembroke's Case* (1636) Clayt. 47, cited at § 3.70.

[27] *Peppin* v. *Shakespear* (1796) 6 T.R. 748, 101 E.R. 806; see also *Duke of Portland* v. *Hill* (1866) L.R. 2 Eq. 765 (right to dig coal limited to *propriis usis*); *Incledon* v. *Burges* (1689) Carth. 65, 90 E.R. 642 (stones for necessary repairs to messuage).

[28] See the case cited in *Hayward* v. *Cunnington* (1668) 1 Lev. 231, 83 E.R. 383.

[29] *Clayton* v. *Corby* (1843) 5 Q.B. 415, 114 E.R. 1306.

[30] See Harris and Ryan, p. 46, n. 84; *Cooke's Inclosures*, p. 40; Elton, p. 109 (cases *contra* cited); *sed* Woolrych, p. 9, doubts. The apparent confusion on the subject seems to have arisen from certain remarks in *Clayton* v. *Corby*, above, n. 29, when Lord Denman C.J. in considering a claim to take clay for sale remarked on the lack of quantification. However, it is suggested that all he was doing was drawing attention to the proposition that the claim was for the entirety of the close. His comments say nothing about converting a fixed right, or part of it, into a right in gross.

[31] C.R.A. 1965, s.15.

[32] *cf.* §§ 3.124–3.126 *et seq.*

[33] *e.g.* Gwent C.L. 1–4.

[34] *cf.* § 3.68 and n. 81.

[35] *cf.* § 3.18.

tenant to land as true rights of common, albeit that there are theoretical difficulties in the way of this conclusion.[36]

(b) *Gaming and shooting rights*

The rights to take game on common land, and sole pastures, are usually **8.12** vested in the owner of the soil: "property *ratione soli* is the common law right which every owner of the land has to kill and take all such animals *ferae naturae*, as may from time to time be found on his land."[37] The owner of a waste prima facie has this right, but after inclosure it will vest in the allottees in severalty in the absence of clear words to the contrary.[38] Neither commoners nor owners of cattlegates, *i.e.* holders of rights over stinted pastures have a right to take game.[39] Owner-occupiers and agricultural tenants have a right to take ground game, *i.e.* hares and rabbits, under the provisions in section 1 of the Ground Game Act 1880, but by proviso (2) to that section holders of rights of common are not occupiers for the purposes of the Act. Holders of sole rights, *i.e.* participators in grazing stinted pastures, are not mentioned in the proviso and, it seems, are able to take ground game. Holders of rights on regulated pastures, in their capacity as beneficial owners of the land, are entitled to all gaming rights subject only to any statutory exception in favour of the previous owner if the pasture originated in an inclosure award. If a commoner takes game without lawful authority the owner of the soil can maintain an action in trespass[40] and an offence under section 30 of the Game Act 1831 may have been committed.[41]

In one case it was said that there is "no good reason why there should not be **8.13** a custom for commoners to take or destroy rabbits or other game," although on the particular facts there was held to be no such custom.[42] Evidence from court rolls had been adduced that over 100 years previously the commoners had been licensed to destroy rabbits "they being likely to overrun all this part of the country." Today it will usually be necessary to rely for rabbit destruction on the powers which the Minister of Agriculture, Fisheries and Food has under the Pests Act 1954 to designate rabbit clearance areas and authorise shooting.

There is, of course, no reason why a right to take rabbits (or other game) **8.14** should not exist as a right of common.[43] In this event the quantity which may be taken will be limited to the domestic needs of the dominant

---

[36] *cf.* § 3.18; see also the comments of Saunders in *Hoskins* v. *Robins* (1671) 2 Wms.Saund. 324 at 327, 85 E.R. 1123 at 1124, denying that *levancy* and *couchancy* can ever apply to a sole pasture.

[37] *Blades* v. *Higgs* (1865) 11 H.L.C. 621 at 631, 11 E.R. 1474 at 1479, *per* Lord Westbury L.C.

[38] *Greathead* v. *Morley* (1841) 3 Scott N.R. 538, 60 R.R. 479.

[39] Game Act 1831, s.10.

[40] *Rigg* v. *Earl of Lonsdale* (1857) 1 H. & N. 923, 156 E.R. 1475.

[41] *Watkins* v. *Major* (1875) 44 L.J.M.C. 164.

[42] *Coote* v. *Ford* (1900) 83 L.T. 482.

[43] *Samford and Havel's Case* (1612) Godb. 184, 78 E.R. 112; *Duke of Portland* v. *Hill* (1866) L.R. 2 Eq. 765.

tenement.[44] Occasionally, it seems, a lord has granted a lease for taking rabbits on a common.[45]

Relationship with other parties

(a) *The owner of the soil*

8.15   **(i) Limited rights of action**   In chapter seven, it was demonstrated that the owner of the soil has available to him, subject to certain statutory limitations, all the rights of any freehold owner providing that he does not use the rights wantonly, or unnecessarily abridge or interfere with the rights of the commoner.[46] Thus, he may graze the land, plant trees, keep rabbits, use the land for sporting purposes and take minerals. In the event of conflict between a use by the owner and use by a commoner there is normally no right of abatement if the acts of the owner are merely an excessive user of lawful right. The commoner is not entitled to distrain the owner's surcharging animals,[47] or cut down planted trees,[48] or kill rabbits[49] or destroy rabbit warrens.[50] But, on the other hand, a commoner is not liable for damage to the owner's property on the common merely by using his right of common so that, for example, damage caused by animals eating a stack made on the common is not actionable by the owner.[51]

8.16   **(ii) Abatement against the owner of the soil**   The commoner is entitled to the self-help remedy of abatement where the act of the owner has no lawful basis. This was explained by Lord Mansfield thus:

> "The lord, by his grant of common, gives everything incident to the enjoyment of it, (as ingress, egress, &c.); and thereby authorizes the commoner to remove every obstruction to his cattle's grazing the grass which grows upon such a spot of ground: because every obstruction is directly contrary to the terms of the grant."[52]

8.17   It has been held that a commoner may remove a hedge planted on the common "for thereby he did not meddle with the soil, but only pulled down the erection."[53] Similarly a fence actually on the common may be removed, but if only blocking ingress and egress may only be abated so as to restore access to the land.[54] A pond made on the common may not be abated by digging

[44] *ibid.*

[45] *Newcombe* v. *Fewins* (1877) 41 J.P. 581.

[46] *cf.* §§ 7.04–7.05.

[47] *Carril* v. *Pack and Baker* (1613) 2 Bulstr. 115, 80 E.R. 996.

[48] *Kirby* v. *Sadgrove* (1797) 1 Bos. & Pul. 13, 126 E.R. 751; *Hope* v. *Osborne* [1913] 2 Ch. 349.

[49] *Bellew* v. *Langdon* (1602) Cro.Eliz. 876, 78 E.R. 1100; *Hadesden* v. *Gryssel* (1607) Cro.Jac. 195, 79 E.R. 170.

[50] *Cooper* v. *Marshall* (1757) 1 Burr. 259, 97 E.R. 303; *Carril* v. *Pack and Baker*, above, n. 47.

[51] *Farmor* v. *Hunt* (1611) Cro.Jac. 271, 79 E.R. 233.

[52] *Cooper* v. *Marshall*, above, n. 50, at 265, 306; followed in *Kirby* v. *Sadgrove*, above n. 48, at 17, 753, *per* Eyre C.J.

[53] *Mason* v. *Cæsar* (1676) 2 Mod. 65, 86 E.R. 944.

[54] 2 Inst.88; *Hambleton's Case* (1627) Litt. 38, 124 E.R. 125; *Arlett* v. *Ellis* (1827) 7 B. & C. 346 at 362, 108 E.R. 752 at 758, *per* Bayley J.

trenches to drain off the water, although it has been said that it would be otherwise if all the common was taken up.[55] However another, and better, view is that even if the right of common is totally destroyed there is no right of abatement against the owner unless it can be done without interfering with his rights.[56] To illustrate the point, if the owner builds a pond which covers the entire common this is an excess of lawful user which cannot be abated, but if the owner wantonly floods the land this would not be an exercise of lawful right and could be abated.

Any alleged right of abatement should be exercised with discretion for, if it **8.18** proves ultimately to have been unlawful, the abator may suffer damages in a trespass action and, of course, the costs of the action.[57]

The equivalent of abatement with regard to animals on the common was **8.19** the, now abolished, action of distress damage feasant. There is ample authority that this form of self help was not available to a commoner against the owner of the soil unless the owner had no right to graze or his entitlement was for a fixed number.[58] The position is now governed by the new actions contained in the Animals Act 1971,[59] and it may be that henceforth a commoner is entitled to detain an owner's surcharging animals.[60] However, there is still the fundamental difficulty confronting such a course of action that the owner's grazing livestock are unquantified, and unregistrable under the provisions of the C.R.A. 1965, with a consequent inherent uncertainty as to his entitlement.

Although the direct action of abatement is not readily available against the **8.20** owner of the soil there are a number of remedies and special forms of statutory action which may be taken as well against the owner as against a stranger to the common.[61]

(b) *Strangers to the common*

(i) Actions against strangers The commoner not being in possession **8.21** of the soil or even of the grass until it is grazed is unable to bring an action in trespass.[62] At one time it was thought that the only remedy available was distress damage feasant, but it was decided in an early case[63] that an action on the case lay, for if distraint failed the commoner might lose all his common and be without remedy. It was the view of the court at the time that the commoner ought to prove actual loss before bringing such an action but

---

[55] *Carril* v. *Pack and Baker*, above, n. 50; *cf. Pelling* v. *Langden*, above n. 8.

[56] *Kirby* v. *Sadgrove* (1797), above, n. 48, at 17, 753, *per* Eyre C.J.

[57] *Hope* v. *Osborne* [1913] 2 Ch. 349.

[58] § 10.21.

[59] Especially ss.4 and 7, for which see §§ 10.8 and 10.14.

[60] § 10.19.

[61] See § 8.28.

[62] 22 Assiz. 48; 5 Vin.Ab. 34(5); *Sir Simon de Harcourt's Case* (1520) Y.B. 12 H8, 2a, *per* Brook J.; *Crogate* v. *Morris* (1611) 2 Brownl. & Golds. 146, 123 E.R. 814

[63] *Robert Mary's Case* (1612) 9 Co.Rep. 111b, 77 E.R. 895; *cf. Crogat* v. *Morris* (1610) 2 Brownl. & Golds. 56, 123 E.R. 812; *Crogate* v. *Morris* (1610) 1 Brownl. & Golds. 197, 123 E.R. 751; *Morris's Case* (1611) Godb. 185, 78 E.R. 112.

succeeding cases make it clear that infringement of right is all that is necessary. The cases were reviewed and summarised in 1899 thus:

> "These cases appear to me to shew that any act of a stranger whereby the commoner is prevented from having the use and enjoyment of his common of pasture in as ample and beneficial manner as he otherwise would, is a legal injury for which an action will lie, even although no actual damage may be proved."[64]

8.22 The rule now is that a right of action depends upon the nature of the defendant's act not on the exercise of the plaintiff's right; that is to say, the cause of action is that the plaintiff has been put in a position where he cannot enjoy his right as well as before.[65] The point is well illustrated by a case where the court held unanimously for a representative commoner in damages of one farthing following removal of manure from a common.[66] A commoner may bring an action not only for unlawful consumption, taking away or destruction of the herbage (or indeed any other product for which he has right) but also anything which if not stopped would grow into a legal right to the prejudice of the commoners.[67] It follows that, in an action against a stranger for grazing his cattle, it is unnecessary for the commoner to allege that there is an insufficiency of grazing left to satisfy his right of common; it is sufficient to prove that the stranger's cattle grazed the common.[68]

8.23 **(ii) Driving the common** A commoner or commoners may drive the common for the purpose of segregating animals which are known to be straying but may not, it seems, in the absence of a custom, merely to view the animals present.[69] The owner of the soil, on the other hand, probably does have a right to drive for a view.[70] The proper course of action for commoners, who wish to drive, is, either, to be authorised as agents of the owner or, alternatively, to obtain the consent of all the persons entitled to graze. If, following a drive, detention of surcharging or straying animals is proposed, the provisions of the Animals Act 1971 should be complied with.[71]

---

[64] *Robertson* v. *Hartopp* (1889) 43 L.R. Ch.D. 484 at 500, *per* Stirling J.; *cf. Bronge* v. *More* (1654) Sty. 428, 82 E.R. 834; *Woolton* v. *Salter* (1683) 3 Lev. 104, 83 E.R. 599; *The Dippers at Tunbridge Wells* (1769) 2 Wils. K.B. 414 at 422, 95 E.R. 892 at 897; *Wells* v. *Watling* (1779) 2 Wm.Bl. 1233, 96 E.R. 726; *Hobson* v. *Todd* (1790) 4 T.R. 71, 100 E.R. 900; *Pindar* v. *Wadsworth* (1802) 2 East. 154, 102 E.R. 328; *Williams* v. *Morland* (1824) 2 B. & C. 910 at 916, 107 E.R. 620 at 622; *Harrop* v. *Hirst* (1868) L.R. 4 Ex. 43 at 46.
[65] *Wells* v. *Watling*, above, n. 64, at 1234, 727, *per* Blackstone J.
[66] *Pindar* v. *Wadsworth*, above, n. 64.
[67] *King* v. *Brown, Durant and Co.* [1913] 2 Ch. 416 at 420, *per* Joyce J. specifically referring to an easement. While it seems that one act in trespass is not actionable by a commoner, continued acts become a disturbance of the right of common.
[68] *Wells* v. *Watling*, above, n. 64 (the commoner need not show that he turned out any cattle of his own at the time of the surcharge).
[69] For the principles involved in driving a common see §§ 10.87 *et seq.*
[70] See §§ 10.89–10.90.
[71] See §§ 10.14 *et seq.*

(iii) Abatement against strangers   A commoner may abate a build- **8.24** ing which is a nuisance on the common, or at least that part which creates a nuisance, by pulling it down, but not a house which is occupied.[72] An occupied house, it has been said, may be pulled down providing that notice of intention to abate is given.[73] However, such action in modern times is likely to be viewed askance by the courts and a counter claim for damages in the event of the act being declared unlawful is likely to be substantial. The very existence of a substantial building erected on common land may lead to a conclusion that the commoners have impliedly released their rights of common.[74]

Nevertheless, under suitable circumstances the courts will uphold the right **8.25** of abatement on common land. In one case commoners were convicted of malicious damage to a notice board erected on common land by a parish council which, it seems, had power to manage the land under the provisions of the Commons Act 1899. The notice merely indicated a route to a building site. The Court of Criminal Appeal quashed the convictions as the notice, on these facts, was unlawful, having nothing whatsoever to do with the common or preservation of order on it.[75]

(c) *Other commoners*

The old action of distress damage feasant was not available to a commoner **8.26** against another commoner for the latter always had some colour of right for grazing his animals.[76] Distress was also not available against cattle present *pur cause de vicinage* having strayed from the common on which they were lawfully turned out even, it seems, if they were surcharging.[77] Distress damage feasant has been abolished and with it the associated doctrine of colour of right, but it may be that something similar will be developed in respect of the new action for detention available under the Animal Act 1971. Pending clarification the most helpful comment which can be made is that commoners should proceed with caution.[78]

In all other respects a commoner may treat another as a stranger to the com- **8.27** mon in respect of his unlawful acts on the common.[79] An action for surcharging has been said to be the most usual form of action between commoners and there is a precedent for such an action in *Atkyn's Court Forms*.[80] There do not, however, seem to be any reported cases in England and Wales in modern times. In the only case which seems to have occurred recently in Ireland, the court was somewhat surprised but awarded an injunction and damages.[81] In an action for surcharging against another

[72] *Perry* v. *Fitzhowe* (1846) 8 Q.B. 757, 115 E.R. 1057, especially, Lord Denman C.J. at 775, 1064; followed in *Jones* v. *Jones* (1862) 1 H. & C. 1, 158 E.R. 777.
[73] *Davies* v. *Williams* (1851) 16 Q.B. 546, 117 E.R. 988; approved in *Lane* v. *Capsey* [1891] 3 Ch. 411.
[74] For implied release, see § 5.43.
[75] *R.* v. *Dyer* [1952] Cr.App.R. 155.
[76] *cf.* § 10.20.
[77] *Cape* v. *Scott* (1874) L.R. 9 Q.B. 269.
[78] *cf.* § 10.22.
[79] *King* v. *Brown, Durant and Co.*, above, n. 67, at 420, *per* Joyce J.
[80] 8 Court Forms (2nd ed., 1981), p. 535.
[81] *O'Sullivan* v. *O'Connor* (1976) 114 I.L.T. 63.

commoner there is no need for the surcharge to be stated[82]; it is sufficient merely to state the wrongful grazing. It has also been said, in an action for damages, that if the plaintiff is himself surcharging this will be no bar to recovery "for one tort cannot be set off against another."[83] However, the position will probably be different if an injunction is sought to prevent further surcharging (the more likely course of action) for the plaintiff will be expected to come to the court with clean hands.

Remedies

(a) Common law

8.28 In all cases of an interference with the rights of the commoner whether by the owner of the soil, a stranger to the common or another commoner the remedy is an action for damages and/or a claim for an injunction.[84]

8.29 If the interference is the result of an approvement by the owner of the soil then the onus of proof that there is a sufficiency of common remaining lies on the owner.[85] If the complaint is an excessive user of otherwise lawful right by the owner, whether it be by grazing animals, planting trees or any other use of the common the commoner must show that he is unable to enjoy his common in as beneficial manner as before or, as it has been put, "must state the surcharge," *i.e.* specific injury must be proved.[86] The reason for the special rule requiring proof of damage in the case of actions against the owner is that, for example, "the lord is entitled to what remains of the grass [or any other product], and may consume it himself, or permit another to do so, provided a sufficiency of common is left for the commoner."[87] It is, therefore, no wrong for the owner to take some of the commoner's entitlement if the commoner himself has not taken it. In the case of an approvement the opposite applies and the owner must leave a sufficiency not only for present need but the sum of all entitlements to rights of common.[88] As against a fellow commoner or a stranger, as shown above, it is unnecessary "to state the surcharge."[89]

8.30 It has been noticed that a commoner may not bring an action in trespass,[89a] but the holder of a sole right, whether of pasture, herbage or vesture, fishing, shooting, or any other product, is in a different position. Such rights are sole

[82] *Atkinson* v. *Teasdale* (1772) 3 Wils.K.B. 278 at 290, 95 E.R. 1054 at 1060, *per* de Grey L.C.J.; s.c. 2 Black. W. 817, 96 E.R. 482; *Smith* v. *Feverell* (1675) 2 Mod. 6, 86 E.R. 909.

[83] *Hobson* v. *Todd*, above, n. 64,, at 74, 901, *per* Buller J.

[84] *King* v. *Brown, Durant and Co.*, above, n. 67.

[85] For approvement, see § 7.47.

[86] See the cases cited above, n. 82.

[87] *Hobson* v. *Todd*, above, n. 64,, at 74, 901, *per* Buller J.; *Arlett* v. *Ellis* (1827) 7 B. & C. 346 at 362, 108 E.R. 752 at 759, *per* Bayley J.; *cf. Malvern Hills Conservators* v. *Whitmore* (1909) 100 L.T. 841 for analogous position in the case of mining and quarrying.

[88] *Robertson* v. *Hartopp* (1889) L.R. 43 Ch.D. 484 at 503, *per* Stirling J. and at 515 *et seq., per curiam* (C.A.).

[89] *cf.* above, n. 82.

[89a] See § 8.21.

profits à prendre and are true incorporeal hereditaments against which an act of trespass may be committed and an action will lie.[90] The owner of a sole profit has property in the product even before taking or severing it. In addition an action in the nature of nuisance brought by the owner of a sole profit will be treated as though it is an action in trespass.[91] In a case where the defendants had polluted a river in which the lessee plaintiffs had a several fishery, an attempt was made to establish the existence of a superior Crown title thus impugning the plaintiff's title.[92] It was held that in this particular form of nuisance action it would be treated similarly to a trespass action and it followed that the defendants could not set up a *jus tertii* even against a possessory title.

The Rules of the Supreme Court provide that one or more of numerous per-   **8.31** sons having the same interest in one cause or matter may sue or be sued on behalf of all the persons so interested. A judgment against a representative defendant will bind other persons who are not parties to the action unless they can show fraud, collusion or that the court was misled or unless there were special circumstances.[93]

(b) *Statutory remedies*

(i) The Law of Property Act 1925, s.194[94]   Under the provisions of   **8.32** this section the erection of any building or fence, or the construction of any other work on land, which was subject to rights of common on January 1, 1926, is unlawful unless the consent of the Secretary of State is obtained. Where a consent has not been obtained a commoner, *inter alia*, may apply to a county court to make an order for the removal of the work and the restoration of the land to the condition in which it was before the work was erected or constructed.[95] The power to make the order is discretionary and it seems may not be exercised if the aggrieved party has failed to make his dissent to the works known to the defendant and/or has stood by and allowed the work to go ahead.[96] Similarly, long delay in instituting action may result in the court refusing to order restoration.[97] Among the parties able to bring action for restoration the commoner may be in special diffi-culty in the event of delay as it has been suggested[98] that standing by and allowing detrimental reliance on the lack of action may lead to a deduction that the commoners have impliedly released their rights.

---

[90] *Holford* v. *Bailey* (1850) 13 Q.B. 426, 116 E.R. 1325; *cf. Smith* v. *Kemp* (1693) 2 Salk. 637, 91 E.R. 537; *Cox* v. *Glue* (1848) 5 C.B. 533, 136 E.R. 987.

[91] *Fitzgerald* v. *Firbank* [1897] 2 Ch. 96 at 97, *per* Kekewich J.

[92] *Nicholls* v. *Ely Sugar Beet Factory* [1931] 2 Ch. 84.

[93] R.S.C. Ord. 15, r. 12; *cf. Phillips* v. *Hudson* (1867) L.R. 2 Ch.App. 243; *Commissioners of Sewers* v. *Gellatley*; (1876) 3 Ch.D. 610, *per* Jessel M.R., especially at 616; *Howard* v. *Maitland* (1883) 11 Q.B.D. 695; *Salmon* v. *Edwards* [1910] 1 Ch. 552; *Walker* v. *Murphy* [1914] 2 Ch. 293, [1915] 1 Ch. 71.

[94] For further discussion, see § 9.34.

[95] s.194(2).

[96] *Symonds* v. *Malvern Hills D.C.* (1978) 248 E.G. 238.

[97] *ibid.*; *Wimbledon and Putney Commons Conservators* v. *Nicol* (1894) 10 T.L.R. 247.

[98] § 5.48.

8.33   It should L. noticed, and it is considered again later,[99] that the granting of a consent under this section merely makes lawful that which would be otherwise unlawful without consent. The consent has nothing to say, nor can it affect, the rights of the parties with legal interests in the land. It follows that any enclosure of part of a common by the owner is actionable by a commoner through abatement or otherwise if it infringes his rights irrespective of the consent given.[1]

8.34   **(ii) Commons Act 1876, s.30**   The county court has jurisdiction under this section to hear a case relating to any illegal inclosure or encroachment of, or upon, any common (as defined in the Act[2]) or part of a common. The court may grant an injunction against such an inclosure or encroachment or make an order for removal. This section is of much wider application than section 194 of the L.P.A. 1925 both in terms of dispute resolution and the classes of land with which it is concerned. The section applies to land "subject to be inclosed"[3] whereas section 194 applies only to land subject to rights of common on January 1, 1926. Thus stinted pastures, regulated pastures and common fields fall within its scope.

8.35   **(iii) Limitation of actions**   It has been said that rights of common are extinguished where a person encroaching on, or otherwise adversely possessing, the land over which the rights are exercised, acquires protection from re-entry by the paper title owner by the effect of the Limitation Acts.[4] Section 15 of the Limitation Act 1980 provides that no action shall be brought for the recovery of land after the expiration of 12 years from the date on which the right of action accrued. Land, however, is defined under the Act so as to exclude incorporeal hereditaments.[5] Indeed, while it is possible to see how a person can take possession of a right of common by user, it is difficult to visualise acts of adverse possession of such a right by an occupier of a common or part of a common, when an owner (or squatter) has a right to that part of the product unused by the commoner.

8.36   In addition, when the adverse possession of the land of a common is accompanied by enclosure without the consent of a Secretary of State under the provisions of section 194 of the L.P.A. 1925, the Limitation Act cannot vitiate the unlawful nature of the enclosure. The relevant part of that section declares that work without consent "shall not be lawful." The unlawful nature, it is suggested, continues indefinitely and protection lies in the reluctance of the courts to interfere in longstanding enjoyment and not in the effect of the Limitation Act 1980.

8.37   The position cannot be said to be altogether satisfactory. A possessory title holder is relatively secure in his title to land after the elapse of the statutory limitation period, but is insecure in respect of any profits exercisable over

---

[99] § 9.35.
[1] For limitations on abatement, see §§ 8.15 *et seq.*
[2] s.37.
[3] The section is also applied to any metropolitan common: Metropolitan Commons Act 1878, s.3.
[4] Harris and Ryan, § 2.96; Joshua Williams, p. 154, but see *Tapley* v. *Wainwright* (1833) 5 B. & Ad. 395, 110 E.R. 836.
[5] s.38(1).

the land. On the other hand commoners may not rely upon the non-operation of the Limitation Act to protect their rights in the event of encroachment for, as has been suggested,[6] under certain circumstances a doctrine of implied release of rights may be applied.

There are exceptions to the general proposition that an encroachment **8.38** accompanied by adverse possession will lead to a possessory title protected by limitation. If there is a statutory prohibition on inclosure without the consent of Parliament applicable to the land, as may be found in connection with land regulated under the Commons Act 1876,[7] an encroacher will not be able to plead the Limitation Act.[8] Further, a person holding the land under statutory authority may not obtain a possessory title,[9] nor may a person claiming against a title to land which contains a statutory bar on alienation,[10] but where there are merely statutory restrictions, such as the need to obtain certain consents, a possessory title may be established.[11]

Management

(a) Commoners associations

The most usual form of management by commoners is through an unincorporated association, which has all the usual difficulties which that type of **8.39** organisation entails.[12] In particular, an association cannot bind a dissenting minority of its members to the agreed plans of the majority whether it be in respect of the regulation of stocking, improvement, changed use of the land or works of a capital nature. An association may not either grant easements,[13] nor join with the owner of the soil in granting easements. This is sometimes partially overcome by an association agreeing not to sue the owner's grantee but this is obviously less than satisfactory for the grantee.

In the context of compulsory purchase of common land, with consequent **8.40** extinguishment of rights, an association may receive statutory recognition as a body authorised to receive and disburse compensation monies.[14] However, the provisions of the relevant statutes do not extend to allow an association to act in the same way if the compensation is for the suspension or disturbance of rights.[15]

---

[6] See § 5.48.
[7] By s.36.
[8] *Collis* v. *Amphlett* [1918] 1 Ch. 232, (C.A.).
[9] *Wimbledon and Putney Commons Conservators* v. *Nicol*, above, n. 97.
[10] *Earl of Abergavenny* v. *Brace* (1872) L.R. 7 Ex. 145.
[11] *Mayor of Brighton* v. *Guardians of Brighton* (1880) L.R. 5 C.P.D. 368.
[12] See further at § 12.150.
[13] *Paine & Co.* v. *St. Neots Gas & Coke Co.* [1938] 4 All E.R. 592 [1939] 3 All E.R. 812.
[14] See further at §§ 5.91 *et seq.*
[15] See further at § 5.107.

(b) *Statutory management*

8.41   There are a number of general statutes enabling various forms of management over common land and these are considered later.[16] Some, such as the Metropolitan Commons Act 1866[17] and the Commons Act 1876[18] allow for instigation by commoners. Others, such as the establishment of statutory regulated pastures, are dependent upon inclosure awards. All are limited in their scope to enable an increase of statutory management for agricultural purposes. An exception can be found in the Dartmoor Commons Act 1985, which has recently made provision for the comprehensive management of commons in Devon largely under the auspices of a council of elected commoners.[19]

8.42   Nevertheless, a not inconsiderable number of commons are regulated under the Commons Acts 1876 and 1899.[20] In addition some commons are managed under specific local statutes. Where there is an Act in force it is comparatively easy to ascertain the duties and responsibilities of the parties involved. Less easy to identify and investigate are powers granted under private Inclosure Acts which, in some cases at least, provide substantial powers of management. An example is where an award granted the "proprietors" powers to regulate rights, levy rates, and sell sand, gravel and earth.[21]

(c) *Manorial courts*

8.43   Upon the abolition of copyhold tenure in 1925 most manorial courts lost their last administrative reason for existence. Most have just ceased to function. Those remaining had their powers defined, and in most cases strictly curtailed, by the Administration of Justice Act 1977.[22] A small number of courts retained powers to manage common land but in most cases, it seems, without the sanctions to make their actions effective.

(d) *Heather and grass burning*

8.44   A management practice frequently carried out by commoners is the burning of grass, heather and other vegetation. Such burning is controlled through the Heather and Grass Burning (England and Wales) Regulations 1986[23] made under the authority of section 20 of the Hill Farming Act 1946. A person contravening the Regulations is liable to a penalty not exceeding level 3 on the standard scale.[24]

8.45   Under the Regulations the burning of heather and grass is prohibited on any land between April 15 and October 1 in any year if situated in specified

---

[16] See Chapter 12.
[17] § 12.34.
[18] § 12.43.
[19] § 12.84.
[20] *cf.* Table 2 at § 1.09 and Appendix 9.
[21] *Paine & Co.* v. *St. Neots Gas & Coke Co.*, above, n. 13.
[22] For which see § 12.147.
[23] S.I. 1986 No. 428.
[24] Hill Farming Act 1946, s.20(2); Wildlife and Countryside Act 1981, s.72(2); Criminal Justice Act 1982, s.46.

upland areas and, additionally, in any lowland area between March 31 and April 16 and between September 30 and November 1, except in accordance with a licence issued by the Minister of Agriculture or the Secretary of State for Wales.[25] It is the duty of an applicant for a licence to notify in writing any other person interested in the land as owner or occupier, any persons in charge of adjacent land, and, if the land is common land, or an open space, or subject to rights of common or similar rights of grazing, the persons responsible for the management of the land and, in any event, the persons entitled to rights of common or grazing, of the application.[26]

In any event no burning shall be commenced between sunset and sunrise **8.46** and the persons mentioned above must be notified in writing of the intention to burn not less than 24 and not more than 72 hours before the commencement.[27] The burning is subject to requirements that sufficient persons and equipment to control and regulate the burning are used and that all reasonable precautions are taken to prevent injury to any persons or things on the land or adjacent land.[28]

Occupiers' Liability

"The rules of occupiers' liability are those rules of law which govern the **8.47** liability of an occupier of premises for injuries to persons who come onto those premises."[29] In the case of the common lands it cannot be said that there is clear liability on commoners as occupiers but, on the other hand, it also cannot be said with certainty that they are free from liability. Nor is there one clear code of rules governing all common land—liability, if it exists, varies from one type of common to another and may vary between classes of entrants on the same common.

(a) *The duties to entrants to land*

(i) Occupiers' Liability Act 1957 A common duty of care to visitors **8.48** to land is laid down in section 2(1) of the Act:

" . . . a duty to take such care as in all the circumstances of the case is reasonable to see that the visitor will be reasonably safe in using the premises for the purposes for which he is invited or permitted by the occupier to be there."

A visitor to premises is a person who, under the common law, was treated as an invitee or licensee.

(ii) Occupiers' Liability Act 1984 Distinguishable from the com- **8.49** mon duty of care is a duty owed to all persons, other than visitors, in respect of any risk of their suffering injury on the premises by reason of any danger

---

[25] S.I. 1986 No. 428, reg. 6.

[26] *ibid.* regs. 7(3), 8.

[27] *ibid.* reg. 5(1), (2).

[28] *ibid.* reg. 5(2).

[29] North, *Occupiers' Liability* (1971), p. 1; also see generally for the law of occupiers' liability.

due to the state of the premises, or things done, or omitted to be done, on them. Under the Occupiers' Liability Act 1984 this duty is only owed by an occupier to another person if

> "(a) he is aware of the danger or has reasonable grounds to believe that it exists;
> (b) he knows or has reasonable grounds to believe that the other is in the vicinity of the danger (in either case, whether the other has lawful authority for being in that vicinity or not); and
> (c) the risk is one against which, in all the circumstances of the case, he may reasonably be expected to offer the other some protection."[30]

The standard of the duty is to take such care as is reasonable in all the circumstances of the case to see that entrants to the land do not suffer injury[31] by reason of the danger concerned.[32] The liability of an occupier is clearly of a more onerous kind in respect of "visitors" and it is necessary, therefore, to decide which persons entering common land come into this category.

(b) *Visitors to common land*

8.50 **(i) National Parks and Access to the Countryside Act 1949** Under this Act an access agreement may be made with, or an access order served upon, the owner of open land.[33] A person entering land under such an agreement or order for the purposes of open-air recreation shall not be treated as a trespasser on that land.[34] But, the liability of a person interested in the land shall not be increased in respect of the state thereof, or of things done, or ommitted thereon,[35] and section 1(4) of the Occupiers' Liability Act 1957 provides expressly that:

> "A person entering any premises in exercise of rights conferred by virtue of an access agreement or order under the National Parks and Access to the Countryside Act, 1949, is not, for the purposes of this Act, a visitor of the occupier of those premises."

8.51 **(ii) Access under "a right conferred by law"** Section 2(6) of the Occupier's Liability Act 1957 provides that:

> "For the purposes of this section persons who enter premises for any purpose in the exercise of a right conferred by law are to be treated as permitted by the occupier to be there for that purpose, whether they in fact have his permission or not."

The context of the section makes it clear that the "right conferred by law" is not a right enjoyed by a commoner, a person using a public way or a per-

---

[30] Occupiers' Liability Act 1984, s.1(3).
[31] In the Occupiers' Liability Act 1984 "injury" means death or personal injury: s.1(9); there is no liability for loss of or damage to property: s.1(8).
[32] s.1(4).
[33] See further at § 11.34.
[34] s.60.
[35] s.66(2).

son exercising an easement.[36] Comment in texts and in a Law Reform Committee report[37] confine the categories of persons concerned to those exercising statutory rights of entry such as the police, employees of public utility undertakings and entrants to public parks. However, it is hardly arguable that persons entering common lands under a statutory right of access for air and exercise granted under section 193 of the L.P.A. 1925, or for exercise and recreation to a regulated common under the Commons Act 1876 are there other than in the exercise of a right conferred by law, thus bringing them within the common duty of care owed to visitors. The position is further complicated as access under the Act of 1876 is most usually confined to the inhabitants of a neighbourhood. Thus, persons entering this class of land will be owed different duties dependent upon their place of residence.

(iii) Implied licences   A licensee (one of the categories of visitor) is a   **8.52**
person entering premises under circumstances where the occupier has no material interest in the entry, *i.e.* the occupier has neither invited entry nor does he derive material benefit therefrom.[38] In the context of the common lands it has to be considered whether a member of the public exercising *de facto* access without *de jure* right may be a licensee. In general it seems that the courts will not accept mere knowledge of the presence of the public on common land as indicating a licence—"a repeated trespass of itself confers no licence" as how can it be said of an occupier "that he had licensed what he cannot prevent."[39] Nevertheless, owners and commoners should be careful not to expressly or impliedly license the public, or sections of the public, to enter the land without recognising that a higher duty of care towards them may arise.

On lands owned by the National Trust it may be simpler to find that the   **8.53**
members of the public are present as implied licensees. The preamble to the National Trust Act 1907 states that the public are admitted to the lands owned[40] and the general purposes of the Trust state that open spaces may be maintained for public recreation or resort. In addition officers of the Trust have stated publicly that access is allowed almost everywhere on the common lands.[41]

(c) *Occupiers of common land*

To this point there has been a tacit assumption that there is an identifiable   **8.54**
occupier of common land for the purposes of occupiers' liability. In many cases this may not be so. It might be expected that the owner is also the

---

[36] s.2 of the Occupiers' Liability Act 1957 merely defines the extent of the duty to "visitors"; which by virtue of s.1 encompasses the pre-existing categories of the licensee and invitee under the common law and not those with legal interests in or over the land. The section should only have relevance to statutorily created licensees.

[37] Third Report of the Law Reform Committee: *Occupiers' Liability to Invitees, Licensees and Trespassers* (Cmnd. 9305 (1954)), paras. 38, 78(x) and recommendation 2(x), at p. 41.

[38] *e.g. Lowery* v. *Walker* [1911] A.C. 10.

[39] *Edwards* v. *Railway Executive* [1952] A.C. 737 at 746, *per* Lord Goddard.

[40] See further at § 12.128.

[41] *ibid.*

occupier subject only to limited rights granted to commoners to use the land in a limited way. The practical reality, however, is frequently very different and it may be the commoners who exercise the main control over the land. Each example will have to be considered on its own facts and there is little doubt that in many there will be no identifiable occupier.

8.55   The courts now seem to take a broad view of the persons constituting occupiers for the purposes of occupiers' liability. In *Wheat* v. *E. Lacon & Co. Ltd.* (1966)[42] the House of Lords held that there could be multiple occupation of premises, with duties varying in nature and extent attributable to the respective occupiers. Before that case it had been thought that the occupier of premises was the person who had "immediate supervision and control and the power of permitting and prohibiting the entry of other persons." In rejecting this test, Lord Denning M.R. proposed a broader approach:

> "Wherever a person has a sufficient degree of control over premises that he ought to realize that any failure on his part to use care may result in injury to a person coming lawfully there, then he is an 'occupier' and the person coming lawfully there is his 'visitor' and the 'occupier' is under a duty to his 'visitor' to use reasonable care. In order to be an 'occupier' it is not necessary for a person to have entire control over the premises. He need not have exclusive occupation. Suffice it that he has some degree of control. He may share the control with others. Two or more may be 'occupiers.' And whenever this happens, each is under a duty to use care towards persons coming lawfully on to the premises, dependent on his degree of control. If each fails in his duty, each is liable to a visitor who is injured in consequence of his failure but each may have a claim to contribution from the other."[43]

This approach seems sufficient to ensure that in some circumstances a commoner or commoners will owe the common duty of care to visitors and the general duty of care to other persons. In the event of injury to an entrant there may be difficulty in identifying a particular tortfeasor, but an injured person may proceed against any one who is liable leaving him to draw in the other joint tortfeasors.[44]

(d) *Limitation of liability*

8.56   **(i) for the common duty of care**   An occupier of premises has no obligation under the common duty of care for "risks willingly accepted as his" by the entrant.[45] Further the obligation is owed to visitors except insofar as the occupier is free to, and does, extend, restrict, modify or exclude his duty to them by agreement or otherwise.[46] Thus, the obligation may be modified or excluded by contractual term or otherwise, *i.e.* by notice, so far as the occupier is free to do so. The significance of the last qualification is that the ability to limit liability is controlled by the Unfair Contract Terms Act 1977. Under that Act obligations and duties arising from the occupation of premises used for business purposes[47] may only be excluded in accord-

---

[42] [1966] A.C. 552.
[43] *ibid.* at 578.
[44] Law Reform (Married Women and Tortfeasors) Act 1935, s.6(1).
[45] Occupiers' Liability Act 1957, s.2(5).
[46] *ibid.* s.2(1).
[47] Unfair Contract Terms Act 1977, s.1(3).

ance with the provisions contained in the Act. Such persons cannot exclude liability for death or personal injury resulting from negligence[48] and, in any other case of loss or damage, except insofar as the term of the notice satisfies a requirement of reasonableness.[49]

Prima facie most, but not all,[50] commoners and owners of common land are **8.57** persons using premises for business purposes, are within the business provision and are restricted in their ability to limit liability towards persons entering as visitors. However, the Occupiers' Liability Act 1984 makes an exception affecting entry to common lands when in section 2 an addition to section 1(3) of the Unfair Contract Terms Act 1977 (which defines business liability) is provided:

> " . . . but liability of an occupier of premises for breach of an obligation or duty towards a person obtaining access to the premises for recreational or educational purposes, being liability for loss or damage suffered by reason of the dangerous state of the premises, is not a business liability of the occupier unless granting that person such access for the purpose concerned falls within the business purposes of the occupier."

The effect of the provision is that on common land any or all liability to **8.58** visitors entering for exercise or recreation may be excluded by contractual term or notice. This does not create the same immunity as applies in the case of persons entering under an access agreement or order[51] who, it will be recalled, are deemed not to be visitors for the purposes of occupiers' liability. Entrants under an access agreement and under the right of access contained in section 193 of the L.P.A. 1925 are lawful entrants to the land but the former are deemed not to be visitors in spite of agreement as to their presence, whereas entrants under the latter provision are deemed to be visitors in spite of the lack of agreement as to their presence. Both, as lawful entrants, will, however, be affected by notices excluding liability. It seems that in either case a trespasser, unlawfully present,[52] cannot be affected by an exclusion notice. The possibility arises that a person suffering injury on common land may seek to claim that his presence was unlawful to escape the effect of an exclusion notice.

(ii) to persons other than visitors The duty owed to persons other **8.59** than visitors applies to dangers due to the state of the premises or things done, or omitted to be done, on them, of which the occupier is aware or has reasonable grounds to believe exist.[53] In the context of the common lands, the additional qualification that a person is only liable if he knows, or has reasonable grounds to believe, that an entrant is in the vicinity of the danger or may come into the vicinity of the danger seems to be met wherever there is *de facto* access to the land.

---

[48] s.2(1): for the purposes of the Act, negligence means *inter alia* occupiers' liability: s.1(1)(c).
[49] s.2(2).
[50] The grazing of animals for commercial profit is something done in the course of business; *aliter* in the case of products taken for domestic purposes.
[51] § 8.50.
[52] The occupier can hardly be seen as giving a trespasser a licence to trespass subject to an exclusion notice.
[53] *cf.* § 8.49.

8.60 As with visitors, an occupier is not liable to an entrant for "risks willingly accepted as his."[54] Further:

> "Any duty owed by virtue of this section in respect of a risk may, in an appropriate case, be discharged by taking such steps as are reasonable in all the circumstances of the case to give warning of the danger concerned or to discourage persons from incurring the risk."[55]

The significance of the phrase "may, in an appropriate case, be discharged" is not entirely clear for there is an implication that on occasions a case may not be appropriate for a warning. Subject to this qualification, it seems that the liability to persons other than visitors may be discharged by suitable notices and/or physical discouragement from entry to a dangerous area by, say, enclosure.

(e) *Dartmoor Commons Act 1985*

8.61 This Act provides a right of public access to finally registered common land on Dartmoor and expressly provides that a person entering the land in accordance with that right is not, for the purposes of the Occupiers' Liability Act 1957, a visitor of any occupier of the commons.[56]

(f) *Proposals for reform*

8.62 The Common Land Forum recommends that future legislation shall provide public access to the common lands and also recommends that the Occupiers Liability Act 1957 should not apply to such land.[57] This recommendation, if implemented, will have the effect of changing the liability over land currently subject to a right of public access under section 193 of the L.P.A. 1925 or the Commons Acts.

---

[54] Occupiers' Liability Act 1984, s.1(6).
[55] s.1(5).
[56] Dartmoor Commons Act 1985, s.10(2).
[57] Common Land Forum Report, p. 27, Recommendation 6.5(11).

9. Fencing on and near the Common Lands

The general duty to contain animals

Under the common law the owner of *manseuetae naturae*[1] was bound to keep them upon his own land and was liable if they escaped and committed a trespass.[2] The principle was laid down as early as 1480 when, in dealing with a trespass from an unfenced common, the defence was held to be bad "for when he puts his beasts in the common he ought to use his common so that they do no wrong to another man; and if the land in which he ought to have his common is not enclosed . . . he ought to keep his beasts in the common and out of the land of another."[3] The liability was strict and independent of negligence: " . . . if a man's beasts without his will or knowledge break into another's close, he is guilty of trespass for a man is bound by law to keep his beasts without doing wrong to anyone."[4] **9.01**

A fence is the term used to describe any form of barrier intended to bar the passage of animals, and for the purposes of the Animals Act 1971 fencing includes the construction of any obstacle designed to prevent animals from straying.[5] The general duty to contain animals does not include an obligation to erect a fence to effect that containment, nor is there any general duty to erect a fence to surround any land: "the law bounds every man's property and is his fence."[6] There are a number of common law and statutory exceptions to the general rule. There is an obligation on mine and **9.02**

---

[1] *cf.* North, *The Modern Law of Animals* (1972), pp. 92–94. In mediaeval times, liability in cattle trespass was limited to "avers" but as time went on the category was extended to include most domestic farm animals, excluding dogs, cats, bees and probably domestic pigeons. The modern forms of statutory action apply to livestock as defined in s.11 of the Animals Act 1971.

[2] The general principles of, and authority for, the now defunct action of cattle trespass were reviewed by Blackburn J. in giving the judgment of the Exchequer Chamber in *Fletcher* v. *Rylands* (1866) L.R. 1 Ex. 265 at 280–282; affirmed *sub nom. Rylands* v. *Fletcher* (1868) L.R. 3 H.L. 330.

[3] *Anon.* (1480) Y.B. 20 Edw. 4, folio 10, pl. 10 (translated in *Read* v. *Edwards* (1864) 34 L.J.C.P. 31 at 32); *cf. Anon.* (1580–1581) 3 Dyer 372b, 73 E.R. 835.

[4] *Anon.* (1496) Keil. 3, 72 E.R. 156 n. 7, *per* Keble J. The trespass need only be technical: for a minimal trespass see *Ellis* v. *The Loftus Iron Company* (1874) L.R. 10 C.P. 10.

[5] s.11.

[6] *Star* v. *Rookesby* (1710) 1 Salk. 335, 91 E.R. 295, *per curiam.*

quarry owners to erect and maintain fences[7]; on tenants to repair fences[8]; and, in the absence of fences, licensees without exclusive possession may be denied a remedy both under common law and statute.[9] There are also statutory obligations to erect and maintain fences under the Inclosure Acts 1845–1882,[10] the Railway Clauses Consolidation Act 1845[11] and the Mine and Quarries Act 1954.[12]

9.03   Additionally, agricultural contracts of tenancy are deemed[13] to include obligations on the part of the tenant "to repair and . . . to keep in good tenantable repair . . . fences, hedges, field walls, stiles, gates and posts, cattle grids . . . "[14] and "to cut, trim or lay a proper proportion of the hedges in each year of the tenancy so as to maintain them in a good and sound condition,"[15] insofar as such obligations are not inconsistent with an agreement in writing.[16] The purpose of the deemed obligations is to clarify the relationship between landlord and tenant, but for the purposes of actions between adjoining occupiers of land in connection with animals straying it will be shown that it matters not to whom an obligation to maintain a fence is owed—the mere existence of a duty to maintain a fence is sufficient.[17]

9.04   The typical area of common land used for grazing is substantial and more often than not is unenclosed except to the extent that it abuts land occupied in severalty. It follows that the problems associated with straying livestock are magnified on the common lands. The duty of the commoner to contain his livestock is broadly the same as it is for any other grazier, in

---

[7] *Groucott* v. *Williams* (1863) 32 L.J.Q.B. 237 (lessee/mine owner liable to lessor/occupier for mare killed by falling down an uncovered mine shaft); *Hawken* v. *Shearer* (1887) 56 L.J.Q.B. 284 (quarry and pasture let to separate tenants, quarry owner liable for injury to grazier's livestock); *M'Morrow* v. *Layden* [1919] 2 I.R. 398 (heir succeeding to lease of mine succeeds to liability for non-fencing by predecessor).

[8] "It is so notoriously the duty of the actual occupier to repair the fences, and so little the duty of the landlord, that, without any argument to that effect, the landlord may maintain an action against his tenant for not so doing, upon the ground of injury done to the inheritance . . . ": *Cheetham* v. *Hampson* (1791) 4 T.R. 318, 100 E.R. 1041, *per* Lord Kenyon C.J.

[9] *Churchill* v. *Evans* (1809) 1 Taunt. 529, 127 E.R. 939. It was admitted in argument that a person with a right to remove paving stones co-extensive with a right to pasturage by another was not able to distrain damage feasant. *Quaere* whether either has a duty to guard against casual damage.

[10] Inclosure Act 1845, s.83; it seems also that, whenever an award has been made under a previous Inclosure Act which did not contain an express power to require maintenance in perpetuity, such a power will be implied: *Garnett* v. *Pratt* [1926] 1 Ch. 897.

[11] s.68.

[12] s.151.

[13] Agriculture (Maintenance, Repair and Insurance of Fixed Equipment) Regulations 1973 (S.I. 1973 No. 1473), reg. 3.

[14] *ibid.* Sched., para. 5(1): "repair involves putting into repair having regard to age, character and condition at the commencement of the tenancy": *Evans* v. *Jones* [1955] 2 Q.B. 58 at 66, *per* Evershed M.R.

[15] *ibid.* para. 9.

[16] A contractual clause prevails over the statutorily implied provisions: *Burden* v. *Hannaford* [1956] 1 Q.B. 142 (C.A.).

[17] *cf.* § 10.43.

other words, to see that his livestock do not stray to the land of another person. With the extensive unenclosed areas involved the task of preventing straying could be, and sometimes is, a major difficulty in the use of the commons. The task of preventing straying is ameliorated only by the widespread acceptance in common land areas that there is a duty imposed on occupiers of contiguous land to fence against the common, which is a reversal of the normal fencing rules. It will be shown that where there is a legal duty to fence, and livestock stray because of a breach of that duty, the owner of the livestock is not liable for damage caused by the straying. It is a matter, therefore, of some importance to determine when a duty to fence will arise, and conversely when it will not. This chapter considers the question of fencing on and around common lands and the next examines liability for straying animals in the light of the fencing obligations established thereby.

Fencing against a common

In spite of the general duty on the part of a commoner, or any landowner, to **9.05** contain his cattle, there is in practice a widespread, if not universal, acceptance that occupiers of land abutting a waste are under a binding obligation to maintain fences so that animals on the common do not stray onto their property. This is so well understood among the rural communities that, in straying cases coming before the courts, it is frequently conceded as being a binding obligation at the outset.[18]

The existence of a duty to fence in case law authorities was noticed by the treatise writers in the nineteenth century. It was categorised in *Gale's Easements* as "a spurious kind of easement obliging an owner of land to keep his fences in a state of repair, not only sufficiently to restrain his own cattle within bounds, but also those of his neighbours."[19] It is suggested later that an obligation to fence as between neighbouring landowners as a form of easement is accurately designated spurious, lacks the characteristics of an easement, and, in particular, is incapable of acquisition by prescription. There has probably never been a general easement of fencing and the cases which allow for an obligation to fence between adjoining landowners can be explained as either being directly concerned with or, arising from, the duty to fence against common land.[20]

(i) The duty explained as a custom The duty to fence has been con- **9.06** sidered in the courts on several occasions in modern times,[21] culminating with the decision in the Court of Appeal in *Egerton* v. *Harding*[22] in 1974. In that case the Court, in effect, affirmed the layman's view that the duty to

---

[18] *e.g. Coaker* v. *Willcocks* [1911] 2 K.B. 124; *Sharpe* v. *Harvey* (1935) 2 L.J.N.C.C.R. 261; *Spry* v. *Mortimore* (1946) 13 L.J.N.C.C.R. 83; *Sutcliffe* v. *Holmes* [1947] K.B. 147.

[19] (2nd ed., 1849), p. 297.

[20] For fencing between adjoining landowners, see § 9.55.

[21] See the cases cited above, n. 18; *Swift* v. *Ellis* (1939) 6 L.J.N.C.C.R. 384; *Cooke* v. *Skinner* (1947) 98 L.J. 38; *Jones* v. *Price* [1965] 2 Q.B. 618; *Crow* v. *Wood* [1971] 1 Q.B. 77.

[22] [1975] Q.B. 62.

fence against the waste land class of the common lands could be founded in customary law and in the particular place be as binding as the common law. The facts were not atypical: the plaintiff owned a cottage, and the defendant occupied a farm adjoining Binwood Common in Hampshire; the defendants exercised grazing rights for cattle over the common; a hedge forming the boundary between the common and the cottage had been kept in repair by the plaintiff for a number of years but was allowed to deteriorate and the defendant's cattle strayed into the cottage garden; the plaintiff sued in cattle trespass[23] and the defendant claimed, in defence, that the plaintiff was under a duty to fence against the common. At first instance the county court judge found that a custom to fence against the common had been proved and, further, that there was no evidence of inclosure, grant or presumption of lost modern grant. The plaintiff's claim was dismissed and he appealed.

9.07 The Court of Appeal affirmed the decision of the county court judge in a reserved judgment delivered by Scarman L.J. It was noted that the judge had considered evidence bringing into view all the lands surrounding and adjoining the common and had concluded that a custom was proved, recognising that for a custom to be upheld as local law it had to be shown to be of immemorial origin, reasonable, continued without interruption and certain. The Court held that—

> " . . . once there be established an immemorial usage of fencing against the common as a matter of obligation, the duty to fence is proved, provided always that it can be shown that such a duty could have arisen from a lawful origin. In the present case we are prepared to assume that the mists of the past obscure the historical origins of the usage. Yet it is plain that the duty could have arisen from one of several lawful origins: as between neighbouring owners it could have derived from grant or prescription: within a manor it could derive from custom by which the lord protected the interests of his copyholders, or from enclosure."[24]

9.08 The case was considered to be analogous to one where a company was held to be under a duty to repair a sea wall. There, Wills J. said "it seems to me that according to all ordinary principles when you find a liability of a very onerous kind asserted and submitted to for a long series of years, although the evidence begins well within modern times, still, you are bound to presume everything which is not manifestly absurd which will support and give a legal origin to the practice."[25]

9.09 It will be noticed that the court did not decide directly that the origin of the obligation lay in custom but accepted the possibility as one alternative. In so doing, a case which had led differently constituted Courts of Appeal to

---

[23] The damage occurred before the abolition of cattle trespass by the Animals Act 1971.
[24] [1975] Q.B. 62 at 71, 72.
[25] *London and North-Western Railway Co.* v. *Fobbing Levels Sewers Commissioners* (1897) 75 L.T. 629 at 632.

believe that there could be no origin in custom for an obligation to fence was explained differently by further consideration of alternative reports.[26]

The way seems open for proof of a custom to fence against the common over **9.10** the majority of the common land wastes. As a custom there is no question of extinguishment by unity of ownership; there is also no need to establish that the right to benefit from the custom passes with title to land. On most wastes there will be little difficulty in establishing that the obligation is of immemorial origin, reasonable, certain and has been continued without interruption.

(ii) The duty explained as an easement   In a previous case heard in **9.11** the Court of Appeal, *Crow* v. *Wood* (1971),[27] it had been concluded, from the case of *Bolus* v. *Hinstocke* (1670),[28] that a customary origin for the obligation to fence against a common could not exist. The Court went on to explain the obligation in the traditional manner as an easement with peculiarly convoluted and unsatisfactory results. The facts were not dissimilar to those in *Egerton* v. *Harding*, except in one respect: the plaintiff's and the defendant's farms adjoined a moor; both had rights to graze over the moor; the plaintiff did not exercise her rights and allowed the boundary fence to deteriorate; the defendant's sheep strayed onto the plaintiff's farm causing damage, and the plaintiff sued in cattle trespass, but the moor and several adjoining farms had been in common ownership for many years. In 1951 a farm was sold to the person from whom the defendant derived title. This was followed by the sale of two farms to the plaintiff in 1956 and 1966. The county court judge found for the plaintiff and the defendant appealed, founding his defence on a duty to fence on the part of the plaintiff arising from an implied grant at common law, and/or by the provisions of section 62 of the L.P.A. 1925.

The case proceeded on the basis that, although the county court judge **9.12** referred to a custom to fence, the duty could not arise from custom by virtue of the court's reading of *Bolus* v. *Hinstocke*. Nor could it have arisen by prescription at common law because of the common ownership: *Kilgour* v *Gaddes* (1904).[29] After reviewing the authorities Lord Denning M.R. concluded that:

> "It seems to me that it is now sufficiently established—or at any rate, if not established hitherto, we should now declare—that a right to have your neighbour keep up the fences is a right in the nature of an easement which is capable of being granted by law so as to run with the land and to be binding on successors. It is a right which lies in grant and is of

---

[26] Diplock L.J. had suggested in *Jones* v. *Price* [1965] 2 Q.B. 618 at 639, in reliance on *Polus* v. *Henstock* (1670) 1 Vent. 97, 86 E.R. 67, that an obligation to fence could not arise by custom. Lord Denning M.R. reached the same conclusion in *Grow* v. *Wood* [1971] 1 Q.B. 77 at 83, relying on another report of the same case *Bolus* v. *Hinstocke* (1670) 2 Keb. 686, 84 E.R. 431. In *Egerton* v. *Harding* it was held that these views of the case were mistaken.

[27] Above n. 26.

[28] *ibid.*

[29] [1904] 1 K.B. 457.

such a nature that it can pass under section 62 of the Law of Property Act 1925."[30]

9.13 It was but a short step to find that the defendant's farm, purchased in 1951, enjoyed a right and advantage, passing under section 62, to graze his sheep on the moor together with a right to require other farmers to keep up their fences. The plaintiff was liable to maintain her boundary fences. This result has the awkward consequence that without an express reservation in the 1951 conveyance later purchasers of land in the common ownership could not be granted a similar right against the 1951 purchaser. Lord Denning, citing Glanville Williams out of context,[31] declared:

> " . . . I would say that in every conveyance it is implied that every farmer who has a right to put sheep on the moor and to have his neighbour repair fences, is under an obligation, ancillary to it, to keep up his own fences. The right and obligation extends to all farmers who buy their farms from the common owner, no matter in what order they buy them."[32]

9.14 This argument of mutual benefit and burden, although attractive in the case in hand, does suffer from grave difficulties. If it is correct then on the particular facts before the court the decision should have been reversed: the plaintiff had in fact abandoned her rights to graze which was the reason she allowed the boundary fences to deteriorate—or does the burden outlive the benefit? Alternatively, if the burden of fencing is only attached to the benefit of grazing, is it the case that had the later sales been without the benefit to graze no obligation to fence would exist? If so, many commons will only be partly fenced by adjoining owners. Further, if the common owner had directed his thoughts to the question could he have not granted rights to graze over the servient land and not burdened the land he was selling with the obligation to fence? If he wished to impose the burden expressly, what is the form of the "grant?" Surely it must take the form of a positive covenant which is not binding on successors in title.[33] Explaining the duty to fence against a common in terms of a traditional type of easement bristles with difficulties. It is necessary, in order to satisfy the reality of all persons expecting, and in practice finding, that an obligation to fence is accepted on the part of all the occupiers of contiguous land, to make so many special provisions that the so-called easement can only be explained as being a *lex loci* or custom.

9.15 It should now be recognised that the source of the generally expected duty to fence against a waste land type of common lies in custom and that no further attempt needs to be made to explain it in terms of a form of easement. Thus, the duty, where it exists, is that all occupiers of land contiguous to a waste must maintain a fence on the boundary of their land for the benefit of those who have a legal right to graze over the land.

[30] *Crow* v. *Wood* [1971] 1 Q.B. 77 at 84.
[31] Glanville Williams, p. 209. The author merely suggested that the grantor of an easement of way might also be able to undertake repair and bind his successors in title (expressly refuted in *Austerberry* v. *Oldham Corporation* (1885) 29 Ch.D. 750 at 773, 774, *per* Cotton L.J.).
[32] *Crow* v. *Wood* [1971] 1 Q.B. 77 at 85.
[33] *Austerberry* v. *Oldham Corporation* (1885), above, n. 31.

(a) *The extent of the duty*

Where land abutting a common is conveyed by reference to an Ordnance **9.16**
Survey map the prima facie presumption that the boundary lies in the
centre of the fence[34] is displaced. In the absence of evidence to the contrary,
where a fenced close adjoins a piece of waste land, the fence can be presumed to belong to the owner of the close.[35]

There is first instance support for the proposition that the duty to fence **9.17**
against a common may extend beyond the perimeter of the common to any
land which may reasonably be expected to be affected by livestock straying
from the common. In *Spry* v. *Mortimore* (1946)[36] it was held that the "occupier of inclosed [*quaere* enclosed] land so near the common that commonable animals may reasonably be expected to trespass upon it must fence the
exposed part of his land adequately against them." The land concerned was
300–400 yards from the boundary of the common down a lane. The extent
of the duty will depend upon the facts. However, it is not unusual to find
that occupiers adjoining highways near common land, and in particular
along highways connecting parts of commons, accept the duty to fence as a
matter of course.

(b) *The standard of fencing*

The standard of fencing required is not such that all animals, under all cir- **9.18**
cumstances, will be contained. In *Coaker* v. *Willcocks* (1911)[37] the defendant had occupied a "newtake"[38] farm in the Forest of Dartmoor and seized
some of the plaintiff's sheep which had strayed from the adjoining common.
It was acknowledged by the defendant that there was a duty, on his part, to
fence against the common and the issue was whether the duty extended to
all sheep or only the moorland sheep traditional to the area. Scottish sheep
had been introduced on the moor in 1907. Darling, holding for the defendant, said:

> " . . . these Scotch sheep are of a peculiarly wandering and saltative dis-
> position, straying and jumping in a way which distinguishes them from
> sheep which have hitherto been turned on the unenclosed land, wan-
> dering as other sheep do not and jumping as other sheep cannot. In my
> judgment the defendant was not bound to fence his land from sheep of
> this description; it was the duty of the plaintiff, if he chose to own such
> sheep, to keep them from trespassing on the defendant's land."[39]

The decision was upheld in the Court of Appeal,[40] where it was held that **9.19**
the plaintiff was under an obligation to keep his sheep off his neighbour's

---

[34] For which, see *Fisher* v. *Winch* [1939] 1 K.B. 666; *Davey* v. *Harrow Corporation*
[1958] 1 Q.B. 60.

[35] *White* v. *Taylor* (No. 2) [1969] 1 Ch.160 at 200, *per* Buckley J.

[36] [1946] 13 L.J.N.C.C.R. 83 at 85.

[37] [1911] 1 K.B. 649.

[38] The term seems to be used in various ways in Dartmoor to mean inclosures under
statute, extra-statutory inclosures from the Forest of Dartmoor, and the lower
slopes of a moor which have been enclosed for the wintering of livestock. In the
latter sense it is broadly equivalent to the Welsh "fridd."

[39] [1911] 1 K.B. 649 at 654.

[40] *Coaker* v. *Willcocks* [1911] 2 K.B. 124, C.A.

land in the absence of proof that the defendant was under an obligation to keep out the particular class of sheep.[41] It seems that the standard of fencing required is only that necessary to keep out the local breed and, although there are indications that a custom may be extended to new practices, the burden on the servient tenant should not thereby be increased.[42] It should perhaps be noticed that the major breed of sheep on Dartmoor today is the Scottish sheep (of saltative disposition) and those persons with land abutting the common now seem to accept the obligation to fence them out.

9.20 Fences only have to be reasonably secure. To contain a pig, for example, the duty is to maintain "such a fence that a pig not of a particularly wandering disposition, nor under any excessive temptation will not get through it . . ."[43] and the courts have not laid down "that there must be a fence so close and strong that no pig could push through it, or so high that no horse or bullock could leap it."[44] It is also unnecessary to take account of the possibility of animals breaking through by the use of exceptional force or under exceptional conditions as might occur when calves have been weaned from cows.[45] Nevertheless, account must be taken of the normal disposition of animals: it must be expected that cattle will rub against gates,[46] sheep will get through small gaps in hedges,[47] horses may develop tricks to break through fences,[48] and horses and cattle may be expected to reach through and over fences.[49] Thus, the duty is not absolute and the commoner may not be able to avoid liability for every escape by pleading the breach of a duty to fence on the part of the person strayed upon.

9.21 The primary duty to prevent straying lies upon the commoner. In the event of an escape through a fence, the onus of proof should therefore lie on the commoner to establish that there has been a breach of a duty to fence.

(c) *Dilapidated fences*

9.22 Where a custom to fence against a waste can be established it might be thought that the obligation to maintain fences will continue, whether the common is used or not, and whatever use is made of the adjoining land. It might also be thought that if the owner of the fence allows deterioration he is at risk and the commoner may ignore the dilapidation. Indeed on the authority of a case in 1442 it has been said that there is no rule *scienti non fit iniuria*.[50]

This does not seem to be the modern view. In a cattle trespass case, *Sutcliffe* v. *Holmes* (1946)[51] the plaintiff sued for damage caused by straying sheep and the defendant claimed that a third party was in default of his duty to

---

[41] At 130, *per* Farwell L.J.
[42] *Mercer* v. *Denne* [1905] 2 Ch. 538 at 581.
[43] *Child* v. *Hearn* (1874) L.R. 9 Ex. 176 at 182, *per* Bramwell B.
[44] *ibid.* at 181–182.
[45] *Cooper* v. *Railway Executive* [1953] 1 W.L.R. 223.
[46] *Page* v. *The Great Eastern Railway Co.* (1871) 24 L.T. 585.
[47] *Bessant* v. *The Great Western Railway Co.* (1860) 8 C.B.N.S. 368, 141 E.R. 1208.
[48] *Spry* v. *Mortimore* (1946) 13 L.J.N.C.C.R. 83 at 86.
[49] *Wiseman* v. *Booker* (1878) 3 C.P.D. 184 at 188; *Ellis* v. *Loftus Iron Co.* (1874) L.R. 10 C.P. 10.
[50] Glanville Williams, p. 214, n. 4.
[51] [1947] K.B. 147.

fence against the common. In a county court case, *Sharpe* v. *Harvey* (1935)[52] it had been held that the wrongful act of a third party provided a defence in cattle trespass. The Court of Appeal approved the principle laid down but considered that it was too widely stated: account should be taken of whether the defendant knew or ought to have known of the defective fences, and ought to have taken steps to have the defects remedied or, otherwise prevented the escape of his sheep.[53] The action of cattle trespass, and with it the defence of wrongful act of a third party, has been abolished by the Animals Act 1971[54] but it may that the state of knowledge of the commoner about defective fences may still be relevant in common law actions where the commoner is seeking recompense for damage to animals following straying.[55]

(d) *Extinguishment*

It was established in the seventeenth century that the general rule is that   **9.23** unity of seisin of adjoining closes serves to extinguish a duty to fence.[56] In *Boyle* v. *Tamlyn* (1827)[57] the question was treated by Bayley J. as beyond doubt and, further: " . . . where the person who has so become the owner of the entirety afterwards parts with one of the two closes, the obligation to repair the fences will not revive unless express words be introduced into the deeds of conveyance for that purpose."[58]

The rule, cannot apply to common land so as to extinguish the obligation on   **9.24** the part of the owner of the soil of the common in relation to his demesne or purchased freeholds.[59] This is much as might be expected if the obligation to fence against a common is customary and owed to graziers by any person abutting a common. Whether the custom will survive unity of seisin of all the dominant tenements with the servient tenement, where the dominant tenements, or some of them, have never been in the actual occupation of the owner, must be considered undecided. It might seem in principle beyond argument but it must be remembered that when tenants of the manor were copyholders the custom continued and if copyholders are replaced by agricultural tenants holding rights in common, instead of rights of common, the need for a mutuality in fencing against the common

---

[52] (1935) 2 L.J.N.C.C.R. 261.
[53] *Sutcliffe* v. *Holmes* [1947] K.B. 147 at 156, *per* Somervell L.J.
[54] Animals Act 1971, s.1(1)(c); see further at § 10.08.
[55] See further at §§ 10.109 *et seq.*
[56] *Drake* v. *Doylye* (1604) Noy 14, 74 E.R. 985; *cf. Polus* v. *Henstock* (1670) 1 Vent. 97, 86 E.R. 67.
[57] (1827) 6 B. & C. 329, 108 E.R. 473; *cf. Erskine* v. *Adeane* (1873) 8 Ch.App. 756; *Jones* v. *Lee* (1912) 106 L.T. 123.
[58] *ibid.* at 337, 476; there were early doubts about whether the duty could revive: *Anon.* (1570) 3 Dyer 295b, 72 E.R. 663; *Drake* v. *Doylye* (1604), above, n. 56; the question seems to have been settled by Crew C.J. in *Sury* v. *Pigot* (1626) Pop. 166 at 172, 79 E.R. 1263 at 1268 and followed in *Polus* v. *Henstock*, above, n. 56; later cases made it clear that express words could not revive the duty: see *Austerberry* v. *Oldham Corporation* (1885) 29 Ch.D. 750.
[59] Nor can the purchase of a strip of land outside the fence extinguish the duty; the suggestion that it could was made in *Egerton* v. *Harding* [1975] 1 Q.B. 62 at 63 by counsel but not taken up by the court.

remains. It may be that the custom will survive until all dominant and servient land is in the same actual occupation.

9.25 If the common is inclosed it is clear that the obligation to fence against the land will continue. In *Barber* v. *Whiteley* (1865),[60] Inclosure Commissioners had allotted a waste and made provision for the erection and maintenance of fences except where the waste adjoined old copyhold enclosures. It was held that the obligation to fence survived the inclosure. Hunt commented soon afterwards[61]:

> "It is quite plain that the principles here laid down apply with equal force to a modern and an ancient approvement; and it appears from this case that, where a liability to repair a fence for the benefit of the commoners of a manor exists, such liability is not taken away by the inclosure of the commons under an Inclosure Act or otherwise, for agreements among the commoners themselves [to allot the common into severalty portions] ought not to affect the liability of third parties."

(e) *Enforcement*

9.26 Enforcement of an obligation to maintain fences used to be through the writ *de curia claudenda*,[62] which was abolished in 1833. Long before then it had fallen into disuse and was effectively replaced by an action on the case. This action lay between adjoining landowners and not, as with the writ of *claudenda*, between adjoining freeholders. It has been said not to lie at the suit of a commoner for "reasons that are difficult to appreciate."[63] The case cited in support for this view is *Smith* v. *Burton* (1674),[64] for which the headnote is not entirely accurate. A commoner complained that the fences adjoining the common were out of repair "whereby he durst not use his common for fear his cattle should stray upon the defendant." The decision was that the action was not good "for if his cattle had trespassed upon him through his own bounds, he might have justified." The court was drawing attention to the rule at the time that, in an action on the case it was necessary to state title to the common, whereas in a justification to an avowry damage feasant it was not. Later this rule was relaxed,[65] and the lack of capability in a commoner to bring an action for disturbance of his right may now be considered defunct. However, it seems that "everyone who would maintain an action on the case must have a particular right, or show special damage,"[66] and a plaintiff commoner cannot demand repair "if he has his

[60] (1865) 34 L.J.Q.B. 212.
[61] Hunt, *The Law relating to Boundaries and Fences* (2nd ed., 1870), p. 67; the decision in the case was in no way innovatory as the inclosure was the result of a private Act in 1828, which would have been governed by the Inclosure (Consolidation) Act 1801, which in s.27 confirms that pre-existing duties to fence survive an inclosure.
[62] For which see Williams, "The Origin of the Prescriptive Duty to Fence" (1938) 54 L.Q.R. 405.
[63] Glanville Williams p. 216; North, above, n. 1, p. 131.
[64] (1674) 1 Freem. 145, 89 E.R. 105.
[65] Note to *Mellor* v. *Spateman* (1669) 1 Wms.Saund. 343 at 346, 85 E.R. 495 at 497, *per* Serjent Williams.
[66] *Wagstaff* v. *Rider* (1719) 1 Com. 341, 92 E.R. 1102, citing *Iveson* v. *Moore* (1699) 1 Salk. 15, 91 E.R. 16, *per* Holt C.J.

right of common only by licence or contract with the defendant; for it does not appear that he has any more right of common than at the will of the defendant . . . "[67] A commoner, properly in possession of a right of common, ought now to be able to bring an action for damages and/or a mandatory injunction to compel repair.

The courts are slow to respond to applications for mandatory injunctions **9.27** and are likely to act only if grave damage is likely, not just feared, or if damages will be insufficient. The cost of compliance will be taken into account but if the action by the defendant is wanton may be disregarded. The likelihood is that the order will be made so as to prevent further loss.[68]

(f) Common fields, stinted pastures, regulated pastures

The obligation to fence the boundaries of common fields, stinted pastures **9.28** and regulated pastures is likely to be altogether different. The general rule in common fields seems to have been that the fields were in much the same position as land held in severalty portions and the liability was to fence against the wastes outside the fields. This is recognised in section 27 of the Inclosure (Consolidation) Act 1801, which makes express provision for common field boundaries to continue to be maintained by the severalty owners with the allotment holders outside the fields relieved of any liability.

Where stinted pastures and regulated pastures have their origin in an inclo- **9.29** sure award, the award must be consulted to discover liability. The Inclosure Act 1845, for example, provides that "the several allotments to be made shall be inclosed, ditched and fenced and the fences so to be made shall for ever afterwards be repaired and maintained by such persons as the valuer shall direct."[69] In spite of the apparently permanent nature of the wording the duty to maintain a fence should not survive unity of seisin and occupation of the separated closes—the purpose of the Act was to define liabilities of adjoining parties for private purposes and not to impose obligations in perpetuity, irrespective of changed circumstances.

Occasionally stinted and regulated pastures may have their origin in grant **9.30** by the lord of a waste or part of a waste. Under these circumstances, there seems no reason why the obligation to fence against the waste should not survive the grant much as in the case of an allotment.[70]

(g) Endorsement of the custom

The Common Land Forum endorses the "custom and practice" of fencing **9.31** adjoining private land against the common, and records its support of the assistance given by public authorities to schemes of fencing, particularly those which form part of urban fringe renewal.[71] The Dartmoor Commons

---

[67] *Wagstaff* v. *Rider* (1719) 1 Com. 341 at 342.
[68] *Morris* v. *Redland Bricks Ltd.* [1970] A.C. 652 at 665F–666G, *per* Lord Upjohn; *cf.* Aldridge, *Boundaries, Walls and Fences* (5th ed., 1982), especially pp. 30–31.
[69] s.83; see further at n. 10, above.
[70] See § 9.25.
[71] Common Land Forum Report, para. 5.11.

Act 1985, for the avoidance of doubt, declares that the custom on the commons concerned is to fence against any animals lawfully depastured there.[72]

Statutory limitations on fencing

(a) *Town and Country Planning legislation*

9.32 Fencing is development within the terms of the Town and Country Planning Act 1971 and requires planning permission.[73] Some fencing is excluded as being a minor operation by the provisions of article 3 and Schedule I to the Town and Country General Development Order 1977[74]: the erection or construction of "gates, fences, walls or other means of enclosure not exceeding one metre in height where abutting on a highway used by vehicular traffic or two metres in height in any other case . . . "[75] is normally exempt. This exemption may itself be excluded by a direction, made under article 4 of the same Order, which may be made so as to apply to a specified area. Article 4 directions are more likely in coastal areas and areas of outstanding natural beauty. Thus, under circumstances of the most relaxed control, planning permission is only required for new fencing over one metre high where it abuts a highway and two metres high elsewhere. No permission is required for repair or renewal of fences unless they are to be taken above the prescribed heights.[76]

9.33 Whether or not a proposed fence abuts a highway is a question of fact not altogether easy to determine. Reliance cannot be placed on finally registered maps drawn under the C.R.A. 1965 which, while showing the boundaries of statutory common land, do not define the boundaries of a highway, which may overlap a common.[77] On some occasions it seems that planning authorities will waive strict compliance with planning requirements provided the siting and type of fence is considered to be suitable.

(b) *Law of Property Act 1925, s.194*[78]

9.34 **(i) Provisions** A measure of statutory control over fencing, and other works, on common land is established by this section which provides in sub-section(1) that:

> "The erection of any building or fence, or the construction of any other work, whereby access to land to which this section applies is prevented or impeded, shall not be lawful unless the consent of the Minister[79] thereto is obtained, . . . "

---

[72] s.9.

[73] s.22: "development . . . means the carrying out of building, engineering, mining or other operations in, over or under land . . . "

[74] S.I. 1977 No. 289.

[75] *ibid.* Sched. 1, Class II, sundry minor operations, s.1.

[76] *ibid.* art. 3.

[77] s.21(2) provides that the conclusive evidence provision contained in s.10 shall not apply for the purpose of deciding whether any land forms part of a highway.

[78] For the full text, see Appendix 3.

[79] The Secretaries of State for the Environment and Wales, for England and Wales respectively: Secretary of State for the Environment Order 1970 (S.I. 1970 No. 1681).

Subsection (3) provides that:

> "This section applies to any land which at the commencement of this
> Act[80] is subject to rights of common:
> Provided that this section shall cease to apply—
> (a) to any land over which the rights of common are extinguished under
> any statutory provision;
> (b) to any land over which the rights of common are otherwise ext-
> inguished, if the council of the county in which the land is situated
> by resolution assent to its exclusion from the operation of this sec-
> tion and the resolution is approved by the Minister."

Proviso (b) is not, in practice, considered to be necessary for fencing alone
but is reserved for cases where an extinguishment of rights has taken place
and the use of the land is to be changed.[81] Subsection 4 of the section
exempts those works which are authorised under statute, works in connection with the taking of minerals, and any telegraphic lines.

The consent of the Minister has no more effect than to make lawful that **9.35**
which would otherwise be unlawful by virtue of the provisions of the section. It has no further implications in relation to other consents or agreements required. In particular, other parties interested in the common are
not inhibited thereby from taking any form of action which may be available to them, as well as an action under section 194.[82]

(ii) Conditions It seems that the draftsman of the 1925 legislation, in **9.36**
making provision for public access to certain "urban" commons, under section 193 of the L.P.A. 1925,[83] thought that the giving of access might inhibit
the owners of the soil from making grants of common land for specific
works such as public buildings.[84] It was decided to enact section 194 with
the intention of facilitating development work of a public nature providing
the consent of a Minister was obtained. The section, however, is worded in
a way which provides a much larger result. The principle requirements for
the section to operate are (a) that the works are such that access is prevented
or impeded, and (b) that the land was subject to rights of common on January 1, 1926.

The meaning of "access" The meaning of the word access came up **9.37**
directly for consideration in *Att.-Gen.* v. *Southampton Corporation*
(1969).[85] A writ was issued on behalf of three objectors seeking to restrain
the local authority from constructing two car parks on an urban common
claiming, *inter alia*, that the Corporation required the consent of the Minister under section 194. It was found, from the evidence given, that rights of
common were in existence on January 1, 1926, but that none were currently
enjoyed. Access of commoners could not therefore be obstructed but Foster
J. considered that:

[80] *i.e.* January 1, 1926.
[81] See further § 7.68.
[82] For this form of action, see § 9.51.
[83] For which see § 11.06.
[84] Royal Commission Report, Minutes of Evidence, Ministry of Agriculture and
Fisheries, p. 71.
[85] (1969) 21 P. & C.R. 281.

"Where the word "access" is used in section 194(1) I think that it refers to the expression "access for air and exercise" in section 193. Will the construction of the two car parks prevent or impede access to the land for air and exercise? . . . It is true that if you consider the car parks without any cars parked upon them a person can exercise upon them but when the car parks have cars parked upon them, it seems to me inevitable that the space so occupied cannot be used for exercise or for air. In my judgment therefore the proposed works will be unlawful unless the Minister's consent is obtained."[86]

The access for the public to take air and exercise, provided by section 193, then is one form which must not be prevented or impeded.

9.38 However, in ordinary language it is hardly arguable that the section can be read other than so as to include any form of access legally exercisable over a common, of which that of the commoners for exercising rights is the most obvious. Thus, if the land is not subject to section 193 access, consent is still required if the access of the legal interests is obstructed but, if these too are not affected, or there are none, then no consent is required. Similarly, it seems probable that, if all the commoners agree that their access to the land is not obstructed, the works may escape the effect of the section.

9.39 It seems that not all works and fences on commons are to be viewed as preventing or impeding access. It has been held that low walls and railings intended to guide vehicular traffic rather than impede or prevent travel on foot do not require consent,[87] but, on the other hand, hard core laid as a way to a private house impeded access to the grazing.[88]

9.40 *Limited to land subject to rights of common* The second limitation to the section is that it can only apply to land which was subject to rights of common on January 1, 1926. It follows that not all statutory common land falls within the ambit of the section. Stinted pastures, regulated pastures and any common fields, subject only to the rights of the owners in severalty, will not usually be subject to the section unless, of course, they happen also to be subject to rights of common. The section may be unsatisfactory to the extent that it is possible, although undecided, that some of these classes of land may be subject to rights of public access under section 193[89] but not subject to the restrictions of section 194. There is probably also land subject to rights at the present date but not so subject at the beginning of 1926 due to unified ownership at that time. There certainly is land registered as statutory common land under the head of waste land of a manor which is not within the purview of the section.

9.41 Thus, not all statutory common land falls within the ambit of section 194. Conversely, the fact that unregistered land is deemed by the Act not to be common land[90] does not necessarily mean that it is not subject to section

---

[86] *Att.-Gen.* v. *Southampton Corporation* (1969) 21 P. & C.R. 281 at 288.

[87] *Hambledon R.D.C.* v. *Hinde* (1968) 19 P. & C.R. 212.

[88] *Eaton* v. *Keaton* (1966), Cheltenham County Court, October 14, 1966: (1967) 17 C.S.J. No. 6.

[89] *cf.* §§ 11.10–11.15.

[90] C.R.A. 1965, s.1(2)(*a*).

194. Being subject to rights of common at the beginning of 1926 is the relevant factor—registration as statutory common land is irrelevant.

Savings in the Commons Registration Act 1965   The C.R.A. **9.42**
1965 contains a purported saving provision referring to section 194. Section
21(1) provides that—

> "Section 1(2) of this Act [unregistered land deemed not to be common
> land and unregistered rights not exercisable] shall not affect the appli-
> cation to any land registered under this Act of section 193 or section
> 194 of the Law of Property Act 1925 . . . "

It is difficult to understand what effect this provision has. It only applies to
land which is registered under the Act. Had the wording of the Act been that
unregistered rights were extinguished, the position might have arisen that
registered land had been subject to extinguishment of rights under statute,
thereby bringing into play subsection 3, proviso (a), which excludes land
where rights have been extinguished by statute. But the Act did not
expressly extinguish rights and merely provides that "no rights of common
shall be exercisable unless registered."[91] The C.R.A. 1965 cannot affect
either of the two requirements of section 194 which bring land within its
purview.

In any event, the provision cannot apply to land which has not achieved **9.43**
registration. Some would argue that it is this class of land which is at most
risk from development and prima facie most needed protection. In the event
that there is unregistered land which was subject to rights of common at the
beginning of 1926 and was also within the purview of section 193, the interest to be protected, in the absence of any registered rights of common, is the
public interest in access. The protection available for this class of land is
considered below.[92]

(iii) Applications   Upon an application to a Minister for consent the **9.44**
procedure he must follow is prescribed in section 194(1):

> " . . . in giving or withholding his consent the Minister shall have
> regard to the same considerations and shall, if necessary, hold the same
> enquiries as are directed by the Commons Act 1876, to be taken into
> consideration and held by the Minister before forming an opinion
> whether an application under the Inclosure Acts 1845 to 1882 shall be
> acceded to or not."

The considerations directed by the Commons Act 1876 are that the Minister shall certify that in his opinion an inclosure "would be expedient, having regard to the benefit of the neighbourhood as well as to such private
interests as aforesaid [persons interested in the common]."[93] The nature of
the enquiries to be made are based on sections 10 and 11 of the Act.

---

[91] C.R.A. 1965, s.1(2)(b); but see *Central Electricity Generating Board* v. *Clwyd County Council* [1976] 1 W.L.R. 151 at 155–156, *per* Goff J.: "cease to be exercis-able" is a synonym for extinguished, but see also the discussion at §§ 11.18–11.22.
[92] §§ 9.51 and 11.18 *et seq.*
[93] Preamble.

9.45 In advice to applicants, given on behalf of the Secretary of State for Wales (the appropriate Minister in Wales),[94] it is stated that:

> "In effect, he can grant consent only if he is satisfied that it would be expedient for him to do so, having regard to the "benefit of the neighbourhood" as well as to "private interests." The Secretary of State is advised that the "benefit of the neighbourhood" means the health, comfort, and convenience of the inhabitants of any populated areas in or near any parish in which the land concerned, or any part of it, is situated in the general context of the enjoyment of the common as an open space; and "private interests" means the advantage of the Lord of the Manor or other owner of the soil and of the commoners."

9.46 It might be taken as an a implication from this advice that the proposed works must benefit the neighbourhood as well as the private interests.[95] However, an opinion in the following terms has been adopted by the Department of the Environment:

> "Counsel has advised that the question on which the Secretary of State has to form an opinion in the context of section 194 is not whether the giving of his consent will be for the "benefit of the neighbourhood" as defined above, but whether, having regard to the "benefit of the neighbourhood" as well as to "private interests," it is expedient that his consent should be given. In Counsel's opinion, the expression "benefit of the neighbourhood" refers to the existing benefit, which is to be protected, rather than to any additional benefit to be expected as a result of the proposed inclosure. Any such additional benefit would be considered generally in assessing the expediency of giving consent, but it would not be given priority as a consideration. The 1876 Act clearly contemplates that any enclosure will involve some encroachment on the common, and some interference with private interests. In other words, Counsel's view is that the Acts do not require that the Secretary of State, before giving his consent, shall form the opinion that the proposed inclosure or work will enure for the benefit of the neighbourhood and private interests but merely that he shall take the "health, comfort and convenience" of the inhabitants and the "advantage of the persons interested in the common" into consideration in making his decision."[96]

9.47 Before submission of an application the proposals have to be published, inviting objections, in the manner prescribed in section 31 of the Commons Act 1876.[97] The Secretary of State notifies informally the Open Spaces Society[98] and seeks to resolve any objection received, by correspondence. In the light of any unresolved objections, or lack of information, a decision is

---

[94] Welsh Office: application for the consent of the Secretary of State under s.194 of the Law of Property Act 1925, 1986.

[95] The impression is perhaps reinforced by an emphasised statement that applicants do not always develop sufficiently their case as to why they regard the proposal as being expedient having regard to the benefit of the neighbourhood.

[96] Correspondence received from the Department of the Environment stating that this opinion will be included in notes to applicants in the future.

[97] Secretary of State for Wales' notes for applicants, above, n. 94.

[98] (1981) C.S.J. no. 1, p. 3; (1984) 22 O.S. no. 1, p. 21.

taken as to the holding of a local inquiry, in which event the procedure laid down in section 11 of the Commons Act 1876 is followed. There is no provision for appeal against the decision of the Secretary of State.

If the common is regulated under the Commons Act 1899, applicants must **9.48** seek the managing authority's agreement to the proposals and ask them either (a) to apply for the Secretary of State's consent under the scheme or, (b) to amend the scheme before his consent is sought by the applicants under section 194, as necessary.[99]

Where a provisional order confirmation Act under the Commons Act 1876 **9.49** is in effect it seems that an application for the consent of the Minister under section 194 is inappropriate as inclosure of such land is prohibited by section 36 of the Commons Act 1876. The principle of *generalia specialibus non derogant* applies as between the 1876 and 1925 Acts. It may be, however, that car parks are not inclosures and require consent under section 194.

Special provisions are made for common and commonable land owned by **9.50** the National Trust.[1] Section 23 of the National Trust Act 1971 requires that the erection of most buildings and, the construction of other work requires the consent of the Secretary of State if access by the public is prevented or impeded thereby. There is no enforcement procedure under the Act.

(iv) Enforcement A special form of action is provided in section **9.51** 194(2) of the L.P.A. 1925:

"Where any building or fence is erected, or any other work constructed without such consent as is required by this section, the county court within whose jurisdiction the land is situated, shall, on an application being made by the council of any county or district concerned, or by the lord of the manor or any other person interested in the common, have power to make an order for the removal of the work, and the restoration of the land to the condition in which it was before the work was erected or constructed, but any such order shall be subject to the like appeal as an order made under section thirty of the Commons Act 1876."[2]

The interest in the common necessary to bring an action is probably restricted to those with a legal interest in the land such as an owner of the soil (or part of it), commoners, and holders of easements or customary rights. The public interest in the land, if any, is represented by the county and district council. In the event that the council is the offender, the course the public can seek to follow is a relator action in the High Court.[3] Limitations on the enforcement of section 194 have already been considered.[4]

---

[99] Notes for applicants, above, n. 94.

[1] See further at § 12.126.

[2] Appeal is now to the Court of Appeal, by words substituted in the Commons Act 1876 by the Administration of Justice (Appeals) Act 1934, Sched., Pt. 1.

[3] *e.g. Att.-Gen.* v. *Southampton Corporation* (1969) 21 P. & C.R. 281; *cf.* R.S.C., Ord. 15, r. 11.

[4] At § 8.32 and §§ 9.36 *et seq.*

9.52   **(v) Practice**   The erection of fencing on common land so as to divide it into severalty portions, although on occasions highly beneficial to the private interests in the land, will usually be considered detrimental to the benefit of the neighbourhood. An application for consent is unlikely to be successful. On the other hand, fencing to protect animals from damage resulting from road traffic accidents can be seen as directly beneficial to the private interests and the inhabitants of the neighbourhood by a reduction in the accident rate and the continued proper stocking of the land. This type of application is more likely to be successful. Section 194 is well used. Some 645 consents were given by Ministers in the period 1956–1986.[5]

9.53   **(vi) Proposals for reform**   The Common Land Forum recommends that future legislation shall provide for section 194 to be applicable to all "commons" including any which come into existence after the passing of a new Commons Act.[6] Further, it is recommended that county councils should have a duty, and the public a power, to take action under the provisions in section 194 against any person carrying out work, which requires the consent of the Minister, without that consent.[7] It is also recommended that temporary fencing on commons be allowed, subject to consent under section 194, where necessary to prevent the spread of disease among farm stock depastured there.[8]

9.54   The Dartmoor Commons Act 1985 also makes provision for the application of section 194 to all registered Dartmoor commons (*i.e.* as they become finally registered under the C.R.A. 1965).[9] The subsection concerned is worded so as to require the Commoners Council to apply for consent in carrying out functions which involve the erection of any building or fence or the construction of any other work on a common. From the wording it seems that it is unnecessary for the works to impede or obstruct access for a consent to be necessary.

Fencing between adjoining landowners

9.55   When animals stray from the common lands it is not unusual for them to travel long distances and stray further onto other lands. As the breach of any duty to fence, regardless of to whom it may be owed, may provide a defence in an action for damage caused by the straying,[10] any duty imposed on landowners outside the immediate common land area is of especial importance to commoners.

(a) *The incidence of the duty in practice*

9.56   It has already been noticed that the duty to fence against a common may survive inclosure of the whole or part of a common.[11] It follows that in any area where there has been inclosure there may be a duty to maintain par-

[5] See Appendix 9.
[6] Common Land Forum Report, para. 5.8.
[7] *ibid.* para. 5.9.
[8] *ibid.* para. 5.12.
[9] C.R.A. 1965, s.9.
[10] Considered at § 10.43.
[11] § 9.25.

ticular fences in spite of the common land having ceased to exist or, the land in severalty no longer abutting a common. Whether this is so in any individual case is a matter of record and at any current date may be difficult to determine. Nevertheless, the point should not be forgotten in considering liability in a straying action.

Where the common land itself has been subject to inclosure, that is to say in **9.57** the case of stinted or regulated pastures, the liability for fencing is once again a matter of record on the particular inclosure award.[12] In the case of common fields notice should be taken of the usually encountered liability for the occupiers of the common fields to maintain their own boundary fences.[13]

Perhaps the most frequently encountered duty will be that imposed on ten- **9.58** ants of agricultural holdings in their contracts of tenancy.[14] These may be express or implied as a result of regulations. It is not unknown for express obligations to be imposed by landlords by sharing liability between adjoining tenants so that, for instance, each tenant maintains, say, his westernmost boundary fence.

(b) *The prescriptive obligation*

It is also frequently remarked in texts that an obligation to maintain fences **9.59** may arise between adjoining landowners by grant or prescription.[15] There is, of course, no reason why such an obligation may not exist as a matter of contract and this is not unusual in contracts between landlord and tenant. Similarly, there is no reason why it should not arise between parties by covenant under seal. However, as is well known such positive covenants are not generally enforcable against successors in title to the original covenantee except by indirect means.[16] Nevertheless, it has generally been supposed that grants to maintain fences may exist in a form to bind successors and that such a grant may be proved by prescription or presumed grant.

Nobody seems to have been able to suggest the form such a grant would **9.60** take and as a doctrine, which must have its own peculiar rules, it bristles with difficulties over principles and consequently has never been fully explained. It is proposed, therefore, to review briefly the authority which exists for the doctrine and suggest that it is susceptible to alternative explanation.

A statement of the law as it has been generally understood may be found in **9.61** *Gale's Easements*,[17] which commences with an extract from the judgment of Willmer L.J. in the Court of Appeal in *Jones* v. *Price* (1965),[18] itself an extract from Gale in the 13th edition:

[12] § 9.29.
[13] § 9.28.
[14] § 9.03.
[15] Megarry and Wade, p. 908.
[16] For further details see Megarry and Wade, p. 767.
[17] (14th ed., 1972) at p. 37; but for later consideration see the 15th ed., 1986 pp. 39–43.
[18] [1965] 2 Q.B. 618.

"A true easement, as has been seen, is either a right to do something or a right to prevent something. A right to have something done is not an easement, nor is it an incident of an easement; for instance, the owner of the site of a right of way is not bound to keep the way in repair. An obligation to do something on one's own land can only arise, speaking generally, by statute or contract, and the burden of a contractual obligation of that kind does not run with the land. Anomalously, however, the courts have recognized what has been called a prescriptive obligation on the owners and occupiers of a piece of land to maintain a fence thereon for the benefit of the owners and occupiers of adjoining land. The obligation has been established by proof of long usage under which the quasi-servient owner or occupier has consistently repaired the fence when told to do so by the quasi-dominant owner or occupier, and therefore inferentially in performance of a binding obligation. The legal justification for subjecting private land to a positive burden does not appear to have been questioned or explained; the right so recognized is not an easement, but if it may be assumed to be enforceable against a purchaser without notice its existence produces the same situation as if an easement had been created. Probably it rests on the presumption of a contract, which is considered or assumed, contrary to modern principle, to be binding on successors in title."

9.62   It has been demonstrated that an obligation to maintain fences does exist on a widespread scale in relation to the duty to fence against a common as a matter of custom, and not as a form of easement between adjoining land owners or occupiers. It has also been shown that this obligation will survive the inclosure of waste lands.[19] It can be anticipated that at times, and in areas where inclosure was occurring on a piecemeal basis, there would be a significant number of fences which local knowledge would recognise had been fenced immemorially by the occupier of the land, although it no longer abutted common land. An individual landowner would prescribe for such an obligation in the form that his neighbour had repaired the fence time out of mind.[20] The plea would be correct but the origin of the duty would have been in the customary duty to fence against common land and not in any grant, express or presumed, between the landowners.[21] There is an extraordinary dearth of cases where acquisition of a duty by user has been successfully pleaded or even discussed.

9.63   It might also be anticipated that while inclosure was proceeding apace the duty to fence as between neighbouring landowners would be frequently

---

[19] § 9.25.

[20] *e.g. Star* v. *Rookesby* (1710) 1 Salk. 335, 91 E.R. 295: the plaintiff declared that the tenants and occupiers of the defendant's close had, time out of mind, made and repaired the fence between the plaintiff's and defendant's close: prescription held sufficiently alleged; *cf. Pomfret* v. *Ricroft* (1669) 1 Saund. 321, 85 E.R. 454, especially n. 1(c) at 456; *Boyle* v. *Tamlyn* (1827) 6 B. & C. 329, 108 E.R. 473.

[21] It is suggested that to view a prescriptive plea as a method of acquisition, almost of an adverse nature, is comparatively modern as the result of the development of the doctrine of lost modern grant. Until the late 18th century it was more a method of proof of rights, which may well have preceded the advent of the common law itself, and although legal theory would have it that all prescription pre-supposes a grant it is a fairly nebulous concept when the rights may have originated before the doctrine of an owner for all land was developed.

recognised and often litigated. As the pace of inclosure abated, as the duty was progressively extinguished by unified ownership of the closes, and as memory of past inclosures faded, fewer duties would be recognised and fewer cases would come to court. This is exactly what seems to have happened. There has been only one successful case where the duty has been accepted as having arisen between adjoining severalty landowners in the last century or so and even in that case the matter was not fully considered. It is therefore possible to explain the prescriptive duty to fence, as described in the older cases, as being derived only from the customary duty to fence against a common. If this is correct, there is a remarkable lack of authority for the so-called anomalous easement of fencing arising by grant or acquisition by prescription.

(c) *Modern authorities*

In view of the approval of the doctrine, albeit in a somewhat qualified form, **9.64** in the Court of Appeal in *Jones* v. *Price* (1965)[22] it is necessary to examine the modern authorities. The first difficulty must be the form of "grant" of a duty to fence. It is difficult to see how it could be framed other than as a positive covenant. Adopting Diplock L.J.'s words in *Jones* v. *Price*,[23] "there is no precedent in the books for such a grant and it is difficult to envisage its form." Secondly, prescription according to the usual rules is difficult. Common law prescription will frequently be defeasible on the grounds of unified ownership—the great majority of fences must have come into existence during the time of legal memory. The duty does not seem to come within the ambit of the Prescription Act 1832. The only judicial comment, which seems to have mystified some writers,[24] is that of Williams J. in *Peter* v. *Daniel* (1848)[25] when he abruptly remarks during counsel's argument about a right to scour a ditch: "if it sets up a duty only, it is not within Lord Tenterden's Act." However, the comment is totally explicable in the light of the Real Property Commissioners Report in 1829,[26] which preceded the Act of 1832. The Report drew a clear distinction between easements and profits on the one hand and "prescriptive obligations arising out of the tenure of lands, such as to make fences or repair roads" on the other. Proof of these obligations was recommended to be subject to a period of reduction in legal memory and the provision was not adopted. Thus proof by prescription is largely dependent on the doctrine of lost modern grant with the inherent difficulty of explaining the form of the grant.

---

[22] Above, n. 18.

[23] *ibid.* at 640.

[24] *cf.* Hunt, p. 51; *Gale's Easements* (4th ed., 1868), p. 467, and especially Glanville Williams, p. 410, where an attempt is made to cast doubt on the comment: "On the other hand Gale (11th ed.), p. 434 quotes a dictum of Vaughan Williams J. that the Act has no application to mere duties. The exact meaning of this observation is obscure, and as applied to fencing it receives no support from other authorities . . . there is no reason why statutory prescription should not be possible." With respect, there is also no positive support from other authorities that it does apply and, as the present text explains, the dictum is in accord with the recommendations leading to the enactment of the Prescription Act 1832.

[25] (1848) 5 C.B. 568, 136 E.R. 1001.

[26] First Report of the Real Property Commissioners (1829), printed by order of the House of Commons, p. 53.

9.65 A case which involved long repair of fences is *Hilton* v. *Ankesson* (1872),[27] which the Court of Appeal in *Jones* v *Price* felt unable to say had been wrongly decided.[28] At Assize it was proved that the defendant had repaired the fence for at least 50 years. The witnesses, when asked why they had repaired, said they thought that every man had to repair his own fences. On hearing this the judge ordered a non-suit with leave for the plaintiff to have it set aside. The Court of Exchequer were unanimous in supporting the judge. Kelly C.B. said that a liability to repair a fence can only be created by Act of Parliament, or some agreement or covenant which will constitute a binding contract between the parties, for if a man chooses to surround his land with a fence, he may pull it down at any time—it would be alarming if the law were otherwise and a person who once set up a fence were compelled to keep it up.[29] Channel B. could see no evidence for liability—the defendants and his predecessors kept up the fences for their own purposes, not for the sake of their neighbours and no legal obligation is to be inferred from such acts of repairing.[30] Pigott and Bramwell B. were in agreement and for it to be otherwise, thought the latter, would involve a very serious state of affairs.[31] Evidence that the defendant had repaired, not under requisition, but because he thought he ought to repair, according to Bramwell B. "shows no obligation to repair."[32] Thus, long repair under a mistaken belief as to the law seems insufficient to establish a legal duty.

9.66 Nevertheless, Kelly C.B., recognising that an obligation could be established by contract or covenant, went on to say:

> "Undoubtedly, there may be evidence of such an agreement or covenant by the acts of the parties, as where a person is called upon to repair, and he has repaired accordingly; in such a case, although the evidence would by no means be conclusive, it would still be evidence for consideration of the jury."[33]

Thus, it seems that it may be possible to evidence a contract between the parties by acts of repair. However, later cases make clear that a positive contractual liability of this nature will not run with the land so as to bind third parties.[34]

9.67 More modern cases have reached similar conclusions. In *Cordingley* v. *Great Western Railway Co.* (1948)[35] a prescriptive duty based on nearly 100 years of repair failed as the maintenance was carried out primarily for the safety of the railway's passengers. Further the clear issue of fencing between adjoining farmers came before the Court of Appeal in *Jones* v. *Price* (1965).[36] A boundary hedge had been maintained partly by one farmer and partly by

---

[27] (1872) 27 L.T.(N.S.) 519.
[28] [1965] 2 Q.B. 618 at 636, *per* Willmer L.J.
[29] *Hilton* v. *Ankesson* (1872) 27 L.J.(N.S.) 519 at 520.
[30] *ibid.*
[31] *ibid.*
[32] *ibid.*
[33] *ibid.*
[34] *Austerberry* v. *Oldham Corporation* (1885) 29 Ch.D. 750; *cf.* also *Potter* v. *Parry* (1859) 7 W.R. 182 (covenant to fence designed to run with the land doubtful).
[35] [1948] E.G.Dig. 177.
[36] [1965] 2 Q.B. 618.

another for 50 years and by succeeding owners. No prescriptive duty was found. The comments made are enlightening:

> "There is nothing . . . to prevent adjoining occupiers from making an agreement between themselves that one or the other shall keep the boundary fence in repair. Such an agreement, however, binds only the parties to it . . . "[37]
>
> " . . . an obligation to maintain a cattle-proof boundary fence upon one's own land to keep out the cattle of one's neighbour is capable of running with the land as a servient tenement in favour of the neighbouring land as dominant tenement . . . It is by no means clear whether such an obligation can today be newly created so as to run with the land, except by Act of Parliament."[38]
>
> "I am . . . reluctant to accept that a prescriptive right to have a boundary fence maintained can be proved only by showing that repairs have consistently been carried out at request . . . "[39]

In *Jones* v. *Price* counsel described the case of *Lawrence* v. *Jenkins* (1873)[40] **9.68** as the first clear formulation of the prescriptive duty to fence. Not only does it seem to have been the first modern successful claim, it also seems to have been the last, and it is an unsatisfactory authority for modern use. The defendant owners of a wood, and his predecessors in estate, had repaired the boundary fence for a period of 19 years after notice by an adjoining farmer. The owners and occupiers had carried out repairs when necessary for more than 40 years. The county court judge found that there was an obligation to repair the fence to exclude the farmer's cattle. The plaintiff was non-suited on the grounds that damage to the fence had been caused by a third party contractor. The issue which came before the Queens Bench was whether the defendant or the contractor was liable, the obligation to fence being admitted at that stage. In his judgment Archibald J. approved the description of the obligation to fence in *Gale's Easements*[41] as a spurious easement. It is not clear that he directed his attention to the method of proof through long requisitioned repair. The details of the proof in the lower court are not reported. It may be that all that was proved was the existence of a contractual right which, at the time it was open to a lower court to hold, could be binding on successors in title. It was not until *Austerberry* v. *Oldham Corporation* (1885)[42] that it was finally decided that positive covenants cannot bind successors in title to the land.

(d) *Abandonment of the doctrine*

All the early cases and all the ones in this century where a duty has been **9.69** found to exist are capable of explanation as arising from the customary duty applicable on common lands: abandonment of the whole doctrine of "the spurious easement of fencing" is now overdue. The comments made in the Court of Appeal in *Jones* v. *Price* indicate the difficulties which exist in providing the doctrine with legal principle or even rational explanation.

---

[37] *Jones* v. *Price* [1965] 2 Q.B. 618 at 633, *per* Willmer L.J.
[38] *ibid.* at 639, *per* Diplock L.J.
[39] *ibid.* at 636, *per* Willmer L.J.
[40] (1873) L.R. 8 Q.B. 274.
[41] (4th ed., 1868) p. 460.
[42] Above, n. 34.

However, if this view is incorrect, enough has been said to indicate the extraordinary difficulty, approaching impossibility, of ever proving the existence of such a duty by means of evidence of requisitioned repair over a long period.

(e) *Policy considerations*

9.70 Some impetus towards the continuation of the doctrine has come from doubts expressed by writers[43] and judges as to the consequences if there is no such prescriptive obligation. It has been felt that there is a policy imperative. In *Jones* v. *Price* it was expressed this way be Willmer L.J.:

> "I feel that our decision [not to find a prescriptive duty] may have somewhat far-reaching results, in that it may have the effect of upsetting well-established arrangements between neighbouring farmers all over the country which, though hitherto regularly acted upon, have no sound basis in law."[44]

His fears were unfounded. Farmers still share fencing where it is to their mutual benefit, keeping in mind their general duty to contain their livestock, and insure against the occasional straying. Had the decision been otherwise the result might have been counter-productive. Any request to fence, following an informal agreement to share fencing, would have been treated as a requisition to repair which might lead to the establishment of a duty encumbering the title. The prudent farmer would always refuse. The policy imperative lies towards dynamic change to reflect the classes of livestock which any farmer wishes to contain and not the ossification of all fences as they are at any given moment. If a farmer chooses, say, to give up keeping sheep he should not be under a duty to fence his neighbour's sheep out simply because at one time they both kept sheep and agreed to fence accordingly. There is the one exception where substantial numbers of persons are, or might be, affected by the actions of one person and that, of course, is on the common lands which are, and ought to be, an exception to the general rule.

---

[43] *cf.* Glanville Williams, pp. 203–209 where the author recognises the existence of an antimony in the cases and seems to throw his weight behind the existence of a prescriptive duty on policy grounds. First, he thinks that having to fence one's boundary is of little significance to a farmer. Few farmers would agree. Secondly, he opines that, without the widespread existence of the duty, double fencing would result. This is not the result in practice. The present text suggests that the policy considerations lie in the opposite direction.

[44] Above, n. 36, at 637.

10. Liability for Animals

Introduction

By provisions contained in the Animals Act 1971 the long-established **10.01** action of cattle trespass has been replaced with new rules for liability for damage caused by, and expenses due to, the straying of livestock.[1] At the same time the common law right to seize and detain any animal by way of distress damage feasant was abolished and replaced with a new form of statutory action described as detention and sale of trespassing livestock.[2] The Animals Act 1971, *inter alia*, also makes provision for liability for damage done by dangerous animals, injury to livestock by dogs, the protection of livestock from injury by dogs and damage caused by animals straying on the highway.[3] Not all liability concerned with straying animals is encompassed. In particular the Act has nothing to say regarding liability for damage *to* straying animals, the indemnity actions which may follow animals straying over several land boundaries, or the general law relating to personal trespass through the agency of animals. It follows that in any particular incident there may be alternative courses of action either under statutory procedures or common law process.

The common lands used for grazing are, more usually than not, unenclosed, **10.02** extensive in area and grazed by untended livestock. Frequently, the land is crossed by unfenced highways, which adds to the risk of straying and increases the possibility of damage to, or by, those using the highway. It follows that it is on, or near, the common lands that many of the problems in connection with liability for animals arise. It cannot, however, be stated with confidence that liability is altogether clear and there are a number of matters which are in doubt and have not been subject to litigation. That there has been little litigation is a tribute to the persons involved or, possibly more likely, to their insurers.

This Chapter attempts first, to outline the various courses of action open to, and liable to be taken against, those concerned with livestock on common

[1] Animals Act 1971, ss.1, 4.
[2] *ibid.* s.7(1).
[3] *ibid.* ss.2, 3, 8, 9.

land[4] secondly, to describe the actions which may be taken against dogs; and thirdly, to outline the criminal sanctions which are applicable.

ACTIONS UNDER THE ANIMALS ACT 1971

Straying animals

1. Preliminary matters

(a) Animals and livestock

10.03 Both animals and livestock are referred to in the Animals Act 1971. Livestock is defined as cattle, horses, asses, mules, hinnies, sheep, goats, poultry and deer not in a wild state.[5] For most practical purposes "livestock" encompasses all normal farm animals with the exception of cats and dogs. Where the term "animal" is used it must be presumed to have the common law meaning which, additionally, includes cats and dogs.[6] In the context of the common lands it should also be noticed that where there is a duty to fence against a common (which as will be seen may form the basis of a defence against an action for liability for straying animals), it may not be a duty which is applicable to all livestock but only those classes which have a right to be present and then only the breeds of those classes which are usually kept there.[7] Thus, in any particular incident the liability for straying may differ from one type of livestock to another.

(b) Straying

10.04 The Act refers to the straying of livestock and seeks to abolish the old principle that in a claim in cattle trespass "reliance was put on the technical trespass to the land with other loss taken into account in estimating the damage."[8] It followed that the straying of livestock was actionable *per se* without proof of damage, but the new approach is designed so that claims have "a real rather than a nominal basis,"[9] *i.e.* an action for damage arises consequent upon a straying and not as parasitical to a trespass. Under the common law action of cattle trespass a mere technical trespass was all that was required, but the term "straying" seems to have the connotation of "wandering away from the custody of the owner on to the land of another person."[10]

---

[4] The concentration in this work is on the duties and liabilities of commoners. For more general discussion see North, *The Modern Law of Animals* (1972), upon which, it is acknowledged, much of this Chapter is based.

[5] Animals Act 1971, s.11; in the same section "poultry" is further defined.

[6] See Glanville Williams, pp. 136–149.

[7] *Coaker* v. *Willcocks* [1911] 1 K.B. 649 [1911] 2 K.B. 124; see further at §§ 9.18–9.21.

[8] Law Commission Report No. 13, *Civil Liability for Animals* (1967), para. 64; the Animals Act 1971 was based on this Report with substantial enactment of all the recommendations contained.

[9] *ibid.*

[10] *Oxford English Dictionary* (1979) (compact edition).

(i) Technical trespass Under the law of cattle trespass all that was   **10.05**
necessary was some element of trespass so that, for example, where a horse
intruded a part of its body over or through a fence this was sufficient.[11] If the
intention of the Animals Act 1971 is to provide a real rather than a nominal
basis for claims for damage caused by animals on the property of another
person it should be unnecessary for there to be even a technical trespass. A
case of the type described should be decided in the same way by giving
straying at least as wide a meaning as trespass. Some support for the view
that the courts will adopt this stance can be gathered from a case where
horses on land adjoining a railway put their heads over and under a fence,
maintained by the railway company, and consumed vegetables. The company was under a statutory duty to maintain the fence for the protection of
neighbouring land from trespass and preventing the cattle of the occupiers
of the land from straying therefrom. The court was satisfied that the horses
were straying from the land "within the fair meaning" of the words.[12]

(ii) Straying as unlawful presence It has been suggested that, where   **10.06**
livestock are lawfully on land but remain there after the permitted period,
"it is difficult to see how such livestock can be said to have strayed."[13] This
draws attention to the method by which the livestock reached the land
rather than their status once there. The wording of the Animals Act 1971
lends some support to this point of view. Both of the relevant sections refer
to "where livestock strays on to any land."[14] However, adoption of the view
that the method of reaching the stage of unlawful presence is the main criterion in deciding whether a straying has occurred has some difficulties. It
can hardly be that an innocent plaintiff, if he is to have an effective remedy,
must first ask if the animals strayed there of their own volition. If the mode
of entry must be of this nature then if the livestock is unlawfully placed
there by the owner, or a third party, they will not have strayed and the Animals Act will not be effective when it is most needed. It must be that straying on to land includes unlawful unaccompanied presence.[15] This is in
accord with the old rules under the common law, where trespass and distress were available once a reasonable time had elapsed after unactionable
entry[16] or when hitherto lawful presence became unlawful.[17] It is particularly important on common land that a wider view of straying, to include

---

[11] *Ellis* v. *Loftus Iron Co.* (1874) L.R. 10 C.P. 10.

[12] *Wiseman* v. *Booker* (1878) 3 C.P.D. 184 at 188, *per* Lindley J.

[13] North, p. 107.

[14] Animals Act 1971, ss.4(1), 7(2); the marginal notes refer respectively to "Liability
for damages and expenses due to trespassing livestock" and "Detention and sale of
trespassing livestock."

[15] If the statutory action is to have a "real rather than nominal basis" any damage
caused by straying, however it occurs, should be potentially actionable. In the case
of an intentional straying occasioned by the owner of the livestock, or a third party,
it seems that an action in personal trespass through the agency of animals will also
lie: see § 10.116.

[16] *Goodwyn* v. *Cheveley* (1859) 4 H. & N. 631, 157 E.R. 989: straying from a highway; where there was a straying caused by the breach of a duty to fence, owed by
the person strayed upon, actions for damage and by distress lay after notice had
been given to the owner of the animals: *Edwards* v. *Halinder* (1594) 2 Leon. 93, 74
E.R. 385, *Poole* v. *Longuevill* (1669) 2 Wms. Saund. 282, 85 E.R. 1063, *Kimp* v.
Cruwes (1695) 2 Lutw. 1578, 125 E.R. 868.

[17] *Stodden* v. *Harvey* (1607–1608) Cro. Jac. 204, 79 E.R. 178.

unlawful presence, be adopted or there is no action available against the sur-charging commoner or intentional trespasser. It can hardly be intended that the Act has deprived commoners of all the remedies formerly available to them.

(c) Commoners as plaintiffs

10.07 An action in cattle trespass could only be maintained by a person in possession of the land. No action could be brought by a passer-by on the highway,[18] or a servant[19] or relative[20] of the person in possession. Anomalously, licensees[21] and the buyers of growing crops[22] were allowed the action, but not a commoner.[23] Under the Animals Act 1971, inferentially, it is owners and occupiers of land who can maintain the new statutory actions.[24] The, now abolished, action of distress damage feasant was available to commoners from an early date but the action in trespass was not. Instead, as has been demonstrated, the action by a commoner lay in nuisance for damage caused which required only nominal damage to his interest.[25] It would be extraordinary if the new actions for straying did not allow an action by a commoner and it seems, therefore, that he must be considered within the category of an occupier of the land for the purposes of this Act.[26]

2. The statutory straying action

(a) Animals Act 1971, s.4

10.08 The rules of the common law imposing liability for cattle trespass were abolished by the Animals Act 1971[27] and replaced by a statutory form of action described in the marginal notes as "liability for damages and expenses due to trespassing livestock."[28] Section 4 provides:

> "(1) Where livestock belonging to any person strays on to land in the ownership or occupation of another and—

---

[18] *Cox* v. *Burbidge* (1863) 13 C.B.N.S. 430, 143 E.R. 171; *Hadwell* v. *Righton* [1907] 2 K.B. 345; *Higgins* v. *Searle* (1909) 100 L.T. 280; *Heath's Garage Ltd.* v. *Hodges* [1916] 2 K.B. 370.

[19] *Cox* v. *Burbidge,* above, n. 18.

[20] See North, p. 94, and cases cited there at n. 11.

[21] *ibid.* at n. 12.

[22] *Wellaway* v. *Courtier* [1918] 1 K.B. 200; *cf. Wiseman* v. *Booker* (1878) 3 C.P.D. 184.

[23] See *Robert Mary's Case* (1612) 9 Co.Rep. 111b, 77 E.R. 895: an action on the case for damage caused was provided in lieu of trespass. Owners of common fields and regulated pastures, and holders of sole rights are in an altogether different position and clearly can maintain an action in trespass (although, since its abolition, not cattle trespass).

[24] Animals Act 1971, ss.4(1), 7(2).

[25] See further § 8.21.

[26] The concept of an occupier varies according to the particular context. For an example where a golf club was held, for the purposes of rating, to be in occupation of a common also used by commoners for grazing, see *Pennard Golf Club* v. *Richards (V.O.)* (1976) 20 R.R.C. 225; for occupation in connection with occupiers' liability, see *Wheat* v. *E. Lacon & Co. Ltd.* [1966] A.C. 552.

[27] Animals Act 1971, s.1(1)(c).

[28] Notice that trespass and straying seem to be used synonomously. The text prevails not the marginal notes.

(a) damage is done by the livestock to the land or to any property on it which is in the ownership or possession of the other person; or

(b) any expenses are reasonably incurred by that other person in keeping the livestock while it cannot be restored to the person to whom it belongs or while it is detained in pursuance of section 7 of this Act, or in ascertaining to whom it belongs;

the person to whom the livestock belongs is liable for the damages or expenses, except as otherwise provided by this Act.

(2) For the purposes of this section any livestock belongs to the person in whose possession it is."

The section is clearly intended to effect the Law Commission recommendation that "the straying of livestock should no longer be actionable *per se* without proof of actual damage."[29] However, while it is no longer possible to bring an action simply for trespassing neither is proof of damage necessary before a cause of action exists. Following livestock straying a person is liable for damage or expenses and it seems that substantial expenses may be recovered in the absence of any damage. In *Morris* v. *Blaenau Gwent D.C.* (1982)[30] a district council recovered a sum of £587 for expenses incurred in connection with a detention in respect of a single straying by five ponies without, it seems, any damage being caused.

(b) Plaintiffs

The plaintiffs in an action are, inferentially, owners and occupiers. It has **10.09** been suggested that commoners are occupiers for the purposes of the Animals Act 1971.[31] A third class of plaintiff on common land would seem to be a local authority where, under the provisions contained in the C.R.A. 1965, the owner of the land is unknown and the land is under the protection of that authority.[32] On common land it is just possible that two causes of action may arise as where the grazing of land by straying animals damages the grazing and also damages, say, heather valuable for sporting purposes. Where the straying is on to other land both owner and occupier of the land may have an action but only one should recover. Liability is for damage but it is, of course, measurable by loss. If, for example, a fence is damaged on tenanted property the tenant may claim as he is due to surrender the fence, at the end of his term, to the landlord "in good tenantable repair."[33] In this situation the tenant should claim and recover but if he fails to do so the landlord may bring the action.

(c) Defendants

It is the person to whom the livestock belongs who is liable in this form of **10.10** action and livestock belongs to the person in whose possession it is. Thus, it is the hirer under a hire purchase agreement, the lessee, the bailee[34] or the

---

[29] Law Commission Report No. 13 (1967), p. 44.
[30] (1982) 80 L.G.R. 793, C.A.
[31] See § 10.07.
[32] C.R.A. 1965, s.9; see further § 7.40.
[33] See § 9.03.
[34] Agisted stock will be in the possession of the person accepting them, in the capacity of bailee.

borrower of livestock who is liable, not the owner. The employee or agent who only controls the livestock escapes liability. It should be noticed that the owner and occupier of the land whence the escape occurs are not necessarily liable although in practice they, or one of them, will most usually be the persons to whom the livestock belongs. It is clear that commoners are potential defendants in respect of any livestock in their possession and suggestions that the rules of cattle trespass did not apply "against the owner of cattle which stray on to adjoining property" or that there was "no obligation to prevent cattle straying from common land" are misconceived.[35]

(d) Actionable damage

10.11 In the Animals Act 1971 "damage" is defined generally as including the death of, or injury to, any person.[36] The action under section 4 is, however, limited to damage to the land, or property on the land, which is strayed upon. There is strict liability for such damage; no element of foreseeability is required. It is sufficient that damage has been caused by straying livestock. The need for adequate insurance is self-evident particularly when straying livestock has been known to derail trains.[37]

(e) Personal injury

10.12 It is not possible to claim under section 4 for personal injury. This does not preclude a common law action on proof of negligence, when the remoteness test of foreseeability on the basis of *The Wagon Mound* decision will apply.[38] Alternatively, an action may lie for damage caused by an animal under section 2 of the Act.[39]

(f) Consequential losses

10.13 The section refers to damage, not losses. thereby excluding consequential losses which may result, other than incidental expenses incurred in connection with the straying. In the event, say, that diseased animals stray and a movement order is imposed on, or a period of quarantine is necessary for, the plaintiff's livestock it will not be possible to claim for the consequential losses incurred. It will be otherwise if the straying livestock infect the plaintiff's animals for then damage to property will have resulted from the straying.[39a] A similar result will ensue if a bull, ram or stallion comes into contact with the females of the species. Any damage done then and there, including an undesired mating, will be recoverable, but not the consequential losses involved in re-arrangement of a breeding programme or delayed sales.

[35] Harris and Ryan, p. 63; North, p. 96, n. 3 and p. 99. The confusion seems to have arisen because usually consent of a Minister is required for fencing on common land under the provisions contained in s.194 of the L.P.A. 1925. However, this provision can have no effect on the liability of the commoner for straying and the one place where consent to fencing is never required is on the boundaries adjoining land in another occupation, as no access can thereby be obstructed: see further at §§ 9.34 *et seq.*
[36] Animals Act 1971, s.11.
[37] *e.g. Cooper* v. *Railway Executive* [1953] 1 W.L.R. 223.
[38] [1967] 1 A.C. 617.
[39] For which, see § 10.51.
[39a] *Theyer* v. *Purnell* [1918] 2 K.B. 333.

3. Detention and sale

(a) Animals Act 1971, s.7

10.14 The mediaeval remedy of distress damage feasant for animals was abolished by the Act. It is replaced by a statutory procedure, described as "detention and sale of trespassing livestock,"[40] contained in section 7 of the Act which provides that:

"(1) The right to seize and detain any animal by way of distress damage feasant is hereby abolished.

(2) Where any livestock strays on to any land and is not then under the control of any person the occupier of the land may detain it, subject to subsection (3) of this section, unless ordered to return it by a court.

(3) Where any livestock is detained in pursuance of this section the right to detain it ceases—

(a) at the end of a period of forty-eight hours, unless within that period notice of the detention has been given to the officer in charge of a police station and also, if the person detaining the livestock knows to whom it belongs, to that person; or

(b) when such amount is tendered to the person detaining the livestock as is sufficient to satisfy any claim he may have under section 4 of this Act in respect of the livestock; or

(c) if he has no such claim, when the livestock is claimed by a person entitled to its possession.

(4) Where livestock has been detained in pursuance of this section for a period of not less than fourteen days the person detaining it may sell it at a market or by public auction, unless proceedings are then pending for the return of the livestock or for any claim under section 4 of this Act in respect of it.

(5) Where any livestock is sold in the exercise of the right conferred by this section and the proceeds of the sale, less the costs thereof and any costs incurred in connection with it, exceed the amount of any claim under section 4 of this Act which the vendor had in respect of the livestock, the excess shall be recoverable from him by the person who would be entitled to the possession of the livestock but for the sale.

(6) A person detaining any livestock in pursuance of this section is liable for any damage caused to it by a failure to treat it with reasonable care and supply it with adequate food and water while it is so detained.

(7) References in this section to a claim under section 4 of this Act in respect of any livestock do not include any claim under that section for damage done by or expenses incurred in respect of the livestock before the straying in connection with which it is detained under this section."

10.15 For an extra-judicial remedy the provision is remarkably free from restraints, considering that the value of the livestock could run into many thousands of pounds. The only requirement of notice is to an officer in

---

[40] *cf.* § 10.08, n. 28.

charge of a police station and as no offence is involved there seems no good reason why he should take any action. There is no requirement for advertisement of an impending sale or any need for the detainor to use his best endeavours, or indeed any endeavour, to find an unknown owner. The provision provides an exception to the rule *nemo dat quod non habet* with remarkably few safeguards.

(b) Limitations on use

10.16 Detention is largely a farmers' remedy. Few ordinary citizens have the facilities to hold animals for any length of time. It is, however, unusual for farmers to detain the animals of their contiguous neighbours as they would normally prefer to return them whence they came and claim against the keeper's insurance policy. In practice the most widespread use seems to be in connection with the common lands both by graziers' associations following "drives" of the common land[41] and local authorities attempting to discourage straying from common land into nearby townships. The use by local authorities of the Animals Act 1971 seems to breach the principle desired by the Law Commission that action for trespassing livestock should be related to the damage caused.[42]

(c) Detainors

10.17 The class of persons entitled to detain is limited to occupiers and it has been suggested that, in the context of this Act, a commoner is an occupier.[43] It can hardly be doubted that stintholders on a stinted pasture, together with occupiers of regulated pastures and common fields, are also occupiers. On the other hand an owner of a common may not be an occupier. Under the old law of distress an owner almost always had the right to distrain the animals of a commoner while a commoner was, in all but a few situations, unable to distrain the animals of the owner.[44] If, as has been suggested, unlawful presence of livestock on land may be equated with straying, it may be now that the commoner can detain the owner of the land's surcharging livestock. This is almost a complete reversal of the former common law rules.

10.18 It must be doubtful whether a commoner exercising a right of vicinage on a contiguous common, or a person exercising a right of intercommonage in a common field may detain straying livestock except where they stray to the site where the substantive right is exercisable.[45] That is to say that the holder of a right of vicinage may only detain on his "home" common and the severalty owner in a common field may only detain for straying on his own land. There is some support for the latter view in connection with distress in the context of common of shack.[46] Under the law of distress it

---

[41] For which see § 10.87.

[42] See the case cited at § 10.08.

[43] See § 10.07; notice that owners of the land are excluded as plaintiffs in this action.

[44] See § 10.20.

[45] The rights of vicinage and intercommonage are not substantive rights to graze but are merely rights not to be sued by those with substantive rights; *cf.* §§ 1.70 and 3.56.

[46] Anon, *Commons* (1st ed., 1698), p. 52 (citing Mich. 8 Jac., B, C, *Broadrig's Case*); 9 Vin.Ab.), 121 (citing *Boderidge's Case*).

seems that in actions between commoners it was no excuse for a surcharging commoner that the distrainor was himself surcharging.[47]

(d) Detainees

Potential detainees are those persons who are in possession of livestock **10.19** which strays. In relation to straying on a common these are prima facie any person whose livestock stray there, including those of the commoners and the owner of the soil, unless they are lawfully present. It has been suggested that straying in the context of common land has the meaning of unlawful presence.[47a] Thus any livestock of owner or commoner present in breach of lawful entitlement may be said to be straying. This includes any "surcharging" livestock, where surcharging means any animals in excess of lawful entitlement. In the case of both commoners and owners this raises problems of distinguishing livestock lawfully and unlawfully present.

(e) Doctrine of colour of right

The same problems of identifying which animals were lawfully present **10.20** arose in connection with the, now abolished, action of distress damage feasant. Rules were developed under the common law which prevented distress by a commoner wherever the potential detainee had some colour of right to graze the common.[48] No fully comprehensive set of rules was developed but the doctrine is well described by Lord Mansfield in *Hall* v. *Harding* (1769)[49];

> " . . . wherever there is a colour of right for putting in the cattle, a commoner cannot distrain, because it would be judging for himself, in a question which depends upon a more competent inquiry; but where cattle are put on the common, without any colour or pretence of right, the commoner may distrain them; and therefore he may distrain the cattle of a stranger. But here the plaintiff had a colour for putting in his cattle; though in fact he might exceed the due number. He might put them in under the idea or pretence of having more acres of land than he really had . . . In cases where a writ of admeasurement lies between commoners, one cannot distrain the other; he cannot for his own benefit admeasure the right of the other."

It is clear that, in the view of Lord Mansfield, a commoner could distrain the **10.21** cattle of strangers who had no colour of right,[50] but not where the number to which a commoner was entitled was related *pro rata* to his acreage of

---

[47] *Hobson* v. *Todd* (1790) 4 T.R. 71 at 74; 100 E.R. 900 at 901, *per* Buller J.
[47a] See § 10.06.
[48] For a full description of the doctrine, see Glanville Williams, pp. 53–58.
[49] (1769) 4 Burr. 2426 at 2432, 98 E.R. 271 at 275; approved and followed *Cape* v. *Scott* (1874) L.R. 9 Q.B. 269. In the case a commoner had distrained the alleged surcharging sheep of another commoner with an accepted right to graze two sheep for every acre of land occupied, which is of a similar nature to appurtenant rights registered under the C.R.A. 1965 today.
[50] This has not been in doubt since the 13th century: see Glanville Williams, p. 46; see also *Thomas* v. *Nichols* (1681–1682) 3 Lev. 40, 83 E.R. 566. It matters not whether the straying livestock were placed on the common or escaped there; *Morris' Case* (1612) Godb. 185, 78 E.R. 112.

land. It was unnecessary on the facts to express an opinion on absolute fixed rights, as may occur on a stinted pasture.[51] The same distinction as between fixed rights and rights *sans nombre* applied where a lord sought to distrain the alleged supernumary animals of a surcharging commoner.[52] There was agreement that the commoner had no general right to distrain the animals of the lord[53] unless, say, there was no right to graze the land until Lady Day,[54] or where the lord was limited to a fixed number.[55]

(f) Colour of right today

10.22   The doctrine, although formally of no relevance due to the abolition of distress damage feasant, has some parallels in the rights of detention under the Animals Act 1971. Only rights of common were registrable under the C.R.A. 1965. The rights of the owner of the soil and his tenants were not registrable and have not, therefore, been quantified under the Act. The rights of commoners still depend, usually, upon the amount of inbye land a particular commoner holds—which under the old doctrine of colour of right prevented distraint. The rights of the owner and his tenants still are uncertain, and this was also a barrier to distraint. The dangers of a wrongful detention, with a consequent action for unlawfully interfering with a person's lawful rights, remain. The subject may only be brought to an entirely satisfactory conclusion by statutorily imposed grazing registers with proper identification of livestock which may be grazed.

(g) Animals which may be detained

10.23   It was not finally settled under the law of distress which animals might be taken in the event of a proven surcharging. In one case it was held that it was the last animals put on which should be distrained[56]; in another it was assumed that any of the total might be taken.[57] It also seems that all animals might be distrained if they had never been *levant* and *couchant* on the land to which the rights were attached.[58]

---

[51] For which see *Dixon* v. *James* (1698) 1 Freem. 273, 89 E.R. 195; *Atkinson* v. *Teasdale* (1772) 3 Wils. K.B. 278 at 287, 95 E.R. 1054 at 1059, *per* Blackstone J.

[52] *Anon.* (1770) 3 Wils. K.B. 126, 95 E.R. 970; *Dixon* v. *James*, above, n. 51; *Follett* v. *Troake* (1705) 2 Ld.Raym. 1186, 92 E.R. 284; *Atkinson* v. *Teasdale*, above, n. 51; *Sloper* v. *Alen* (1619) 1 Brownl. & Golds. 171, 123 E.R. 735; *Fulcher* v. *Scales* (1738) 1 Sel.N.P. (13th ed.), 389; *Atthill* v. *Atthill* (1622–1623) Winch's Entries 970; *Hoskins* v. *Robins* (1671) 2 Wms.Saund. 324, 85 E.R. 1123; *cf.* Serjent Williams' note to *Mellor* v. *Spateman* (1669) 1 Wms.Saund. 346, 85 E.R. 500.

[53] For the latest view, see *Hall* v. *Harding* (1769) above, n. 49, at 2430, 274, *per* Lord Mansfield.

[54] *Trulock* v. *White* (1638) 5 Vin.Ab. 33.

[55] *Kenrick* v. *Pargiter* (1608) Cro.Jac. 208, 79 E.R. 181 (but see doubts expressed in judgments); *cf. Hoskins* v. *Robins* (1671) 2 Saund. 324, 85 E.R. 1123; *Hall* v. *Harding* (1769), above, n. 49.

[56] *Ellis* v. *Roakes* (1750) Willes 638, 125 E.R. 1361.

[57] *Hall* v. *Harding* (1769), above, n. 49; *Ellis* v. *Roakes* (1750), above, n. 56.

[58] Note to *Mellor* v. *Spateman*, 1 Wms.Saund. 346c, 85 E.R. 500; *cf. Atthill* v. *Atthill* (1622–1623), above, n. 52.

(h) "not under control"

Straying livestock may only be detained if "not then under the control of **10.24** any person."[59] It was suggested earlier that "straying" incorporates the concept of unlawful presence whether following an intentional act or initial lawful presence.[60] In allowing detention only where livestock is not under control, the law of distress is followed. Under the common law, for instance, it was clear that a horse could not be taken while a rider was upon it,[61] but the mere presence of the servant of an owner was insufficient to protect an animal from distraint.[62]

(i) Damage by the livestock detained

Under the law of distress it was clear that "if ten head of cattle are doing **10.25** damage, one cannot take one of them and keep it till he be satisfied for the whole damage."[63] This rule is reflected in the Animals Act 1971, which provides in section 7(3) that livestock may only be detained until an amount is tendered sufficient to satisfy any claim in respect of the damage those livestock have done and not any other. In addition, section 7(7) expressly provides that the claim under a detention allows only for instant damage and not any caused by previous strayings.[64] However, there seems no reason why instant damage should not be recovered through detention and a concurrent action started for recovery under section 4 for previous damage.

(j) The act of detention

The right to detain determines at the end of a 48-hour period unless notice **10.26** is given to an officer in charge of a police station.[65] It is not necessarily clear when detention commences. Section 4 allows for the recovery of expenses incurred in keeping livestock while it cannot be restored to the person to whom it belongs and additionally while it is detained under section 7. From this it may be inferred that keeping and detention may be separate acts. It follows that there may be a keeping followed later by a detention.

Under the law of distress it was said that "no precise acts or forms of words **10.27** is essential to distress,"[66] which seems to indicate that distraint occurred when it was intended to occur. The general rule was that there was no legal right for a possessor to enter land for the purposes of recovering straying animals,[67] unless they strayed through fences which the person strayed upon

---

[59] Animals Act 1971, s.7(2).

[60] See § 10.06.

[61] *Storey* v. *Robinson* (1795) 7 T.R. 138, 101 E.R. 476; *Field* v. *Adames* (1840) 12 Ad. & E. 649, 113 E.R. 960.

[62] *Bunch* v. *Kennington* (1841) 1 Q.B. 679, 113 E.R. 1291.

[63] *Vaspor* v. *Edwards* (1702) 12 Mod. 658 at 660, 88 E.R. 1585 at 1586, *per* Holt C.J.

[64] Also repeating the common law as described in *Vaspor* v. *Edwards* (1702), above, *per* Holt C.J. 130 E.R. 1154.

[65] Animals Act 1971, s.7(3)(a).

[66] *Knowles* v. *Blake* (1829) 5 Bing. 499, 113 E.R. 1291.

[67] See Glanville Williams, p. 111 and n. 3 thereto; entry can only be justified, it seems, if it can be shown that danger to property is imminent and it is reasonably necessary to enter for the prevention of damage: *Cope* v. *Sharpe (No. 2)* [1912] 1 K.B. 496.

was under a duty to repair[68] or if the straying has been caused by the act of a third party.[69] The possessor will always be in a dilemma: he has a duty not to harm his neighbour but to enter his neighbour's land is an act of personal trespass. It is probably the case that the duty not to continue damage is the primary one and that entry to recover livestock is permissible unless they have been detained.

10.28 If they have been detained it is not sufficient for the possessor to point to a defence that he may have against an action for damages caused (such as a breach of duty to fence owed by the person strayed upon), for a right to detain accrues to a person strayed upon merely if the livestock is straying and is not then under the control of any person. Where livestock has been detained and the possessor has a complete defence to an action under section 4 of the Animals Act 1971 the detainor must release the livestock on request. If the detainor refuses to release the detained animals the possessor can and should apply to the court[70] for an order for the return of the livestock which will prevent the procedure in section 7 being followed through to sale.[71]

(k) The site of detention

10.29 By analogy with the law of distress it seems that the livestock must be taken into detention on the site where the damage occurred,[72] or at least the detainor and the livestock must be together in the *locus in quo* before pursuit, in order to make the detention justifiable.[73] The Animals Act is silent as to where detention may continue but in the absence of any rules there seems no reason why it should not be at the place of the detainor's choice.[74]

(l) Duty to the detained livestock

10.30 After detention the detainor is liable, under section 7(6) of the Act, in a counter claim by the possessor for failure to treat the detained livestock with reasonable care and supply it with food and water. It is also an offence, under the Protection of Animals Act 1911, s.7, for any person who impounds or confines animals not to supply a sufficient quantity of food and water. Any person may enter a pound to supply food and water if an ani-

---

[68] *Goodwyn* v. *Cheveley* (1859) 4 H. & N. 631, 157 E.R. 989; 20 Vin.Ab., 465 citing 10 E.4, 7, (a), pl. 19. Both cases were concerned with straying from a highway which is not breach of a duty to fence but a form of excused trespass.

[69] *Chapman* v. *Thumblethorp* (1584) Cro.Eliz. 329, 78 E.R. 579; *Baker* v. *Andrews* (1652) Style 357, 82 E.R. 774; *Sorlie* v. *McKee* [1927] 1 D.L.R. 249.

[70] To the High Court or county court under R.S.C. 1, Ord. 29, r. 6.

[71] Animals Act 1971, s.7(4).

[72] *Vaspor* v. *Edwards* (1702) above, n. 63 at 661, 1586, *per* Holt C.J.; *cf. Lindon* v. *Hooper* (1776) 1 Cowp. 414 at 417, 98 E.R. 1160 at 1162, *per* Lord Mansfield.

[73] *Clement* v. *Milner* (1800) 3 Esp. 95, 170 E.R. 550, *per* Lord Eldon; and see *Knowles* v. *Blake* (1829) above, n. 66, at 500, 1155, where Best C.J. indicates that distraint is effected by intention not capture.

[74] For the nature of pounds, see Glanville Williams, pp. 93 *et seq.* The rule for cattle was that distrained animals had to be impounded within the hundred or no more than three miles from the site of the distraint; *cf. Coaker* v. *Willcocks* [1911] 2 K.B. 124; Distress Act 1554 (now repealed).

mal has been without for six successive hours and the cost is recoverable as a civil debt.[75]

(m) The proceeds of sale

After a sale the detainor must account to the person who would, but for the sale, be entitled to possession of the livestock for the proceeds, but may first deduct the costs of the sale and any claim he may have under section 4 of the Animals Act 1971. This is straightforward where the value of the live-stock exceeds the damage, expenses and costs. The Act does not refer to the converse position where after sale the detainor still has an unsatisfied claim. Under the common law distress was an alternative to action[76] but the Animals Act does not seem to preclude an action under section 4 for any amount due after the section 7 procedure has been exhausted. **10.31**

(n) Sale where possessor is not liable

It will be seen that detention and sale may take place even where there has been no damage to land or property and where the possessor of the livestock has a complete defence which will free him from any liability for damage and/or associated expenses.[77] If the possessor of livestock is not ascertain-able there may be little alternative for the detainor but to proceed to sale. In this situation the proceeds of sale, or part of them, will be recoverable by the possessor, providing he starts proceedings within the limitation period pre-scribed for recovery of money due under statute, *i.e.* six years from the date of the sale.[78] **10.32**

4. Exceptions from liability

(a) Animals Act 1971, s.5

The defences available in the action of cattle trespass tended to be complex but had moved some way towards the modern development of fault based liability.[79] The Animals Act 1971 has revived a more strict liability by pro-viding only limited exceptions. Section 5 (in so far as it effects section 4) provides that: **10.33**

> "(1) A person is not liable under sections 2 to 4 of this Act for any damage which is due wholly to the fault of the person suffering it . . .

---

[75] Animals Act 1911, s.7.

[76] "If a beast has done more damage than he is worth, let him not distrain but rather take his action": *Vaspor* v. *Edwards* (1702), above, n. 63 at 661, 1586, *per* Holt C.J.

[77] *cf.* § 10.34, exceptions (ii), (iii).

[78] Limitation Act 1980, s.9(1).

[79] In particular the acts of third parties had become acceptable as defences to other-wise strict liability actions; see further §§ 10.109 *et seq.*

(5) A person is not liable under section 4 of this Act where the livestock strayed from a highway and its presence there was a lawful use of the highway.

(6) In determining whether any liability for damage under section 4 of this Act is excluded by subsection (1) of this section the damage shall not be treated as due to the fault of the person suffering it by reason only that he could have prevented it by fencing; but a person is not liable under that section where it is proved that the straying of the livestock on to the land would not have occurred but for a breach by any other person, being a person having an interest in the land, of a duty to fence."

10.34 The section provides three distinct exceptions:

(i) By subsections 1 and 6 there is no liability for damage which is due wholly to the fault of the person suffering it but the damage shall not be treated as his fault by reason only that he could have prevented it by fencing. The common law rule that there is no general duty to fence animals out is re-enacted.

(ii) By subsection 5 there is no liability under section 4 where livestock lawfully using the highway stray therefrom.

(iii) By subsection 6 there is no liability under section 4 where straying would not have occurred but for a breach of a duty to fence by a person having an interest in the land strayed upon.

It will be noticed that (i) provides an exception to liability for damage whereas (ii) and (iii) provide exceptions to all liability under section 4, which it will be recalled includes damage and expenses in connection with detention.

(b) The extent of the exceptions

10.35 It might be thought inconsistent that the quality of exception varies according to who is responsible for causing the straying. However, this is not necessarily the case. Consider circumstances where a plaintiff's land is reached via a roadway through the defendant's land and a gate in the boundary fence. If the gate is left open by a third party and livestock stray on to the plaintiff's land, the defendant is strictly liable for damage caused to, and expenses incurred by, the plaintiff. The defendant's general duty is to prevent his livestock straying. If the plaintiff is under a duty to maintain the fence and gate, the duty to prevent livestock straying is reversed and he will have no claim for damage caused or expenses against the defendant. Where the plaintiff is under no duty to maintain the fence but he, himself, leaves the gate open (or, say, accidentally destroys the defendant's fence) the defendant is relieved from liability for damage caused, but not from payment of expenses incurred. This seems correct in principle: while the defendant should not be liable for damage he, nevertheless, has a general continuing duty not to allow his livestock to stray and if the straying does continue he is in breach of the duty and is liable for any expenses incurred. Straying from a highway is treated in the same way as where the plaintiff is in breach of a duty to fence. It is suggested later that no defendant may allow his livestock to continue to stray after a reasonable time has elapsed even where the Animals Act 1971 seems to except him totally from liability under section 4.[80]

(c) Fault of the plaintiff

Fault is defined by reference to the Law Reform (Contributory Negligence) **10.36**
Act 1945[81] so that a plaintiff has no claim for damage where it is wholly due to his own negligence, breach of statutory duty or any other act or omission which would give rise to a defence of contributory negligence, including breach of contract.[82]

By a somewhat tortuous route a counterclaim for the contributory negli- **10.37**
gence of the plaintiff is introduced into an action under section 4, thus ameliorating the otherwise strict liability. Section 10 of the Animals Act 1971 provides:

> "For the purposes of . . . the Law Reform (Contributory Negligence) Act 1945 . . . any damage for which a person is liable under sections 2 to 4 of this Act shall be treated as due to his fault."

"Fault" has the same meaning as in the Law Reform (Contributory Negligence) Act 1945,[83] and is as described above.[84] Section 1(1) of the 1945 Act provides:

> "Where any person suffers damage as the result partly of his own fault and partly of the fault of any other person or persons, a claim in respect of the damage shall not be defeated by reason of the fault of the person suffering the damage, but the damage recoverable shall be reduced to such extent as the courts think just and equitable having regard to the claimant's share in the responsibility for the damage."

Thus, where, by virtue of section 5(6) of the Animals Act 1971, a plaintiff is **10.38**
not to be held at fault for, say, leaving a gate open in a fence which he is under no duty to maintain, and prima facie the owner of straying livestock is strictly liable for all damage caused, a counterclaim for contributory negligence is possible. This is similar in nature to the defence of "leave and licence" which existed under the common law: leaving a gate open "would be evidence in support of a plea of leave and licence as to the damage done on that day."[85] In spite of some criticism of the doctrine[86] it seems not unreasonable that a livestock owner may place some reliance on the continued existence of his neighbour's fences. The view that he may do so was endorsed by Lord Greene M.R. in *Park* v. *Jobson* (1945).[87]

---

[80] See further § 10.42.
[81] Animals Act 1971, s.11.
[82] *cf. Quinn* v. *Burch Bros.* [1966] 2 Q.B. 370.
[83] Animals Act 1971, s.11; Law Reform (Contributory Negligence) Act 1945, s.4.
[84] See § 10.36 above.
[85] *Wellaway* v. *Courtier* [1918] 1 K.B. 200 at 203 *per* Lawrence J.
[86] Glanville Williams, p. 180: "it would be odd if one who leaves his land entirely unfenced should be able to recover damages for cattle trespass, while one who fences but leaves a gate open should not."
[87] [1945] 1 All E.R. 222 at 225.

(d) Straying from a highway

10.39 It was well established under the common law that the owner of animals lawfully on the highway was not liable, in the absence of negligence,[88] for straying on to adjacent lands.[89] The principle underlying the exception was that of inevitable accident, not an obligation to fence against the highway. Indeed there is no general obligation to fence any land boundary. In some circumstances, near the common lands, the position may be different. There is some slight authority that the customary duty to fence against a waste may extend along a highway and away from the common land itself.[90] It has also been suggested that, where a waste has been partially enclosed resulting in severed portions, the obligation may exist along the highway adjoining one part of a waste and another.[91] Where the existence of a duty to fence against the highway can be established, an exception from liability under the second part of section 5(6) of the Animals Act 1971 may be maintained irrespective of whether or not the livestock is lawfully present on the highway.

10.40 Further, it may be that, where livestock is travelling unaccompanied along a highway from one part of a waste to another, this is a lawful use of the highway sufficient to invoke the exception under section 5(5) of the Animals Act 1971.[92] There is limited authority that unaccompanied animals may be lawfully using the highway. In *Hadwell* v. *Righton* (1907)[93] Phillimore J. put it thus: "if fowls are kept near a highway, and there is a corn stubble belonging to their owner on the other side of the road to which they might naturally and properly go, I am not prepared to say that to allow them to go there by themselves would be an unlawful use of the highway by their owner."

10.41 It may not always be possible to determine whether land is common land with a highway passing over it. The registers maintained under the C.R.A. 1965 are not definitive on this point. The Act required the registration of common land which is within the definition under the Act but excluded any land which forms part of a highway.[94] It follows that there is land which is common land under the common law but which is not registrable under the C.R.A. 1965 as it is also highway land. This class of land is unaffected by

---

[88] "Traffic on the highways, whether by land or sea, cannot be conducted without exposing those whose persons or property are near to it to some inevitable risk . . . In neither case, therefore, can they recover without proof of want of care or skill occasioning the accident"; *Fletcher* v. *Rylands* (1866) L.R. 1 Ex. 265 at 286, *per* Blackburn J.

[89] *Dovaston* v. *Payne* (1795) 2 H.Bl. 527, 126 E.R. 684; *Goodwyn* v. *Cheveley* (1859) 4 H. & N. 631, 157 E.R. 989; *Tillett* v. *Ward* (1882) 10 Q.B.D. 17; *Gayler and Pope Ltd.* v. *Davies* (1924) 2 K.B. 75.

[90] *Spry* v. *Mortimore* (1946) 13 L.J.N.C.C.R. 83; considered at § 9.17.

[91] See § 9.17.

[92] Particularly if the reason for the division of the waste is occasioned by inclosure by the lord: *Barber* v. *Whiteley* (1865) 34 L.J.Q.B. 212 at 216; or an inclosure award: Inclosure Act 1845, s.83.

[93] [1907] 2 K.B. 345 at 348.

[94] C.R.A. 1965, s.22(1): "common land" does not include land which forms part of a highway; s.21(2): s.10 (the conclusive evidence provision) shall not apply for the purpose of deciding whether any land forms part of a highway.

the provision in the Act deeming unregistered land not to be common land as it is not land which is capable of being registered under the Act.[95]

When a straying has occurred, arising out of lawful use of the highway, and **10.42** the section 5(5) exception from liability has been invoked, it cannot be that no liability will arise however long the straying is allowed to continue. There must be a moment when the straying becomes an unlawful presence. Under the common law the owner of animals straying from the highway was allowed a reasonable time to remove the animals following which a distress damage feasant was lawful. In *Goodwyn* v. *Cheveley* (1859),[96] where a herdsman had left some straying animals in order to take the remainder to their destination, it was held that what was a reasonable time was a question for the jury. It seems inevitable that this same doctrine of unlawful presence after a reasonable time has elapsed must have application to the current statutory action. Thus, once such a reasonable time has elapsed the exception in section 5 ceases to be operative and the plaintiff suffering damage may rely on sections 4 and 7 for recovery, or may exercise the right of abatement,[97] or bring an action in personal trespass through the agency of animals.[98]

(e) Breach of a duty to fence

A person is not liable under section 4 of the Animals Act 1971 for either **10.43** damage caused or expenses incurred where it is proved that the straying would not have occurred but for a breach by any other person, being a person having an interest in the land [strayed upon], of a duty to fence.[99] The most frequent occurrences of such a duty are found on the boundaries of land adjoining wastes, on land let on agricultural tenancies or affected by inclosure awards, and in connection with statutory undertakings or operations controlled by statute. Certain features of the exception to liability should be noticed:

(i) It only applies when the straying would not have occurred but for the breach of the duty. If, for example, livestock is driven through a fence there will be no exception available on the ground that the plaintiff was under a duty to maintain the fence.

(ii) There only has to be a breach of the duty to fence by a person with an interest in the land strayed upon. Thus, a duty owed by a tenant to his landlord or one owed by the landlord to a derivative title holder, or a statutory undertaking owing a duty to specified classes of persons is sufficient. Under the common law a defence to cattle trespass was only available to the person to whom the duty was owed[1] and under this circumstance it was usually relevant to

---

[95] C.R.A. 1965, s.1(2)(a); no land *capable of being registered under the Act* shall be deemed to be common land unless it is so registered.

[96] n. 89, above.

[97] For which see § 10.91.

[98] For which see § 10.116.

[99] See § 10.33. The position may be different where adjoining tenants are mutually responsible for a fence through which livestock stray: *Holgate* v. *Bleazard* [1917] 1 K.B. 443.

[1] The distinction must still be made in connection with common law actions for which see § 10.87.

consider the relationship between parcels of land in terms of dominant and servient tenements. The position now is that, however unmeritorious the result may be, any person whose livestock stray, whether or not they are lawfully on the land from which the straying occurs, may take advantage of the exception.

(iii) The Act does not purport to alter the standard of fencing required. Thus, the duty is not absolute but remains one to maintain a reasonable fence to contain animals behaving normally and, in respect of a fence adjoining a waste, to a standard to contain animals consistent with the usual breeds for the locality.[2] There is no need to fence against animals not commonable on a particular waste. For example, it is unlikely that there is ever a requirement to fence against poultry.[3]

Damage by animals

1. Straying on to a highway

(a) Common law

10.44 There is no rule at common law that an occupier of land is under a duty to fence his land against a highway.[4] This seems sound in principle if, as applies in many cases, the owner of the land also owns the land *ad medium filum* over which the highway runs and the public merely has a right to travel over it. In the light of this it is perhaps hardly surprising that the rule developed that at common law the occupier of land adjoining a highway could not be found negligent in failing to provide, or having defective, fences which allowed cattle to stray to the highway. In the days of high speed traffic the rule can be seen as anachronistic, if not actually bizarre. Nevertheless, the rule was confirmed by the House of Lords in *Searle* v. *Wallbank* (1947)[5] after a motor cyclist collided with a horse which had strayed from a field adjoining a highway. The plaintiff's claim in negligence failed on the grounds that there was no general duty of care on the defendant to prevent his horse straying.

(b) Abolition of the common law rule

10.45 The rule in *Searle* v. *Wallbank* was abrogated by section 8(1) of the Animals Act 1971 which provides:

"So much of the rules of the common law relating to liability for negligence as excludes or restricts the duty which a person might owe to others to take such care as is reasonable to see that damage is not caused by animals[6] straying on to a highway is hereby abolished."

Thus, the ordinary rules of negligence involving reasonable standards of care towards those foreseeably likely to be affected apply to animals stray-

[2] See discussion at §§ 9.16 and 9.18.
[3] *cf.* § 3.39; also Glanville Williams, p. 215.
[4] *Potter* v. *Parry* (1859) 7 W.R. 182; *Goodwyn* v. *Cheveley* (1859) above, n. 89; *cf.* Glanville Williams, p. 371.
[5] [1947] A.C. 341.
[6] *i.e.* dogs and cats are included.

ing on to a highway. It seems that a higher standard of care will be required where land adjoins a high speed traffic highway than a quiet bridleway. It should be noticed, however, that there is no strict liability for the consequences of straying and the ordinary defences of acts of a third party and inevitable accident apply, and a counterclaim for contributory negligence is possible. The non-negligent defendant is not liable.[6a]

(c) Highways over unfenced land

Special provision is made in section 8(2) for highways adjoining unfenced **10.46** land, of which the common lands are the most important example:

> "Where damage is caused by animals straying from unfenced land to a highway a person who placed them on the land shall not be regarded as having committed a breach of the duty to take care by reason only of placing them there if—
> (a) the land is common land, or is land situated in an area where fencing is not customary, or is a town or village green; and
> (b) he had a right to place the animals on that land.

The section does not have the effect of providing livestock keepers with an exception from liability but merely disallows a presumption of failure to take care by reason only of placing the animals on unfenced land.

The section only applies to unfenced land of certain classes. "Common **10.47** land" and "town or village green" have the same definitions as apply under the C.R.A 1965.[7] Upon completion of the registration procedure under the C.R.A. 1965 the usual position will be that the only land which will qualify under these headings will be land which is registered, for most, but not necessarily all, other land will then be deemed not to fall into the class concerned. Land which is provisionally registered under the C.R.A. 1965 may still require investigation to establish whether it falls within the definitions under the Act.[8] The remaining category, of "land situated in an area where fencing is not customary," is not altogether certain in definition. The term "area" is, at the best, vague, and "customary" must have a colloquial meaning for there can hardly be a *lex loci* requiring fencing. It must be that the section applies to land which is not, by the standards of the vicinity, usually fenced.[9] This seems to be a question of fact in the particular case. Animal owners should be wary of relying on the section wherever fencing in the

---

[6a] *cf. Pike* v. *Wallis, The Times,* November 6, 1981; *Upton* v. *John Reed Partnership* (1977) (C.A., March 25, 1977, unreported).

[7] C.R.A. 1965, s.22(1); notice that the land has to fall within the definitions of common land and town and village greens in the Act. It is not necessary for the land to be registered as such. It seems, *e.g.* that land which is waste land of a manor but which has not been registered is affected by the section. The C.R.A. 1965 deems that such land, being unregistered, is not common land but then it, perhaps, never was.

[8] It is entirely possible for land to be provisionally registered under the Act and not to comply with the definitions.

[9] Some land was fenced at times of agricultural optimism and shortly thereafter abandoned. It is suggested that remnants of old fences are insufficient for a presumption that fencing is or was "customary." Examples may be seen today in the Brecon Beacons and on Dartmoor where self-evidently it has never been the practice to fence open grazings.

area has been carried out in the past or the area is one where the practice of fencing is developing.

(d) "Enclosed" common land

10.48 It is not entirely certain that all common land may be considered unfenced. Consider a waste entirely surrounded by farm land in severalty with access ways leading to a highway. Is the land unfenced? In a case before the Court of Appeal the plaintiff raised the question in respect of an area of some 2,000 acres.[10] The Court seems to have given little, if any, attention to the matter, being more concerned with the evidence of negligence relating to sheep on the highway with little interest in how they got there. This seems correct; negligence is required and the C.R.A. 1965 merely says that, in respect of unenclosed land, placing livestock there is not in itself a breach of the duty to take care. Thus, even proof that the land, although common land, is not to be considered unenclosed does not, in itself, necessarily imply negligence.

(e) The animals affected

10.49 The only straying animals which are affected by the section are those placed there by a person with a right so to do. Thus, a trespasser or surcharging commoner will be unable to take advantage of the section.[11] Similarly, a person who has some right but not a right at the time of the event is probably also outside the provisions.[12] Similarly, those who use rights claiming title from the owner thereof should ensure that they are properly authorised.[13] In *Davies* v. *Davies* (1975),[14] a road traffic accident case, the entitlement of the grazier to use rights of common was challenged. The rights of common registered under the C.R.A. 1965 were in the names of Mrs. Davies and her brother, but were exercised by Mrs. Davies' son, the defendant. The defendant's rights to turn animals to the common were upheld by the Court of Appeal and it is clear that where there is an informal licensing of rights between members of the family this is acceptable to the court. This proposition may only be accurate where both the rights and the land to which they are appurtenant are used together.[15] It follows that a person licensing rights without the dominant land to which they are attached may not be able to take advantage of the provision in section 8.

(f) Excessive grazing

10.50 It has been contended that a right to graze land may be exceeded merely by keeping animals too long on the land or by grazing too many animals.[16] However, this does not seem to have any effect on the legal right to place

---

[10] *Rudyard* v. *Owen* (1980) C.A. Lexis, Enggen Library, Cases; the case may not have been fully argued as the plaintiff was a litigant in person.

[11] The surcharging commoner may be entirely outside the purview of the section even if he can show that some of the livestock is lawfully present.

[12] Thus, it is suggested, that the licensee who leaves livestock on the common beyond the time of his licence or the commoner who grazes in a closed season has some right but none at the time of the event.

[13] For which see § 4.35 and §§ 4.72 *et seq.*

[14] [1975] Q.B. 172; see further at § 6.27.

[15] See § 6.30.

[16] North, p. 160.

them on the land which is the criterion required by the section. In a road traffic accident case a plaintiff sought to establish that the defendant had lost his right to graze animals on common land, and, consequently, the protection of section 8(2) of the Animals Act 1971, because there was substantially no grazing or no adequate grazing on the common for his sheep.[17] This was described in the main judgment of the Court of Appeal as "quite misconceived."

2. Damage by animals to persons and property

(a) Preliminary

A keeper of livestock may be liable for damage to land and property caused **10.51** by the livestock straying on to the land of another person.[18] He is not liable under that provision for the death of or injury to any person. The general rule is that the keeper of an animal not belonging to a dangerous species may rely on the presumption that the animals are harmless. However, there is a further provision in the Animals Act 1971 making a keeper of animals liable for all classes of damage, including personal injury and death, caused by certain types of non-dangerous animals, whether or not they are straying, in specified circumstances. It follows that commoners may be held liable for damage to another person's animals, another commoner, and members of the public exercising rights of access to the commons, and personal injury, as well as damage to land and property, where animals stray from the common.

(b) Liability for non-dangerous animals

Section 2(2) of the Animals Act 1971 provides: **10.52**

> "Where damage is caused by an animal which does not belong to a dangerous species, a keeper of the animal is liable for the damage, except as otherwise provided by this Act, if—
> (a) the damage is of a kind which the animal, unless restrained, was likely to cause or which, if caused by the animal, was likely to be severe; and
> (b) the likelihood of the damage or of its being severe was due to characteristics of the animal which are not normally found in animals of the same species or are not normally so found except at particular times or in particular circumstances; and
> (c) those characteristics were known to that keeper or were at any time known to a person who at that time had charge of the animal as that keeper's servant or, where that keeper is the head of a household, were known to another keeper of the animal who is a member of that household and under the age of sixteen."

It is animals not livestock which are referred to in this section—dogs and cats are included.[19] The types of animals concerned of particular relevance to common land are horned breeds of animals, the aggressive male, and the

---

[17] *Rudyard* v. *Owen* (1980), above, n. 10.
[18] § 10.08.
[19] Glanville Williams, pp. 136–149 *cf.* § 10.03.

female which may be temporarily aggressive at or after parturition. Before an action will lie three cumulative conditions must be satisfied.

10.53   **(i) The kind of damage required**   For an action to be brought the damage must be of certain kinds:

   (a) Of a kind which the animal, unless restrained, is likely to cause, *i.e.* it has abnormal behavioural characteristics making it likely that it will attack animals, property or persons. This class of damage is concerned with "attacks" by animals. The damage must also be of a type which the animal is likely to cause so that an abnormal tendency to kick cars will not necessarily be evidence of a tendency to kick animals or humans.[20] Probably the converse also applies, but there is some authority that a tendency to attack one class of animals indicates a tendency to attack others[21] and proof of a tendency to attack humans may be evidence of a generally aggressive nature.[22]

   (b) Of a kind which if it was caused would be of a serious nature. An attack is not necessary for this class of damage. The animal may have physical characteristics which make any damage, however caused, likely to be severe. For example, animals with abnormally long horns may, intentionally or otherwise, cause severe damage. Secondly, the animal may be diseased and passively do damage of a serious nature to other animals of the same species. Thirdly, it might be possible to bring the ineffectually castrated, or the abnormally precocious, male of the species mating with females into this class.[23]

10.54   **(ii) Abnormal characteristics required**   The second condition to be satisfied in order to bring an action under the section is that the likelihood of the damage or of its being severe is abnormal to the species or is abnormal at certain times or under certain circumstances. There are four possible, but not necessarily distinct, situations where a keeper may be liable for damage caused:

   (a) The animal may have behavioural characteristics which are abnormal to the species. At common law there was some discussion as to whether there could ever be liability for any injury caused by behaviour which might be considered natural to the species but there does not seem to have been a case where a claim has been defeated on this ground alone. The words "characteristics of the animal which are not normally found in animals of the same species" were considered directly in *Wallace* v. *Newton* (1982)[24] when it was held that they were to be given their ordinary and natural meaning. The plaintiff in the case did not have to show that the horse, which had crushed her arm suddenly while being loaded into a trailer, had a vicious and abnormal tendency to injure people.

---

[20] *Glanville* v. *Sutton* [1928] 1 K.B. 571; *cf. Osborne* v. *Chocqueel* [1896] 2 Q.B. 109, *Hartley* v. *Harriman* (1818) 1 B. & Ald. 620, 106 E.R. 228.

[21] *Brock* v. *Richards* [1951] 1 K.B. 529 at 537.

[22] *Gething* v. *Morgan* (1857) 29 L.T.O.S. 106; *Worth* v. *Gilling* (1866) L.R. 2 C.P. 1.

[23] But see the additional characteristics required at § 10.54.

[24] [1982] 1 W.L.R. 375.

It was sufficient to show that the horse was unpredictable, unreliable in behaviour and, in that way, dangerous.

(b) The animal, although behaviourally normal, may have special physical characteristics which make it liable, if it does cause damage, to cause severe damage. Examples of this class of animal have already been given above.[25]

(c) The animal may have behavioural characteristics of a kind where it is not likely to cause damage except at particular times or in particular circumstances. Into this category might fall the aggressive behaviour of the male at mating or, the female at parturition or in defending her offspring.

(d) Finally there is the category where the physical characteristics of the animal are such that if damage is caused it will be severe but the characteristics are not normally found except at particular times and in particular circumstances. The non-contagious animal, capable of infecting other animals at, say, parturition or the very large animal capable of causing severe damage upon being affected by an extraneous event may fall within this category.

(iii) Knowledge The final condition for liability is that the keeper **10.55** must have actual knowledge, knowledge imputed from the knowledge of his servant, or deemed knowledge where the knowledge is that of another keeper of the animal who is a member of his household and is under the age of 16, of the characteristics.

(c) Defendants

It is the keeper of an animal as defined in section 6(3), (4) who is liable for **10.56** the damage caused:

"(3) Subject to subsection (4) of this section, a person is a keeper of an animal if—
 (a) he owns the animal or has it in his possession; or
 (b) he is the head of a household of which a member under the age of sixteen owns the animal or has it in his possession;
 and if at any time an animal ceases to be owned by or to be in the possession of a person, any person who immediately before that time was a keeper thereof by virtue of the preceding provisions of this subsection continues to be a keeper of the animal until another person becomes a keeper thereof by virtue of those provisions.

(4) Where an animal is taken into and kept in possession for the purpose of preventing it from causing damage or of restoring it to its owner. a person is not a keeper of it by virtue only of that possession."

It will be seen that in the cases of abandoned animals and animals detained under section 7 of the Animals Act 1971 liability for damage under section 2 continues to be that of the original keeper or possessor as the case may be.

[25] At § 10.53 example (b).

(d) Plaintiffs

10.57 On common land an action will be available to all persons lawfully present on the land whether they be owners of the land, commoners, users of public rights of way or easements or, usually, members of the public exercising rights of access over the land. Under most circumstances a trespasser will be unable to bring an action.

(e) Exceptions from liability

10.58 The basis of liability is strict but not absolute. The various exceptions are contained in section 5 of the Act:

"(1) A person is not liable under sections 2 to 4 of this Act for any damage which is due wholly to the fault of the person suffering it.

(2) A person is not liable under section 2 of this Act for any damage suffered by a person who has voluntarily accepted the risk thereof.

(3) A person is not liable under section 2 of this Act for any damage caused by an animal kept on any premises or structure to a person trespassing there, if it is proved either—

(a) that the animal was not kept there for the protection of persons or property; or

(b) (if the animal was kept there for the protection of persons or property) that keeping it there for that purpose was not unreasonable."

As with liability under section 4 a person is not liable for any damage which is due wholly to the fault of the person suffering it and contributory negligence may be introduced as a counterclaim.[26] Additionally, there is no liability where a person has voluntarily accepted the risk of damage.

10.59 On the common lands commoners will generally have a defence available as against trespassers, as animals kept on the land are self-evidently not kept there for the purposes of protection of persons or property. However, it may not be altogether clear which persons gaining access to common lands are trespassers. Under some statutory provisions it is only "inhabitants of the neighbourhood" who are strictly entitled to enter the land for exercise and recreation.[27] On National Trust owned commons, and possibly some other common lands, entrants may be present by the express or implied licence of the owner of the soil.[28] Where public or private rights of way cross common lands entrants may be present for the purpose of exercising those rights and be outside the status of trespasser.

(f) Entrants under access orders and agreements

10.60 Under provisions contained in the National Parks and Access to the Countryside Act 1949 access orders and agreements may be made which provide for a right of public access to open land.[29] Under section 60(1) of that Act a

[26] See § 10.37.
[27] See §§ 11.28, 11.29. Even where there is a statutory right of access for air and exercise under provisions contained in s.193 of the L.P.A. 1925 entry for an unlawful purpose will involve trespass: *cf.* §§ 11.25 *et seq.*
[28] For access on National Trust land, see §§ 8.53, 11.42 and 12.125; for implied rights of access generally, see §§ 8.52.
[29] See further § 11.34.

person so entering land "shall not be treated as a trespasser on that land or incur any other liability by reason only of so entering or being on that land." It is clear that such a person does not commit the tort of trespass nor incur any other liability.

This leaves open the question of whether he may be treated as a trespasser **10.61** for the purposes of an exception from liability in a claim under section 2 of the Animals Act 1971. It seems that he may be so treated for section 66(2) of the National Parks and Access to the Countryside Act 1949 provides that the operation of section 60(1) "shall not increase the liability, under any enactment not contained in this Act or under any rule of law, of a person interested in that land . . . in respect of the state thereof or of things done or omitted thereon." In the case of occupiers' liability this section is reinforced by express provision in the Occupiers' Liability Act 1957 declaring that for the purposes of that Act entrants under the 1949 Act are not to be treated as visitors to the land.[30]

3. Damage by dogs

(a) Damage by killing or injuring livestock

In the event that damage is caused by any animal, including dogs, an action **10.62** may lie under section 2 of the Animals Act 1971, and a commoner may just as well be a plaintiff as a defendant under that section. The Act of 1971, however, also contains express provision where the damage to livestock is caused by a dog. Section 3 provides:

> "Where a dog causes damage by killing or injuring livestock, any person who is a keeper of the dog is liable for the damage, except as otherwise provided by this Act."

(b) The type of damage

It is an essential prerequisite for an action that there shall have been the **10.63** killing or injury of livestock, and that it was caused by a dog. Thus, it seems, that the killing or injury does not have to be direct; chasing a sheep over a quarry edge, for example, will suffice. It is perhaps not quite so clear whether consequential damage is also recoverable. Suppose a cow is bitten by a dog, runs into the path of a vehicle and is killed, it would seem that the dog has caused the damage, including the death of the cow, and probably has caused any damage sustained by the vehicle. If the vehicle is forced into the path of another vehicle and the driver is killed can it still be said that the dog has caused that damage? There seems no reason why not, as there is an unbroken chain of events, and the Animals Act 1971 includes personal injury and death in the term "damage."[31] The view is somewhat reinforced by the use of the expression "causing damage" when the preceding equivalent legislation spoke only of "injury done to any cattle by a dog."[32]

---

[30] Occupiers' Liability Act 1957, s.1(4), cited at § 8.50.
[31] Animals Act 1971, s.11.
[32] Dogs Act 1906, s.1(1).

(c) Defendants

10.64 Liability for damage is placed on the keeper of a dog as is the case under section 2 of the Animals Act 1971.[33] In the case of a dog which has "gone wild" the fact that the original keeper may claim to have abandoned the dog will not absolve him from liability as he remains the keeper until another person takes up the role.[33a] Nor does the status of keeper pass to a person who has custody of a dog if the purpose of the custody is to prevent it causing damage or to restore it to its owner.[33b]

(d) Strict liability

10.65 Liability is strict although not absolute. Neither negligence nor fault on the part of the defendant has to be proved, and the qualifying conditions applicable to an action under section 2 are irrelevant.[34]

(e) Plaintiffs

10.66 A plaintiff does not have to be the owner or possessor of livestock although, more often than not, he will be. He merely has to be a person suffering damage caused by a dog killing or injuring livestock which brings into the possible category of plaintiffs persons beyond the primary participants.[35]

(f) An exception to liability

10.67 One class of person is excepted from liability under section 3 by virtue of section 5(4):

> "(4) A person is not liable under section 3 of this Act if the livestock was killed or injured on land on which it had strayed and either the dog belonged to the occupier or its presence on the land was authorised by the occupier."

10.68 For the purposes of the Animals Act 1971 the commoner must be classed as an occupier[36]: this means that a commoner may use his dog to control and drive straying livestock on the common without risk of an action against him under section 3. Where livestock have strayed from the common on to other land the occupier similarly may use his dog to drive them even if the commoner has a full defence to an action under section 4 because of a breach of a duty to fence by the person strayed upon. However, if in so doing the livestock is killed or injured the commoner may bring an action against the person strayed upon for being in breach of his duty to fence and may claim for all losses naturally resulting including damage to the livestock.[37]

---

[33] Animals Act 1971, s.6(3), (4), cited at § 10.56.
[33a] *ibid.* s.6(3)(b).
[33b] *ibid.* s.6(4).
[34] See §§ 10.53 *et seq.*
[35] See § 10.63.
[36] See § 10.07.
[37] See further at § 10.99.

4. Protection of livestock against dogs

(a) A statutory defence available in civil actions

A statutory defence is available in any civil proceedings[38] brought against a   **10.69**
person for killing or causing injury to a dog, while acting for the protection
of livestock. Section 9 of the Animals Act 1971 provides:

"(1) In any civil proceedings against a person (in this section referred to
as the defendant) for killing or causing injury to a dog it shall be a
defence to prove—
> (a) that the defendant acted for the protection of any livestock and
was a person entitled to act for the protection of that livestock;
and
> (b) that within forty eight hours of the killing or injury notice
thereof was given by the defendant to the officer in charge of a
police station.

(2) For the purpose of this section a person is entitled to act for the protection of any livestock if, and only if,—
> (a) the livestock or the land on which it is belongs to him or to any
person under whose express or implied authority he is acting;
and
> (b) the circumstances are not such that liability for killing or caus-
ing injury to the livestock would be excluded by section 5(4) of
this Act.

(3) Subject to subsection (4) of this section, a person killing or causing
injury to a dog shall be deemed for the purposes of this section to
act for the protection of any livestock if, and only if, either—
> (a) the dog is worrying[39] or is about to worry the livestock and
there are no other reasonable means of ending or preventing the
worrying; or
> (b) the dog has been worrying livestock, has not left the vicinity
and is not under the control of any person and there are no practicable means of ascertaining to whom it belongs,

(4) For the purposes of this section the conditions stated in either of
the paragraphs of the preceding subsection shall be deemed to have
been satisfied if the defendant believed that it was satisfied and had
reasonable grounds for that belief.

(5) For the purposes of this section—
> (a) an animal belongs to any person if he owns it or has it in his
possession; and
> (b) land belongs to any person if he is the occupier thereof."

It should be noticed that it is livestock which may be protected and that the   **10.70**
section does not apply where a dog worries other dogs or cats. Included
within the definition of livestock are all the main farm animals and poultry,

---

[38] For the defence in a criminal action, see § 10.128.

[39] "Worrying" is not defined in the Animals Act 1971. The description contained in
the Dogs (Protection of Livestock) Act 1953, s.1(2) is appropriate: "(a) attacking
livestock or (b) chasing livestock in such a way as may reasonably be expected to
cause injury or suffering to the livestock or, in the case of females, abortion, or loss
of or dimunition in their produce": cf. *Hanlin* v. *O'Sullivan* [1954] S.A.L.R. 286.
Direct injury as required by s.3 of the Animals Act 1971 is not necessary.

which are further defined, for the purposes of the section, to include pheasants, partridges and grouse while in captivity.[40] Thus, a person is not entitled to act where the worrying is of game running free.

10.71   The method of protection is not specified and while the use of guns is most likely it might be by any available method such as striking with an instrument or throwing missiles.

(b) Persons entitled to act

10.72   A person is entitled to act if either the livestock or the land on which the livestock is belongs to him. For the purposes of this section, an animal belongs to a person if he owns it or has it in his possession and land belongs to any person if he is the occupier thereof. Persons acting on the express or implied authority of persons entitled are also entitled. It will be noticed that land does not "belong" to the owner of the soil *qua* owner and to be entitled to act an owner must also be an occupier. In the context of common land it seems that a commoner must be taken to be an occupier of the land[41]; in which case he is entitled to act for the protection of *any* livestock on the land as the land is deemed to belong to him.

10.73   There seems to be no judicial interpretation to confirm that a commoner is an occupier for the purposes of this section and as a matter of caution commoners might consider expressly authorising one another to act for the protection of any livestock. Similarly, estate gamekeepers could be authorised expressly. It is not only commoners who may act as any person whose livestock is worried is brought within the section, but licensees and trespassers will not be occupiers able to act for the protection of livestock other than their own.

(c) An exception

10.74   The Animals Act 1971 does not directly require that there shall be lawful use of the land by the livestock. Instead a person is not entitled to act for the protection of livestock if the circumstances are such that liability for killing or injuring the livestock would be excluded by section 5(4) of the Act.[42] The result on the common lands of this provision is that the owner of livestock straying (or present through surcharging) may protect the livestock against all dogs except those owned by the occupiers of the land, *i.e.* dogs owned by commoners or other persons entitled to graze.

(d) Acting for protection

10.75   To claim the benefit of the statutory defence a person must not only be entitled to act but also must be acting in protection of the animals in accordance with the circumstances prescribed. A person may act:

> (i) if the dog is worrying or about to worry livestock *and* there are no other reasonable means of ending or preventing the worrying; *or*

---

[40] Animals Act 1971, s.11.
[41] See § 10.07.
[42] Cited at § 10.67.

(ii) if the dog has been worrying livestock, has not left the vicinity, is not under the control of any person and there are no practicable means of ascertaining the owner.[43]

It is sufficient to satisfy any of these conditions that the defendant believed the condition to be satisfied and had reasonable grounds for that belief.[44]

It seems clear that a person with land or livestock belonging to him may act to protect his livestock even if the initial worrying has been on another person's land or to another person's livestock. **10.76**

(e) Common law

This part of the Animals Act 1971 and its predecessors in legislation are clearly intended to, at least, reinforce the common law rules about the protection of property from attack by dogs. However, the Act does not purport to replace the common law rules and there seems no reason why, in the event of failure to satisfy fully the rules under the statute, the defendant should not fall back on a common law defence.[45] **10.77**

(f) Criminal liability

Apart from the civil liability which the dog owner may attract for damage to animals and the rights given to owners to protect their livestock the worrying of livestock may as well attract criminal sanctions.[46] In addition, in some circumstances, it is an offence for dogs merely to be at large in a field or enclosure where there are sheep unless under close control.[47] **10.78**

Multiple strayings

(a) Liability under the common law

Where straying occurs from the common lands it is not unusual for livestock to travel considerable distances and complex liability can arise as between a number of parties. Under the common law if the straying was caused by the breach of a duty to fence liability for damage applies to "not only an injury which is the necessary consequence, but also an injury which is the not unnatural consequence of the breach of the duty," and "if cattle stray over a large district, the person whose neglect first caused them to **10.79**

---

[43] Animals Act 1971, s.9(3).

[44] *ibid.* s.9(4).

[45] *Cresswel* v. *Sirl* [1948] 1 K.B. 241: the onus of proof is on the defendant to justify shooting and by way of proof must establish (i) that the dog was attacking or, if left at large, would renew the attack, and (ii) that, either there was no alternative other than shooting of stopping the attack or preventing the renewal or, the defendant in all the circumstances acted reasonably in regarding the shooting as necessary to prevent attack or renewed attack, *per* Scott L.J. at 249; *cf.* Glanville Williams, pp. 91, 252.

[46] Dogs (Protection of Livestock) Act 1953, s.1(1), considered at § 11.63.

[47] Wildlife and Countryside Act 1981, s.12, Sched. 7, para. 3, considered at § 11.64; Dartmoor Commons Act 1985, s.10(6), considered at § 12.111.

stray is responsible for the consequences."[48] There may, of course, be an intervening event which will interrupt the chain of causation flowing from the breach of the duty. In *Singleton* v. *Williamson* (1861)[49] Bramwell B. foresaw such events:

> "There may be cases where a person would not be liable for all the consequences of his neglect, as, for instance, if a bull got into a close through defect of fences, and being irritated by some person, rushed through a hedge into an adjoining field; or if cattle were tempted to break through the hedge by some person offering them food."

Whether the possessor of straying livestock will have a defence under the Animals Act 1971 against an action for damage to land and property when animals stray further will depend upon the particular circumstances. He may or may not be directly liable to the person suffering damage. Where he is liable he may be able to seek an indemnity under the common law from the person originally in breach of a duty to fence.[50]

(b) Straying to one person's land

10.80 Clearly if livestock stray from A's land to B's land, where B is in breach of his duty to fence, the exception under section 5(6) of the Animals Act 1971 is effective and A is not liable to B for damage. If the livestock strays further to C's land, and C is a derivative title holder from B, then A is not liable to C, as there has been a breach of a duty to fence by a person with an interest (as superior title holder) in the land upon which damage has been done. If C, under his tenancy agreement,[51] also owes a duty to B to maintain his boundary fence, A will not be liable to C for the additional reason that C, a person interested in C's land, is in breach of his duty to fence, albeit that the duty is owed to B.

10.81 Considering the same circumstances where B is the owner of the land in his occupation and landlord of C's land, and B is not in breach of a duty to fence, A will be liable to B but not to C if C owes a duty to fence to B.

10.82 If the ownership and tenancy are reversed so that B is the tenant owing a duty to fence and C is the landlord, where B is in breach of the duty and A's animals stray to B's land and then C's land, A is clearly not liable to B. He is also not liable to C for damage on C's land because C is the paramount title holder of the B and the C land and there has been a breach by a person interested in that land. C, it is suggested, cannot avoid his liability to maintain a fence merely by letting the land to somebody else. To hold otherwise would

---

[48] *Singleton* v. *Williamson* (1861) 7 H. & N. 410 at 416 and 413, 158 E.R. 533 at 535 and 534, *per* Bramwell B. and Pollock C.B. For modern expositions as to liability, which may be summed up as "any loss naturally flowing from the trespass" see *Theyer* v. *Purnell* [1918] 2 K.B. 333 at 341 *per* Avery J.: infection with sheep scab, *Buckle* v. *Holmes* [1926] 2 K.B. 125 at 130, *Wormald* v. *Cole* [1954] 1 Q.B. 614 at 627; *Eustace* v. *Ayre* (1947) 14 L.J.N.C.C.R. 106: plaintiff's bull sustaining injury attempting to mate with straying cow.
[49] *Singleton* v. *Williamson* (1861), above, n. 48, at 416, 535.
[50] See § 10.101.
[51] The tenancy agreement will usually require the tenant to maintain his fences in "good tenantable repair"; see § 9.03.

enable any person with a duty to fence against a common to avoid all liability for the duty by the device of letting the strip of land containing the fence to a man of straw or a person outside the jurisdiction of the court. No doubt C has his remedy against his tenant B for breach of contract, or under the indemnity action,[52] but he has no action against B under section 4 of the Animals Act 1971, for that action only lies against "the person to whom the livestock belongs" and that person is A.

(c) Straying to more than one person's land

Where B and C are independent persons, and there is no duty to fence on the part of B or C, A will be liable to both B and C for damage caused by straying to the land of either as the exception from liability under section 5(6) is not available to him. In the quite likely situation where straying occurs from a waste and B has a duty to fence against the waste but is in breach of that duty, A is not liable to B but is liable to C, who is not in breach of a duty to fence. Nevertheless, the person whose neglect first caused the straying is responsible for the consequences[53] and there is authority that A will be able to claim an indemnity from B in respect of C's claim.[54] **10.83**

There seems no reason, if A's livestock stray to B's land, as a result of B being in breach of a duty to fence, and thence to other land of A (who clearly cannot claim from himself under the Animals Act action), why A should not use the indemnity action against B. **10.84**

(d) Multiple fencing obligations

Occasionally multiple fencing obligations may exist. This is quite likely where B and C are tenants and are under express or implied agreements to maintain their fences in good tenantable repair.[55] Where A's livestock stray to B's land and thence to C's land, A is liable to neither B nor C both of whom are in breach of a duty to fence. **10.85**

The Animals Act 1971 has changed the very peculiar common law position which existed previously. Under the common law, advantage could only be taken of a breach of a duty to fence where the duty was owed to the person whose animals strayed. Thus if C owed the duty only to B and B owed a duty only to A, when A's animals strayed to B and C's land, only C had an action in cattle trespass against A. A was, however entitled to claim an indemnity from B for being the person whose neglect first caused the animals to stray and B in turn could claim an indemnity from C for being in breach of his duty to fence. As Glanville Williams has pointed out, barring insolvency, a classical example of circuitous action existed.[56] It will be shown later that the common law requirement that a breach of a duty to fence may only be of advantage to the person to whom the duty is owed is still of relevance in actions concerned with straying where the straying animals are damaged.[57] **10.86**

[52] See § 10.101.
[53] See § 10.79.
[54] See § 10.101.
[55] cf. above, n. 51.
[56] Glanville Williams, p. 221.
[57] See § 10.102.

COMMON LAW ACTIONS

(1) Actions by the person strayed upon

(a) The right to drive a common

10.87 On the common lands any form of self-help by graziers against straying animals, whether it takes the form of detention or abatement by ejection of the livestock, usually has to be preceded by separation of the offending animals from those lawfully present. This may be accomplished by driving all the livestock to a suitable point where they may be individually identified. This procedure is usually known as "driving the common" or, in the older cases, as "making a drift." Who may, and under what circumstances one may, drive a common is not entirely certain. Joshua Williams asserts:

> "In many places the lord exercises, and I apprehend that he always has, a right of *driving the common*, as it is said, that is, the right, once a year or oftener if he thinks fit, of driving all the cattle and sheep upon the common into some corner or inclosed place, for the purpose of ascertaining whose sheep and cattle they are, and whether or not they have been rightfully put upon the common, in exercise of a lawful right of common."[58]

The proposition no doubt describes the practice in the past but very few owners today exercise the right to carry out, or accept responsibility for, such a drive.

10.88 **(i) Beasts of a stranger** In *Thomas* v. *Nichols* (1681–1682)[59] it was resolved by all the justices present except one that:

> " . . . the lord or any commoner seeing a stranger's beasts there may impound or drive them out of the common without custom; and to sever them from the beasts of the commoners, if it cannot be otherwise done, may drive them and the beasts of the commoners together, to a convenient place to separate them."

The position was considered to be less clear when it was uncertain whether strangers' animals were present or in the case of suspected surcharging by commoners: "But where the usage is at certain times of the year to *drive a common for a view*, if the beasts of strangers are found there; or if the common be over-charged, in such case the party must prescribe and show the custom . . . "[60]

The court clearly thought that an investigative drive—driving for a view—required a custom.

10.89 **(ii) Driving for a view** However, in *Follett* v. *Troake* (1705),[61] the custom was thought always to exist, at least in favour of the owner of the soil:

> "In case of common sans nombre, if there be a surcharge, it must be

---

[58] Joshua Williams, p. 151.
[59] (1681–1682) 3 Lev. 40 at 41, 83 E.R. 566 at 567.
[60] *ibid.*
[61] (1705) 5 Lord Raym. 1186 at 1187, 92 E.R. 284 at 285.

remedied by a writ of admeasurement.[62] But where the common is for a certain number, there a drift is very reasonable. For until a drift is made, it is hard to know whether there be a surcharge or no. And for that reason drifts of commons may be by custom, and there are such customs in all wastes. And it is unreasonable to say, the drift shall not be, unless there is a surcharge, because till the drift is made, it is not possible to know, whether there be a surcharge or no; and the intent of the drift was to discover the surcharge. This is also more reasonable than a custom to drive the common at a certain time; because if that were the custom, the commoners would surcharge the common all the rest of the year, except at those times; and so the custom would be ineffectual for the end it was intended."

In the case before the court a custom for the reeve appointed by the lord's **10.90** steward to make a drift at any time was held good. In other cases a master forester on Dartmoor was the competent authority to make a drift[63] but a surveyor, elected by copyholders to view the animals on a common and distrain those damage feasant, was unable to justify in his own right in an action for replevin.[64] It seems, therefore, that there is sufficient authority to assert that the owner of the soil, or his agent, may drive the common for a view but that commoners may only drive to separate the known straying animals of strangers. Since the enactment of the Animals Act 1971 the appropriate procedure would seem to be for the commoners, or an association of commoners, to drive for a view as authorised agents for the owner and to detain in their own right as occupiers of the land.

(b) Ejectment

It can hardly be doubted that a person entitled to the drastic self-help remedy of detention and sale is also entitled to the lesser remedy of ejection. **10.91** Indeed they are often coupled together in consideration by the courts. In *Thomas* v. *Nichols* (1681–1682),[65] for example, the court held that: "the lord or any commoner seeing a stranger's beasts there may impound or drive them out of the common without a custom; . . . "

It has been stated that where cattle have strayed and "a person is not under **10.92** any obligation to repair fences, he is justified, it would seem, in driving cattle which come into his close out into the highway[66] and leaving them there; but if he is bound to repair he must drive them back into the close from which they escaped in consequence of his neglect."[67] In *Mitten* v. *Faudrye* (1626)[68] Jones J. is reported as saying that the animals may not be driven back to the land of a stranger, but only to a highway, a common or the land of the owner of the animals. He also refused to admit that there was

---

[62] The writ, now abolished, to ascertain the rights of each commoner at any one time.

[63] *Mortimer* v. *Moore* (1845) 8 Q.B. 294, 115 E.R. 887.

[64] *Stephens* v. *Keblethwayt* (1617) Cro.Jac. 436, 79 E.R. 372.

[65] See above, n. 59, at 41, 567.

[66] But see the doubts expressed at §§ 10.95 *et seq.*

[67] Hunt, p. 255, citing and approving *Carruthers* v. *Hollis* (1838) 8 Ad. & E. 113, 112 E.R. 778.

[68] (1626) Popham 161, 79 E.R. 1259.

a right to return animals to the land of the owner if it was sown with corn unless it was a matter of necessity.[69]

10.93 **(i) Returning animals to a common** It seems certain that where animals have strayed from a common through a boundary fence which a contiguous occupier is under a duty to maintain the occupier of the land strayed upon may not turn them to a highway: "it is perfectly clear that the least to be expected from a party in that situation . . . is, that he should put back the sheep into the place in which they were before they quitted it in consequence of his neglect."[70]

10.94 **(ii) The use of dogs** The owner of land strayed upon is not expected to attempt ejection unaided. He may use a "little dog"[71] to help him but not "mastiffs"[72] which might damage the livestock.

(c) The right to turn to a highway doubted

10.95 There is ample judicial[73] and academic[74] support for the view that "if the occupier of the land on to which the animals stray is under no obligation to repair his fences then he is permitted to drive the straying animals out of his land even on to the highway."[75] Indeed, the ordinary householder may have little alternative when animals stray from the highway. Where, however, the action is by a farmer, the courts today will not necessarily take the same view today as they did when the normal traffic on a highway was an occasional horse-drawn carriage.

10.96 The person strayed upon may be in something of a quandary. Returning the animals whence they came, without repairs to the fence, is likely to result in a repeated straying. While an action may lie against the owner of the animals most farmers would prefer an unsullied crop to a legal action even if insurers pay without argument. A decisive way of dealing with the problem is to turn them "down the road." However, in so doing it is evident that two results ensue. First, the person strayed upon has taken the animals under his control and secondly, by turning them on to the highway he has almost certainly committed an act of personal trespass against the owner of the highway. That owner may not wish to take action but the mere act of turning them to the highway, it can hardly be doubted, is unlawful. A person who assumes control of another person's animals and then knowingly commits an act of trespass with them may be in some difficulty in pointing to cases a century or two old and claiming that, whatever the consequences today, the result should be the same as it would have been then.

10.97 If a third party, damaged on the highway, has recourse against the owner of straying animals, the owner is prima facie liable for all the natural conse-

---

[69] s.c. *Millen* v. *Fawdrey* (1626) Latch. 119, 82 E.R. 304; there is also no right of abatement available to the owner of the soil of a common for damage done to his property if the animals are lawfully present: *Farmor* v. *Hunt* (1611) Cro. Jac. 271, 79 E.R. 233.
[70] *Carruthers* v. *Hollis* (1838), above, n. 67, *per* Lord Denman.
[71] *Tyrringham's Case* (1584) 4 Co.Rep. at 38b, 76 E.R. at 981.
[72] *King* v. *Rose* (1673) 3 Keb. 228, 84 E.R. 691.
[73] See cases cited at §§ 10.91 and 10.92.
[74] Hunt, p. 255, Glanville Williams, pp. 90–92.
[75] North, p. 134.

quences flowing from the straying.[76] This, however, can hardly include the results of the action of a third party intervening and, say, turning a herd of cattle into the middle of a high speed stream of road traffic. The action may well be an intervening act sufficient to prevent liability for the traffic accident falling on the livestock owner, and the actor may find himself held to have assumed control of the animals and liable for a negligent act causing the accident.

10.98

Similarly, if straying animals are turned on to a highway and are there injured it is unwise to assume that old cases will necessarily be followed if there was any alternative course of action available to the person strayed upon. Turning animals into a stream of traffic becomes more like inflicting damage on the animals than the protection of property from animals. In at least one of the old cases there are indications that the person strayed upon is not entitled to inflict damage unnecessarily on the crops of the defaulting owner of the animals.[77] It seems but a short step to say that nor may he be instrumental in inflicting damage on the straying animals themselves.

(d) The duty to fence and non-feasance

10.99

The duty to fence includes a duty to contain animals as well as to keep them out, so that a breach of the duty causing straying from the servient land is actionable for non-feasance. Usually, where the servient tenant's animals stray, the statutory tort action under section 4 of the Animals Act 1971 will be available to the person strayed upon. Where the livestock is already straying on the servient tenement no action lies against the servient tenant as the livestock is not in his possession but in that of a third party, against whom the action will lie.[78] Sometimes it may be the case that the possessor of the animals is unknown or the livestock escapes from the land where damage has been done before it is identified. In this situation the duty to contain animals may be invoked against the defaulting servient tenant.[79]

10.100

The first clear exposition of this principle can be seen in the case of *Star* v. *Rookesby* (1710)[80] where it is stated that trespass, or an action on the case lies,: "trespass, because it was the plaintiff's ground and not the defendant's; and case because the first wrong was a non-feasance and neglect to repair, and that omission is the gist of the action; and the trespass is only consequential damage." It is clear that the liability for this aspect of the duty to fence lies on the occupier and not the owner out of occupation.[81]

---

[76] See § 10.79.

[77] *Millen* v. *Fawdrey* (1626), cited at § 10.92.

[78] Animals Act 1971, s.4.

[79] The action may only be brought by the dominant tenant as under the common law it lies only between contiguous closes: see the discussion at §§ 10.102–10.104.

[80] (1710) 1 Salk. 335, 91 E.R. 295, *per curiam*.

[81] *Cheetham* v. *Hampson* (1791) 4 T.R. 318 at 319, 100 E.R. 1041 at 1042, *per* Lord Kenyon.

(e) The indemnity action

10.101   It has been shown that if A's livestock stray to B's land, where B is in breach of a duty to fence, and thence to C's land, where C is under no duty to fence, A is liable to C for damage to land and property and those expenses specified in section 4 of the Animals Act 1971.[82] However, the person who first caused the livestock to stray is responsible for the consequences and, as has been shown above, is liable for his non-feasance.[83] A may recover for his losses against B under the indemnity action. In *Holbach* v. *Warner* (1622)[84] the claim was for such an indemnity, and, although the case went off on pleading, was accepted by the court. In *Right* v. *Baynard* (1674)[85] the court refused to accept that A should be excused his liability to C because of B's default for "if this were a good plea, the right of repairing the fences between [B] and [C] would be tried between [A] and [C] but . . . [A] must be put to his special action on the case against [B] for not repairing." It has been suggested[86] that in order to avoid circuitous actions C should be allowed to recover directly from B, but the argument has been rejected judicially[87] and, further, the statutory action under section 4 of the Animals Act 1971 does not allow it.

(2) Damage to animals

10.102   The statutory tort in section 4 of the Animals Act 1971 deals only with damage caused *by* livestock straying and leaves untouched the question of damage caused *to* the livestock. The pre-existing common law actions available for damage to animals are entirely distinct from the statutory tort and different rules apply. Where the straying is the result of a breach of a duty to fence it has been shown that, under the Animals Act exceptions, it is only necessary to ask whether there is a breach of that duty[88] whereas in the common law actions the criterion is to establish to whom the duty is owed.[89] This usually prevents strangers from taking advantage of the duty in a common law action although it should be kept in mind that some Inclosure Awards seem to create a duty *simpliciter*, without specifying to whom that duty is owed.[90] It is valid, therefore, in most actions to think in terms

---

[82] § 10.08.

[83] *cf.* §§ 10.79 and 10.99; an order for reinstatement of the fence may also be sought: see § 9.26.

[84] (1622) Cro. Jac. 665, 79 E.R. 576; cited and approved *Powell* v. *Salisbury* (1828) 2 Y. & J. 391, 148 E.R. 970.

[85] (1674) 1 Freem. 379 at 380, 89 E.R. 283 at 283, *per* Twisden J.; *cf.* s.c. *semble Smith* v. *Baynard* (1674) 3 Keb. 388, 84 E.R. 782 and *Baynard* v. *Smith* (1674) 3 Keb. 417, 84 E.R. 798: cases explained in *Jones* v. *Robin* (1847) 10 Q.B. 620 at 638, 116 E.R. 235 at 242, *per* Parke B.; *cf.* also Fitz.N.B. (8th ed., 1755), 128, C, note (a).

[86] Glanville Williams, p. 223.

[87] *Sutcliffe* v. *Holmes* [1947] 1 K.B. 147 at 156, *per* Somervell L.J.

[88] See § 10.43.

[89] Glanville Williams, pp. 218 *et seq.*

[90] Inclosure Act 1845, s.83. However, the intention of the section must surely be to establish liability for fencing between contiguous landowners and not to create a general duty of which any person may take advantage.

of a dominant and servient tenement as it is well established that the duty, for common law purposes, can only exist as between contiguous closes.[91]

(a) Straying from the dominant to the servient tenement

Where cattle lawfully on the dominant tenement stray on to the servient **10.103** tenement due to a breach of the duty to fence the dominant tenant can recover damages for injury to his animals suffered on the servient tenement.[92] Thus, damages may be claimed for the death of, or injury to, cattle resulting from eating yew tree leaves,[93] falling into a ditch,[94] being hit by a train,[95] drinking contaminated water,[96] hitting their heads on a viaduct,[97] falling into a quarry,[98] falling from one field to another[99] or by suffering a haystack falling on them.[1] The dominant tenant may claim in respect of all animals lawfully on the tenement if he is responsible for them. The degree of responsibility required seems to be quite minimal with a gratuitous bailee entitled to recover.[2] If the animals stray further then, on the principle that the servient tenant is liable for all the not unnatural consequences flowing from the breach of his duty to maintain a fence, he will be liable for all the damage caused to the livestock.[3]

(i) Liability limited to animals lawfully present If animals are **10.104** unlawfully on the dominant tenement they are regarded as being unlawfully present on the servient tenement in spite of the servient tenant's breach of a duty to fence and no action will lie for any damage they suffer there. In cattle trespass it was said that "if cattle of one man escape into the land of another, it is no excuse that the fences were out of repair, if they were trespassers in the place from whence they came."[4] It follows that if the cattle stray from A's land to B's land, where A is in breach of the duty to

[91] *Dovaston v. Payne* (1795) 2 H.Bl. 527, 126 E.R. 684, *per* Heath J.
[92] *Gale's Easements* (2nd ed., 1849) p. 297; Hunt, p. 251, North, p. 131; *cf. Wilson v. Newberry* (1871) L.R. 7 Q.B. 31, *Wiseman v. Booker* (1878) 3 C.P.D. 184, *Ponting v. Noakes* [1894] 2 Q.B. 281; the fence itself must not damage livestock on the dominant tenement, so that, where decayed pieces fall off, and are consumed by animals causing death, the servient tenant is in actionable breach of the duty to repair: *Firth v. Bowling Iron Co.* (1878) 3 C.P.D. 254.
[93] *Lawrence v. Jenkins* (1873) L.R. Q.B. 274; *Clune v. Clare County Council* (1972) 114 I.L.T. 58.
[94] *Anon.* (1675) 1 Vent. 264, 86 E.R. 177.
[95] *Bessant v. Great Western Railway Co.* (1860) 8 C.B.N.S. 368, 141 E.R. 1208; *Dawson v. Midland Rail Co.* (1872) L.R. 8 Ex. 8; *Luscombe v. Great Western Railway Co.* [1899] 2 Q.B. 313; *Symons v. Southern Rail Co.* (1935) 153 L.T. 98.
[96] *Harrison v. M'Culvey* (1840) 2 Cr. & Dix. 1.
[97] *Dixon v. Great Western Rail Co.* [1897] 1 Q.B. 300.
[98] See cases cited at § 9.02, n. 7.
[99] *Rooth v. Wilson* (1817) 1 B. & Ald. 59, 106 E.R. 22.
[1] *Powell v. Salisbury* (1828) 2 Y. & J. 391, 148 E.R. 970.
[2] *Rooth v. Wilson* (1817) above, n. 99 *a fortiori* a licensee: *Dawson v. The Midland Rail Co.* (1872) above, n. 95; *cf. Broadwater v. Blot* (1817) Holt. 547, 171 E.R. 336 for duties of agisters and *Coggs v. Barnard* (1703) 2 Ld.Raym. 909 at 912, 92 E.R. 107 at 109, *per* Holt C.J. for categories of bailee.
[3] *cf.* § 10.79 and especially the cases cited there at n. 48.
[4] *Dovaston v. Payne* (1795) 2 H.Bl. 527 at 531, 126 E.R. 684 at 686, *per* Heath J.; *Sackville v. Milward* (1444) 2 H.6, 7, 8, 13 Vin.Ab. 163, 164; *Anon.* (1770) 3 Wils. K.B. 126, 95 E.R. 970, *per* Wilmot C.J.

fence, and thence into C's land, where C is in breach of a duty to fence owed to B, and are there damaged, A has no action against C as C is not liable for animals unlawfully present on his dominant tenement, namely B's land.

10.105 Where multiple obligations to fence exist the position should be different. Where B has to fence against A, and C has to fence against B, and animals stray from the land of A to that of B and thence to the land of C the animals may be regarded as lawfully present on B's land as he has consented to their presence by being in breach of his duty owed to A. It is clear that A can claim from B for all the not unnatural consequences of being in breach of the duty owed to A which will include the damage caused to the animals on C's land.[5] However, in the absence of any intervening event, B should be able to claim an indemnity from C for the breach of his duty to fence, *i.e.* his failure to prevent the straying of animals lawfully present on B's land. It has been suggested that the double action, by both A and B, is undesirable and circuitous.[6] It is not circuitous as C has no action against A and separate actions seem inevitable if the issues between A and B, on the one hand, and B and C, on the other, are to be properly tried. An action between A and C could produce the result that C is held liable when B had a defence which would prevent A's animals from being lawfully present on B's land.

10.106 **(ii) The surcharging commoner** Where the dominant tenement is common land, it is clear that both a stranger to the common and a surcharging commoner have a defence against an action for damage to land or property under the Animals Act 1971 if livestock strays through a boundary fence and the duty to fence against the common exists.[7] It was also clear under the common law that the animals of a surcharging commoner which so strayed could not be distrained as the commoner had some colour of right for their presence.[8] It cannot be said, however, that the position today is that the animals of a surcharging commoner will necessarily be viewed as lawfully present, in an action against the person in default of the duty to fence, if the animals are damaged consequent upon the straying. The C.R.A. 1965 required the registration of the maximum number of animals which might be grazed and declared the right to be exercisable only in relation to animals not exceeding that number.[9] To graze in excess of the maximum number is to exercise in a way forbidden by statute and it seems that the surcharging commoner can no longer be viewed as exercising a lawful right.

10.107 **(iii) Common pur cause de vicinage** There is no doubt that a person exercising a right of common *pur cause de vicinage* may take advantage of the exception of a breach of a duty to fence where the animals stray and an action would otherwise lie for damage to land and property caused by the straying animals.[10] The origin of this class of common right is in a mutual agreement of the commoners on contiguous commons not to sue in trespass where the animals stray over the unfenced boundaries of the adjacent

---

[5] *Singleton* v. *Williamson* (1861) 7 H. & N. 410, 158 E.R. 533.
[6] North, p. 146.
[7] § 10.43.
[8] *Vivian* v. *Dalton* (1896) 41 S.J. 129, (D.C.).
[9] C.R.A. 1965, s.15.
[10] See § 10.43.

lands.[11] It is difficult to see any reason why such an agreement should have any effect on the duties of third parties and in particular the duty to fence against one of the commons. It seems that the correct analysis is that the duty to fence is owed to those with a substantive right to graze a common and any separate agreement those persons may reach with their neighbouring commoners should not increase the *quantum* of that duty. It follows that, for the purposes of the common law actions following a straying by animals grazing only by right of vicinage, while they may be lawfully present on the land sufficiently to prevent detention or an action for damage on that land, they are not animals of persons to whom the duty to fence is owed. They may be treated by a person in breach of a duty to fence against a common as though they were animals of strangers to the dominant tenement and trespassing there.

(b) Straying from the servient to the dominant tenement

Principle seems to require that a person who allows his animals to stray **10.108** should never recover for damage caused to them. However, if the dominant tenant entices the animals on to his land he will be liable for any damage they suffer. This can be seen most clearly in events somewhat unlikely today. At one time a person was entitled passively to place "dog spears" on his land to trap straying dogs[12] but he was not free to set baited traps with strong smelling flesh to entice dogs on to his property to ensnare them.[13] In the latter case Lord Ellenborough C.J. said that:

> "Every man must be taken to contemplate the probable consequences of the act he does . . . What difference is there in reason between drawing the animal into the trap by means of his instinct which he cannot resist, and putting him there by manual force?"[14]

In modern times the wilful placing of a bull in a field adjoining another containing heifers might be considered an enticement sufficient to make the dominant tenant liable for any damage caused to the heifers.

(c) Defence of act of a third party

Prior to the enactment of the Animals Act 1971 the strict liability of cattle **10.109** trespass had been mollified somewhat by the acceptance of a defence of the unknown act of a third party.[15] It was also acceptable in the derivative action of cattle trespass, concerned with the escape of non-natural things brought on to land, known as the rule in *Rylands* v. *Fletcher*.[16]

It might be expected that the same defence would be available in the anal- **10.110** ogous common law action of damage caused to animals consequent upon a breach of a duty to fence. Such case authority as exists indicates otherwise

---

[11] See § 3.47.

[12] *Jordin* v. *Crump* (1841) 8 M. & W. 782, 151 E.R. 1256; *Deane* v. *Clayton* (1817) 7 Taunt. 489, 129 E.R. 196.

[13] *Townsend* v. *Wathan* (1808) 9 East. 277, 103 E.R. 579.

[14] Above, n. 13, at 281, 581.

[15] Following the Animals Act 1971 the defences under cattle trespass are no longer applicable as s.1 of the Act replaced the rules imposing liability for cattle trespass, thus reimposing stricter liability.

[16] For which see *Charlesworth and Percy on Negligence* (7th ed., 1983) paras. 13.01–13.150.

but it will be suggested that this may now be anomalous. In *Lawrence* v. *Jenkins* (1873)[17] the plaintiff's cattle strayed through a defective fence which was admittedly subject to a duty to fence on the part of the defendant. The plaintiff's cattle died as a result of eating yew leaves and the question before the court was whether the defendant or his contractor, who had damaged the fence, was liable. It was held that the duty to maintain a fence was absolute, act of God or *vis major* only excepted, and that the act of a third party or lack of notice was no defence. Archibald J., giving the judgment of the court, held that a fence upon which an obligation to maintain exists "renders it, we think, incumbent on the party upon whom the prescriptive obligation is imposed to repair the fence in time to prevent its becoming defective, and subjects him to all risks of injury that may be done to it by strangers or trespassers."[18]

10.111 Glanville Williams has described the early development, and vagaries, of the defence of act of a third party in cattle trespass.[19] In the middle of the seventeenth century Rolle J. seems inconsistent: "He that drives my cattel into another man's land is the trespasser against him, and not I who am the owner of the cattel"[20] but "if cattel be stolen and put into my ground, I may take them damage feasant, or bring an action of trespass against the owner."[21]

By the middle of the nineteenth century there seemed but little scope for the defence in cattle trespass. Blackburn J. in giving the judgment of the Exchequer Chamber in *Fletcher* v. *Rylands* (1866)[22] said that the law "seems to be perfectly settled from early times; the owner must keep them in at his peril, or he will be answerable for the natural consequences of their escape" and the defendant can only excuse himself "by shewing that the escape was owing to the plaintiff's default; or perhaps that the escape was the consequence of *vis major*, or the act of God; but as nothing of this sort exists here, it is unnecessary to inquire what excuse would be sufficient."

10.112 An excuse which would be sufficient was found in *Rickard* v. *Lothian* (1913)[23] when it was held that the malicious act of a third party provided a defence in an action under the rule in *Rylands* v. *Fletcher*. This was taken in *Smith* v. *Great Western Railway Co.* (1926)[24] to include all damage caused by the wrongful acts of third persons. A plea of the wrongful act of a third party in a cattle trespass action was considered in the Court of Appeal in *Sutcliffe* v. *Holmes* (1946)[25] and the development of the defence in *Rylands* v. *Fletcher* actions was examined. Somervell L.J. giving the judgment of the court said: "The reasoning in both cases [*Rickard* and *Smith*] seems to me to be based on findings that the defendant was unaware of the act or default

---

[17] (1873) L.R. 8 Q.B. 274.
[18] *ibid.* at 280.
[19] Glanville Williams, p. 181.
[20] *Smith* v. *Stone* (1647) Style 65, 82 E.R. 533.
[21] *Topladye* v. *Stalye* (1649) Style 165, 82 E.R. 615.
[22] (1866) L.R. 1 Ex. 265 at 279–280; affirmed *sub nom. Rylands* v. *Fletcher* (1868) L.R. 3 H.L. 330.
[23] [1913] A.C. 263 at 278, *per* Lord Moulton. The first formulation of the defence can be found in *Box* v. *Jubb* (1879) 4 Ex.D. 76.
[24] [1926] 135 L.T. 112 at 115.
[25] [1947] 1 K.B. 147.

at the time, was guilty of no negligence in being unaware of it, and could not reasonably have foreseen and guarded against it or its consequences."[26]

The attention of the court was drawn to a judgment in *Sharpe* v. *Harvey* (1935)[27] where it had been laid down as a general principle that if the defendants' animals enter the plaintiff's land owing to the wrongful act of a third party, the defendant is not liable. Somervell L.J. thought the principle too broadly stated: "The learned judge should, I think, have considered the question whether the defendant knew or ought to have known of the defect and ought to have taken steps to have it remedied or seen that the sheep did not escape as a result.[28]

Thus, in both cattle trespass and *Rylands* v. *Fletcher* cases in the absence of **10.113** negligence by, or the knowledge of, the defendant, a defence of wrongful act of a third party is admissible. In both classes of case strict liablity was vitiated but not, it seems, in the anologous type of case where the defendant is the person under a duty to fence as in the case of *Lawrence* v. *Jenkins*. That case, however, was long before the modern trend towards amelioration of strict liability and would probably be decided differently today. While strict liability has been reimposed for straying animals, by statute, it would be odd if under the common law the duty to maintain a fence to keep animals out was higher than the duty imposed on a person to contain unnatural things on his land in *Rylands* v. *Fletcher* liability.

It is probable that, while a commoner may rely entirely on a breach of the **10.114** duty to fence as an exception to liability for damage caused by his straying livestock, in any action he may bring for damage to his animals following straying through defective fences he may be met by the defence that the fence was damaged by the unknown act of a third party.[29] Further, on the authority of *Sutcliffe* v. *Holmes* a commoner's actual or constructive knowledge of defects in, and acquiescence in the condition of, fences will prevent him recovering for the damage received.

(3) Other common law actions

(a) General application

While the majority of actions in connection with animals on or near the **10.115** common lands will now be concerned with the statutory action for cattle straying, provided by the Animals Act 1971, it should not be forgotten that the only common law actions abolished by the Act were cattle trespass and the extra-judicial remedy of distress damage feasant. It follows that in all

[26] *Sutcliffe* v. *Holmes* [1947] 1 K.B. 147 at 155.

[27] (1935) 2 L.J.N.C.C.R. 261.

[28] [1947] 1 K.B. 147 at 156 a defendant is required to prove that the act of a third party caused the trespass: *Morris* v. *Curtis* (1947) L.J.N.C.C.R. 284.

[29] It may be over simplistic to say that any wrongful act, occasioned by a third party, without the knowledge of the defendant, is without negligence by him. It may or may not have negligent connotations to leave cattle in a field where there is a gate depending upon the incidence of strangers who may leave it open. Non-negligent behaviour might be to erect a stile or cattle grid in place of, or in addition to, the gate. The point does not appear to have occurred to the court in *M'Gibbon* v. *M'Curry* (1909) 43 I.L.T. 132 (trespass caused by stranger on right of way through defendant's field leaving gate open; defendant not liable).

cases consideration should be given to the possibility that additionally, or instead of, the statutory actions an alternative is available under the common law actions of nuisance,[30] negligence, or the rule in *Rylands* v. *Fletcher*.[31]

(b) Personal trespass

10.116   It is clear that it is possible to commit a personal trespass through the agency of animals much as it is possible to trespass on land in and by the means of motor vehicles. A clear enunciation of the principle is contained in the judgment of Murray C.J. in *Hunt* v. *Shanks* (1918):[32]

> "A man is answerable for the trespass of his cattle, if they stray without his knowledge and against his will into another person's land; but he is also answerable for his own acts of trespass, and if he unlawfully drives his cattle into another's land or permits them to remain there for an unreasonable time after he has become aware that they are trespassing, or breaks a fence, or opens a gate, with a view to inducing them to pass through, and they do pass through, the resulting trespass, in my opinion, is his trespass and not merely the trespass of his cattle."

Thus, a personal trespass may occur not only when a person's animals are driven or induced to stray, but also when an excused straying occurs, once the owner becomes aware that the animals are so straying. This is in accord with the common law rule that where animals strayed as the consequence of a breach of a duty to fence the person strayed upon could bring an action or distrain once notice was given to the owner.[33]

10.117   No doubt the driving of animals on to the land of another person or recklessness as to whether damage may occur is also an offence under the Criminal Damage Act 1971 providing that there was an intention to destroy or damage, or recklessness as to whether that would be the result.[34] Mere negligence will not be sufficient.

CRIMINAL OFFENCES

(a) Regulated commons

10.118   It is usual, wherever a common is "regulated" under statute, for by-laws to control behaviour to be in force. Although these are primarily intended to control the public exercising rights of access to the land they almost univer-

---

[30] *cf.* Glanville Williams, Chapter 14; Pearce and Maston, *Law relating to Nuisances* (1926), Chapter 8; for statutory nuisances see the Public Health Act 1936, ss.92–100, especially s.92(1)(b).
[31] See *Charlesworth and Percy on Negligence* (7th ed., 1983) paras. 13.01–13.150.
[32] [1918] S.A.L.R. 254 at 261.
[33] *Edwards* v. *Halinder* (1594) 2 Leon. 93, 74 E.R. 385; *Poole* v. *Longuevill* (1669) 2 Wms.Saund. 282, 85 E.R. 1063; *Kimp* v. *Cruwes* (1695) 2 Lutw. 1578, 125 E.R. 868.
[34] Criminal Damage Act 1971, s.1(1): "A person who without lawful excuse destroys or damages any property belonging to another intending to destroy or damage any such property or being reckless as to whether any such property would be destroyed or damaged shall be guilty of an offence." By s.4 the offence is punishable by imprisonment for 10 years. However, note that by s.10(1) "property" means property of a tangible nature but "not including mushrooms growing wild on any land or flowers, fruit or foliage of a plant growing wild on any land."

sally prohibit unlawful grazing by animals, which may affect both strangers to the common and the commoners. The statutes may be local and common specific, or made under the enabling legislation contained in the Metropolitan Commons Acts 1866–1898[35] and the Commons Acts 1876[36] and 1899.[37] There is no standard code for all the legislation and to ascertain the extent of the by-laws it is necessary to examine the provisions for each particular common. A lesser measure of control is contained in Orders of Limitations which may be imposed on land subject to a right of public access under section 193 of the L.P.A. 1925.[38] Such Orders usually contain a prohibition on unlawful grazing.

(b) Control of dogs

Of general application to agricultural land but of especial importance on common lands are the provisions contained in the Dogs (Protection of Livestock) Act 1953, which creates an offence for worrying of livestock and in certain circumstances makes it an offence for a dog to be at large (that is to say not on a lead or otherwise under close control) in a field or enclosure in which there are sheep.[39] **10.119**

(c) Regulation by commoners

In two situations the commoners themselves are entitled to make by-laws and regulations controlling livestock, the breach of which is an offence. Where land has been allotted as a statutory regulated pasture in an Inclosure Award made under the Inclosure Act 1845 regulations, which may include control of grazing livestock, may be made by the stintholders.[40] By virtue of section 33 of the Inclosure Act 1852 it is an offence for any person to have any stock or animals on any regulated pasture contrary to such regulations. The owners of regulated pasture may, at an annual general meeting, make by-laws to control the management of animals on the pasture.[41] The penalty which may be imposed under such regulations or by-laws may not exceed level 1 on the standard scale for any one offence.[42] **10.120**

Of a similar nature is the control which may be exercised by commoners through a scheme made under the Commons Act 1908.[43] The regulation in this case is concerned only with entire animals and allows the persons entitled to turn out animals on the common to regulate the times at which, and the conditions under which, such animals may be grazed. Contravention of regulations made under such a scheme, or obstructing an officer appointed under the scheme in the execution of his duties, is an offence on **10.121**

---

[35] See further § 12.34.

[36] See further § 12.43.

[37] See further § 12.64 and Appendix 6.

[38] See further § 11.26.

[39] See further § 11.64.

[40] Powers of appointed reeves: Inclosure Act 1845, s.118; offence of wilful or malicious damage to any fences: Inclosure Act 1848, s.10; for a fuller discussion, see § 12.18.

[41] Commons Act 1876, ss.15, 16.

[42] *ibid.* s.16; Criminal Justice Act 1982, ss.40, 46.

[43] See further § 12.76.

conviction for which a person is liable to a fine not exceeding level 1 on the standard scale.[44]

(d) Highways Act 1980

10.122 Of particular relevance to many areas of the common lands or other open grazings is the provision contained in section 155 of the Highways Act 1980, which makes it an offence for horses, cattle, sheep, goats or swine to be found straying on a highway or lying on or at the side of a highway.[45] The penalty upon conviction is an amount not exceeding level 2 on the standard scale.[46] A person convicted is also liable to pay the reasonable expenses of removing any animal so found to the keeper's premises or to the common pound or other place where it is impounded, and the fees and charges of the pound keeper.[47] An offence of "pound breach" exists for unlawful release of any animals seized under the section.[48]

10.123 The section does not apply in relation to any part of the highway passing over any common, waste or unenclosed ground.[49] It has been said, *obiter dicta*, that the exception applies not only to a highway passing over a common but also to a highway abutting a common.[50] This seems correct as the highway, in abutting unenclosed land, is *ex hypothesi* passing over unenclosed land. It was held, however, in *Rees* v. *Morgan* (1976)[51] that this interpretation of the exception does not apply if the animals stray down the highway and away from the point where the common land and highway co-exist. Again this is correct in principle if there is a definite termination of the boundary of the common. On occasions, however, a common may have been divided by inclosure which in effect creates parcels of common land separated by highway corridors. These corridors may still be common land although unregistered under the C.R.A. 1965. That Act forbids registration of any land which forms part of a highway,[52] but also does not deem such land to have ceased to be common land as it is not land capable of being registered under the Act.[53] It may be possible to establish, in some circumstances, that the highways adjoining severed parts of common land are unenclosed land over which a highway passes.

10.124 The offences under the Highways Act 1980 are provided for the protection of the public and do not necessarily render the keeper of the animals liable to an action at law.[54]

---

[44] Criminal Justice Act 1967, s.92, Sched. 3, Pt. I; Criminal Justice Act 1982, ss.38, 46.

[45] The offences of "straying" and "lying" are distinct: *Lawrence* v. *King* (1868) L.R. 3 Q.B. 345; *cf. Morris* v. *Jeffries* (1866) L.R. 1 Q.B. 261, *Sherborn* v. *Wells* (1863) 3 B. & S. 784, 122 E.R. 293, *Golding* v. *Stocking* (1869) L.R. 4 Q.B. 516, *Horwood* v. *Goodall* (1872) 36 J.P. 486.

[46] Highways Act 1980, s.155(2).

[47] *ibid.* s.155(3).

[48] *ibid.* s.155(4).

[49] *ibid.* s.155(1).

[50] *Davies* v. *Davies* [1975] Q.B. 172 at 178, *per* Lord Denning M.R.

[51] (1976) 240 E.G. 787, (D.C.); 120 S.J. 148 [1976]; Crim.L.R. 252.

[52] C.R.A. 1965, ss.22(1), 21(2).

[53] *ibid.* s.1(2)(a).

[54] *Heath's Garage Ltd.* v. *Hodges* [1916] 2 K.B. 370; *cf. Davies* v. *Davies* [1975], above, n. 50.

(e) Town Police Clauses Act 1847, ss.24–27

By virtue of section 24 of this Act a police officer or any resident in a district **10.125**
council area may seize and impound any cattle found at large in any street.
A penalty not exceeding level 1 on the standard scale is prescribed[55]
together with liability for the reasonable expenses of impounding and keeping the cattle. If the penalty and expenses are not paid within three days the
council may proceed to sell the cattle following notice to the owner, if
known or, if not known, following public notice seven days before the
sale.[56] A council is empowered to purchase land and to erect and maintain a
pound thereon.[57] Damaging a pound or releasing or attempting to release
impounded cattle is an offence and upon summary conviction a person is
liable to be committed to prison for a term not exceeding three months.[58]

The provisions in the Act have been widely used by local authorities in **10.126**
South Wales[59] but there are indications that some now prefer the civil procedures under the Animals Act 1971.[60]

(f) Bulls in fields crossed by public rights of way

Section 59 of the Wildlife and Countryside Act 1981 prohibits the keeping **10.127**
of a bull in a field crossed by a public right of way unless it is under 10
months old or, is not of a recognised dairy breed and is at large with cows or
heifers. The penalty for a breach of this provision is a fine not exceeding
£200.

(g) Criminal damage and dogs

It is an offence under section 1 of the Criminal Damage Act 1971 if a person **10.128**
without lawful excuse destroys or damages any property belonging to
another intending to destroy or damage any such property or being reckless
as to whether any such property would be destroyed or damaged. Thus, killing or injuring dogs on common land is an offence unless it is done with
lawful excuse, defined in section 5(2)(b) of the Act as where the person "destroyed or damaged . . . in order to protect property belonging to himself or
another . . . and at the time of the act . . . he believed that the property . . .
was in immediate need of protection and that the means of protection were
or would be reasonable having regard to all the circumstances" and the
belief "is honestly held."[61]

It seems that where a defence is available in civil proceedings under section **10.129**
9(3)(a) of the Animals Act 1971, a defence is also available under the

---

[55] Criminal Law Act 1977, s.31(6); Criminal Justice Act 1982, s.46.
[56] Town Police Clauses Act 1847, s.25.
[57] *ibid.* s.27.
[58] *ibid.* s.26.
[59] For an account of the scale of impounding in the South Wales valleys, see Lewis,
Stock Trespass and Straying in the Townships of Glamorgan and Monmouthshire
(1965) (private publication by the National Farmers Union).
[60] See the case cited at § 10.08, n. 30.
[61] An honest belief may be held to exist even if it is the result of self-induced intoxi-
cation: *Jaggard* v. *Dickinson* [1981] 1 Q.B. 527 (D.C.).

Criminal Damage Act 1971, that is to say, in circumstances where a dog is worrying or about to worry livestock and there are no other means of ending or preventing the worrying. However, there may be no defence to a criminal action where the civil defence is based on section 9(3)(b), that is to say where a dog has been worrying livestock, has not left the vicinity, is not under the control of any person, and there are no practicable means of ascertaining to whom it belongs.

11. Public Access to the Common Lands

Introduction

In spite of the undoubted fact that the general public has *de facto* access to a very high proportion of the common lands there is no more a general legal right of access than there is to any other land. In the absence of a special right to enter common land, granted by statute, or dedication by the owner, the general rule is that the owner is entitled, if he wishes, to take an action against a stranger who walks, rides or "takes his carriage" upon the common.[1]

11.01

(a) Common land

It has been estimated that about one fifth of the one and a half million acres of common land is subject to a *de jure* right of public access.[2] Most of this is the result of an express provision contained in the L.P.A. 1925, s.193, which affects certain lands in "urban" areas.[3] Of growing importance for public access are the extensive common land areas owned by the National Trust. In 1983, the Trust owned and managed some 135,000 acres of registered common land, half of it in the Lake District, and there have been substantial purchases since that date.[4] It will be shown that under the National Trust Acts there is strictly no legal right in the public to enter the lands but, by a combination of the duties imposed under the Acts and Trust policy, access is almost totally uninhibited.[5]

11.02

Under provisions contained in the National Parks and Access to the Countryside Act 1949, legal rights of access may be acquired over certain classes of open land, through the medium of agreement or by compulsory order. In spite of the obvious applicability of these provisions to the common lands,

11.03

---

[1] *Blundell* v. *Catterall* (1821) 5 B.& Ald. 268 at 315, 106 E.R. 1190 at 1207, *per* Abbott C.J.

[2] *Common Land, Preparations for Comprehensive Legislation, Report of an Inter-Departmental Working Party 1975–1977* (1978), para. 1.1, (published by the Department of the Environment).

[3] See § 11.06.

[4] *e.g.* 16,000 acres at Abergwesyn Common, Powys.

[5] See § 11.42.

little use seems to have been made of them for this purpose except in special and unusual circumstances.[6]

11.04 A further source of a public right of access is a number of Acts dealing with particular commons. These are of two types: special Acts with their own common specific legislation,[7] and confirmation Acts and schemes under the Metropolitan and Commons Acts which provide control and regulation under standard procedures.[8] Many of these Acts, however, do not provide a general right of access but access limited to inhabitants in a particular "neighbourhood."

(b) Town and village greens

11.05 Both town and village greens may be subject to access for exercise and recreation by way of customary right, presumed dedication or following inclosure awards. In these cases also, any rights are likely to be limited to 'the inhabitants of the locality.'[9]

General statutory rights of access

1. Law of Property Act 1925, s.193[10]

11.06 The most important single source of public access over common lands is contained in this section, which provides that:

> "Members of the public shall . . . have rights of access for air and exercise to any land which is a metropolitan common within the meaning of the Metropolitan Commons Acts 1866 to 1898, or manorial waste, or a common, which is wholly or partly situated within [an area which immediately before 1st April 1974 was] a borough or urban district, and to any land which at the commencement of this Act is subject to rights of common and to which this section may from time to time be applied . . . "[11]

(a) The land concerned

11.07 **(i) Metropolitan commons** The section is applied to all land which qualifies as a metropolitan common, *i.e.* any land subject to rights of common at the passing of the Metropolitan Commons Act 1866 and any land

---

[6] At Itchingwood Common, Surrey it seems that in the absence of any commoners and in view of the wish of the owner to crop the land an agreement was reached, and compensation paid, for the owner to crop only with hay and public access continued: *cf.* Clayden, *Our Common Land* (1985), p. 6; for the statutory provisions, see further § 11.34.

[7] See further §§ 11.37, 11.38.

[8] See §§ 11.31–11.33.

[9] See § 11.40 and Chapter 13.

[10] For the full text, see Appendix 3.

[11] The Act came into force on January 1, 1926, so most rights of access commenced on that date. The wording of the section, however, is such that any land which becomes or has become a qualifying "common" after that date still attracts rights of access. For what constitutes a "common," see § 11.11.

subject to be inclosed under the provisions of the Inclosure Act 1845,[12] the whole or part of which is situated within the Metropolitan Police District as defined at the passing of the Act of 1866.[13] The section, therefore, applies to all such land whether or not it is regulated under the Acts.

(ii) Urban and rural commons   Whether the remaining land defined   **11.08** in section 193 is included can only be ascertained by reference to local authority areas which no longer exist. In spite of some difficulties caused by the punctuation in the initial printing of the Act,[14] it is now clear that all manorial waste and commons, which are partly or wholly situated in the former borough or urban districts, are encompassed. These classes of land have become known as "urban commons" and those outside the requisite areas are frequently referred to as the "rural commons." To some extent these are misnomers for some of the urban commons are in rural areas, because of the extent of the former urban district and borough boundaries, and, conversely, some rural commons are now in built-up areas. Of particular note are the Lake District, which is largely composed of urban commons in spite of its open rural nature and, the indiscriminate mixture of rural and urban commons in South Wales depending on the now defunct local authority boundaries.

(iii) Dedicated rural commons   A lord of the manor or other owner of   **11.09** the soil may by revocable or irrevocable deed apply the section to a rural common which is subject to rights of common at the time of the execution of the deed.[15] Some 137 deeds were executed between 1926 and 1955, affecting some 118,500 acres.[16] Since 1956 a further 90 have been lodged with the Secretaries of State.[17] If a deed is subsequently revoked then the right of public access ceases. Revocation is unusual but not unknown.[18] A deed may only effectively be made in respect of land which is within the class for which dedication is possible. In *Att.-Gen.* v. *Brock Brothers (Transport) Ltd.* (1972)[19] a deed reciting that the lands were unenclosed wastes of a manor was considered: the Court of Appeal held that the land was not waste land of the manor and the deed of dedication had no effect.

(b) Definitions uncertain

(i) "manorial waste"   The term "manorial waste," used in the L.P.A   **11.10** 1925, is not defined nor seems to have been directly the subject of judicial interpretation. It has been shown earlier that the term "waste land of a manor," which has been judicially defined, has been viewed by the courts with some doubt which, put shortly, revolves round the question whether

[12] Metropolitan Commons Act 1866, s.3, as amended by the Metropolitan Commons Act 1869, s.2.
[13] See further § 12.34.
[14] The original printing of the L.P.A. 1925 omitted a comma after the words "or a common," thereby substantially changing the meaning. This has been repeated in some current printings. The text shows the correct punctuation.
[15] L.P.A. 1925, s.193(2); for a precedent see 7 Forms & Precedents (4th ed.) 125.
[16] Royal Commission Report, para. 93, Minutes of Evidence, pp. 37–38.
[17] See Appendix 9.
[18] For an example, see (1985) 22 O.S.S., Vol. 4, p. 6.
[19] (1972) (unreported); cited in *Re Badenhill Common, Tytherington, Avon* (1978) 13/D/9, 8 D.C.C. 79.

the land currently needs still to be parcel of a manor or alternatively whether it is sufficient for it to have its historical origin in waste of a manor.[20] The Court of Appeal ultimately held that waste land of a manor means land still held of the manor.[21] If the term "waste land of a manor" has such a marginal meaning today it seems not unreasonable to suggest that manorial waste has an ordinary meaning, whereby manorial is an adjectival description displaying the historical origin of waste land, much as industrial waste land might indicate its former use. Pending statutory or judicial interpretation this wider interpretation is to be preferred in order to effect the purpose of section 193, which was clearly intended to provide a right of public access to those open spaces in urban areas which have survived the inclosure movement. Argument in *R. v. Doncaster Metropolitan Borough Council, ex p. Braim* (1986)[22] seems to have proceeded on the assumption that "manorial waste" has the same meaning as "waste land of a manor" but nothing turned on it as the owners of the soil in that case were the lords of the manor.

11.11   **(ii) "a common"**   Similarly, the term "common" has no precise meaning and is more of a colloquial term than a term of art. It cannot be said that the wording of the section is of great assistance in elucidating the intention of the L.P.A. 1925. In section 193(1) access is granted to a "common" in an urban area and also to any "land subject to rights of common" which is dedicated to the section. In making provision, in the same subsection, for cessation of rights the reference is to "any land over which commonable rights are extinguished under any statutory provision." It is possible to infer that commonable rights can be distinguished from rights of common and that, as rights of common has a narrow technical meaning, commonable rights has a wider meaning. Perhaps it follows that commonable rights are exercisable over a common and the latter term includes land which is not strictly subject to rights of common.

11.12   At the time the L.P.A. 1925 was passed the immmediately preceding statutory definitions of the term "common" were in the Metropolitan Commons Act 1866 and the Commons Act 1876. In both a common is defined as land subject to be inclosed under the Inclosure Acts.[23] If this is the meaning of a common in section 193 all land subject to be inclosed is included and the only land, used agriculturally in common and still uninclosed, which falls outside the definition is land subject only to rights held under the owner of the soil.[24] However, even this land may subsequently fall within section 193 if at a date after 1925 it has become, or becomes, within the definition, for the Act provides that access applies to a common which *is* wholly or partly within the prescribed districts.

[20] See §§ 2.36 *et seq.*

[21] *Re Box Hill Common* [1980] Ch.109.

[22] (1987) 85 L.G.R. 233.

[23] Metropolitan Commons Act 1866, s.3; Commons Act 1876, s.37. In the Commons Act 1899 the definition was widened even further to include town and village greens: s.15. For the details of land subject to be inclosed, see § 1.33.

[24] *i.e.* where the common is grazed only by tenants of the owner.

(iii) Stinted pastures, common fields, regulated pastures If this **11.13**
view of the meaning of the term "common" is correct, stinted pastures and
common fields are within the ambit of the section but will not be subject to
the corresponding control provisions contained in the L.P.A. 1925, s.194.[25]
Lands which have been inclosed under the Inclosure Act 1845, and in this
connection the statutory regulated pastures are the most important lands in
point, are not included as they can hardly still be subject to be inclosed. The
same remark does not apply to regulated pastures established before 1845 as
they appear to be included within the definition of land subject to be
inclosed.[26]

(iv) Inconsistent wording in the Act It cannot be said that section **11.14**
193 or section 194 of the L.P.A. 1925 are worded in a wholly satisfactory
manner. Section 194 which was, at the least, designed to prevent works on
land subject to access under section 193 does not, for example, by its wording have any application to manorial waste.[27] There is, therefore, no inconsistency in suggesting that the term common in section 193 may include
land which is not subject to rights of common simply on the grounds that
some of the land will not be subject to control under section 194. Further
inconsistencies arise from the differential treatment of registered and
unregistered land under the C.R.A. 1965.[28]

(v) Difficulties for the public There are considerable difficulties in **11.15**
the way of members of the public wishing to ascertain which land is subject
to a right of access under section 193. Status depends upon historical local
authority boundaries; interpretation of the terms in the Act; deeds of dedication which may or may not be revocable; the correctness of a deed of dedication; and, not least, the boundaries of a common which may be
contiguous to, and unenclosed from, another common not subject to access.
When the status of the land may decide criminal liability for certain acts the
position can only be described as highly unsatisfactory.

(c) Excepted land

The section does not apply to any common or manorial waste which is for **11.16**
the time being held for the purposes of the Armed Forces and in respect of
which rights of common have been extinguished or cannot be exercised.[29]
The rights of any person to take minerals and to let down the surface of the
soil are not prejudiced or affected by the section.[30]

(d) Extinguishment

The rights of access cease to apply if the commonable rights are **11.17**
extinguished under any statutory provision or if the county council of the
area concerned by resolution assent to the exclusion of the land from the

---

[25] The section only applies to land subject to "rights of common" on January 1, 1926.
See further §§ 9.40 and 11.30.
[26] See the Inclosure Act 1845, s.11, cited at § 1.33.
[27] See § 9.40.
[28] See §§ 11.18 *et seq.*
[29] L.P.A. 1925, s.193(6).
[30] *ibid.* s.193(5).

section and the resolution is approved by the Secretary of State.[31] The most frequent occasion for the section to be set aside will be where a compulsory purchase order is in effect which includes a statutory extinguishment of commonable and other rights. It is, however, not unknown for a council resolution to be passed excepting land from the provisions of sections 193 and 194.[32] Such a resolution is unlikely to be passed unless the land is required for some publicly beneficial purpose.

(e) Saving of the section in the Act of 1965

11.18   Section 21(1) of the C.R.A 1965 expressly provides that section 1(2)(*b*) of the Act (non-exercisability of unregistered rights) shall not affect the application of section 193 (and section 194) of the L.P.A. 1925 to any registered common land. This seems to be a cautious inclusion to preserve public access (and the control of works on common land) in the event that non-exercisability is deemed to be equivalent to extinguishment.[33]

11.19   Section 21 does not apply to land which did not achieve registration under the Act and, if non-exercisability can be equated with extinguishment, it might be possible to establish that the C.R.A. 1965 has extinguished commonable rights under a statutory provision, with a resulting termination of the right of public access. This is, however, to fly in the face of the express words of the Act of 1965 that unregistered rights are merely not exercisable. In the alternative, however, if non-exercisability is equivalent to extinguishment, it may be difficult in many cases to establish that rights have been extinguished for the inference to be drawn from non-registration might just as well be that the rights had been abandoned. In this event no rights existed for the extinguishment provision to work on.[34]

11.20   In *R. v. Doncaster Metropolitan Borough Council, ex p. Braim* (1986)[35] it was contended that any rights of public access derived from section 193 were extinguished because the land had not been registered under the C.R.A. 1965. The matter may not have been fully considered because the main purpose of the appellants was to establish that the land was held in trust as an open space to bring the land under the provisions of the Local Government Act 1972, s.123(2A)[36] and the court was able to find that public rights of recreation had existed before 1860. Nevertheless, McCullough J., in an *obiter dictum*, preferred the view that the existence of the saving provision in section 21(1) relating to registered land, provided a clear implication that rights of access were extinguished following non-registration of the land, to the argument that, once public rights had been granted in 1925,

---

[31] *ibid.* s.193(1), proviso (*d*).

[32] See Appendix 9.

[33] This was held to be the case in *Central Electricity Generating Board* v. *Clwyd County Council* [1976] 1 W.L.R. 151 at 155–156, *per* Goff J.

[34] The argument has equal application to s.194 of the L.P.A. 1925, for which, see §§ 9.34 *et seq.*, especially § 9.42.

[35] (1987) 85 L.G.R. 233.

[36] Which requires a local authority holding land on trust as an open space and intending to dispose of the land to advertise the proposal and consider any objections made to them.

express words in a succeeding statute were required for their extinguishment.[37]

It should be noticed that non-registration of land under the C.R.A. 1965 also **11.21** carries with it the provision, contained in section 1(2)(a), that, if the land was capable of being registered under the Act, it was henceforth deemed not to be common land. This does not, however, mean that all land unregistered under the C.R.A. 1965 is deemed to be of changed status. It is only land capable of registration under the Act, but unregistered, which is deemed not to be "common land." That is to say, that such land may no longer be registered as common land under the Act. There seems no reason why land which was not capable of registration under the Act should not retain the status of a "common" for the purposes of public access under the L.P.A. 1925 and under certain circumstances it almost certainly will. Consider, for example, land in an urban area which was subject to rights of common on January 1, 1926, was made subject to a right of access on that date, and over which all rights of common were abandoned before 1965. Neither of the circumstances prescribed in the L.P.A. 1925 for cessation of public rights subsist, namely a statutory extinguishment of rights or a resolution of the county council assenting to exclusion from the operation of section 193,[38] and the land, providing it is not also waste land of a manor, is not within the registrable categories of land under the C.R.A. 1965. Clearly, deeming the land not to be "common land" under the Act of 1965 has no effect because prior to the Act it was not common land as defined in the Act. The land seems to retain its status as "a common" for the purposes of the L.P.A. 1925. The same result occurs in the case of land which was waste land of a manor at the beginning of 1926 but which had lost its status as such before the registration periods under the C.R.A. 1965. Section 193 of the Act of 1925 is expressly worded so that rights of access apply only to land which *is* a metropolitan common, manorial waste or a common but it is clear that "common land" in the C.R.A. 1965 cannot be equated with "a common" or "manorial waste" in the L.P.A. 1925. There is no reason why land should not remain manorial waste or a common and not be "common land."

The matter cannot be considered completely settled, however, and there **11.22** must be considerable force in the argument that once Parliament had provided important public rights to certain land in 1925, subject only to highly restricted circumstances for cessation of those rights, of which non-registration of land for other purposes under a later statute were self-evidently not one, a clear intention from Parliament to terminate those rights is necessary. This is not evinced in the wording of the C.R.A. 1965.[39]

(f) The nature of the access

The section speaks of a right of public access for "air and exercise," an **11.23** expression which is undefined and not, it seems, subject to any definitive judicial interpretation. It may be contrasted with the usual provision in a provisional order confirmation Act under the Commons Act 1876 which

[37] [1987] 85 L.G.R. 240.
[38] See § 11.17.
[39] The C.R.A. 1965 merely states that "no rights of common shall be exercisable . . . unless they are registered . . . ": s.1(2)(b).

was likely to provide something in the nature of "a right of free access to the said common, and a privilege of playing games, and enjoying reasonable recreation thereon."[40] It is at least arguable that the right under section 193 is no more than to enter and walk upon the land—a species of *jus spatiandi*. There can be little doubt that the playing of games, in an organised event, is not included.

11.24   The main point of contention, currently, is whether exercise taken on horseback is permitted. The right to do so was at issue before the Divisional Court in *Miens* v. *Stone* (1985)[41] when a respondent appealed, by way of case stated, against a conviction for an offence contrary to a by-law made under sections 12 and 15 of the Open Spaces Act 1906. The offence was allegedly committed by riding a horse on common land which was subject to section 193 access. It was submitted that a right of access under section 193 imparts a right for any member of the public to ride a horse on any land to which access is given. Tudor Price J. was prepared to accept, without deciding, that, because access on horseback is not expressly excluded, the section confers such a right. While not founding his judgment on the point, Farquharson J., in the main judgment, dealt directly with the submission as follows:

> "I take the view that the terms of section 193(1), simply reading them as they stand and in the context of the proviso of that same sub-section, do not give a right to any member of the public to use a horse in enjoying or exercising the right of access for air and exercise."

The balance, on the basis of the two indeterminate views, is marginally in favour of the exclusion of horseback riding from the meaning of air and exercise,[42] but the question cannot be said to be decided.

11.25   **(i) General limitations on rights**   In respect of all land to which the section applies, any person who, without lawful authority, draws or drives any carriage, cart, caravan, truck or other vehicle, or camps, or lights fires on the land shall be guilty of an offence and is liable, on summary conviction, to a fine not exceeding level 1 on the standard scale.[43] The land may also be subject to a district council's good rule and government by-laws which have general application[44] and, any by-laws made for the regulation of the common or, under any statutory authority.[45]

11.26   **(ii) Orders of limitation**   The rights of access may, on application to the Secretary of State by the owner of the soil or any person entitled to commonable rights, be made subject to limitations and conditions as to the

---

[40] See the Commons Act 1876, cited at § 11.32.

[41] [1985] D.C., CO/1217/84, April 30, 1985; Lexis, Enggen Library, Cases.

[42] Marginally because Farquharson J. decided without founding his case on the point, while Tudor Price J. accepted without deciding. For an opposing view see Montgomery, *Note* [1985] Conv. 415. Access on horseback is allowed on the commons of Dartmoor: Dartmoor Commons Act 1985, s.10(1).

[43] L.P.A. 1925, s.193(4): fine increased and converted to a level on the standard scale by the Criminal Justice Act 1982, ss.37, 38 and 46.

[44] Local Government Act 1972, s.235(1).

[45] L.P.A. 1925, s.193(1), proviso (a); for examples, see the Wimbledon and Putney Commons Act 1871 (c.cciv), s.84 and *Miens* v. *Stone* (1985), above, n. 41.

exercise thereof.[46] The terms imposed are those which in the opinion of the Secretary of State are necessary or desirable for protecting the legal interests in the land, the land itself, and any object of historical interest from being injuriously affected.[47]

Such an order is known as an "Order of Limitations" and in its application **11.27** to particular land is variable in content. Among the matters usually considered for inclusion are prohibitions, without lawful authority, on removal of soil, minerals or turf; taking fish; discharging firearms or missiles; destroying, catching or attempting to take wild animals; permitting dogs to chase birds or animals or otherwise failing to keep dogs under control; permitting animals to graze; bathing; posting notices; training or exercising horses; holding any shows or exhibitions on the land; and erecting any temporary building or fence on the land.[48] Occasionally, an Order may modify the nature of access to part of the land. A recent Order restricted access to an area to be used as a golf course in the following terms: "that without lawful authority no person shall in or upon the land (i) play or attempt to play golf on any portion of the common laid out as a golf course and (ii) loiter upon the greens, tees or bunkers, or wilfully obstruct any fairway."[49] Any person who fails to observe the limitations contained in an Order commits an offence and is liable to a fine not exceeding level 1 on the standard scale.[50] The general effect of an Order, apart from preventing access to certain sites, is to impose criminal liablity for a number of matters which would, otherwise, be subject only to civil action.

When an Order of Limitations is made the applicant shall publish the terms **11.28** in such a manner as the Secretary of State may direct.[51] This usually takes the form of a requirement to erect and maintain permanent notices on specified parts of the land in a prescribed form, which may include references to the relevant offences under the general law.[52]

It should perhaps be noticed that the control of activities under the L.P.A. **11.29** 1925 and the sanctions involved apply as much to commoners as to the general public unless a particular activity, otherwise forbidden, forms part of the lawful exercise of a right of common.

(g) Protection of the right

Protection lies primarily in the enforcement provision contained in section **11.30** 194 of the L.P.A. 1925. Under that section, in relation to land which was subject to rights of common on January 1, 1926, the erection of any building or fence, or the construction of any other work which prevents or impedes access is unlawful without the consent of a Minister.[53] Where any such

---

[46] L.P.A. 1925, s.193(1), proviso (b).

[47] *ibid.*

[48] From the set form of limitations prepared for the convenience of applicants by the Welsh Office.

[49] Maltby Far and Low Commons, Maltby, Near Rotherham: decision of the Secretary of State for the Environment; *cf.* (1987) 22 O.S.S. No. 8, p. 12.

[50] L.P.A.1925, s.193(4), and see above, n. 43.

[51] *ibid.* s.193(3).

[52] From notes for the guidance of applicants supplied by the Welsh Office.

[53] L.P.A. 1925, s.194(1). See further § 9.34.

works are carried out without consent, the county court shall, on the application of a county or district council, the lord of the manor or, any other person interested in the common, have power to make an order for the removal of the works and the restoration of the land to the condition in which it was before the works were carried out.[54] It should be noticed that the principal criterion for the section to have effect is that the land was subject to rights of common when the L.P.A. 1925 came into effect, *i.e.* January 1, 1926. It follows that any of the land affected by section 193 which was not subject to rights of common on that date is unaffected by section 194. Within this class is at least the category of manorial waste and possibly, depending upon the construction which is placed upon the term "common," all stinted and regulated pastures and some common fields.[55]

2. Metropolitan Commons Act 1866

11.31 This Act defined metropolitan commons with the primary intention of enabling schemes of regulation to be applied to them. By virtue of the provisions of section 193(1) of the L.P.A. 1925 a right of public access for air and exercise was applied to all metropolitan commons whether or not regulated.

3. Commons Act 1876

11.32 Under the provisions of this Act any particular common may be regulated or inclosed following the enactment of a provisional order confirmation Act.[56] Frequently the confirmation Act will provide either a general, or a spatially limited right of access to the public or, perhaps more usually, to the inhabitants of the neighbourhood. A typical provision is:

> "That there be reserved to the inhabitants of Bishops Cleeve, Cheltenham, and the neighbourhood, a right of free access to the said Common, and a privilege of playing games, and enjoying reasonable recreation thereon, subject to such by-laws and regulations as may from time to time be made by the Conservators and confirmed by the Secretary of State."[57]

4. Commons Act 1899

11.33 A common may be regulated under this Act and brought within the control of a local authority. The form of a scheme is controlled under Regulations made by the Secretaries of State.[58] The model form of scheme contains the provision that:

> "The inhabitants of the neighbourhood shall have a right of free access

---

[54] L.P.A. 1925, s.194(2), and see § 9.51.

[55] Common fields may or may not be subject to rights of common: *cf.* § 1.65.

[56] See further § 12.43.

[57] Commons Regulation (Cleeve) Provisional Order Confirmation Act 1890 (c.lxxviii), Sched.

[58] Commons (Schemes) Regulations 1982 (S.I. 1982 No. 209). See further at Appendix 6.

to every part of the common and a privilege of playing games and of enjoying other kinds of recreation thereon, subject to any bye-laws made by the Council under this Scheme."[59]

5. National Parks and Access to the Countryside Act 1949

Under this Act public access to land for open air recreation may be provided **11.34** through the medium of an agreement with the owner of the land or by the application of an access order.[60] The provisions apply to "open country," which means any area appearing to a local authority to consist wholly or predominately of mountain, moor, heath, down, cliff or foreshore.[61] A high proportion of the common lands fall within the meaning of open country but it seems that only a small number of agreements, and possibly no orders, have been made in respect of them.[62] Where there is already *de facto* access they have but little practical advantage except inasmuch as the status of the entrant to the land is changed to that of a lawful visitor from, prima facie, that of a trespasser.

(a) Entrants not treated as trespassers

Where an agreement or order is in effect, a person who enters the land for **11.35** the purpose of open-air recreation without breaking or damaging any wall, fence, hedge or gate, or who is on the land having so entered, shall not be treated as a trespasser thereon or incur any other liability by reason only of so entering or being on the land.[63] It will be noticed that the mode and purpose of entry qualifies the right and effectively changes the status from that of trespasser to that of lawful entrant. The sanction for failure to comply with the conditions is to restore the possibility of an action in trespass rather than to impose criminal liability (although, of course, damage to property may create liability for an offence under the Criminal Damage Act 1971[64]). The status of lawful entrant under the National Parks and Access to the Countryside Act 1949 does not import the status of visitor for the purposes of the Occupiers' Liability Act 1957.[65]

(b) Restrictions on activities

The same sanction of re-imposed liability for an action in trespass is **11.36** incurred for non-compliance with a list of restrictions on activities contained in the Second Schedule to the Act.[66] The restrictions are similar in nature to those imposed by an Order of Limitations made under section 193 of the L.P.A. 1925,[67] which incorporates liability for a criminal action for

---

[59] *ibid.* Sched., art. 4.
[60] National Parks and Access to the Countryside Act 1949, Pt. V, especially ss.59, 64, 65.
[61] *ibid.* s.59(2)
[62] *cf.* Royal Commission Report, para. 94.
[63] National Parks and Access to the Countryside Act 1949, s.60(1).
[64] See § 11.52.
[65] Occupiers Liability Act 1957, s.1(4), cited at § 8.50.
[66] For which see Appendix 4.
[67] See § 11.26.

the breach thereof. To many owners of common lands access through a revocable deed under section 193, coupled with criminal sanctions under an Order of Limitations, might seem preferable to an access agreement under the National Parks and Access to the Countryside Act 1949, with civil remedies for breach of the conditions. However, the Act of 1949 has the added incentive for the persons interested in the land, whether as owners or otherwise, that compensation payments may be made.[68]

Local Acts

(a) Acts for particular commons

11.37 There is a substantial number of local Acts dealing expressly with one common or a group of commons. They may or may not provide a right of public access and each must be examined to discover the particular terms. One of the earliest Acts to provide a right in the public to enjoy common land as an open space for recreation was the Epping Forest Act 1878.[69] This may be contrasted with the duty imposed on conservators under the Wimbledon and Putney Commons Act 1871 "to keep the commons for ever open and unenclosed and unbuilt on . . . and to preserve the same for public and local use, for the purposes of exercise and recreation."[70] This is not unequivocally a legal right vested in the public but it is of much the same effect.

(b) Water undertakings

11.38 During the second half of the nineteenth century, and into the twentieth century, the larger local authorities sought and were granted compulsory powers to purchase substantial upland areas for use as water catchment areas. To control pollution they frequently also sought control of the land and the exclusion of the public. Under the Manchester Corporation Waterworks Act 1879, however, the corporation was prohibited from restricting or interfering with "the access heretofore actually enjoyed on the part of the public and tourists to mountains and fells surrounding Lake Thirlmere."[71] Land controlled by water authorities may or may not be common land or statutory common land. An example of land which is neither, although subject to extensive rights of grazing in common by tenants of the Welsh Water Authority, is 45,000 acres of land near Rhayader in mid-Wales in the Elan and Claerwen valleys. The land was acquired under the Birmingham Corporation Water Act 1892, which provides the public with:

> " . . . a privilege at all times of enjoying air exercise and recreation on such parts of any common or unenclosed land acquired by the Corporation . . . [in the catchment area] whether any common or commonable rights in or over such lands shall have been acquired or relinquished under the provisions of the Act or not . . . "[72]

---

[68] National Parks and Access to the Countryside Act 1949, ss.64(2), 70.

[69] (41 & 42 Vict. c.ccxiii), s.9.

[70] (34 & 35 Vict. c.cciv), preamble and s.34. However, s.103 preserved the land as a metropolitan common under the Metropolitan Commons Act 1866 and the L.P.A. 1925, s.193(1) provided a right of access to metropolitan commons.

[71] s.62.

[72] s.53.

The Welsh Water Authority sought before the High Court to establish that **11.39** some limited fencing and reseeding to extend the area of uneconomic inbye lands did not infringe this provision. It was held that any fencing or ploughing of the land would offend the section.[73]

(c) Recreational allotments

Where an allotment has been made under the Inclosure Acts for exercise **11.40** and recreation it is necessary to examine the particular award to discover the exact terms. It is likely, in the case of an allotment since the Inclosure Act 1845, to be in the form of the words in the Act: " . . . an allotment for the purposes of exercise and recreation for the inhabitants of the neighbourhood."[74]

(d) Dartmoor commons

The most notable recent addition to the right of public access, through the **11.41** means of a local Act, is contained in the Dartmoor Commons Act 1985 which provides a right of access to all commons registered finally under the C.R.A. 1965 and situate in the area of Dartmoor. This right of access is peculiar inasmuch as it includes expressly a right to take exercise on horseback.[75]

National Trust Acts

The Trust is under a statutory duty to keep common lands unenclosed and **11.42** unbuilt upon as open spaces for the recreation and enjoyment of the public.[76] The Acts, however, contain no express grant of rights of access to the public. It is the practice of the Trust to allow, and encourage, public access to common lands but an officer of the Trust has stated that it has never been admitted that there is a *de jure* right of access.[77] It seems that the Trust has not been in the practice of dedicating common land to access under the provisions contained in section 193 of the L.P.A. 1925. The general public is entitled to use Trust owned common lands as places for recreation without fear of being treated as trespassers, subject to by-laws imposed by the Trust, but may not object if restrictions are imposed upon the access. Recreation on Trust land probably does not include the playing of games or holding meetings or gatherings for athletic sports for there are special provisions in the National Trust Act 1907 allowing common land to be set aside for these purposes.[78]

---

[73] *Welsh Water Authority* v. *Paul Clayden* (1984) (unreported), Ch.D., January 13, 1984, before Whitford J.

[74] Inclosure Act 1845, s.30; see further at §§ 13.09 *et seq.*

[75] Dartmoor Commons Act 1985, s.10. See further at § 12.106.

[76] See further § 12.128.

[77] Workman, "The National Trust Experience," in *the Future of Common Land and its Management*, Open Spaces Society (1983), p. 26.

[78] See § 12.125.

Proposals for a general right of access

11.43   The Common Land Forum Report recommends that future legislation should provide for a right of public access to all statutory common land from an appointed date, which shall be not more than five years after the passing of the Act.[79] The purpose of the delay is to allow time for management schemes, incorporating public access, to be formulated. One of the duties of a management association for a "grazing common" shall be the promotion of access to it for the purpose of quiet enjoyment.[80] Any access authorised under a scheme, affecting land already subject to section 193 of the L.P.A. 1925, must not limit the access already in existence.[81]

(a) Nature of access

11.44   The public access proposed is to be defined as "a right of access to common land by persons on foot for the purpose of quiet enjoyment."[82] A model scheme of management must allow casual, informal and local horse-riding on commons where it already occurs, subject to regulation, and elsewhere may permit such horse-riding at its discretion.[83]

(b) Control of dogs

11.45   On amenity commons, not used for grazing, dogs shall be kept under proper control.[84] On commons used for grazing and/or the preservation of game any person who takes a dog there or allows it to enter and remain shall prevent it from disturbing, worrying or chasing any bird or animal and shall keep it on a leash.[85]

(c) Compensation for legal interests

11.46   The Common Land Forum Report includes a recommendation that, where the public's access adversely affects the other lawful uses to which the common may be put, central government should make funds available for the payment of compensation to owners of the land and holders of rights.[86]

Public rights and the common law

(a) Presumed dedication

11.47   Until recently it had been generally assumed that the public could not acquire a *jus spatiandi* over privately owned land.[87] The reasoning behind this view is not altogether convincing, for if an owner of land can dedicate

---

[79] Common Land Forum Report, para. 4.2.
[80] *ibid.* para. 4.11.
[81] *ibid.* para. 4.24.
[82] *ibid.* para. 2.8.
[83] *ibid.* para. 4.17.
[84] *ibid.* para. 4.35 (i).
[85] *ibid.* para. 4.35 (ii).
[86] *ibid.* para. 4.38.
[87] See *Att.-Gen.* v. *Antrobus* [1905] 2 Ch. 188 at 189, *per* Farwell J.; approved in *Re Ellenborough Park* [1956] Ch. 131 at 144, *per* Danckwerts J. and at 182–184, *per* Evershed M.R.

land to public access there seems no reason why a dedication should not be presumed from long user.[88] This seems to have been the conclusion reached in *R.* v. *Doncaster Metropolitan Borough Council, ex p. Braim* (1986),[89] when McCullough J. held that Doncaster Common constituted an open space within the meaning of section 123(2A) of the Local Government Act 1972. Use by the public before 1860 had not been on sufferance and the owners, the Council, had never asserted a right to end the user. The only factual inference to be drawn was that from some date prior to 1860 the public had used the common for recreation as of right. Had an express grant of the rights claimed been produced the law would have recognised their validity and, further, the law allowed the court to presume that some time before 1860 they had been validly granted.

(b) Customary rights of access[89a]

Distinguishable from rights in the general public are customary rights exercisable by members of a local community. For a custom to be recognised it must be ancient, certain, reasonable and continuous.[90] In most cases where it has been possible to establish a customary right there are usually two distinct features involved: they have been limited to a particular close and a particular activity. Examples of successful claims are to hold a fair or wake,[91] dance round a maypole,[92] dry fishing nets,[93] enter one day for horse racing[94] and dance on a close at all times of the year.[95] One, of a more general nature, held good was a custom for "all inhabitants of a parish to play at all kinds of lawful games, sports and pastimes in the close of A, at all seasonable times of the year at their free will and pleasure."[96] A difficulty confronting any further claims to such customary rights is that the C.R.A. 1965 required registration of town and village greens, which, *inter alia*, are defined as "land . . . on which the inhabitants of any locality have a customary right to indulge in lawful sports or pastimes."[97] The result of not registering land in this category under the mandatory procedure, which ended in 1970, was that "no land capable of being registered . . . shall be deemed to be . . . a town or village green unless it is so registered."[98] However, although customary rights cannot now be claimed, if user continues there seems no reason why after twenty years a claim may not be made by the inhabitants of a locality based on that user instead of custom. The

11.48

[88] *cf. Goodman* v. *Mayor of Saltash* (1882) 7 App.Cas. 633: corporation entitled to a profit held on trust for the inhabitants.
[89] (1987) 85 L.G.R. 233.
[89a] Considered further at §§ 13.02 *et seq.*
[90] *Hammerton* v. *Honey* (1876) 24 W.R. 603, *per* Jessel M.R.
[91] *Wyld* v. *Silver* [1963] Ch. 243.
[92] *Hall* v. *Nottingham* (1875) 1 Ex.D. 1.
[93] *Mercer* v. *Denne* [1905] 2 Ch. 538; this right is not, of course, a general public right but resides only in those members of the public who are, or become, fishermen.
[94] *Mounsey* v. *Ismay* (1865) 1 H. & C. 729, 158 E.R. 1077.
[95] *Abbott* v. *Weekly* (1665) 1 Lev. 176, 83 E.R. 357.
[96] *Fitch* v. *Rawling* (1795) 2 H.Bl. 393, 126 E.R. 614; *cf. New Windsor Corporation* v. *Mellor* [1975] 1 Ch. 380; *contra*, as claim too uncertain, *Millechamp* v. *Johnson* (1746) Willes 205n, 125 E.R. 1133, *Edwards* v. *Jenkins* [1896] 1 Ch. 308 (doubted in the *New Windsor* case, above).
[97] C.R.A. 1965, s.22(1).
[98] *ibid.* s.1(2)(a).

C.R.A. 1965 does not require the registration of rights to indulge in lawful sports and pastimes and consequently has no effect on unregistered rights which may continue unabated—providing, of course, that they are not challenged in the meantime by the owner of the soil.[99]

(c) Private rights

11.49   There seems no reason in principle why a private right appurtenant to dominant land should not exist for access to land for exercise or recreation in the form of an easement. In *Re Ellenborough Park* (1955)[1] it was put thus by Evershed M.R.:

> "A *jus spatiandi* cannot be acquired by public user as an easement, and this is clearly so, if only for the reason that there can be no dominant tenement to which the easement could be said to be appurtenant. It does not necessarily follow from this, however, that no such *jus* could be acquired by individuals by prescription, and still less does it follow . . . that no such *jus* could be created in favour of an individual for the better enjoyment of his property by a grant which was express in its terms."[2]

An easement of this nature is unaffected by the provisions in the C.R.A. 1965.

Criminal offences on common land

11.50   There are a number of criminal offences which apply directly to common lands. At the same time the general law applies as much on the common lands as it does anywhere else. The offences apply to commoners as well as the public, unless they are excepted because the particular activity is in connection with the lawful exercise of rights over the land. It can be unusually difficult to discover which activities on common lands will attract criminal sanctions for all will depend upon the legal status of the particular common concerned. It has been demonstrated that a right of access may exist consequent upon various general and local Acts and, usually, by-laws for such commons will be in force. In addition, common land may also be subject to a district council's good rule and government by-laws which have general application. There is no uniform code of behaviour, or standard by-laws, applicable to all common land. A special complication arises when access is limited to "the inhabitants of the neighbourhood" for, apart from obscurity as to criminal liability, the civil status of an entrant may be in doubt.

(a) General law

11.51   There are a number of provisions in the general law of particular relevance to common lands. In considering any special provisions or by-laws affecting common lands it should always be borne in mind that they are additional to the general measures which are applicable.

---

[99] See further § 13.25.

[1] [1955] Ch. 131.

[2] *ibid.* at 183, but see 182–184

(i) Damage to property Damage to property on the common lands is   **11.52**
liable to be an offence under the provisions contained in the Criminal
Damage Act 1971. Section 1 makes it an offence for a person to destroy or
damage property belonging to another, and property belongs to a person if he
has a proprietary interest in it.[3] For the purposes of this Act, property does
not include mushrooms growing wild or the flowers, fruit or foliage of a
plant growing wild.[4] A plant includes a shrub or tree.[5] If the destruction is
done by fire the offence is to be charged as one of arson.[6] An offence under
the Criminal Damage Act 1971 is prima facie committed in the event of
damage or destruction of trees, saplings, gorse or underwood or setting fire
to heath, gorse or fern. Any other property on a common including notice
boards, seats, rubbish receptacles and any buildings, fences or equipment is
protected by the same provision.

(ii) Ancient monuments Under provisions contained in the Ancient   **11.53**
Monuments and Archaeological Areas Act 1979 any injury to, or disfigure-
ment of, any object of historical, scientific or antiquarian interest is an
offence and, if the object is recognised as an ancient monument any injury
or defacement of it will also be an offence.[7]

(iii) Plants and animals The Wildlife and Countryside Act 1981 con-   **11.54**
tains comprehensive provisions for the protection of birds, animals and
plants. It is an offence to kill or injure any wild bird, to take, damage or destroy nests or, to take or destroy eggs of any wild bird.[8] Certain animals *ferae
naturae* are protected.[9] Certain plants are listed[10] and it is an offence to
pick, uproot or destroy such plants.[11] In addition it is an offence for a person, not being an authorised person, to intentionally uproot any wild plant
which is not listed.[12]

(iv) Litter It is an offence under the Litter Act 1983 to deposit anything   **11.55**
in any place to which the public have access without payment which causes
or tends to cause defacement.[13] The penalty is a fine not exceeding level 3
on the standard scale.[14] It is also an offence to abandon on open land, or any
land forming part of a highway, a motor vehicle, part of a motor vehicle or
any thing.[15] A person who leaves any thing on the land, in circumstances in
which he may reasonably be assumed to have abandoned it, is deemed to
have abandoned it there.[16]

---

[3] Criminal Damage Act 1971, s.10(2).
[4] *ibid.* s.10(1)(*b*).
[5] *ibid.* s.10(1).
[6] *ibid.* s.1(3).
[7] Ancient Monuments and Archaeological Areas Act 1979, s.28.
[8] Wildlife and Countryside Act 1981, s.1(1).
[9] *ibid.* s.9.
[10] *ibid.* Sched. 8.
[11] *ibid.* s.13(1)(*a*).
[12] *ibid.* s.13(1)(*b*).
[13] Litter Act 1983, s.1. In sentencing regard must be had to the risk of injury to persons and animals: s.14.
[14] *ibid.* s.1(3).
[15] Refuse Disposal (Amenity) Act 1978, ss.2(1), 19(1).
[16] *ibid.* s.2(2).

11.56   **(v) Threatening, abusive or insulting behaviour** It is an offence, in a public or private place, to use threatening, abusive or insulting words or behaviour towards another person with intent to cause that person to believe that immediate unlawful violence will be used against him or another by any person or to provoke the immediate use of unlawful violence by that person.[17]

11.57   **(vi) Mass trespass** The Public Order Act 1986, s.39 attempts to deal with the problem of mass trespass, which has received much publicity in recent years and can often affect common land. A power is given to the senior police officer present to direct persons to leave land and, if a person fails to leave the land as soon as reasonably practicable or, having left the land, enters again as a trespasser within three months, he commits an offence. A person committing the offence is liable on summary conviction to imprisonment for a term not exceeding three months or, a fine not exceeding level 4 on the standard scale or, both.

11.58   A number of conditions must be satisfied before the section can be invoked:

(i) two or more persons must have entered as trespassers (the section, therefore, cannot be used against a person or persons who enter originally as licensees);

(ii) the senior police officer present must reasonably believe that the persons concerned are there with the common purpose of residing for any period; and

(iii) the same officer must reasonably believe that reasonable steps have been taken by or on behalf of the occupier of the land to ask the persons to leave (unreasonable steps involving, say, the use of any form of violence by the occupier probably vitiates the effect of the section).

11.59   In addition, one of three aggravating conditions is required:

(i) that the persons have caused damage to property on the land; or

(ii) that they have used threatening, abusive or insulting words or behaviour towards the occupier, a member of his family or an employee or agent; or

(iii) that the persons have between them brought twelve or more vehicles on to the land.

11.60   Certain definitions should be noticed. "Property" means property within the meaning of section 10(1) of the Criminal Damage Act 1971.[18] "Land" does not include buildings other than agricultural buildings or scheduled monuments. "Occupier" means the person entitled to possession of the land by virtue of an estate or interest held by him.[19] Commoners probably do not have a sufficient interest in possession to act in spite of their interest in the land by virtue of their rights of common. There is no reason, however, why the owner of the soil should not appoint commoners, or an association of commoners, to act on his behalf to take the reasonable steps necessary to

---

[17] Public Order Act 1986, s.4. See also the offence of causing harassment, alarm or distress contained in s.5.
[18] For which, see § 11.52.
[19] Public Order Act 1986, s.39(5) (definitions).

ask the persons trespassing to leave the land. Beneficial owners of regulated pastures, on the other hand, seem to have the necessary interest in possession. Local authorities, responsible for the protection of common land, by virtue of the provisions contained in section 9 of the C.R.A. 1965, clearly have power to act under section 39 of the Public Order Act 1986 as they "may take such steps for the protection of land against unlawful interference as could be taken by an owner in possession of the land."[20]

(b) Motor vehicles on common land

It is an offence under the Road Traffic Act 1972 to drive a motor vehicle, **11.61** without lawful authority, to or upon any common land, moorland or other land of whatever description not being land forming part of a road.[21] It is also an offence to take a motor vehicle on any road being a footpath or bridleway.[22] A person shall not be convicted of an offence if he proves, to the satisfaction of the court, that the vehicle was taken on the land for the purpose of saving life, extinguishing fire or meeting any other like emergency,[23] or if the motor vehicle is taken on land within 15 yards of a road for the purpose of parking only.[24] The latter exception does not create a right to take a vehicle on to land, nor does it provide a right to park there and a person entitled to any right or remedy in trespass is unaffected.[25] Further, the operation of any by-laws and section 193 of the L.P.A. 1925 are expressly saved.[26] Thus, a relatively law abiding citizen may take care not to drive more than 15 yards onto a common to avoid the offence under the Road Traffic Act 1972 only to find that an offence has been committed under section 193 of the L.P.A. 1925. The penalty for an offence under the Act of 1972 is an amount not exceeding level 3 on the standard scale.[27]

A further offence under the Road Traffic Act 1972 relates to heavy commer- **11.62** cial vehicles, which may not be parked wholly or partly on the verge of a road unless parked by permission of a constable in uniform or, it is placed there for the purpose of saving life, extinguishing fire or meeting any other like emergency or, for the purpose of loading or unloading.[28]

(c) Control of dogs

Of general application to agricultural land is the offence of worrying live- **11.63** stock created by section 1(1) of the Dogs (Protection of Livestock) Act 1953. "Worrying" is defined widely to include attacking, chasing as may be reasonably expected to cause injury or suffering and, in the case of females, abortion or loss or diminution in their produce.[29] "Livestock" means cattle,

[20] See further § 7.40.
[21] Road Traffic Act 1972, s.36(1).
[22] *ibid.*
[23] *ibid.* s.36(3).
[24] *ibid.* s.36(2).
[25] *ibid.* s.36(4).
[26] *ibid.*
[27] Criminal Justice Act 1982, ss.38, 46.
[28] Road Traffic Act 1972, s.36A (added by the Heavy Commercial Vehicles (Controls and Regulations) Act 1973, s.2(2)).
[29] Dogs (Protection of Livestock) Act 1953, s.1(2).

sheep, goats, swine, horses or poultry.[30] "Agricultural land" means land used as arable, meadow or grazing land[31] and therefore includes common lands used for grazing. The Minister may by order direct that the subsection shall not apply to an area consisting of mountain, hill, moor, heath or down land[32]: however, no order to this effect has been made at the time of writing. A person shall not be guilty of an offence if the livestock worried are trespassing at the time and, the dog is owned by, or in the charge of, the occupier of the land or a person authorised by him, unless the person causes the dog to attack the livestock.[33]

11.64   **(i) Deemed worrying**   The offence of actual worrying of livestock clearly has application to all the common lands used for grazing but, in addition, a second class of offence may arise if the particular land can also be classified as a field or enclosure. Section 1(2)(c) of the Dogs (Protection of Livestock) Act 1953 extends the meaning of worrying livestock on agricultural land to "being at large (that is to say not on a lead or otherwise under close control) in a field or enclosure in which there are sheep."[34] This deemed worrying provision does not apply to a dog of the owner or occupier of the field, the owner of the sheep or any person authorised by him, a police dog, a guide dog, a trained sheep dog, a working gun dog or a pack of hounds.[35] No proceedings may be brought under the Act except by or with the consent of the chief officer of police of the area concerned, the occupier of the land, or the owner of the livestock in question.[36] The maximum penalty for dogs worrying livestock under section 1 of the Act is a fine not exceeding level 3 on the standard scale.[37]

11.65   **(ii) Seizure by the police**   Where a dog is found on any agricultural land and a police officer has reasonable cause to believe that the dog has been worrying livestock on that land and no person is present who admits to being the owner or in charge of it, he may seize it and detain it until the owner has claimed it and paid the expenses of detention.[38] If the dog is not claimed it may be disposed of under the same conditions as are provided in the Dogs Act 1906, s.3(4)–(9).[39]

11.66   **(iii) Dartmoor commons**   For the purposes of the protection of livestock the Dartmoor Commons Act 1985 contains a provision which allows the Park Authority, following notices posted in such places on the commons as they think fit, to apply the Dogs (Protection of Livestock) Act 1953, s.1(2)(c) to the commons, or any part thereof specified in the notices, as if the commons, or that part, were a field or enclosure.[40]

---

[30] Dogs (Protection of Livestock) Act 1953, s.3(1); cattle, horses and poultry are further defined.
[31] *ibid.*; land is further defined for additional purposes not relevant here.
[32] *ibid.* s.5.
[33] *ibid.* s.1(3).
[34] *ibid.*: added by the Wildlife and Countryside Act 1981, s.12 and Sched. 7, para. 3.
[35] *ibid.* s.1(2A).
[36] *ibid.* s.2(1).
[37] See the Criminal Justice Act 1982, s.37(1), (2).
[38] Dogs (Protection of Livestock) Act 1953, s.2(2).
[39] *ibid.* s.2(3), as amended by the Police Act 1964, s.64(3), Sched. 10, Pt. I.
[40] Dartmoor Commons Act 1985, s.10(6).

(iv) Civil actions for damage to livestock Where a dog has caused   **11.67**
damage to livestock the owner may bring an action for damages against the
owner[41] and he may also take direct action for the protection of livestock.[42]

(v) Proposals for reform The Common Land Forum Report recom-   **11.68**
mends an increased right of public access to the common lands but accom-
panies that recommendation with a requirement for more stringent control
than before in respect of dogs taken to the common lands.[43]

---

[41] See further § 10.62.
[42] See further § 10.69.
[43] See § 11.43.

12. Management

12.01   The management of the common lands is a complex task when a substantial number of persons are capable of acting independently in pursuit of their individual rights over the land of some other person. Achieving a particular management target under these circumstances frequently depends upon an agreement among all the parties concerned and, more often than not, this is not forthcoming. It follows that on the common lands it is usually necessary to have statutory support to compel compliance. There are a number of general statutory provisions which do provide regulatory powers directly for various classes of the common lands. In addition a significant number of local Acts have been passed which provide powers related to particular areas of common land. Of particular importance in this category is the Dartmoor Commons Act 1985, which not only regulates a high proportion of the common lands in Devon but also, possibly, indicates the way in which management will develop in the future. Finally there are a number of statutes not primarily directed at common land but which have a part, albeit somewhat indirectly, in the management of common lands through control of specified activities.

12.02   Arguably the most widespread form of management over the majority of the area of the common lands, however, is through various forms of local, and mainly informal, associations of persons interested in the land. These are frequently known as commoners' or graziers' associations. They suffer from the disadvantage of being unable to bind dissenting minorities. In spite of this many have developed and improved common lands, particularly in relation to fencing and the provision of cattle grids. Suffering from the same disadvantage of lack of coercive power are the remnants of the manorial courts.

STATUTORY MANAGEMENT

General Management Acts

1. Inclosure Act 1773

12.03   The Inclosure Act 1773 is primarily directed towards the improved management of common arable fields which form but a tiny minority of the common lands. This part of the Act is virtually obsolete. There are some provisions affecting common meadows, stinted pastures and wastes and, although these might be expected to be of some assistance today, they seem not to have been invoked in modern times.

(a) Enforcement

The Act largely works on the principle of specified majority agreements **12.04**
being enforcable at law providing the agreement is entered into in a prescribed manner.[1] Thus, enforcement depends upon civil actions between
the parties concerned. Where rules and regulations have been agreed the
owners and occupiers of land in common fields may bring an action in trespass or case[2] against any person breaching the regulations prescribed, in
which the offending party shall answer in damages to the aggrieved party.[3]

(b) Open and common fields

The most comprehensive part of this Act deals with open and common **12.05**
fields, by which are meant the composite of open arable fields and common
grass fields, used in severalty for part of the year and grazed in common for
the remainder. Open arable fields are virtually unknown today but there are
several examples still in existence of common meadows.

The general scheme is that, where three-quarters of the occupiers[4] agree, **12.06**
the open arable lands may be "ordered, fenced, cultivated and improved" in
accordance with an acceptable plan,[5] providing that any such plan shall not
last for longer than six years or two rounds[6] of crops, whichever is the
lesser.[7] The participators, with the same majority agreeing, are also empowered to postpone the opening times of the fields for common grazing, determine how long the fields shall remain open, and regulate the stints of
livestock which may be grazed.[8]

Detailed provisions allow for the removal of balks, meers and slades,[9] sub- **12.07**
ject to the retention of roadways,[10] with other land to be used in common
allocated in exchange.[11] Where balks are removed stone boundary markers
shall be inserted in their place.[12] Common grazing may be suspended with
each occupier enjoying his grazing in severalty.[13]

The rights of grazing enjoyed by cottagers with no land in the fields[14] and **12.08**
the graziers of sheepwalks[15] are protected by providing that they shall enjoy

---

[1] ss.24, 26.
[2] Now commenced by a writ of summons indorsed with a statement of the nature of
the claim made; see R.S.C., Ord. 6, r. 2.
[3] s.26.
[4] In all cases tenant occupiers require the consent in writing of their landlords: s.25.
[5] s.1.
[6] Round = a single rotation of crops.
[7] s.2.
[8] s.7.
[9] s.11. The unploughed land between the strips in an open field are known variously
as balks, meers and slades. Sometimes the unploughed strips also form access ways
round and through the fields.
[10] s.12.
[11] s.13.
[12] s.14.
[13] s.9.
[14] s.8.
[15] s.10. In this context "sheepwalk" is probably a synonym for a foldcourse; for which
see § 3.116.

the rights as fully as before unless agreeing to an annual payment or advantage in lieu. Where the pre-existing common grazing is to be enjoyed in severalty the cottagers, or a majority of those who have not accepted compensation, may accept an equivalent piece of land upon which they may continue to enjoy their rights of common.[16]

12.09 A field master or reeve shall be appointed annually to supervise the scheme and there is power to finance expenditure by a levy on occupiers, which is recoverable on default by distress and sale.[17]

12.10 The provision for postponing the opening times of fields, determining how long the fields shall remain open and regulating stints seems to have application to common meadows as much as to arable lands.[18]

(c) Wastes

12.11 Drainage, fencing and other improvements to a waste may be effected by a lord of the manor[19] by raising a sum of money from a demise of part of the waste, not exceeding a twelfth part for a period of not more than four years. To be lawful three-quarters of the persons having rights of common must agree to the demise and one-half of the lord's tenants must agree the method of improvement.[20]

(d) Stinted commons

12.12 An alternative to leasing part of the waste exists for those manors which include stinted pastures. At a properly constituted meeting, one-half of the stintholders present and the lord may agree to levy an assessment on the lord, and all the stintholders, for the same purposes of drainage, fencing and other improvements.[21] The inclusion of the lord of the manor in the provision is sufficient to prevent regulated pastures from being affected, and the section can only apply to the stinted pasture of the sole rights nature.[22]

12.13 A second provision relates to "stinted commons of pasture," which are never enjoyed in severalty but are shut up for certain times of the year. A majority in numbers and value of stintholders at a properly constituted meeting may, with the consent of the lord, his steward or agent, agree to postpone the opening of the pastures for not more than 21 days.[23] Again the regulated pastures seem to be unaffected.

12.14 Thirdly, there is a provision allowing two-thirds in number and value of commoners, with the consent of the lord of the manor or his steward or agent, to direct in any year a closed grazing period.[24] Dissenters to the

---

[16] s.9.
[17] ss.3, 4, 5, 6.
[18] s.7.
[19] Note, not any other owner of the soil.
[20] s.15.
[21] s.16; note that in the sections relating to stinted commons it is the lord of the manor who is mentioned and not any other owner of the soil.
[22] For which see §§ 3.90 *et seq.*
[23] s.17.
[24] s.18.

arrangement may require the setting apart of a portion of a common for their own use.[25] The land to which these provisions apply is described as "common pastures, with stinted or limited rights therein, which are open the whole year." It seems that the usual form of stinted pasture is included together with any common field where the rights are fixed. Thus a town common, for example, where inhabitants have a fixed allowance of right, will be within the ambit of the section.[26]

(e) Commonable animals variation

Provision is made for holders of rights of common in "stinted common pas- **12.15** tures" to vary the classes of animals grazed from horses, beasts or neat cattle only to allow the grazing of sheep.[27] This provision must be considered to have been impliedly overruled by section 15 of the C.R.A. 1965.

(f) Inclosure of strips

There is a saving provision for the customary right, where it exists, to **12.16** inclose strips.[28] The customary right can only apply where there are no rights of common exercisable by persons without land in the fields.[29] As has already been suggested, such land is not properly registrable under the C.R.A. 1965 as statutory common land.[30] Also, the land is not subject to the provisions of section 194 of the L.P.A. 1925 as it is not land which was subject to rights of common on January 1, 1926.[31] It follows that the customary right of inclosure survives to the present day and is not affected by either the L.P.A. 1925 or the C.R.A. 1965. However, if the land has been registered under the Act of 1965, section 10 provides conclusive evidence that at the time of registration it was subject to rights of common. There seems no reason why the land should not be enclosed under the custom and an application for removal of the land from the commons registers sustained on the grounds that the land has ceased to be subject to such rights.

(g) Control of rams

One general provision affects wastes and common fields. There is an unqua- **12.17** lified prohibition on turning rams to, or suffering them to remain upon, such land between August 25 and November 25 in every year.[32] For many years, under powers contained in the Hill Farming Act 1946,[33] the Minister of Agriculture made, and still may make, regulations for the control of rams and uncastrated ram lambs on designated land, which was defined as land not fenced in such a way as to prevent rams from straying between flocks in different ownerships. The regulations applied to most of the common lands, and provided a licensing system for approved animals to be turned out for

[25] s.19.
[26] e.g. R. v. Churchill (1825) 4 B. & C. 750, 107 E.R. 1240.
[27] s.20.
[28] s.27.
[29] §§ 1.29 and 1.70.
[30] § 2.33.
[31] § 9.40.
[32] s.21.
[33] s.18 as extended by the Livestock Rearing Act 1951, s.7.

specified periods.[34] While the regulations were in force it seems that the ban contained in the Inclosure Act 1773 was impliedly, and temporarily, over-ruled by a later provision authorising what would be otherwise unlawful. Since the revocation of the Regulations[35] it seems that the Act of 1773 is now effective to provide a total ban on turning out rams in the specified period. There is no provision in the Act of 1773 for any enforcement which must depend upon civil action by a person aggrieved by a breach of the section concerned.

2. Inclosure Act 1845

12.18 The main thrust of the Inclosure Act 1845 was towards the inclosure of wastes and common fields. Included within the provisions for an inclosure award is further statutory recognition of the practice under the older private inclosure Acts of throwing together smaller allotments into one enclosure and allowing continued grazing in common, by the allottees, of an appropriate stint of animals. This class of the common lands is known here as a regulated pasture and, recognising the added refinements for management available through the Inclosure Act 1845, a regulated pasture awarded under that Act is known as a statutory regulated pasture.

12.19 The management provisions available for an ordinary regulated pasture depend upon the particular inclosure award and can only be ascertained by study of that award.[36] The statutory regulated pasture awarded under the Inclosure Act 1845, on the other hand, provides directly applicable statutory powers of management. In this section it is those powers under the Act of 1845 which are considered.

(a) The award of a regulated pasture

12.20 On receiving a request from persons whose interests exceed one-half in value of the whole interest in the land to be allotted, the Inclosure Commissioners are empowered to direct that the land, or part of it, be converted into a regulated pasture to be stocked and grazed in common by the persons specified in an award.[37] The incentive for seeking this option is self-evident—allotments may be of less value than the cost of fencing them individually.[38]

12.21 The nature of a regulated pasture is not a redistribution of common land for it is an allotment "to be in full bar of and satisfaction and compensation for . . . rights of common."[39] Rights of common are extinguished and an entirely new form of land and tenure is created.

---

[34] See the Control of Rams Regulations 1952 (S.I. 1952 No. 1800).

[35] See the Control of Rams Regulations (Revocation) Regulations 1981 (S.I. 1981 No. 892).

[36] Some regulated pastures are derived from direct grant by a lord and have no statutory basis.

[37] s.113.

[38] See the Brecknock Forest Acts 1815 and 1818 for an example where an award into severalties was found too expensive to effect.

[39] ss.106, 114.

In establishing a regulated pasture the valuer making the award is required **12.22** to set out the land to be used, ascertain and allot the stints or rights of pasturage to each allottee, specifying the animals which may be grazed and, if he thinks fit, the period during the year when the animals may be kept on the pasture.[40]

(b) Fencing

The valuer is also required in his award to direct how and at whose expense **12.23** the pasture shall be fenced from other land.[41] Such fences ordered to be erected "shall for ever afterwards be repaired and maintained by such persons as the valuer shall direct."[42] It follows that in the case of these pastures there is no room for the customary obligation to fence against a common.[43] It is a statutory offence wilfully or maliciously to damage a fence (or any other work) directed to be erected by a valuer.[44] The obligation to maintain the fences survives so long as the regulated pasture remains in being.

(c) Property in the soil

The valuer is required to determine the proportionate liability of each stin- **12.24** tholder in respect of any rate raised at the time of the inclosure or any rate raised thereafter.[45] It is the proportionate value of the rate ascribed to each allottee which provides the value of the stint taken into account in any voting procedures required in management.[46] The ownership of the pasture is vested in the stintholders in proportion to their share of the total rate,[47] in undivided shares. Since 1925, the legal estate to land may not be held in undivided shares[48] and in most cases today the legal estate is vested in the Public Trustee.[49]

(d) Management

Wide powers of management and control are vested in the stintholders and **12.25** are exercisable by the majority in value of those persons present at an annual general meeting. The powers include—

    (i) regulating the times when stock are admitted to, and excluded from the pasture;

    (ii) the maintenance, or the provision, of fences, ditches, drains, watercourses, embankments, jetties and weirs;

    (iii) the erection and maintenance of buildings on the pasture for the

---

[40] s.113.
[41] *ibid.*
[42] s.83.
[43] *cf.* §§ 9.28 *et seq.*
[44] Inclosure Act 1848, s.10; the maximum penalty is level 1 on the standard scale: Criminal Law Act 1977, s.31(6); Criminal Justice Act 1982, s.46.
[45] s.115.
[46] *ibid.*
[47] s.116.
[48] L.P.A. 1925, s.1(6), s.39(4), Sched. 1, Pt. IV, para. 1(1), Sched. 1, Pt. V, para. 2 (application of the Act to undivided shares in land). The Act is of no effect if the legal estate was vested in trustees before January 1, 1926.
[49] *cf.* §§ 7.87 *et seq.*

shelter or stall-feeding of stock with power to let them from year to year at a rent[50];

(iv) the right to disburse the residue of rents, after paying annual expenses, to the owners of stints in proportion to their respective liability for rates[51]; and

(v) the making of by-laws and regulations for the prevention of, or protection from, nuisances or for keeping order on the pasture, and for general management, occupation and enjoyment of the pasture, provided that the consent of the lord and confirmation by the Secretary of State are obtained.[52]

(e) Appointment of reeves

12.26 The major part in value of stintholders present at an initial meeting shall elect a field reeve or reeves and "shall ever after the first meeting meet for the election of a field reeve or reeves on the first Monday in February in every year." The reeve may appoint such herds and assistants as he thinks fit.[53] A certificate in writing under the hands and seals of two justices of the peace shall be evidence of appointment of a reeve.[54] The appointed reeve is empowered to put into effect the decisions of the stintholders in annual meeting.[55]

(f) Regulation of stints

12.27 When it appears to the majority in values of the owners of the stints present at annual meeting that it is expedient to do so, they may direct that the stints shall be increased or diminished rateably.[56]

(g) Financial contributions

12.28 All salaries and expenses incurred in managing the pasture are payable from time to time by a rate leviable on the stintholders in proportion to their rateable interest in the pasture. The rates are payable to the reeve on demand; if unpaid, after 14 days have elapsed, the reeve may exclude the stock of any owner or his tenant from the pasture until the arrear is fully paid; and any demand or distress may be made on the occupier of a stint as if he were the owner.[57] Any money so paid by an occupier is deemed to be a payment of rent on account and shall be allowed by the landlord accordingly.[58] It should be noticed that the rights and obligations under the Inclosure Act 1845 fall to the owner of the stint, not the occupier.

---

[50] s.118.
[51] *ibid.*
[52] Commons Act 1876, ss.15, 16, 17; "skirts" in s.15 must be a misprint for "stints." The consent of the lord of the manor to the making of by-laws seems today to be somewhat anachronistic.
[53] Inclosure Act 1845, s.117.
[54] *ibid.*
[55] s.118.
[56] s.119.
[57] s.120.
[58] *ibid.*

(h) Penalties

The reeve may distrain all stock and animals found on the pasture in contra- **12.29** vention of any regulations.[59] Unlike the distress for non-payment of rent, distraint for contravention of regulations seems to be distress damage feasant which has now been abolished.[60] Detention under the Animals Act 1971 now seems more appropriate, with the reeve viewed as the authorised agent of the owners and occupiers of the stints.[61]

It is a statutory offence for any person to have any stock or animals on any **12.30** regulated pasture contrary to the regulations of the pasture,[62] and is punishable on summary conviction by a fine, not exceeding the current amount at level 1 on the standard scale, in respect of each head of stock found on the pasture.[63] The penalty for any breach of the by-laws is a penalty not exceeding level 1 on the standard scale.[64] Further, as we have seen,[65] it is an offence to damage fences directed to be erected by a valuer in the allotment award.

(i) Deemed regulated pastures

The Inclosure Act 1857 allows Inclosure Commissioners to make an award **12.31** without requiring allotments to be fenced on the boundary, or otherwise, and instead to direct that they shall be known by metes and bounds.[66] In this event the land is held in divided shares unenclosed one from another. Such allotments are deemed to be regulated pastures[67] provided, nevertheless, that any person interested in an allotment may at any time fence the same at his own expense.[68]

(j) Commons Registration Act 1965

As discussed above,[69] statutory regulated pastures are not properly regis- **12.32** tered under the C.R.A. 1965. Many have been registered and currently attract the conclusive evidence provision in that Act.[70] It is clear that section 15 of the C.R.A. 1965, which limits the number of animals which may be grazed over registered common land, is incompatible with section 119 of the Inclosure Act 1845, which allows stintholders to increase the number of animals which may be grazed. The deemed regulated pastures of the Inclosure Act 1857 seem even more inappropriate for registration under the C.R.A. 1965 when there is a reserved right for each owner to withdraw from

---

[59] s.118.
[60] Animals Act 1971, s.7(1).
[61] cf. §§ 10.14 et seq.
[62] Inclosure Act 1852, s.33.
[63] Statute Law Revision (Substituted Enactments) Act 1876, s.1; Criminal Law Act 1977, s.31(6); Criminal Justice Act 1982, s.46.
[64] Commons Act 1876, s.16; Criminal Justice Act 1982, ss.40,46.
[65] § 12.23.
[66] Inclosure Act 1857, s.1.
[67] s.2.
[68] s.1.
[69] §§ 2.30–2.32.
[70] s.10.

the arrangement at any time. There is some small amount of empirical evidence that deemed pastures have been registered.[71]

(k) Dealing in the legal estate

12.33   Where the legal estate to the land has become vested in the Public Trustee[72] on the statutory trusts the trusts may only be executed with the consent of the court. Any person interested in the trust may apply to the court for an order declaring the rights and interests effective under the Act and the court may make an order as it thinks fit.[73]

3. Metropolitan Commons Act 1866

12.34   The Metropolitan Commons Act 1866 applies to any common, as defined,[74] which is situated within the Metropolitan Police District as defined at the passing of the Act.[75] Such commons are known as metropolitan commons.[76] Apart from management of metropolitan commons, the Act also completely prohibits any metropolitan common, or part of a common, being included in an inclosure award.[77] Further, irrespective of whether a management scheme has been established, all the metropolitan commons are subject to a right of public access for air and exercise under the provisions in section 193 of the L.P.A. 1925.[78] Thirty-three schemes of management have been approved under the Act.[79]

(a) Promotion of a scheme

12.35   A scheme for the local management of a metropolitan common may be made on a memorial presented to the Secretary of State by the lord of the manor, any commoners, the local authority (as defined[80])[81] or 12 or more ratepayers, inhabitants of the parish or parishes where the common is situate.[82] Under the Metropolitan Commons Act 1866 neither the lord of the manor nor commoners have power to veto a proposal but may object at an

---

[71] *Re Tenants Meadow, Duddon, Cumbria* (1975) 262/D/4–7, 3 D.C.C. 214.

[72] L.P.A. 1925, Sched. 1, Pt. V, para. 2 and see further §§ 7.87 *et seq.* and § 12.24.

[73] *ibid.* para. 3.

[74] "Land subject at the passing of the Act to any right of common and any land subject to be included [*sic*: misprint for inclosed as *any* land could be included in an inclosure award] under the provisions of the Inclosure Act 1845": Metropolitan Commons Act 1866, s.3; Metropolitan Commons Amendment Act 1869, s.2; for land subject to be inclosed, see the Inclosure Act 1845, s.11 cited at § 1.33.

[75] As defined in the Metropolitan Police Acts 1829 and 1839 and an Order in Council made thereunder.

[76] Thus all land within the definition is affected by subsequent statutes controlling metropolitan commons whether they are regulated under the Act or not.

[77] s.5.

[78] For which, see § 11.6.

[79] See Table 2 at § 1.09 and Appendix 7.

[80] See Sched. 1 to the Act, as amended and partially repealed by the Local Government Act 1985, ss.16, 102(2) and Scheds. 8, 17.

[81] Metropolitan Commons Act 1866, s.6.

[82] Metropolitan Commons Amendment Act 1869, s.3; for draft schemes see, 7 Forms and Precedents (4th ed.) 86, 94.

initial stage[83] or petition Parliament at the draft Bill stage with an appearance before a Select Committee as is provided in the case of a private Bill.[84]

A scheme may be promoted to include the expenditure of money on the **12.36** drainage, levelling and improvement of a common and to make by-laws and regulations for the prevention of nuisances and the preservation of order thereon.[85] The provisions relating to any particular common may only be ascertained by reference to the particular supplemental Act concerned.

On presentation of a memorial the Secretary of State may, if he thinks fit, **12.37** prepare a draft scheme and shall cause it to be published.[86] Two months must elapse after publication to allow time for suggestions and objections following which a public enquiry may be held. A scheme is then prepared and if any person with a legal interest in, over or affecting the land is dissatisfied with any determination made he may bring an action at law, by means of a feigned issue, against the person in whose favour the determination is made or against the Secretary of State as provided in section 56 of the Inclosure Act 1845.[87] A prepared scheme shall not of itself have any operation until confirmed by Act of Parliament by means of a Metropolitan Commons Supplemental Act.[88]

(b) Financing a scheme

All expenses incurred in relation to any memorial or subsequent scheme **12.38** shall be defrayed by the memorialists, or the ratepayers, or inhabitants of the parish or district willing and offering to defray those expenses, or the local authority.[89] A local authority may contribute an amount by a gross sum or annual payment towards the execution of a scheme including the provision of compensation moneys.[90]

The Metropolitan Commons Act 1866 originally provided a second method **12.39** of raising money to finance a scheme by allowing the raising of a local rate but this provision has now been repealed.[91]

(c) Amendment

The Secretary of State may approve and certify a scheme for amending any **12.40** scheme confirmed by Act of Parliament and all the original provisions apply to an amendment scheme.[92]

---

[83] Metropolitan Commons Act 1866, s.10.
[84] s.23.
[85] s.6.
[86] ss.7, 8, 9.
[87] s.16.
[88] s.22.
[89] s.24.
[90] s.25.
[91] Repealed by the Local Government Act 1939, ss.207–208 and Sched. 5.
[92] s.27.

(d) Protection of legal interests

12.41 No estate, interest, or right of a profitable or beneficial nature in, over or affecting a common shall be taken away or injuriously affected without compensation except with the consent of the person affected.[93]

(e) Purchase of rights of common

12.42 A London borough is empowered to purchase any saleable rights in common or any tenement having rights of common annexed thereto to prevent the extinction of rights of common.[94]

4. Commons Act 1876

12.43 Under the Inclosure Act 1845, if the Commissioners were of the opinion that it was necessary for the health, comfort and convenience of the inhabitants of any cities, towns, villages or populous places in or near which land was proposed to be enclosed, they were required to set out the terms and conditions under which the inclosure was recommended including allotmemts for recreation, exercise and for the labouring poor.[95] The Commissioners were required to certify, in reporting to Parliament, that in such circumstances the scheme was expedient having regard as well to the health, comfort and convenience of the inhabitants as to the private interests in the land.[96]

12.44 The Commons Act 1876 took the matter one stage further declaring that "inclosure in severalty as opposed to regulation of commons should not be herein-after made unless it can be proved to the satisfaction of the said Commissioners, and of Parliament that such enclosure will be of benefit to the neighbourhood as well as to private interests, and to those who are legally interested in any such commons."[97] The main result of the Act was to prevent further inclosure on a large scale and to change direction towards what is known as regulation of commons.

(a) Regulation

12.45 A provisional order for the regulation and/or inclosure of a common (as defined in the Commons Act 1876[98]) may provide for the adjustment of rights and for improvement of a common.[99] Adjustment of rights comprises the following[1]:

(1) on waste land of a manor[2] the determination of persons by whom

---

[93] s.15.

[94] Metropolitan Commons Act 1878, s.2 as amended by the Local Government Act 1985, s.16 and Sched. 8, para. 10(2).

[95] *cf.*Inclosure Act 1845, s.27 (now repealed).

[96] *cf.* Commons Act 1876, preamble.

[97] *ibid.*

[98] Land subject to be inclosed under the Inclosure Acts 1845 to 1868: s.37; but not any metropolitan common: s.35.

[99] s.3.

[1] s.4.

[2] Waste land of a manor includes land not parcel of a manor if the rights may be exercised at all times of the year, and are for cattle *levant* and *couchant* or are other rights not limited by stints: s.37.

and the stock by which, and the times at which common of pasture is to be exercised;

(2) as respects rights of turbary, estovers, taking gravel, stone or otherwise interfering with the soil—

    (a) the determination of by whom, where and when such rights may be taken with provisions for compensation for aggrieved persons by a grant of equal value, or with the consent of the person, money; and

    (b) the restriction, modification, or abolition of all or any such rights which may permanently injure the common;

(3) as respects rights of common over land which is not waste land of a manor

    (a) the stinting or determination of rights together with the persons by whom, the mode in which and the times at which such rights are to be exercised, with the same compensation provisions as in (2) above for aggrieved persons, and

    (b) the restriction, modification or abolition of all or any such rights which may be injurious to the general body of commoners or to the proper cultivation of the land;

(4) in all cases the determination of the rights of the lord of the manor, owner of the soil of the common or other severalty owners with the same provisions as to compensation or abolition as are contained in (2) and (3) above; and

(5) the settlement of boundary or other disputes between the parties interested in the land.

A scheme of improvement may comprise any or all of the following[3]: **12.46**

    (a) The draining, manuring or levelling of the common;

    (b) the planting of trees on part of the common, or in any other way improving or adding to the beauty of the common;

    (c) the making of by-laws and regulations for the prevention of, or protection from, nuisances or for keeping order on the common;

    (d) the general management of the common;

    (e) the appointment of conservators.

It will be seen that the adjustment of rights is a once and for all procedure **12.47**
involved at the award stage of inclosure and regulation.[4] It is clearly of less relevance today and is to some extent otiose following the provision for registration of rights under the C.R.A. 1965.

(b) Making an application

An application for a provisional order may be made to the Secretary of State **12.48**
by persons who appear to him to represent at least one-third in value of the interests in the land affected.[5] The application may relate to any land

---

[3] s.5.

[4] The conservators are frequently given a power to regulate rights for management purposes but it would be *ultra vires* to exercise this power so as to adjust rights between one commoner and another.

[5] s.2(2).

subject to be inclosed[6] and may be for regulation and/or inclosure.[7] If both inclosure and regulation are included the application will be treated as if it were for two separate commons.[8] This provision has the result of bringing the "benefit of the neighbourhood test"[9] to bear separately on each proposal. A proposed provisional order may provide generally, or otherwise, for adjustment of rights and management of the common or may state that all or any such matters are to be provided for in the proceedings subsequent to the confirmation of the provisional order by Parliament.[10]

12.49 Sufficient support for the application is necessary for at every stage of the procedure consent has to be obtained from persons representing two-thirds in value of the interests in the common, the lord of the manor if the land is waste land of any manor[11] and, where freemen, burgesses or inhabitant householders of any city, borough or town are entitled to rights of common, two-thirds of their number.[12]

(c) Procedure in outline

12.50 An application must be advertised and accompanied by detailed evidence of the proposals.[13] The evidence supporting the application must include maps, details of which provisions are to be put into effect, and information bearing on the expediency of the application with regard to the benefit of the neighbourhood as well as private interests.[14] If the Secretary of State is satisfied that a prima facie case has been made out he shall order a local inquiry to be held[15] and may make personal enquiries.[16] A draft provisional order is then prepared at which stage the Secretary of State may insert any of the statutory provisions contained in the Act of 1876,[17] which are designed to benefit the neighbourhood, and provisions to protect private interests.[18] The draft provisional order is deposited in the locality for study by interested persons,[19] and thereafter the Secretary of State must satisfy himself that the requisite persons have consented.[20] At any time before the draft order is certified as expedient by the Secretary of State, the proposals may be modified.[21] When certified as expedient to be passed by Parliament it has no validity in law until enacted in a provisional order confirmation Act,[22] but before enactment the order may be referred to a committee of either House

[6] See above, n. 98.
[7] s.2.
[8] s.2(2).
[9] See § 12.52.
[10] s.3.
[11] s.12(5).
[12] s.12(6).
[13] s.10(1).
[14] s.10(2), (3), (4), (5).
[15] s.11.
[16] s.11(6).
[17] s.7.
[18] s.12(1), (2), (3).
[19] s.12(4).
[20] s.12(5), (6).
[21] s.12(8).
[22] s.12(9), (10).

of Parliament where further modifications may be made.[23] Any modifications then made are subject to the same required consent of persons interested in the land or rights over it.[24] The final stage is for the order to be brought into effect by a Provisional Order Confirmation Act.

A provision is usually inserted into the provisional order confirmation Act **12.51** allowing for a valuer to be appointed to make an award to effect the purposes of the order and the procedure under the Inclosure Act 1845 is followed.[25] The award therefore follows some time after the passing of the Act.[26]

(d) Benefit of the neighbourhood

In considering the expediency of any application for a provisional order, the **12.52** Secretary of State is required to take into consideration whether the application will be for the benefit of the neighbourhood. With a view to such benefit the Secretary of State may insert such of the following terms and conditions as are applicable to the case:

"(a) that free access is to be secured to any particular points of view; and
(b) that particular trees or objects of historical interest are to be preserved; and
(c) that there is to be reserved, where a recreation ground is not set out, a privilege of playing games or of enjoying other species of recreation at such times and in such manner and on such parts of the common as may be thought suitable, care being taken to cause the least possible injury to the persons interested in the common; and
(d) that carriage roads, bridle paths, and footpaths over such common are to be set out in such directions as may appear most commodious; and
(e) that any other specified thing is to be done which may be thought equitable and expedient, regard being had to the benefit of the neighbourhood."[27]

Consideration of the benefit to the neighbourhood is a concept adopted **12.53** from the Commons Act 1876 for application in several other statutes. It is considered more fully in connection with applications under section 194 of the L.P.A. 1925 where it is in comparatively constant use at this day.[28]

Whether any or all of the particular features which may be inserted are **12.54** actually included may only be ascertained by examination of the relevant provisional order confirmation Act. In particular, a considerable variation between Acts has been noticed in respect of the access provisions. Some provide a general public right, some a right restricted to the inhabitants of the neighbourhood, some provide rights restricted to a defined area and some include none at all.[29]

[23] s.12(11).
[24] ibid.
[25] Inclosure Act 1845, ss.34–38; cf. Commons Act 1876, s.13.
[26] Usually one or two years later.
[27] s.7.
[28] See §§ 9.44–9.46.
[29] Berger, *Management Schemes for Commons* (1985) p. 48, Table 11.

(e) Suburban commons

12.55 A separate class of land known as a suburban common was recognised by the Commons Act 1876 in a provision which now has been repealed.[30] Some of the orders which have been made were under this provision. The commons were those situated wholly or partly within a town with more than 5,000 inhabitants and having a sanitary authority, or a common or part of a common within six miles of the centre of such a town. The sanitary authority was empowered to enter into an undertaking to pay moneys towards certain matters which would be for the benefit of the inhabitants of the town. Further, an authority was empowered to pay compensation in respect of rights of common for the purpose of securing greater privileges for the benefit of the town.

12.56 The section also empowered a sanitary authority (later a district council[31]) to acquire by gift and hold on trust for the benefit of the town any common within their area. Powers were also given for an authority to purchase any saleable rights in common or any tenement with rights of common annexed thereto with a view to preventing the extinction of rights of common.[32]

(f) Financing regulation

12.57 When a provisional order confirmation Act has been passed to regulate a common the subsequent proceedings are, so far as is practicable, the same as they would be if the common were to be inclosed instead of being regulated and the provisions of the Inclosure Acts 1845 to 1868 apply.[33] Thus, the expenses of the regulation "shall be borne and defrayed by the several persons interested in the lands to be [regulated]."[34] The Secretary of State may, if he thinks fit, insert in any provisional order for regulation, a provision for the raising and payment of the expenses of, and incidental to, the regulation of the common, either wholly or partly, by the sale of a portion of the common.[35]

12.58 A provisional order may provide for the raising of money from time to time by such persons as are interested in the common, and for such amounts as the Secretary of State thinks fit, to be applied towards the improvement or protection of the common, either by means of rates levied on the persons, and in respect of the property, who or which will be benefited by the improvement or regulation, or by means of the sale of any outlying or other small portion of the common not exceeding one-fortieth part of the total area.[36] Where a provision for the sale of part of a common is included the Secretary of State shall specify the situation and maximum quantity of the portion so to be sold.[37] Further, he may, if he thinks fit, also insert a provision for the investment of the proceeds of sale with the application of

---

[30] Commons Act 1876, s.8 (repealed by the Local Government, Planning and Land Act 1980, ss.1(3), 194 and Sched. 3, para. 1; Sched. 34, Pt III).

[31] Local Government Acts 1894 and 1972.

[32] A similar provision is still in force for metropolitan commons: § 12.42.

[33] s.13.

[34] Inclosure Act 1845, s.124; cf. ss.124–132.

[35] Commons (Expenses) Act 1878, s.2.

[36] Commons Act 1876, s.14.

[37] Commons (Expenses) Act 1878, s.3.

annual income from the investment to be applied to the improvement or protection of the common, coupled with provision for sale of the investments from time to time with the application of the proceeds of sale for the same purposes.[38]

(g) General management

A provisional order will usually contain provision for the appointment of a **12.59** Board of Conservators to manage the common and the Commons Act 1876 envisages that this will always be done, although not directly required.[39] The constitution and membership of the Board will vary from one Act to another. It seems that, where an Act relates primarily to upland grazings and its regulation, it will not be unusual for the Board to consist of only persons entitled to rights to graze. On the other hand, when the main use to which the common is put is mainly of an amenity nature, the Board is more likely to include representatives of local inhabitants and local authorities. A representative of the owner of the soil is almost invariably included as one of the Conservators.[40] The powers of the Conservators are circumscribed by the terms of the valuer's award made after the provisional confirmation order Act is passed.

(h) Protection of legal interests

(i) Mineral and other rights Where the rights of a lord of the manor **12.60** in the soil of a common or in mineral or other rights may be affected by a provisional order a statement shall be inserted in the order as to an allotment, or otherwise, as compensation. If mineral property or other rights are vested in persons other than the lord of the manor and are likely to be affected by the order, there shall be inserted such provisions and reservation as are required to be inserted by the Inclosure Acts 1845 to 1868 or as shall appear to the Secretary of State proper to be inserted.[41]

(ii) Rights of common As has been shown, an order which includes **12.61** adjustment of rights may make provision for compensation.[42] The Board of Conservators may also be given powers of management which include the regulation of grazing or the exercise of other rights of common.[43] It will be usual to include in a valuer's award a condition that in exercising the power of regulation no by-law may be made which prejudicially affects rights of common or requires a charge to be made for the exercise of rights.

(i) Enforcement

Regulation of a common is enforceable through by-laws, the making and **12.62** altering of which are subject to confirmation by one of Her Majesty's Principal Secretaries of State.[44] Breach of the by-laws is a statutory offence[45] with

---

[38] *ibid.*
[39] Under s.5 the improvement of commons includes, *inter alia*, the appointment of conservators.
[40] Berger, *Management Schemes for Commons* (1985), p. 32, Table 11.
[41] s.12(3).
[42] § 12.45.
[43] As a feature of general management allowed under s.5(4).
[44] s.16.
[45] *ibid.*

a maximum penalty on summary conviction not exceeding level 1 on the standard scale.[46]

(j) Prohibition on inclosure

12.63 Where a provisional order confirmation Act has been passed affecting regulation of any common no such common or part thereof shall be inclosed without the consent of Parliament.[47]

5. Commons Act 1899

12.64 The Commons Act 1899 provides a simpler method of regulating a common through a district council adopting a model form of scheme laid down under regulations. Instead of the positive assent required in the Commons Act 1876, a proposal under the 1899 Act is subject to a veto by the owner of the soil, or persons representing one-third in value of the interests in the common. It is, therefore, much easier to assess at an early stage whether the legal interests in the common are prepared to accept the proposal. The Commons Act 1899 has been widely used,[48] mainly on common lands which have ceased to be of great agricultural use and in respect of comparatively small areas of land.[49]

(a) Powers of a district council

12.65 A district council may make a scheme for the regulation and management of any common within its district.[50] The scheme shall be in a prescribed form laid down in Regulations.[51] In making the Regulations the Secretary of State is limited to the inclusion of matters specified in the Act but, on the other hand, may, and in fact has excluded some matters authorised by the Act.[52]

(b) Procedure for making a scheme

12.66 Not less than three-months before the making of a scheme the council shall cause the draft scheme to be published.[53] During the three-month period any person may make an objection or suggestion.[54] After the expiry of the three month period the council shall consider any objections and suggestions and may require an officer of the council to hold an inquiry.[55] The

---

[46] Criminal Justice Act 1982, ss.40 and 46.
[47] s.36.
[48] See Table 2 at § 1.09 and Appendix 9.
[49] Less than 70 acres on average: see Table 2 at § 1.09.
[50] s.1(1); *cf.* § 12.75.
[51] Commons (Schemes) Regulations 1982 (S.I. 1982 No. 209), Sched. for which see Appendix 6.; Commons (Schemes) (Welsh Forms) Regulations 1982 (S.I. 1982 No. 667), Sched. (in English and Welsh).
[52] There is no provision in the Commons (Schemes) Regulations 1982 for the laying out of ways allowed by the Commons Act 1876, s.7.
[53] Commons Act 1899, s.2; Commons (Schemes) Regulations 1982, art. 4.
[54] s.2(2)
[55] s.2(3).

council may then by order approve the scheme, with or without modification, and thereupon the order becomes effective.[56] If before approval the
council receives a written notice of dissent from the lord of the manor, or
other person entitled to the soil of the common, or from persons representing at least one-third in value of such interests in the common as are affected by the scheme, the council shall not proceed any further.[57]

(c) Regulation and management

The management of any common regulated by a scheme made by a district **12.67**
council shall be vested in the district council.[58] A scheme is made with a
view to the expenditure of money on the drainage, levelling and improvement of the common, and to the making of by-laws and regulations for the
prevention of nuisances and the preservation of order on the common.[59] It
may include any of the statutory provisions for the benefit of the neighbourhood mentioned in the Commons Act 1876, s.7.[60]

The powers given in the draft scheme, prescribed in Regulations,[61] may be **12.68**
summarised as:

(a) to execute necessary works of drainage, raising, levelling or other
works for the protection of the common;
(b) to fence quarries, pits, ponds and streams;
(c) to preserve vegetation including a power to erect temporary fencing;
(d) to plant trees and shrubs and otherwise improve the common for
exercise and recreation;
(e) to conserve trees or objects of historical, scientific or antiquarian
interest[62];
(f) to make, revoke or alter by-laws to prevent nuisances and to preserve order on the common.[63]

(d) Public rights

The draft scheme provides for a right of free access, and a privilege of play- **12.69**
ing games and of enjoying other kinds of recreation restricted to "the
inhabitants of the neighbourhood."[64] To effect the recreational privilege
there is power to set apart any portion or portions of the common for organised games which may be temporarily enclosed to prevent cattle and horses
(note not sheep) from straying thereon but not so as to affect prejudicially
enjoyment as an open space, the lawful exercise of any rights of common, or
so as to create a nuisance or be a nuisance to inhabitants of houses or users
of roads.[65]

[56] s.2(4).
[57] s.2, proviso.
[58] s.3.
[59] s.1(1).
[60] s.1(2); cf. § 12.52.
[61] Commons (Schemes) Regulations 1982 (S.I. 1982 No. 209) for which see Appendix
6.
[62] Sched., para. 2.
[63] Sched., para. 8.
[64] Sched., para. 4.
[65] Sched., para. 6.

12.70 Under a scheme, a council is also empowered to set apart temporarily and fence a portion or portions of a common for the parking of motor and other vehicles and may make charges for the use thereof.[66] The area set aside shall not be so near to any dwelling house as to create a nuisance or be an annoyance to the inhabitants of the house. The consent of the owner or owners of the soil must first be obtained, and that of the Secretary of State, who in giving or witholding his consent is required to have regard to the same considerations and shall, if necessary, hold the same enquiries as are directed by the Commons Act 1876 to be taken into account before forming an opinion as to whether an application under the Inclosure Acts 1845 to 1882 shall be acceded to or not.[67] The same consent must be obtained, and regard had to the same considerations and, if necessary, the same enquiries may be made before a council erects any shelter, pavilion, drinking fountain or other building on the common.[68]

12.71 In exercising its power to improve the common for exercise and recreation a council may plant trees and shrubs for shelter or ornament and may place seats upon and light the common, and otherwise improve the common for these purposes.[69]

(e) Legal interests

12.72 The Commons Act 1899 provides that no estate, interest or right of a beneficial nature in, over or affecting a common shall, except with the consent of the person entitled thereto, be taken away or injuriously affected without compensation being made.[70] A council may not set apart for games any part of a common which will prejudicially affect rights over the common without making compensation,[71] but, it seems, may set apart car parks without doing so.[72] It also appears that the making of by-laws regulating the use of rights of common to take part of the soil of the common or, trees or, underwood may trigger the compensation provisions.[73]

(f) Financing a scheme

12.73 All expenses incurred in the making and execution of a scheme, and any compensation, are payable by the council,[74] but one council may contribute to the cost of another executing a scheme and may enter into an undertaking so to do.[75] A parish council[76] may agree to contribute the whole or part of the cost of a scheme for a common within their parish.[77]

---

[66] Sched., para. 7.
[67] cf. §§ 12.50–12.53.
[68] Sched., para. 2.
[69] ibid.
[70] Commons Act 1899, s.6.
[71] Commons (Schemes) Regulations 1982 (S.I. 1982 No. 209), Sched., para. 6.
[72] Sched., para. 7.
[73] Sched., para. 8(b).
[74] s.11(1).
[75] s.12.
[76] In Wales a community council: Local Government Act 1972, ss.20(b), 179(1), (4).
[77] s.5.

(g) Byelaws

The draft scheme includes a list of model by-laws which provide extensive **12.74**
control over interference with the land or any part of it, (including the regulation of some legal rights over the land[78]), the prohibition of certain activities over the land and the regulation of others.[79] The provisions with respect
to by-laws are governed by the general rules contained in the Local Government Act 1972, s.236[80] and are enforcable on summary conviction by a fine
not exceeding level 2 on the standard scale and, in the case of a continuing
offence, by a further fine not exceeding £5 for each day the offence continues after conviction.[81]

(h) Excluded land

A common is defined to include any land subject to be inclosed under the **12.75**
Inclosure Acts 1845 to 1882 and any town or village green.[82] But a scheme
may not be made on any common which is, or might be, the subject of a
scheme made under the Metropolitan Commons Acts 1866 to 1878, or is
regulated by a Provisional Order under the Inclosure Acts 1845 to 1882, or
has been acquired or is managed under the Corporation of London (Open
Spaces) Act 1878, or is the subject of a private or local and personal Act
intended to preserve a common as an open space, or is subject to by-laws
made by a parish council under section 8 of the Local Government Act
1894.[83] Thus excluded, *inter alia*, are commons regulated under the Commons Act 1876 and statutory regulated pastures created under the Inclosure
Act 1845.

6. Commons Act 1908

This Act sets out only to provide for the control of entire (*i.e.* uncastrated) **12.76**
animals on certain common lands. It has already been noticed that under
the Inclosure Act 1773 it is unlawful to turn out rams during an autumn
period.[84] In contrast the 1908 Act deals with all animals at all times of the
year. The general scheme is that the persons entitled to turn animals out on
the land may appoint a committee with powers to act, make regulations,
appoint an officer to enforce the regulations and collect annual contributions from the persons entitled to graze.

(a) Persons entitled to act

The persons entitled to instigate a scheme of regulation are "the persons **12.77**
entitled to turn out animals on a common."[85] Thus, it is users of rights over
the land and not the fee simple owners who may act. A "common" is not

---

[78] Sched., para. 8(b).
[79] Sched., para. 8.
[80] s.10.
[81] Local Government Act 1972, s.237, as amended by the Criminal Justice Act 1982,
    s.46.
[82] s.15.
[83] s.14.
[84] § 12.17.
[85] s.1(1).

defined but includes "commonable land."[86] In the Acts immediately preceding the 1908 Act, the Commons Acts 1876 and 1899, a common is defined as land subject to be inclosed[87] and it seems not unreasonable to make the presumption that it has the same meaning in the 1908 Act. As has been shown "commonable land" has no precise meaning[88] and it seems that its express inclusion is an attempt to ensure that all the classes of land subject to be inclosed were brought within the scope of the Act—an admittedly cumbersome device. It does, however, ensure that an attempt to limit the word "common" merely to land subject to rights of common is prevented. The only land used in common agriculturally which may not be within the scope of the Commons Act 1908 is probably land which has become a statutory regulated pasture because it has already been inclosed under the provisions in the Inclosure Act 1845.[89] This has no effect on the scope of the Act of 1908 as all land subject to by-laws, which may regulate the turning out of animals, is excluded from the ambit of the Act and statutory regulated pastures are so affected.[90]

(b) Procedure

12.78 The Secretary of State[91] may convene a meeting for the purposes of the 1908 Act on the request of three persons claiming to be entitled to turn out on a common, or the council of the county, or the metropolitan district,[92] in which any part of the common is situated.[93] By order of the Secretary of State two or more adjoining commons may be declared to be one for the purposes of the Act.[94]

12.79 The persons entitled to turn animals out may resolve, by a majority in value of interest of the persons present at a meeting,[95] to:

  (1) make, alter or revoke regulations for determining the times, if any, at which and the conditions under which entire animals of any class[96] may be upon the common;
  (2) appoint officers to enforce the regulations and to detain and dispose of any animal removed from the common; and
  (3) raise such sums of money as are necessary to defray expenses by either,
    (a) annual contributions payable by the persons for the time being entitled to turn out animals; or
    (b) by way of an annual payment in respect of each animal turned out,
    prescribing a person entitled to receive and sue for sums due; and

[86] s.1(9).
[87] For which see the Inclosure Act 1845, s.11, cited at § 1.33.
[88] See §§ 1.44 *et seq.*
[89] Inclosure Act 1845, s.114.
[90] Inclosure Act 1845, s.118; Commons Act 1876, s.15.
[91] The Secretaries of State for the Environment and Wales.
[92] Added by the Local Government Act 1985, s.16; Sched. 8, para. 10(4).
[93] s.1(3); for an application to the Secretary of State see 7 Forms and Precedents (4th ed.) 81.
[94] s.1(7).
[95] The form of such a meeting and the methods of calculating the value of interests are prescribed in the Commons Rules 1966 (S.I. 1966 No. 96).
[96] s.1(9): horses, asses, cattle, sheep, goats, swine.

(4) appoint a committee and delegate powers to it.[97]

The regulations made are of no effect until approved by the Secretary of State.[98]

(c) Enforcement of regulations

12.80 Animals present on a common in breach of the regulations may be removed and disposed of by the appointed persons.[99] It is suggested that the provisions of the Animals Act 1971 apply to such a removal and disposal.[1] In addition, the owner of any animal found on a common in contravention of a regulation and any person who obstructs an officer appointed under the Act in the execution or enforcement of a regulation shall be liable on summary conviction to a fine not exceeding level 1 on the standard scale or, in the case of a continuing offence, a fine of 50 pence per day for every day during which the offence continues.[2]

(d) Excluded land

12.81 The Act applies to the Crown Estates, but not to the New Forest or to any common, in respect of which the conservators or other body appointed by, or under, any Act of Parliament to regulate the common have powers to make by-laws in respect of the same matters for which regulations may be made under this Act.[3]

(e) Dartmoor

12.82 The powers exercisable by persons entitled to turn animals out under the Act were in the case of the forest or chase of Dartmoor to be exercised by the Duke of Cornwall, but a regulation could not be submitted for confirmation by the Secretary of State until it had been approved by a resolution passed by the majority in value of interest of the persons for the time being entitled to turn out animals on the forest or chase.[4] This part of the Act must be taken to have been impliedly repealed by the Dartmoor Commons Act 1985 which brings the whole of Dartmoor within the exclusion that it consists of commons for which powers of making by-laws exist.[5]

Local Acts

12.83 There is a not insignificant number of local Acts effecting management of various tracts of the common lands of which those for the New Forest,[6] Epping Forest,[7] and the Malvern Hills[8] are perhaps the best known. As each

---

[97] s.1(1).
[98] s.1(1), proviso; for draft regulations, see 7 Forms and Precedents (4th ed.) 85.
[99] s.1(1)(a).
[1] For which see § 10.14.
[2] s.1(2), as amended by the Criminal Justice Act 1982, s.38.
[3] s.1(8).
[4] s.2.
[5] See § 12.92.
[6] The New Forest Acts 1854, 1949 and 1970.
[7] The Epping Forest Acts 1878, 1880, supplemented by the City of London (Various Powers) Act 1977.
[8] The Malvern Hills Acts 1884, 1909, 1924, 1930.

Act has been drawn up with the particular land in mind it is impossible to consider them in the present work. In many cases they are detailed and comprehensive.

Dartmoor Commons Act 1985

12.84 One of the most recent local Acts to deal with a tract of the common lands is that affecting Dartmoor. It is comprehensive and affects a very substantial proportion of the total common land acreage in the country. As it may well come to be regarded as a model for future legislation it deserves special attention.

12.85 Dartmoor is one of Britain's 10 National Parks. It covers about 350 square miles of which the core is 150 square miles of common land. The commons registrations under the C.R.A. 1965 originally included 280 land units with many hundreds of rights entries—one unit of 11,284 hectares has 948 rights entries finally approved.[9] Dartmoor is clearly an area of considerable agricultural importance. However, most would also consider that its importance for recreational and amenity use is equally great. The Dartmoor Commons Act, designed to effect control and management, reflects both interests.

12.86 The main features of the Act are the establishment of a self-regulating, self-financing and largely elected Commoners' Council charged with a duty to maintain the commons and promote proper standards of livestock husbandry; the extension of a right of public access to all the land encompassed by the Act[10]; and to provide the National Park Authority with powers to manage and control the extended and now *de jure* right of access.

(a) The Dartmoor Commoners' Council

12.87 **(i) Constitution** The Council consists of not less than 24 and not more than 28 members, of whom 26 shall be appointed as follows:

(a) 16 by the commoners following election at four geographically located commoners' meetings with only commoners recorded as grazing not less than 10 livestock units[11] being eligible for election;
(b) two by the Park Authority, one of whom shall be from amongst members of the Authority appointed by the Secretary of State;
(c) one by the Duchy of Cornwall (the major landowner on Dartmoor);
(d) two, being persons appearing to represent the landowners, by the Park Authority;
(e) one veterinary surgeon, by the members appointed pursuant to paras. (a) to (d) above and (f) below;

---

[9] Aitchison, Hughes and Masters, *The Common Lands of England and Wales*, (unpublished report for the Countryside Commission), Appendix 2(c).

[10] s.2(1); so much of the land in the districts of South Hams, Teignbridge and West Devon in the county of Devon as is finally registered in the commons registers under the C.R.A. 1965, excepting certain lands, for which see s.10(3)(a) and the National Parks and Access to the Countryside Act 1949, s.60(5)(b)–(g) (for which see further at § 12.107).

[11] s.2(1): a livestock unit means one horse, one cattle beast or five sheep.

(f) four being commoners entitled to graze less than ten livestock units and recorded on the graziers register as normally grazing an animal or animals, following election at four geographically located commoners' meetings.[12]

A further two members may be co-opted by the Commoners' Council, as elected and appointed.[13]

The definition of "commoners" is those persons entitled to exercise rights   **12.88** of common upon the commons, being rights registered (whether for the time being provisionally or finally) under the C.R.A. 1965 or registered under the Land Registration Acts 1925 and 1936.[14] To be eligible for election a commoner under (a) and (f) above also needs to be recorded as a grazier under the Dartmoor Commons Act 1985.[15]

(ii) The functions of the Council   The functions of the Council are: **12.89**

(a) to take such steps as appear to them to be necessary and reasonably practicable for the maintenance of the commons; and

(b) the promotion of proper standards of livestock husbandry including an assessment of the number of animals which can be properly depastured.

In discharging its duties the Council is required to have regard to the enhancement of the natural beauty of the commons and their use as a place of resort and recreation for enjoyment by the public.[16]

In particular the Council may: **12.90**

(a) protect the commons and render assistance to any commoner in the maintenance of his rights of common;

(b) undertake heather, gorse, grass, and bracken burning operations;

(c) plant clumps of broad leaved trees (not more than one acre in extent) for the protection of animals but so that each clump is not less than one mile from another, and fence and enclose as necessary for as long as may be necessary to protect the trees from animals;

(d) enter into agreements with owners of the soil for the grazing management of the commons; and

(e) shall have power to do anything which is calculated to facilitate the discharge of any of its functions including expenditure of money or the acquisition or disposal of any property or rights.[17]

The Council may arrange for the discharge of any of its functions (other than those relating to the control of finance or the making of regulations) by a commoners' association, an association of commoners' associations or any local authority whose area includes any part of the commons.[18] Where the functions are so delegated the exercising of the power to undertake

[12] s.3(2) and Sched. 1.
[13] s.3(3).
[14] s.2(1).
[15] Sched. 1, para. 12(1) and s.3(2)(f).
[16] s.4(1).
[17] s.4(2).
[18] s.4(6)(a).

burning operations and plant trees requires the prior approval of the Commoners' Council.[19]

12.91 In any event, in respect of burning operations and tree planting, the Council may not proceed without the consent of the owner of the soil which shall be deemed to have been given if there is no response to a notice served on the owner or, in a case where the owner is unknown, a notice has been placed on the land.[20]

12.92 **(iii) Regulations** In order to fulfil their functions the Council shall make regulations affecting the whole or any part of the commons for the following purposes:

(1) to ensure the good husbandry and maintenance of the health of animals depastured;

(2) to ensure that the commons are not overstocked and to effect that purpose may fix the number of animals which may be depastured by virtue of a right of common or of any other right or privilege (regulations to this effect shall also provide that a person, aggrieved by a regulation fixing the numbers which he may depasture, shall have a right of appeal to an arbitrator[21]);

(3) to ensure that animals newly introduced are hefted or flocked and are permanently marked;

(4) to control entire animals and to prescribe conditions under which such animals are depastured;

(5) to ensure that dead commonable animals are removed from the commons as soon as possible;

(6) to exclude from grazing:
  (a) bulls exceeding the age of six months, shod ponies or horses, and other animals not entitled to be on the commons;
  (b) any unthrifty animals and those likely to suffer unnecessarily if they remain on the commons;

(7) to regulate or prohibit burning[22]; and further may make regulations.

(8) to exclude all animals or animals of a particular class from grazing where the Council are satisfied that such exclusion is necessary for the maintenance of the commons or for the promotion of proper standards of livestock husbandry; and

(9) to regulate the exercise of rights of common of all kinds and rights of a similar nature, not being rights of common, and to prohibit the use of the commons by persons purporting to exercise rights in excess of their entitlement by persons not entitled to such rights either as commoners or otherwise.[23]

12.93 Regulations made are subject to certain restrictions:

(a) in fixing the number of animals which may be depastured from time to time in so far as a restriction operates to reduce the number

---

[19] s.4(6)(b).
[20] s.4(3).
[21] s.5(5).
[22] s.5(1)(a).
[23] s.5(1)(b).

below that which would otherwise be exercisable the Council must, so far as is reasonably practicable, impose on all holders of like rights a proportionally similar restriction;

(b) subject to certain exceptions the regulations shall not alter the area over which any right of common may otherwise be exercised;

(c) the Council shall not reduce an entitlement to depasture to less than two animals; nor

(d) discriminate between rights of the same class or character; and

(e) in fixing the number of animals which may be depastured the Council may not increase a grazing right to a number exceeding a commoner's entitlement under the C.R.A. 1965.[24]

Regulations made by the Council shall not have effect unless and until con- **12.94** firmed by the Secretary of State, who shall determine the date on which they shall come into operation. Before making regulations the Council shall consult the Park Authority and not less than 90 days before making application to the Secretary of State for confirmation shall serve copies on the Park Authority, the owners of the commons and all the commoners' associations. Representations received shall be forwarded with the application to the Secretary of State. If the representations are not withdrawn the Secretary of State may cause a local inquiry to be held or afford a representor an opportunity to be heard by an appointed person.[25]

It will be noticed that the Council has power to regulate rights of common **12.95** other than pasturage and also rights which are not rights of common. Thus the unquantified rights of the owner of the soil in respect of his demesne or purchased freeholds are controllable together with rights in common exercisable through a leased or licensed grant by the owner of the soil. Thus some persons are affected who have no part to play in the electoral process which is restricted to commoners.[26] It will also be necessary to regulate some rights which have not been subjected to the registration quantification under the C.R.A.1965.

(iv) Enforcement   The Council is required to appoint such persons as **12.96** they think necessary to act as reeves for the purpose of enforcing or securing compliance with the Regulations and generally for carrying into effect the powers and duties of the Council.[27] The Regulations may also provide for the detention, by any authorised person, of animals found on the commons in contravention of the Regulations, for the recovery of the costs of detention and for the sale of detained animals.[28] Additionally, Regulations may provide that persons in contravention thereof shall be guilty of an offence and liable on summary conviction to a fine not exceeding level 3 on the standard scale and for a continuing offence, following conviction, to a fine not exceeding £40 per day for each day the offence continues.[29]

[24] s.5(2).
[25] s.5(6)(7).
[26] See § 12.88.
[27] s.6.
[28] s.5(3).
[29] s.5(4). By the provisions in s.5(8), s.236(3)–(6), (8), (9) and s.238 of the Local Government Act 1972 are applied with modifications.

12.97   **(v) Register of graziers and commoners** It is graziers of the commons, not only commoners, who are subjected to regulation of rights, and it is commoners who are also graziers who may be elected to the Council. The two classes of persons will most usually coincide but it is not necessary for all graziers to be commoners. In addition to be effective in grazing management it is the rights used by graziers which have to be controlled and not legal entitlements which may or may not coincide. An essential pre-condition for both elections and control of grazing is that there shall be a record of user in addition to the record of right maintained in the commons registers under the C.R.A. 1965. The Dartmoor Commons Act 1985 makes provision for the establishment of a new register of graziers and commoners.

12.98   The Park Authority initially,[30] and the Council after establishment,[31] are charged with initiating and maintaining such a register showing the following particulars:

  (a) the name and address of each person who, by virture of a right to do so, grazes animals on the commons;
  (b) the name and address of every other person who is a commoner and who applies to have his name entered on the register;
  (c) in respect of each person within category (a) the number of animals for the time being grazed on the commons and the mark by which the ownership of the animals may be identified; and
  (d) such other particulars as to the Council seems fit.[32]

12.99   A statutory duty was imposed on any person who had grazed on any part of the commons in the 12 months ending March 31, 1986, or who subsequently graze on the commons, to supply to the Park Authority such particulars as are required for his registration in the register.[33] Further, there is a continuing duty for every person whose name is recorded in the register to notify any event warranting deletion or alteration of the particulars to the secretary of the Council within 28 days of the occurrence of that event.[34] Breach of either of the duties or the supply of false particulars is an offence with liability to a fine not exceeding level 2 on the standard scale.[35]

12.100   The register differs substantially from the commons registers maintained under the C.R.A. 1965.[36] The combination of categories (a) and (b) of the register records graziers and the numbers of animals being grazed from time to time in any year. This is a new concept as it records actual user and not legal right. The C.R.A. 1965, in contradistinction, records legal rights and (unless the right is held in gross) the land to which the rights are attached,

---

[30] s.7(2).
[31] s.7(1): the appointed day for the establishment of the Commoners' Council was June 30, 1986: s.2(1).
[32] s.7(3).
[33] s.7(5)(a).
[34] s.7(5)(c).
[35] s.7(5)(e).
[36] Unusually the county of Devon has maintained an extra-statutory register of derivative interests alongside the commons registers to record, *inter alia*, changes of ownership.

and not the owners or necessarily the users of the rights.[37] Further, persons who are not holders of rights of common registrable under the 1965 Act may qualify for an entry on the Dartmoor Commons Act 1985 register. These latter users of rights will not, of course, have been subjected to the statutory quantification of rights required by the C.R.A. 1965. The secretary of the Council may amend registrations as he thinks fit and any person aggrieved by such a decision, shall be heard by the Council, and may appeal against the Council's decision within 21 days by way of complaint for an order to a magistrates' court.[38]

A commoner who is not currently a grazier may register under category (b) **12.101** but is not compelled to do so. Thus a non-grazier commoner may, as will be seen,[39] escape all financial liability for the scheme. There is no provision for owners of rights, who have let farms and rights, to register as it is commoners (and a commoner is a person entitled to exercise a right of common[40]) and graziers who may register. Thus, the out-of-occupation owner of rights of common has no direct way of influencing events.

Finally, it should be noticed that under category (b) of the persons entitled **12.102** to an entry on the register a commoner holding rights of common other than pasturage may register but may not be elected to the Commoners' Council.

(vi) Financial provisions The Council shall cause to be kept proper **12.103** accounts which shall be audited annually[41] and has borrowing powers as if it were a local authority.[42] To meet the Council's annual net revenue requirement a power is provided to require contributions from commoners who are graziers, commoners who have grazing rights which are not currently in use, and other commoners.[43] Any amount demanded is a debt due to the Council[44] and may, therefore, be recovered by an action in debt.

The method by which contributions are raised is to set a "prescribed sum," **12.104** calculated as follows:

    (a) in the case of a person grazing by virtue of his right of common, 30 pence for each livestock unit;
    (b) in the case of a person who has a right of common to graze animals but who does not exercise that right, 5 pence for each livestock unit which he is entitled to graze or the sum of £1 (whichever is the greater);
    (c) in the case of any other person having a right of common, the sum of £1.[45]

[37] The commons registers under the C.R.A. 1965 record only applicants who registered rights and there is no provision for updating this section of the registers unless the land to which rights are attached is divided or rights in gross have been transferred; see further §§ 4.79 *et seq.*
[38] s.7(6), (7).
[39] See § 12.104.
[40] See § 12.88.
[41] s.15.
[42] s.17.
[43] s.16(3) and *cf.* § 12.98.
[44] s.16(4).
[45] s.16(3).

The Council may resolve to raise the prescribed sum or such other sums as may be determined. If the amount determined is less or more than the amounts prescribed in the Dartmoor Commons Act 1985 any other sums shall bear the like proportion one to another as laid down in the categories in the Act.[46]

12.105   It will be noticed that the classes of persons required to contribute are not co-extensive with the categories entitled to graze the commons. Thus excluded from contribution are any persons "who, by virtue of a right to do so, grazes or depastures an animal or animals on the commons" who is not also a commoner.[47] Secondly, there is no provision for a distinction between moneys required for works of an income or capital nature. Thus, a tenant grazier may find that he is required to contribute to works of a capital nature, such as the provision of shelter belts, the advantage of which will accrue to his landlord after the termination of his term. Thirdly, there is no provision for raising differential contributions to reflect expenditure on individual commons which at any one time may vary substantially as between one common and another.

(b) Public access

12.106   Subject to the provisions of the 1985 Act and compliance with all rules, regulations and by-laws for the time being in force the public shall have a right of access to the commons on foot and horseback for the purpose of open-air recreation.[48] The "commons" are defined in the Act to mean so much of the land in the districts of South Hams, Teignbridge and West Devon in the county of Devon as is finally registered in the register of common land under the C.R.A. 1965.[49] It follows that the provisions for access will only come into force in stages. In a survey of the commons of Devon carried out in 1984 it was estimated that it would take some five years for all the Devon commons registers to be brought to finality.[50]

12.107   Certain land which may occur on the commons is excluded from the right of access by reference to the corresponding sections in the National Parks and Access to the Countryside Act 1949 relating to access agreements under that Act.[51] Thus, excluded is land managed as a nature reserve, land covered by buildings and their curtilages, parks, gardens and pleasure grounds, land used for getting minerals, processing minerals and depositing of waste, railways, tramways, golf courses, racecourses, aerodromes, works by statutory undertakings and land in the course of development for some of these purposes.

12.108   A person who enters a common which is subject to the right of public access for the purposes of open-air recreation without breaking any wall, fence,

---

[46] s.16(3).
[47] *cf.* s.7(3)(*a*).
[48] s.10(1).
[49] s.2(1).
[50] Aitchison, Hughes and Masters, *The Common Lands of England and Wales* (unpublished report for the Countryside Commission), p. 16.
[51] s.10(3)(*a*), (*b*); *cf.* National Parks and Access to the Countryside Act 1949, s.60(5)(*b*)–(*g*).

hedge, gate or other thing shall not be treated as a trespasser or incur any other liability by reason only of so entering or being on the common.[52] Nevertheless a person so entering is not, for the purposes of the Occupiers' Liability Act 1957, a visitor of any occupier of the commons.[53] The Act also incorporates, by reference, Schedule 2 to the National Parks and Access to the Countryside Act 1949 which provides a list of prohibited activities applicable to public access.[54] An entrant to a common who is in breach of the provisions in the Act of 1949 forfeits his privilege under the Dartmoor Commons Act 1985 of not being treated as a trespasser.[55]

(i) Nature of access The right of access granted seems to be of a dif- **12.109** ferent nature to that referred to in previous general statutes. Under the L.P.A. 1925, s.193 it is access for "air and exercise" which is allowed on metropolitan and urban commons; in the Commons Act 1876 it is a "privilege of playing games and enjoying other species of recreation"; and in the Commons Act 1899 it is "a right of free access and a privilege of playing games and of enjoying other kinds of recreation." It seems clear that the open-air recreation is something more than the access for air and exercise of the L.P.A. 1925 but something less than a privilege of playing games, at least in an organised event. By express mention access on horseback is clearly incorporated.

(ii) Regulation The Park Authority may regulate or prohibit access by **12.110** all, or part of the public, to the whole, or part of the commons by public notices to effect:

(a) protection of ancient monuments, or areas of archaeological, historical or scientific interest;
(b) protection and restoration of the natural beauty of the commons and their suitability for rough grazing and recreation;
(c) preservation of trees planted for shelter;
(d) protection of animals on the commons;
(e) prevention of fire risks on the commons; and
(f) prevention of accidents at any source of man-made danger on the commons.

Whether the Park Authority regulates or prohibits access or not any powers under any other enactment whereby access is regulated or prohibited are preserved.[56]

To protect animals on the commons, the Park Authority, by notice, may **12.111** bring into effect section 1(2)(c) of the Dogs (Protection of Livestock) Act 1953,[57] which provides that it is an offence if a dog in the charge of an owner worries livestock and, for the purposes of that Act, worrying livestock includes "being at large (that is to say not on a lead or otherwise under close

[52] s.10(1).
[53] s.10(2) cf. §§ 8.47 et seq.
[54] s.10(3)(a) cf. National Parks and Access to the Countryside Act 1949, ss.66, 68, 78 and Sched. 2 cf. Appendix 4.
[55] See s.10(3)(a) and s.60(1) of the National Parks and Access to the Countryside Act 1949.
[56] s.10(4).
[57] See further, §§ 11.63 et seq.

control) in a field or enclosure in which there are sheep." The Dartmoor Commons Act 1985 provides that a notice shall have effect as if the commons or the parts specified in the notice were a field or enclosure.[58]

12.112   Provision is made for notices of proposals of regulation or prohibition to be made public before they come into force except in cases of emergency or where the regulation or prohibition is for less than 28 days.[59] Contravention of a requirement in a notice will constitute an offence under by-laws made by the Park Authority.[60] The existing powers of the Park Authority to make by-laws and to appoint wardens is extended to all the land to which the right of public access is applicable.[61] No by-laws may, however, be made so as to apply to any act done in pursuance of the exercise of any right of common or any act done by the owner of the soil or a person acting on his behalf.[62]

12.113   **(iii) Physical damage to the commons**   Where a member of the public enters upon the commons for the purpose of open-air recreation and causes damage to the commons or any thing therein the Park Authority may make good that damage.[63]

12.114   **(iv) Unlawful interference with the commons**   The Park Authority may take such steps as are necessary, whether by civil proceedings or otherwise, for the protection of the commons against unlawful interference as could be taken by an owner in possession. Before taking proceedings the Authority shall consult the lord of the manor, or other owner of the soil, of the common concerned.[64]

12.115   **(v) Control of horses let for hire**   The Park Authority is empowered to give directions to the owners of horses, which are, or are intended to be, let to members of the public for hire or reward as to the tracks on the commons which these horses may use.[65] Before giving such directions the authority shall consult the lord of the manor or other owner of the soil, the Commoners' Council and the owners of the horses.[66] A person who fails, without reasonable excuse, to comply with a direction is liable on summary conviction to a fine not exceeding level 3 on the standard scale.[67]

(c) Confirmation of common law and custom

12.116   Notwithstanding any enactment or rule of law it is provided that a right of common shall not be severable from any land with which it was held at the passing of the Act.[68] This has no effect on abandonment or release of rights, or apportionment on division of the dominant land.

[58] s.10(6).
[59] s.10(9), (10), (11).
[60] ss.10(12), 11.
[61] s.11(1); *cf.* National Parks and Access to the Countryside Act 1949, ss.90, 92.
[62] s.11(4).
[63] s.14.
[64] s.13.
[65] s.12(1).
[66] s.12(3).
[67] s.12(2).
[68] s.8.

For the avoidance of doubt it is also declared that on the commons con- **12.117**
cerned there is a custom that the owner of lands abutting the commons
fences that land against the commons.[69] This declaration has no extending
or limiting effect so that if in a particular case it can be proved that the custom is more or less extensive it is unaffected.

(d) Application of Law of Property Act 1925, s.194

In carrying out its functions under the Dartmoor Commons Act 1985 the **12.118**
Commoners' Council must seek the consent of the Secretary of State under
the provisions contained in section 194 of the L.P.A. 1925 in respect of the
erection of any buildings or fence or the construction of any other work.[70] It
seems from the wording in the Act of 1985 that it is unnecessary for the
works to actually prevent or impede access for a consent to be required.

(e) Saving of legal estates in or over the commons

It is provided that nothing in the 1985 Act shall affect prejudicially or alter **12.119**
any estate, right, interest, privilege, exemption or authority of, or enjoyed
by, any person as the owner or other holder of any manorial right, or any
other legal estate (except a right of common) in or over any part of the commons in respect of mineral or sporting rights, or a right similar in subject
matter to a right of common (except to the extent that a right of common is
affected by the Act).[71]

Before making any by-laws the Park Authority is required to notify the **12.120**
owners of the soil of the commons affected and if requested shall give any
such person an opportunity of appearing before and being heard by the
Authority.[72] In making by-laws the Authority is not authorised to regulate
or prohibit access to any part of the commons by the owner, his servant or
agent.[73]

The Park Authority is empowered to protect the commons by taking civil or **12.121**
criminal action but shall consult the lords of the manor or other owners
before so doing.[74]

The owner of the soil of a common is entitled to be notified of any burning **12.122**
operations or tree planting proposed by the Commoners' Council and the
operations may only proceed with his consent.[75]

Management by control

Apart from the Acts described above, all of which are of particular appli- **12.123**
cation to the common lands, there are a number of enactments which deal
somewhat more indirectly with control of activities. Although mostly not

[69] s.9. For the custom and its extent see §§ 9.05 et seq.
[70] s.4(4); cf. §§ 9.34 et seq.
[71] s.20.
[72] s.11(3).
[73] s.10(8).
[74] s.13, and see § 12.114.
[75] s.4(3).

directly designed to aid overall management, by controlling certain activities, agricultural management is influenced to the extent that the use to which the land is put is altered. They are of particular relevance in the context of the control of various forms of public access.

1. National Trust Acts

12.124 The National Trust owns very considerable acreages of common land particularly in some of the prime amenity areas. In 1983 it owned 135,000 acres, half of it in the Lake District. As active agricultural areas the Lake District, Long Mynd, the Brecon Beacons and Exmoor may be cited.[76] Recently, other substantial blocks of land have been acquired.

12.125 **(i) Powers and duties over common land** As might be expected, there are wider powers given to the National Trust than is usual with other management bodies. The main powers and duties relating to common lands owned by the Trust are contained in the National Trust Act 1907, s.29. The duty of the Trust in respect of common or commonable lands is that "they shall at all times keep such property unenclosed and unbuilt on as open spaces for the recreation and enjoyment of the public." Additionally the Trust is required to resist and abate all enclosures and encroachments on the land or the appropriation of the soil, timber or roads thereof for any purpose inconsistent with the Act. The powers granted by the section are:

(a) to plant, drain, level and otherwise improve or alter any part of a common, and to make temporary enclosures for these purposes, for the protection or renovation of turf and to protect trees and plantations;
(b) to make and maintain roads, footpaths, ways and ornamental ponds and waters over the property;
(c) to erect, maintain and repair sheds for tools and materials; and
(d) to set apart parts of the property upon which persons may play games or hold meetings or gatherings for athletic sports.

12.126 Additional powers are contained in section 23(1) of the National Trust Act 1971:

"(a) to provide or arrange for the provision of facilities and services for the enjoyment or convenience of the public, including meals and refreshments, parking places for vehicles, shelters and lavatory accommodation;
(b) to erect buildings and carry out works."

The extension of powers in 1971 was accompanied, in section 23(2), by a special version of the provision contained in the L.P.A. 1925, s.194, which makes the erection of works which prevent or impede access on common land unlawful without the consent of the Secretary of State.[77] The Trust is required on the same terms and conditions as apply to section 194 to seek

---

[76] cf. Workman J., "The National Trust Experience" in *Report of Conference on the Future of Common Land and its Management* (1983) (Open Spaces Society), pp. 26 and 28.
[77] For which see §§ 9.34 *et seq.*

the consent of the Secretary of State to the erection of any building or the construction of any other work which prevents or impedes access to the common, with the exception of the erection of sheds for tools and materials (the works directly authorised by section 29 of the National Trust Act 1907). Unlike the L.P.A. 1925 provisions, there is no direct mention of fences but they can hardly escape being "other work" which prevents or impedes access. It seems that the temporary enclosures for protecting alterations to the common, turf renovation and trees authorised by the 1907 Act now require the consent of the Secretary of State.

It has been remarked in connection with section 194 of the L.P.A. 1925 that **12.127** there are circumstances when that section does not apply to some land presently in the category of statutory common land and further that the section may sometimes be avoidable by the legal interests in the land.[78] The same qualifications do not apply to section 23(1) of the National Trust Act 1971 as any erection on land owned by the National Trust will inevitably prevent or impede the access to the open spaces for the recreation and enjoyment of the public which the Trust is under a duty to maintain.

(ii) Rights of the public   The purpose of the National Trust Act 1907 **12.128** was to take over the properties of a non-profit making association incorporated under the then Companies Acts and to create the National Trust for Places of Historic Interest or Natural Beauty as a statutory corporation. In the preamble to the Act it is recited that the Association has acquired "considerable property comprising common park and mountain land" and "that the public are admitted to the lands, building and property owned by the Association." The general purposes of the new corporation, contained in section 4 of the Act, provide that the Trust "may maintain and manage or assist in the maintenance and management of lands as open spaces or places of public resort and buildings for purposes of public recreation resort or instruction." It will be seen that the purpose of holding open spaces is public recreation and the practice of the Association was to admit the public. The section of the Act dealing with common lands merely imposes a duty to keep such property unenclosed. Thus, no additional right of public access was granted directly. Nevertheless common lands may be subject to rights of public access granted by other enactments[79] or dedication to access by an owner before acquisition by the Trust. The right of the individual member of the public on common land owned by the National Trust, in the absence of a right derived from a source other than the National Trust Acts, seems to be no higher than that of a licensee subject to control and regulation by the conditions laid down by the Trust. In the words of an officer of the Trust, "the Trust in owning the commons for the benefit of the public has never conceded that there is a total right of access everywhere though it is de facto almost everywhere."[80]

(iii) By-laws   The Trust has extensive and wide ranging powers to **12.129** make by-laws for the regulation and protection of, suppression of nuisances on, the preservation of order upon, regulation of conduct on and securing

---

[78] § 9.40.

[79] *e.g.* L.P.A. 1925, s.193.

[80] Workman J., "The National Trust Experience" in *Report of Conference on the Future of Common Land and its Management* (1983), p. 26.

the safety of any person resorting to their land or property.[81] The procedures for making by-laws, creating offences and establishing levels of fines under the by-laws are those applicable to local authorities.[82] A breach of the by-laws is a statutory offence punishable on summary conviction by a fine not exceeding level 2 on the standard scale, and in the case of a continuing offence, the sum of £5 for each day during which the offence continues after conviction.[83]

12.130   **(iv) Charges for entry**   Under the National Trust Act 1907 the Trust was not permitted to make charges for admission to any common or commonable land to which the public had a right of access at the date when such property was acquired, except where a portion had been set apart to play games or hold meetings or gatherings for athletic sports.[84] The Act of 1971 empowers the Trust to charge the public for use of any facilities, services, parking places or other accomodation and for playing games, sailing, boating, bathing, fishing and other forms of recreation on any lands, or property or waterway.[85]

12.131   **(v) Protection of rights of common**   The Act of 1907 contains a saving provision for rights of common in the following terms:

> "All rights of common commonable or other like rights or rights of way in over or affecting the Trust property shall remain and be unaffected by the provisions of this Act and save as in this Act expressly provided nothing contained in or done under or in pursuance of this Act shall take away abridge or prejudicially affect any estate vested in or any right belonging to and previously to the passing of this Act exercisable by any person."[86]

While there is an apparent intention in the section to prevent any prejudicial effect or abridgment of rights over the land it is subject to the exception of those matters "in this Act expressly provided." As has already been seen, the matters which are expressly provided for common lands are wide ranging including, for instance, powers to plant trees, make footpaths, setting land apart for games, providing facilities for meals, building shelters and lavatories, laying out car parks and the erection of buildings.[87] In some circumstances there will be an uneasy compromise between the need of the Trust to respond to their obligations and the duty not to affect the rights over the land. The safeguard for the commoners lies primarily in the overriding duty of the Trust to preserve the commons as open spaces and

---

[81] National Trust Act 1971, s.24(1). At the time of writing the additional powers available under this section have not been invoked; the by-laws in force and applicable generally to all Trust property are those of 1965 relying on the National Trust Acts 1907–1953.

[82] The National Trust Act 1937, s.12, as amended by the National Trust Act 1971, s.24(4), applies the provisions of the Local Government Act 1933, s.250(2)–(7), (10), ss.251, 252 (now replaced by the Local Government Act 1972, ss.235–237) to by-laws made by the Trust.

[83] Local Government Act 1972, s.237, as amended by the Criminal Justice Act 1982, ss.38, 46.

[84] National Trust Act 1907, s.30(2).

[85] National Trust Act 1971, ss.23(3), 30(2).

[86] s.37.

[87] §§ 12.125–12.126.

secondly, by the need for the consent of the Secretary of State where any access to the land is prevented or impeded by any works erected. Unlike the erection of works on common land owned by persons other than the Trust, it seems that the commoner has no right to abate such works, providing the consent of the Secretary of State has been obtained, as they constitute work authorised under statute. Should the works deprive the commoners of a sufficiency of common, however, there seems no reason why an action should not be brought against the Trust for exceeding their statutory powers.

For the same reason, that the Trust may not prejudicially affect the rights **12.132** over the land, on principle they may not charge commoners for the exercise of rights of piscary when making provision for charging the public for fishing, or charge for motor vehicles on the land if a commoner is lawfully taking his vehicle there in the exercise of his right of common.[88]

2. Open Spaces Act 1906

Under the provisions of this Act a local authority may acquire open spaces **12.133** in its district, by purchase or otherwise, and "undertake the entire, or partial care, management, and control of any such open space . . . whether any interest in the soil is transferred to the local authority or not."[89] Where a local authority has acquired an interest or estate in, or control over, the land, by-laws may be made for its regulation, admission to the land and for the preservation of order and prevention of nuisances.[90] The same powers are available to a London borough in relation to any park, heath or common under its control or management.[91]

The expression "open space" means any land, whether inclosed or not, on **12.134** which there are no buildings or of which not more than one-twentieth part is covered with buildings and the whole or remainder of which "lies waste and unoccupied."[92]

Upon acquisition of any estate or interest or control over land under the **12.135** Open Spaces Act 1906 the local authority shall hold and administer it in trust to allow the enjoyment thereof by the public as an open space under proper regulation and control.[93] It must be maintained in a good and decent state and the authority may enclose with railings and gates, drain, level and turf the ground and provide ornaments, lights and seats.[94]

In its application to common land it is clear that statutory common land **12.136** which has fallen to registration under the head of waste land of a manor will qualify as land which lies waste and unoccupied. It is less clear that land subject to rights of common may similarly be considered as unoccupied but it seems that some land of this nature has been placed under the provisions

[88] For when a commoner may lawfully take a vehicle on common land, see § 8.05.
[89] s.9.
[90] s.15.
[91] *ibid.*
[92] s.20.
[93] s.10.
[94] *ibid.*

of the Open Spaces Act 1906. Where land subject to rights is brought within the purview of the Act the local authority is restricted by the requirement that "no estate, interest or right of a profitable or beneficial nature in, over or affecting an open space . . . shall, except with the consent of the persons entitled thereto, be taken away or injuriously affected by anything done under this Act without compensation being made for the same."[95]

12.137 The Act seems to envisage the taking of control of land where the owner is unknown for control may be undertaken whether any interest in the soil is transferred to the local authority or not.[96] It will be recalled that statutory common land is placed under the "protection" of a local authority where the owner is unknown in accordance with the terms of section 9 of the C.R.A. 1965.[97] It is just possible to argue that land of this class is taken under the control of the authority sufficiently for the Open Spaces Act 1906 to be invoked. In the case of land registered as a village green under the C.R.A. 1965 the matter is put beyond doubt. Following an unknown owner hearing, if the Commons Commissioner is not satisfied that any person is the owner, he is required to vest the land in a local authority.[98] After vesting, the land is treated as if acquired under the Open Spaces Act 1906 and the powers under sections 10 and 15 to manage and make by-laws apply, providing that the land is not already subject to regulation under the Commons Act 1899.[99]

3. Law of Property Act 1925, s.193

12.138 Where common land is subject to a right of public access for air and exercise either directly under this section or by deed of dedication to the section by the owner of the soil, the owner or any person entitled to commonable rights over the land may apply to the Secretary of State for an "order of limitations." The matter has been considered fully earlier[1] and it needs only to be said now that the rights of the public exercising rights of access are circumscribed by such an order.

4. The Ministry of Housing and Local Government Provisional Order Confirmation (Greater London Parks and Open Spaces) Act 1967

12.139 The law in relation to open spaces in the Greater London Council and the London Borough Council areas was brought together into a Provisional Order confirmed by this Act and annexed thereto as a schedule. The aim of the Act is to secure uniformity in the law applicable to parks and open spaces. An open space is defined in the Act to include heaths and commons, so has application to statutory common land.[2]

[95] s.13.
[96] s.9.
[97] See § 7.40.
[98] C.R.A. 1965, s.8(1)–(3).
[99] ibid. s.8(4).
[1] See §§ 11.06 et seq.
[2] Sched., Pt. II, para. 6.

There are wide powers of management and control of open spaces contained **12.140**
in the Act.[3] They may not, however, be used in such a manner as to contra-
vene any right which a person may have otherwise than as a member of the
public.[4] In the case of a common (undefined in the Act) there are restrictions on the provision of facilities, the erection of buildings and permanent
inclosure without the consent of the Secretary of State for the Environment.[5]

5. Caravan Sites and Control of Development Act 1960

Under the provisions contained in section 23 of the Caravan Sites and Con- **12.141**
trol of Development Act 1960, a district council may make an order, either
absolute or conditional, prohibiting the stationing of caravans for the purposes of human habitation on a common. In the section a common is
defined so as to include any land which is subject to be inclosed under the
Inclosure Acts 1845 to 1882 and any town or village green except:

  (a) land to which the L.P.A. 1925, s.193 applies;
  (b) land which is regulated under the Commons Act 1899; and
  (c) land in respect of which a caravan site licence is in force.

A statutory offence for contravention of an order is created.[6]

6. Countryside Act 1968

The Countryside Act 1968 allows local authorities to make provision for **12.142**
country parks, that is to say, a park or pleasure ground for the purpose of
providing or improving opportunities for the enjoyment of the countryside
by the public.[7] An authority may extend, maintain and manage a country
park[8] and do all things appearing to them to be desirable including the erection of buildings and the provision of facilities.[9] The powers may only be
exercised on (a) land belonging to the authority or (b) on terms agreed with
the owners and other persons whose authority is required for the purpose.[10]
There is, therefore, no reason why a park should not be established on common land by agreement with the owner of the soil and the commoners.

---

[3] *ibid.* paras. 7, 8, 9, 10; the powers formerly exercised by the Greater London Council have been largely transferred to the London boroughs: see the Local Government Reorganisation (Property etc.) Order 1986 (S.I. 1986 No. 148), art. 23(5) and
the Local Government Reorganisation (Property etc.) No. 2 Order 1986 (S.I. 1986
No. 413), art. 4(2).
[4] *ibid.* para. 11.
[5] *ibid.* para. 12.
[6] Once an order has been made the onus for proving that the land concerned is not
common land lies on a defendant prosecuted under the Act: *Sawyer* v. *Giles* (1966)
200 E.G. 855.
[7] s.7(1).
[8] s.6(1).
[9] s.6(2).
[10] s.6(3).

Alternatively an authority may acquire any land required by them by compulsory purchase.[11] The effect of such a purchase if accompanied by extinguishment of rights will result in the land ceasing to be statutory common land.

12.143   However, the cessation of statutory common land status will not necessarily take the land outside the purview of some other statutes affecting common land,[12] nor affect any right of public access to the land. Section 9 of the Countryside Act 1968 makes special provision for common land[13] to which the public has rights of access[14] and for this class of land the section is mandatory.[15] The Minister[16] is empowered to authorise a local authority to "appropriate" the land either by compulsory purchase including the extinguishment of commonable or other rights over the land or where the authority already owns the land by the acquisition of all such rights.[17] Where the land has been appropriated under authority of the Minister the land shall be held by the authority free of public rights of access but shall be used for the benefit of the public resorting to the land.[18] No restriction applying to commons generally or to any particular common contained in or having effect under any enactment shall prevent an authority from taking land under the Act.[19] Where land is taken out of common land under this provision an exchange of land equally advantageous to the persons entitled to commonable or other rights and to the public is required unless it seems unnecessary.[20]

12.144   Once land is acquired or appropriated under the Act and taken out of the common lands wide powers are available to the authority to do anything which appears desirable to effect the purposes of the enjoyment of the countryside by the public, including erecting buildings, providing facilities and services and doing any other works.[21]

---

[11] s.6(4).

[12] A power granted to a council to acquire land does not include statutory extinguishment of rights sufficient to exclude the operation of ss.193 and 194 of the L.P.A. 1925.

[13] Common land has the meaning given to it in s.22(1) of the C.R.A. 1965: s.9(6).

[14] Common land to which the public has rights of access means (a) land to which s.193 of the L.P.A. 1925 applies other than by a revocable instrument or, (b) common land comprised in an access agreement or order under Pt. V of the National Parks and Access to the Countryside Act 1949 other than a revocable agreement or one for a specified period or, (c) any other common land to which the public have rights of access permanently or for an indefinite period: s.9(6). It seems that the provisions may not apply to certain common lands regulated under the Commons Acts 1876 and 1899 where the land is subject not to a right of access in the public but instead in the inhabitants of the neighbourhood.

[15] Sched. 2, para. 4(1).

[16] Now the Secretaries of State for the Environment and Wales.

[17] Sched. 2, para. 1(1), (2).

[18] *ibid.* para. 1(3).

[19] *ibid.* para. 5.

[20] *ibid.* para. 1(4).

[21] s.9(2), (3).

NON-STATUTORY MANAGEMENT

(a) Manorial courts

A study of court rolls will indicate the important part which many manorial **12.145** courts played in commons management until comparatively recent times. The functions of the various types of court do not need to be distinguished for the present purposes[22] and it is sufficient to say that the imperative for customary courts to sit disappeared with the abolition of copyhold tenure following the property legislation of 1925.[23] Neither manors as institutions nor manorial courts as administrative organisations for the manors have been abolished,[24] and in theory the courts may still be held. Their jurisdiction, however, has been so restricted as to make most of them obsolete in practical terms.

The nineteenth century saw a steady erosion in the use and effectiveness of **12.146** the manorial courts. Real property actions were abolished by the Real Property Limitation Act 1833, s.36. Under the County Courts Act 1846, s.14 lords were entitled to surrender the right of holding any court where debts and demands might be recovered to a county court and the County Courts Act 1867, s.28 provided that henceforth no action or suit which could be brought in any county court shall be commenced in any hundred or other inferior court not being a court of record. Criminal jurisdiction seems to have withered away following the increased jurisdiction of justices of the peace after the enactment of the Summary Jurisdiction Act 1848. By the L.P.A. 1922, s.188(6) the jurisdiction for enforcing a liability arising under a court leet regulation or otherwise for such matters as the maintenance of dykes, ditches, sea walls and ways was transferred to the county or High Court. Nevertheless, courts leet and courts baron were saved expressly by the Sheriff's Act 1887, s.40(1) and customary courts were not abolished in the course of the 1925 property legislation.

Following a Law Commission Report,[25] section 23 of the Administration of **12.147** Justice Act 1977 restricted the jurisdiction of most remaining manorial courts. The general scheme contained in the section is to recognise that a number of courts appear to have, but not exercise, jurisdiction to hear and determine legal proceedings, to provide that such courts shall cease to have that jurisdiction, but to allow the courts to continue to sit and transact such other business, if any, as was customary immediately before the section came into force. Three categories of court are recognised and dealt with in different ways[26]:

   (a) the Estray Court for the Lordship of Denbigh and the court leet for the manor of Laxton are excluded from the provisions of section 23;
   (b) courts of certain descriptions which include courts baron, courts leet and customary courts of the manor (Part I of the Schedule to

---

[22] See *Scriven's Copyholds*.

[23] L.P.A. 1922, s.128, Sched. 12: enfranchisement of copyholds.

[24] *cf.* L.P.A. 1925, s.201(1): express application of provisions to manors, reputed manors and lordships.

[25] Law Commission Report No. 72, *Jurisdiction of Ancient Courts*, Cmnd. 6385, (1976).

[26] For the complete list, see Appendix 5.

the 1977 Act) together with a named list of courts (Part II of the Schedule) were subject to abolition of jurisdiction but are allowed to continue the business, if any, as was customary; and

(c) a third list of courts (Part III of the Schedule) were also deprived of jurisdiction and the business that is to be treated as customary is that specified in column 2 of that part of the Schedule.

12.148 Apart from the two courts excluded from the effect of the section the general result is that a number of courts can point to the Administration of Justice Act 1977 as evidence of the customary business which they are entitled to transact albeit that they have no jurisdiction to hear and determine legal proceedings. All other courts, of the types specified in the Act, are also deprived of jurisdiction but are not abolished and if they wish to transact business will have to evidence that it was customary for them to do so immediately prior to the passing of the Act.

12.149 The customary business of the courts specified in Part III of the Schedule to the Act frequently contains reference to management of common land but it is difficult to see how such management or control can be fully effective without a power to hear and determine in legal proceedings.

(b) Associations of commoners and graziers

12.150 Far more numerous than the vestiges of the manorial courts are the voluntary associations of commoners or graziers some of which evolved from manorial institutions and still bear some such title as "the homagers" of the manor. They are to be distinguished from graziers' organisations established under Inclosure Awards. Many were revived or established to regulate and agree the registration of rights under the C.R.A. 1965. They vary from the purely nominal to active organisations. All share the substantial disadvantage that they have no power to bind a dissenting minority.

12.151 The liability of the individual member is restricted to the subscription, if any, which he has agreed to pay and possibly contracts entered into on his behalf by the association if he has acquiesced in the transaction. It is not possible for a majority of members to bind a person who dissents to financial contributions or such matters as the regulation of numbers of animals grazed. An association may not grant easements,[27] or bind the individual members in acquiescence to the owner of the soil granting easements. This particular problem is sometimes dealt with by the association entering into an agreement with the owner's grantee that the association will not sue, but this is not entirely satisfactory to the grantee.

12.152 Of particular difficulty is the position when the majority of members of an association wish to carry out works of a capital nature such as the erection of fencing or the placement of cattle grids on roads. It is not possible to demand contributions from a dissenting minority. Nor is it clear that, when sums of money are paid to an association for matters such as opencast coal mining or any use of the common which causes temporary interference with the rights of the commoners, an association is satisfactorily empow-

---

[27] *Paine & Co.* v. *St. Neots Gas and Coke Co.* [1938] 4 All E.R. 592; [1939] 3 All E.R. 812.

ered to hold or distribute the payments received.[28] On the other hand an association may be fully authorised to receive and distribute capital sums received for the extinguishment of rights over common lands.[29]

PROPOSALS FOR NEW FORMS OF STATUTORY MANAGEMENT

The Common Land Forum in its Report to the Countryside Commission reached the view that a new Commons Act should provide for a right of public access to those common lands registered under the C.R.A. 1965, and that it should be regulated in its exercise. It was further agreed that encouragement should be given to the better management of commons for the combined objectives of agriculture, woodland, recreation and conservation.[30] The Act, it is suggested, should provide for public access to be granted on all registered common land not more than five years from a date to be stated in a statutory instrument. During the five-year period specified, management schemes for commons may be submitted for approval, but if no scheme is submitted for a particular common it will be treated as if it were subject to a model management scheme.[31] **12.153**

A number of persons and authorities, it is proposed, shall have *locus standi* to initiate a management scheme: the owner of the soil; a commoner; a local authority; a National Park Authority where the Authority is not also the county council; and the owner of minerals if he is not also the owner of the soil.[32] **12.154**

Two forms of standard management scheme are suggested: one primarily for "amenity commons," *i.e.* those commons where grazing rights are no longer, or not substantially exercised, and the other for "grazing commons."[33] **12.155**

(a) Amenity commons

In the case of amenity commons the adoption of the management scheme already available under the Commons Act 1899, and its subordinate Regulations, is accepted as being suitable, with some minor modifications. It is recognised that without adequate finance an authority is unlikely to carry out satisfactory management and it is proposed that the new Act should facilitate the input of local authority financial, management and technical resources.[34] **12.156**

---

[28] § 5.107.
[29] § 5.91.
[30] Common Land Forum Report, para. 2.6.
[31] *ibid.* para. 4.4.
[32] *ibid.* para. 4.5.
[33] *ibid.* para. 4.7.
[34] *ibid.* paras. 4.8–4.10.

(b) Grazing commons

12.157 For grazing commons it is proposed that a model form of management scheme shall be prepared broadly on similar lines to the one contained in the Dartmoor Commons Act 1985,[35] although with significant variations in matters of detail.[36] For example, the proposals would allow the afforestation of up to one-quarter of a common.[37] A scheme which adopted the model proposals could receive approval of the Secretary of State, delegated to a county council.[38] Where, however, significant variations from the model form of scheme are desired by the promoters, a draft scheme would be forwarded to the Secretary of State who, following a public inquiry, if it seems necessary to him, would decide whether the special circumstances peculiar to the particular common justified a departure from the model scheme.[39]

12.158 The financing of a grazing common is expected to be the responsibilty of the management association. Whether the method adopted is through licence fee, stint levy, special levy or grant from a local authority the raising of money shall be approved by specific resolution at a general meeting.[40] Those entitled to attend and vote at a general meeting, it is suggested in the Report, are the owners of the soil, lessees of sporting and mineral rights for terms exceeding one year, persons having registered rights in the common, and representatives of the county, district and local councils.[41]

12.159 Where the right of access granted to the public adversely affects the other uses to which the land could be put, it is recommended that central government should provide funds to make compensation available to the owners and rights holders.[42]

---

[35] *cf.* § 12.84.
[36] Common Land Forum Report, paras. 4.11 *et seq.*
[37] For example, the Report proposes that up to one quarter of a common may be planted with trees (see para. 4.17 (viii)) whereas the Dartmoor Commons Act 1985 allows only the planting of clumps of one acre (see § 12.90, above).
[38] *ibid.* paras. 4.15 and 4.29.
[39] *ibid.* para. 4.27.
[40] *ibid.* Appendix F, art. 16.
[41] *ibid.* Appendix F, art. 1.
[42] *ibid.* para. 4.38.

13. Town and Village Greens

Introduction

In popular language, the village green is a well-known social phenomenon. **13.01**
It is a small area of open land in the middle of a village where the inhabitants can rest or play, the children run around and, archetypally, the village
cricket team holds its matches. The term is so well known that is has found
its way into a number of statutes, usually in the joint form of town and village greens. Nevertheless, until the C.R.A. 1965 required registration of
greens there was no statutory definition of the classes of land involved and
no strict common law meaning. The protection of greens from inclosure
depended upon proof that the activities on the land by inhabitants of a locality were such as would be recognised by the courts as being of customary
origin and indeed many such rights have been recognised. However, the
land over which the courts have confirmed rights is quite frequently very
different in nature from the typical green, often being an enclosure or very
extensive in area.[1] Thus, a town or village green may mean a relatively
small area geographically located in a town or village but, if it has a common law meaning is probably any land subject to customary rights of exercise and recreation. If then a town or village green depends upon the rights
exercisable over the land rather than its location it is sensible to refer to
such land merely as a green, as here.

(a) Land subject to customary rights

The courts have long recognised that privately owned land may be subject **13.02**
to a custom for the inhabitants of a parish or other locality to enjoy rights to
enter for recreational purposes. In so doing, a distinction has always been
made between specific activities on the land and a right merely to wander
about on it, a *jus spatiandi*, which has been held to be a right unknown to
the law.[2] As early as the seventeenth century a right to dance at all times
of the year on a certain close was accepted.[3] The conditions necessary to

---

[1] *Virgo* v. *Harford, The Times,* March 30, 1893 (Walton in Gordano, Somerset, 65
acres); *Lancashire* v. *Hunt* (1894) 10 T.L.R. 310 (Stockbridge Common Down,
Hants., 165 acres).
[2] *Att.-Gen.* v. *Antrobus* [1905] 2 Ch. 188; but see *R.* v. *Doncaster Metropolitan
Borough Council, ex p. Braim* (1987) 85 L.G.R. 233, cited at § 11.47.
[3] *Abbot* v. *Weekly* (1665) 1 Lev. 176, 83 E.R. 357.

establish a customary right were considered in the case of *Fitch* v. *Rawling* (1795),[4] when the playing of cricket was justified under a custom for "all the inhabitants of the parish to play at all kinds of lawful games, sports and pastimes on the ground in question at all seasonable times of the year at their free will and pleasure." In that case one defendant pleaded a similar custom "for all persons for the time being, being in the said parish": this was held to be bad, for what was claimed was a custom for all mankind. Subsequent cases have confirmed that, for a custom to exist, the beneficiaries must be restricted to a certain local area of which the parish is most usually mentioned.[5] Occasional use by persons other than inhabitants will not prevent the recognition of a custom[6] nor, once a custom is established, will more general use, although the fact of persons present without strict right may have implications for such matters as occupiers' liability.[7]

13.03   **(i) Types of activity**   Activities which have been upheld in the courts as customary include a right to dance round a maypole and otherwise enjoy recreation,[8] enter for horse racing,[9] dance at all times of the year,[10] take recreation including horse riding,[11] play cricket,[12] practice archery[13] and play all lawful village sports, games and pastimes.[14] On the other hand, claims by inhabitants of a right to exercise and train racehorses in a place outside the parish,[15] and to train and exercise horses taken in and not owned by inhabitants of the parish or for the purposes of a business have been rejected.[16] Thus, it seems that for a right of recreational use to be upheld there must be no commercial activity. This is not to say that commercial activities may not be recognised under customary law[17] but the land will not be in the nature of a green.

13.04   **(ii) The locality**   A customary right may not be claimed for the public at large[18] or, in the words of Sir George Jessel M.R., "if the custom alleged is for certain persons to dance on a green, and the evidence proves that anyone, whether belonging to that class of persons or not, has done so, it is too wide."[19] In *Edwards* v. *Jenkins* (1895)[20] it was held that a custom claimed for inhabitants of three parishes was bad. Three parishes could not be

---

[4] *Fitch* v. *Rawling* (1795) 2 H.Bl. 393, 126 E.R. 614.

[5] See further, §§ 13.04–13.05.

[6] *Hammerton* v. *Honey* (1876) 24 W.R. 603, *per* Sir George Jessel M.R.

[7] See further, § 8.47.

[8] *Hall* v. *Nottingham* (1875) 1 Ex.D. 1.

[9] *Mounsey* v. *Ismay* (1865) 1 H. & C. 729, 158 E.R. 1077.

[10] *Abbott* v. *Weekly* (1665), above, n. 3.

[11] *Lancashire* v. *Hunt, Lancashire* v. *Maynard and Hunt* (1894) 10 T.L.R. 310 and 448.

[12] *Fitch* v. *Rawling* (1795), above, n. 4.

[13] *New Windsor Corporation* v. *Mellor* [1975] 1 Ch. 380.

[14] *Virgo* v. *Harford* (1893), above, n. 1.

[15] *Sowerby* v. *Coleman* (1867) L.R. 2 Ex. 96.

[16] *Lancashire* v. *Hunt* (1894), above, n. 11; *sub proc.* 11 T.L.R. 49.

[17] *Mercer* v. *Denne* [1905] 2 Ch. 538 (fishermen drying nets); *Tyson* v. *Smith* (1838) 9 Ad. & E. 406, 112 E.R. 1265 (victuallers pitching stalls at a fair).

[18] *Fitch* v. *Rawling* (1795), above, n. 4; see also *Earl of Coventry* v. *Willes* (1863) 9 L.T. 384, *per* Cockburn C.J.

[19] *Hammerton* v. *Honey* (1876), above, n. 6.

[20] [1896] 1 Ch. 308, *per* Kekewich J.

regarded as one district. However, that case was disapproved by Lord Denning M.R. in *New Windsor Corporation* v. *Mellor* (1975)[21] and in the same case Brightman L.J. considered, without deciding the point, that one locality might provide facilities for surrounding localities.[22]

From these observations, which are, at the least, highly persuasive it seems **13.05** clear that the courts are not restricted in modern times to the narrow concept of one parish alone and indeed it is difficult to see how this can now be so when settlements may straddle more than one parish. The recognition in some cases of the rights of inhabitants of towns (which may well encompass more than one parish)[23] indicate that it ought to be a question of fact in each case as to the extent of the locality which is relevant. There would seem, for example, to be no reason why a housing estate, whatever its extent, should not be regarded as a locality. Perhaps the test today is that the court is able to identify the inhabitants of a particular locality, together with the ability to identify those persons not included.

(iii) Extinguishment of customary rights In claiming the existence **13.06** of a customary right, evidence of prolonged non-user may go towards indicating that the custom never existed,[24] but there is no presumption that non-user leads to abandonment. In *New Windsor Corporation* v. *Mellor* (1975)[25] a customary right of archery was established but had been unused since 1875. The Court of Appeal confirmed that the right could not be lost by disuse or abandonment. Once established a customary right may only be extinguished by statute.[26]

(iv) Greens and rights of common No doubt a substantial number of **13.07** greens were originally part of the waste land of a manor and some are, it seems, merely a recognised part of such a waste.[27] It follows that some greens are also subject to rights of common.[28] On principle it must be that the recreational use in such circumstances is subservient to the rights of the owner of the land and the commoners. Although it now seems clear that recreational use may be claimed at all times of the year there may be circumstances still where the use is limited in time. In the event of conflicting priorities, the original property rights of owners and commoners should

---

[21] [1975] 1 Ch. 380 at 387.

[22] *ibid.* at 396.

[23] *Mounsey* v. *Ismay* (1865), above, n. 9 (the freemen and citizens of a town).

[24] *Hammerton* v. *Honey* (1876), above, n. 6: "persistent interruption of the user, as by the inclosure of the land and the exclusion of the persons claiming the right for some time, is strong evidence against the existence of the custom," *per* Sir George Jessel M.R.

[25] *New Windsor Corporation* v. *Mellor* [1975] 1 Ch. 380.

[26] *Hammerton* v. *Honey* (1876), above, n. 6, *per* Sir George Jessel M.R.

[27] *Ratcliff* v. *Jowers* (1891) 8 T.L.R. 6 (Barnes Green, a portion of Barnes Common, subject to rights of recreation); *Forbes* v. *Ecclesiastical Commissioners for England* (1872) L.R. 15 Eq. 51 (Pear Tree Green, Southampton); for an example of a recreational allotment "indistiguishable" from a moor, see *Re (1) Bowes Moor, Bowes and (2) a recreational allotment, Bowes, Teesdale D., Durham* (1975) 44/D/53–61, 4 D.C.C. 223.

[28] Some still exist in this form today, although since registration under the C.R.A. 1965 (for which see § 13.18) it is more usual to find land subject to rights registered as common land and village greens registered without rights.

prevail. Thus, for example, if the land is traditionally cut for hay, the existence of the recreational use will not allow inhabitants to enter and spoil the hay.[29] On the other hand it also seems, as a matter of principle, that the owners of the land, or rights over the land, may not exercise their rights in such a way as to wilfully inhibit or prevent the rights of recreation.

13.08   **(v) Allotted greens**   Greens are expressly excluded from allotment in an inclosure award by section 15 of the Inclosure Act 1845, which declares that no town or village green is land subject to be inclosed under the Act. Nevertheless, where already in existence, they may be included in an inclosure award for allotment to the church wardens and overseers of the poor of the parish (at the time of the Act of 1845; now the parish or community council) to hold in trust to allow the use for purposes of exercise and recreation, providing that the extent of the green is not thereby reduced. The trustees have the same duties as trustees allotted new land for recreational purposes, and the Inclosure Commissioners (now the Secretaries of State) are required to set out a boundary line between the green and adjoining inclosed land.[30] The effect of such an allotment is to extinguish any rights of common over the land.[31]

(b) Land allotted for recreational use

13.09   During the nineteenth century it became the practice to allot some land in an inclosure award as a place of exercise and recreation for the inhabitants of the parish and neighbourhood. The Inclosure Act 1845 required the Inclosure Commissioners to consider, in the case of any allotment affecting a waste (but not one of stinted pastures or common fields), the allocation of between four and ten acres according to the size of the parish population.[32] In the event that the Commissioners decided not to make such an allotment the grounds on which they had so decided had to be stated in their annual general report.[33] After 1845 practically all inclosure awards included an allotment for recreation and after 1876 most schemes of regulation included a general right of access for recreation.[34]

13.10   It seems that, in some cases where inclosure awards were made in mountainous areas and the inclosure was of great extent, instead of setting out specific allotments for recreation a public right to roam over the land to be

---

[29] *Fitch v. Fitch* (1797) 2 Esp. 543, 170 E.R. 449. It seems that an *extension* of rights of ownership is an offence: see the Commons Act 1876, s.29, considered at § 13.42.

[30] Inclosure Act 1845, s.15; but not necessarily fenced: see the Inclosure Act 1852, s.14 (allotments for recreational purposes on town and village greens may be set out, distinguished by metes and bounds, and not fenced).

[31] *ibid.* s.106. There is no reason why new rights may not have been expressly re-granted: see *Re Bowes Moor*, above, n. 27.

[32] *ibid.* s.31. The provision specifying acreages relative to population was repealed by the Commons Act 1876, s.34.

[33] *ibid.*

[34] See further §§ 12.54 and 12.69; such rights of access, however, are not allotments for recreation.

inclosed, so long as is not actually tilled or planted, was reserved.[35] It is not known whether such rights have survived and, if they have, they may be viewed more as limited rights of access to land than as a form of recreational allotment.

(i) Allottees By virtue of section 73 of the Inclosure Act 1845, allot- **13.11** ments for recreation were usually awarded to the churchwardens and over-seers of the parish to hold the land as a place of exercise and recreation for the inhabitants of the parish and neighbourhood. As an alternative, under section 74 of the same Act, it was possible for a consenting allottee to per-mit his allotment to be used for exercise and recreation in which case the herbage belonged to him. This alternative procedure, with a private owner of the land, was repealed in 1876.[36]

(ii) Owners today The functions of churchwardens and overseers of **13.12** the poor (except so far as they relate to church affairs or ecclesiastical char-ities) are now exercisable in parishes by parish councils or meetings, in communities by community councils, in the City of London by the Com-mon Council, in Greater London (except the City and Temples) by London borough councils and otherwise by rating authorities.[37]

(iii) Powers and duties of the owners Section 73 of the Act of 1845 **13.13** lays down in detail the powers and duties of the allottees. The primary duty is to hold the land for the benefit of the inhabitants and in the first instance to fence, drain and level the land. There is a continuing duty to maintain the fences as directed in the award and to keep the land in good condition. The grass and herbage may be let from time to time and the proceeds, and any amount received from the general rate,[38] may be applied to the main duties of maintenance,[39] improving the recreation ground or any other recreation grounds in the same parish or neighbourhood, purchasing or hiring additional ground for recreational purposes,[40] improving or maintaining field gardens in the same parish or neighbourhood,[41] and the redemption of any land tax, tithe rentcharge or other charge on the ground.[42]

Where the land is allotted to an individual person the same duties of main- **13.14** taining the fences and of preserving the surface of the land in good condition

[35] See, *e.g.* the Provisional Order Confirmation (Hendy Bank Common, Radnor) Act 1880 (c. lxxxvii) and the Provisional Order Confirmation (Llandegley Rhos Com-mon, Radnor) Act (c. lxxxix); in both Acts rights are reserved to the *public* of free access at all times to land which is for the time being unplanted or uncultivated for arable purposes.
[36] Commons Act 1876, s.25.
[37] Local Government Act 1894, ss.5(2), 6(1)(c), London Government Act 1899, ss.11, 23; City of London (Union of Parishes) Act 1907, s.11; Rating and Valuation Act 1925, s.62; Overseers Order (S.R. & O. 1927 No. 55); 1927 London Government Act 1963, s.1(6); Local Government Act 1972, ss.1,2,20, 179, Scheds. 1, 4.
[38] The Act refers to the poor rate which now, except in application to the City of Lon-don and Temples, is to be construed as a reference to the general rate: General Rate Act 1967, s.116(2).
[39] Inclosure Act 1845, s.73.
[40] Commons Act 1876, s.27.
[41] Commons Act 1879, s.2.
[42] Commons Act 1899, s.16.

apply but the other powers available to the churchwardens and overseers have no application for the herbage, in this type of case, belongs to the allottee.[43]

13.15   **(iv) A power to sell**   The trustees of any recreation ground may, with the approval of the Secretary of State, sell all or any part of the allotment vested in them and out of the proceeds purchase any fit and suitable land in the parish or neighbourhood. The new land must be held in trust for the same purposes as the land so sold. The Secretary of State shall not give his consent unless it is proved to his satisfaction that the land purchased is more suitable for the purposes of the trust than the allotted land.[44] If the trustees are paid monies in compensation for compulsory purchase under any Act of Parliament the money shall be applied as provided in the Inclosure Acts 1845 to 1878 as amended by the Commons Act 1879.[45] Where the allotment is less than convenient the Secretary of State may authorise an exchange of land which is more suitable if a person owning such land is willing to exchange it.[46]

13.16   **(v) A scheme of the Charity Commissioners**   The owners of a recreational allotment may apply to the Charity Commissioners to provide a scheme of management in the exercise of their ordinary jurisdiction, as if the provisions in the award had been established by the founder in the case of a charity having a founder.[47] The powers of the Charity Commissioners are laid down in the Charities Act 1960 and include the power to order the sale and exchange of land.[48]

13.17   **(vi) Periodic reports by owners**   Section 28 of the Commons Act 1876 requires the owners/trustees of a recreational allotment to make reports to the Secretary of State at intervals of not less than three nor more than five years, as the Secretary of State shall direct, with such particulars of rents received as are required by him.

Registration

(a) The classes of land registrable

13.18   Town and village greens are required to be registered under the C.R.A. 1965 by the same procedures, already described,[49] as apply to common land. They are defined for the purposes of the Act as:

> " . . . land which has been allotted by or under any Act for the exercise or recreation of the inhabitants of any locality or on which the inhabitants of any locality have a customary right to indulge in lawful sports

---

[43] Inclosure Act 1845, s.74.

[44] Commons Act 1876, s.27

[45] Commonable Rights Compensation Act 1882, s.3; *cf.* § 13.11 for purposes concerned.

[46] Inclosure Act 1845, s.149.

[47] Commons Act 1899, s.18; and see the Charities Act 1960, s.4, especially subs. (10).

[48] Charities Act 1960, s.29.

[49] See §§ 2.02 *et seq.*

and pastimes or on which the inhabitants of any locality have indulged in such sports and pastimes as of right for not less than twenty years."[50]

Any land which was capable of registration under the Act during the mandatory registration period, which ended on July 31, 1970, is deemed not to be a town or village green unless so registered.[51] It will be seen that three distinct classes of land were registrable at the time of the initial mandatory registration procedure.

(i) Allotted land Under the first head of the definition all land allotted **13.19** for the exercise and recreation of the inhabitants of a locality, whether before or after the Inclosure Act 1845, was registrable. Included within this category are also those greens which were subject to customary rights and brought in to an inclosure award by virtue of section 15 of the 1845 Act. Not registrable was land set aside as a public park under a private Act,[52] acquired as a public pleasure ground under section 164 of the Public Health Act 1875[53] or held on trust under the Open Spaces Act 1906.[54] The head only has reference to land allotted under an inclosure award and then only where the allotment was for exercise and recreation and not any other purpose.[55] Some of the land which was allotted seems to have been almost useless for the purposes of exercise and recreation.[56]

(ii) Land subject to customary rights The second head of registrable **13.20** land, that is to say land on which the inhabitants of any locality have a customary right to indulge in any lawful sports and pastimes, is clearly intended to bring within registration the class of land which had previously been considered as the common law green. It follows that the law relating to customary rights described above has relevance to the eligibility for registration of this category of land.[57] The category clearly overlaps the third head of the definition and in some of the Commissioners' decisions it is not altogether clear which one is being discussed.

(iii) Land used as of right for twenty years The inclusion of this **13.21** category is analogous to the establishment of easements by prescription although, under the common law and statute, prescription has no application to public rights.[58] It is presumably included to facilitate registration of land where use in the nature of customary rights to indulge in sports and

---

[50] C.R.A. 1965, s.22(1).
[51] *ibid.* s.1(2)(a).
[52] *Re The Rye, High Wycombe, Bucks.*[1977] 3 All E.R. 521.
[53] *Re The Downs, Herne Bay, Kent* (1980) 219/D/2, 9 D.C.C. 417.
[54] *Re Gateacre Green, Gateacre, Merseyside* (1980) 89/D/1 (land conveyed as a public walk or pleasure ground; children playing games on it since 1913 not "as of right" but as members of the public using a public open space).
[55] *Re Mill Hill, Belton, Leics.* (1977) 221/D/4–5, 5 D.C.C. 178 (land allotted under an Act of 1812 for holding a public horse fair not registrable).
[56] See the *Re Bowes Moor* case, above, n. 27, and remarks of the Commons Commissioner there to this effect.
[57] §§ 13.02 *et seq.*
[58] A decision by a Commissioner that land qualified as a village green under the Prescription Act 1832 and, if necessary, under the doctrine of a lost modern grant must be considered *per incuriam*: *Re part of Carreg Sawdde, Llangadog, Dyfed* (1981) 272/D/166, 11 D.C.C. 293.

pastimes existed but could not be proved as customary. It was accepted, albeit *obiter dicta*, in *New Windsor Corporation* v. *Mellor* (1975)[59] that the correct period of 20 years user to be taken into account was that preceding the passing of the Act on August 5, 1965. This view certainly bars the use of a period of 20 years which has been succeeded by non-user (and possibly another use) but there must be some doubt as to whether a strict adherence to the period laid down in that case is altogether appropriate.[60]

13.22   As was pointed out by Lord Denning M.R. in the *New Windsor Corporation* case 20 years user gives no right to local inhabitants under the common law.[61] However, lest it be thought that the owner of land which has achieved registration under this head of the definition may be in a position to prevent the use of the land for the purposes of sports and pastimes it should be noticed that registration could only have been achieved where the user was as of right. That is to say, the owner following objection to the registration, or by lack of objection, has failed to establish that the inhabitants of the locality did not have a right and final registration provides conclusive evidence of the matters registered as at the date of registration.[61a] Further, there are, as will be seen, statutory provisions which prevent interference with rights over town and village greens[62] and once again the C.R.A. 1965 provides conclusive evidence that the land registered under this head of the definition has that status.

(b) Commissioners' decisions

13.23   In considering the possible existence of customary rights and rights proved by 20 years user the Commissioners have tended to follow the common law decisions relating to customary rights with some modifications. Generally, they have adopted a fairly restrictive view of a locality for the purposes of heads (ii) and (iii) of the C.R.A. 1965 (see above), with *Edwards* v. *Jenkins* (1895)[63] sometimes cited in support for the contention that the meaning is a parish. In one decision it was held that the use of 10 acres by the side of a river by persons from two villages and surrounding areas was wider than the use allowed by the inhabitants of a locality and the registration was annulled.[64] In another a building estate had been laid out in 1850 and the land in question provided for the use of the owners and occupiers on the estate. It was concluded that the recreational use to which the land had

---

[59] [1975] 1 Ch. 380 at 391.

[60] It would be less than appropriate for land registered, say, in 1970 on the basis of 24 years user to be rejected on the basis of only 19 years before 1965 when it is clearly registrable at the time of registration and may well be eligible for registration as "new land" after July 31, 1970. The more appropriate dates for the termination of the 20 year period would be the date of registration (which was an alternative suggested by Lord Denning M.R.) or even the date of a hearing if there is one.

[61] [1975] 1 Ch. 380 at 391.

[61a] C.R.A. 1965, s.10.

[62] §§ 13.30–13.31; but see the doubts there expressed as to whether a town or village green registered under the C.R.A. 1965 is necessarily of the same status for the purposes of other statutes.

[63] [1896] 1 Ch. 308; cited at § 13.04.

[64] *Re River Bank, Heddon on the Wall, Northumberland* (1973) 27/D/6, 2 D.C.C. 34.

been put was sufficient but it was held that the estate was not a locality as required by the Act.[65]

It is clear that the type of activity which will be accepted has to be some-   **13.24** thing more than a mere wandering on the land[66] for it is "lawful sports and pastimes" which are required and not the "exercise and recreation" of the allotted recreational allotment. In early decisions the Commissioners seem to have accepted that children playing on a piece of open land was sufficient basis to establish a full customary right without any requirement that there should be any sort of formal organisation of the sports or pastimes.[67] Children playing "cowboys and indians" and informal games of cricket and football has been held sufficient.[68] Later there was some resistance to this approach: mere playing on the land by children has since been held insufficient.[69] It has also been doubted whether such informal use can be viewed as being as of right when tolerance by the land owner is an alternative explanation.[70] The question has also been considered as to whether children alone can be properly representative of the inhabitants of a locality.[71]

(c) Effect of non-registration

The C.R.A. 1965 declares that "no land capable of being registered under   **13.25** this Act shall be deemed to be . . . a town or village green unless it is so registered."[72] The intention of the Act seems clear: a once and for all registration of the classes of land concerned was to be achieved and any land not registered was to lose its pre-existing status. It seems evident that the true village green subject to customary rights, if not registered, is deemed no longer to have that status and reverts to an unincumbered condition.

The provision, however, seems less than appropriate in respect of land allot-   **13.26** ted by or under an Act of Parliament for specific and restricted purposes. Can it be that the provisions have converted land, allotted under an Inclosure Award, into unincumbered freehold land free from any public rights? The public rights (unlike rights of common) were not required to be registered and have not suffered the non-exercisability provision contained in section 1(2)(b) of the C.R.A. 1965. All that seems to have happened is that the land itself is deemed no longer to be a town or village green—a status which it did not have before the Act of 1965. The matter cannot be considered decided but it seems possible that the land retains its pre-existing status.[73] A number of statutory provisions still affect the land,[74] the land

---

[65] *Re Silverhill Park Pleasure Ground, St. Leonards-on-Sea, East Sussex* (1979) 83/D/ 1, 8 D.C.C. 266.
[66] See further, § 13.02.
[67] *Re The Village Greens, Waddingham, Lincolnshire* (1972) 24/D/3, 1 D.C.C. 34.
[68] *Re Bridge Green, Hargrave, West Suffolk* (1972) 35/D/1. See Campbell, *Decisions of the Commons Commissioners* (1972).
[69] *Re Towan Green, St. Merryn, Cornwall* (1979) 206/D/2, 8 D.C.C. 89.
[70] *Re The Field, Smailes Lane, Rowlands Gill, Gateshead Borough* (1984) 266/D/1, 15 D.C.C. 27.
[71] *Re Towan Green case*, above, n. 69.
[72] C.R.A. 1965, s.1(2)(a).
[73] *Contra* Clayden, *Our Common Land* (1985), p. 64.
[74] See §§ 13.39 *et seq.*

may be subject to a scheme under the Charities Act 1960,[75] and it is difficult to see how the Act can have affected the trust on which a parish council (most usually) holds the land.

13.27 No sensible comparison can be made with the equivalent provisions for common land where it has been held that statutory awards of rights over land are extinguished by non-registration[76] for in that event the land was allotted for private purposes subject only to those rights, which have been expressly deemed unexercisable. On a recreational allotment the land was allotted only for recreational purposes and the recreational rights have not been similarly treated. It should also be noticed that, if the land is still in recreational use and has been for 20 years, there seems no reason why, in the absence of registration in the initial registration period, it should not now fall to registration as a "new" village green under the provisions contained in section 13 of the C.R.A. 1965.[77]

(d) New town or village greens

13.28 Section 13 of the C.R.A. 1965 provides for the registers maintained under the Act to be amended where "any land becomes a town or village green." By Regulations made under the Act[78] any person may make an application for land to be registered and the procedure followed is the same as that for the registration of new common land.[79] The notes to the application form[80] suggest four ways in which land may become a town or village green:

> "(1) By or under an Act of Parliament otherwise than as substituted land (as to substituted land, see category (4) below).
> (2) By customary right established by judicial decision.
> (3) By the actual use of the land by the local inhabitants for lawful sports and pastimes as of right for not less than 20 years
> (4) By substitution or exchange for other land which has ceased to be a town or village green under—
> > (a) sections 147 and 148 of the Inclosure Act 1845[81]; or
> > (b) paragraph 11 of Schedule 1 to the Acquisition of Land (Authorisation Procedure) Act 1946[82]; or
> > (c) any other enactment providing, on the exchange of land, for the transfer of rights, trusts or incidents attaching to the land given in exchange from that land to the land taken in exchange and vice versa."

---

[75] See § 13.16.
[76] *Re Turnworth Down, Dorset* [1978] Ch. 251.
[77] See § 13.28.
[78] Commons Registration (New Land) Regulations 1969 (S.I. 1969 No. 1843) especially regs. 3–6.
[79] *cf.* § 2.56.
[80] Commons Registration (New Land) Regulations 1969 (S.I. 1969 No. 1843), Form 30, n. 5.
[81] In the case of greens, s.149 of the Inclosure Act 1845 seems more applicable than s.148 which is concerned with the exchange of intermixed lands. For exchange of lands, see § 2.59.
[82] Now the Acquisition of Lands Act 1981, s.19 and Sched. 3; for compulsory purchase, see § 5.85.

The suggestions under (1) and (4) are self explanatory and the suggestion **13.29** under (2) is unlikely to be possible for the reasons given above, namely, that the Act by deeming unregistered land not to be a town or village green must have had the effect, at least, of extinguishing any customary rights exercisable.[83] It is difficult to see how a court could decide that land is a village green subject to customary rights in the face of a statute deeming otherwise. It follows that applications for new registrations are likely always to be based on the 20 years of user as suggested in (3), apart, of course, from statutory creation and exchanges.

The registration authority (providing that after preliminary consideration it **13.30** does not consider the application not duly made) must notify interested parties and publish notices of the application in the concerned area.[84] After receiving statements in objection the authority must consider the application, and the objections, and shall dispose of the application by acceptance or rejection. The writer is aware of four applications for new registrations—at Whitstable, Kent; Welwyn Garden City, Hertfordshire; the city of Cardiff, South Glamorgan; and at Worthing, West Sussex. The first and the last were successful. In both of the last two, at least, the registration authority adopted a procedure similar to a Commons Commissioner's hearing and considered the matter in public, although there is no statutory requirement so to do.[85]

(e) Greens and common land

For the purposes of registration under the C.R.A. 1965 common land and **13.31** greens are mutually exclusive: " 'common land' does not include a town or village green."[86] Nevertheless, sections 1(1) and 4(2) of the Act seem not to preclude the registration of rights of common over greens. The rather odd result ensues that rights of common may be registered and exercisable over land which is deemed not to be common land. There is little doubt but that this situation is the exception rather than the rule.[87]

(f) Greens and highways

For the purposes of registration a highway may not be registered as common **13.32** land,[88] or if it has been so registered mistakenly the entry is not conclusively evidential as to whether the land forms part of a highway.[89] There is no corresponding prohibition in respect of greens and it follows that land may be both a village green and a highway. There may be rights to indulge in lawful games and pastimes over a highway but registration of land as a green does not affect the status of land as a highway.[90]

---

[83] See § 13.25.

[84] Commons Registration (New Land) Regulations 1969 (S.I. 1969 No. 1843), regs. 5, 6.

[85] For further details of the procedures adopted, see Clayden, *Our Common Land* (1985), pp. 73–74; also (1981) 21 C.S.J., No. 2, 14.

[86] C.R.A. 1965, s.22(1).

[87] *e.g. Re Broad Heath Common, Presteigne, Powys* (1974) 58/D/9, 3 D.C.C. 130.

[88] C.R.A. 1965, s.22(1).

[89] *ibid.* s.21(2).

[90] *ibid.; cf. Re The Green, Hargrave, Suffolk* (1979) 234/D/79, 9 D.C.C. 18; *Medstead Village Green, Medstead, Hants.* (1979) 214/D/113, 9 D.C.C. 165.

(g) Ownership of greens

13.33   It has been shown that, generally, land allotted for recreational purposes has vested in the parish or community council.[91] In respect of other land it may be owned by any person but is perhaps more usually found to be owned by a local authority. Where no person was registered as owner under the C.R.A. 1965, following a Commissioner's hearing, the land is vested in a parish or community council by virtue of the provisions in that Act.[92] Where such a vesting has taken place the land is treated as though the council had acquired the land under the Open Spaces Act 1906 and sections 10 and 15 of that Act giving the council powers to manage and make by-laws apply.[93]

Management

13.34   Greens may be brought under various statutory provisions most of which are more appropriate to control by local authorities with the occasional exception available to private owners.[94]

(a) Metropolitan Commons Acts 1866–1878[95]

13.35   A scheme of regulation under these Acts may be promoted only in respect of land which is subject to be inclosed or was subject to rights of common when the 1866 Act was passed.[96] As land classed as a town or village green is not land subject to be inclosed[97] it follows that a scheme under the Metropolitan Commons Acts for a green, or including a green, may now only be entered into if the land was subject to rights of common in 1866.

(b) Commons Act 1899[98]

13.36   A district council may make a scheme of regulation under this Act including or consisting of land registered as a green.[99]

(c) Open Spaces Act 1906[1]

13.37   A local authority, including a parish or community council, have wide powers to manage, and control through by-laws, an open space acquired under or dedicated to the purposes of this Act. The powers of management are largely concerned with the provision of amenities to further public recreation but it must be doubted whether those powers extend to such mat-

---

[91] See § 13.12.
[92] See further, § 7.37.
[93] See further, § 12.133.
[94] But see § 13.37, n. 2.
[95] See further, § 12.34.
[96] Metropolitan Commons Act 1866, s.3 as amended by Metropolitan Commons Amendment Act 1869, s.2.
[97] Inclosure Act 1845, s.15.
[98] See further, § 12.64.
[99] Commons Act 1899, s.15.
[1] See further, § 12.133.

ters as the provision of car parks on a green resulting in the inhibition of lawful activities of the inhabitants over the site concerned. Under certain circumstances trustees or other persons having the care and management of an open space to which the public is admitted for enjoyment may also have powers to make by-laws.[2]

(d) Law of Property Act 1925, s.193[3]

A private owner, or a commoner if there is one, may seek an Order of Limi- **13.38** tations[4] on any land subject to section 193 of the L.P.A. 1925, (which provides a right of public access on urban commons and any rural commons dedicated to the section). Such an Order is likely to be less than comprehensive and it follows that local authorities are unlikely to use this provision if they are the owners of a green.

Criminal offences on greens

(a) Inclosure Act 1848, s.10

Where a green has been allotted under an inclosure award it is an offence if **13.39** any person shall wilfully or maliciously commit any damage, injury, or spoil to or upon any fences, ditches or other works made or done for the purposes of the inclosure, or to or upon any such allotment. Upon summary conviction a person committing such an offence is liable to pay such sum of money as shall appear to be reasonable compensation for the damage not exceeding level 1 on the standard scale.[5]

(b) Inclosure Act 1857, s.12

This section applies to town and village greens and any land allotted upon **13.40** inclosure as a place for exercise and recreation. It seems, therefore, to have application to any land registered as a green under the C.R.A. 1965 except possibly the class of land registered consequent upon 20 years enjoyment of a right to play lawful sports and pastimes, which would not have been viewed as a green at the time of the passing of the 1857 Act. It is not certain whether the effect of the 1965 Act is to convert this class of land into a green for all purposes or merely for the purposes of registration. There is the added complication that it may not be altogether clear whether land, proved to be capable of registration by this method, was also capable of being registered as land subject to customary rights. It is a question which may well need to be resolved in future legislation.[6]

The offences created by the section are several: it is an offence wilfully **13.41** to lead, drive or draw any cattle or animal on the land without lawful

[2] Open Spaces Act 1906, s.15(3): trustees or other persons having the care or management of any open space shall have the powers to make by-laws conferred by s.4 of the Town Garden Protection Act 1863; for a precedent for by-laws and consent thereto see 15 Forms & Precedents, (4th ed.) 486.
[3] For which see further, § 11.06.
[4] See §§ 11.26 et seq.
[5] Criminal Law Act 1977, s.31(6); Criminal Justice Act 1982, ss.37, 46.
[6] For reform, see § 13.49.

authority, lay any manure, soil, ashes, rubbish or other matter or thing thereon, or to do any other act whatsoever (whether wilfully or not) to the injury of the land or to interrupt the use or enjoyment thereof as a place for exercise and recreation. On summary conviction a person committing an offence is liable to a penalty not exceeding level 1 on the standard scale and a sum for damages. The person who may lay an information before the justices under the section are a churchwarden or overseer of the parish or the owner of the soil, and, by virtue of section 29 of the Commons Act 1876, any inhabitant of the parish.

(c) Commons Act 1876, s.29

13.42   This section applies to any town or village green or recreation ground (*i.e.* land allotted for recreational purposes) which has a known and defined boundary. Since the registration of greens under the C.R.A. 1965 the boundaries of all greens should be known or defined. The same measure of doubt exists as to the class of land established by 20 years enjoyment of lawful sports and pastimes as applies in the case of the Inclosure Act 1857, s.12.[7] It is unclear whether this section applies to that type of land.

13.43   The section extends the classes of persons who may lay an information before the justices, in respect of an act for which a person is liable to pay damages or a penalty under the Inclosure Act 1857, s.12, to any person who is an inhabitant of the parish where the green or recreational ground is situated.

13.44   Further, first, any encroachment on, or inclosure of, a green and secondly, any erection on, or disturbance or interference with, or occupation of the soil which is made otherwise than with a view to better enjoyment, shall be deemed to be a public nuisance. An action may be taken by the Attorney-General to restrain a person committing a public nuisance and a member of the public may sue if he suffers special damage. A public nuisance is also a common law offence.[8]

13.45   Rather obscurely, within the section is a prohibition on "occupation of the soil thereof which is made otherwise than with a view to the better enjoyment of such town or village green or recreation ground." As a matter of principle, this section cannot prevent pre-existing uses of occupation by the owner or commoners but it seems sufficient to prevent an owner from providing any new form of occupation as might be illustrated by, for example, the granting of easements over the land. It would also seem that no new rights of common may be acquired by prescription, *i.e.* by the presumed grant of the owner.

13.46   The section is not altogether happily worded. Any encroachment or inclosure on a green is forbidden but by implication an erection on a green with a view to enhancing better enjoyment (for example, a cricket pavilion) is

---

[7] *cf.* § 13.40.

[8] For public nuisance see, as a tort, Buckley, *The Law of Nuisance* (1981), p. 56 and, as a crime, Smith and Hogan, *Criminal Law* (5th ed., 1983), p. 746. A public nuisance is a misdemeanour at common law triable either way: Criminal Law Act 1977, s.16, Sched. 2.

allowed. The erection of a building for better enjoyment is also unlikely to interrupt the use or enjoyment of the place for exercise and recreation, which is an offence under the Inclosure Act 1857, s.12, but it can hardly be other than an encroachment or an inclosure. Perhaps the intention of the Act is that encroachments and inclosures are only deemed to occur when they are carried out by a person intending to deprive the inhabitants of rights over part of the land without any countervailing benefit. Thus, it will be unlawful to enclose any part of a green for private purposes or to interfere with the surface by, say, establishing a car park or to take possession by, say, driving an entranceway to a house across a green. While it may be permissable to erect buildings which are directly related to the enjoyment of the place for exercise and recreation, such as a bandstand, cricket pavilion, changing rooms or toilets, other buildings, which might be considered desirable community facilities, such as, say, a village hall, are unlawful.

(d) Vehicles on greens

It is an offence under the Road Traffic Act 1972, s.36, to drive off a road, **13.47** unless the driving is no more than 15 yards from the highway with the sole purpose of parking.[9] However, the section expressly excludes the operation of the 15 yard exception where section 193 of the L.P.A. 1925 or any by-laws apply to the land.[10] However, even where there is neither section 193 dedication nor by-laws in operation a person driving on to a green would appear to be committing an offence under the Inclosure Act 1857, s.12 as this forbids any act whatsoever which interrupts the use or enjoyment of a green or a recreation ground as a place for exercise or recreation.[11]

Change of use

Commons Act 1876, s.19

The section provides that nothwithstanding anything contained in any **13.48** other Act it shall not be lawful to authorise the use of or to use any recreational allotment or any part thereof for any other purpose than those declared by the act or award. The recital to the provision declares the mischief to be prevented as being powers under other Acts to divert such allotments from the uses declared by Parliament and, it seems, does not overrule the provision for exchange of land available under the Inclosure Act 1845, ss.147–149.[12] Nor, on the principle of implied repeal can it have any effect on later express provisions for a change of use for the land. An allotted recreational ground may, therefore, be subject to compulsory purchase under the Acquisition of Land Act 1981,[13] regulation under the Commons Act 1899[14] and, somewhat anomalously, may be sold under an order of the Charity Commissioners.[15]

---

[9] See § 11.61.
[10] Road Traffic Act 1972, s.36 (4).
[11] There is no requirement in this particular offence for the act to be wilful. It seems enough merely for it to be done whether in ignorance or not.
[12] See further, § 2.59.
[13] See §§ 5.85 *et seq.*
[14] See § 12.64.
[15] *cf.* § 13.16.

Proposals for reform

13.49 The Common Land Forum Report recommends a number of changes to be included in a second stage of legislation.

(1) The inhabitants of the locality, it is recommended, should be granted a statutory right to indulge in lawful sports and pastimes on every registered green in the locality concerned. This is to remove the doubt which exists over the extent of rights which have been established merely by proof of 20 years enjoyment.[16] At the same time it is also recommended that the test for a "locality" should be a "neighbourhood" rather than parish based as at present.[17] This latter change will, of course, have little effect on registered greens, most of which have, by now been considered on the parish basis, but a changed basis will assist the creation of "new" greens.

(2) Provision , it is recommended, should be made for the removal of greens "incorrectly registered" under the C.R.A. 1965 where the term incorrect registration has the meaning that the land:

(a) consists and did consist of, at the date of provisional registration, land on which a private dwelling house stands, or part of or the whole of the garden or other land enjoyed with a private dwelling house; or

(b) it is land which is used, and which was in use at the date of provisional registration, for a purpose incompatible with, or to the exclusion of, the use of the land as a town or village green.[18]

In the case of incorrect registrations of common land a similar provision envisages disputes being heard by an Agricultural Land Tribunal.[19] Where a village green is concerned it is recommended that the appropriate body to deal with both incorrect registrations and also clerical and administrative errors is the county court.[20]

(3) Where the ownership of a green has vested in a local authority, it is recommended that a power be given to the county court to make a divesting and re-vesting order in favour of the original owner.[21]

(4) If the provision at (1) above is enacted, that is to say a lawful right for inhabitants to indulge in lawful sports and pastimes is deemed to exist over any registered green, the Forum foresees the possibility of conflict between the use of the land for that purpose and, say, organised games. It is recommended that councils be given statutory powers to manage the land in such circumstances, such powers to be exercised in conjunction with the landowner where the council is not that person.[22] It is further recommended that local councils should have the power to purchase a green compulsorily where it cannot be used for its statutory purposes due to the

---

[16] Common Land Forum Report, Appendix D, para. S 9.

[17] *ibid.* para. S 11.

[18] *ibid.* paras. S 13–S 16.

[19] *ibid.* Appendix C, para. 013.

[20] *ibid.* Appendix D, para. S 16.

[21] *ibid.* paras. S 18–S 20.

[22] *ibid.* paras. S 21–S 22.

default or act of the owner,[23] but accepts that this power is inappropriate where the owner is the Crown Estates.[24]

(5) It is recommended that criminal sanctions be retained for damage to, or encroachment on, greens through the repeal, and re-enactment in modern form, of the Inclosure Act 1857, s.12 and the Commons Act 1876, s.29.[25]

(6) New management powers, it is proposed, should make provision for the temporary use of land for car parking where it is in connection with recreational use. It is also recommended that desirable facilities, not connected with recreational use, such as bus shelters and village halls, should be permitted subject to safeguards similar to those in the L.P.A. 1925, s.194.[26] The same section is proposed as a suitable medium to adjudicate on whether a landowner should be permitted to allow, or confirm, a right of way for access to adjoining properties.[27]

(7) It is recommended that the powers of the Charity Commissioners to authorise the sale or lease of a recreation allotment should be removed.[28]

---

[23] Common Land Form Report, Appendix D, para. S 21.
[24] *ibid.* note at the end of Appendix D.
[25] *ibid.* para. S 24.
[26] *ibid.* para. S 26.
[27] *ibid.* para. S 25.
[28] *ibid.* para. S 30.

14. Commons Commissioners

Preliminary matters

(a) Functions of the Commons Commissioners

14.01 Following the initial registration objection periods,[1] section 5 of the C.R.A. 1965 requires the registration authority concerned to refer any registration of land or rights which has not become final to a Commons Commissioner. The Commissioner to whom any such matter has been referred shall inquire into it and shall either confirm the registration, with or without modification, or refuse to confirm it.[2] If the registration is confirmed it becomes final and, if refused, becomes void, unless an appeal is brought against the decision.[3]

14.02 Additionally, wherever any land registration as a common or a town or village green has become final but no person is registered as owner of the land then, unless the land is registered under the Land Registration Acts 1925 and 1936, the registration authority shall refer the question of ownership to a Commissioner.[4] Following inquiry the Commissioner shall, if satisfied that any person is the owner of the land, direct the registration authority to register that person as owner.[5] If not so satisfied, and the land is a town or village green, the Commissioner shall direct the authority to register a local authority as owner[6] and, if the land is common land, shall take no action, with the result that the land remains protected, that is to say a local authority may take such steps for the protection of the land against unlawful interference as could be taken by an owner in possession.[7]

(b) Appointment

14.03 The Lord Chancellor is required to appoint to be Commons Commissioners such number of barristers or solicitors, of not less than seven years standing, as he may determine, and is required to draw up, and from time to time

---

[1] For which see §§ 2.05, 2.06.
[2] C.R.A. 1965, s.6(1).
[3] *ibid.* s.6(1)(a), (b).
[4] *ibid.* s.8(1).
[5] *ibid.* s.8(2); see further § 7.36.
[6] *ibid.* s.8(3), (4); see further § 7.37.
[7] *ibid.* s.9; the section applies to any finally registered land for which no person is registered as owner.

revise, a panel of assessors to assist the Commissioners in dealing with cases requiring special knowledge.[8] One of the Commissioners is appointed to be Chief Commons Commissioner. The first appointment as Chief Commons Commissioner took effect early in 1972 and since then there have been between one and four Commissioners sitting at any one time. They have almost invariably held their inquiries without the assistance of assessors and few occasions have been identified when an assessor has been involved.[9] The Commissioners and assessors are tribunals under the direct supervision of the Council of Tribunals.[10]

(c) Referral of matters to a Commissioner

The preliminary stages of registration and referral to a Commissioner have been discussed earlier and it is sufficient to say that, where there was no objection to a land or rights registration, the entry became final.[11] However, where there was an objection, and neither the registration nor the objection was withdrawn in the periods allowed, the entry remains provisional only, until such time as a Commissioner has inquired into the matter and issued a decision.[12] The majority of disputed registrations have been settled, following an inquiry, but in certain parts of the country, notably parts of South and West Wales, many disputes remain to be heard.[13] It seems that it may be several years before all the outstanding matters have been resolved. **14.04**

The referral of a matter to the Commons Commissioners by a registration authority is effected by the use of specified forms accompanied by the relevant documentation and plans.[14] Where the matter is one of unclaimed ownership of land the authority is further required, as soon as possible after referral, to display and publish notice of the referral, in prescribed form, in one or more local newspapers.[15] **14.05**

(d) A residual jurisdiction in the court

The dispute resolution procedure having taken in excess of 20 years already, and it being inevitable, in some cases, that there will be a further period of delay, it is worth considering whether hardship might allow the Commissioners' jurisdiction to be set aside and exercised immediately by the **14.06**

---

[8] C.R.A. 1965, s.17(1).
[9] e.g. Re Knacker's Hole Common, Puncknowle, Dorset (1972) 10/D/5, 1 D.C.C. 9; Re Erringdon Common or Bellhouse and Erringdon Moor, Calderdale D., Yorks. (W.R.) (1975) 45/D/34–35, 3 D.C.C. 66.
[10] Tribunal and Inquiries Act 1971, Sched. 1, para. 5.
[11] §§ 2.05–2.07.
[12] C.R.A. 1965, s.6(1), (2).
[13] Certain counties were noted in a survey as having a large area of land still recorded as provisional. The situation is partly due to a time lag between Commissioners decisions and amendment of the registers. Two with very large areas outstanding in South Wales were Dyfed and Powys: see the comment and tables in Aitchison, Masters and Hughes, The Common Lands of England and Wales (1984) (unpublished report to the Countryside Commission), pp. 4–5. The reconstitution of other registers in South Wales is proceeding under the provisions contained in the Commons Registration (Glamorgan) Act 1983 (c. ix).
[14] Commons Commissioners Regulations 1971 (S.I. 1971 No. 1727), regs. 8, 9.
[15] ibid. reg. 11.

courts. Before the Commissioners were appointed it was held that the courts would intervene and the question might arise in the future whether there was residual jurisdiction "for instance, to deal with cases where the registration, on the face of it, represents an abuse of the right of registration conferred by the Act."[16] Megarry J. could not see "what there is in the Act of 1965 which so plainly excludes the jurisdiction of the courts that the remedy of declaration and injunction is taken away. The matter seems to me to be one not of jurisdiction but of discretion."[17] The Court of Appeal, while not deciding that a residual jurisdiction lay in the courts, thought that it could be used only "in a case in which it was established beyond a peradventure that the applicant for registration was at the time of the application, or has since become, other than *bona fide* in his suggestion that this is, or may turn out to be when the whole matter comes before a commons commissioner, common land."[18]

14.07 It seems that it still may be possible to seek dispute resolution through the courts where, say, bad faith in an applicant for registration can be shown to exist. However, even then the court is likely to exercise its inherent residual jurisdiction only where a Commissioner's hearing is incapable of being brought about at an early date.[19] It should perhaps be remarked that a provisional registration of land or rights, in itself, confers no status on the land nor does it protect the rights. Thus, for example, a provisionally registered applicant for common rights is unable merely to point to the entry on the register to obtain an injunction to prevent a gravel company from removing top soil and working the land. To be successful he must at least produce prima facie evidence of the existence of the rights.[20]

(e) Legal aid

14.08 The Legal Aid (Extension of Proceedings) Regulations 1972 provide for the extension of legal aid to any proceedings before a Commons Commissioner.

(f) Assistance in proceedings by public bodies

14.09 A district council, with the consent of the county council, may assist a commoner in maintaining rights of common where, in the opinion of the council, the extinction of such rights would be prejudicial to the inhabitants of the district.[21] Similar powers to assist commoners are sometimes provided to Conservators appointed under local statutes regulating commons.[22]

[16] *Booker* v. *James* (1968) 19 P. & C.R. 525 at 530, *per* Pennycuick J.: court held land registered had cease to be common land in 1817; land ordered to be removed from the register.

[17] *Trafford* v. *Ashby* (1969) 21 P. & C.R. 293 at 297 (declaration granted that the land was not subject to any common right of piscary and was not registrable as common land). This view was confirmed in *Thorne* v. *Bunting* [1972] 1 Ch. 470 at 475, *per* Megarry J.

[18] *Wilkes* v. *Gee* [1973] 1 W.L.R. 742 at 747, *per* Russell L.J.

[19] Such circumstances do exist in parts of Glamorgan where all commons registers are being reconstituted and though the Commissioners have jurisdiction it cannot be exercised, perhaps for several years.

[20] *Cooke* v. *Amey Gravel Co.* [1972] 1 W.L.R. 1310.

[21] Local Government Act 1894, s.26(2).

[22] *e.g.* Ashdown Forest Act 1974, s.16 (a duty to protect rights of common).

Commons Commissioners' hearings

(a) Preliminary matters

The duties and powers of, together with the procedure to be followed by, the **14.10**
Commissioners are contained in the Commons Commissioners Regula-
tions 1971.[22a]

(i) **Duty to arrange a hearing** Where any matter is referred to a Com- **14.11**
missioner by a registration authority, the Commissioner is required, subject
to the one exception mentioned below,[23] to arrange a hearing for the purpose of inquiring into it.[24]

(ii) **Notice of hearing for inquiry into a dispute** Where a hearing **14.12**
has been arranged the Commissioner is required to give at least 28 days'
notice to persons entitled to such notification of the date, time and place of
the hearing.[25] Further, at least 10 days before the hearing a notice giving particulars of the hearing must be published in one or more local newspapers.[26]
The persons entitled to notification are, in the case of a land registration,
the applicant and a person who made an objection together with any person
whose application has been noted under section 4(4) of the C.R.A. 1985[27]
and, where the dispute was occasioned by a registration treated as an objection under regulation 7(1) of the Regulations,[28] the person, if any, who made
that registration.

In the case of a rights registration, the persons entitled to be notified are the **14.13**
applicant for the registration and an objector to it, together with any person
whose application has been noted under the General Regulations of 1966
and any person whose registration has been treated as an objection under
regulation 7(1).[29] It should be noticed that, as it is not possible to amend the
rights registers in favour of a new owner, where all the dominant land
together with the rights have been conveyed, or otherwise transferred, a current owner of rights is not necessarily a person entitled to be notified. It is
otherwise where there has been an amendment following either the transfer
of rights in gross or where the dominant land in the original registration has
been divided.[30]

Where the inquiry is concerned with a dispute over the registration of a per- **14.14**
son as owner of the land, the persons entitled to be notified are the person
registered as owner, a person who has made an objection, in the case of

---

[22a] S.I. 1971 No. 1727.
[23] See § 14.32 (decisions by consent).
[24] The Commons Commissioners Regulations 1971 (S.I. 1971 No. 1727), reg. 13, subject to reg. 31.
[25] *ibid.* reg. 14(1).
[26] *ibid.*
[27] *ibid.* reg. 14(2) (*i.e.* persons attempting to register land which has previously been
registered).
[28] *ibid.* (conflicting registrations treated as objections).
[29] *ibid.* reg.14(3) and see Commons Registration (General) Regulations 1966 (S.I 1966
No. 1471), reg. 9(5): second registration of a right of common to be noted.
[30] For which see §§ 4.79–4.81.

substituted land, the owner of that land, and, if the dispute was occasioned by a registration treated as an objection under regulation 7(1), the person registered as owner of that land.[31]

14.15   **(iii) Notice of hearing as to unclaimed ownership**   The same 28 days' notice to persons entitled to notification and 10 days' notice published in local newspapers as are required for the hearing of a dispute are also required for a hearing into an unclaimed ownership of the land.[32] The persons entitled to notification are every person on whose application a subsisting registration affecting the land has been made, every person whose application has been noted in respect of any such registration, any person who has written to the Commissioner claiming either ownership or information as to ownership and any person appearing to the Commissioner to be likely to have information relevant to the question of ownership of the land.[33]

14.16   **(iv) Postponed hearings**   Where a Commissioner alters the published arrangements for a hearing a further 28 days' notice to the persons entitled to such notice and 10 days' notice through publication in newspapers is required.[34]

14.17   **(v) Hearings in public**   A Commissioner is required to sit in public except when hearing an application for an order or directions of an interlocutory nature.[35]

(b) Procedure

14.18   In general, and subject to the provisions in the Regulations, the procedure at any hearing shall be such as the Commissioner shall in his discretion determine.[36] The degree of formality adopted seems to vary according to the particular hearing but invariably makes adequate provision for persons appearing without representation. There is no provision for routine pre-trial hearing or pleadings[37] but the Commissioner may, on the application of any person entitled to be heard, order any point of law which appears to be in issue to be disposed of at a preliminary hearing conducted in public.[38]

14.19   **(i) Persons entitled to be heard**   The persons entitled to be heard are those persons entitled to receive notification of the hearing (for which, see above)[39] and additionally, in the case of a disputed land registration or an unclaimed ownership hearing, the registration authority and any concerned authority[40]; and, in the case of a rights registration or disputed ownership registration, any person who gives his name and address to the Com-

---

[31] Commons Commissioners Regulations 1971 (S.I. 1971 No. 1727), reg. 14(4).
[32] *ibid.* reg. 15(1).
[33] *ibid.* reg. 15(2).
[34] *ibid.* reg. 13.
[35] *ibid.* reg. 17(2).
[36] *ibid.* reg. 18.
[37] But see provision for orders and directions described at § 14.17.
[38] Commons Commissioners Regulations 1971 (S.I. 1971 No. 1727), reg. 28.
[39] See §§ 14.12–14.14.
[40] Commons Commissioners Regulations 1971 (S.I. 1971 No. 1727), reg. 19(1), (4).

missioner at or before the hearing and satisfies the Commissioner that he has succeeded to the interest, or part of the interest, of any of the persons entitled to notification of the hearing.[41]

The Commissioner has discretion at the hearing of a dispute as to the regis- **14.20** tration of land, or at a hearing relating to the question of the ownership of any unclaimed land to take evidence from any person who gives his name and address and volunteers to give evidence.[42] It is now clear that a person who has failed to make an objection to a land registration may take advantage of one made by another person to some part of the land, for the result is to throw the whole registration into dispute requiring the applicant for registration to substantiate his application. It may be, therefore, that a person who has made no direct objection is a person able to give evidence and throw light upon the validity of the applicant's claim. A Commissioner, as has been shown, has discretion to hear such a person and, in some circumstances, may be under a duty to hear such evidence.[43]

A Commissioner may, if he thinks fit, proceed with a hearing in the absence **14.21** of a person entitled to be heard but, on receiving an application from such a person being absent, may reopen the hearing and set aside any decision on such terms as he thinks fit, if he is satisfied that such a person had sufficient reason for his absence. A person wishing to have a hearing reopened must so request the Commissioner within 10 days of the decision being sent to him.[44]

(ii) **Representation at the hearing** A person entitled to be heard may **14.22** be represented by counsel or solicitor or, with the leave of the Commissioner, by any other person.[45] It is not unusual for persons to be represented by land agents, surveyors, officers or members of farmers' unions, representatives of local councils or officers of local or national organisations.

(iii) **Evidence** Evidence may be given orally or, with the consent of **14.23** the persons entitled to be heard or where the Commissioner so orders, by affidavit, but the Commissioner may at any stage of the proceedings make an order requiring personal attendance for examination and cross-examination of any deponent.[46] A Commissioner may require evidence to be given on oath and for that purpose has power to administer oaths and take affirmations.[47] The Clerk for the time being of the Commissioners has power to administer oaths and take affirmations for the purpose of affidavits to be used in proceedings before a Commissioner.[48] No person shall be required to give any evidence or to produce any document which he could not be required to give or produce on the trial of an action in the High Court.[49]

---

[41] Commons Commissioners Regulations 1971 (S.I. 1971 No. 1727), reg. 19(3)(4).
[42] ibid. reg. 23(5).
[43] Re West Anstey Common [1985] Ch.329 (C.A.); considered at 14.27.
[44] Commons Commissioners Regulations 1971 (S.I. 1971 No. 1727), reg. 21.
[45] ibid. reg. 20.
[46] ibid. reg. 22(1).
[47] ibid. reg. 22(2).
[48] ibid. reg. 22(3).
[49] ibid. reg. 23(2).

14.24 The following Practice Direction was issued by the Chief Commons Commissioner on May 1, 1972[50]:

> "1. Where any person relies on an inclosure award at a hearing, he should produce at the hearing:–
> (1) (i) The original award (together with the map, if any, referred to in it) and a copy of the relevant portion of the award or
> (ii) Copies certified by the person having the custody of the award and of the map, if any, referred to in it.
> (2) If available, a copy of the relevant Inclosure Act, which will be returned after the decision has been given.
> 2. In cases in which more than one party is entitled to be heard the parties should ensure that there is no duplication of copies."

14.25 The Chief Land Registrar shall not be required to produce any document in his custody but there is provision for a Commissioner, upon an application by a person entitled to be heard at the hearing, to require any person who is entitled to authorise the production by the Chief Land Registrar of any document to do so.[51]

14.26 **(iv) Attendance of witnesses** A Commissioner has power to issue a witness summons requiring the attendance of any person to give oral evidence or produce any document subject to the person requiring the attendance paying to the witness a sum sufficient to cover his expenses for attending the hearing and, where appropriate, the production of the document.[52] It seems that this power is used very infrequently.

14.27 **(v) Expert witnesses** No more than one expert witness may be called in support of or against a disputed registration unless leave to call more than one is granted by the Commissioner before or at the hearing.[53]

14.28 **(vi) Rights of persons entitled to be heard** A person entitled to be heard at a hearing may give evidence, address the Commissioner, tender documentary evidence, call witnesses and examine them.[54] In disputed cases the person is entitled to cross-examine the witnesses who are in support of, or objecting to, the registration as the case may be.[55] Where the hearing relates to the question of the ownership of unclaimed land, a person claiming ownership may cross-examine another person claiming ownership.[56] A person who is represented at a hearing may exercise his rights to address the Commissioner and examine and cross-examine witnesses only by his representative.[57]

14.29 **(vii) Grounds of objection** Where a dispute is occasioned by an objection the person making the objection may only rely upon the grounds stated in his objection unless the Commissioner allows him to put forward such

---

[50] [1972] C.L.Y. 354.
[51] Commons Commissioners Regulations 1971 (S.I. 1971 No. 1727), reg. 14(4).
[52] *ibid.* reg. 22(1) and see reg. 22(3).
[53] *ibid.* reg. 24.
[54] *ibid.* reg. 25(1).
[55] *ibid.* reg. 25(2).
[56] *ibid.* reg. 25(3).
[57] *ibid.* reg. 25(4).

additional grounds as appear to the Commissioner to be material. Where the Commissioner allows any additional grounds to be put forward he may do so on such terms, whether as to adjournment or otherwise, as he thinks fit.[58]

It is unusual, but not unknown, for a Commissioner to allow an amend-   **14.30** ment. This is largely due to the wide nature of the objections which were usually made. By far the commonest words used to make an objection follow suggestions made in the Forms prescribed in the Commons Registration (Objection and Maps) Regulations 1968.[59] Examples are "that the land was not common land at the date of the registration," "that the right of common does not exist," "that the right of common should consist of fewer animals," and "that the person named as owner was, at the date of registration as such, not the owner of the land."

(c) Decisions

The decision of a Commissioner upon any matter referred to him under the   **14.31** C.R.A 1965 must be given in writing and (except where the decision is given by consent)[60] must include a statement of the reasons for the decision and an explanation in general terms of the right to appeal.[61] As soon as possible after a Commissioner has decided any matter he is required to send a copy of the decision to the registration authority, to every person entitled to be heard at the hearing or, where the decision is by consent (see below) to every person who consented, and, where the decision relates to the question of ownership of any unclaimed land, also to any person who has written and asked to be informed.[62]

(i) Decisions by consent   Where all the persons entitled to be heard at   **14.32** the hearing of a dispute have agreed upon the terms of the decision to be given by the Commissioner and the particulars are reduced to writing and signed by all the persons concerned the Commissioner may, if he thinks fit, give a decision in accordance with those terms without a hearing. He shall not give his consent to such a decision where the dispute concerns either a right of common or the ownership of land unless he is satisfied that there is no person who, if a hearing were held would be entitled to be heard as a person suceeding to the interest or part of an interest, of any other person, or that every person so interested has consented in writing.[63] A decision in this form contains no reasons for the decision but merely records the terms of the agreement.

There is no appeal against such decisions as all the parties entitled to be   **14.33** heard are in agreement. However, if a party did find himself aggrieved by a decision the appropriate procedure is an application for judicial review of the actions of the Commissioner.[64] The procedure of decision by consent is

---

[58] Commons Commissioners Regulations 1971 (S.I. 1971 No. 1727), reg. 26.
[59] (S.I. 1968 No. 989), Sched. 1, Form 26.
[60] For which see § 14.32
[61] Commons Commissioners Regulations 1971 (S.I. 1971 No. 1727), reg. 30.
[62] *ibid.* reg. 30(3).
[63] *ibid.* reg. 31.
[64] For judicial review of the decisions of a Commissioner, see § 14.36.

not widely used but is by no means unknown. It is a useful procedure where an incorrect registration of land, without rights, has been made and the applicant for registration subsequently accepts that this has occurred.

14.34 **(ii) Clerical errors** A Commissioner has the power to correct, in any document prepared by him or under his authority, any clerical mistake or error arising from any accidental slip or omission.[65] This power clearly does not extend to the amendment of errors occasioned by the registration authority or applicants, except where the matter is the subject of a dispute.[65a]

(d) Appeals

14.35 An appeal, by way of case stated by the Commissioner, may be made to the Chancery Division of the High Court within six weeks of the date on which the decision is sent to any aggrieved person.[66] An appeal lies only on a point of law. The decision of the court may be to vary the Commissioner's decision or to remit for rehearing, usually before another Commissioner. No appeal to the Court of Appeal may be brought against the decision of the High Court except with the leave of that Court or the Court of Appeal.[67] For the purposes of an appeal from a Commissioner's decision "any aggrieved person" may include persons other than those entitled to be heard at the hearing. In R. v. *Chief Commons Commissioner, ex p. Constable* (1977)[68] an order of mandamus was issued on the Commissioner compelling him to state a case on the application of a person claiming rights which had been transferred to a parish council for registration purposes.

(e) Judicial review

14.36 The actions and decisions of a Commissioner may be subject to review by the court. In R. v. *Commons Commissioner, ex p. Bostock G.S.* (1982)[69] there had been some confusion over the decision of a Commissioner to adjourn proceedings. The decision was quashed and remitted with an order to rehear the matter. In his judgment Comyn J. said:

[65] Commons Commissioners Regulations 1971 (S.I. 1971 No. 1727), reg. 33.
[65a] Thus, serious clerical errors by a registration authority cannot be rectified by a Commissioner. In one case, an authority had registered an applicant's rights on the wrong C.L. unit, effectively extinguishing the rights over the correct land: *Re Newton Fell, Newton in Bowland, Lancs.* [1987] 220/D/326–327, 17 D.C.C. 302. Current proposals for reform in second stage legislation take no account of such injustices.
[66] C.R.A. 1965, s.18(1). The proceedings in the High Court are assigned to the Chancery Division and are to be heard by a single judge: R.S.C., Ord. 93, r. 16(1),(3). The time within which a person aggrieved by a decision may appeal is six weeks from the date on which the person was sent the decision: R.S.C., Ord. 93, r. 16(2). A case is stated by a Commissioner under R.S.C., Ord. 56, r. 9. The action is commenced by an originating notice of motion; cf. R.S.C., Ord. 93 rr. 10 and 16, R.S.C., Ord. 55, r. 3, R.S.C., Ord. 56, r. 10. See *Practice Direction* [1984] 1 W.L.R. 1216. An application for leave to appeal out of time may be made to the High Court: *e.g.* see *Re West Anstey Common* [1984] Ch. 172 and R. v. *Chief Commons Commissioner, ex p. Winnington* [1982] Lexis, Enggen Library, Cases.
[67] C.R.A. 1965, s.18(2).
[68] (1977) 76 L.G.R. 127, (D.C.).
[69] [1982] C.L.Y. 288; May 27, 1982, before Comyn J; Lexis. Enggen Library, Cases.

"The usual method of challenging a Commons Commissioner is by case stated to the Chancery Division. I am satisfied that this is not an appropriate remedy in this particular matter where no errors of law, or indeed any errors are alleged against the Commons Commissioner, but where the court is being moved on the basis that all parties were under different misapprehensions, so that in the end justice is not achieved. Even though there were alternative means of procedure still open to the applicant, that would not prevent him choosing one rather than another."

An application for review will also lie where it can be established that a **14.37** Commissioner has exceeded his jurisdiction or failed to exercise it. An example can be seen in the case of *R. v. Chief Commons Commissioner, ex p. Winnington* (1982).[70] The facts were that there were two owners of common land at the time of registration, one as to a small part, the other as to the remainder. The owner of the small part made an objection to the land registration and the owner of the larger part objected to the registration of rights. At the time of the Commissioner's hearing in 1979 the larger part of the common had been sold and the successor in title to the original objector to rights appeared before the Commissioner. The Commissioner held the rights registrations to be unsustainable. The objector to the land registration did not appear to support his objection. The Commissioner confirmed the registration of the land stating: "there was no appearance by or on behalf of the objector. In these circumstances I confirm the registration." Some time after the Commissioner's decision Walton J. in *Re Sutton Common, Wimborne* (1982)[71] held that "the matter" referred to a Commissioner is not the particular dispute which occasioned the reference but, rather, the validity or otherwise of the land registration. The owner of the land applied for relief by way of judicial review to the Queens Bench Division. Adopting the approach laid down in *Re Sutton Common*, Woolf J. held that as a matter of law it was necessary to require clear proof of the land registration from the applicants and, in the circumstances, the Commissioner failed to exercise his jurisdiction. Relief was granted by way of an order of certiorari.

(f) Practice at the hearings

The Commissioners, it hardly needs to be said, are bound by the decisions **14.38** of the superior courts. It seems, however, that they do not feel themselves bound, or on some occasions even persuaded by, decisions of other Commissioners. This may be illustrated by reference to one of the major issues which confronted the Commissioners—the interpretation of the term "waste land of a manor."[72] In 1975 in the decision *Re Yateley Common, Hampshire* (1975)[73] Commissioner Baden Fuller declared that in his opinion the words should be given the meaning they commonly had in 1965: "that is not as describing land which is known or reputed to fulfil two conditions (i) being 'waste land' and (ii) being 'of' (in the sense of belonging to a lord of) a manor; but as describing land which is 'free to be used by everyone, public' and which is such by reason of it being waste land of a

[70] *The Times*, November 26, 1982, Lexis, Enggen Library, Cases.
[71] [1982] 1 W.L.R. 647.
[72] For which see §§ 2.36 *et seq.*
[73] (1975) 214/D/9–13, 3 D.C.C. 153.

manor historically." The following day Chief Commons Commissioner G.D.Squibb issued his decision in *Re The Green, Woodford, Wilts.* (No. 1) (1975)[74] in which he refused to accept that the land concerned fell under the head of waste land of a manor as "there was no evidence that the Church Commissioners the supposed owners are the lords of any manor of which this land forms part." It follows that the decisons of the Commissioners are not always consistent.

14.39 Nevertheless, persons appearing before the Commissioners might wish to consult past decisions of the Commissioners for guidance. It is a difficult task when only a small number have been reported out of the many thousands which have been made. The most prolific sources available are the Current Law Year Books, the Journals of the Open Spaces Society and a small number included in *Decisions of the Commons Commissioners.*[75] Individual copies of the full decisions may be obtained from the Public Record Office or on application to the Clerk to the Commons Commissioners but, in either case, it is necessary to know the title of the decision or its reference number.

14.40 **(i) The date at which the status of a land registration must be considered** In the earlier hearings it was the common practice to consider the status of the land for registration as at the date of the registration. Where substantiated rights over the land were in evidence at the date of the hearing this had little effect but where the land was claimed to be registrable as common land subject to rights of common, but no rights had been registered, retrospective consideration of rights which could not be proved at any current date was involved. For example, it was held that sole rights of pasture vested in a parish council, but unregistered, had existed over the land at the date it was registered and the land was confirmed in registration.[76] The precarious nature of some of the rights found acceptable may be seen in a decision where land had been registered but no rights, and evidence was given by the chairman of the parish council that he used to cut bracken for litter for a pig and gorse for the family bread oven up to the late 1920s and that he had seen bracken cut since. The Commissioner was satisfied that the taking of bracken and gorse must be attributed to a right of common of estovers attached to the cottage in which it had been used and, further, that the right had not been abandoned. The land registration was confirmed.[77]

14.41 A more complex case came before a Commissioner in *Re Dee Marsh Saltings, Flint* (1974)[78] where a parcel of land had been registered by the registration authority, after the closing date for applications had passed,[79] on July

[74] (1975) 241/D/13–15, 3 D.C.C. 203.
[75] Selected by Campbell (1972) (published by the Commons, Open Spaces and Footpaths Preservation Society). These are not to be confused with the decisions compiled under the same title and held at University College, Cardiff.
[76] *Re Halling Common, Halling, Kent* (1973) 19/D/13, 1 D.C.C. 348; for technical reasons the decision was in fact *obiter dicta*, but the parties seem to have accepted it.
[77] *Re Shottisham Poor's Common or the Bowling Green, E.Suffolk* (1973) 34/D/15–16, 1 D.C.C. 436.
[78] (1974) 52/D/3–4, 2 D.C.C. 183.
[79] As they were entitled to do, *i.e.* between the closing date for application on January 2, 1970 and the final date for registration on July 31, 1970.

17, 1970. No rights were, or at that date could have been, registered. It was submitted on behalf of the objector that there were no rights of common at the date of registration as the closing date for applications for registrations of rights had passed. This submission, and others, were rejected by the Commissioner who said:

> "It seems to me that, for the purpose of deciding whether to confirm or to refuse to confirm the registration, I must consider whether the land in question was subject to rights of common immediately before the registration i.e. on 17th July 1970. The fact that no rights of common had been registered at that date, or the fact that no commoner could after 2nd January 1970 apply for the registration of any right of common, appears to me to be irrelevant. The rights of common (if any) over the land had not been extinguished for want of registration on 18th July 1970. I do not think that I am required to consider whether any rights of common affecting the land on 17th July 1970 ceased to be exercisable after 31st July 1970. Section 10 of the Act, as I read it, operates to establish conclusively the status of the land from the moment when the registration becomes final, whether or not rights of common have been registered in respect of the land.

The registration was confirmed and the objector appealed by way of case stated to the High Court.

The appeal was heard in 1975 and is reported *sub nom. Central Electricity* **14.42** *Generating Board* v. *Clwyd County Council* (1975).[80] Goff J. thought that, if the Commissioner were right in looking at the date of registration in deciding whether to confirm land as subject to rights, it would become conclusively evidential that it was common land at that date and nothing more. It followed that "when the rights ceased to be exercisable, it would lead inevitably to an application, an unanswerable application, to amend the register" unless, of course, it had fallen to registration as waste land of a manor not subject to rights of common. The appeal was allowed and Goff J. refused to confirm the registration:

> "In my judgment, at the time when the commissioner heard the matter the land was not subject to rights of common, and on that short ground he ought to have refused to confirm the registration. What is referred to him under section 5(6) is 'the matter' and the matter in my view is whether or not the land is common land. To confirm the registration because at that time it might have been right, when one knows at the hearing that it is wrong, leaving the objector to apply to amend the register, seems to be a wrong course to pursue."[81]

Although it is now clear that Goff J.'s "unanswerable application" is not **14.43** correct and land which has, for whatever reason and irrespective of its true common law status, fallen to registration without rights registered over it will be deemed to be waste land of a manor,[82] the rationale of his judgment has been accepted and it is now correct only to consider the state of the land

---

[80] [1976] 1 W.L.R. 151.
[81] *ibid.* at 157.
[82] *Corpus Christi Colleg* v. *Gloucs. County Council* [1983] 1 Q.B. 360, considered at § 2.76.

as at the date of the hearing. It makes no difference whether the original registration was under the head of land subject to rights or, alternatively, as waste land of a manor.[83] In either case it is the status at the date of the hearing which must be considered. It follows that, where at the date of the hearing the land is not subject to registered rights the only consideration is whether the land is waste land of a manor. This has not escaped the notice of some owners who have been able to take action between registration and the hearing of an objection to ensure that the land falls outside the registrable categories.[84]

14.44   **(ii) The "matter" before the Commissioner**   Where an objection to a registration was made, and not cancelled or withdrawn in the periods allowed, the registration authority is required to refer the matter to a Commons Commissioner.[85] The effect of an objection to, say, a small proportion of the total land area registered results in the whole of the registration of land and rights being provisional only. In most of the early cases the Commissioners took the view that, where this situation applied, the resolution of the dispute on the small area was sufficient to dispose of the matter.[86] However, following an appeal from a Commissioner's decision heard in the High Court in 1982,[87] it is apparent that the effect of any objection, whether to a part or the whole of the land, following the wording in regulation 5(4)(b) of the Commons Registration (Objection and Maps) Regulations 1968,[88] which contemplates that while an objection may relate to part of the land it will, nevertheless, be an objection to the whole of the land and any rights registered over it. Thus, any objection will result in the whole matter being referred to a Commissioner, *i.e.* the validity or otherwise of the registration which has been put in question by the objection. It follows that a person who has not himself objected may take advantage of the provisional nature of the registration and make his objections known at a hearing, a Commissioner must hear those objections and take them into account, and that all provisional registrations of rights require to be proved before and confirmed by the Commissioner.

14.45   The main authority on the points at issue is the Court of Appeal decision in *Re West Anstey Common* (1985).[89] A parcel of land was registered provisionally as common land and the main dispute which ultimately came before a Commissioner for decision related to an objection to only part of the land. The Commissioner, and the judge on appeal from his decision,[90] regarded the matter as being simply a dispute concerning the part of the land to which objection had been made. The dispute was resolved by a com-

---

[83] The *C.E.G.B.* case was concerned with land only claimed to be subject to rights of common, but in *Re Burton Heath; Bellord* v. *Colyer* (1983) Lexis, Enggen Library, Cases, Nourse J. followed it in respect of waste land of a manor.

[84] *Re Trewden Moors, Pendle, Lancs. (No. 1) and (No. 2)* (1982) 220/D/218–220, 217, 13 D.C.C. 114, 115 cited at § 3.12, n. 29.

[85] C.R.A. 1965, s.5(6).

[86] For a typical late decision to this effect, see *R.* v. *Chief Commons Commissioner ex p. Winnington* (1982) Lexis, Enggen Library, Cases, considered at § 14.37.

[87] *Re Sutton Common, Wimborne* [1982] 1 W.L.R. 647.

[88] S.I. 1968 No. 989.

[89] [1985] Ch.329.

[90] *Re West Anstey Common* [1984] Ch. 172, before Whitford J.

promise between the parties resulting in the removal of the part objected to from the register. Another landowner, who had not objected to the land registration, was refused a hearing by the Commissioner. The practical result was that his land was encumbered by a higher stocking rate of live-stock entitled to graze following the compromise which removed some of the land originally registered. In the Court of Appeal, Slade L.J. reviewed the cases and concluded that "the provisions of s.5(6) [of the Act] which envis-age a 'matter' being referred to the commissioner and those of s.6(1) [of the Act] which envisage him 'inquiring into it' presuppose that he must address his mind to a question. That question is, I think, *what is to be done about the registration to which objection has been taken?* That is the matter which is referred to him."[91] It followed that the objection made to part of the land raised wider issues. It put in question the status of all the land and, as an objection to the land fell under section 4 of the C.R.A. 1965 to be treated as an objection to any rights over the land, all the rights.

Once a registration of rights requires confirmation it appeared to Slade L.J. **14.46** that "the onus of proving his case inevitably falls on the person making the registration." This has been the opinion of the judges in several cases and only Lord Denning M.R. has expressed a contrary view.[92] As to the amount of proof required Slade L.J. was content to adopt a passage[93] from the judg-ment of Walton J. in *Re Sutton Common, Wimborne* (1982)[94]:

"Of course, in many situations extremely little in the way of proof will be required. To take an example at the hearing in this case, if there is a large area of land which is registered as a common, and an objection is taken as to a small piece on the fringes of the land, which happens to be somebody's back garden, then although the objection of that person theoretically puts in question the status of the whole of the area, pro-viding that nothing else arises to cast the slightest doubt on the status of the remainder of the land, the commissioner will, I think, be fully entitled to rely on the original statutory declarations made by the regis-trant pursuant to reg. 8(1) of the Commons Registration (General) Regulations 1966, S.I. 1966/1471, as discharging the necessary burden of proof. I do not, of course, intend to lay down any general rules as to how the burden of proof is to be satisfied in any case where the matter is not so simple. That must depend on precisely how the matter pres-ents itself to the commissioner in any particular set of circumstances, which may, of course, vary almost infinitely. But if it is borne in on the commissioner, as the result of information which is before him or which is sought to be placed before him and which, if correct, is rel-evant that the registration is questionable, then he should, in my view, insist that the burden of proof is properly discharged to his satisfaction

[91] [1985] Ch. 329 at 340. The emphasis is that of Slade L.J.
[92] See *Re Sutton Common, Wimborne* [1982] 1 W.L.R. 647 at 656, *per* Walton J.; *Cor-pus Christi College* v. *Gloucs. County Council.* [1983] Q.B. 360 at 379, *per* Oliver L.J. (*contra* Lord Denning M.R. at 367); adopted in *Re Ilkley and Burley Moors* (1983) 47 P. & C.R. 324 and *R.* v. *Chief Commons Commissioner, ex p. Winn-ington* (1982) Lexis, Enggen Library, Cases; for the same onus of proof for manorial waste see *Re Burton Heath; Bellord* v. *Colyer* (1983), Lexis, Enggen Library, Cases.
[93] [1985] Ch. 329 at 342.
[94] [1982] 1 W.L.R. 647 at 656–657.

so as to establish (if possible) that the registration has, in effect, been properly made."

14.47 Slade L.J. went on to consider whether the Commissioner should have heard the landowner who had not formally objected. It was noted that he had no formal right to be heard as one of the categories of persons "entitled to be heard," but it was further noticed that a Commissioner is required to give public notice of a hearing, which indicated that persons not "entitled to be heard" may have an interest in attending the hearing, and the Commissioner has discretion to admit the evidence of any person who volunteers to give evidence. It was concluded that, though it was a matter for his discretion, on the facts of the case the Commissioner should have admitted the evidence of the landowner as to the validity of the relevant land and rights sections in so far as they affected his land.[95] The appeal was allowed and the matter remitted for a further hearing before another Commissioner.[96]

14.48 **(iii) Costs** A Commissioner may order any party to any proceedings before him to pay to any other party to the proceedings any costs incurred by that party.[97] Costs do not follow the event, *i.e.* it is not the practice for a "losing party" to be called upon to pay "the winning party's" costs. As the Commissioner's discretion is absolute it is not possible to predict with certainty when costs will be awarded.[98] It is quite clear, however, that a person with an honest belief in a claim or an objection will not be penalised for being wrong—and indeed when many registrations have been made with an eye to protecting public rights it could hardly be otherwise. In one decision it was put thus: making a mistake is not enough to bring down costs; it must appear that the applicant was acting not in good faith or unreasonably after having a mistake pointed out or did some other thing putting persons to unnecessary expense.[99]

14.49 The occasions when it seems that costs are likely to be awarded are when the application can be viewed as being frivolous and is not supported at a hearing by attendance, or where conclusive evidence is offered before a hearing to an applicant or objector indicating that the application or objection is unsustainable and the person refuses to withdraw or fails to attend the hearing. Further, it seems that a litigant pursuing an application or

---

[95] [1985] Ch. 329 at 343–344. The decision can have quite far reaching effects under some circumstances. In *Re Ilkley and Burley Moors* (1983) 47 P. & C.R. 324, two contiguous unfenced commons were registered as one common land unit. A rights claimant on one of the commons was not objected to by the owner, but the owner of the *other* common was a person aggrieved by the decision of a Commissioner to confirm the rights and was able to appeal (successfully) against rights over land other than his own. In the circumstances the only rights of grazing exercisable over this person's land must have been rights of vicinage, which are determinable by enclosure and seem to be outside the scope of the C.R.A. 1965.
[96] Subsequent proceedings before a Commissioner: *Re West Anstey Common, West Anstey, North Devon D., Devon* (1986) 209/D/234–243, 17 D.C.C. 100.
[97] C.R.A. 1965, s.17(4).
[98] *Re Yateley Common, Hampshire* [1977] 1 W.L.R. 840 at 854, *per* Foster J., disapproving (1972) 122 N.L.J. 1137.
[99] *Re Aislaby Moor and Gally Hill, Aislaby, N.Yorks.* (1987) 268/D/501–502, 17 D.C.C. 212, *per* Cmr. Baden Fuller

objection at a hearing with little or no evidence in support or in the face of decided cases known to him may be liable to costs.[1]

(g) Disposal of disputed registrations

When a disputed registration has become final (with or without modifica- **14.50** tion) or has become void, the Commissioner is required to inform the registration authority under seal and send a copy to the persons entitled to receive copies of his decisions.[2]

Where a notification of finality is received from a Commissioner by a regis- **14.51** tration authority, the authority is required to indicate the fact in the registers as appropriate with such adaptations and modifications as the case may require and shall make any necessary amendment to the register map and any supplemental map.[3] Where any final registration of land contains no indication of area the authority shall enter the area, and enter any new area whenever there is any alteration. The area must be stated in hectares to three decimal places.[4]

[1] *Re Cuxton Common Marsh, Cuxton, Kent* (1979) 219/D/10, 9 D.C.C. 158.
[2] Commons Commissioners Regulations 1971 (S.I. 1971 No. 1727), reg. 32 *cf.* § 14.35.
[3] Commons Registration (Disposal of Disputed Registrations) Regulations 1972 (S.I. 1972 No. 437), regs. 3, 4, 5.
[4] *ibid.* reg. 6.

Appendix 1

COMMONS REGISTRATION ACT 1965

C. 64

An Act to provide for the registration of common land and of town or village greens; to amend the law as to prescriptive claims to rights of common; and for purposes connected therewith. [5th August 1965]

BE IT ENACTED by the Queen's most Excellent Majesty, by and with the advice and consent of the Lords Spiritual and Temporal, and Commons, in this present Parliament assembled, and by the authority of the same, as follows:—

1.—(1) There shall be registered, in accordance with the provisions of this Act and subject to the exceptions mentioned therein,—

> (a) land in England or Wales which is common land or a town or village green;
> (b) rights of common over such land; and
> (c) persons claiming to be or found to be owners of such land or becoming the owners thereof by virtue of this Act;

and no rights of common over land which is capable of being registered under this Act shall be registered under the Land Registration Acts 1925 and 1936.

(2) After the end of such period, not being less than three years from the commencement of this Act, as the Minister may by order determine—

> (a) no land capable of being registered under this Act shall be deemed to be common land or a town or village green unless it is so registered; and
> (b) no rights of common shall be exercisable over any such land unless they are registered either under this Act or under the Land Registration Acts 1925 and 1936.

(3) Where any land is registered under this Act but no person is registered as the owner thereof under this Act or under the Land Registration Acts 1925 and 1936, it shall—

> (a) if it is a town or village green, be vested in accordance with the following provisions of this Act; and
> (b) if it is common land, be vested as Parliament may hereafter determine.

2.—(1) The registration authority for the purposes of this Act shall be—

(a) in relation to any land situated in any county [. . .]¹ the council of that county [or, if the county is a metropolitan county, the council of the metropolitan district in which the land is situated]² or county borough; and

(b) in relation to any land situated in Greater London, the [council of the London borough in which the land is situated]²;

except where an agreement under this section otherwise provides.

(2) Where part of any land is in the area of one registration authority and part in that of another the authorities may by agreement provide for one of them to be the registration authority in relation to the whole of the land.

3.—(1) For the purpose of registering such land as is mentioned in section 1(1) of this Act and rights of common over and ownership of such land every registration authority shall maintain—

(a) a register of common land; and

(b) a register of town or village greens;

and regulations under this Act may require or authorise a registration authority to note on those registers such other information as may be prescribed.

(2) Any register maintained under this Act shall be open to inspection by the public at all reasonable times.

4.—(1) Subject to the provisions of this section, a registration authority shall register any land as common land or a town or village green or, as the case may be, any rights of common over or ownership of such land, on application duly made to it and accompanied by such declaration and such other documents (if any) as may be prescribed for the purpose of verification or of proving compliance with any prescribed conditions.

(2) An application for the registration of any land as common land or as a town or village green may be made by any person, and a registration authority—

(a) may so register any land notwithstanding that no application for that registration has been made, and

(b) shall so register any land in any case where it registers any rights over it under this section.

(3) No person shall be registered under this section as the owner of any land which is registered under the Land Registration Acts 1925 and 1936 and no person shall be registered under this section as the owner of any other land unless the land itself is registered under this section.

(4) Where, in pursuance of an application under this section, any land would fall to be registered as common land or as a town or village green, but the land is already so registered, the registration authority shall not register it again but shall note the application in the register.

---

¹ Words repealed by the Local Government Act 1972, Sched. 30.
² Words inserted by the Local Government Act 1985, s.16 and Sched. 8.

(5) A registration under this section shall be provisional only until it has become final under the following provisions of this Act.

(6) An application for registration under this section shall not be entertained if made after such date, not less than three years from the commencement of this Act, as the Minister may by order specify; and different dates may be so specified for different classes of applications.

(7) Every local authority shall take such steps as may be prescribed for informing the public of the period within which and the manner in which applications for registration under this section may be made.

5.—(1) A registration authority shall give such notices and take such other steps as may be prescribed for informing the public of any registration made by it under section 4 of this Act, of the times and places where copies of the relevant entries in the register may be inspected and of the period during which and the manner in which objections to the registration may be made to the authority.

(2) The period during which objections to any registration under section 4 of this Act may be made shall be such period, ending not less than two years after the date of the registration, as may be prescribed.

(3) Where any land or rights over land are registered under section 4 of this Act but no person is so registered as the owner of the land the registration authority may, if it thinks fit, make an objection to the registration notwithstanding that it has no interest in the land.

(4) Where an objection to a registration under section 4 of this Act is made, the registration authority shall note the objection on the register and shall give such notice as may be prescribed to the person (if any) on whose application the registration was made and to any person whose application is noted under section 4(4) of this Act.

(5) Where a person to whom notice has been given under subsection (4) of this section so requests or where the registration was made otherwise than on the application of any person, the registration authority may, if it thinks fit, cancel or modify a registration to which objection is made under this section.

(6) Where such an objection is made, then, unless the objection is withdrawn or the registration cancelled before the end of such period as may be prescribed, the registration authority shall refer the matter to a Commons Commissioner.

(7) An objection to the registration of any land as common land or as a town or village green shall be treated for the purposes of this Act as being also an objection to any registration (whenever made) under section 4 of this Act of any rights over the land.

(8) A registration authority shall take such steps as may be prescribed for informing the public of any objection which they have noted on the register under this section and of the times and places where copies of the relevant entries in the register may be inspected.

(9) Where regulations under this Act require copies of any entries in a register to be sent by the registration authority to another local authority

they may require that other authority to make the copies available for inspection in such manner as may be prescribed.

6.—(1) The Commons Commissioner to whom any matter has been referred under section 5 of this Act shall inquire into it and shall either confirm the registration, with or without modifications, or refuse to confirm it; and the registration shall, if it is confirmed, become final, and, if the confirmation is refused, become void—

   (a) if no appeal is brought against the confirmation or refusal, at the end of the period during which such an appeal could have been brought;
   (b) if such an appeal is brought, when it is finally disposed of.

(2) On being informed in the prescribed manner that a registration has become final (with or without modifications) or has become void a registration authority shall indicate that fact in the prescribed manner in the register and, if it has become void, cancel the registration.

(3) Where the registration of any land as common land or as a town or village green is cancelled (whether under this section or under section 5(5) of this Act) the registration authority shall also cancel the registration of any person as the owner thereof.

7.—(1) If no objection is made to a registration under section 4 of this Act or if all objections made to such a registration are withdrawn the registration shall become final at the end of the period during which such objections could have been made under section 5 of this Act or, if an objection made during that period is withdrawn after the end thereof, at the date of the withdrawal.

(2) Where by virtue of this section a registration has become final the registration authority shall indicate that fact in the prescribed manner in the register.

8.—(1) Where the registration under section 4 of this Act of any land as common land or as a town or village green has become final but no person is registered under that section as the owner of the land, then, unless the land is registered under the Land Registration Acts 1925 and 1936, the registration authority shall refer the question of the ownership of the land to a Commons Commissioner.

(2) After the registration authority has given such notices as may be prescribed, the Commons Commissioner shall inquire into the matter and shall, if satisfied that any person is the owner of the land, direct the registration authority to register that person accordingly; and the registration authority shall comply with the direction.

(3) If the Commons Commissioner is not so satisfied and the land is a town or village green he shall direct the registration authority to register as the owner of the land the local authority specified in subsection (5) of this section; and the registration authority shall comply with the direction.

(4) On the registration under this section of a local authority as the owner of any land the land shall vest in that local authority and, if the land is not

regulated by a scheme under the Commons Act 1899, sections 10 and 15 of the Open Spaces Act 1906 (power to manage and make byelaws) shall apply in relation to it as if that local authority had acquired the ownership under the said Act of 1906.

(5) Subject to subsection (6) of this section, the local authority in which any land is to be vested under this section is—

(a) if the land is in a parish or community where there is a parish or community council, that council, but, if the land is regulated by a scheme under the Commons Act 1899, only if the powers of management under Part I of that Act are, in accordance with arrangements under Part VI of the Local Government Act 1972, being exercised by the parish or community council;

(b) if the land is in a London borough, the council of that borough; and

(c) in any other case, the council of the district in which the land is situated.

(6) Where—

(a) any land has been vested in a district council in accordance with subsection (5)(c) of this section, and

(b) after the land has been so vested a parish or community council comes into being for the parish or community in which the land is situated (whether by the establishment of a new council or by adding that parish or community to a group of parishes or communities for which a council has already been established),

then, if the circumstances are such that, had the direction under subsection (3) of this section been given at a time after the parish or community council had come into being, the land would in accordance with subsection (5)(a) of this section have been vested in the parish or community council, the district council shall, if requested to do so by the parish or community council, direct the registration authority to register the parish or community council, in place of the district council, as the owner of the land; and the registration authority shall comply with any such direction.

(7) The council of any district, parish or community affected by any registration made in pursuance of subsection (6) above shall pay to the other of those councils so affected such sum, if any, as may be agreed between them to be appropriate to take account of any sums received or to be received, or any expenditure incurred or to be incurred, in respect of the land concerned, and, in default of agreement, the question of what sum, if any, is appropriate for that purpose shall be determined by arbitration.]³

9. Where the registration under section 4 of this Act of any land as common land has become final but no person is registered under this Act or the Land Registration Acts 1925 and 1936 as the owner of the land, then, until the land is vested under any provision hereafter made by Parliament, any local authority in whose area the land or part of the land is situated may take such steps for the protection of the land against unlawful interference as could be taken by an owner in possession of the land, and may (without

---

³ subss. (5)–(7) were inserted by the Local Government Act 1972, s.189, and substituted subs. (5).

prejudice to any power exercisable apart from this section) institute proceedings for any offence committed in respect of the land.

10. The registration under this Act of any land as common land or as a town or village green, or of any rights of common over any such land, shall be conclusive evidence of the matters registered, as at the date of registration, except where the registration is provisional only.

11.—(1) The foregoing provisions of this Act shall not apply to the New Forest or Epping Forest nor to any land exempted from those provisions by an order of the Minister, and shall not be taken to apply to the Forest of Dean.

(2) The Minister shall not make an order under this section except on an application made to him before such date as may be prescribed.

(3) The Minister shall not make an order under this section with respect to any land unless it appears to him—

(a) that the land is regulated by a scheme under the Commons Act 1899 or the Metropolitan Commons Acts 1866 to 1898 or is regulated under a local Act or under an Act confirming a provisional order made under the Commons Act 1876; and

(b) that no rights of common have been exercised over the land for at least thirty years and that the owner of the land is known.

(4) The Minister shall, before dealing with any application under this section, send copies thereof to the registration authority and to such other local authorities as may be prescribed, and shall inform those authorities whether he has granted or refused the application; and those authorities shall take such steps as may be prescribed for informing the public of the application and its grant or refusal.

(5) If any question arises under this Act whether any land is part of the forests mentioned in subsection (1) of this section it shall be referred to and decided by the Minister.

12. The following provisions shall have effect with respect to the registration under the Land Registration Acts 1925 and 1936 of any land after the ownership of the land has been registered under this Act, that is to say—

(a) section 123 of the Land Registration Act 1925 (compulsory registration of title on sale) shall have effect in relation to the land whether or not the land is situated in an area in which an Order in Council under section 120 of that Act is for the time being in force, unless the registration under this Act is provisional only; and

(b) if the registration authority is notified by the Chief Land Registrar that the land has been registered under the Land Registration Acts 1925 and 1936 the authority shall delete the registration of the ownership under this Act and indicate in the register in the prescribed manner that it has been registered under those Acts.

13. Regulations under this Act shall provide for the amendment of the registers maintained under this Act where—

   (*a*) any land registered under this Act ceases to be common land or a town or village green; or

   (*b*) any land becomes common land or a town or village green; or

   (*c*) any rights registered under this Act are apportioned, extinguished or released, or are varied or transferred in such circumstances as may be prescribed;

[. . .]⁴

14. The High Court may order a register maintained under this Act to be amended if—

   (*a*) the registration under this Act of any land or rights of common has become final and the court is satisfied that any person was induced by fraud to withdraw an objection to the registration or to refrain from making such an objection; or

   (*b*) the register has been amended in pursuance of section 13 of this Act and it appears to the court that no amendment or a different amendment ought to have been made and that the error cannot be corrected in pursuance of regulations made under this Act;

and, in either case, the court deems it just to rectify the register.

15.—(1) Where a right of common consists of or includes a right, not limited by number, to graze animals or animals of any class, it shall for the purposes of registration under this Act be treated as exercisable in relation to no more animals, or animals of that class, than a definite number.

(2) Any application for the registration of such a right shall state the number of animals to be entered in the register or, as the case may be, the numbers of animals of different classes to be so entered.

(3) When the registration of such a right has become final the right shall accordingly be exercisable in relation to animals not exceeding the number or numbers registered or such other number or numbers as Parliament may hereafter determine.

16.—(1) Where during any period a right of common claimed over any land was not exercised, but during the whole or part of that period either—

   (*a*) the land was requisitioned; or

   (*b*) where the right claimed is a right to graze animals, the right could not be or was not exercised for reasons of animal health;

that period or part shall be left out of account, both—

   (i) in determining for the purposes of the Prescription Act 1832 whether there was an interruption within the meaning of that Act of the actual enjoyment of the right; and

   (ii) in computing the period of thirty or sixty years mentioned in section 1 of that Act.

(2) For the purposes of the said Act any objection under this Act to the registration of a right of common shall be deemed to be such a suit or action as is referred to in section 4 of that Act.

⁴ Words repealed by the L.P.A. 1969, s.16(2) and Sched. 2, Pt. I.

(3) In this section "requisitioned" means in the possession of a Government department in the exercise or purported exercise of powers conferred by regulations made under the Emergency Powers (Defence) Act 1939 or by Part VI of the Requisitioned Land and War Works Act 1945; and in determining in any proceedings any question arising under this section whether any land was requisitioned during any period a document purporting to be a certificate to that effect issued by a Government department shall be admissible in evidence.

(4) Where it is necessary for the purposes of this section to establish that a right to graze animals on any land could not be or was not exercised for reasons of animal health it shall be sufficient to prove either—

(a) that the movement of the animals to that land was prohibited or restricted by or under the Diseases of Animals Act 1950 or any enactment repealed by that Act; or

(b) that the land was not, but some other land was, approved for grazing under any scheme in force under that Act or any such enactment and the animals were registered, or were undergoing tests with a view to registration, under the scheme.

17.—(1) The Lord Chancellor shall—

(a) appoint to be Commons Commissioners such number of barristers or solicitors of not less than seven years standing as he may determine; and

(b) draw up and from time to time revise a panel of assessors to assist the Commons Commissioners in dealing with cases calling for special knowledge;

and shall appoint one of the Commons Commissioners to be Chief Commons Commissioner.

(2) Any matter referred under this Act to a Commons Commissioner shall be dealt with by such one of the Commissioners as the Chief Commons Commissioner may determine, and that Commissioner may sit with an assessor selected by the Chief Commons Commissioner from the panel appointed under this section.

(3) If at any time the Chief Commons Commissioner is for any reason unable to act, the Lord Chancellor may appoint another Commons Commissioner to act in his stead.

(4) A Commons Commissioner may order any party to any proceedings before him to pay to any other party to the proceedings any costs incurred by that party in respect of the proceedings; and any costs so awarded shall be taxed in the county court according to such of the scales prescribed by county court rules for proceedings in the county court as may be directed by the order, but subject to any modifications specified in the direction, or, if the order gives no direction, by the county court, and shall be recoverable in like manner as costs awarded in the county court.

(5) The Minister shall pay to the Commons Commissioners and assessors appointed under this section such fees and such travelling and other allowances as the Minister may, with the approval of the Treasury,[5] determine,

[5] Now exercised by the Minister for the Civil Service by virtue of S.I. 1968 No. 1656.

and shall provide the Commons Commissioners with such services and facilities as appear to him required for the discharge of their functions.

18.—(1) Any person aggrieved by the decision of a Commons Commissioner as being erroneous in point of law may, within such time as may be limited by rules of court, require the Commissioner to state a case for the decision of the High Court.

(2) So much of section 63(1) of the Supreme Court of Judicature (Consolidation) Act 1925 as requires appeals to the High Court to be heard and determined by a Divisional Court shall not apply to an appeal by way of case stated under this section, but no appeal to the Court of Appeal shall be brought against the decision of the High Court in such a case except with the leave of that Court or the Court of Appeal.

19.—(1) The Minister may make regulations—

(a) for prescribing the form of the registers to be maintained under this Act and of any applications and objections to be made and notices and certificates to be given thereunder;

(b) for regulating the procedure of registration authorities in dealing with applications for registration and with objections;

(c) for prescribing the steps to be taken by registration authorities for the information of other local authorities and of the public in cases where registrations are cancelled or modified;

(d) for requiring registration authorities to supply by post, on payment of such fee as may be prescribed, such information relating to the entries in the registers kept by them as may be prescribed;

(e) for regulating the procedure of the Commons Commissioners and, in particular, for providing for the summoning of persons to attend and give evidence and produce documents and for authorising the administration of oaths, and for enabling any inquiry or proceedings begun by or before one Commons Commissioner to be continued by or before another;

(f) for enabling an application for the registration of rights of common attached to any land to be made either by the landlord or by the tenant and for regulating the procedure where such an application is made by both;

(g) for enabling the Church Commissioners to act with respect to any land or rights belonging to an ecclesiastical benefice of the Church of England which is vacant;

(h) for treating any registration conflicting with another registration as an objection to the other registration;

(i) for requiring, before applications for registration are entertained, the taking of such steps as may be specified in the regulations for the information of persons having interests in any land affected by the registration;

(j) for the correction of errors and omissions in the registers;

(k) for prescribing anything required or authorised to be prescribed by this Act.

(2) The regulations may make provision for the preparation of maps to accompany applications for registration and the preparation, as part of the

registers, of maps showing any land registered therein and any land to which rights of common registered therein are attached, and for requiring registration authorities to deposit copies of such maps with such Government departments and other authorities as may be prescribed.

(3) The regulations may prescribe the payment of a fee not exceeding five pounds on an application made after the end of such period as may be specified in the regulations.

(4) The regulations may make different provision with respect to different circumstances.

(5) Regulations under this Act shall be made by statutory instrument which shall be subject to annulment in pursuance of a resolution of either House of Parliament.

20.—(1) Any order made by the Minister under any provision of this Act may be varied or revoked by subsequent order made thereunder.

(2) Any such order, other than an order made under section 11 of this Act, shall be made by statutory instrument.

(3) Any statutory instrument made under this section shall be subject to annulment in pursuance of a resolution of either House of Parliament.

21.—(1) Section 1(2) of this Act shall not affect the application to any land registered under this Act of section 193 or section 194 of the Law of Property Act 1925 (rights of access to, and restriction on inclosure of, land over which rights of common are exercisable).

(2) Section 10 of this Act shall not apply for the purpose of deciding whether any land forms part of a highway.

22.—(1) In this Act, unless the context otherwise requires,—
"common land" means—

> (a) land subject to rights of common (as defined in this Act) whether those rights are exercisable at all times or only during limited periods;
> (b) waste land of a manor not subject to rights of common;

but does not include a town or village green or any land which forms part of a highway;
"land" includes land covered with water;
"local authority" means [. . .]⁶ the council of a county, [. . .]⁷ London borough or county district, the council of a parish [. . .]⁷;
"the Minister" means the Minister of Land and Natural Resources⁸;
"prescribed" means prescribed by regulations under this Act;
"registration" includes an entry in the register made in pursuance of section 13 of this Act;
"rights of common" includes cattlegates or beastgates (by whatever name

⁶ Words repealed by the Local Government Act 1985, s.102(2) and Sched. 17.
⁷ Words repealed by the Local Government Act 1972, Sched. 30.
⁸ Now the Secretaries of State for the Environment and Wales by virtue of S.I. 1967 No. 156 and S.I. 1970 No. 1681.

known) and rights of sole or several vesture or herbage or of sole or several pasture, but does not include rights held for a term of years or from year to year;

"town or village green" means land which has been allotted by or under any Act for the exercise or recreation of the inhabitants of any locality or on which the inhabitants of any locality have a customary right to indulge in lawful sports and pastimes or on which the inhabitants of any locality have indulged in such sports and pastimes as of right for not less than twenty years.

(2) References in this Act to the ownership and the owner of any land are references to the ownership of a legal estate in fee simple in any land and to the person holding that estate, and references to land registered under the Land Registration Acts 1925 and 1936 are references to land the fee simple of which is so registered.

23.—(1) This Act shall apply in relation to land in which there is a Crown or Duchy interest as it applies in relation to land in which there is no such interest.

(2) In this section "Crown or Duchy interest" means an interest belonging to Her Majesty in right of the Crown or of the Duchy of Lancaster, or belonging to the Duchy of Cornwall, or belonging to a Government department, or held in trust for Her Majesty for the purposes of a Government department.

24. There shall be defrayed out of moneys provided by Parliament any expenses of the Minister under this Act and any increase attributable to this Act in the sums payable under any other Act out of moneys so provided.

25.—(1) This Act may be cited as the Commons Registration Act 1965.

(2) This Act shall come into force on such day as the Minister may by order appoint, and different days may be so appointed for different purposes; and any reference in any provision to the commencement of this Act is a reference to the date on which that provision comes into force.

(3) This Act does not extend to Scotland or to Northern Ireland.

Appendix 2

COMMONS REGISTRATION ACT 1965

EXEMPTION FROM REGISTRATION UNDER SECTION 11

Date of Order	Name and location of exempted land	Approx. area
22.7.66	The Links Common, Whitley Bay, North-umberland	33 acres
25.11.66	The Stray, Harrogate, Yorks	215 acres
2.12.66	Part of West End Road, Recreation Ground, Southampton	1.6 acres
2.12.66	Cippenham Village Green Common, Slough, Bucks.	9.6 acres
6.12.66	Ten pieces of land known collectively as the "Coventry Commons", City of Coventry.	357 acres
9.12.66	Otterbourne Hill Common, Otterbourne, Hampshire	21 acres
12.12.66	Victoria Gardens, Portland, Dorset	4.2 acres
13.12.66	Cassiobridge Common, Watford, Herts.	1.85 acres
14.12.66	Shenfield Common, Brentwood, Essex	33 acres
15.12.66	Thorpe Green, Egham, Surrey	36 acres
16.12.66	Ley Hill Common,	98 acres
	Coleshill Common,	12 acres
	Austenwood Common,	16 acres
	Gold Hill Common,	17 acres
	Hyde Heath Common all in Amersham R.D., Bucks	22.5 acres
20.12.66	Upper Tilt, Lower Tilt, Brook Hill and Leigh Hill Commons,	22 acres
	Little Heath Common,	15.5 acres
	Old Common,	33.5 acres
	Downside Common all in Esher U.D., Surrey	17.5 acres
20.12.66	West Wickham Common, London Borough of Bromley	26 acres
20.12.66	Kenley Common, partly in the London Borough of Croydon and partly in the Caterham and Warlingham U.D., Surrey	87 acres
21.12.66	Coulsdon Common, London Borough of Croydon	103 acres

Date of Order	Name and location of exempted land	Approx. area
21.12.66	Spring Park, West Wickham, London Borough of Bromley	51 acres
22.12.66	Oxshott Heath, Esher, Surrey	228 acres
22.12.66	Micklegate Stray, York	420 acres
22.12.66	Farthingdown Common, Coulsdon, London Borough of Croydon	121 acres
22.12.66	Riddlesdown Common, Purley, London Borough of Croydon	88 acres
3.1.67	Mitcham Common, London Borough of Merton	430 acres

Appendix 3

LAW OF PROPERTY ACT 1925

Commons and Waste Lands

193.—(1) Members of the public shall, subject as hereinafter provided, have rights of access for air and exercise to any land which is a metropolitan common within the meaning of the Metropolitan Commons Acts 1866 to 1898, or manorial waste, or a common, which is wholly or partly situated within [an area which immediately before 1st April, 1974 was][1] a borough or urban district, and to any land which at the commencement of this Act is subject to rights of common and to which this section may from time to time be applied in manner hereinafter provided:

Provided that—

(a) such rights of access shall be subject to any Act, scheme, or provisional order for the regulation of the land, and to any byelaw, regulation or order made thereunder or under any other statutory authority; and

(b) the Minister shall, on the application of any person entitled as lord of the manor or otherwise to the soil of the land, or entitled to any commonable rights affecting the land, impose such limitations on and conditions as to the exercise of the rights of access or as to the extent of the land to be affected as, in the opinion of the Minister, are necessary or desirable for preventing any estate, right or interest of a profitable or beneficial nature in, over, or affecting the land from being injuriously affected, or for protecting any object of historical interest and, where any such limitations or conditions are so imposed, the rights of access shall be subject thereto; and

(c) such rights of access shall not include any right to draw or drive upon the land a carriage, cart, caravan, truck, or other vehicle, or to camp or light any fire thereon; and

(d) the rights of access shall cease to apply—

　(i) to any land over which the commonable rights are extinguished under any statutory provision;

　(ii) to any land over which the commonable rights are otherwise extinguished if the council of the county or [. . .][2] or Metropolitan district[3] in which the land is situated by resolution

---

[1] Words inserted by the Local Government Act 1972, s.189(4).
[2] Words repealed by the Local Government Act, s.273(1), (3), Sched. 30.
[3] Words inserted by Local Government Act 1985, s.16, Sched. 8, para. 10(5).

assent to its exclusion from the operation of this section, and the resolution is approved by the Minister.

(2) The lord of the manor or other person entitled to the soil of any land subject to rights of common may by deed, revocable or irrevocable, declare that this section shall apply to the land, and upon such deed being deposited with the Minister the land shall, so long as the deed remains operative, be land to which this section applies.

(3) Where limitations or conditions are imposed by the Minister under this section, they shall be published by such person and in such manner as the Minister may direct.

(4) Any person who, without lawful authority, draws or drives upon any land to which this section applies any carriage, cart, caravan, truck, or other vehicle, or camps or lights any fire thereon, or who fails to observe any limitation or condition imposed by the Minister under this section in respect of any such land, shall be liable on summary conviction to a fine not exceeding [£20][4] for each offence.

(5) Nothing in this section shall prejudice or affect the right of any person to get and remove mines or minerals or to let down the surface of the manorial waste or common.

(6) This section does not apply to any common or manorial waste which is for the time being held for Naval, Military or Air Force purposes and in respect of which rights of common have been extinguished or cannot be exercised.

194.—(1) The erection of any building or fence, or the construction of any other work, whereby access to land to which this section applies is prevented or impeded, shall not be lawful unless the consent of the Minister thereto is obtained, and in giving or withholding his consent the Minister shall have regard to the same considerations and shall, if necessary, hold the same inquiries as are directed by the Commons Act, 1876, to be taken into consideration and held by the Minister before forming an opinion whether an application under the Inclosure Acts, 1845 to 1882, shall be acceded to or not.

(2) Where any building or fence is erected, or any other work constructed without such consent as is required by this section, the county court within whose jurisdiction the land is situated, shall, on an application being made by the council of any county [. . .][5] or district concerned, or by the lord of the manor or any other person interested in the common, have power to make an order for the removal of the work, and the restoration of the land to the condition in which it was before the work was erected or constructed, but any such order shall be subject to the like appeal as an order made under section thirty of the Commons Act, 1876.

(3) This section applies to any land which at the commencement of this Act is subject to rights of common:
Provided that this section shall cease to apply—

[4] Figures substituted by Criminal Justice Act 1967, Sched. 3, Pt. I; now converted to level 1 on the standard scale: Criminal Justice Act 1982, ss.37, 38 and 46.
[5] See n. 2 above.

(a) to any land over which the rights of common are extinguished under any statutory provision;

(b) to any land over which the rights of common are otherwise extinguished, if the council of the county [. . .]^5 or metropolitan district^6 in which the land is situated by resolution assent to its exclusion from the operation of this section and the resolution is approved by the Minister.

(4) This section does not apply to any building or fence erected or work constructed if specially authorised by Act of Parliament, or in pursuance of an Act of Parliament or Order having the force of an Act, or if lawfully erected or constructed in connexion with the taking or working of minerals in or under any land to which the section is otherwise applicable, or to any [telecommunication apparatus for the purposes of a telecommunications code system].^{7}

---

^{6} See n. 3 above.

^{7} Words substituted by the Telecommunications Act 1984, Sched. 4, para. 16.

Appendix 4

NATIONAL PARKS AND ACCESS TO THE COUNTRYSIDE ACT 1949

SECOND SCHEDULE

GENERAL RESTRICTIONS TO BE OBSERVED BY PERSONS HAVING ACCESS TO OPEN COUNTRY OR WATERWAYS BY VIRTUE OF PART V OF ACT

1. Subsection (1) of section sixty of this Act shall not apply to a person who, in or upon the land in question,—

 (a) drives or rides any vehicle;
 (b) lights any fire or does any act which is likely to cause a fire;
 (c) takes, or allows to enter or remain, any dog not under proper control;
 (d) wilfully kills, takes, molests or disturbs any animal, bird or fish or takes or injures any eggs or nests;
 (e) bathes in any non-tidal water in contravention of a notice displayed near the water prohibiting bathing, being a notice displayed, and purporting to be displayed, with the approval of the local planning authority;
 (f) engages in any operations of or connected with hunting, shooting, fishing, snaring, taking or destroying of animals, birds or fish, or brings or has any engine, instrument or apparatus used for hunting, shooting, fishing, snaring, taking or destroying animals, birds or fish;
 (g) wilfully damages the land or anything thereon or therein;
 (h) wilfully injures, removes or destroys any plant, shrub, tree or root or any part thereof;
 (i) obstructs the flow of any drain or watercourse, opens, shuts or otherwise interferes with any sluice-gate or other apparatus, breaks through any hedge, fence or wall, or neglects to shut any gate or to fasten it if any means of so doing is provided;
 (j) affixes or writes any advertisement, bill, placard or notice;
 (k) deposits any rubbish or leaves any litter;
 (l) engages in riotous, disorderly or indecent conduct;
 (m) wantonly disturbs, annoys or obstructs any person engaged in any lawful occupation;
 (n) holds any political meeting or delivers any political address; or
 (o) hinders or obstructs any person interested in the land, or any person acting under his authority, in the exercise of any right or power vested in him.

2. In the application of the foregoing provisions of this Schedule to waterways,—

 (a) for references to land there shall be substituted references to a waterway;
 (b) sub-paragraphs (a) and (b) of paragraph 1 of this Schedule shall not apply; and
 (c) sub-paragraph (f) of the said paragraph 1 shall have effect as if the words from "or brings" to the end of the sub-paragraph were omitted.

Appendix 5

ADMINISTRATION OF JUSTICE ACT 1977

SCHEDULE 4

CURTAILMENT OF JURISDICTION OF CERTAIN ANCIENT COURTS

PART I

DESCRIPTIONS OF COURTS

Courts Baron.
Courts Leet.
Customary Courts of the manor.
Courts of Pie Poudre.
Courts of the Staple.
Courts of the clerks of the markets (or clerk of the market).
Hundred Courts.
Law Days.
Views of Frankpledge.
Common law (or Sheriffs') county courts as known before the passing of the County Courts Act 1846.

PART II

SPECIFIC COURTS

The Basingstoke Court of Ancient Demesne.
The Coventry Court of Orphans.
The Great Grimsby Foreign Court.
The King's Lynn Court of Tolbooth.
In the City of London, the Court of Husting and the Sheriffs' Courts for the Poultry Compter and Giltspur Street Compter.
The Macclesfield Court of Portmote.
The Maidstone Court of Conservancy.
The Melcombe Regis Court of Husting.
The Newcastle-upon-Tyne Courts of Conscience or Requests and Conservancy.
The Norwich Court of Mayoralty.
The Peterborough Dean and Chapter's Court of Common Pleas.
The Ramsey (Cambridgeshire) Court of Pleas.
The Ripon Court Military.
The Ripon Dean and Chapter's Canon Fee Court.
The St. Albans Court of Requests.
The Court of the Hundred, Manor and Borough of Tiverton.

The York Courts of Husting, Guildhall and Conservancy.
The Ancient Prescriptive Court of Wells.
The Cheney (or Cheyney) Court of the Bishop of Winchester.

PART III

BUSINESS CUSTOMARY FOR CERTAIN COURTS

Court	Business which the court may sit to transact
The Alcester (Warwickshire) Court Leet, Court Baron and View of Frankpledge.	The taking of presentments with respect to matters of local concern. The presentation of audited accounts of the manor.
The Ashburton Courts Leet and Baron.	The appointment of a portreeve and other officers. The taking of presentments with respect to matters of local concern.
The Bideford Manor Court.	The appointment of a people's warden, tything man and way-wardens. The taking of presentments with respect to matters of local concern.
The Court Leet and Court Baron of the Ancient Manor of Bowes in the County of Durham.	The taking of presentments with respect to matters of local concern. The presentation of audited accounts of the manor. The management of the commons in the manor.
The Ancient Court Leet and Court Baron of the Manor of Bromsgrove.	The appointment of a bailiff, reeve and other officers. The taking of presentments with respect to matters of local concern. The annual proclamation of the ancient charter granted in or about 1199. The observance of the ancient custom of the Midsummer Fair.
The Bucklebury Court Baron.	The taking of presentments with respect to matters of local concern. The appointment of tythingmen and haywards.
The Courts Leet and Baron of the Barony of Cemaes in the County of Dyfed.	The taking of presentments with respect to matters of local concern. The management of the common lands on the Preseli Hills in the County of Dyfed.
The Clifton Courts Leet and Baron and View of Frankpledge.	The taking of presentments with respect to matters of local concern. The appointment of pasture masters of byelaw men and other officers.
The Manorial Court for the Hundred and Borough of Cricklade.	The appointment of a hayward. The management of the common lands in the Hundred and Borough of Cricklade.
The Croyland View of Frankpledge, Court Leet and Great Court Baron.	The management of the commons and village greens within the Lordship of Croyland.

Court	Business which the court may sit to transact
The Danby Court Leet and Court Baron.	The management of the commons in the manor of Danby.
The Manor of Dorney with Boveney Court Leet with Court Baron and View of Frankpledge.	The taking of presentments with respect to matters relating to Dorney and Lake End Commons.
The Manor Court of Dunstone (otherwise Blackslade).	The appointment of a foreman and reeve. The taking of presentments with respect to matters of local concern. The management of the commons in the manor.
The Court Baron of East Horndon.	The management of the commons in the manor of East Horndon.
The Courts Leet and Baron of the Manors of Eton-cum-Stockdales in Colenorton.	The appointment of a bailiff and hayward. The taking of presentments with respect to the management of the commons in the manors and other matters of local concern.
The Manor of Flying Court Leet.	The management of the commons in the manor.
The Court Baron for the Manor of Heaton in the City of Bradford.	The annual appointment of a foreman. The taking of presentments with respect to matters of local concern. The occasional perambulation of boundaries.
The Court Leet and Court Baron of the Manor of Henley-in-Arden in the County of Warwick.	The taking of presentments with respect to matters of a local concern.
The Town and Manor of Hungerford and Manor and Liberty of Sanden Fee Hocktide Court and Court Leet.	The appointment of a constable, portreeve, tithingmen and other officers. The administration and regulation of common rights and matters connected therewith.
The City of London Court of Husting.	The enrolment of wills and deeds.
The Manor of Mickley Court Leet and Court Baron.	The taking of presentments with respect to matters of local concern.
The Court Leet and Baron of the Manor of Mynachlogddu in the county of Dyfed.	The management of the common lands in the Parish of Mynachlogddu.
The Norwich Court of Mayoralty.	The admission of freemen of the City of Norwich.
The Court Leet of the Island and Royal Manor of Portland.	The taking of presentments with respect to the common wastes of the manor.
The Southampton Court Leet.	The taking of presentments with respect to matters of local concern.
The Southwark Courts Leet and Views of Frankpledge for (respectively) the King's Manor of Southwark, the Guildable Manor and the Great Liberty Manor.	The pronouncement of an address by the High Steward of the Southwark Manors and the appointment of traditional Officers.
The Manor of Spaunton Court Leet and Court Baron with View of Frankpledge.	The taking of presentments with respect to matters of local concern. The control and management of various common rights over Spaunton Moor, North Yorkshire.

Court	Business which the court may sit to transact
The Spitchwick Courts Leet and Baron.	The appointment of a foreman, reeve and other officers. The taking of presentments with respect to matters of local concern. The managment of the commons in the manor of Spitchwick.
The Courts Leet and Baron of Stockbridge.	The appointment of a bailiff, serjeant at mace and hayward. The taking of presentments with respect to matters of local concern. The management of the commons in the borough of Stockbridge.
The Court Leet of the Manor and Borough of Wareham.	The taking of presentments with respect to the common, the town walls, the town pound and other matters of local concern.
The Warwick Court Leet.	The taking of presentments with respect to matters of local concern.
The Manor of Whitby Laithes Court Leet.	The management of the commons in the manor.

Appendix 6

THE COMMONS (SCHEMES) REGULATIONS 1982

(S.I. 1982 No. 209)

The Secretary of State for the Environment, as respects England, and the Secretary of State for Wales, as respects Wales, in exercise of the powers conferred by sections 1, 2 and 15 of the Commons Act 1899 and now vested in them, and of all other powers enabling them in that behalf, hereby make the following regulations:—

1. These regulations may be cited as the Commons (Schemes) Regulations 1982, and shall come into operation on 25th March 1982.

2. In these regulations, "council" means the council of a district, and "scheme" means a scheme made under the Commons Act 1899 for the regulation and management of a common.

3. A scheme made by a council shall be in the form set out in the Schedule to these regulations, subject to such modifications as appear to the council to be necessary or expedient.

4. Notice of the intention to make a scheme shall be given by—

(a) inserting a notice in the form set out in the Schedule to these regulations, or a form to the like effect, in at least one newspaper circulating in the neighbourhood of the common to which the proposed scheme relates, the notice to be inserted twice with an interval of not less than one week between the insertions;

(b) displaying copies of the notice at two or more places on the common;

(c) serving a copy of the notice upon the council of every county and of every parish and, in Wales, of every community in which the common, or any part of the common, to which the proposed scheme relates is situate;

(d) sending a copy of the notice to every person entitled to the soil of the common, whether as Lord of the Manor or otherwise;

(e) sending a copy of the notice to every commoner:

Provided that, where a copy of the notice is required to be sent,—

(i) it shall be sent by pre-paid registered letter, or by the recorded delivery service;

(ii) in a case where Her Majesty is entitled to the soil of the common, the copy of the notice shall be sent to the Crown Estate Commissioners or, where Her Majesty is entitled as Duke of Lancaster, to the Chancellor of the Duchy of Lancaster;

(iii) in a case where the Duke of Cornwall is entitled to the soil of the common, the copy of the notice shall be sent to the Lord Warden of the Stannaries.

(iv) in a case where the council is satisfied after reasonable inquiry that it is not practicable to ascertain the name or address of any person or commoner, it may dispense with the requirement to send a copy of the notice to that person or, as the case may be, to that commoner;

(v) in a case where the council considers that the commoners are too numerous, it may dispense with the requirement to send a copy of the notice to the commoners.

5. Copies of a draft scheme shall be placed on sale at the offices of the council which intends to make the scheme for such reasonable price as the council may determine.

6. The plan referred to in a draft scheme shall be deposited at the offices of the council which intends to make the scheme, and shall be available for inspection during office hours.

7. The Commons Regulations 1935 are hereby revoked.

SCHEDULE

FORM I

FORM OF SCHEME

1. The piece of land with ponds, streams, paths and roads thereon, commonly known as   , situate in the [parish] [community] of   in the County of   and hereinafter referred to as "the common", as shown on a plan sealed by, and deposited at the offices of the   District Council of   hereinafter called "the Council" and thereon coloured green, being a common within the meaning of the Commons Act 1899, shall henceforth be regulated by this Scheme, and the management thereof shall be vested in the Council.

2. The Council may execute any necessary works of drainage, raising, levelling or other works for the protection and improvement of the common, and may, for the prevention of accidents, fence any quarry, pit, pond, stream or other like place on the common, and shall preserve the turf, shrubs, trees, plants and grass thereon, and for this purpose may, for short periods, enclose by fences such portions as may require rest to revive the same, and may plant trees and shrubs for shelter or ornament and may place seats upon and light the common, and otherwise improve the common as a place for exercise and recreation. Save as hereinafter provided, the Council shall do nothing that may otherwise vary or alter the natural features or aspects of the common or interfere with free access to any part thereof, and shall not erect upon the common any shelter, pavilion, drinking fountain or other building without the consent of the person or persons entitled to the soil of the common and of the Secretary

of State [for the Environment] [for Wales]. The Secretary of State, in giving or with-holding his consent, shall have regard to the same considerations and shall, if necess-ary, hold the same enquiries as are directed by the Commons Act 1876 to be taken into consideration and held by the Secretary of State before forming an opinion whether an application under the Inclosure Acts 1845 to 1882 shall be acceded to or not.

3. The Council shall maintain the common free from all encroachments and shall not permit any trespass on or partial enclosure thereof or of any part thereof.

4. The inhabitants of the neighbourhood shall have a right of free access to every part of the common and a privilege of playing games and of enjoying other kinds of recreation thereon, subject to any byelaws made by the Council under this Scheme.

5. The [here insert description of any particular trees or objects of historical, scien-tific or antiquarian interest] are, so far as possible, to be conserved by the Council.

6. The Council may set apart for games any portion or portions of the common as it may consider expedient and may form grounds thereon for cricket, football, tennis, bowls and other similar games, and may allow such grounds to be temporarily enclosed with any open fence, so as to prevent cattle and horses from straying thereon; but such grounds shall not be so numerous or extensive as to affect prejudi-cially the enjoyment of the common as an open space or the lawful exercise of any right of common, and shall not be so near to any dwelling-house or road as to create a nuisance or be an annoyance to the inhabitants of the house or to persons using the road.

7. The Council may, with the consent of the person or persons entitled to the soil of the common, and of the Secretary of State, temporarily set apart and fence such por-tion or portions of the common as it may consider expedient for the parking of motor and other vehicles, and may make such charges for the use of such part as it may deem necessary and reasonable: provided that any area so set apart shall not be so near to any dwelling-house as to create a nuisance or be an annoyance to the inhabi-tants of the house. The Secretary of State, in giving or withholding his consent, shall have regard to the same considerations and shall, if necessary, hold the same enquir-ies as are directed by the Commons Act 1876 to be taken into consideration and held by the Secretary of State before forming an opinion whether an application under the Inclosure Acts 1845 to 1882 shall be acceded to or not.

8. The Council may, for the prevention of nuisances and the preservation of order on the common, and subject to the provisions of section 10 of the Commons Act 1899, make, revoke or alter byelaws for any of the following purposes, namely—

(a) prohibiting any person without lawful authority from digging or taking turf, sods, gravel, sand, clay or other substance on or from the common, and from cutting, felling or injuring any gorse, heather, timber, or other tree, shrub, brushwood or other plant growing on the common;

(b) regulating the place and mode of digging and taking turf, sods, gravel, sand, clay, or other substance, and cutting, felling and taking trees or underwood on or from the common in exercise of any right of common or other right over the common;

(c) prohibiting the removal or displacement of seats, shelters, pavilions, drink-ing fountains, fences, notice-boards, or any works erected or maintained by the Council on the common;

(d) prohibiting any person without lawful authority from killing, molesting or intentionally disturbing any animal, bird or fish or engaging in hunting, shooting or fishing or the setting of traps or nets or the laying of snares;

(e) prohibiting the driving, drawing or placing upon the common or any part thereof without lawful authority of any motor vehicle, motor cycle, carriage, cart, caravan, truck or other vehicle (including any aircraft), except in the case of accident or other sufficient cause;

(f) prohibiting—

(i) the flying of any model aircraft driven by the combustion of petrol vapour or other combustible substances;

(ii) the taking off or (except in the case of accident or other sufficient cause) landing of any glider or any other aircraft;

(iii) the flying of any glider or aircraft in such a manner as to be likely to cause undue interference with the enjoyment of the common by persons lawfully on it;

(g) prohibiting or, in the case of a fair lawfully held, regulating the placing on the common of any show, exhibition, swing, roundabout or other like thing;

(h) regulating games to be played and other means of recreation to be exercised on the common;

(i) regulating assemblies of persons on the common;

(j) regulating the use of any portion of the common temporarily enclosed or set apart under this Scheme for any purpose;

(k) prohibiting or regulating the riding, driving, exercising or breaking in of horses without lawful authority on any part of the common;

(l) prohibiting any person without lawful authority from turning out or permitting to remain on the common any cattle, sheep or other animals;

(m) prohibiting any person from bathing in any pond or stream on the common, save in accordance with the byelaws;

(n) prohibiting camping or the lighting of any fire;

(o) prohibiting or regulating any act or thing which may injure or disfigure the common, or interfere with the use thereof by the public for the purposes of exercise and recreation;

(p) authorising any officer of the Council, after due warning, to remove from the common any vehicle or animal drawn, driven or placed, or any structure erected or placed thereon in contravention of this Scheme or of any byelaw made under this Scheme;

(q) prohibiting any person on the common from selling or offering or exposing for sale or letting to hire or offering or exposing for letting to hire, any commodity or article, unless in pursuance of an agreement with the Council or otherwise in the exercise of any lawful right or privilege;

(r) prohibiting the fixing of bills, placards or notices on trees, fences, erections or notice boards on the common;

(s) prohibiting the hindrance or obstruction of an officer of the Council in the exercise of his powers or duties under this Scheme or under any byelaw made thereunder.

9. Copies of all byelaws made under this Scheme shall be displayed on notice boards placed on such parts of the common as the Council think fit.

10. Nothing in this Scheme or any byelaw made under it shall prejudice or affect any right of the person entitled as Lord of the Manor or otherwise to the soil of the common, or of any person claiming under him, which is lawfully exercisable, in, over, under or on the soil or surface of the common in connection with game, or with mines, minerals, or other substrata or otherwise, or prejudice or affect any right of the commoners in or over the common, or the lawful use of any highway or thoroughfare on the common, or affect any power or obligation to repair any such highway or thoroughfare.

11. Printed copies of this Scheme shall be available for sale at the offices of the Council for such reasonable price as the Council may determine.

Form II

Form of Notice

Commons Act 1899

Notice is hereby given that the   Council intend to make a Scheme under the above Act for the regulation and management of   in their district with a view to the expenditure of money on the drainage, levelling and improvement of the Common, and to the making of byelaws for the prevention of nuisances and the preservation of order.

Copies of the draft Scheme may be purchased and the plan therein referred to may be inspected at the offices of the Council.

Any objection or representation with respect to the Scheme or plan shall be sent to the offices of the   District Council of   within three months from the date of this notice.

If, at any time before the Council have approved the Scheme, they receive a written notice of dissent, which is not subsequently withdrawn, from either a person entitled to the soil of the common or from persons representing at least one third in value of such interests in the common as are affected by the Scheme, then the Scheme cannot be made.

Appendix 7

Commons which have been the subject of Schemes approved and certified pursuant to the Metropolitan Commons Acts, 1866 to 1898, and confirmed by Parliament

Year	Name of Common	County
1869	Hayes Common	Kent
1871	Blackheath	Kent
1871	Shepherd's Bush Common	Middlesex
1872	Hackney Commons	Middlesex
1873	Tooting Beck Common	Surrey
1876	Barnes Common	Surrey
1877	Ealing Commons	Middlesex
1877	Clapham Common	Surrey
1877	Bostall Heath	Kent
1880	Staines Common	Middlesex
1881	Brook Green &c.	Middlesex
1882	Acton Commons	Middlesex
1882	Chiswick and Turnham Green Commons	Middlesex
1882	Tottenham Commons	Middlesex
1884	Streatham Common	Surrey
1886	Chislehurst Common	Kent
1888	Chislehurst and St. Paul's Cray Commons†	Kent
1888	Farnborough Commons	Kent
1891	Mitcham Commons	Surrey
1893	Banstead Commons	Surrey
1893	Orpington Commons	Kent
1898	Barnes Common†	Surrey
1898	East Sheen Common	Surrey
1899	Harrow Weald Common	Middlesex
1900	Petersham Common¶	Surrey
1901	Orpington Commons†	Kent
1901	Ham Common¶	Surrey
1904	Farnborough Commons†	Kent
1904	No Man's Land	Middlesex
1908	Malden Green	Surrey
1909	Keston Common and Leaves Green	Kent

† Amending Schemes
¶ Schemes amended by Richmond, Petersham and Ham Open Spaces Act 1902

Sources: Board of Agriculture and Fisheries, Annual Report of Proceedings under the Tithe, Copyhold, Inclosure, Commons, Land Drainage and other Acts for the year 1911, (1912), Cd.6150; etc.

Appendix 8

Commons which have been the subject of Regulation under the Commons Act 1876

Date of Provisional Order Confirmation Act	Name of Common	County
1879	Matterdale	Cumberland
1879	East Stainmore	Westmorland
1880	Clent Hill	Worcester
1880	Abbotside	Yorks. N. Riding
1880	Lizard	Cornwall
1881	Beamsley Moor	Yorks. W. Riding
1881	Langbar Moor	Yorks. W. Riding
1881	Shenfield	Essex
1882	Stivichall	Warwick
1882	Crosby Garrett	Westmorland
1884	Redhill and Earlswood	Surrey
1885	Ashdown Forest	Sussex
1885	Drumburgh	Cumberland
1886	Stoke	Warwick
1886	Totternhoe	Bedford
1887	Ewer	Southampton
1887	Laindon	Essex
1888	Therfield Heath and Greens	Hertford
1889	Amberswood	Lancaster
1890	Cleeve Hill	Gloucester
1893	West Tilbury	Essex
1894	Luton Moors	Bedford
1895	High Road Well Moor	Yorks. W. Riding
1895	Bexhill Down	Sussex
1895	Darwen Moor	Lancaster
1898	Wolstanton Marsh	Stafford
1898	Runcorn Heath and Hill	Chester
1901	Skipwith	Yorks. E. Riding
1902	Sodbury	Gloucester
1904	Oxshott Heath	Surrey
1904	Merrow Down	Surrey
1908	Towyn Trewan	Anglesey
1911	Burrington	Somerset
1911	Winton and Kaber	Westmorland
1914	Gosford Green	City of Coventry
1919	Coity Wallia	Glamorgan

Sources: Board of Agriculture and Fisheries, Annual Report of Proceedings under the Tithe, Copyhold, Inclosure, Commons, Land Drainage and other Acts for the year 1911, (1912), Cd.6150; etc.

Appendix 9

Applications decided under major commons enactments 1956–1986

Year	Commons Act 1876	Commons Act 1899		LPA 1925, s.193		MHLGPO†	LPA 1925, s.194		Acq. of Land Act 1981 s.19*	National Trust Act 1971, s.23	Incl. Acts Exchanges
		Schemes	s.22	Deeds	Orders		Consents	Resolutions			
ENGLAND											
1956	—	3	1	1	—	N/A	9	—	4	N/A	2
1957	—	3	3	1	1	N/A	10	—	10	N/A	2
1958	—	8	—	7	2	N/A	10	2	15	N/A	—
1959	—	8	8	1	—	N/A	14	—	22	N/A	—
1960	—	11	3	2	—	N/A	14	—	11	N/A	1
1961	—	15	8	4	—	N/A	11	—	14	N/A	1
1962	—	12	15	2	—	N/A	17	—	11	N/A	—
1963	—	14	4	6	—	N/A	6	—	7	N/A	—
1964	—	13	7	—	—	N/A	9	—	22	N/A	1
1965	—	10	7	3	1	N/A	14	—	10	N/A	1
1966	—	13	18	1	—	N/A	15	—	17	N/A	—
1967	—	4	15	11	1	N/A	14	—	13	N/A	2
1968	—	15	11	6	—	N/A	13	—	19	N/A	4
1969	1	6	10	2	3	1	21	—	15	N/A	—
1970	—	15	16	—	1	1	16	—	25	N/A	1
1971	1	7	12	4	1	1	19	—	16	1	1
1972	—	15	14	3	—	2	24	—	32	1	3
1973	—	11	11	—	—	1	17	—	25	3	4
1974	—	4	11	1	—	2	21	—	18	1	—
1975	—	5	9	—	1	1	15	—	22	2	1
1976	—	13	7	—	—	—	19	—	19	3	—
1977	—	5	6	4	—	1	16	—	18	—	5
1978	—	6	4	1	1	—	19	—	18	1	1
1979	—	2	3	3	1	2	13	—	19	1	4
1980	—	4	4	2	1	—	20	—	11	—	2
1981	—	1	1	6	—	1	12	1	8	—	2
1982	—	—	2	4	—	—	13	—	4	1	4
1983	—	‡	4	4	—	2	17	—	10	—	4
1984	—	1	1	—	—	2	18	—	12	1	4
1985	—	—	1	—	—	1	29	—	10	—	7
1986	—	—	3	—	1	1	21	—	12	—	2
England	2	224	219	79	14	17	486	3	469	14	56

Year	Commons Act 1899		LPA 1925, s.194		LPA 1925, s.193		Resolns	Acquisition of Land Act 1981		Commons Act 1908	Pembs. C.C. Act 1965, s.57
	s.22	Schemes	Consents	Refusals	Deeds	Orders		Auth. Proc. Act 1946	1981		
WALES											
1965	—	—	2	—	—	—	—	—	—	—	—
1966	—	—	2	1	—	—	—	—	—	—	—
1967	1	1	1	—	—	—	—	1	—	—	—
1968	—	—	8	—	3	1	—	—	—	—	—
1969	2	—	4	2	—	—	—	—	—	—	—
1970	1	—	12	1	—	—	1	2	—	—	—
1971	—	—	6	—	—	—	2	1	—	—	—
1972	1	1	6	1	—	—	1	—	—	—	—
1973	—	1	11	—	—	—	—	—	—	—	—
1974	—	—	4	—	4	1	—	—	—	—	—
1975	1	—	1	1	—	—	2	—	—	—	—
1976	2	—	8	—	—	—	1	2	—	1	1
1977	1	—	9	1	—	—	—	1	—	—	—
1978	—	—	5	—	—	—	2	—	—	—	—
1979	1	—	12	—	—	—	—	—	—	—	—
1980	—	—	11	1	—	—	1	1	—	—	—
1981	—	—	6	1	—	1	—	2	—	—	—
1982	4	—	13	—	—	—	1	2	—	—	—
1983	1	‡	8	—	—	—	2	1	—	—	—
1984	1	—	14	—	3	—	1	—	1	1	—
1985	1	—	8	—	1	—	—	—	3	3	—
1986	3	—	8	2	—	—	—	—	—	—	1
Wales††	20	3	159	11	11	3	14	13	4	5	2

† Ministry of Housing and Local Government Provisional Order Confirmation (Greater London Parks and Open Spaces) Act 1967

†† Figures since the establishment of the Welsh Office: 1964–86

‡ Since 1982 new schemes have not required the consent of a Secretary of State

* Until 1982 consents under the Acquisition of Land (Authorisation) Procedure) Act 1946.

[Sources: Department of the Environment and Welsh Office]

Glossary

The language of the law of commons is a mixture of legal and agricultural terms which can be confusing to laymen and legal practitioners respectively. The purpose of the list below is to provide an initial guide to some of the more troublesome words used in the text or encountered in practice. The numbers in brackets refer to the paragraphs in the text where the word or expression may be seen in context.

Agistment:	the pasturing of one person's animals on the land of another for the payment of money, with control of the animals by the landowner (7.12); *see also* **animals on tack**.
Animals *ferae naturae*:	feral, not domesticated (3.86).
Appendant:	attached to land by privilege of law (3.28); *cf.* **appurtenant**.
Approvement:	the right of the owner of the soil of a common to inclose any part of the common not needed to satisfy the rights of the commoners (7.47).
Appurtenant:	attached to land by express or implied acts of the parties (3.36); *cf.* **appendant**.
Arosfa:	Welsh variation of sheepwalk.
Award (Inclosure):	the final and binding document controlling statutory inclosure or regulation of any, but mainly common, lands (12.22).
Balk:	the unploughed piece of land between adjoining ploughed strips in a common field (12.07).
Beastgate:	*see* **stint**.
Bona vacantia:	goods without an owner (5.66).
Cattlegate:	*see* **stint**.
Commonable:	appertaining to use in common; variable according to context (1.44).
Common in the soil:	the right of common which allows the taking of part of the soil of another person's land, *e.g.* gravel, stone, marl, etc. (3.77).
Copyhold:	a form of tenure peculiar to a manor, now obsolete (3.102).
Corporeal:	capable of physical possession (3.04); *cf.* **incorporeal**.
Covenant:	a promise contained in a deed (9.64).
Cullet flock:	the flock of the lord of a manor in which his tenants might place sheep; obsolete (3.116).
Cynefin:	Welsh variation of sheepwalk.
Deed:	a document signed sealed and delivered (4.36).

Deed poll:	a deed with only one party (5.93).
Demesne:	the land of a manor retained by the lord for his own use (1.06).
Demise:	the grant of a lease (6.46).
Detain:	*see* **detention**.
Detention:	the statutory equivalent of distress damage feasant, provided by the Animals Act 1971 (10.14).
Disseisin:	the loss of seisin (1.02); *see* **seisin**.
Distress:	*see* **distrain**; especially distress damage feasant (seizure following damage by especially animals) (10.14).
Distrain:	the lawful extra-judicial seizure of goods including animals (10.14).
Dominant tenement:	the land to which the benefit of a right is attached (10.102); *cf.* **servient tenement**.
Drift:	*see* **drive**.
Drive:	gathering animals on a common to detect strays (10.87).
Easement:	a right over land for the benefit of other land (5.08); in some early cases used to describe any right over or in land; *cf. profit à prendre*.
Enclosure:	a field or other close which has been fenced; *cf.* **inclosure**.
Encroachment:	the unlawful enclosure of part of a common (8.34).
Enfeoffment:	the act of granting a corporeal hereditament by livery (*i.e.* delivery) of seisin (3.29).
Enfranchise:	the statutory right which exists for certain classes of lessees, and copyholders, to purchase the fee simple to land (5.67).
Escheat:	a lord's right to property without an owner.
Estate contract:	a contract for the sale or lease of land (4.91).
Estoppel:	prohibition on a person denying facts which he has led another person to assume to be true (4.37).
Estovers:	a right which a tenant, or a commoner may have to take certain products from the land of another person, especially timber, firewood, bracken and rushes (3.64).
Fealty:	loyalty due to a feudal lord (2.45 n.97).
Foldage:	the right of a lord to have his tenant's sheep folded on his demesne land (obsolete) (3.115).
Foldcourse:	the right of the lord to graze his flock of sheep over the land of the tenants of a manor (obsolete) (3.116).
Fridd:	Welsh word for the lower enclosed parts of a hill.
Gate (also gait):	*see* **stint**.
Hafod à hendre:	the practice in Wales of transhumance for people, flocks and herds from the lowlands to the uplands in the summer (1.07).

442

Half year land:	land which is occupied, and cultivated in serveralty for half a year with grazing in common for the remainder (1.70); *see also* **shack**.
Hefted flock:	an upland flock settled on and acclimatised to a recognized part of common grazing (3.105).
Herbage:	a sole profit to take grass by grazing or cutting (3.96).
Hereditament:	an inheritable right in property (3.02).
Inbye land:	the enclosed land of an upland farm (3.107).
In gross:	a right existing independently of attachment to land (3.43).
Inclosure:	the extinguishment of common and other rights by legal process, usually an inclosure award, coupled, usually with enclosure of the land into severalty holdings (1.33).
Incorporeal:	incapable of physical possession (3.02); *cf.* **corporeal**.
Intercommonage:	the right shared by occupiers of strips in common fields to graze in common the entirety of the land in an open season without fear of being sued in trespass (1.29).
Joint ownership:	the ownership of land by more than one person entitled to the whole jointly with the other(s); *cf.* **undivided shares**.
Jus spatiandi:	a right to wander at will over the land of another person (11.47).
Jus tertii:	the title of a third party (8.30).
Lammas land:	land cropped in severalty by one or more persons for hay and opened for grazing in common on Lammas Day, *i.e.* August 1, on the new calendar or August 12, on the old (1.06).
Leared:	*see* **hefted flock**.
Legal memory:	the time since the coronation of Richard I in 1189 (9.64).
Lex loci:	local law, to be distinguished from the common law (1.04).
Levant and couchant:	literally getting up and lying down; the limitation of numbers of grazing animals by the requirement that they must be maintained on the dominant tenement in winter (3.123).
Limitation:	(of actions), a statutory bar of a right of action after a period of time (8.35).
Lot meadow:	hay meadows owned in severalty where the owners draw lots periodically to ascertain the individual parcel(s) to be cut for hay by each owner (1.69 n.46).
Manorial court:	a private court of the lord of a manor, *e.g.* courts baron, leet and customary (12.145).
Manorial waste:	*see* **waste land of a manor**; but the term may have a different meaning in some statutes (11.10).

Meadow:	land used for cutting hay; *cf.* **pasture**.
Metes and bounds:	measurement and boundaries (1.66).
Novel disseisin:	the recent loss of seisin; applied in the now obsolete action for recovery of land through an assize of novel disseisin (1.02).
Pannage:	a right of common to graze pigs on acorns and beech mast in a wood or forest (3.62).
Pasture:	land used for grazing; *cf.* **meadow**.
Pasturage:	the right to use land as pasture, thus common of pasturage (3.59).
Piscary:	a right to fish (3.74).
Prescription:	usually acquisition of easements and profits by long user (4.57); also user for the time of legal memory (4.64).
Profit à prendre:	a right to take some part of, the produce of, or the wild animals on the land of another person (3.05).
Pur autre vie:	for the life of another person (7.47 n.34).
Pur cause de vicinage:	the mutual right of commoners on contiguous unfenced commons not to be sued in trespass if animals stray across the boundary of the lands (3.46).
Quia Emptores:	a statute of 1289/1290 which forbade further subinfeudation; thereafter alienated lands were held of the superior lord, frequently the Crown (3.30).
Regulated common:	land controlled by the Metropolitan Commons 1866, the Commons Acts 1876, 1899 and 1908 (10.118).
Regulated pasture:	a pasture owned in undivided shares by the graziers, usually established by an inclosure award more especially by an award under the Inclosure Act 1845 (1.75).
Right of common:	a *profit à prendre* held for an interest equivalent to a fee simple and shared with the owner of the land over which it is exercisable (3.11); *cf.* **right in common** and **sole profit**.
Right in common:	a *profit à prendre* held for an interest less than a fee simple and shared with the owner of the land over which it is exercisable (3.11); *cf.* **right of common** and **sole profit**.
Sans nombre:	a right of common of pasturage not limited by numbers (3.137).
Seignory:	the rights or holdings of a feudal lord, usually one holding direct of the Crown.
Seisin:	the possession of land in fee simple, *i.e.* freehold.
Servient tenement:	the land burdened by a right over it (10.102); *cf.* **dominant tenement**.
Severalty:	land held by an individual as opposed to ownership or use in common (3.108).

Shack:	a right to graze in common after harvest of arable crops in a common field thus common of shack and shack land (1.70); *see also* **intercommonage**.
Sheepheaf:	*see* **sheepwalk**.
Sheepwalk:	the distinct part of a waste where a hefted flock is established (3.105).
Sole pasture:	the right to take a sole profit of pasturage; usually found on stinted pastures but may be exclusive to one person (3.97).
Sole profit:	a *profit à prendre* held for a legal estate where the owner of the land over which it is exercised retains no interest in the product or part of the land concerned (3.16), cf. **right of common and right in common**.
Stint:	a fixed number of animals entitled to graze over, usually, a stinted pasture (1.60); *see also* **beastgate, cattlegate, gate, gait**.
Stinted pasture:	the land over which a sole profit of pasturage is exercised (1.60).
Straying right:	variable; a right of common appurtenant; a sole profit of pasture; a right of common *pur cause de vicinage* (4.19).
Subinfeudation:	alienation of land by creation of a tenure subsidiary to that of a lord (3.30).
Suit of court:	a lord's privilege to require the attendance of tenants at a manorial court (2.45 n.97).
Surcharging animals:	animals grazed by a commoner in excess of his lawful entitlement (8.26).
Tack:	colloquial for agisted, thus to take sheep on tack (3.109).
Tenement:	the property held by a tenant.
Time immemorial:	the time of legal memory.
Toftstead:	the site of a homestead even if derelict (1.45 n.86).
Turbary:	a right of common to take peat or turf for fuel (3.71).
Undivided shares:	land owned collectively by a number of persons each of whom owns a distinct, but unidentified, portion of the whole (2.27); distinguish from joint ownership.
Vesture:	a right to all the products of land apart from mines, minerals and timber (3.92).
Vicinage:	used variably as abbreviation for common of shack or common *pur cause de vicinage* (1.70).
Waste land of a manor:	the unenclosed lands of a manor (2.38).

Index